The Building Systems Integration Handbook

The Building Systems Integration Handbook

Richard D. Rush, AIA, Editor

The American Institute of Architects

John Wiley & Sons
New York Chichester Brisbane Toronto

Library of Congress Cataloging-in-Publication Data
Main entry under title:

The Building systems integration handbook.

Includes index.
1. Building. 2. Architecture. I. Rush, Richard, 1944–
TH145.B844 1985 720 85–22550
ISBN 0–471–86238–X

Printed in the United States of America

10 9 8 7 6 5 4 3 2 1

To Bill Caudill, with warm thanks

Contents

Acknowledgments

Writing this book has taken five years, from inception to completion. During that time, it is certain that many people's lives have touched and been touched by the effort. It has been a huge task and far from a simple one. Many people have participated and many have donated their time. It is not often that the opportunity arises to direct such an effort. For the last three years that privilege has been mine.

Each chapter has its own legacy. Chapter 1 began as background material and a source document for the roundtable that became Chapter 2. All of the professionals who attended the roundtable discussion were volunteers dedicated only to clarifying the notion of building systems integration. Each of the four—Irwin Cantor, John Pile, Joseph Loring, and William Caudill—participated in the panel and in our follow-up requests for review with great enthusiasm. This book is dedicated to the memory of Bill Caudill, who died just two weeks after he reviewed the draft of his comments. The participation and encouragement of such men went a long way toward generating the momentum necessary for an endeavor of this magnitude.

Chapter 3 was written by Robert Miller, and the basic layout of the chapter was his creation. Although we all participated in the selection of the buildings, it was his consistent dedication that provided continuity for the chapter from its beginning.

Chapter 4's author is Thomas Vonier. His chapter was a particularly difficult one because of the amount of research necessary, including finding architects and designers willing to contribute working drawings from which the generic examples could be derived. Tom is an exceptionally consistent professional whose support has been vital to the project. The graphics for the chapter were assembled and drawn by Darrel Rippeteau with Rick Vitullo as designer in charge.

Chapter 5 was written by Barbara Heller with the assistance of Doris King. The size of the chapter (25 products) made the writing task one of the largest in the book. A broad range of product knowledge was mandatory, and Barbara's experience as a specifications writer suited her perfectly to the task.

Chapter 6 is probably the most intellectually ambitious of the book, although the authors—Volker Hartkopf, Vivian Loftness, and Peter Mill—had been working as a team in the general field of performance criteria for several years prior to this book.

Chapter 7 is unique to this book. It was begun by William Miner and McCain McMurray and completed by Stephanie Stubbs and myself. Although the final version of this chapter contains only Stephanie's and my writing, the theoretical foundations were influenced by both Bill and McCain.

For the last three years a task force has reviewed and helped to guide our work. Their efforts have been purely voluntary. They are Jack Hartray, FAIA (chairman); Thomas Moreland, AIA; Marvin Suer, AIA; and James Cowan, FAIA. Special thanks go to Marvin Suer who was particularly generous in his participation as a reviewer of Chapters 4 and 7 and took on the project as if it were his own.

The graphic quality of this book is due largely to the supervision of Darrel Rippeteau and Allen Assarsson, with drawings by Karin Buchanan and Rick Vitullo. Timothy McDonald and Gary Mills also participated at various times throughout the work. The design for the book itself was conceived and developed by Leonard Johnson of Johnson Design. Special thanks are due to Janine Ward of Johnson Design for her hard work and dedication to the project. Typography was supplied by Carver Photocomposition Inc.

Copyediting and rewriting for the book was done under the supervision of Joseph Dundin, and was executed by him and a team composed of Janet Rumbarger and Lynne Jennrich. Catherine Coughlin was also instrumental in the early stages of the book in setting our standards of copy excellence. To the extent that the book's somewhat specialized language is handled clearly and consistently, it is thanks to Joe Dundin and this team. Gretchen Bank has served as our researcher for nearly all of the chapters and has maintained her quality of work through our three-year effort. Maxine Parker and her word processing staff have done their best not only as typists but as professionals ingenious at calming editors.

Thanks are due to Thurman Poston, the original editor in charge of the book for John Wiley & Sons, and to Carol Beasley, the publisher in charge of the book, for their faith and support throughout the project.

The architects of the buildings in Chapter 3 have our gratitude for their courtesy and support. We also wish to thank the many reviewers and contributors of Chapters 4 and 5. Of particular note are Walter Rosenfeld, who reviewed the entirety of Chapter 5 in its early stages; Harry Misuriello for his mechanical engineering counsel in Chapters 3 and 4; and Zivan Cohen for his structural engineering expertise in Chapter 4. Similar thanks go to Robert Dean for his year-long contribution to Chapter 6 and to Janet Nairn for her help with Chapter 5. William A. Webb of Rolf Jensen & Associates served as our fire protection reviewer for Chapters 4, 5, and 6.

I also wish to thank Professor William Wright and his students at the Massachusetts Institute of Technology, who used the book as a text for a course in mechanical system integration and provided a review of it for us.

Very special thanks is extended from those who made this book a reality to those who made it possible, the members of the American Institute of Architects, without whose financial support this book would not have been possible, and without whose technical and moral support it would not have been attempted. A final thanks goes to Robert T. Packard, director of the editorial department of the AIA, and the rest of the staff for their constant encouragement. It was Robert Packard who gave the task to me in the beginning and whose vision of such a book I inherited.—*Richard D. Rush*

Preface

Work on this book began with an assertion, as early as 1980, that a book on the subject of systems was long overdue. The success of *Architectural Graphic Standards* was evident, as was the need to do for building systems what *Architectural Graphic Standards* had done for architectural detailing and component design. Numerous chapters were outlined and authors were sought.

Very early in the project, it was decided that the subject would be best dealt with through an integrated approach, with all systems delineated in great detail. What was missing was a clear concept of integration. There were so many systems that a thorough discussion of them was truly impossible in the space and time provided. What was needed was a shorthand; we therefore reduced all building systems to a set of four overall systems—structure, envelope, mechanical, and interior. At first they were diagramed as the corners of a square, with the diagonals and sides representing the six possible pairs of systems. It was Bill Caudill's coaching that brought about the tetrahedron; Bill simply preferred triangles. His encouragement brought the four corners of the square into three dimensions, and the square became a tetrahedron with its sides representing the six pairs of system combinations.

At the time of the roundtable discussion in Chapter 2, only the 11 system tetrahedrons had been invented. It was agreed that some sort of scale from simple to complex was needed, but it was not yet clear how to represent the levels. John Pile helped crystalize the level discussion with his remarks presented in Chapter 2.

After much experimentation both with the definitions of the levels and with their symbolic representation, five levels emerged: remote, touching, connected, meshed, and unified. Combining the system definitions with the notion of levels produced the first integration diagrams. They represented the four main systems in a building as well as the five levels of combination. In order to represent the combinations of the systems more rapidly, we developed a simpler two-dimensional diagram.

Although we had succeeded in inventing a way of describing the four main systems and their integration, such a method was mainly of use in the early stages of conversation about a building. Cutting a building open exposed many different subsystems, sometimes several within the same overall system. We began to abbreviate the section of a building with a two-dimensional drawing of a two-story shell, much like the graphic representation of a two-story frame used for structural analysis. The diagram described a roof, an interior floor, side walls, and a foundation floor. At the same time we began drawing ball diagrams wherein each system used was represented as an individual ball that could be labeled according to its overall system.

The building section presented us with the most suitable way to analyze the nature of the diagrams. By cutting the frame of the building in half, an "E" shape was developed, with four points designated as points of origin for clusters of system balls representing the integration present. Each individual subsystem could be represented both by its generic system designation and by the level of integration present when it combined with other subsystems.

The final development in diagrammatic method occurred in the graphic presentation process of the cross-sections arising out of Chapters 3, 4, and 5. The final integration that a building represents in these chapters is devoid of material and main system designation. It is only represented by the conventional name of the subsystem and by the level of integration that the various systems represent. Since the products in Chapter 5 emanate from Chapters 3 and 4, the same letters of the alphabet are used in the diagrams in Chapter 5 as in Chapters 3 and 4.

The development of the six performance mandates proceeded alongside that of the diagrammatical procedures. With the greater awareness of integration technology being invented, the ease of discussing the different interactive characteristics of performance criteria became apparent. The development of the visible integration concepts also had a clarifying effect on the diagrams, and especially on the discussion of the interior system. The diagrams are documents of the physical truth of system interaction. Visible integration represents the visible results of the esthetic decisions that influence the integration process.

It is important to note that the research into the subject matter for this book occurred simultaneously with the writing of the chapters, which were begun with only the most general ideas about what was to be discussed. The entire process of clearly defining building systems integration with words and diagrams grew out of the process of writing about it.

This book represents an integrative team effort. The number of individuals who have served as consultants, reviewers, panelists, authors, assistants, and contractors is over one hundred. It is important to note that only a large volunteer group like the American Institute of Architects could have produced this book. Only a large organization could have funded the effort, and only volunteers made the effort feasible in terms of professional time.

On behalf of the many people who devoted their talents to this book, I invite you, the reader, to enjoy its pages. It is my personal assertion that understanding the concepts developed in this book will improve your practice. Our commitment is to your continued excellence and creativity. —Richard D. Rush

The Building Systems Integration Handbook

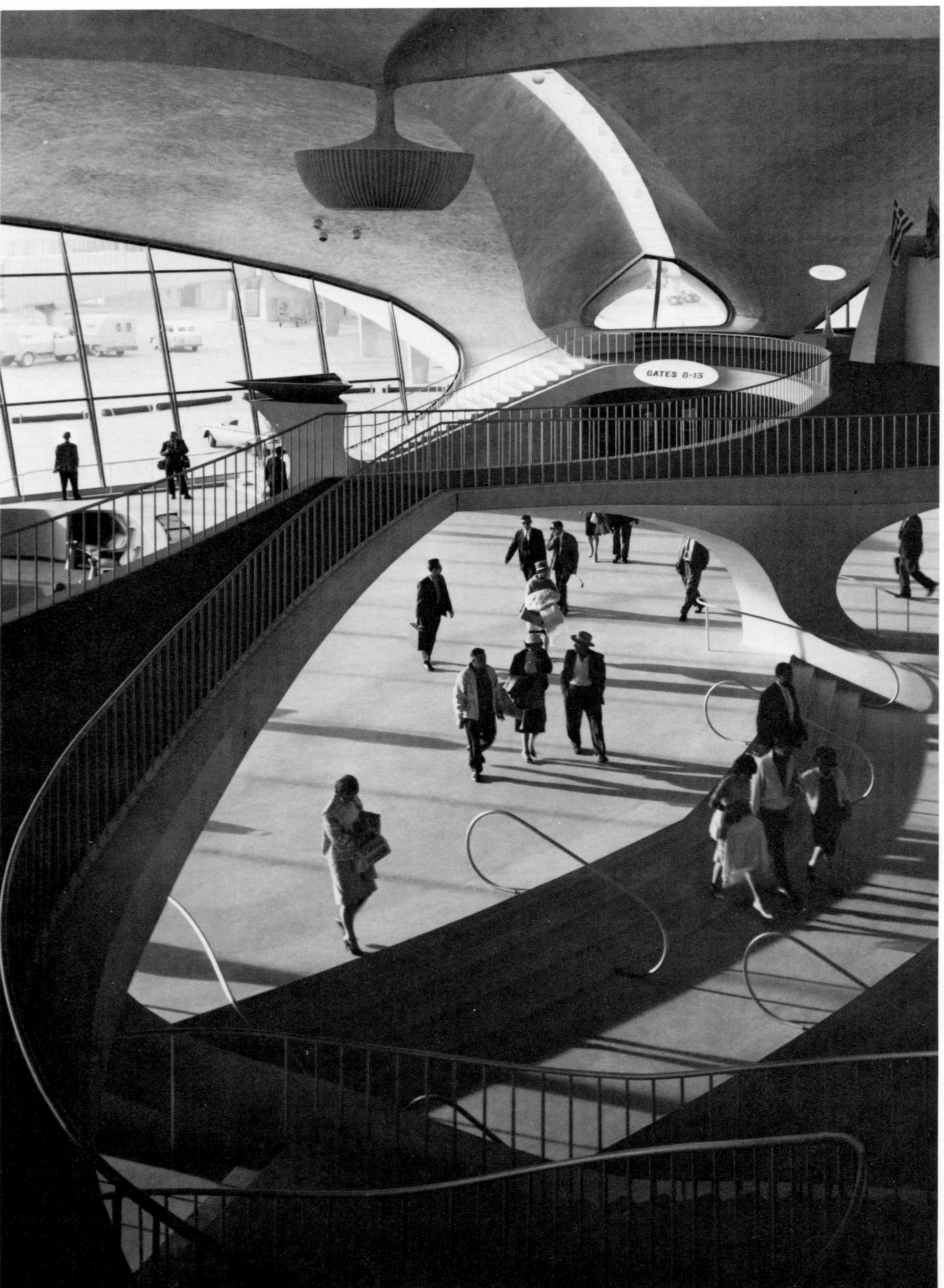
GATES 8-15

Chapter 1
Introduction

Author:
Richard D. Rush, AIA

The premise of this book is that building design is a creative process, one for which the architect is uniquely suited. The precise quality that determines this standing among design professionals is the ability to produce the result we define as building systems integration.

Every building that has ever been used has been integrated, but integration has rarely been a conscious process. The word integration has not had a precise meaning in the domain of building, and for this reason integration has not been consciously sought. Integration results without intention because the criteria that serve as the basis for design are not specific to systems; they are specific to the building as a whole. When criteria come into play through the building, they integrate the physical form automatically. This book, therefore, is not necessary for the achievement of building systems integration. Systems integration occurs in every building, deliberately or not.

How, then, can the analysis and study of integration benefit the designer? This book is intended to provide a context in which designers can examine the nature of the integration that commonly occurs in building design. The design produced by a conscientious architect after reading this book may not differ significantly from those produced before. What can occur when the descriptive technology in this book is applied is an increase in the ability to recognize appropriate integration, with a corresponding increase in efficiency, effectiveness, and depth of detail. One result may be to permit the designer to choose more quickly and easily the solution that would have been chosen anyway. The opportunity also exists for changing the integrative aspects of individual building design methodologies.

The general subject of this book is creativity. Creativity in buildings extends from the facades to the depths of the mechanical room, but it is most apparent in the surfaces of the building that are exposed to view. Without creativity in the hidden aspects of the building design, however, the building literally cannot exist. A vocabulary for discussing creativity in the visual arts has been developed over the centuries, and its present refinement allows the visual aspects of a building to be described in some detail. What is needed is a vocabulary for discussing the creativity involved in the less obvious aspects of building design.

This book offers the reader a tool for discussing creativity in terms of building systems. A discussion of the disposition of the systems and components of a building requires a vocabulary simple enough and universal enough to be used effectively. The definition of building systems integration requires clear differentiation of the various integration situations and an awareness of the choices that have been or can be made. Further, the clear delineation of the task of the architectural designer will make the task itself more apparent to the layman, and may bring greater appreciation for the professional skills involved in designing buildings. Selling services in the absence

Eero Saarinen's TWA Terminal at Kennedy Airport in New York exemplifies the high level of systems integration possible in shell structures. Photo: Ezra Stoller, ESTO.

of such distinctions is the equivalent of trying to sell apples without being able to identify the various species.

We believe that this book offers the first clear definition of building systems integration. It will be obvious that other definitions are possible, and eventually some will be formulated. But for the moment, and in the absence of competition, we offer the following: building systems integration is the act of creating a whole functioning building containing and including building systems in various combinations.

When does the process of integration begin? Without the client, there is no building. The client's need for a building generates a choice: either select a building that has already been built or select an architect. The more specific the need, the less chance there is that the client will find an existing building that fits that need. Often the client is in search of a specific building identity. This too reduces the chance that a suitable building will be found to exist.

When a client chooses an existing building, it is already integrated. The selection of an architect for a new building carries with it a greater degree of uncertainty. The architect is retained for the duration of the design and presumably succeeds in achieving the goal of a completed building. In selecting the architect, the client insures that integration will be achieved. Integration, therefore, begins with a leap of faith in the architect. The choice of the architect is the first in a series of creative acts that result in a built building.

For the architect, the process of integration begins when he or she is selected for the job. It ends when the working documents are complete, including changes in the documents during construction. An essential ingredient of the architect's responsibility, like the client's, is choice. Part of the task is selecting from existing products and services; another part is integrating and originating systems.

In this book, our definition of a system differs from that of integration. A system is a coherent set of physical entities organized for a particular purpose. It works when its results correspond to the intentions or goals, based upon identified needs, established for it. The success of a system, like that of integration, is evaluated by comparison of the intention with the result, but different methods are used for achieving the result.

A system relies on deductive reasoning. Errors in system use result either from false or inaccurate assumptions or from faulty reasoning. A true system is designed and constructed in a rational manner; seeming contradictions and inconsistencies that occur at random cannot easily be built into it. In this realm, given the same assumptions and structure of logic, two different designers can arrive at the same solution. Creativity is involved in the design of a system, but the dominant force is logic.

Integration is another procedure entirely. The dominant force is not logic but creativity, causing something to occur without precedent. All precedents can be analyzed and a solution deduced from them. Creativity, therefore, includes situations where logic is not sufficient to conceive the solution and where new possibilities are brought forth. In these circumstances, the problem can be logically stated and the facts logically recorded, but the act of finding the solution reaches beyond the conscious mind and into the realm of what we don't know we don't know. The ability to evoke new possibilities is necessary, and the ability to recognize the best solution when it appears is essential.

A building must be rationally drawn in order to be built at all. However, the choice of its elements' color, shape, and even location may be made without any reason capable of being expressed in words. Because these elements are visible, their treatment may arise out of a visual perception rather than a verbal perception. Whenever a question of taste, judgment, or experimentation enters the process, there is potential for disagreement and for making a particular design appear unsystematic. The final integration that a design for a building becomes, therefore, is an order that includes systems but is not itself a system.

While creating the context for an integrative design choice involves logic, the act of choosing may not. The choice itself must be recognized simply as solving the problem, and the experience of recognition may or may not be communicable. It is for this reason that we describe integration in physical terms. The integration of the whole building is complete when all of the links between all of the systems have been established.

It is possible to choose the link between systems when one of the systems is still undefined; the choice springs from one system into seeming oblivion. The choice of link can create the missing system. The most daring type of integration occurs when the link is chosen before either of the two systems it is destined to join. It is a bridge between two roads that do not yet exist. The choice is either outside logic or is such pure logic that it attracts two systems that justify it. Such a choice is what birds are to flight; it is the thrill of good design.

The act of integration is less easily, and perhaps less usefully, defined than described. This book is an attempt to generate a coherent method of recognition and description. It is also an attempt to create a context in which integration can intentionally occur. We do not believe it is the only way to recognize and describe, much less achieve, integration. The camera is not to be confused with the photograph.

Architects don't learn to design by reading books. Every architect's learning process is by direct experience and takes a lifetime. Each building design is a lesson, and it usually offers substantial proof that the architect still has unanswered questions about the subject. Improving design skills requires the architect's recognition of the flaws in his or her own work. It is a result of comparison with the work of others and analysis of ways each individual achieves integration of systems. The corresponding goal is to improve one's ability to appreciate integration opportunities.

BEGINNING AT THE END

The task of designing a building has always been complicated. As buildings increase in complexity, the introduction of consultants, performance standards, or whole predesigned systems enters into the design or selection process. To understand completely all of the various systems necessary to operate and construct all buildings is an impossible task. Happily, it is rarely necessary to understand all aspects of all systems in order to integrate particular building systems. An edited body of information, however, is necessary, which can emanate from the issues involved, the specific decisions necessary, and the vocabulary used by experts to converse about the particular building systems.

At the outset, it was our intent that this book discuss all of the significant issues necessary for any building design. After artificially reducing all building systems to four primary systems, it became clear that to do justice to all of the possible combinations and subsystem criteria, several hundred thousand bits of information would have to be included. An idealized mathematical model can be algebraically derived and can even serve as a computerized model, permitting space and time for every possibility. As a practical matter, however, that quantity of information exceeded this book's capacity. In actual practice, the whole array of possible bits of information is considerably reduced by the selection of systems and combinations of certain systems that are particularly rich in potential and have been proven in the field to be economical. Conceptual approaches to specific design problems often produce integration solutions that are inappropriate to existing building problems, i.e., particular functions, sites, climate, scale, and so on. By contrast, an attitude toward integration used in one building can be applied to other buildings having various uses or different environmental foci.

Similarly, an examination of economical buildings of various types and scales yields a set of system combinations that can be considered the bread and butter of building systems—the "cliches" of our current technology. These generic systems are applicable across building-type lines and problem demands. We began planning the book by trying to isolate those integration situations having the richest potential for buildings. The task was analytical, not synthetic. We therefore arranged the book as follows.

Chapter Two: In order to produce the context of experience in the construction industry, we called upon four design professionals who could represent the state of the art in each major division of effort toward integration: structural engineer Irwin Cantor, mechanical and electrical engineer Joseph Loring, interior designer John Pile, and architect William Caudill. Through their participation, these professionals were able to capture what was for them, at the time of the roundtable discussion, the state of the art of systems integration. This book is, to no small degree, a refinement of the thoughts expressed by the people who participated in that discussion. Chapter 2 also serves as an effective introduction to the subject in the language of the practicing professional, complete with examples drawn from the reservoir of recent architectural history.

Chapter Three: There are many books and magazines that serve as a portfolio of designs within a given frame of reference. Many of the 19 built buildings chosen for this book have also been published elsewhere. As built buildings, they all have clients, sites, programmatic requirements, costs, and architects. The purpose of the case studies is to create a context of specific building form in which we are likely to find systems and discover integration. It is believed that these particular buildings will yield information of broad general application, although they are all innovative and nonconventional in their own way. The choices represent a keen interest in the uniqueness that often manifests itself in the form of exposed mechanical or structural systems. Some buildings even embody a level of whimsy that no systematic process could reproduce.

Chapter Four: There is no such thing as a conventional building. Every building incorporates innovation or imagination to some degree. We found it useful, however, to look at building systems integration without the distraction of the particular issues that might influence a specific building. For the 15 generic examples in Chapter 4 there are no specific sites, clients, programs, or architects in the normal sense. The purpose is to explore building systems configurations in the context of the criteria by which they are selected. Each generic example was created by a small group of architects in consultation with an architect of particular expertise in the subject of the example.

Chapter Five: While a building is an integration, a major system is usually a collection of subsystems. In that light, components or products can be subsystems. By disassembling the building and looking at a specific subsystem, the criteria governing selection of the product begin to surface along with possible options and applications. All of the products discussed in this book originate in either Chapter 3 or Chapter 4. We have attempted to concentrate not only on the immediate considerations that usually influence the selection, but also on general considerations that may not be immediately apparent but may eventually become extremely important. It is in the all-encompassing general criteria that the seeds of creativity usually lie.

Chapter Six: A building satisfies a wide array of human goals. Sometimes the criteria emanate specifically from a designated function of the building, and sometimes they originate in the universal nature of building. Such criteria are specific to the successful function of the total built space, not to the systems individually. Comfort is a product of all five senses, and no small function of the individual perception of each person. To evaluate the performance of a building, it is necessary to define individual criteria as well as their interrelationships. It is important to note that true comfort and delight from a building is an integration of criteria, not a systematic assemblage.

Chapter Seven: The number of combinations of systems that a building represents is enormous. Just how complex the situation is and how many possibilities there are has never been represented before. Such a representation is forced by its sheer size to be abstract. The intent in Chapter 7 is to provide the reader with both a handbook (through examination of available options) and an experience with a new technology for describing and analyzing building systems integration.

If the book is to work as a design aid, it must inform the creative choice that design represents. As far as possible, we have tried with this book to augment the cyclical process of design. The cycle could be described simply as follows:

Disposition of experience in the context of vision
Disposition of vision in the context of form
Disposition of form in the context of systems
Disposition of systems in the context of criteria
Disposition of criteria in the context of value
Disposition of value in the context of experience

The cycle begins and returns to the context of experience. To this extent, experience can create new experience.

HOW TO DESCRIBE SYSTEMS

The more unified a building is, the more difficult it is to call out its distinct systems; parts often have more than one purpose and defy simple generic classification. An example is an African mud and thatch dwelling. The mud walls are thick enough to give structural strength and construction stability, using available building materials, while also insulating the occupants from heat and protecting them from the weather. When complete, the roundness reflects the sun and deflects the wind. The circular geometry also reduces the material usage (and construction time) to a minimum for the maximum space enclosed.

The thatched roof has similar redundancy: the thatch sheds water but permits ventilation and allows smoke from an indoor cooking fire to escape. Individual bundles of thatch conform to the geometry of the wall. The soot from the fire inside coats the thatch for water protection.

Integration in this setting does not end with the physical needs of the structure; it extends to the cultural necessity of separate houses for individuals and clusters of houses for the extended family. An entire village of such houses visibly integrates into the savannah not only because the materials are the same but also because the scale of the residential cluster is appropriate to its environment.

The formal prototype for such architecture is often found in nature. The large mushroom-shaped termite constructions of the African savannah are miniatures very similar in exterior appearance

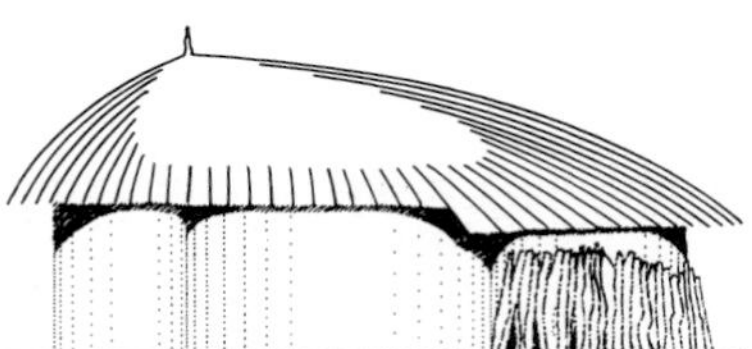

ELEVATION: HOUSE FOR A SENUFO WOMAN

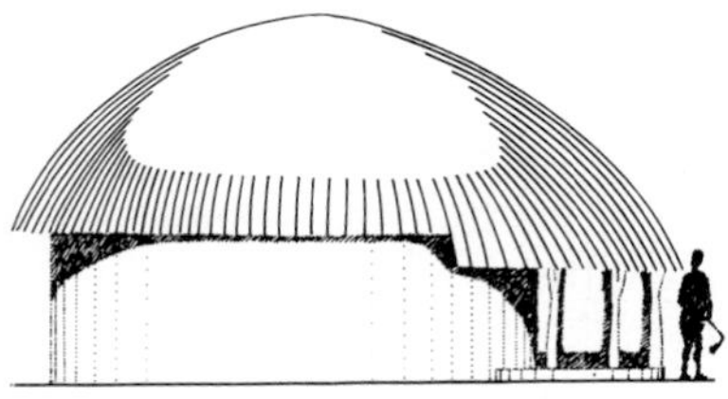

ELEVATION: HOUSE FOR A SENUFO MAN

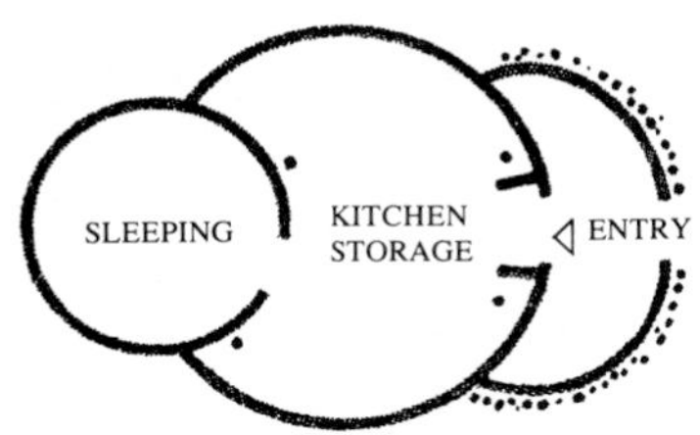

HOUSE PLAN FOR A SENUFO WOMAN

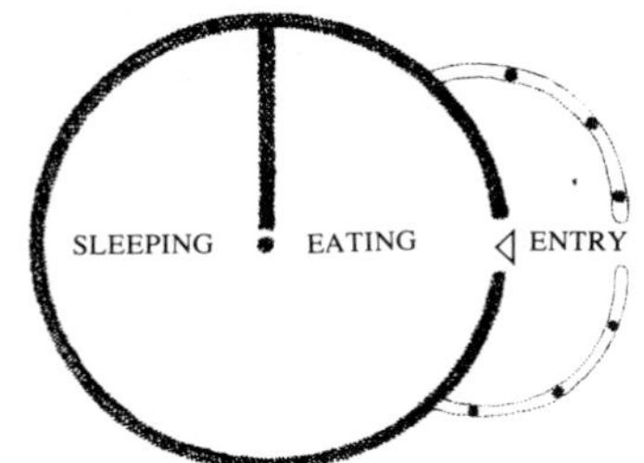

HOUSE PLAN FOR A SENUFO MAN

The photos and drawings above depict the traits of economy of materials, structure, and construction. Directly above is a photo of a termite construction, which closely resembles the form of the houses themselves. The buildings represent Senufo dwellings in the Korhogo region of the Ivory Coast. Photograph of termite dwelling by Richard Sidy, others by Richard Rush.

to the mud huts. This kind of integration and other indigenous examples by both man and other animals approach an integration ideal. In human societies, however, they have sometimes taken centuries to evolve. Such efficiency and high levels of integration are difficult to accomplish in modern buildings. Part of the reason is the added complexity; part is the speed of design; and part is the materials and machinery with which we construct our buildings.

The design process is frequently the effort of a team of professionals or consultants who lend their particular expertise to the design. At the outset no single professional understands the system possibilities of the other, and hence the design often begins only in parts. For the purpose of this book we are defining those parts as structure, envelope, mechanical, and interior.[1]

1. Systems defined, p. 318.

Four Distinct Systems

Structure: The structure creates the equilibrium necessary to allow the building to stand. It includes frames, shells, slabs, bearing walls, and so on. By definition, a structural member supports load other than its own. The structural engineer personifies the structural system of the building, both in knowledge and experience, and can portray any aspect of the design upon which the structural integrity of the building depends—from the foundation to the roof deck.

Envelope: The function of the envelope is to protect the building from penetration by the climate and physical degradation by natural forces. An envelope rarely exists in isolation. A roof assembly, for example, such as a steel frame covered by a metal deck covered by insulation and a built-up roof, is always a structural and envelope combination. Wall assemblies and foundation floors can also be structural, envelope, or interior combinations. The envelope is what is visible on the exterior of the building.

Mechanical: Mechanical systems provide services to the building and its occupants. They control heat transfer, power supply, water supply, and waste disposal. Mechanical systems also include fire safety, security systems, control systems, and conveyances. The mechanical systems' tasks are frequently divided among various professionals, especially in large buildings.

Interior: For purposes of this book, interior systems are simply what is visible from inside a habitable building. Exposed ducts and exposed waffle slabs are included along with "pure" interior systems like hung ceilings and carpet squares. The interior and the envelope are usually interdependent. Each can be treated separately in the sense that the interior systems of a building can change after construction of the exterior, and the exterior skin of the same building can be altered without affecting the interior. Nevertheless, a cross section taken through any part of a habitable building always includes a description of the interior system adjacent to the envelope. Envelope and interior systems are unified in window glass.

The architect usually has total responsibility for the integration of the systems in a building, including responsibility for the participa-

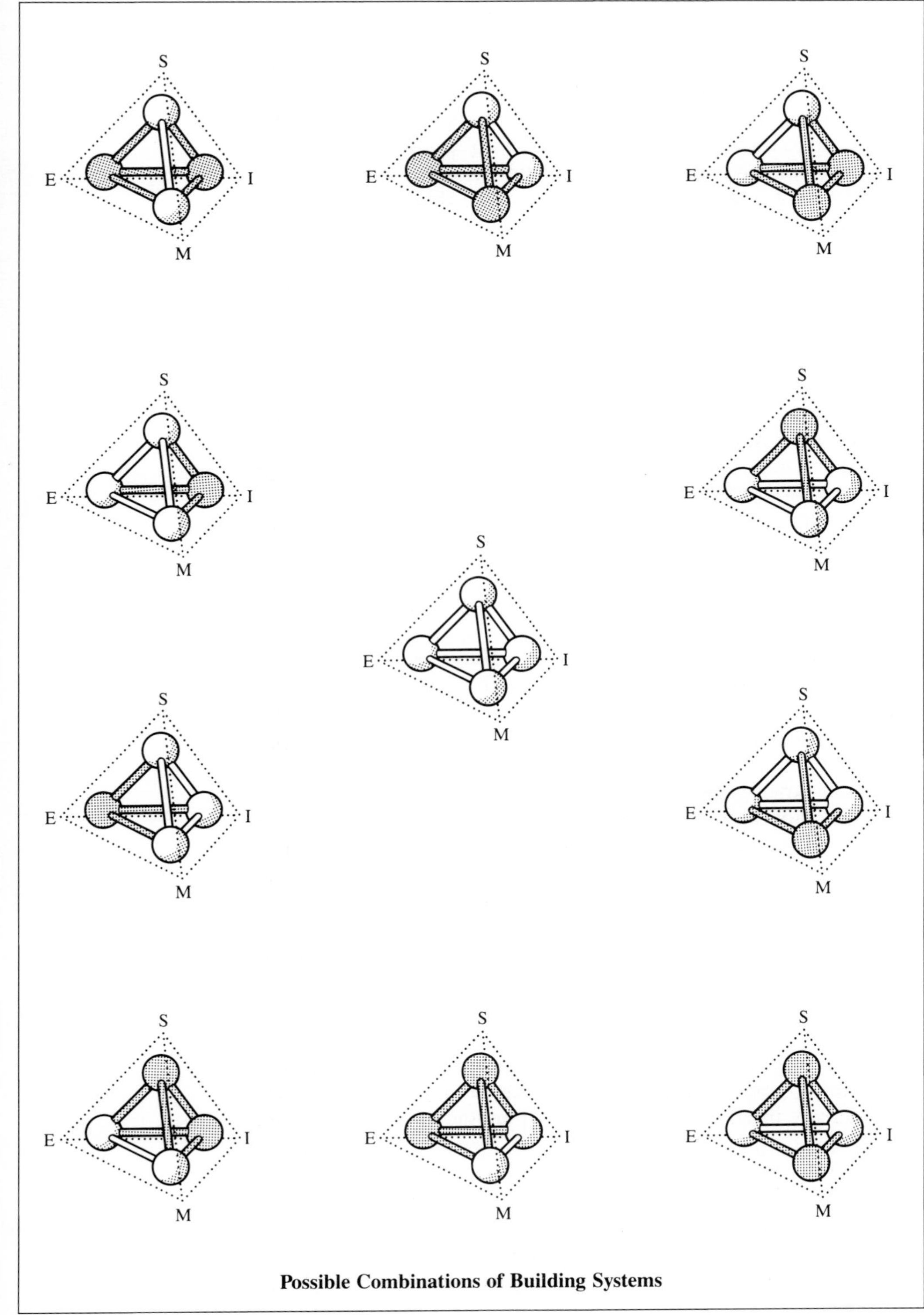

Possible Combinations of Building Systems

tion of others, no matter who performs the calculations. Usually the architect relies more heavily on consultants in the area of structure and mechanical systems than for interior and envelope decisions, although the architect may request an interior designer or a curtain wall consultant. Each major system can have its own integrity; that is to say, once the individual requirements of the overall program have been isolated, an individual system can be independently designed to solve them from the outset. The design professional with a thorough understanding of the design theory identifies the system appropriate to the program needs and then selects the exact materials, products, or machines that satisfy the design criteria. Often the major system is so complex that subsystems produce integration within the major system, as for example when heat is reused from light fixtures to help condition air for the building.

If the major systems in a building are in fact conceived to be four distinct entities, the possible combinations of those systems are exactly eleven.[2] A four-pointed figure with each corner connected to every other yields the tetrahedron as shown. Although there are only six paths between the four points, the possibility of two-, three-, or four-system combinations creates a total of eleven possibilities. The design effort is rarely a simple chronological or sequential process of investigation of such possibilities; however, using the tetrahedron as a key makes the combinations simpler to isolate, analyze, and discuss.

2. System combinations, pp. 318–320.

It is certainly possible to imagine four different systems as separate and autonomous to the extent that they are independently initiated. The possibility of incompatibility is always present. When the four systems come together it is possible to eliminate the "walls" between them and to evaluate the system interdependencies. This can simplify overall performance.

At one end of the theoretical integration continuum, therefore, is a building whose parts are completely independent but coordinated within a designated tolerance. At the other extreme is a building whose components perform multiple tasks that are inseparable. Any discussion that attributes the highest value to the highest degree of integration constitutes a value system; a high level of integration should only be an objective if it is "appropriate." Maximum integration can minimize flexibility. Parts cannot be interchanged when worn out; spaces may become too specific to use when the function of the building changes. It is a judgment of the architect, therefore, to consciously seek a level of integration that is appropriate, both to the immediate intended function of the building and to its possible future uses.

Levels of Integration

For the purposes of this book, we have defined five levels of integration: remote, touching, connected, meshed, and unified. All of the levels are based upon an identifiable physical relationship.

Remote: When two systems are *remote* from each other, they do not physically touch.

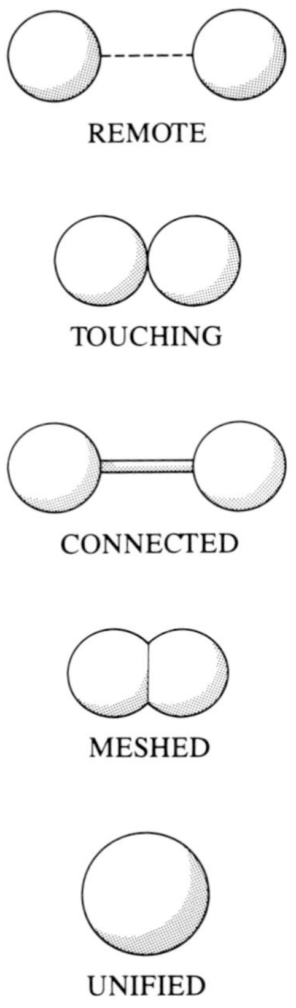

REMOTE

TOUCHING

CONNECTED

MESHED

UNIFIED

Five Levels of Integration

Two-system combinations
1. S+E
2. S+M
3. S+I
4. E+M
5. E+I
6. M+I

Four-system combinations
S+E+M+I or
1. S+E
2. S+M
3. S+I
4. E+M
5. E+I
6. M+I

Three-system combinations
1. S+E+M or
   S+E
   S+M
   E+M

2. S+E+I or
   S+E
   S+I
   E+I

3. E+M+I or
   E+M
   E+I
   M+I

4. S+M+I or
   S+M
   S+I
   M+I

Two-System Versions of All Combinations

The drawings and charts shown on this page are meant to simplify a very complex realm of integration possibilities. By reducing all of the various possibilities of two-system, three-system, and four-system combinations down to two-system combinations and then further judging the probability of occurrence of the two-system combinations, it is possible to concentrate on the most valuable combinations and eliminate the more hypothetical cases.

BSIH Matrix

	remote	touching	connected	meshed	unified
S+E		●	●		●
S+M			●	●	
S+I		●	●		●
E+M			●	●	
E+I	●		●		●
M+I		●	●	●	●

Touching: This relationship involves contact without a permanent connection between the systems.
Connected: This category applies when two systems are permanently attached, either by welds, bolts, or adhesives, directly to each other or through the intermediary of an additional connecting device.
Meshed: The *meshed* category refers to systems that interpenetrate and occupy the same space. The systems can also be physically *connected,* so a value judgment sometimes needs to be made. Usually, two *meshed* systems represent a more restrictive situation which is therefore preferred over *connected* as a category.
Unified: When two systems are *unified*, they are no longer distinct; the same material is applied to more than one use.

When systems are combined in any of the eleven different ways and at any of the five different levels, the task of sorting out the correct resulting integration appears enormously complex.

The BSIH Matrix

Two-system, three-system, and four-system combinations can all be conceived of as being collections of two-system combinations. A three-system combination consists of three pairs of systems; a four-system combination consists of six pairs of systems. As long as the interrelationship between all of the two-system combinations is understood, the potential exists for understanding all of the three- and four-system combinations. If a combination of two systems is not probable as a pair, that relationship is less likely to occur as part of a three- or four-system combination. To reduce, therefore, the total number of possible combinations of systems to a reasonable number, all that is necessary is to evaluate the probable occurrence of all of the combination levels for each possible two-system combination. To accomplish this task, we have created a matrix.[3]

3. The BSIH Matrix. pp. 320–322.

The BSIH Matrix matches each possible level of combinations to each pair of systems and scores the occurrence of the level as either probable or not in the normal context of buildings. If the level is evaluated as probable, a dot is placed in the designated square. In our matrix, there are 17 dots. In other words, we conclude that out of the 30 possibilities, there are only 17 that are most likely to occur in conventional buildings. In fact, these probable conditions do match the situations found in Chapter 4, which illustrates conventional building systems.

The Ball Diagrams

Once the actual materials are chosen or components selected, the generic diagrams that depict each system as a single piece must give way to a more exact kind of diagram wherein each subsystem is called out and the level of combination between each pair of systems expressed. At this point the matrix is probably least strict. What may be remote in a particular part of the building may not be remote, for example, in the context of the whole building and its generalized description. In fact, many of the combinations of systems ultimately found in the buildings in Chapter 3, when diagramed and compared

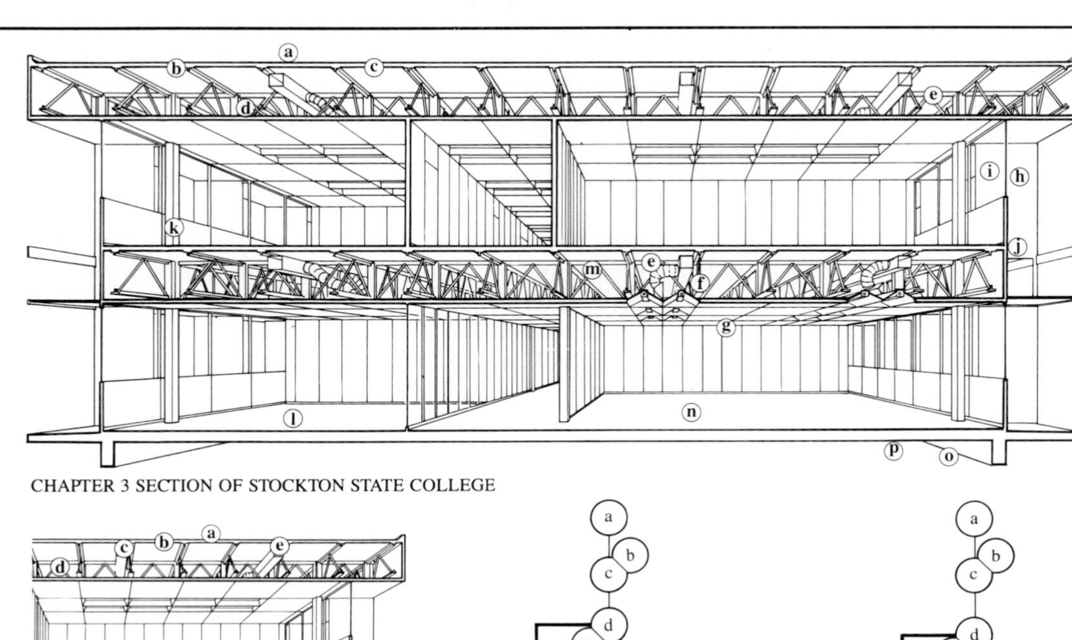

CHAPTER 3 SECTION OF STOCKTON STATE COLLEGE

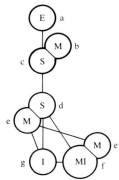

CH. 7 DIAGRAM

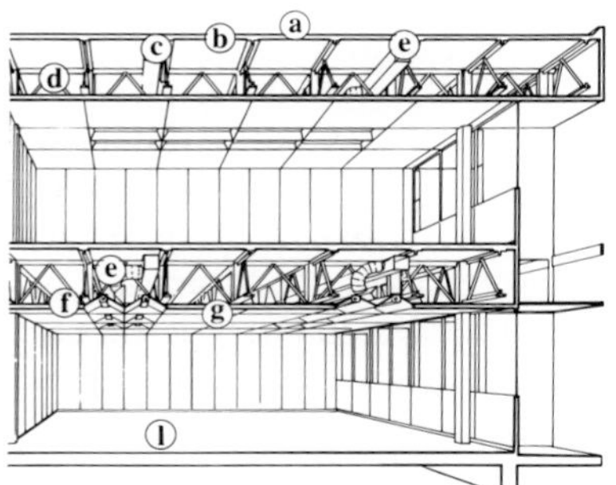

INTEGRATED CEILING

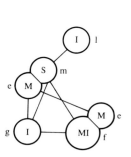

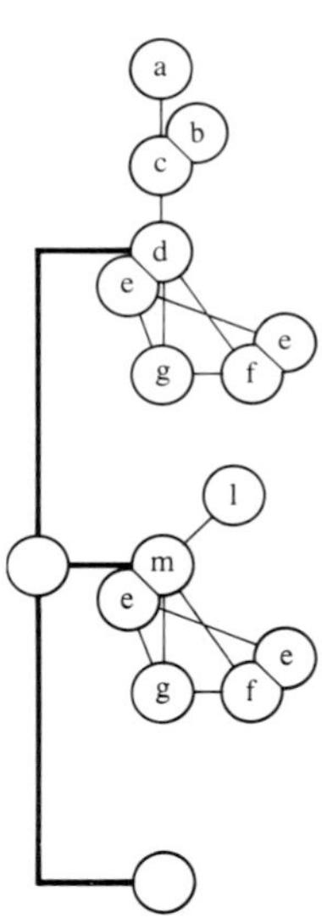

CH. 5 DIAGRAM

a. *Roofing*
b. *Batt insulation*
c. *Metal roof deck*
d. *Steel bar joists*
e. *Ducts*
f. *Air-handling luminaires*
g. *Lay-in ceiling*
l. *Ceramic tile*
m. *Steel bar joists and metal floor deck*

Diagram detail page 182

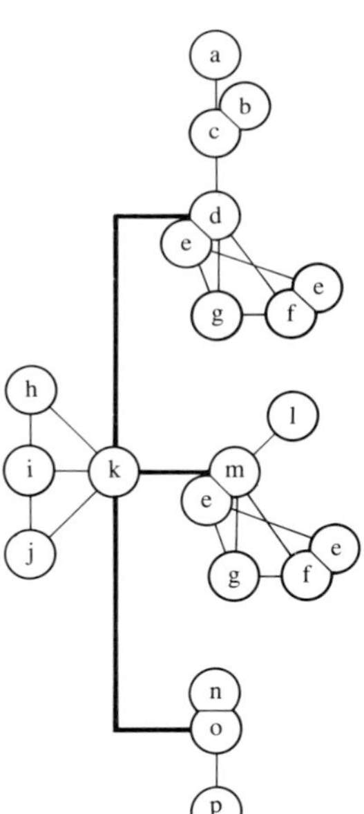

CH. 3 DIAGRAM

a. *Roofing*
b. *Batt insulation*
c. *Metal roof deck*
d. *Steel bar joists*
e. *Ducts*
f. *Air-handling luminaires*
g. *Lay-in ceiling*
h. *Sunscreens*
i. *Window wall assembly*
j. *Lightweight insulating panels*
k. *Steel frame*
l. *Ceramic tile (in gallery)*
m. *Steel bar joists and metal floor deck*
n. *Floor covering*
o. *Cast-in-place concrete foundations*
p. *Waterproof membrane*

Diagram detail page 79

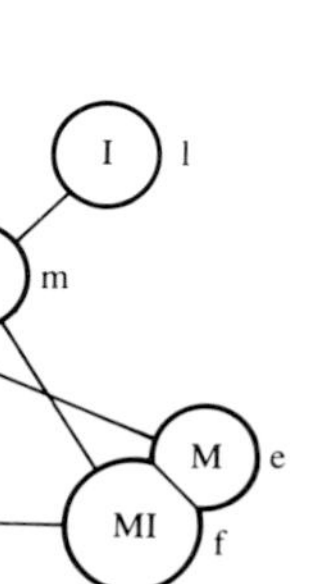

CH. 7 DIAGRAM

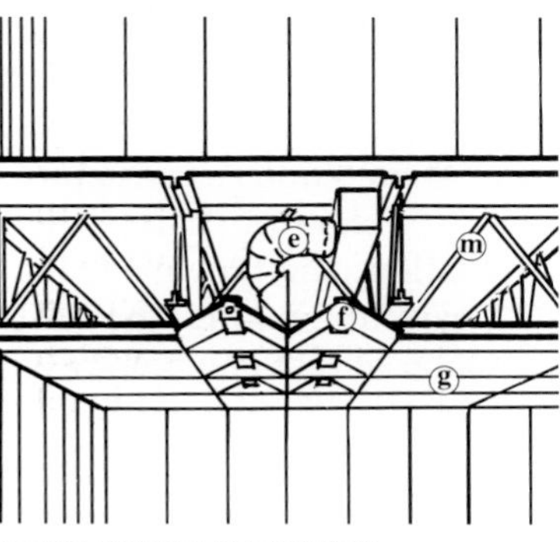

AIR-HANDLING LUMINAIRE

The flow of information in this book, for the most part, is forward. The building shown above is Stockton State College from Chapter 3. Both integrated ceilings and air-handling luminaires are taken from that building and discussed in Chapter 5 as products. Parts of the integration diagrams originating in Chapter 3 are used in Chapter 5; they then reappear in Chapter 7 for comparison with their counterparts from Chapter 3. The callouts and alphabetical designations carry forward in the book as well. In Chapter 7, the system designation is included with the description of the integration level. Unification of systems is also reflected in the Chapter 7 diagrams; larger circles are used to depict two-system unification, and still larger ones are used to depict three-system unification.

to the matrix, will not be found probable. It should be clear at this point that the diagrams are only a point of departure in the context of the matrix. The matrix is not the only one that can exist, and each architect can fabricate a new matrix for each job if the need arises. By using the matrix and the diagrams, the designer allows a symbol to represent the kind of integration desired among the systems without prejudging precisely the materials or systems involved and perhaps being hamstrung by the inherent configuration or geometry of those systems or materials. Very simply, the system diagrams that we propose do for the building systems what the bubble diagram does for planning the layout for a building.

Words Are Not Enough

One difficulty in writing a book on the subject of integration is that words eventually fail at the task. In order to discuss integration, what is being integrated must be defined and the way integration takes place must be defined. As soon as the definitions are fixed, the clock starts on the definitions reaching extinction. If we start with the components and move toward integration, we eventually reach a problem. If we start with the integration and work back to the components, we eventually reach a problem. Ductwork is a good example. No one has difficulty distinguishing a section of ductwork from anything else when the ducts are made of sheet metal and are 2 ft wide in cross section. When the duct becomes a ceiling plenum,[4] a trombe wall,[5] or a double envelope,[6] the physical "duct" cannot be isolated as easily.

4. Aid Association for Lutherans, pp. 62–63.

5. Vocational Technical Education Facility, pp. 98–101.

6. Occidental Chemical, pp. 94–97.

Another example occurs in envelope systems. A window mullion at a small scale has limited structural value. It is literally designed to keep the window panes in place. As the windows increase in size and the surface in which they are placed expands, the wind forces increase, and the window mullions often receive additional steel reinforcing. Eventually the scale of reinforcing reaches a stage where there are benefits from thinking of the mullions as structure. A similar situation occurs with stair shafts or elevator shafts. Their initial placement may be purely for circulation, and they may actually be a liability to the structure. With careful thinking, the walls that enclose the shaft can be seen as a material that can help resist horizontal loading for the whole structure.

Word distinctions of this nature occur constantly in code literature. The designation of commercial or residential, for example, can change the laws relating to buildings and have gross ramifications on the building form, not to mention the eventual use of the building.

Our definitions of the various levels of integration can also suffer. A bolted connection is clearly *connected* in its level. Some adhesives, however, are permanent and others are temporary; how then do we make a universal distinction? A similar example is a protected membrane roof.[7] The great percentage of the roof's surface is held in place by ballast; we call this a *touching* condition. At

7. Protected membrane roofing, pp. 167–168.

the edge, however, the membrane is often physically tied down.

When ductwork is woven through the structure in the ceiling space, it occupies the same space as the structure and is designated *meshed*. When a light fixture is placed into the hung ceiling, it can be said to occupy the same space as the ceiling. We judge the situation *connected* because the two systems do not impede each other.

In the context of integration, therefore, it is possible to get entangled in a semantic game, which serves no immediate purpose, for its own sake. The goal may be stated rather simply. When the task of integration is obstructed by the language, the language needs to be massaged. When the integration task is unformed and confused, the definitions become extremely valuable ways of identifying barriers and opportunities. What is imperative is that the language serve the integration task and not the reverse.

Pictures Are Not Enough

Some of the same problems that occur when we discuss integration also occur when we try to represent integration diagrammatically or photographically. At the outset of a design, it might be important to represent systems as distinct and separate, with no geometry implied. In order to draw the representation, a shape must be used; in our case the shape is a sphere. Then the geometry of size and configuration enter the question, along with the visual description of the connections.

The description of our discussion of levels originates in the translation of systems into spheres and spherical geometry. The distinctions are perhaps more easily seen in terms of circles converging upon one another than through a description in words. The most powerful distinction comes from both words and pictures. Deciding which connection to use between circles is analogous to making the distinction between connections in the systems themselves, and sets the stage for the most relevant discussion. The simple circles converging upon one another tempt the designer to find the equivalent possibilities in the real world.

Before systems are actually chosen, diagrams are helpful to a discussion of possibilities. If the integration has already taken place, diagrams are important to the analysis of the integration. Circle diagrams or ball diagrams[8] give way rapidly in the design process to sketches of physical reality. As with words, when the pictures start to limit the creation of the integration, other pictures are sought.

8. Ball diagrams, pp. 331–335.

Simply stated, the words and the pictures are not ends in themselves, but means to an end. Like X's and O's in the diagram of a football play, they allow us to coach the players before and after the play. The goals and purposes of a building start in the unconscious needs of people; realizing these goals requires communication, both in words and pictures. All of the communication that occurs up to the moment of building is temporary. Once the building is built, the actual experience of the building can be tested against the original goals, with nothing added in words or pictures.

HOW TO USE THE BOOK

It is our hope that there are as many ways to use this book as there are people who will use it. We expect that very few people will read it from cover to cover. Chapter 2 is the only chapter other than this one that is designed to be read as a narrative. The order of the chapters is logical as a description of the analytical process that the book represents. Generally speaking, references within the book flow forward; the reader will normally be referred from earlier chapters to later chapters. Products in Chapter 5 originate in Chapters 3 and 4. The majority of examples in Chapter 6 come from Chapter 3. The specific details in Chapter 7 come from Chapters 3, 4, and 5, and so on. There is a complete table of contents at the front of the book; a chapter table of contents may be found on the opening pages of Chapters 3, 4, 5, and 6. An index is located at the end of the book.

The basic principle at work in the book is that it is simpler and quicker to show someone how to take a mechanism apart than to explain how to put the same object together from scratch. We would further argue that if the right object is dissected, the creative act of reassembly is contained in the dissection itself. In fact, in architectural offices throughout the world there is a process that occurs daily within the design process that is analytical and not synthetic. When an elevator is needed in a building, for example, the architect calls in a consultant to answer whatever questions arise. The architect learns enough to be able to insert the elevator into the building. The designer does not need to understand all of the mechanics involved in elevators in order to design a building that contains one. There may in fact be only two elevators made that will do the job. The complex task of choosing the elevator for the building is rendered simple.

By analyzing a representative sample of buildings, generic case studies, and building components, a high percentage of the most likely built combinations has been generated. The spectrum of practical possibilities has been represented here. The integration characteristics found in those possibilities have been discussed in great detail. The tools are presented that will permit anyone to examine any system or type of integration that is likely to occur.

What we have invented is a logical methodology for translating an existing condition into a universal language, devoid of geometry and material. The only qualities present are a description of the system distinctions and the relationships between them. How then does this work to aid in the design process?

There are two major ways in which this system can be used. One is in the preliminary design process, and the other is after some design choices have been made. In the preliminary design process, there are several questions to ask:

9. Performance criteria, permanence, pp. 237–239.

1. How is the selection of the systems for this building affected by the criteria for the building? How does time affect the choice of systems?[9] Does the building need to be constructed rapidly, used for

a brief time, and demolished quickly? Is the building intended to last forever?

2. Is there a need for a compact building? How can the selection of the systems help to conserve space and material?[10] Is there an opportunity for dual purpose elements? Is there a need for change in the building that will oppose the desire to provide dual purposes?

3. Is there an apparent economic restriction that will vastly influence the choice of systems?[11] The word apparent is important here because the economics of each individual system may be very different from the economics of the final integration.

10. Performance criteria, conservation, pp. 235–236.

11. Performance criteria, economics, p. 237.

The same questions can now be asked of the levels of integration between systems. As the choices are made, thought about the temporary character of the building may result in the need for connections that are easily disassembled. A unified level of integration may provide for the whole building to be moved or may enhance the permanence of the structure.

Such a conversation is useful to have at the outset of the design when the basic discussion about building materials, site planning, orientation, building height, and building geometry is taking place. The structural, envelope, mechanical, and interior systems may be conceptually whole entities.

It is essential to note that our terminology allows the designer to ask questions and to communicate about the nature of the decisions being made. The system provides the questions, but the architect provides the answers. This is a very important distinction to make about this book. It is *not* designed to provide answers. It is designed to provide good, relevant questions. The creativity lies in the answers. It is not the intent to stifle creativity. On the contrary, it is our intent to promote creativity. Our creation is the questions.

Once the preliminary selection of materials and systems has been made, a second level of our terminology and diagraming technique comes into play.[12] Assuming that a construction section can be drawn of the preliminary design, a ball diagram can be made to depict the result. The creation of the ball diagram causes the designer to specifically determine the system and level of integration involved in the design. What follows merely from the description of the integration is a natural series of questions: How can I change the system character to improve the integration? What level of combination other than the one chosen might also be appropriate? The performance mandates discussed in Chapter 6 can all influence the design at this point. Spatial performance, thermal performance, air quality, acoustical performance, and building integrity impact both the selection of the systems and their levels of combination. Note that the question, thus posed, is devoid of material qualities.

12. How to construct a systems ball diagram, pp. 331–335.

There are five possibilities in altering the integration character of the design:

A. Alter the location of the systems.
B. Alter the proximity of the systems.
C. Alter the orientation of the systems.

D. Alter the connection between the systems.

E. Alter the physical make-up of the systems.

The value here is in the domain of response to specific criteria that the building must meet. There is another level of alteration that applies to the design of a building which has nothing to do with the explicit criteria of the building. We call this visible integration.

No two architects will design the same building. Two architects may work within the same constraints of criteria, and both may produce buildings that work well, but the two buildings that result may in fact look very different. Enough books have been written about esthetics that no defense of the artistic role of design needs to be made here. Every architect has an innate ability to produce buildings that have a certain appearance, regardless of their building type, material, or location. The reflection of the personality of the architect is always present, if only because the same mentality has been at work throughout the building design. This presence of personality in the building is rarely completely conscious, and it seems to be less and less universal. Regardless of where it emanates from, the result on the physical decision-making process can be *described* in a universal way. We call this method visible integration. It has to do with the visible consequences of an esthetic decision.

Levels of Visible Integration

We define five levels of visible integration, three of which may occur simultaneously:[13]

13. Visible integration, pp. 381–409.

Level One: Not visible, no change.

The decision has been made, for esthetic reasons, to hide the system completely. Example: HVAC equipment in the mechanical room.

Level Two: Visible, no change.

The choice is to let the system show completely as the function of the system determines its form. Example: exposed structure in a parking garage.

Level Three: Visible, surface change.

In this case the system is in full view, but the surface has been altered to allow it to conform to other surface conditions of the space or enclosure. Example: colored pipes or ductwork.

Level Four: Visible, with size or shape change.

This decision is made to accentuate or allow the system to conform to some predetermined geometry or composition that in itself has nothing directly to do with the correct or efficient functioning of the system. Example: octagonal columns.

Level Five: Visible, with location or orientation change.

The purpose of this kind of change would be to influence the total composition of the space created by the systems in question. Example: relocation of columns or ducts.

Caution

This is not intended to be a book on design methodology. No matter how you presently design your buildings, the integration technology can be of use to you. The questions asked can only clarify the design in a way that clear terminology or diagraming techniques can. The use of free body diagrams permits the structural analysis which eventually results in steel beams. Bubble diagrams for spatial layout allow the client and the architect to discuss the proximity of uses before the building geometry is determined. A computer flow chart allows the programmer to map the logic of a task prior to writing the program. These are all ways of simplifying a very complex process to the degree that the human mind can actually conceive of the process.

Finally, the use of this book will provide the reader with an integration coach. Whatever the design and however it is determined, it can be discussed in terms of integration. The questions raised by the integration technology will clarify the design.

SUMMARY

We believe that all the significant opportunities for building systems integration available with the current technology are presented in this book. We also believe that we have created a context in which it is possible to discuss the task of architectural design. This context may be summed up as follows.

1. Building systems integration is not a purely rational process. Systems by their nature are rational. Integration inevitably involves an informed choice; that is, a consideration of all of the relevant facts and a judgment about the best answer. Vision, intuition, and experience always accompany the logic. Building systems integration applies to all buildings.

2. The underlying building criteria can be presented in isolation from systems or integration. The connection of building elements can also occur without the concept of either building systems or integration. Building systems integration theory is a vehicle the designer can use for translating human needs into physical reality. It is a means of communication that creates a conscious context in which the integration can occur.

3. Building systems integration can also be used as a means of visual expression. The visual manipulation of the building elements to alter the levels of combination is the primary means of this expression. We call this visible integration.[14]

14. Visible integration, pp. 381–409.

4. We assume that exposing the structure or the mechanical system to view immediately transforms it into a unification with either the interior or the envelope, and therefore the structure and the mechanical systems are never in view. Under that definition, the engineering professionals never have responsibility for what is in view for the building's occupants, whether inside or outside the building. The responsibility is always that of the architect.

5. Without the consciousness of building systems integration, there can be no commitment to it. Unless the definitions are produced and the level of awareness raised, communication of commitment cannot take place. Life has a way of making room for commitment. As stated earlier, all buildings that function are integrated;

they become integrated with or without the conscious commitment. The entire design process is one of conscious discussion with the purpose of producing a more perfect match between the request for a building and the promise of one. As architects who promise buildings and end up producing integration, it is time that we clarified what we excel at and commit ourselves to it. Building systems integration, because it is a creative leap and not deductive, has to be accomplished by the architect alone.

6. The choice whether to expose the mechanical systems and structure to the interior space is major from the point of view of integration.[15] That choice usually depends upon the refinement of detail demanded by the activity in the space.

15. Visible integration, pp. 381–409.

7. The mechanical systems are the most versatile; they can be located within or connected to almost any surface in the building. Of the mechanical system decisions, the most significant one is the selection of an air handling solution to the HVAC part of the mechanical systems. Ductwork is the only mechanical system of a size sufficient to cause large-scale alterations in the other systems (holes in the beams, dropped ceilings, etc.).

8. There is a range of possibility for the integration of various systems, subsystems, and components. Some systems can only be combined in one or two ways; others seem to possess an infinite number of possibilities. The more demanding the system is in its physical characteristics, location, orientation, or proximity to other systems, the fewer options there are for its use.

Unused Ideas

We feel confident that this book contains all of the questions about systems integration. It can certainly provide the spark that will generate all the answers. It is our hope that those people who use this book will have clearer answers about building systems integration. The context in which the problem is solved will be improved. Like the subject matter itself, this book integrates a massive amount of experience and expertise, from scratch.

This book represents the best and most fruitful ideas we have had on the subject of building systems integration during the last three years. It does not represent all our ideas. The search for a way to diagram integration included many other viable ways than the one chosen. We gave thought to the economic representation of systems and to an algebraic model for representing system choices; most especially, we tried valiantly to produced a method of deriving all of the ways that were both possible and fruitful to put buildings together.

It is possible to work from the BSIH Matrix and derive all of the possible four-system combinations that result from its two-system logic. It may be worthwhile someday to cost-estimate large jobs based on such logic. It may even be possible to use the system logic to choose systems in other fields than architecture.

Many of our early efforts were spent trying to reduce building design to a completely logical process. A tantalizing assumption is that the same tool that can be used to take a building apart analytically can logically synthesize the parts. We were not the first to fail at this task, and probably will not be the last. People are inclined to try to reduce the unknowns in the way of what they do. The perception is that the risk is reduced, and one feels comfortable as a result.

All of these efforts to reduce creativity to a logical process failed. Our history of assembling buildings in the past only prepares us for the possibilities of the future; it does not determine the future buildings. We shifted our research from deriving design solutions to informing the process. We believe that it is useful for architects to apply their creativity to the context for the discussion of integration. We believe architects are seeking ways to consciously create whole buildings.

History is full of systems that were replaced by better systems. The old systems were not abandoned because they were not good logic; they were abandoned because the logic environment in which they were created changed, and they became invalid.

This book is a technology, no more and no less. Our intentions will be realized if it enriches the production of environmental design. We request that no one use the rigor of this book to reduce the creative possibilities available in the environment. Our promise and intent is that it will not do this. Our further request is that you extend our work by using this book to expand your creative domain. We also request that you share with others the positive value you get from such work, as we have done.

William W. Caudill, FAIA, was a founding partner of the architectural firm of Caudill Rowlett Scott (CRS) in Houston, Texas. Well-known CRS buildings include the U.S. Embassy in Riyadh, Saudi Arabia. Mr. Caudill taught at Rice University and Texas A&M University. His publications include *Architecture by Team* and *Architecture and You*. Mr. Caudill died on June 25, 1983.

Joseph R. Loring is a mechanical engineer and principal of Joseph R. Loring & Associates in New York City. The firm's portfolio includes the World Trade Center and the Citicorp Building, both in New York City, and the Spanish Pavilion at the 1964 World's Fair. Mr. Loring has taught at Columbia University and the Massachusetts Institute of Technology.

Irwin G. Cantor is a structural engineer and heads his own firm in New York City. Among the firm's recent structural work is the design for the Trump Tower, currently the tallest reinforced concrete building in New York City. Mr. Cantor has coauthored several publications, including *Reshore and Preshore Procedures for Flat Plate Floors: Forming Economic Concrete Buildings*.

Photos: Andre Barbeau

John Pile is an interior designer and writer in New York City. He is Professor of Design at Pratt Institute in Brooklyn, and an independent consultant as well. His publications include *Modern Furniture*; *Interior Design: An Introduction to Architectural Interiors* (with Friedman and Wilson); *Drawing Interior Architecture*; *Open Office Planning*; and *Open Office Space*.

Chapter 2 Integration in Practice

This chapter presents the text of a roundtable discussion on building systems integration with a particular emphasis on examining implications and realities for integration in practice. Irwin Cantor, William Caudill, Joseph Loring, and John Pile, as spokesmen for the four major systems—structure, envelope, mechanical, and interior respectively—have identified a range of specific concerns that they have encountered in their years of experience.

Although the panelists agreed at the outset that integration as a design concept is a fundamental priority, it was immediately apparent that there were varying interpretations of the word "integration" as a design intention. A range of practical considerations evolved during the course of the discussion which will be amplified in the material on building types, theory, criteria, and products found in later chapters. The panelists also cited numerous built examples of integration, supplementing the case studies presented in Chapter 3.

The panelists briefly reviewed the motivations and forces for integration in the design professions and devoted considerable attention to identifying building types and systems where integration is critical. Some of the questions concerning the implications of integrated design that were addressed during the course of the roundtable included the following:

Are the levels of integration lower where the program is less demanding, for example, in churches as compared to laboratories or hospitals?

What types of buildings are especially appropriate for high levels of integration?

Why are office buildings good candidates for integration?

How is system efficiency affected by integration?

The panelists examined considerations such as the availability of products for integrated design; the role of energy in directing new approaches to integration; the ramifications of single- and multi-tenant occupancy for integration; and the problems that occur when efforts are made to technologically upgrade parts of integrated systems.

The panel discussion did not always produce a consensus; rather, there emerged a divergence of ideas and experiences that should help to put this book and its subject matter in perspective for the design professional regardless of informational discipline.

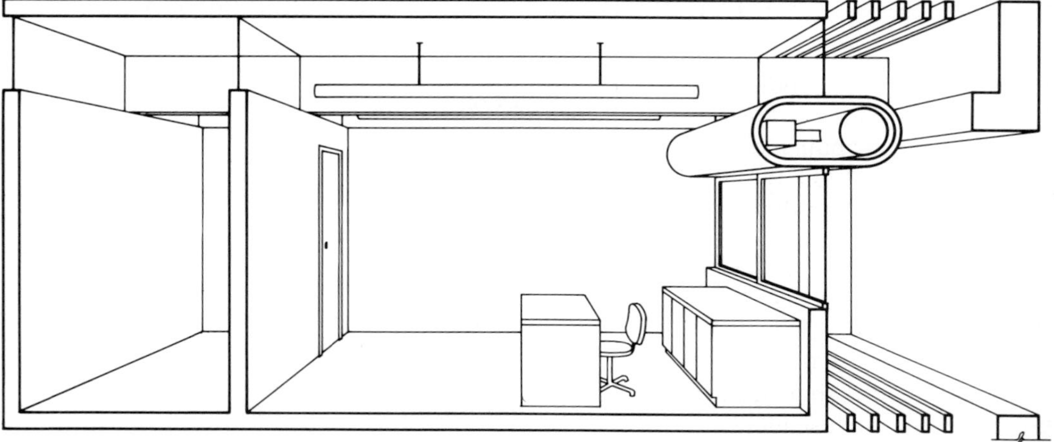

Integration opportunities can emerge from the earliest conception of the building form. The desire for maximum perimeter office space and energy conservation in the Shell Oil Building led to the design of its unique light shelf/window system for control of daylighting. Shell Oil Building, Houston, TX. Architects: CRS/Sirrine, Inc., Caudill Rowlett Scott Division.

INTEGRATION OPPORTUNITIES

RUSH: In your experience, are there certain building types more prone to a high level of integration?

CAUDILL: Integration is a design problem relating to all building types. The mechanical system of a building, for example, more often than not goes counter to the structural system. They work against each other physically and esthetically. This is a challenge to the creative architect who looks upon the problems as an opportunity for integrated design. He or she knows that the design problem might well lead to a solution whereby the mechanical system and the structural system may end up having a symbiotic relationship—that the skillful integration of systems can produce new, fresh architectural form. In short, systems are form-givers.

RUSH: How do you recognize a system or a building that is highly prone to integration?

LORING: In some buildings the design concept mandates systems integration. However, the age-old question applies here: which comes first, the chicken or the egg—the building concept or systems integration? We believe that the building form comes first—this sets the stage for the extent to which systems integration is either feasible or desirable. In our experience we have rarely been invited to participate in the initial conceptual configuration of a project. The program generally strongly influences the configuration. The resulting design, which usually incorporates a structural concept, will also begin to suggest to the mechanical/electrical engineer the opportunities for systems integration.

CAUDILL: The fault lies in the process. You should have been involved in the design process during the conceptual stage.

CANTOR: Many years ago, especially, the architect would draw "his pictures" and then call the structural engineer. I think what you're really approaching here isn't the creation of integrated systems but the emphasis upon the need for an integrated system. The various disciplines must be working together from inception. We're not talking about anything new. I think it's a matter of putting it in perspective so that everybody recognizes that we're part of a team.

RUSH: So the team concept is absolutely necessary to a high level of integration?

CANTOR: It took us a number of years to convince clients that they would pay us the same fee if they brought us in during the conceptual phase of the job as they would if they brought us in after all their sketches were completed. And the more involved the structure is, particularly in taller buildings where structure is such an integral portion of the architecture, the more important it is for the engineer to be "brilliant" right up front.

RUSH: What about building size? Obviously the smaller the building the smaller the budget; sometimes it has to be designed more quickly and built more quickly. A project like the Shell Oil Building, which is a fairly integrated building, used mock-ups and people living in model spaces, working in these spaces to see how they perform; that's a lengthy process. I have a friend in Pittsburgh and at one time, I think, he said he had designed 1,300 buildings. If a building takes him more than a week to design, he's probably going to lose money on it. He does banks, you know, shopping-center-type things.

CAUDILL: This sounds like the architect who designed one bank and repeated it 200 times—with slight modifications. That's dilution of services. We should not waste our time at this low level. Let's keep integrated design on a creative plane.

RUSH: Are we saying that integration *per se* is good?

CAUDILL: Architectural design *is* integration of systems, contrary to the popular belief of the press that architecture is some kind of sauce architects pour over buildings to give them historic flavor.

BUILDING TYPES

RUSH: In our research, when we were looking for integration potential in buildings, we found lots of highly integrated office buildings.[1] We found a fair number of museums. We found very few housing projects, very few libraries, but quite a few campus-type buildings that were integrated to this degree. Maybe it's because an office building is so simple inside. It doesn't make as many demands on the interior. We had to limit the number of office buildings and stretch to find a housing project.

LORING: I believe this is because an office building has the most open program, especially in the case where the building is being designed for multiple tenant occupancy, and the requirements of the future tenants are unknown. In these cases, architects have great flexibility. Depending upon the location and size of the site, and a design configuration to encourage system integration, virtually all tenant layouts can generally be accommodated to pre-established disciplines such as modules, column spacing, floor system spacing, and the like. A laboratory building or library, on the other hand, has a very rigid program which dictates, to a great extent, the direction of the architecture.

RUSH: So the degree of integration would be less where the program is very demanding?

LORING: The buildings which, in our practice, are most fully integrated are almost invariably office buildings, for the reasons previously mentioned.

CANTOR: If an element at one time serves as a structural element and as a raceway for mechanical or electrical[2] (or a floor system incorporating air supply which is serving two trades simultaneously), that would impress me as fully integrated.

LORING: The two examples that you mentioned, electrified floors and floors incorporating air, are diminishing in our practice. We find that electrified cellular floor systems, while they are great during their early periods of use, after ten or more years the telephone cells can be clogged with cabling which is no longer being used. The flexibility of the system can be greatly diminished. We have found that poke-through wiring systems, even with the restrictions imposed by the new fire codes, appear to be a viable alternative, especially in combination with open office landscape layouts. It appears that we're getting away from some forms of integration, or what used to be considered integration.

CANTOR: We are finding particularly in the downtown areas, now, the owners are recog-

1. Office building examples in this book include Aid Association for Lutherans, pp. 62–63, Georgia Power, pp. 86–89, National Permanent, pp. 90–91, Occidental Chemical, pp. 94–97, and Equitable Life, pp. 102–105.

2. Structural/Electrified Floors, pp. 207–208.

3. Access Floors, pp. 202–204.

nizing that very problem, but they are approaching it by raised access floors[3] rather than going back to poke-through.

CAUDILL: Spaces below floors are essential to flexibility if wires are still to be used in the future. A wireless building may be an eventuality. However, as it stands today, some spaces below floors are being gradually filled up with wires that are not being used. The telephone company rarely removes the unused lines. It just adds new ones. We have some buildings where raceways are so full of useless wires there is no room for new lines.

A TEAM OF SYSTEMS

CAUDILL: Design is a team endeavor. We're all partners in the design process. We? Architects, structural engineers, mechanical engineers, electrical engineers, acousticians, estimators—you name it. But I must add the users. The users should be considered part of the team. Buildings are becoming so complex that it takes a team of specialists to design them. The team is the new genius. Members of the team must be committed to the notion that "together we can do a better job than we can separately." Empathy should prevail. The design team's prime goal must be to search and find *appropriateness*—total solution, if you prefer. A well-balanced team assures appropriateness and quality of integrated design. A successful building results when the various systems respect each other, have that empathy, and work together to do a better job as a team of systems. It's believing in the concept of $1+1+1+1 = 5$.

An example of the team of systems concept can be found in the CRS Office Building in Houston. It's an economical, parking garage building type with precast concrete double T's spaced 40 ft on centers. Why 40 ft? It was the mechanical system telling the structural system that the appropriate span should be 40 ft. Fifty feet would have been more economical for structure alone, but for the total cost and overall architectural effect the 40 ft spacing performed more efficiently and economically. The reason is simple. We can shoot air 20 ft from each end of the 40 ft double T beams without ductwork. The double T's were chosen primarily to create an economical lighting system where the concrete T's served as lighting coffers. The result is a very wonderful architectural effect without contrived decoration. It's $1+1+1+1 = 5$.

RUSH: We should discuss the whole question of whether the interior designer and a mechanical engineer are sitting in your office or whether you farm out for services. That situation creates an integrated concept of design in the sense that it all takes place in the same office.

CAUDILL: I don't think it makes a difference where they live or what firm they belong to, just so they're together. To me, a building requires a partnership of many specialists. Obviously there must be a project design concept from the very beginning. This means the different disciplines, structure, mechanical and so forth, should be there and involved in the derivation of that concept.

RUSH: Joe, do you agree with that? Would you like to work in his office rather than being in your own office?

LORING: I don't think it makes a difference. As a matter of fact, we are fighting this concept, in a sense, because we compete against the so-called full-services or integrated services firms from time to time. Many corporations, particularly pharmaceutical firms, have been using full services firms for years, and only recently have begun to retain A/E teams comprised of individual, independent entities—the principle being, deal with the devil you know rather than the devil you don't know.

RUSH: It seems to me one clear way to get integration in a building is to have the individual sitting there eight hours a day.

LORING: Before we moved to our new offices, we were in a building with our offices split between the 26th and 28th floors. I would often comment, only partially in jest, that I got to Philadelphia more frequently than our offices on the 28th floor. In my judgment, if a full-services firm has a two-floor or multiple-floor operation, they may as well be in separate cities.

PILE: At the other extreme, however, I think that some of the absurdities of the world of interior design result from a lack of this kind of communication. So when you find a floor in the Seagram Building that's been done with Georgian paneling or something like that, you feel that it is a monumental absurdity which clearly is because there was no contact between people.

CAUDILL: When we go after a job we always think that there will be perfect integration. But we have used outside consultants if we go beyond our competence.

CANTOR: I started in this business working for an A/E, and the general attitude over there among the E's was, "What the hell, the A's want it and we'll give them whatever they want."

RUSH: I think that's a very good point. The independent specialist has an ability to defend the interests of a specialty intelligently, not in opposition but with good reason, whereas the captive specialist constantly thinks about the fact that he or she is captive, and the answers to the questions have to be the expected answers rather than the true answers.

CANTOR: In the New York area generally the architects and engineers have separate offices and they each run their own operations. I think that there's really a tremendous opportunity that exists when everybody is separate. There's really, to use an old word, a cross-fertilization of ideas.

Joe will work with seven different owners and twelve different architects and so will I, and so will everybody else. We pick up ideas and bits and pieces from different clients. You can walk into client A and say, "This is what I did with client B and client C." Somehow, in those integrated offices, total services offices, they don't seem to have that opportunity to learn from the outside.

One of the first tall glass and steel towers, the Seagram Building was presented with integration issues on the interior and exterior. Georgian paneling inside was perhaps as cacophonous as the sleek glass and steel facade outside was to its neighbors of the era. Seagram Building, New York, NY. Architects: Mies van der Rohe and Philip Johnson. Photograph: Johnson/Burgee Architects.

RUSH: Who is responsible for controlling the level of integration?

LORING: The architect controls, ultimately, either the degree of innovativeness or the level of integration.

CAUDILL: If you wish, let the architect be the team captain—as a coordinator of the design team, but I contend that a team of specialists is required to develop the "team of systems" that is necessary in successful buildings.

Tall buildings, such as the John Hancock Center in Chicago (right) and the Citicorp Center in New York (far right), require that structure and envelope be closely integrated. The cross bracing is visible on the facade of John Hancock and hidden in the Citicorp Center. These solutions in turn suggested opportunities for mechanical and interior integration. John Hancock Center, Chicago, IL. Architects: Skidmore, Owings & Merrill. Photograph: ESTO. Citicorp Center, New York, NY. Architects: Hugh Stubbins and Associates, Inc. Photograph: Edward Jacoby.

DEFINING INTEGRATION

RUSH: How do we get the varying degrees of content? There are certain buildings that you can point to and say, "That's a well-integrated building." There are other buildings you can point to and say, "That's a building where the designers never got together." With the Hancock Building or Citicorp, almost everywhere you look there's been sensitivity to integration. What's the difference in the design approach of those buildings? Why do some have high levels of integration, maybe even with the same problem?

CAUDILL: This depends upon your definition of integration. Does integration mean that all systems should be hidden from view? Or does it mean a building where the systems are overtly expressed visually[4] within its own "system" of esthetics? The former notion is exemplified in CRS's Olin Hall of Science, Colorado College, an exoskeletal design. The bones and guts are in the skin like a grasshopper's. The latter notion of integration would be CRS's Fodrea Elementary School, Columbus, Indiana. All the bones and guts show.

PILE: I think there's a clarification we need to make. It seems to me that integration could be used as a term to refer to physical integration, and there is something else that you could call theoretical or conceptual integration. I take it we're at least all in favor of conceptual integration. So far, everybody seems to be in favor of it.

Whether or not one is in favor of physical integration seems to me to be more involved in questions of building type and use and so forth, because I think there are many situations where you can question the merit of physical integration.

4. Visible integration is discussed on pp. 381–385. Note that visual integration and visible integration are not interchangeable; and that the concept of visible integration as it evolved later in this book differs from the discussion here. The context remains the same.

RUSH: Perhaps we need an example to clarify the difference between physical and conceptual integration.[5] Take an office building with an exposed concrete frame. The mechanical engineer says he wants the spandrel beam lowered to 7 ft 6 in. to reduce window heat gain. The interior designer says why not make it 7 ft 0 in., like the doors? The structural engineer says if the beam is that deep he can use it to take wind load instead of using shearwalls. The builder says that will speed up construction. The mechanical engineer asks what is to be done about heat loss through the concrete. The architect suggests pulling the window back to the plane of insulation on the back side of the wall, which will give us a shadow as well as a continuous thermal break. This is an example of conceptual integration.

CANTOR: What's the difference between integration and coordination if we're trying to establish that? In Mies van der Rohe's work, everything is hidden in the floor; what you really do is either coordinate or integrate everything.

RUSH: Well, one of the distinctions that we've come up with is that systems can be coordinated while remaining separate, independent systems. You have integration in the sense that if you start taking something away from the mechanical, you're already changing structural systems and the interior of the building.

LORING: As I reviewed the reference material that was sent to me to prepare for this panel, I realized that the new energy-efficient building facades, coupled with the dramatic reduction in lighting levels, have rendered many of the original integrated systems obsolete. The heat-of-light system, for example, one of the truly integrated systems, is no longer viable. There is not enough heat obtainable from the lighting to make the system work. The air-floor system has also all but disappeared due to the high static pressures and energy inefficiency of these systems.

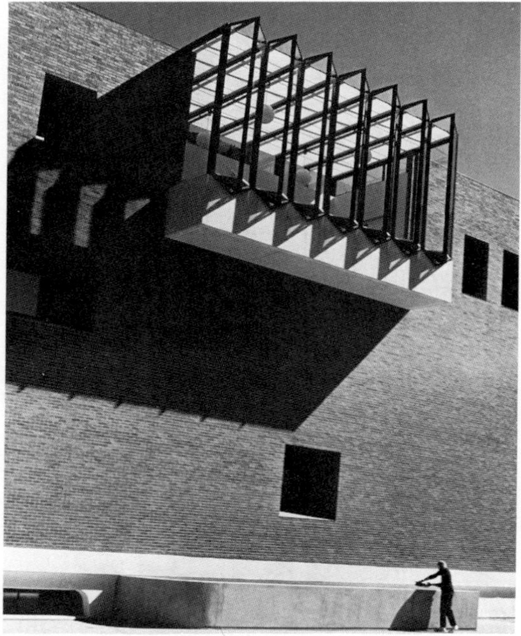

The Olin Hall of Science (left) conceals its structural and mechanical systems within its envelope system. A quite different view of integration is evident in the Fodrea Community School (below left), where exposed structural and mechanical systems become visual design elements. Olin Hall of Science, Colorado Springs, CO. Architects: CRS/Sirrine, Inc., Caudill Rowlett Scott Division. Photographer: Ron Partridge. Fodrea Community School, Columbus, IN. Architects: CRS/Sirrine, Inc., Caudill Rowlett Scott Division. Photograph: Balthazar Korab.

Other basic design changes have taken place. The energy efficiency or thermal opaqueness of the new facades have all but eliminated perimeter systems utilizing induction units, and in many cases fan coil

5. The hierarchy of five levels of integration that is central to this book resulted in part from the distinction made here between physical and conceptual integration.

units cannot be justified. The potential for systems integration, and its direction, is changing.

LEVELS OF INTEGRATION

PILE: I wonder if we don't have to accept a rather complicated definition? On the way to this meeting, doing my homework, I tried as many as five levels of physical integration, and maybe there are ten kinds arranged in a hierarchy.[6] Unification is what I think you were talking about where one thing does two things, maybe even does four things; an example would be a hollow column which is an air conditioning duct. At the opposite extreme is independence, where there's absolutely no physical relationship—for example, like a piece of furniture relative to the room it sits in.

6. Actual definitions of the five integration levels vary from what was discussed at the roundtable, although inspired by that series of questions and responses.

Between these extremes, from unity to independence, you could talk about a tight-fit relationship—the skin to the structure, for example. You could go to a loose-fit relationship, which would describe attached but interchangeable. Next could be relationships which we talked about before where all you're talking about is dimensional coordination or connection; and then finally independence, where you have no connection. All of those are types of integration, actually, even including independence.

RUSH: To exemplify the extreme of total integration you might use a natural force, the ocean or any natural organic system.

CAUDILL: Let's expand our thoughts to architecture that responds to nature. Classic examples are: the cliff dwellings, the teepees, and the igloos. That's my kind of architecture. With the technology we have at our disposal today, it's a shame that we can't recapture the principles of those energy-saving buildings. If so, we would have new forms and new esthetics that express the twentieth century.

RUSH: A total organic relationship is at one end of the integration spectrum.

CAUDILL: That may be perfection.

RUSH: The other extreme would be Manhattan at 8:30 in the morning in a traffic jam: a stream of vehicles that are totally unrelated. They do nothing but pollute each other. They're driven by people with independent destinations. When they're through with the car it goes to some place that has no living relationship to the system at all.

PILE: The only thing that makes me nervous about this is that I keep hearing the approach to unified integration as seen as "good" and separation, independence of systems, as being labeled "bad." And I'm not sure that's reliable. You already have talked about several instances where, if one of the elements becomes obsolete or inappropriate, it becomes hurtful to the unity. That's true for biological systems too. If your liver goes bad, you've gone bad, even though your heart and lungs may still be in good shape. Some of these can be replaced with spare parts, but the ones that can't be replaced with spare parts lead to fatal breakdown. That's true of buildings too. If the heating system becomes obsolete, if it's easy to come back in and put in a new heating system, your building has another 40 years of life ahead of it.

RUSH: That calls to mind something I've discovered with my little boy when I play blocks with him. He likes to build a tower using all of the blocks until it's about five feet high and he comes up and whap, he destroys it. He loves it. When we build a zoo, we build a horizontal structure that's really all over the floor and he can't knock it down at one swipe. He can wipe out the gorilla cage or the lions' area but he leaves some part still standing.

When we build systems that support each other to such a high degree that knocking down one system destroys the whole, we introduce a certain risk.

CAUDILL: Is this the danger of integration?

PILE: I think that's one of the problems we certainly need to look at.

CAUDILL: What about integration in respect to the time element? What about the qualities of flexibility, versatility, and changeability?

RUSH: The degree of integration affects those qualities. Timeliness is also critical to the book. Information itself is changeable. Any information that's living can't be permanently contained in a book. It can be contained in a series of books, but no single book can contain living information that's changing. We'll be stuck with the state-of-the-art technology that we have by the time we write the book. Ten years from now, or maybe even in five years, we're going to write another one that may be computerized on the current state-of-the-art technology.

Let's take a look at incentives for integration. Each member of the building team wants the time invested in research or conceptualization to yield tangible value, in terms of both design and economics. The architect, after all, is looking for a return on the time he invests in the concept of the design. A speculative owner is looking for a direct payback on building design decisions. Different people are looking for different returns. The architect actually may be trying to economize on the structural engineer's time he may be paying for. What types of systems are most easily combined? Can you provide an example of high returns for the extra time that might be required for more conscious effort to integrate?

LORING: The original pressure to integrate, I believe, stems from a desire to reduce the cost of structures by compressing the cube.[7] In the case of a highrise building of, say, 30 stories, the reduction of six inches per floor would buy another floor. This pressure resulted in the development of the light/air troffer, which is the first building element that I can recall as being integrated; namely combining lighting and air distribution in a single device. Then we began to talk about the floor/ceiling sandwich and the structure. Then mechanical engineers and structural engineers began to communicate.

OBSTACLES TO INTEGRATION

RUSH: There are a couple of obvious examples that have not yet been profitable. One is the use of potable sprinkler water; another is reusing gray water. There are systems where integration just doesn't frequently happen. Maybe the roofing system is a system that you'd avoid tampering with because the roof has got enough problems already. To go to the other extreme, what about compatible systems—lighting systems, furnishing systems, security systems? I know that in control systems the fire marshal would rather see the fire system completely independent.

LORING: And so would the people responsible for security.

RUSH: They want to keep their security system completely independent. The other situation that seems to be difficult is artificial illumination directly coordinated with photoelectric cells. I was in a building one day where it was necessary to close the blinds to turn on the light.

CAUDILL: Are you talking about opposites? Integration versus independence?

RUSH: Well, the fire and the security—they need to be independent because they need to work in a crisis situation. Are there other ones?

CAUDILL: I have this hang-up of insisting on visual order. The worst thing I can think of is a tacked-on sprinkler system that destroys visual integration. I think of integrated design as systems "dwelling together in unity," to quote from the Bible.

RUSH: What about the fact that, especially in older buildings, the interiors may undergo not only different tenants but different schemes completely? Could one say that, of the systems we're talking about, the least dependent of the four systems is interior?

PILE: The most tied-in of systems is the structural system, because if you remove that everything falls down, you have nothing. Skin would be the next level, because if

7. Conservation of space, p. 236.

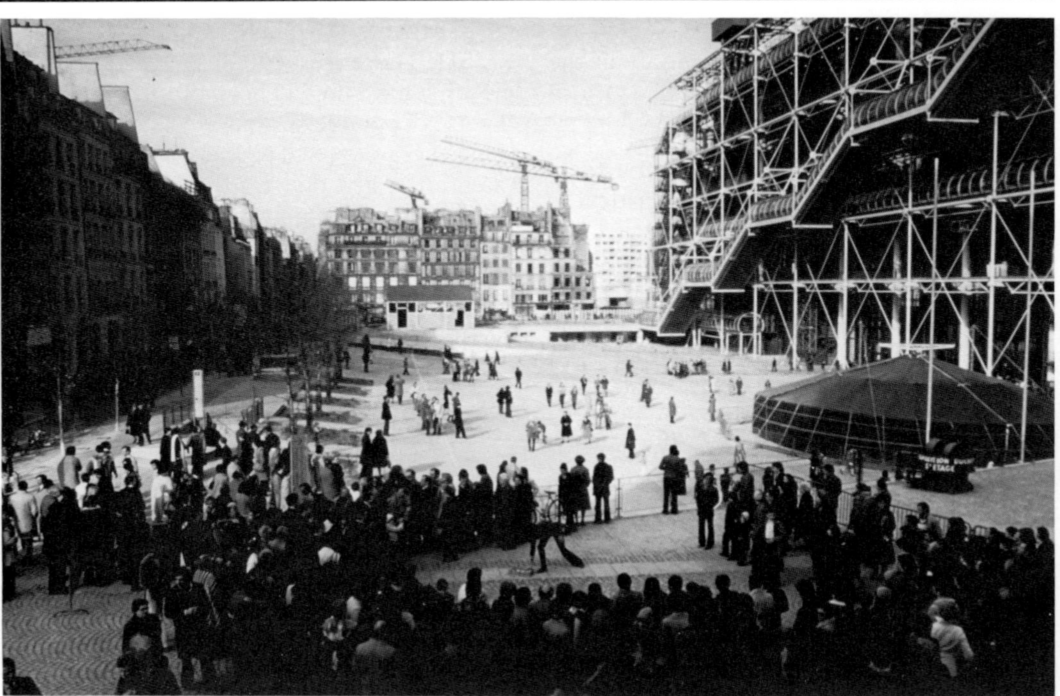

Centre Pompidou derives its esthetic from exposed structural and mechanical systems on both the exterior (right) and the interior (below right). The exterior circulation system and the water-filled trusses for fire protection are two examples of how the Centre integrates systems visually and functionally. Centre Pompidou, Paris, France. Architects: Piano and Rogers. Photograph: Tim Street-Porter.

you remove the skin you're not in a building anymore; you have a pavilion or something. Mechanical, electrical, etcetera becomes a third level and interior, as we usually understand it, becomes the fourth level. Interiors are certainly dependent on the others but least supportive of the others, because you can take out the furniture without the building falling down and without upsetting the plumbing.

RUSH: We were talking about building types before. If you're building the Cathedral of San Francisco, it is a building type that no one is going to come in at some time and transform into an office building. We rejected buildings like monuments, cathedrals, and national galleries for this book because of their uniqueness, both in geometry and in purpose. We think of these buildings and their uses as being "forever." We are less likely to talk about flexibility and things of that nature.[8]

8. Permanence versus flexibility, pp. 237–239.

I used to live in Pittsburgh and remember distinctly one day walking by the site of a huge church the day after it had been demolished. It was about 85 years old and had been for sale for about a year and a half. No further use was found for it. I guess the stigma of having office space or a bar—whatever—in a church was just too much. That says something fundamental about building use and building type in relationship to these systems.

What buildings, historic or otherwise, do you think of when you think of systems being appropriately integrated?

CAUDILL: The first building that comes to mind is the Centre Pompidou. You see structure; you see mechanical; you see the elec-

Nassau Community College is based on a structural system of precast cruciform columns and ledger beams that accept slabs, T's, or double T's. This structural system also serves to coordinate the mechanical, electrical, and lighting systems. Nassau Community College, Garden City, NY. Architects: The Eggers Group P.C., Architects and Planners. Photograph: Otto Baitz.

trical system; you see everything all in one. That's overt integration. That is the esthetic system. That is the architecture.

RUSH: Well, in addition to seeing it, though, you have the water—the fire protection system—in the trusses.

CAUDILL: That's an intellectual thing, not a visual thing.

PILE: I think we have to be careful not to define integration so narrowly as to favor one of these directions. Pompidou is integrated in esthetic ways; the parts are all on display. The more traditional esthetic, which I guess most of us tend to think of as integrated, has concealment as its goal. The structure is all hidden, the mechanical is all hidden, and you wish the walls could be hidden, in effect. That's another kind of integration.

RUSH: If you can't see the integration then it's probably not a building that we're going to choose for this book, because it can't be discussed easily.[9]

PILE: You could take the opposite point of view, that that's the very reason why it needs to be talked about and studied.

RUSH: If it is there. I think that's definitely an ideal. If the drawings reviewed do not express the integration in some way, showing a blowup of the structure, a blowup of the mechanical systems, a blowup of the interior systems, or whatever—we probably passed it over.

CAUDILL: It's an intellectual thing—something to talk about.

CANTOR: Nassau County Community College was a project on Long Island some years back by the Eggers partnership where they used precast cruciform columns. The ledge beams accepted either slabs, single T's, or double T's. The mechanical, the electrical, and the lighting system were all integrated into the structure. The buildings were also set up for growth and change. You could add classroom wings to them. That might be considered integrated structure insofar as the components are concerned.

9. Visible integration, pp. 381–407.

In the Spanish Pavilion at the 1964 New York World's Fair (right), lighting and air conditioning ducts hidden above the small wooden blocks of the decorative ceiling resulted in a formally and mechanically integrated ceiling and interior space. The building represents a classic example of tight physical integration that resists alteration or modification. In contrast, the Hyatt Regency Hotel in Macau (below right) demonstrates that tight physical integration need not be a problem if the entire unit is self-contained and functions as "one complete building block." Three hundred prefabricated guest rooms were shipped from the U.S. to Macau and installed in place in record time and at low cost. Spanish Pavilion, New York, NY. Architect: Javier Carvajal. Photograph: Ezra Stoller, ESTO. Hyatt Regency Hotel, Taipa Island, Macau. Architects: CRS/Sirrine, Inc., Caudill Rowlett Scott Division. Rendering: CRS/Sirrine, Inc., Caudill Rowlett Scott Division.

Like the Hyatt Regency's, the individual housing units of Habitat are based on the total integration concept of "one complete building block." The clear articulation of the boxlike components allows them to express their individuality. Habitat, Montreal, Canada. Architects: Moshe Safdie and Associates Inc. Photograph: Moshe Safdie and Associates Inc.

LORING: I don't know whether anyone remembers the Spanish Pavilion at the New York World's Fair. The building had an unusually decorative ceiling made of small wooden blocks with narrow spaces between each block. The ceiling was designed to function not only as a luminous ceiling but also as a pressurized air plenum. Lighting and air conditioning ducts were installed above the wooden ceiling. There were no visible air distribution devices. The result was a beautiful ceiling and a space with a minimum of general lighting and poor air distribution.

The display lights served to supplement the very low level of general lighting; the effect was what I called "well-distributed darkness." It was extremely effective, however, for display purposes, and it was an example of total integration. It was an incredibly beautiful space. The building was designed to be dismantled, and was ultimately taken down and rebuilt in St. Louis. While the systems were fully integrated they did not lend themselves to being dismantled and were ultimately discarded. I'm beginning to see integration, from this conversation, as something that is rather inflexible.

RUSH: If a building is designed to expand, and maybe even be moved someplace, it might be less prone to this unifying kind of total integration. Unless you can pick it up like the Habitat and take a whole house like a building block and transport it bodily.

CAUDILL: CRS's Hyatt Regency Hotel, located in the Portuguese colony of Macau, is a "building block and transport" system. The prefab concrete blocks were manufactured in Mobile, Alabama. Each block is a guest room, completely finished and furnished. Three hundred of these prefab rooms were packed in a huge freighter, then sailed through the Panama Canal, crossed the Pacific to Southern China, landed at Macau, and lifted and installed in place at the job site in record construction time. This system paid off in design quality and relatively low cost.

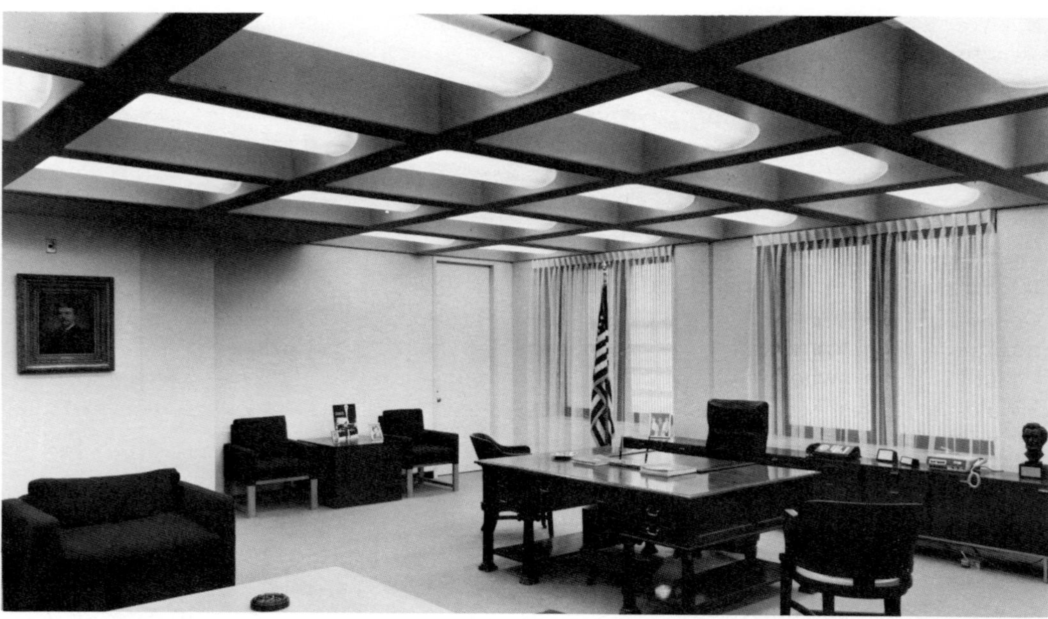

The New York City Police Headquarters Building was originally designed with an air plenum floor resting on an exposed concrete waffle slab. Due to construction union objections, the design was modified to include sheet metal ducts in the floor space. New York City Police Headquarters Building, New York, NY. Architects: The Gruzen Partnership. Photograph: David Hirsch.

LORING: Bill, if you tried to put that building up in Mobile, Alabama, they wouldn't let you. The construction unions would not permit it. You couldn't put that building up in any city in the United States. That's the problem with total integration.

CONSTRUCTION PROBLEMS

RUSH: What role does the construction methodology play — the contractor, the client, the set of building codes, and so forth?

LORING: The Police Headquarters Building in New York City is an example of where the construction methodology frustrated the integration process. The design concept was based upon an exposed concrete waffle slab with an air plenum floor above. The local sheet metal workers union indicated, unequivocally, that they would see to it that no mechanical contractor would bid the job. We ended up by putting sheet metal ducts in the floor space that was designed to be an air plenum.

RUSH: So from the standpoint of the codes, safety monitoring, and of the construction sequence of the building, a highly integrated concept is at a disadvantage. Who's going to build it and what code is responsible for it? And somebody might say, "Well, it says here on page 96 that you're not allowed to have ducts in there and I don't want to hear it."

The only philosophical approach proceeding in a more integrated direction is the performance specifications. In the case of a curtain wall, for example, you're likely to find the performance specifications. The people who want to do the job bid on it and in so doing assemble a group of products which is appropriate to the job. The actual detailing and the actual product selection and so forth are done by a contractor who actually gets the job done to the general esthetic criteria of the architect.

CANTOR: Who assumes responsibility for that assembly when it's in place?

RUSH: It's usually a consortium.

PILE: Everybody takes the responsibility as long as it works, and if it doesn't work nobody takes the responsibility.

CANTOR: Those curtain wall systems that you're talking about, essentially the first couple of steps go in the way you describe.[10] Ultimately, however, the owner is going to turn around to the architect and say, "Hey,

10. Glass and aluminum curtain wall, pp. 212–215.

it's your wall. You accepted it and your structural engineer accepted the curtain wall criteria and everything else." So it's a fine story, but it's not a consortium. It's one person that ultimately gets the responsibility. And it doesn't address the problem of union reactions to integrated systems.

THE MANUFACTURER'S ROLE

RUSH: What about the manufacturers? We can see that codes and so forth probably do not actively encourage integration. What about the people who are making products? Would they rather see an integrated system or individual pieces?

PILE: I think manufacturers in every field have a lot of ambivalence about this, in that they see making an extended system unique as a way of holding the business for themselves. At the same time they would like to sell their product to other people, so they have a certain incentive toward unification. You see all kinds of problems. For example, if the only tires you can put on your car are ones you buy from the car manufacturer, that seems good to that car manufacturer until he realizes he'd like to sell those tires for other people's cars. Then he begins to get interested in organizing a conference on dimensional standardization or something like that. And I think that goes on in endless cycles in business.

CANTOR: It creates a whole new series of problems. Once a system is integrated, it is probably proprietary. No architect is going to be in a position to design a proprietary system into a set of plans early in design. Certainly with governmental projects and even with a private client, we're not going to design a specific system into a building at the outset unless our client has come to an agreement with a certain vendor. Otherwise we've created a box. We're six months down the road, the plans are drawn, and now the price, the budget that the vendor gave our project manager of $6.50 a square foot, is raised to $9.95.

RUSH: Safety issues create similar problems. A manufacturer wants the product to be used as he intended, and that's the only acceptable way in terms of liability. The same is true with almost anything that affects people directly.

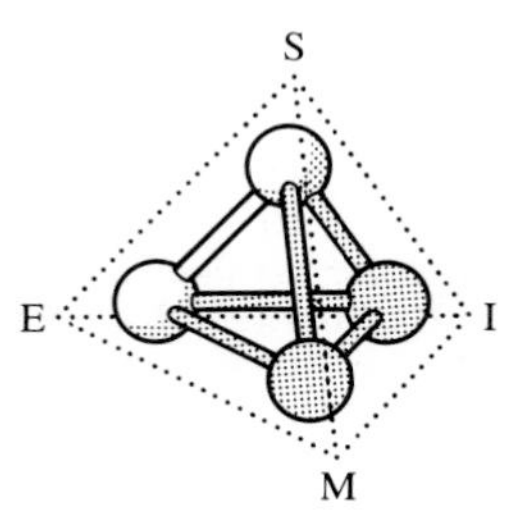

STRUCTURE PLUS ENVELOPE

RUSH: I would like to home in on integration possibilities one by one. What is the potential, for example, of structure and envelope?[11] Do you like to see a building where the structure and the envelope are well integrated, or would you rather that they let your structure alone and let you design as good a structure as you possibly can?

CANTOR: In a two- or three- or ten-story building, it doesn't really matter to me from a purely structural point of view whether the architect wants to make the exterior wall a functional wall or a work of art. However, once a building is going up 50, 60, 70 stories, we've got some trading to do.

There's really no reason that the structure and the architecture shouldn't work together on the exterior of any wall, because basically it's very easy to make the exterior wall serve a dual purpose as a bearing wall and as an enclosure wall. So in that case I would say let's talk for very high levels of integration.

In terms of actual structural need versus desirability, the need doesn't occur until the building gets tall enough to where I've got to take advantage of the perimeter of the building in one manner or another to resist wind and/or earthquake forces.

RUSH: So the more demanding structurally the building is, the more you would argue for integration of those disciplines.

CANTOR: Yes—but in certain respects, they're the easiest buildings in the world. At the other extreme, one of the most economical buildings to build is a one-story tilt-up building.[12] There's a perfect instance of integration of structural engineering, architecture, and to an extent mechanical in terms of insulation.

11. Structure and envelope combination, pp. 323–324.

12. Tilt-up wall, pp. 136–137.

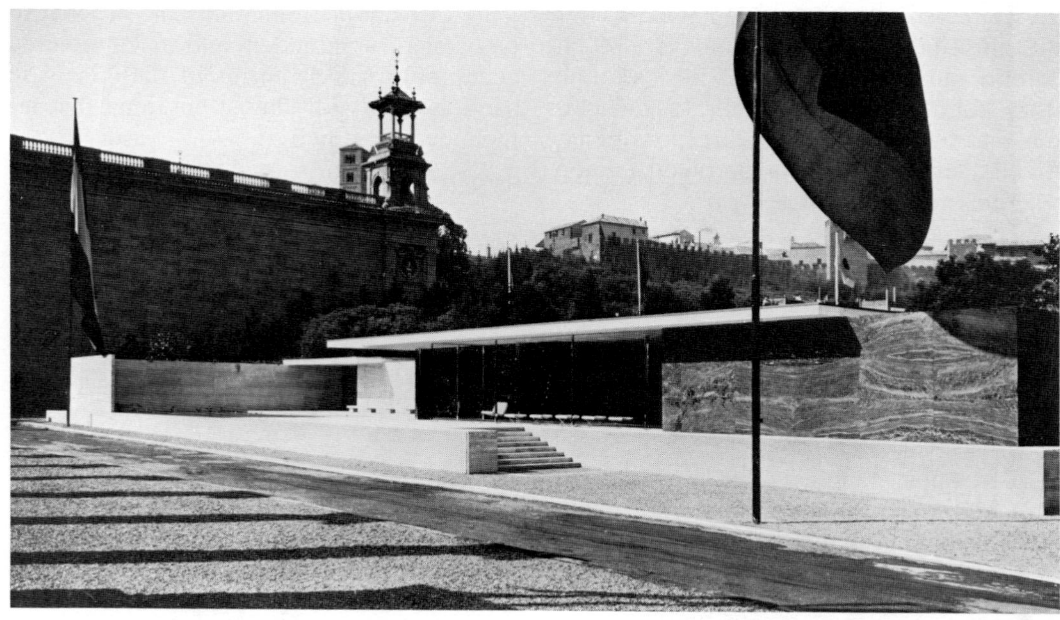

The freestanding walls and the floor and roof slabs of Mies van der Rohe's German Pavilion at the 1929 International Exposition in Barcelona exemplify architecture visually dominated by planar form. The structural module and spatial module are both coordinated with precise elevation proportions, geometrically integrating the building. German Pavilion, 1929 International Exposition, Barcelona, Spain. Architect: Mies van der Rohe. Photograph: Hedrich-Blessing.

PILE: It's almost as if the two extremes are where the integration is of the highest priority. In a balloon frame house there is total integration of skin and structure, and it comes on again as a big factor as the building gets tall.

CANTOR: What about the question of designing the envelope of the building? Do you want to be hamstrung with having it constrained by structural criteria? Some architects want a freedom of expression unfettered by structural considerations.

CAUDILL: From the beginning of our firm, it became clear we needed engineers as partners—not only to be available as we needed them, but to be involved in the conceptual design of every project. There were, and still are, good reasons for this. Structural design, mechanical design, electrical design, acoustical design—to name a few—are major form-givers that can make or break architectural form.

Let me give you a primer on architectural forms: One, there's *plastic* form. Plastic in this sense means sculpture. The accent is primarily on the skin. The bones and guts generally are covered up with some kind of fabric like brick, stone, panels, and glass. Two, there is *skeletal* form. The accent here is showing off the structural frame or bones. The frame is the main thing esthetically. Three, there is *planar* form—an architecture of planes, if you please. Mies' Barcelona Pavilion is a classic example. One type is no better than another; however, if you insist on hiding the structural and the mechanical elements, which is an easy way out, plastic form is used predominantly.[13]

13. Mr. Caudill's definitions of form were not applied to the book's system of categorizing integration levels and types.

RUSH: Why haven't we seen any exposed cross bracing since the Hancock Building and the Maritime Building in San Francisco?

CANTOR: Well, those things take out windows from high-priced exterior offices. There is a new one at 780 Third Avenue in Manhattan where every other window is omitted. Okay, it's going to be 50 some-odd stories. Somebody made a concession.

With Citicorp, for example, the structure is dominating. They're getting away with it because, if you've been in Citicorp, it's a huge, open floor. But take that space and divide it into 10- or 20-foot offices and somebody's going to be looking at the window wall.

Exposed cross bracing in the Alcoa Building (far left) presents a clear example of structure visibly integrated with envelope. The exposed cross bracing in the 780 Third Avenue office building (left) illustrates the sort of trade-off that can occur when building systems are integrated. In this case, the bracing eliminated numerous window locations in the envelope. Alcoa Building at One Maritime Plaza, San Francisco, CA. Architects: Skidmore, Owings & Merrill. Photograph: Morley Baer. 780 Third Avenue, New York, NY. Architects: Skidmore, Owings & Merrill. Rendering: Skidmore, Owings & Merrill.

CAUDILL: When CRS was a baby firm, we designed a small house for one of the chemistry professors at Texas A&M. We designed a second-story bedroom on stilts with a sheltered terrace underneath. The problem was, the bedroom vibrated when someone heavy walked across it. It was strong enough; it just wiggled. I spent a long weekend on the job (it was about 85 percent complete), eating aspirins, thinking up ways to take out the wiggle without ruining the predetermined architectural effect. What would I say to the client who knew what his house should look like? Would he raise hell when I told him that he would have to live with ugly steel cross bracing, which goes counter to the clean, cubistic lines as planned? I learned a great lesson from that experience. Sure, I learned something about vibrations in structures, but that's not the one I'm talking about. The great lesson was twofold: one, don't underestimate the client's appreciation for form and space; and two, to some people the structure can fulfill certain intellectual needs and should be considered as an esthetic element, even decoration. My client said, "Bill, the cross bracing might enhance the beauty of the house." Then he added a real bomb. "Did you consider tying it down with guy wires as in circus tents?" He had an innovative sense of esthetics relating to structures.

CANTOR: Our discipline gets less important in terms of holding up the building as the building gets smaller. Its importance returns in terms of trying to respond to an esthetic requirement. An architect may want the

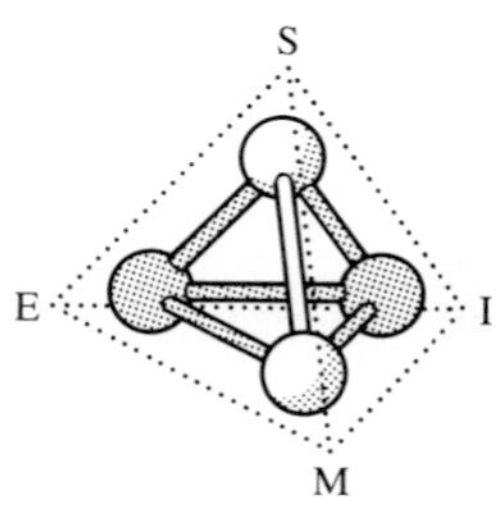

Combining columns and ducts on the building facade has long been a common method of integrating structural and mechanical systems. The Blue Cross/Blue Shield Building (top right) employs alternating columns and mechanical risers. Louis Sullivan used exposed columns and ducts on the Wainwright Building (right) in 1890. Blue Cross/Blue Shield Building, Boston, MA. Architect: Paul Rudolph, Architect. Photograph: Fred Stone. Wainwright Building, St. Louis, MO. Architect: Louis Sullivan. Photograph: Hastings Chivetta.

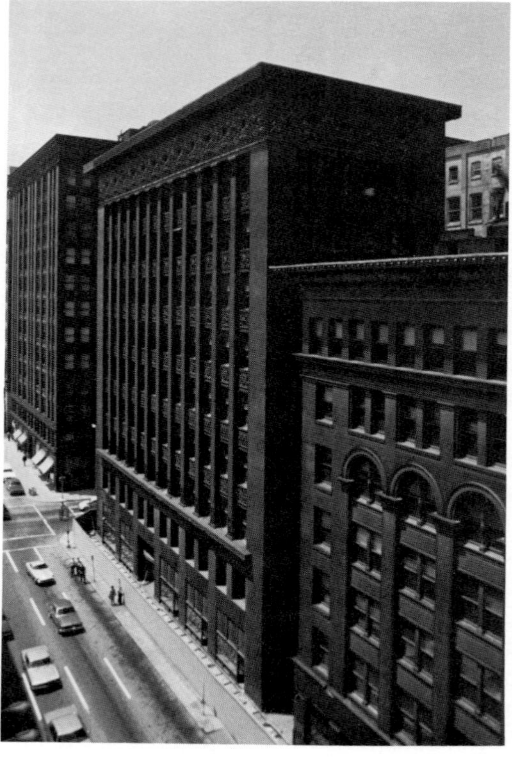

14. Structure and mechanical combination, pp. 324–325.

structural engineer to do some gymnastics. But fundamentally what you said is correct: on a lower-rise building the structural engineer just would fit it in.

STRUCTURE PLUS MECHANICAL

RUSH: What about structure and mechanical?[14] That's the next integration type. The one I think of most often in this area is the Blue Cross-Blue Shield Building in Boston, where every other column is a duct on the outside of the building. The difference isn't apparent until you look down the building and they're coming together at the base of the facade. The Blue Cross-Blue Shield system of alternate mechanical risers was used by I.M. Pei on the Mile-High Center in Denver in a clearer and more subtle expression. It was also used by Louis Sullivan in the Wainwright Building.

LORING: I think that that has historical interest only. No one is doing that anymore, because it implies high velocity, high static pressure, high horsepower systems—which are not energy-efficient.

RUSH: All right. What about water-filled columns?

CANTOR: The only water-filled columns I know about are U.S. Steel in Pittsburgh, I think, and there's one other that came to mind.

RUSH: Consider the columns in the Mercantile Bank Building in Kansas City, and also the trusses in the Centre Pompidou.

CANTOR: I don't know if it has a good monetary bottom line for the client.

RUSH: Do you have that same problem of domain, territoriality?

CANTOR: No, no. A column built with water in it is instantly a perimeter column. The water will supply the fire rating and hopefully Joe Loring will find use for it at the same time. Obviously it has no structural advantage.

RUSH: What are the differences in attitude

Variations on the concept of structural and mechanical integration involving columns and exterior ducts are seen in the U.S. Steel Building (far left) and the Mercantile Bank Building (left), where water-filled columns provide both structure and fire protection. In Centre Pompidou, water-filled trusses perform the same function. U.S. Steel Building, Pittsburgh, PA. Architects: Harrison, Abromovitz and Abbe. Photograph: Harrison, Abromovitz and Abbe. Mercantile Bank Building, Kansas City, MO. Architects: Harry Weese & Associates. Photograph: Hedrich-Blessing.

by building type? A few years ago when laboratories were discussed, ductwork in channel beams was the solution.

LORING: As we see it, the most advantageous type of structural system for a laboratory building today is the flat slab, if it can be justified. If the laboratory contains highly sensitive equipment which requires a vibration-free structure, the structural engineer may be forced into closer column spacing, thicker slabs, and ribbed flooring to effect a more rigid structure. Since the mission of a laboratory may change dramatically, the integrated elements may also have to be modified or removed. We see cube, in the form of higher floor-to-floor heights, as the most important element that provides for future changes in the laboratories.

In other building types there are different attitudes. In the case of hotels, major hotel operators know exactly what they want structurally, mechanically, and electrically. On a hotel project for owners such as Marriott or Hilton, the design criteria are very specific, affording very few design options. They've got their own staff of architects and engineers. Moreover, they've done it thousands of times and they know exactly what they want.

STRUCTURE PLUS INTERIOR

RUSH: How often does the structural engineer talk to the interior designer?[15]

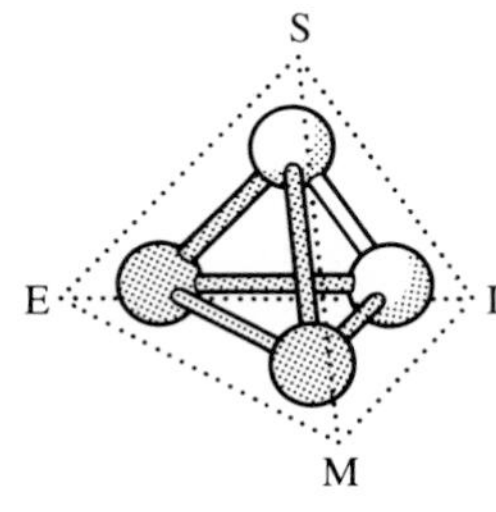

CANTOR: The day that an architect decides to go ahead, that's the day I'm behind schedule. And the interior design groups are those that really require time to think through a project. We haven't had time to negotiate with them. We're busy coming to agreement as to where the columns are going, where the beams are going, and where the job is going.

If you will, the biggest problems that we've run into were the interior design peo-

15. Structure and interior combination, pp. 325–327.

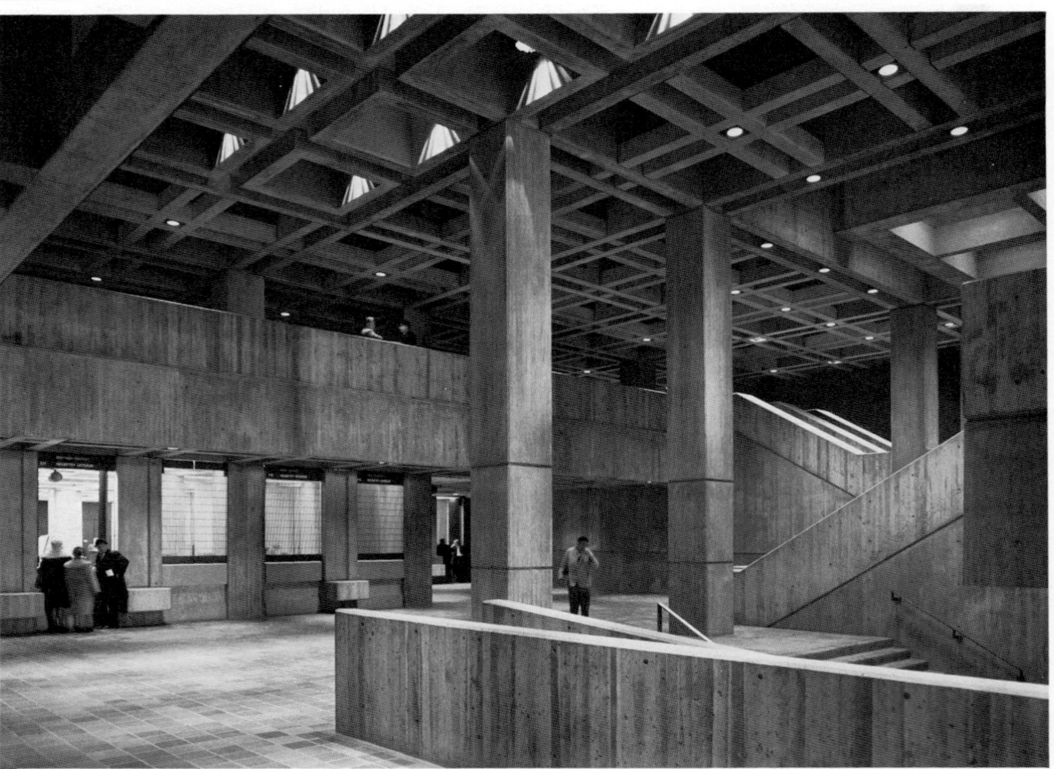

Exposed precast concrete ceilings and columns formally define the interior esthetic of Boston City Hall. Interior circulation elements and countertops are also precast concrete. Boston City Hall, Boston, MA. Architects: Kallman, McKinnell & Wood, Architects. Photograph: Cervin Robinson.

ple (timing-wise, not personality-wise). In hotel work, the owner is in a big rush to get the job done, and will oftentimes bring the interior designer on late in the process or else the designer will be massaging the interior—each time requiring structural change, but in the meantime the structure's going up.

RUSH: What about the fact that a building, until it's bid, can be either steel or concrete? It's hard for an interior designer to come in and say, "Well, do you want me to do two different systems?"

CANTOR: It's interesting that you asked that question. The situation in several cities, in New York particularly, is such that two similar buildings can be bought within a month of each other, one steel and one concrete. The idea of alternates is one that we've been pressing clients to consider. Invest in alternates. We have an office building right now that was engineered in structural steel. For reasons best known to the owner, he wants the entire configuration of the building changed and, because of setback requirements, the best approach to the revised project is reinforced concrete.

LORING: It's going to make a tremendous difference to us from a design standpoint, however.

CANTOR: No question about it, Joe. We did a job in steel with a 12 ft 4 in. story height. The owner came back and said, "Let's try the concrete building." We got it down to 11 ft, changed the number of floors, and everything changed.

RUSH: The classic example of the structure/interior thing that I can think of is Boston City Hall. You have concrete countertops and light soffits. Everything is precast concrete.

PILE: Well, you have to admit that the classic buildings are generally exceptional cases, in that the interior is so tightly inte-

In addition to their striking presence as interior elements, the structural mushroom-cap columns of the Johnson Wax Administration Center provide placement of the top-lit lighting system for the vast open office space. Johnson Wax Administration Center, Racine, WI. Architect: Frank Lloyd Wright. Photograph: Johnson Wax.

grated with the design of the building. The Johnson's Wax Office Building—you can't imagine what an interior designer would do to that.

CANTOR: Boston City Hall is a one-tenant building. I don't know whether the interiors were bought at the same time as the rest of the job or not, but you're talking about different kinds of things now. Museum buildings are also one-tenant buildings.

ENVELOPE PLUS INTERIOR

RUSH: Let's discuss envelope and interior. When one stops performing, the other one starts performing. If you provide shading devices on the envelope of your building—exterior shading devices—maybe the blind system can be eliminated. Or, obviously, if you don't provide the windows you don't have the problem of the carpet fading. There is an interchange. What are the opportunities for coordination? Let's assume it's an owner-tenant building.

PILE: Well, in the case of owner-occupied buildings, things like the basic dimensional coordination become an issue. The window module is a control on the size of the spaces that can be conveniently partitioned. Given a module in a pre-planned building, the interior design has to adjust to it for better or worse. Sometimes it's somewhat for the worse, where the partitions meet up with a perimeter wall in an awkward way. We expect very good control of heat, cold, and glare at the envelope. Glare becomes somewhat less of an issue because interior controls are readily available and easy to use.

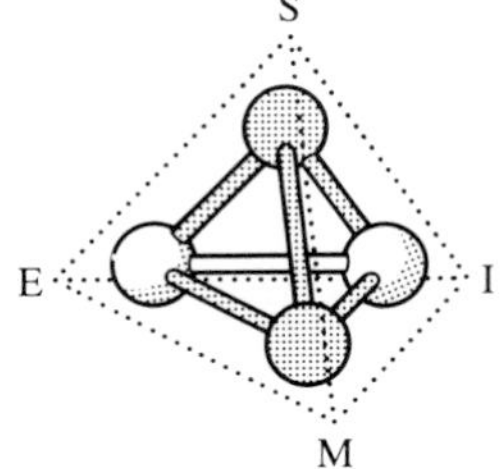

RUSH: What about the Shell Oil Building, Bill? Obviously you couldn't design the light shelf halfway through the design. Somebody very early in the design said, "Okay, we're going to use natural daylighting to best advantage."

CAUDILL: In Shell Oil, daylighting was a programmatic concept that emerged before

Integration of envelope and interior systems is clearly visible in the CBS Building, where a 5 ft interior module governed the placement of windows in the curtain wall. The structure is also integrated with the interior; square columns placed on a diagonal change dimension in the upper floors, until the column itself is cut in half diagonally. CBS Building, New York, NY. Architects: Eero Saarinen and Associates. Photograph: CBS.

any sketches were made. Five hundred offices, by demand and by programmatic concern, required windows. This is no speculative office building. This project was designed for the specific functions of the corporation.

I usually think of buildings as being either "flex" buildings or "fix" buildings. A flex building allows the function to change without much trouble and cost, but a fix building, like a church, like a science lab, like a concert hall, has no innate quality of flexibility. Now we're trying to get our fix buildings to flex. That's hard to do. Interior change is costly.

RUSH: To the interior designer, daylighting introduces a whole realm of problems in addition to solutions. The relationship, I gather, is often that of the envelope being designed while the interior compensates.

CAUDILL: Not on complex buildings. On simple office buildings.

PILE: Even in simple office buildings, the interior design profession is always trying to make a case for the idea that the module, for instance, should be controlled by interior considerations. Everyone admires the CBS Building, for example, saying "Isn't this remarkable—they started with a 5 ft module, developed out of the interior of an office, and built the building to suit." But those are rare cases, and the interior design profession, I think, is getting adjusted to making do.

RUSH: In the case of the Shell Building, Bill, did you have an interior designer in the room when you were designing?

CAUDILL: We are all interior designers—architects, mechanical engineers, lighting engineers, structural engineers, as well as specialists in color, fabrics, and furnishings. Yes, we made test models for daylighting and a full size mock-up of a typical office to test daylighting performance. Later the mock-up was used to test fabrics, color, and furniture.

RUSH: So there was someone saying, "Hey, the carpet's going to fade," at the same time as another person was saying, "Well, have you got enough light?"

CAUDILL: I think also you have to recognize that the role of an interior designer in some of these special purpose buildings is

Perimeter mechanical systems are often integrated with the building envelope. In the Manufacturer's Hanover Building, fan coil units penetrate the skin, enabling the building to use reclaimed and stored heat. Manufacturer's Hanover Building, New York, NY. Architects: Skidmore, Owings & Merrill. Photograph: Ezra Stoller, ESTO.

often small. When you're talking about a concert hall or a church you don't often think about who was the interior designer of the church. The church is its own interior.

MECHANICAL PLUS ENVELOPE

RUSH: What about the integration possibility of combining envelope and mechanical?[16]

LORING: As I've mentioned before, we are increasingly getting away from perimeter systems, because the facades have become so energy-efficient. The "skin" load can be handled from the ceiling, although at times a perimeter radiation system may be installed to maintain heat at night during the winter months without periodically having to run large fan systems.

While I've been saying that we've been getting away from perimeter systems, there are still cases where perimeter systems are the proper solution, such as in the case of the new Manufacturers Hanover Corporation Building where fan coil units were used throughout and where the heating is virtually all reclaimed and stored heat.

CANTOR: But you know, it's interesting: if the mechanical engineer gives up the perimeter, the structural engineer gets something additional to work with. We've gone into this on a couple of projects. By the mechanical disappearing from the perimeter of the building, now we can put in an upturned beam. So here's a perfect instance of evolution, if you will. The building skin situation has changed the approach mechanically and in so doing has given the structural engineer some room to manipulate.

PILE: I would raise the question again of whether we don't need to talk about two

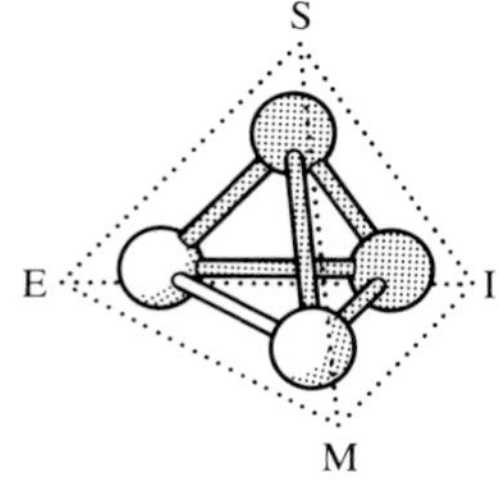

16. Envelope and mechanical combination, pp. 327–328.

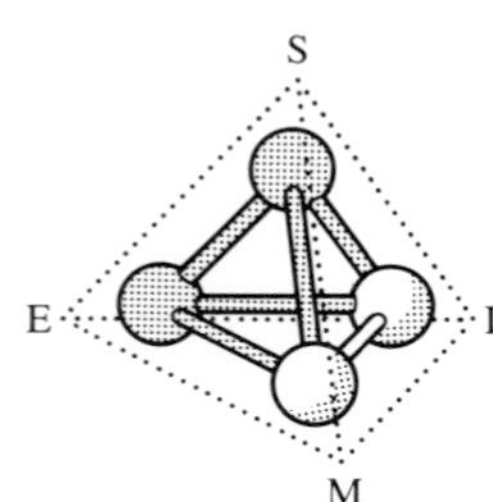

kinds of integration, which you'd perhaps call positive and negative, because in a way becoming independent of the skin is a form of integration, again. The skin is what gives you the independence. And it may not be your responsibility.

LORING: I think the single most important element of a building, from my point of view, is the skin. It either makes or breaks a job from an energy and cost standpoint.

PILE: You have a very strong relationship even though the relationship eventually leads to divorce.

CAUDILL: When you say skin, do you imply panels? Glass? Something that's tacked on to the structural frame? What about utility walls, where most of the utilities fall on the perimeter, or those mechanical elements that hang on the outside of the building as decorations? The skin, the bones, the various systems cannot be considered in isolation. They all go together to achieve a total architectural effect, hopefully reinforcing each other. It's rather foolish for us to talk about a part, or a technique, without the context and total performance and effect we seek. It's better to discuss conceptual design—conceptual integration, if you prefer—than to dwell on a system. From one programmatic concept may spring ten architectural or engineering design concepts.

PILE: Or zero.

CAUDILL: Or zero physical integrations. Or zero depending on what you mean by integration. But if it's integration it's conceptual integration—and surely there's a physical integration or you wouldn't have a conceptual integration.

PILE: I am arguing that you might have a situation where the nature of the conceptual integration brought about physically independent systems. There's a dependence, but if the mechanical system is going to be independent of the skin, close integration is required between the skin and the mechanical of the conceptual sort but not the physical sort. I am arguing that there would be zero physical integration but a very high level of conceptual integration.

RUSH: In a two-story office building, the structure might not be as demanding. We're saying to the structural engineer when he gets to the envelope, "Hey, wait a minute, don't use diagonals because I need to see out and it's going to cost me space. Give me a system that's more compatible with the other aspects of designing an envelope." Then we're coming to the mechanical engineer, and he's either saying, "Well, leave me out of it entirely," or "I'm not going to cause too much trouble; you want a floor-to-ceiling window there, I can handle it."

MECHANICAL PLUS INTERIOR

RUSH: Let's go to the interior-mechanical interface.[17] What opportunities are there from the standpoint of interior design? Is there a high potential or low potential for, let's say, unifying systems or integration?

PILE: Well, it would seem to me the potential is high, a necessity almost. Lighting, for example, is of the essence in the interior. What you're going to do with HVAC is vital. Now, if you talk about private homes, for example, the furniture, which is what most people think is the dominant aspect of interior design, is not usually closely integrated. Maybe it should be. It seems to me that part of the theory of the early Modern Movement was that we ought to integrate as much furniture as possible. Built-in furniture was very important. But in current practice it's not very important in residential architecture.

RUSH: What about electrifying panel systems in the open office, combining a desk and a task light, or bouncing light off the ceiling such as in the John Deere & Company addition?

PILE: It's risen to a new high of importance recently, I think, because of energy concerns and the like. Again, 30 years ago in office design the ceiling took care of everything and the furniture was just loose furni-

17. Mechanical and interior combination, pp. 329–330.

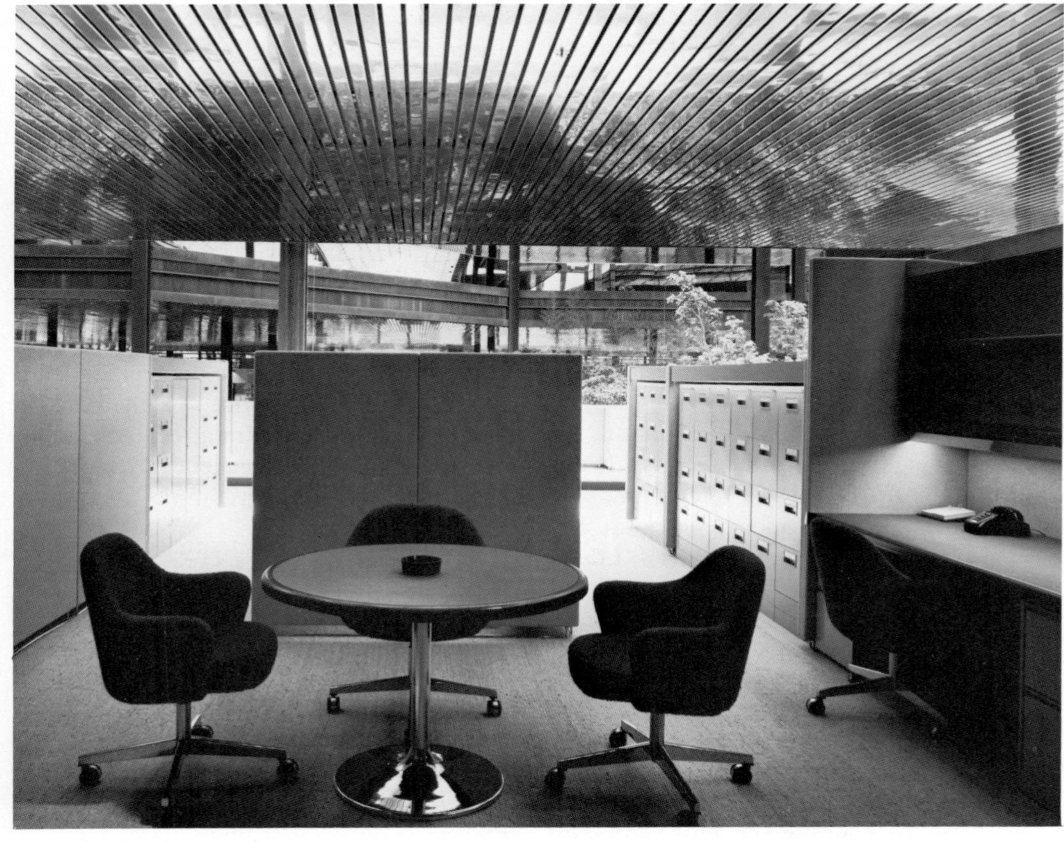

Integration of mechanical and interior often involves a mechanical function provided by an interior element, such as the reflected lighting system incorporated into the desk shelves of the Deere & Company West Office addition. Deere & Company West Office Building, Moline, IL. Architects: Kevin Roche John Dinkeloo and Associates. Photograph: Kevin Roche John Dinkeloo and Associates.

ture. But that's not true now. Everybody asks, "What can furniture do for us in terms of lighting?" I hear rumors of concern about heating and air conditioning in furniture rather than in the building systems.

RUSH: What about flat conductor cable, and the related need to use carpet squares?[18]

PILE: The whole question of wiring, access to wiring for both light and communication, is very important in certain building types. Again, there are people who don't worry so much about it in residential architecture. Even highrise apartment buildings don't go beyond having convenience outlets scattered around the rooms. But in offices it certainly becomes important, and peaks in importance in spaces like computer rooms.

RUSH: Actually, it sounds like it's so integrated that it's almost impossible to conceive of an interior system that doesn't include something to do with electricity or mechanical systems.

PILE: There has been discussion, especially in Europe, of localized heat and air conditioning under individual control, with the idea that that would be both economical and comfortable.

RUSH: Radiant panels in the ceiling?[19]

PILE: Yes. And it's amusing to see the way secretaries or typists use a little electric heater under the desk, saying, "It's too cold in here." In summer, if the air conditioning isn't adequate, people get a little fan at the stationery store and put it on their desks.

LORING: I think you could have as many zones as you have people in a building. Once people are told that all of the heating or

18. Flat conductor cable, pp. 205–206.

19. Radiant heat panels, pp. 177–178.

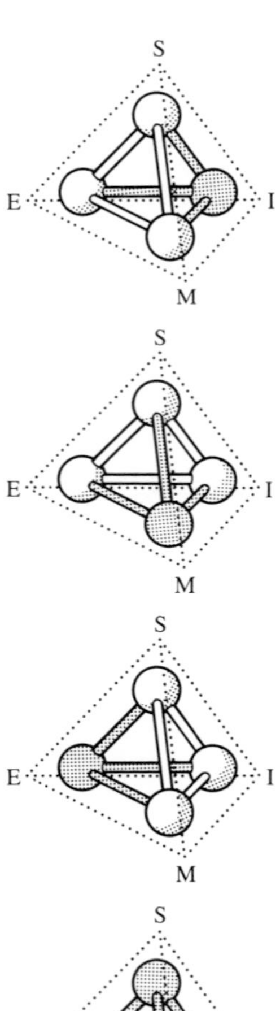

cooling comes from the ceiling, their feet, which happen to be under a desk, immediately are going to get cold or hot.

The use of indirect lighting built into office furniture has not proliferated because totally indirect lighting systems have been found to use considerably more energy than a conventional energy-efficient ceiling lighting system supplemented by task lighting.

RUSH: Where do you draw the line between doing interior design and saying, "That's his job"?

LORING: I think one has to talk about the process, which varies with the client. It varies with each job. But the integration process evolves; no one works in a vacuum. The process has been going on for years. I think what you are trying to do with this handbook is put in organized form alternative approaches and methodologies so that someone who may just be beginning, or may not be familiar with the alternatives, will have a place to start the research process.

Basically, it can be compared to a tug-of-war where each of the design professionals is attempting to achieve the most for their share of the budget dollar. Most decisions, as far as the owner is concerned, will be based upon where the better trade-offs are. Some terrific ideas, insofar as integration is concerned, fall by the wayside because another less sophisticated system may cost less and accomplish almost as much.

RUSH: We're seeing the same kind of thing we've talked about earlier with the trades. Because of this consultant relationship, we might lose the benefit of integration just from people carving out their territory.

LORING: Right.

PILE: I think the interior area perhaps has a particular problem on this front, in that engineering and architecture have had a necessary marriage almost as far back as you can look, while historically interior decorating, as people used to call it, was thought of as entirely separate and disconnected. When the architect was finished the owner brought in this other person who picked out furniture.

I think there is a certain hangover about that into modern times. Maybe we always think there's more problem in our own area, but I always sense more hostility and conflict between architects and interior designers or office planners than there is between architects and engineers. It shouldn't be so, but to some extent I think it is a fact of life.

RUSH: In a building like Citicorp, for example, the interiors are not designed by the architect. They are designed to be completely flexible for any client for five or ten years to come.

LORING: Right. And in that building we have a floor system with flush floor outlets. In many instances, the floor system dictated the discipline of the office layouts which, in effect, was the tail wagging the dog.

RUSH: In a speculative building, it's highly likely that the architect and the mechanical engineer will get together to decide what basic needs they're going to supply for the interior designer as well as the client.

LORING: Yes, and mechanically, the trend is away from large central mechanical systems towards local fan rooms located on individual floors. This is in response to the recognition by the real estate community that tenants are concerned about the utility costs and want to be responsible for the control of their own systems. In some cases, heat pumps or individual chillers are being installed on each floor. Now you may have thirty mechanical equipment rooms instead of one or two.

RUSH: That's decentralization.

LORING: Decentralization is something that seems to be happening.

THREE-PART COMBINATIONS

RUSH: Let's talk about three-part combinations,[20] because actually in many of the cases that we come up with, more often than

Tensile fabric structures, such as Bullock's Department Store, provide unique opportunities for three-part integration of structure, envelope, and interior systems. Cable-supported fabric forms both the structure and envelope of the roof, and admits diffused natural light to the interior. Bullock's Department Store, San Mateo, CA. Architect: L. Gene Zellmer Associates, Inc. Photograph: Steve Proehl.

I would have thought, there is three-part integration. What usually happens is that there's two-part integration with a minor partner. It's an open-sided triangle instead of a closed-sided one. The first integration is a spectator on the other two. Sometimes the relationships are highly meshed.

In something like an inflated structure,[21] for example, the translucent roof, as well as being mechanically determined and structurally sound, can have very large acoustical problems or acoustical and lighting issues. In the case of Bullock's Department Store, for example, where a tensile structure with Teflon coated fiberglass is used, the light is very even. There are no shadows. In a very large structure, maybe a field house and buildings of that type, you almost have to think about those kinds of things. Again, there is no interior designer, perhaps, but you're definitely thinking about the interior.

PILE: You're affecting the interior, yes.

RUSH: What about if you leave out structure? Do you find combinations of envelope, mechanical, and interior only?

PILE: It would seem a somewhat unusual case. Again, I can visualize the kind of case that occurs now and then when somebody decides to convert an old building and strips the structure; then that's a given. And then these other three factors have to be established new and fresh. I remember, for instance, a parking garage that was converted to an office building and the only thing that wasn't changed was the existing structure.

RUSH: What if we leave out the envelope on the next one? Structural, mechanical, and interior. That's similar. What would that be?

PILE: Any landmark building. Well, usually the structure survives with the envelope. I mean it's an unusual case where it would be modifying the structure in a major way while retaining the envelope.

CANTOR: Well, in some old buildings we maintain the envelope and demolish the middle of an old building for a new atrium.

RUSH: Another example is the California Capitol Building in Sacramento, where they left the icing and replaced the cake.

What about structure, envelope, and interior? What have we left out? Take mechanical, where you change the structure and the envelope. That's not an impossibility. Do you have an integrated situation where you integrate structure, envelope, and interior and not the mechanical system?

PILE: That might describe a lot of old buildings that didn't have mechanical systems in the first place.

20. Three-part combinations, p. 318.

21. O'Connell Center, pp. 108–111.

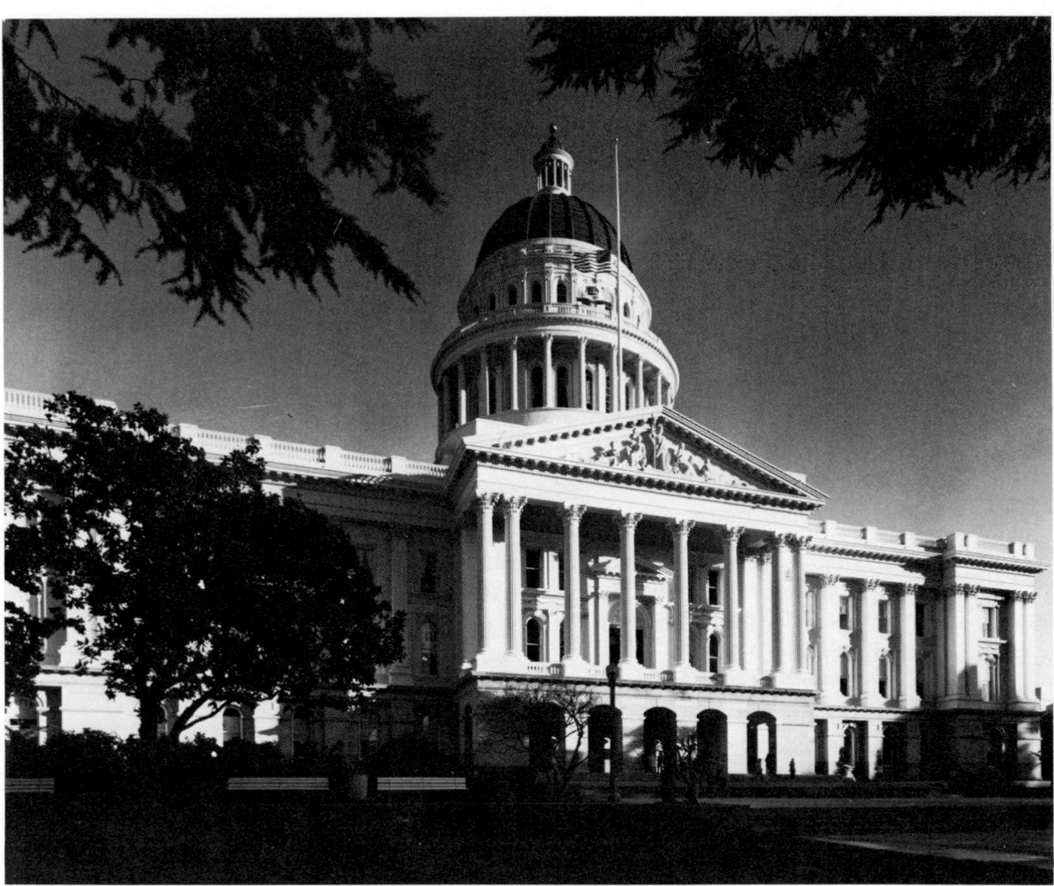

Retrofit and restoration projects often embody three-system integration by emphasizing the portion of the existing building that is to be preserved. The restoration of the California State Capitol saved the envelope and much of the interior, while replacing most of the original structure to resist seismic load. California State Capitol, Sacramento, CA. Architects: Welton Becket Associates. Photograph: Welton Becket.

RUSH: Or a building that doesn't need mechanical.

PILE: Yes, or one that didn't have lighting or plumbing.

RUSH: A stadium.

CAUDILL: There are places where you change the envelope and nothing else.

RUSH: Okay, an architect is reading this book and says, "Hey, I've never read a book on integration before. What am I going to get out of it? I expect two things: to know where the opportunities are, and what opportunities are appropriate for the building I'm designing. All these experts came in and discussed the subject. The second chapter helps in evaluating whether or not these kinds of integration are appropriate to the building that I'm designing." Building types *per se* will be eliminated finally from the generic types. The only thing we're trying to do from the case studies point of view is to try not to eliminate important prototypical building types. The hope is that the watershed from these case studies will fall into all building types, and that the book will be useful no matter what building type is being designed.

The generic case studies will discuss building system types and call attention to them by reference symbols. In the criteria chapter and elsewhere, when we're talking about a particular kind of integration, we'll call it out so it's readily identifiable. This reference system to different kinds of integration allows an architect to say "Well, I do this all the time but I don't ever do it like this. Maybe I ought to. Maybe I ought to call in an interior designer." The criteria charts, to my way of thinking, don't tell you much about what to do; they tell you more about what not to do, opportunities you're missing. What was the last instance in your practice when you saw building integration happening on a very high level, and a unified type of integration?

PILE: It seems to me that the situation where the highest level of integration is across all of these systems is very rare.

CONCLUSIONS

The following are a few of the theoretical and practical premises about which the roundtable participants found themselves in agreement:

1. Integration as a concept is fundamental both in generating a design and in the approach to its implementation.
2. Integration may be construed as a continuum which spans from total system unification to complete independence.
3. Buildings designed for flexible programming, such as those with multiple clients—speculative rental space, for example—are not as good candidates for high integration as owner-occupied buildings, such as corporate headquarters.
4. Implementing an integrated design requires clear lines of communication, whether among the members of an A/E firm or of a team of specialists from a variety of independent sources. Communication lines must allow for two-way communication and feedback during the design process. A highly structured communication system proceeding independently from form to structure to mechanical to interiors often does not result in highly integrated design.[22]
5. Integration may occur on a conceptual level or a physical level or both.
6. Some systems, such as fire safety and security systems, may face unacceptable functional compromise if they are integrated.
7. One important problem with excessive integration is the critical dependence of system combinations and their components; as one part fails or becomes outmoded, all other systems or components may be affected.
8. The taller a building is, the more likely it is that structure and envelope will be highly integrated.
9. Interiors are most integrated in one-tenant buildings such as museums, cathedrals, or municipal buildings.
10. One advantage of full-service A/E firms on a project is ease of communication; an advantage offered by a team of independent specialists is cross-fertilization of ideas among free agents.
11. Many considerations can restrict the range of design options available for a highly integrated project, including: building codes, labor unions, costs, prescriptive specifications, system limitations, technological changes, and program requirements. At the outset of a project, particular attention should be devoted to analyzing the relative importance of these factors and to assigning responsibility for them to appropriate team members.
12. Heavily integrated buildings often do not lend themselves to being dismantled or expanded.

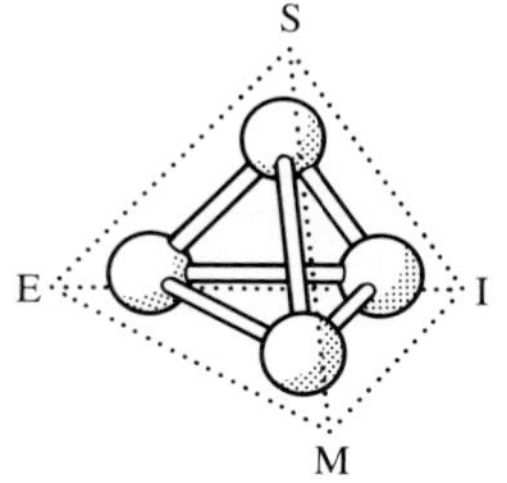

22. Communication is discussed on p. 268.

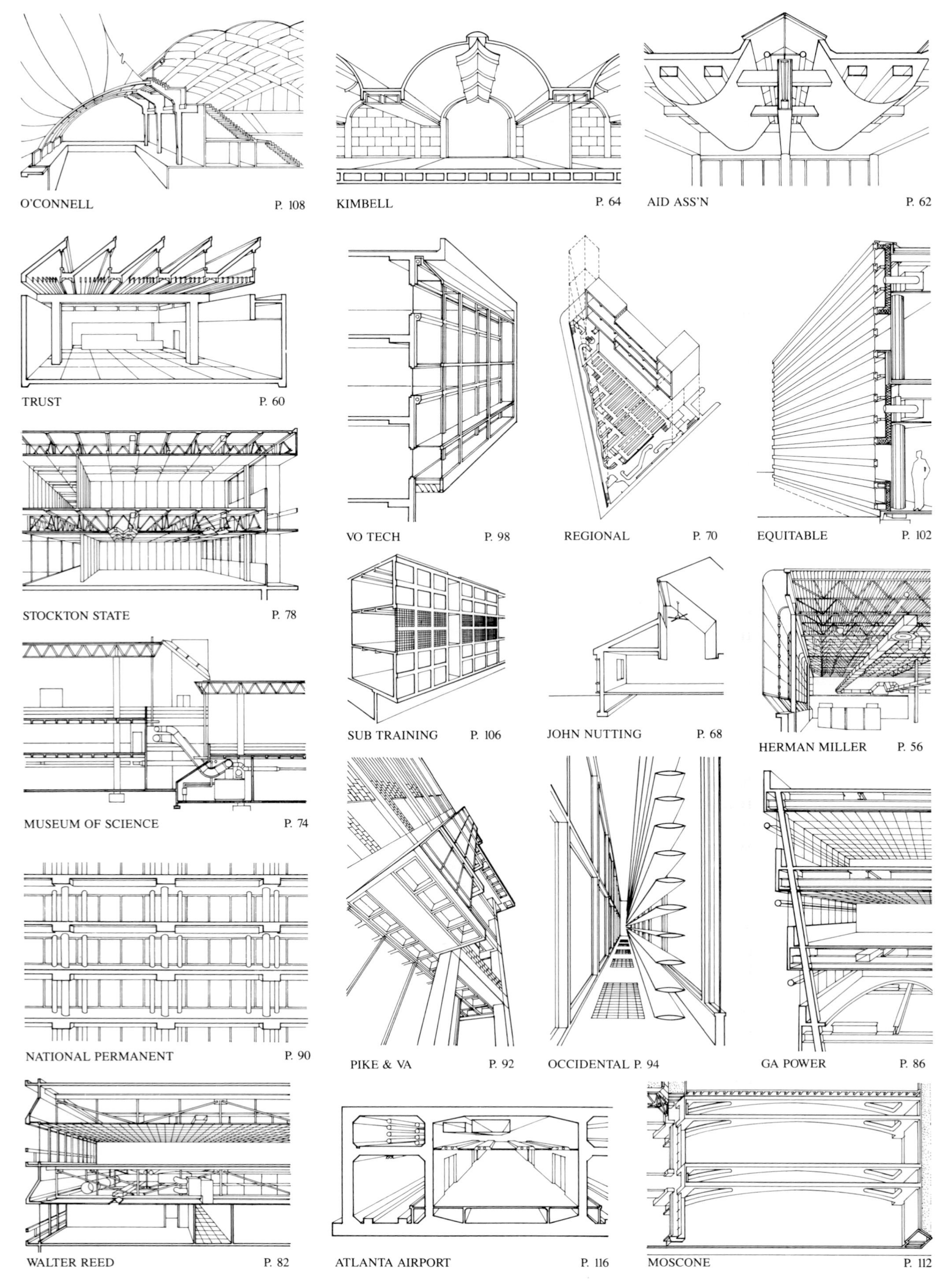
O'CONNELL P. 108
KIMBELL P. 64
AID ASS'N P. 62
TRUST P. 60
VO TECH P. 98
REGIONAL P. 70
EQUITABLE P. 102
STOCKTON STATE P. 78
SUB TRAINING P. 106
JOHN NUTTING P. 68
HERMAN MILLER P. 56
MUSEUM OF SCIENCE P. 74
NATIONAL PERMANENT P. 90
PIKE & VA P. 92
OCCIDENTAL P. 94
GA POWER P. 86
WALTER REED P. 82
ATLANTA AIRPORT P. 116
MOSCONE P. 112

Chapter 3
Case Studies

Author:
Robert L. Miller, AIA

Architectural drawings:
Allen Assarsson

A spectrum of building types, systems, and levels of integration is represented here by nineteen contemporary buildings. The emphasis both in choosing and presenting these examples is on integration ideas. This chapter looks at a project's overall design concept, but it also begins to analyze integration ideas according to system design criteria, integration theory, and products used. References are made to later chapters that explore these topics in more depth.

This stated, it becomes easier to say what this chapter is not. It is not a compilation of the latest integration ideas. That many of the buildings are widely published award-winners has more to do with accessibility—an advantage both for the authors and for users of this handbook—than it does with any desire to set up an Integration Hall of Fame. There has been an attempt, however, to select buildings of quality that bear out in performance the promise of their design concept.

Office and assembly buildings outnumber smaller projects and housing here. An explanation for this is suggested in Chapter 2's roundtable, where it is intimated that large, flexible programs (e.g., offices) are more amenable to a highly integrative approach than tight, conventionalized programs (e.g., housing).[1] Another explanation, that only corporate and institutional budgets are able to support the extra design effort needed to achieve high levels of integration, can be supported or refuted by dozens of examples—including several on these pages. Finally, any rational theory of integration must be balanced by the untidy facts of changing tastes and ideologies. Since the nineteenth century, a designer's way with systems has been an acid test of architectural beliefs. Some have tried to recapture the natural integrity of pre-industrial materials, while others have sought to learn and transform the engineer's unselfconscious way with industrial products. Still others have insisted that the architect's primary role is one of shaping and decorating interior and exterior spaces, with a conscious indifference to whether the building technology of the age happens to be brick or stone or pressurized air. Of these, the third group is under-represented here, not because their buildings do not demonstrate systems integration, but because photographs rarely reveal it.

The reader is invited to enjoy the particularity of these examples, their representation of a building type or a style or a moment in history, and urged to compare them to the examples discussed in Chapter 4, which unlike these do not have a specific architect, site, and function.

1. See discussion of building types, p. 27.

Herman Miller Seating Manufacturing Plant
Holland, Michigan

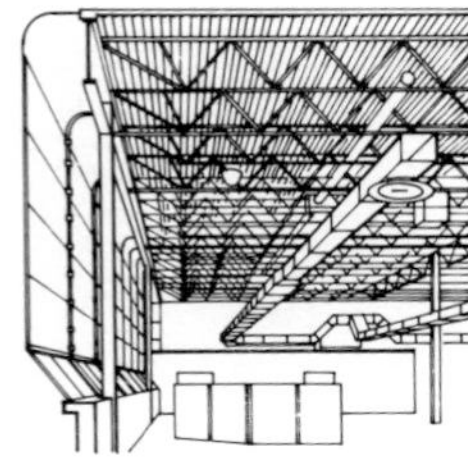

The Herman Miller Seating Manufacturing Plant represents a refined solution to a common building problem: the one-level, steel-frame factory/warehouse. As usual in this type of building, the design criteria included expandability, energy efficiency, flexibility, and speed and economy of construction. But in this project the conventional strategy of using interchangeable elements is transformed by an integrative process.

CRS has pioneered collaborative procedures that involve users—both workers and owners—from the outset of the design process. Herman Miller's management welcomed this innovative approach. The result is not a radical rethinking of the modern factory, but rather a thoughtful reuse of elements found in many large commercial and industrial buildings. Everyday products such as operable strip windows, steel wall panels, exposed open-web steel joists, steel deck roof, and exposed steel ducts[1] take on multiple uses and unexpected formal qualities.

An intermediate degree of visible integration is achieved by exposing and painting elements of the structural and mechanical systems.[2] This strategy helps conserve materials while getting maximum usable space from the enclosed volume.

PROGRAMMATIC INTEGRATION

Functionally expressive, high-quality design was in itself a major project criterion, given the client's well-known commitment to enhancing employee morale and productivity. This commitment can be read in the design for the glass-enclosed, landscaped "People Place" commons, as yet unbuilt, and in the decision to treat both office and manufacturing areas consistently—under the same roof and with comparable design attention. Offices and manufacturing are programmatically integrated as well. They are further interrelated by the Herman Miller furniture system,[3] both in use and as it is being manufactured.

The integration focus in this building is on

A nighttime corner view emphasizes the sleek, streamlined quality of the envelope.

the envelope and particularly the exterior wall. The wall section incorporates a bright, streamlined skin, daylighting, natural cooling, earth sheltering, insulation, and structure. It complements the multihued exposed structural steel, mechanical, and electrical systems that in turn are visibly integrated with the interior. The base of the wall is cast-in-place concrete, integral with the floor slab and rising four feet above it. It acts as a retaining wall for an earth berm—an appropriate response to site, energy conservation, and visual criteria. Since the building is located on a flood plain, the berm helps protect the building from water damage. It also provides a significant amount of earth-sheltered perimeter, helping to stabilize building temperatures. The concrete wall and berm visually erase any visible evidence of the foundation, producing a "floating" effect.

On the interior, this same 4 ft concrete wall forms a durable wainscot and a convenient sill for a 2 ft strip of operable vision glass, canted out for self-shading. This window provides the building's sole source of cooling—one that is usually adequate in this climate. The decentralized floor plan responds to the criterion that no worker should be more than 100 ft from a window.

While the wall's lower strip window provides ventilation and views, the upper strip, a curved acrylic clerestory, is functionally

1. Exposed ducts, pp. 179–181.
2. Visible integration, pp. 381–385, 404.
3. Open plan office furniture, pp. 196–199.

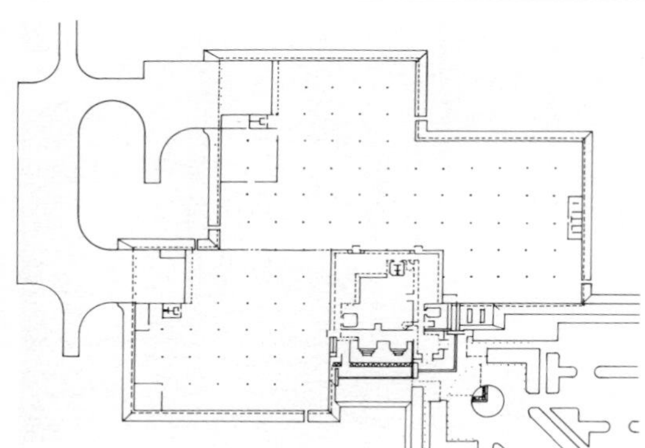

FACTORY FLOOR PLAN

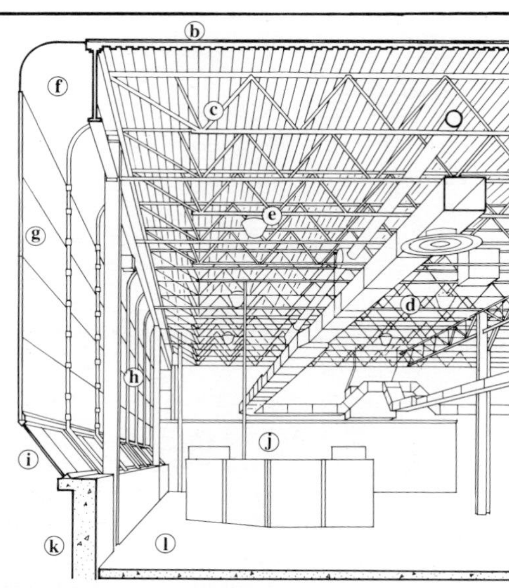

PERSPECTIVE WITH INTEGRATION DETAILS

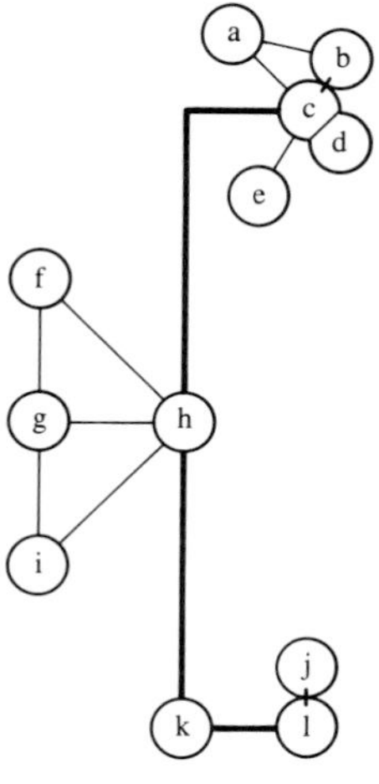

a. *Plastic-dome skylights (see photo at left)*
b. *Protected membrane roof*
c. *Exposed steel bar joists and roof deck*
d. *Exposed ducts and heaters*
e. *High-pressure sodium lighting*
f. *Barrel-vault skylights*
g. *Lightweight metal insulating panels*
h. *Steel curtain wall frame and columns*
i. *Window assembly*
j. *Open office furniture*
k. *Concrete retaining wall (integral with floor slab)*
l. *Exposed concrete floor slab*

Diagram detail page 366

The floor plan (top left) indicates the relationship of manufacturing, warehouse, and office spaces. The section perspective (above) shows the wall's concrete base, outriggers, operable strip windows, and metal wall panels. The panels, clipped together and sealed with a silicone gasket, may be demounted and reused. An interior view (left) shows the roof structure and one of the plastic-domed skylights. A view across the loading area (below) shows the earth berm raised against the concrete base of the envelope.

Structural and mechanical elements, exposed to the interior and painted, allow the enclosed volume to deliver the maximum usable space. Note chair parts stored at left.

part of a flat single-ply roof that also incorporates some 80 acrylic dome-type skylights.[4] Seen from the highway, clerestory and skylights outline the roof and complement the building's sleek imagery. They also contribute acceptable levels of solar heat gain and daylighting, and will vent the building in case of fire.

DEMOUNTABLE WALL PANELS

Between upper and lower windows the wall panels appear to float; they are in fact hung on the same structure that supports the windows, a series of tubular steel outriggers that span vertically between a structural steel roof beam and the concrete sill. The wall panels themselves are of stainless steel with polystyrene insulation and aluminum interior finish.[5] In addition to their insulation value they offer relatively low maintenance and a streamlined look. Since they are clipped together and sealed with an extruded silicone gasket, they can be quickly demounted, moved, and reused. Herman Miller plans to make use of this feature when it expands the present facility, adding two more identical factory units.

Herman Miller's wall integrates envelope with interior finishes, insulation, natural lighting, and ventilation; the wall panels are connected to the building's structure, accomplishing a four-system integration. A similar integration is visible at the connection of the acrylic clerestories, and the decoratively painted, triangulated steel roof structure.[6]

In this building type, the dominant envelope can be highly integrated physically with everything but structure, to which it must be attached independently in order to remain flexible. There is an advantage, however, in removing structural support from the task of the wall panels: it allows them to mesh envelope, passive mechanical, and interior elements in a highly portable unit. Their appropriateness may be measured by the savings realized in time and materials when the complex is expanded. Given this designed-in impermanence, the means used to achieve a high degree of warmth, style, and sense of place merit close study.

4. Plastic-domed skylights, pp. 164–166.
5. Lightweight insulating metal panels, pp. 219–222.
6. Visible integration, pp. 381–385, 404.

Office areas are detailed in the same way as manufacturing spaces. Strip windows 2 ft high and tipped outward for self-shading provide views and the building's only source of cooling. Skylights (not shown) and clerestory contribute solar heat gain and daylighting.

Project: Herman Miller Seating Manufacturing Plant.
Architects: CRS/Sirrine, Inc., Caudill Rowlett Scott Division, Houston, TX. Paul Kennon, FAIA, design principal; Jay Bauer, AIA, senior design architect.
Structural Engineers: CRS/Sirrine, Inc., Caudill Rowlett Scott Division, Houston, TX.
Mechanical Engineers: Geo. T. Crothers, East Grand Rapids, MI; CRS/ Sirrine, Inc., Caudill Rowlett Scott Division, Houston, TX.
Electrical Engineers: B.J. Kempker and Associates, Grand Rapids, MI; CRS/ Sirrine, Inc., Caudill Rowlett Scott Division, Houston, TX.
General Contractor: Owens-Ames-Kimball, Grand Rapids, MI.
Civil Engineers: Holland Engineers, Holland, MI.
Cost: $8.5 million; $40 PSF. Completed June 1980.
Photographs: Balthazar Korab (courtesy of CRS/ Sirrine, Inc., Caudill Rowlett Scott Division).

Trust Pharmacy
Grants, New Mexico

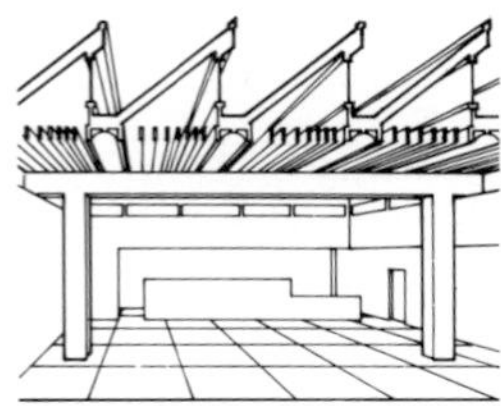

Trust Pharmacy proves that it doesn't take a big building, or a big budget, to produce a convincing and sophisticated level of systems integration. Despite the rows of modern display counters, the main space has the quality of an open-air market.[1] Low, shallow ancillary spaces surround the high, naturally lighted central space. The strategy is to use a massive perimeter masonry envelope to temper extremes of heat and cold, while the trellised central space diffuses the strong direct sunlight.

PASSIVE SOLAR STRATEGY

Roof envelope and structure offer the opportunity for a four-system integration which defines the interior and provides the major portion of the building's heating, cooling, and lighting needs. The roof structure takes the form of a series of four south-facing skylight monitors parallel to the building's long axis. These sawtooth clerestories are spaced to admit relatively more low-angled winter sunlight, and shaded to restrict light from the intense summer sun. The clerestories incorporate white painted wood baffles that diffuse all direct sunlight and provide a non-directional ceiling daylighting system. The use of insulating glass allows the clerestories to function as more efficient barriers to heat loss. Visibly and structurally integrated with the sawtooth roof are glued laminated wood beams,[2] supported both by the concrete masonry exterior walls and by rows of wood columns spaced inside the walls of the envelope. The beams, spanning the building's short axis, intersect and support the long rows of monitors and baffles, while they provide a warmly colored, light-diffusing surface. Because such wood structures are usually exposed, other system elements can be conveniently exposed as well; in this case, the structure supports elements of the daylighting system while helping to diffuse light.

The exposure of these elements conserves space by creating the illusion of more space. In addition, the 18 in. depth of the beams defines a shallow clerestory between the top of the bearing wall and the bottom of the roof structure, admitting a continuous band of natural light around the whole space. Low winter sunlight comes through this clerestory to warm the concrete and tile floors and block walls. Strip lighting is integrated with the roof structure, in the space between beams which corresponds to the gutters between the sawtooth monitors. The wood beams themselves frame eggcrate diffusers for these light fixtures.

DAYLIGHTING

Daylighting levels, along with the temperature stabilizing effect of the masonry, are sufficient to allow the use of nonstandard mechanical systems, although these systems are not themselves directly meshed with the building form. Since electric lights are seldom used, interior heat load is greatly reduced and a low-energy evaporative cooler suffices. Similarly, winter heat gain is substantial enough to allow a small gas-fired heater to be used only as a supplement. Light levels and temperature comfort levels are comparable to those in conventional buildings in the area. The emphasis on energy conservation in this design is appropriate to its integration potential, in that space and resources are conserved and the building is responsive to its climate.[3] The daylighting criteria are the underpinnings of the entire design.

Trust Pharmacy integrates envelope, structure, and interior in a way that is formally straightforward and economical as well as functionally elegant. The two-way span of the wood framing system atop the masonry bearing wall almost automatically defines the space for the clerestory strip window; the clerestory, defined by the top of the wall, is ideally placed to heat the masonry. The fact that envelope is occasionally used as structure contributes to conservation of materials.

The building's responses to energy cost-saving criteria, through daylighting and passive solar design, are readily apparent. Less obvious is its real economy as a formal de-

1. Visible integration, pp. 381–385, 402.
2. Laminated wood post and beam, pp. 144–145.
3. Conservation of space and resources, p. 236.

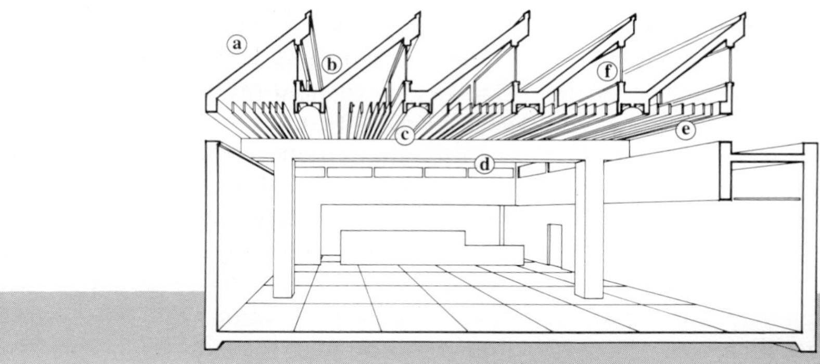

PERSPECTIVE SHOWING ROOF INTEGRATION

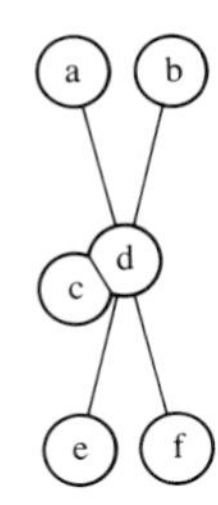

a. *Asphalt shingles*
b. *Clerestories*
c. *Fluorescent lighting*
d. *Exposed, glued laminated rigid frame and deck*
e. *Wood baffles*
f. *Drywall ceiling*

Diagram detail page 379

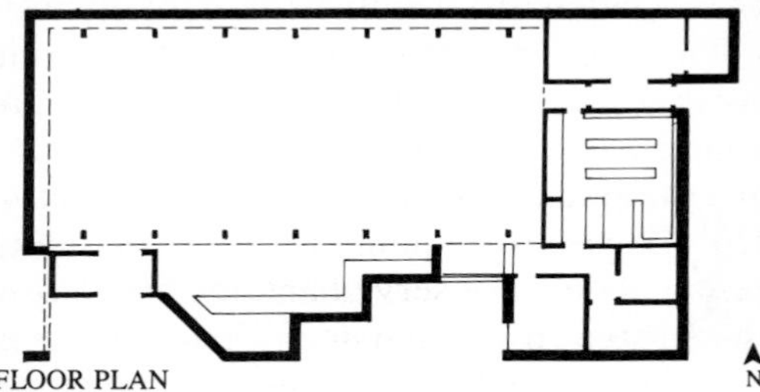

FLOOR PLAN

Clerestory details and strip lighting integrated with the roof appear in the section perspective (top). The low, massive masonry perimeter and high central space are clearly evident on the exterior (center left). In the building plan (above left), ancillary spaces line the south and west sides. An interior view (above right) shows the high, naturally lighted central space of the pharmacy. Glued laminated wood beams support the south-facing skylight monitors and wood baffles.

sign. The conventional alternative, the "cheap" flat-roofed box, would not only have required energy-intensive systems, but would also no doubt have received a decorative interior shell—suspended ceiling, ornate shelving, graphics—as well as exterior appliques. At Trust Pharmacy, the structure and envelope *per se* are admittedly more expensive, but they create their own finishes, allowing the use of the very simplest store fixtures and graphics.

While not appropriate for all contexts, the idea that the building envelope can form its own interior decoration is more than appropriate for a location in New Mexico, where the adobe and heavy timber tradition offers many models. The use of skylights in place of artificial light suggests possibilities for many similar commercial applications.

Mazria/Schiff here use a contemporary technological version of tradition—concrete masonry units and laminated beams—to achieve results that fit several definitions of "economy."

Project: Trust Pharmacy.
Architects: Mazria/Schiff & Associates, Albuquerque, NM.
Project team: Edward Mazria, AIA; Marc Schiff, AIA; Thomas Cain, RA; Steven Yesner, AIA.
Structural Engineers: Engineering Associates, Albuquerque, NM. James Innis, PE; August Mosimann, PE.
Mechanical and Electrical Engineers: Mazria/Schiff & Associates, Albuquerque, NM.
General Contractor: Andrew Mirabal, Grants, NM.
Cost: $150,000; $44 PSF. Completed September 1981.
Photographs: Mazria/Schiff & Associates.

Aid Association for Lutherans Headquarters
Appleton, Wisconsin

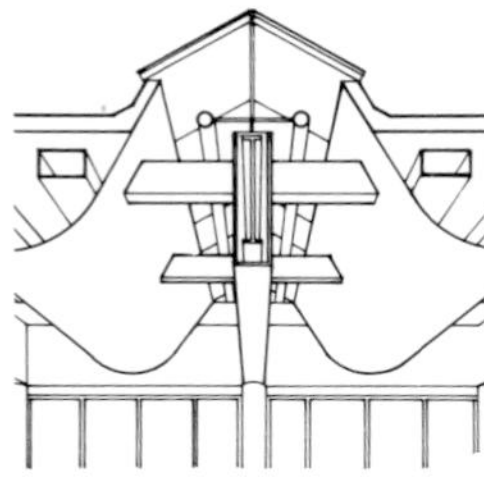

The program for the Aid Association for Lutherans Headquarters stressed flexibility, potential for expansion, and a sense of the concepts of Christianity and community in everyday working situations. The result, a formally organized building of 524,900 sq ft, is an ingenious solution to program requirements. In addition, its daylighting strategy demonstrates how an extraordinary mechanical systems design may develop out of a single strong interiors idea.

The ceiling of the two-story building's upper floor is crucial in terms of systems integration.[1] Almost every ceiling element does double or triple duty. Long strip skylights integrate envelope and interior, and also incorporate fluorescent lighting and electric strip heaters. Directly below each skylight, the building's main structural steel girders carry the light fixtures and some of the sprinkler lines, at the same time helping to baffle and conceal both light sources. Most distinctive of all is the finish ceiling, a series of half-cylindrical "socks" slung between the strip skylights. Formed of foil-backed fiberglass over which white fabric is stretched and anchored, the socks help modulate and spread the light from above while trapping and absorbing sound in large open office areas. They also serve as return-air plenums and conceal air-handling equipment, roof drains, sprinkler lines, and sound-masking speakers. Plastic hoops spaced regularly along the lengths of the cylinders allow the socks to be hinged open in sections for ready access to the concealed systems.

CEILING INTEGRATION

These strong ceiling shapes respond to both visual and energy-saving criteria. They also integrate interior and mechanical elements at the *meshed* level, as do the access floors[2] which make up over a third of the total floor area. Girders paralleling the socks support light fixtures and lend articulation to the ceiling. The skylights represent a unification of envelope and interior. The open plan office furniture system[3] responds to the daylighting strategy of gaining maximum use of the light reflected off the socks. The socks also absorb sound and allow for speech privacy in the office.[4]

Continuous mechanical penthouses, corresponding to the main interior corridors below, are set at right angles to the rows of skylights. The penthouses contain air intakes and other mechanical equipment, with HVAC feeders concealed in the socks branching out to either side, and a variety of VAV air-handling systems are used.

ENERGY MANAGEMENT

The HVAC system consists of 28 subsystems, which respond to widely variable conditions created by the building's daylighting strategy. The three major ones are a single-zone perimeter subsystem, a standard interior subsystem, and a multi-zone subsystem capable of handling those areas with wide swings in heat load. Electric wall heaters are used near perimeter and courtyard windows.

Three electrically driven chillers, one serving as an internal-source heat pump, are supplemented by two electric boilers with a 50,000-gallon hot water storage capacity. Hot water storage tanks are charged during the occupied hours with heat reclaimed from the lighting fixtures, which is then used to heat the interior of the building during the night by means of a turbine-driven electric generator. Reclaimed heat from the exhaust gases is accumulated in a boiler to heat the building during power outages. Temperature and light levels are monitored by an energy management control system[5] especially designed to respond to daylighting conditions.

The sheer number of systems involved and the high levels at which they are integrated required a correspondingly high level of coordination, especially in dimensions. Nevertheless, the design is essentially an outgrowth of the daylighting strategy and the lowrise construction on which this depends. As in the case of the Equitable Life building,[6] the large site obviated the need to conserve space.

1. Visible integration, pp. 381–385, 396–397.
2. Access floors, pp. 202–204.
3. Open plan office furniture, pp. 196–199.
4. Acoustical performance, pp. 254–256.
5. Energy management control systems, pp. 158–160.
6. Compare Equitable Life, pp. 102–105.

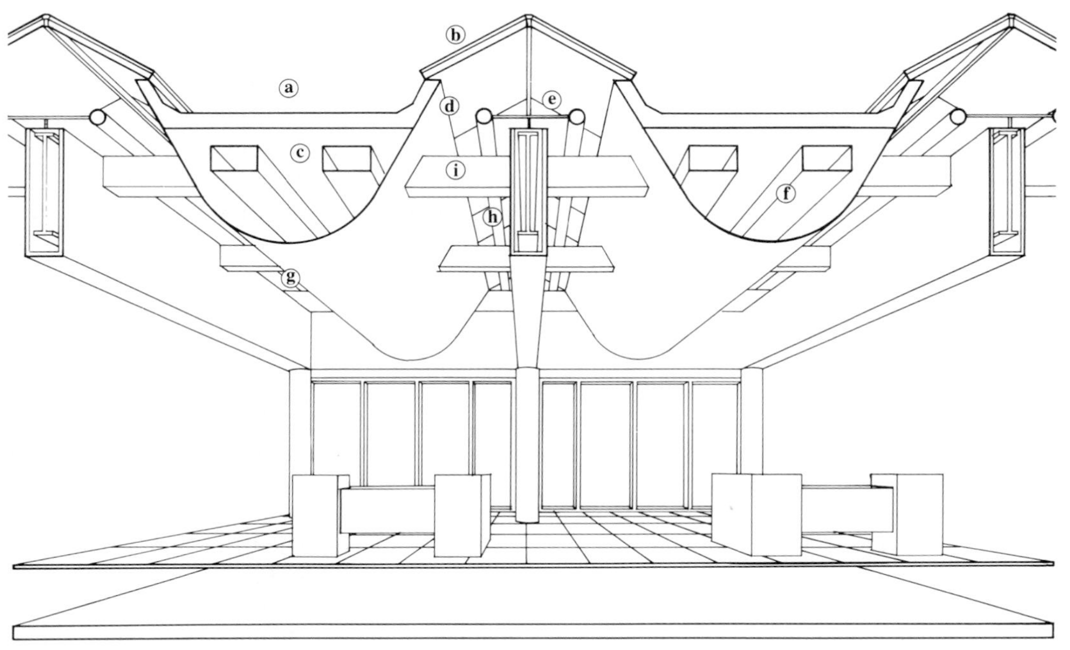

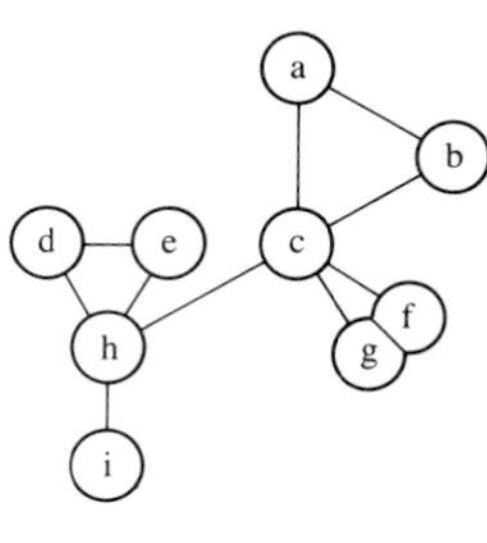

a. *Built-up roof and rigid insulation*
b. *Skylights*
c. *Metal deck and steel beams*
d. *Fluorescent lights*
e. *Strip heaters*
f. *Ducts*
g. *Socks/return air plenum*
h. *Steel beam*
i. *Drywall*

Diagram detail page 379

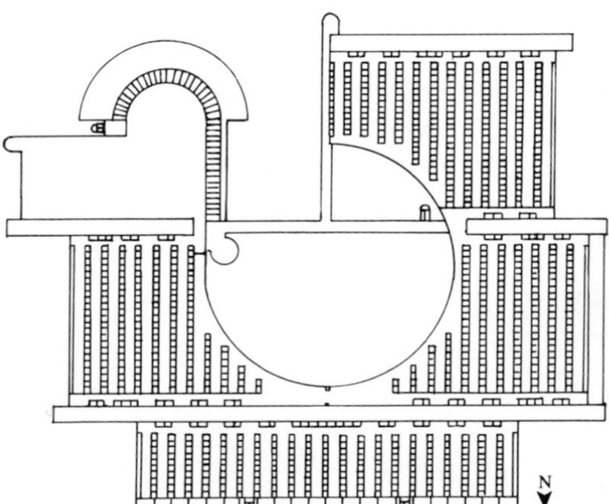

ROOF PLAN

The section perspective (top) shows the half-cylindrical "socks" in relation to the strip skylights and steel girders. In addition to their role in the daylighting scheme, the socks conceal mechanical equipment and serve as return-air plenums. Formal organization and potential for expansion are evident in the building plan (above). The design is an outgrowth of the daylighting strategy and lowrise construction made possible by the 1200 acre site. Skylights and mechanical penthouses are clearly visible in an exterior view (above right). An interior view (right) shows the effect of mechanical-interior integration on second-floor office spaces.

Project: Aid Association for Lutherans Headquarters.
Architects: John Carl Warnecke & Associates, New York, NY. John Carl Warnecke, principal; A.E. Kohn, partner-in-charge; Walter A. Rutes, project director; William E. Pedersen, project designer; John Smart, senior designer; Michael J. Koenen, project planner; Lee Hamptian, project manager; Horst Herman, job captain.
Structural Engineers: Paul Weidlinger, New York, NY.
Mechanical and Electrical Engineers: Joseph R. Loring & Associates, New York, NY.
Interiors Consultant: George Nelson & Co., Inc., New York, NY.
General Contractor: Oscar J. Boldt Construction Co., Appleton, WI.
Cost: $40,000,000; $68 PSF. Completed March, 1977.
Photographs: Harr, Hedrich-Blessing.

Kimbell Art Museum
Fort Worth, Texas

The Kimbell Art Museum's 9.5-acre site is part of a city park and cultural complex that includes the Amon Carter Museum of Western Art as well as other museums and theatres. Conceived and built as the bequest of Fort Worth industrialist Kay Kimbell, the finished product is the result of close and early collaboration between museum director Richard Brown and architect Louis Kahn.

This collaboration is reflected in the high level of integration apparent throughout the building. Lighting criteria, a prime consideration for any museum, dominates Kahn's design scheme. He and the director felt strongly that public gallery spaces should be naturally lighted. To accomplish this, each of the 13 vault-like shells over the interior spaces is split down the center, with double-domed acrylic skylights covering the 2½ ft wide aperture. Additional daylighting is provided by glass lunette bands in the end walls. Exterior glass walls are of 1 in. insulating glass[1] in stainless steel thermal break frames.

LIGHTING CRITERIA AND STRUCTURE

A measure of the influence of lighting criteria is the fact that the skylights deprive the roof shells of most of their "vault action." The shells are not vaults structurally; they are beam-like in that they span lengthwise. In this respect the structure is significantly modified while maintaining the visual reference to vaults; this parallels Kahn's reference in concrete masonry to Roman monolithic construction.

Light from above is diffused within the space by a perforated aluminum reflector, a gull-wing in cross section, which reflects daylight upward toward the cycloid shell as well as transmitting it downward into the space.[2] Kahn referred to this reflector as a "modifier of the light." Because the concrete shell's geometric purity precludes the attachment of lighting fixtures and the concealment of electrical conduit, artificial lighting is attached to a continuous light track at the lower lip of the reflector, and at the low ceiling between the edges of the shells.

Each shell is a clear-span cycloid shape of post-tensioned reinforced concrete 4 in. thick, 23 ft wide, 100 ft long, and 7½ ft high. The shells, each one supported by four 2 x 2 ft columns at the corners, also serve as beams carrying intermediate flat-slab roof

Photo: Marshall D. Meyers

1. Insulating glass, pp. 209–211.
2. Visual performance, pp. 256–257.

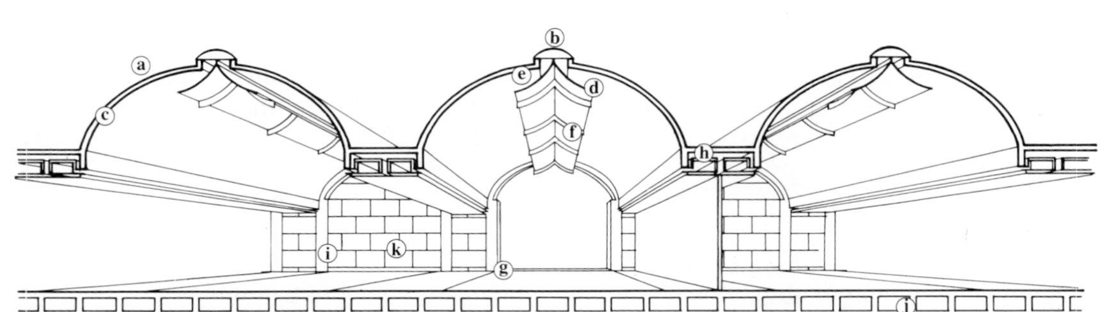

PERSPECTIVE SHOWING GALLERY SPACE

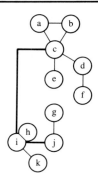

a. *Sheet lead roof*
b. *Acrylic skylights*
c. *Post-tensioned concrete shell*
d. *Reflectors*
e. *Supply ductwork*
f. *Incandescent track lighting*
g. *Wood flooring*
h. *Return air ducts*
i. *Exposed concrete masonry*
j. *Waffle slab*
k. *Travertine infill*

Diagram detail page 364

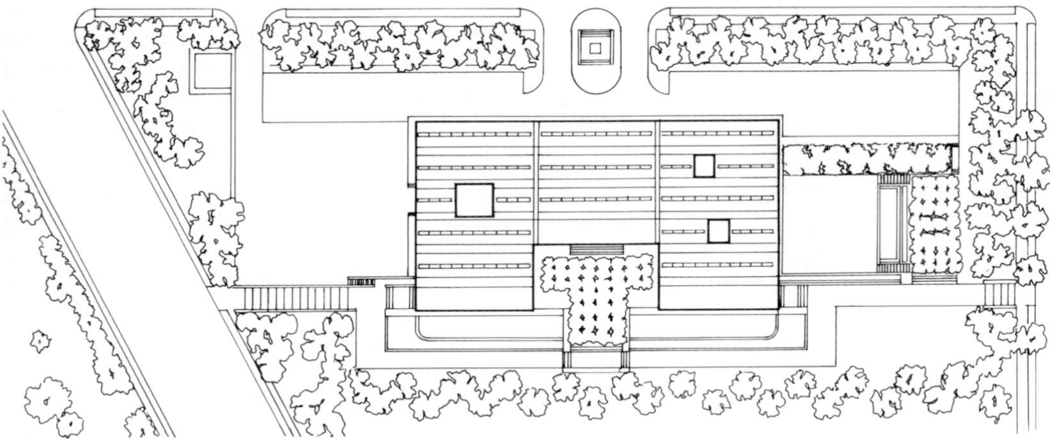

UPPER LEVEL PLAN

◄N

Reflectors and lunette bands appear in a view of the museum lobby (left). The beamlike quality of the shells is emphasized in the section perspective (top). The plan of building and grounds (center) shows the three courtyards, which further integrate envelope and interior. The plan clearly suggests the potential for expansion. A view of the entry sequence (above) shows envelope/interior integration and adaptation to the gently sloping 10 acre site.

Travertine marble sheathes the infill, echoing the as-cast appearance of the concrete structure. The collection's traditional character argued against such visible integration solutions as exposed piping and ductwork.

sections. The main gallery-level floor, a two-way post-tensioned waffle slab 14 in. deep, forms the ceiling of the museum support spaces below. Expanded polystyrene blocks are cast into the slab to form the waffle which, for visual reasons, remains concealed. Three of the concrete gallery walls also act as post-tensioned upturned beams, spanning the 100 ft width of the building as they carry the gallery-level floor slab above the east vehicular entrance and the west shop/office window walls.

Height restrictions dictated the building's 40 ft overall height, so pedestrian access to the main gallery floor is on the upper level, with offices, conservation studios, storage space, and service and vehicular entrances below. Three courtyards which appear at intervals in the plan allow natural light to further influence visitors' experience of the interior of the building. The design makes use of the sloping site in the entry sequence and in the 186-seat auditorium. The latter is a double-height space that uses both gallery and lower levels. The desire to have it roofed by a concrete shell similar to those in the gallery overrides ideal acoustical criteria.

3. Visible integration, pp. 381–385, 404–405.

CONCRETE AS INTERIOR FINISH

Throughout the museum's interior spaces, structural concrete is left exposed, its as-cast appearance echoed by the travertine marble used to sheath non-bearing infill wall surfaces. The building's exterior juxtaposes concrete and travertine as well; exterior travertine walls conceal a thin reinforced concrete diaphragm between columns which braces the columns laterally.

A high level of visible integration is critical in a building intended to provide a unified, coherent environment for the appreciation of the visual arts, and the color and texture of interior surfaces, as well as lighting and spatial organization, all reflect this.[3] At the same time, certain modes of integration, such as exposed ductwork, were rendered inappropriate by the traditional esthetic demands of the collection. Much of the me-

The extension of the form of the cycloid shell to the porticoes represents an instance of visible integration, providing visual clues to the interior layout.

Project: Kimbell Art Museum.
Architects: Louis Kahn, FAIA; Marshall D. Meyers, AIA, Philadelphia, PA, project architect. Associate architect:
Preston M. Geren & Associates, Ft. Worth, TX; Frank R. Sherwood, Ft. Worth, TX, project coordinator.
Structural Engineers: August Komendant, Upper Montclair, NJ; Preston M. Geren & Associates, Ft. Worth, TX.
Mechanical and Electrical Engineers: Cowan, Love and Jackson, Ft. Worth, TX.
Consultants: Richard Kelly, New York, NY, Edison Price, New York, NY—lighting; C.P. Boner & Associates, Houston, TX—acoustics; George E. Patton, Inc., Philadelphia, PA—landscaping; Laurence Channing, Philadelphia, PA—graphics and exhibition design; Thomas Electronics, Ft. Worth, TX—electronics.
General Contractor: Thomas S. Byrne, Inc., Ft. Worth, TX.
Cost: $5,500,000; $55 PSF. Completed October 1972.
Photographs: Ezra Stoller, ESTO, unless otherwise noted.

chanical and electrical equipment is conventionally located in the basement. However, supply air ductwork is incorporated into the concrete roof system, while return air is located between columns within the exterior walls. Attachment points for moveable partitions for changing exhibits are located in the edges of the aluminum soffits under the supply air distribution system.

Several mechanical and electrical subsystems are specifically related to museum functions. For example, the interior humidity level is controlled by sprayed-coil elements in the air distribution system, while equipment vibrations and noise are regulated by the placement of inertial pads and isolators on all rotating machinery. Natural light control is required for conservation purposes and is coupled with the necessity of flexible space for various exhibits. Finally, a central monitoring and control panel, custom-designed for the museum, responds to security demands.

It should be emphasized that the Kimbell Museum is intended as a "permanent" building, one of the few discussed in this chapter. In this respect it bears comparison with the Moscone Center;[4] it might also be contrasted with the Museum of Science and Industry,[5] a building meant to house timely, rather than timeless, exhibits, and to be in itself an experimental, changing exhibit. Permanence does not preclude expansion, such as might be accomplished if additional bays were added to the Kimbell (although this was not intended by the architect). It does mean that the building's useful life is seen as being "forever," as suggested by the very high quality materials and workmanship used in its construction. The museum tends to confirm the assertion that high levels of integration occur frequently in buildings intended to last indefinitely.[6]

Note that buildings of the caliber and intended permanence of the Kimbell Art Museum are by no means commonplace. Its beauty lies not only in its elegance but also in its clarity of concept.

4. Compare Moscone Center, pp. 112–115.
5. Compare Museum of Science and Industry, pp. 74–77.
6. See discussion of permanence, p. 239.

John C. Nutting Apartments
Amherst, Massachusetts

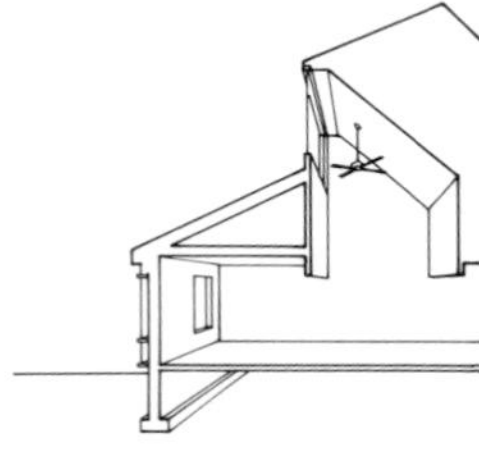

The John C. Nutting Apartments in Amherst, Massachusetts, a five-unit rental apartment complex for disabled but independent residents, is one of the first new buildings in the United States to combine energy-consciousness with barrier-free design. Located adjacent to existing housing for the elderly, this is a pilot project for housing the severely disabled.

In single-family house design, solar energy has often provided a rationale for highly original and even bizarre forms. Similarly, wealthy handicapped clients have been able to commission houses that offer compensatingly rich architectural experiences. The John Nutting Apartments project, on the other hand, started with the dual constraints of a low budget (under $500,000) and the requirement that it fit the context of a small, historic New England community.

The envelope of each of the five units (four three-bedroom and one four-bedroom) takes its form from the historic context, especially traditional rural New England sugar sheds and connected farm buildings. Cedar clapboard siding completes the reference, and visible integration of the envelope arises from this adaptation of an existing formal vocabulary.[1] The envelope accommodates passive solar features, and these mechanical system requirements are in turn reflected in the design of the interiors.

TROMBE WALLS

Heated air, trapped between glass and concrete block in south-facing Trombe walls, is circulated into the units by damper-controlled registers in the block walls. The use of insulating glass makes direct solar gain possible in the New England climate;[2] canvas awnings, when drawn, reduce this heat gain during the summer. Like many passive solar designs, this one represents a relationship among envelope, interior configuration, and the size of the mechanical equipment. Although not connected, these systems are integrated to the point where the distinctions between them become blurred. The air space between the window

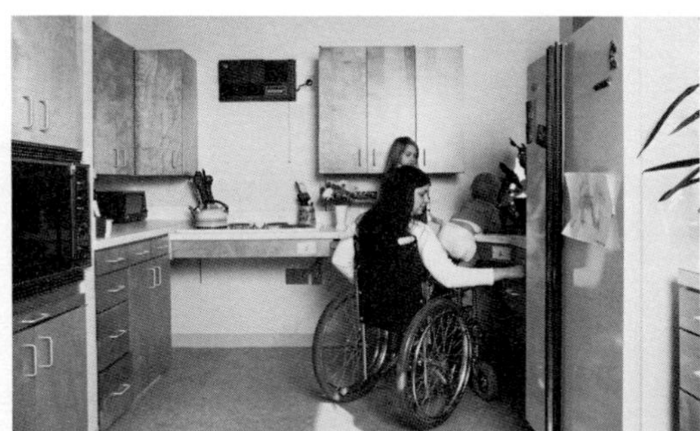

Kitchens are designed with generous proportions, wheelchair-accessible counterspace, and conventional placement of appliances and storage units.

and masonry wall is, in effect, a duct. The interior wall serves as a heater.

In addition, each unit has one or two solar chimneys, or "sun scoops"; the clerestory wall mass collects heat which is then circulated by fan. In summer the scoops act as thermal siphons, venting hot air out of the buildings. The clerestory spaces represent four-system integration; the mechanical element is *connected* in the form of the fans. The sun scoops provide extra light and a feeling of space for the tenants, who often spend long periods of time in their apartments.

CIRCULATION REQUIREMENTS

The interior plans, which are completely generated by user needs, do not involve elaborate circulation spaces for wheelchairs; traffic is simply zoned near one corner of each main room, removing the possibility of placing furniture in the way. Each space is designed with proportions generous enough to accommodate both wheelchair turns and the conventional placement of cabinets, appliances, and furnishings.[3] The building envelope is detailed with batt insulation between 6 in. wood studs, plus 1 in. foam insulating sheathing, to prevent solar loss, and is oriented for solar gain. The interior follows this orientation and gains natural light. Supplementary heating and cooling are provided by individual heat pumps.[4] Each of these strategies supplements the

1. Visible integration, pp. 381–385, 392–393.
2. Insulating glass, pp. 209–211.
3. Spatial performance, pp. 249–250.
4. Heat pumps, pp. 161–163.

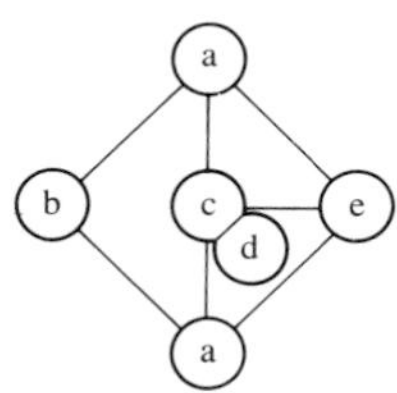

a. *Wood stud frame*
b. *Window assembly*
c. *Masonry thermal mass*
d. *Trombe wall vents*
e. *Drywall*

Diagram detail page 380

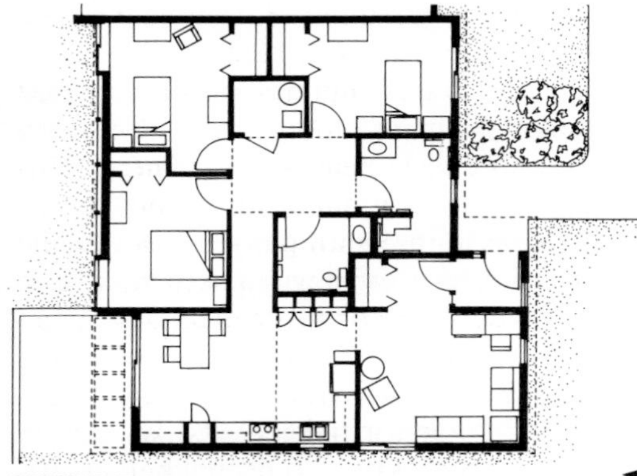

TYPICAL FLOOR PLAN

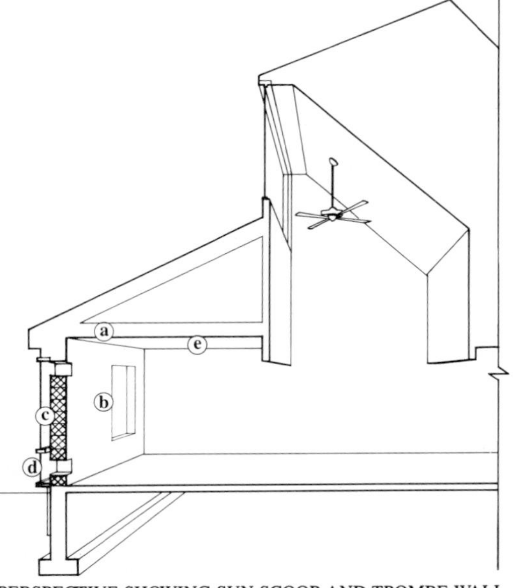

PERSPECTIVE SHOWING SUN SCOOP AND TROMBE WALL

Trombe walls and "sun scoop" clerestories appear in an exterior view (top). Clapboard siding helps the buildings relate to their regional context. The plan of a typical unit (above) shows how traffic is zoned near one corner of each main room. The section perspective (right) is taken through one of the sun scoops.

mechanical design and is extensively integrated with it, resulting in a solution which performs at very high levels in response to basic building performance criteria.

Wherever possible, tenants are encouraged to adjust and control their living spaces for themselves. This can mean opening and closing Trombe vents, placing or removing the fabric Trombe covers, running the air-to-air kitchen heat exchangers, or simply opening and closing windows and doors (each unit has an air lock entry). Kitchens and baths offer counters with adjustable height and a variety of both high and low storage spaces. Aiding independence, too, are roll-in shower stalls, low window sills, and side-hinged appliances, to cite a few examples among many details.

The John Nutting Apartments are successful on several levels. Handicapped access and passive solar features are combined effectively for efficient use of space, time, energy, and materials. The envelope fits the existing historic context and energy requirements, while it is fully integrated with the mechanical system.

Project: John C. Nutting Apartments.
Architects: Juster Pope Associates, Shelburne Falls, MA. Design team: Earl Pope, Jack L. Frazier, AIA, Norton Juster, AIA, Nancy Schwartz.
Structural Engineers: Juster Pope Associates, Shelburne Falls, MA.
Mechanical and Electrical Engineers: Robert W. Hall Consulting Engineers, Inc., Agawam, MA.
Landscape Architects: V. Michael Weinmayr Associates, Boston, MA.
Site Engineers: Gordon E. Ainsworth & Associates, South Deerfield, MA.
General Contractor: Palazzesi Construction Corp., Wilbraham, MA.
Cost: $460,430; $63 PSF ($54 PSF exclusive of site work). Completed October 1981.
Photographs: D. Randolph Foulds (courtesy of Juster Pope Associates).

Illinois Regional Library for the Blind and Physically Handicapped
Chicago, Illinois

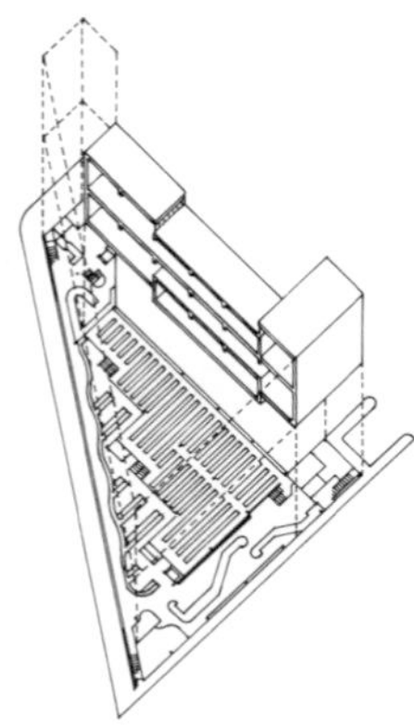

In the Illinois Regional Library, lighthearted forms embody a highly serious attempt to understand, and integrate into the design, the kinetic and perceptual experience of being blind or otherwise physically handicapped. Orientation by feel, memory, sound, and residual vision, as well as difficulty in negotiating complicated spaces, have been accommodated at all levels of building design, from overall *parti* to the details of furnishings. At the same time, the design exhibits built-in flexibility appropriate to a generic library.

This complex identity reflects an integrated programming process that included the Chicago city architect, state officials, library staff, community groups, and representatives of the National Federation of the Blind. In addition to serving handicapped patrons on-site and providing administrative and operations headquarters for a statewide network, the building was required to serve the non-handicapped residents of the immediate neighborhood as a branch library. A particular integration issue in this type of project is the necessity of satisfying the needs of diverse user groups which together form "the client."

ACCESSIBILITY AND SYMBOLISM

The architects responded both practically and intuitively with a design that acknowledges the special problems of the building's users.[1] Within the limitations of its site and budget, it is explicitly what prior facilities were not. Typically such facilities have been found in basements, with operations and handling centers treated as "back rooms." The Illinois Regional Library, on the other hand, is straightforwardly accessible and symbolically almost blatant. It is a bright, morale-building workplace, with public and service spaces as open as possible. Additional benefits include relatively low first cost and a designed-in capability for future expansion.

The architect achieved a compact, unified solution by slipping three stack levels into what is otherwise a two-story building. This space-conserving strategy places more stacks next to the book-handling area while freeing site area for future expansion. The stack arrangement and the largely open floors, combined with the exposed structural, mechanical,[2] and lighting systems, give the building a warehouse-like quality that is appropriate to its primary materials

The cast-in-place, post-tensioned window wall integrates structure, envelope, and interior. The undulations of the window head correspond to librarians' stations in the circulation desk facing it.

1. Compare John Nutting Apartments, pp. 68–69.
2. Exposed ducts, pp. 179–181.

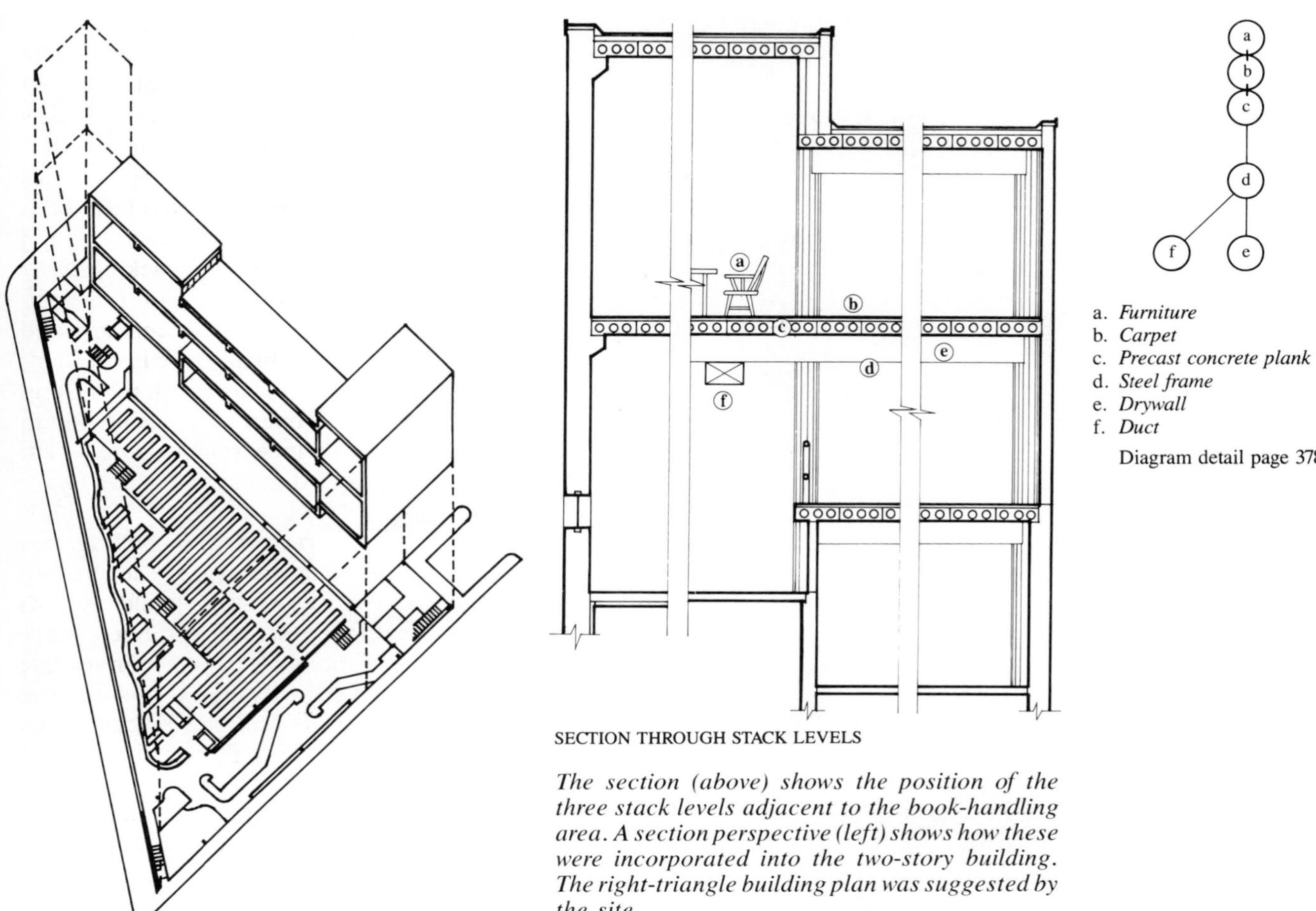

SECTION THROUGH STACK LEVELS

The section (above) shows the position of the three stack levels adjacent to the book-handling area. A section perspective (left) shows how these were incorporated into the two-story building. The right-triangle building plan was suggested by the site.

EXPLODED VIEW SHOWING PLAN AND SECTION

handling function. This image is made acceptable in a public building by visible integration that includes dimensional and color coordination of all these systems.[3] Most integration occurs at a *connected* level between the mechanical and interior systems. For instance, all exposed electrical conduit is alternated vertically with the HVAC down-feeds in the stack area, and horizontal duct runs are organized to have a constant cross-section within each bay. The color-coding of the various systems—red for envelope, yellow for structure, blue for ductwork, etc.—has a practical as well as a visual function, in that bright colors can be seen by the partially sighted. Exposed ductwork has been altered in size as well as painted, resulting in a high level of visible integration at relatively low cost and with little sacrifice in mechanical efficiency.

Given the right triangle building plan suggested by the site, the designers chose the hypotenuse as the location for the circulation desk, defining a primary public area that is long, straight, and easily memorized. The desk is 170 ft long and incorporates such details as cassette player outlets and a Braille card catalog. Hard surfaces are favored throughout, for maximum sound reflection, and guidance for blind users is formal rather than textural. The desk curves inward and downward to define areas out of the main flow of circulation, for wheelchair users and others, at the points where librar-

3. Visible integration, pp. 381–385, 398, 402–403.

The rounded corner at the entrance (top left) reflects curvilinear shapes used throughout the interior to prevent edge collisions. An interior view (left) shows card catalog files at wheelchair level. In a reading area (above), visible integration is achieved through dimensional and color coordination of structural, mechanical, and lighting systems. Recesses in the circulation desk (right) identify librarians' stations and allow wheelchair users to move out of the traffic path.

ians sit; other curved indentations show the way to reading areas and restrooms. Like the curved wall corners and the round steel columns, the desk's curves protect against edge collisions. Throughout, the architect's consideration for the building's users is evident in the emphasis on tactile, as well as visual, cohesiveness. In this, and in its siting and in compatibility with its neighborhood, the building addresses the physiological, psychological, and sociological criteria of performance.[4]

The desk shape and the use and circulation patterns which it creates are mimicked in elevation by the butt-glazed and silicone-sealed window in the hypotenuse wall.[5] For a wheelchair occupant, this window is at eye level for all of its 165 ft length; it widens to normal window heights opposite the librarians' stations. The window wall itself is a huge cast-in-place, post-tensioned concrete beam that creates a monumental image and effectively integrates structure, envelope, and interior.

4. Physiological, psychological and sociological criteria, p. 232.

5. Silicone sealants, pp. 225–226.

PERIMETER WALLS

The remaining perimeter walls are constructed of panels of ¼ in. cold-rolled steel plate, 5 ft wide and 30 ft high, that form their own vertical jambs. These panels can be

Project: Illinois Regional Library for the Blind and Physically Handicapped.
Architects: Stanley Tigerman & Associates, Chicago, IL, in association with the Bureau of Architecture, City of Chicago. Stanley Tigerman, designer; Robert E. Fugman, associate-in-charge.
Structural Engineers: Raymond Beebe, Chicago, IL.
Mechanical and Electrical Engineers: Wallace & Migdal, Chicago, IL.
General Contractor: Walsh Construction Co., Chicago, IL.
Cost: $1,900,000; $59 PSF. Completed August 1977.
Photographs: Howard N. Kaplan (courtesy of Stanley Tigerman & Associates).

removed to accommodate future expansion, greatly enhancing the flexibility of the design. Each steel plate is backed with a sandwich of insulation and an interior drywall finish, with large expansion beads 5 ft on center. This 5 ft module is also dimensionally coordinated with other interior elements. Visually, the striking contrast between the almost windowless curtain wall and the window in the massive concrete facade may be understood as a comment on the paradox of blindness.

The library integrates two approaches to geometry—the very specific, curvilinear circulation areas which bring together several surprising building elements in response to the physical experience of handicap; and the flexible, expandable, and rectilinear areas for employees and non-handicapped users, which transform ordinary elements through careful placement and detail. Clearly, the widely divergent performance demands presented by these user groups were extremely difficult to satisfy in a building as specific as a library. The solution that emerged from the highly integrated design process is quite effective, and the seemingly overwhelming emphasis placed on visible integration actually contributes to the fulfillment of the stated performance criteria.

Museum of Science and Industry
Tampa, Florida

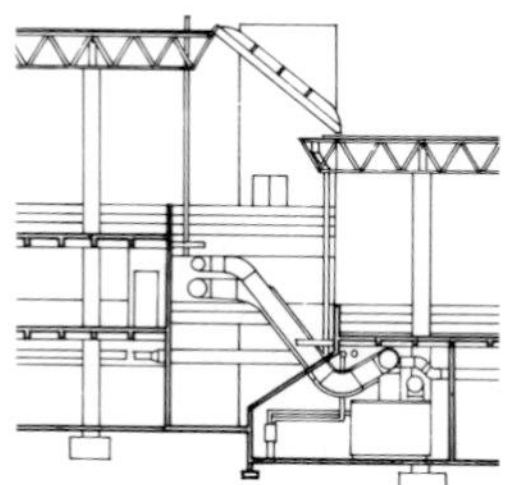

Since London's Crystal Palace of 1851, exhibit buildings have themselves often become exhibits of the latest in building technology. Tampa's Museum of Science and Industry, although designed as a permanent structure, retains this quality of a pavilion, engaging and expanding upon the visitor's idea of what such a museum should be.

The museum's program helped produce an award-winning design that responds to Tampa's distinctive regional climate, with the hoped-for gains in energy efficiency. In addition, all major energy systems for the building function as integral parts of various exhibits, at the same time satisfying their usual performance requirements. Structural, mechanical, electrical, plumbing, and fire protection systems are exposed and color-coded. Their treatment represents a level of visible integration in which system components are exposed without being relocated or reshaped.[1]

While this may seem at first to be integration for its own sake, rather than the outgrowth of real program needs, the results are both practical and applicable to other building types. Combinations of bare and brightly painted structural members, ducts,[2] pipes, and conduits result in both a formally consistent and a functionally open-ended design, allowing new mechanical and electrical components to be introduced and old ones removed without upsetting the visual or spatial order.

ROOF CONFIGURATION

The exposed space frame roof canopy, which by its nature integrates envelope, structure, and interior, is crucial to the final effect of the building; it controls and defines the spaces and systems that flow both indoors and outdoors. The light weight and rigidity of this off-the-shelf roof framing system allow a larger area and wider overhangs than the building structure would otherwise support. Appropriately, it is this versatile, scientifically generated shape, rather than the relatively ordinary, fully enclosed volumes below it, that reads as "the building"

The south-facing roof slope, supported by the space frame, acts as sunshade and porte cochere, and is intended to support photovoltaic cells.

and exhibits the form and scale suitable for a major public facility.

The roof achieves the economic and instructional goal of energy efficiency by reducing the number of spaces that require air conditioning, while its passive solar capabilities supplement air conditioning in the spaces that require it. There are 23,700 sq ft of semi-enclosed space and 15,500 sq ft of open area under roof. Fully conditioned spaces total 30,300 sq ft. The extensive south-facing roof slope acts as a sunshade for the entire building as well as a car and bus drop-off, and is designed to carry photovoltaic cells. The projected photovoltaic installation will eventually contribute up to 15 percent of the building's electric power needs and become part of the museum's research and education program. The roof's north slope is a skylight over an atrium, which lights the building's interior spaces and gives visitors unexpected views of museum support functions.

Through analysis of the site's microclimate and an east/west orientation, the architects were able to take advantage of prevailing east and northeast winds for cooling. Vented openings near the skylight between the two main horizontal roof planes augment this air movement, producing a wind ve-

1. Visible integration, pp. 381–385, 398–400, 406–407.

2. Exposed ducts, pp. 179–181.

All major energy systems are exposed and color-coded, as in the semi-outdoor atrium (above). The relationship of the various levels to the atrium space is indicated in the section (top right). The section perspective (center) shows how the roof configuration, generated by the space frame, gives the building its form. The "inner envelope" shown in the plan (bottom) contains offices, work areas, classrooms, and auditoriums.

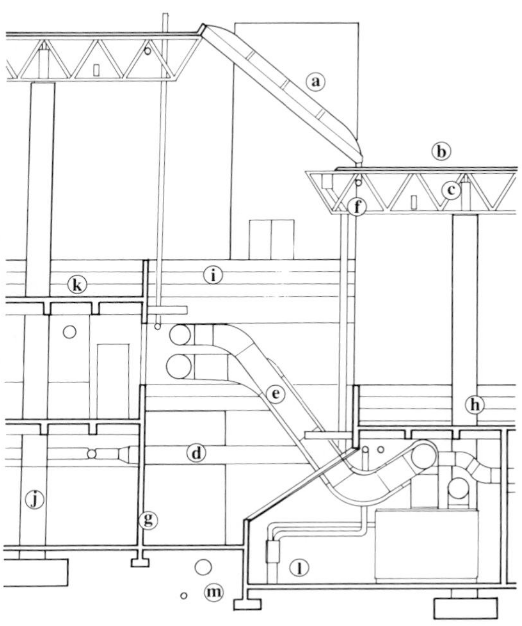

SECTION FACING EAST

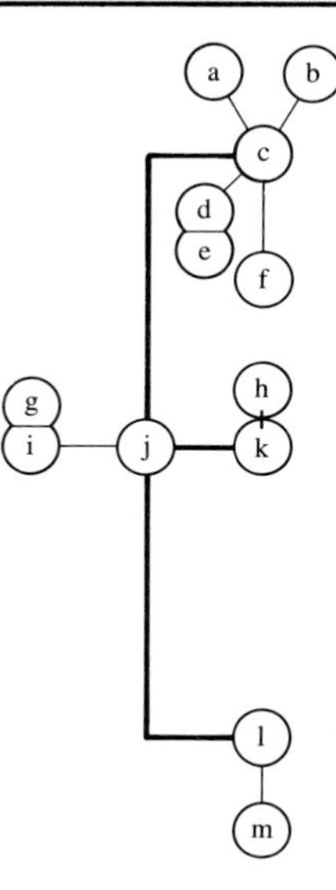

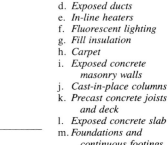

a. *Skylights*
b. *Built-up roof and rigid insulation*
c. *Metal space frame and metal roof deck*
d. *Exposed ducts*
e. *In-line heaters*
f. *Fluorescent lighting*
g. *Fill insulation*
h. *Carpet*
i. *Exposed concrete masonry walls*
j. *Cast-in-place columns*
k. *Precast concrete joists and deck*
l. *Exposed concrete slab*
m. *Foundations and continuous footings*

Diagram detail page 367

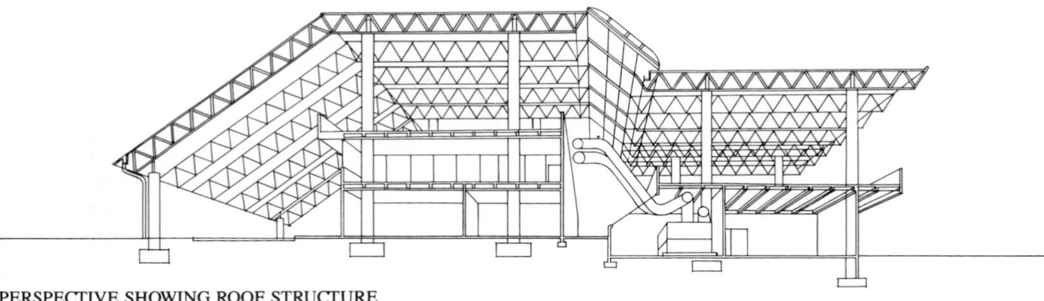

PERSPECTIVE SHOWING ROOF STRUCTURE

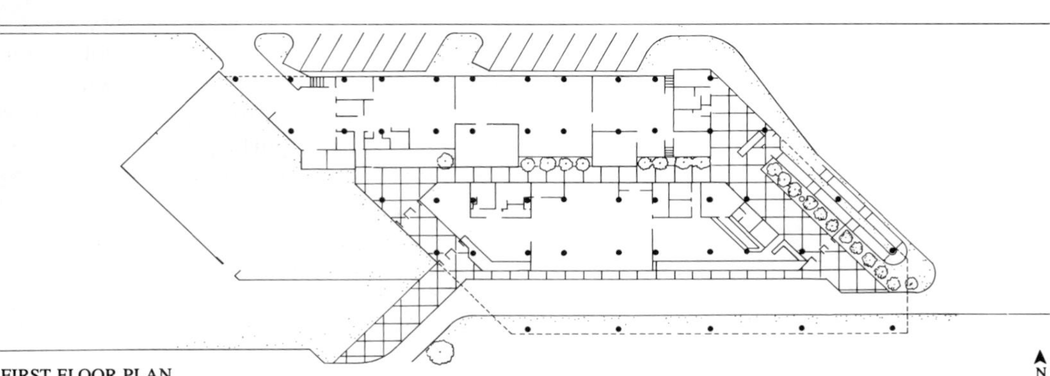

FIRST FLOOR PLAN

locity increase of up to nine miles per hour. As a result, the temperature in the unconditioned areas of the building can be 20°F cooler than outside. The north roof surface also acts as a rainwater collector, serving a system that stores, treats, and distributes water as part of the museum's program on water conservation.

INTERIOR SPACES

The building's enclosed and air-conditioned areas, comprising somewhat less than half of the project's 61,000 sq ft, represent a different level of integration. Precast concrete joists are used with cast-in-place concrete floor slabs, beams, and columns. These elements combine with insulated concrete block walls, based on an 8 in. module, to create an energy-conserving "inner envelope" for offices, work areas, classrooms, and an auditorium. In general, the concrete elements remain unfinished, providing a backdrop for the brightly colored exposed pipes, ducts, light fixtures, and the museum exhibits themselves.[3]

Small packaged metal building units have been designed to house enclosed, air-conditioned exhibits in the semi-outdoor, unconditioned loft areas. The space frame can support a rooftop air conditioning unit above each of these "pods" with visible ductwork leading to it. The pods may be moved or removed, thus conserving time used in changing exhibits.

The Museum of Science and Industry teaches lessons in design and construction by displaying a wide range of active and passive environmental control systems, and an equally wide range of construction types, each used for a specific function: cast-in-place concrete for short-span structures, precast concrete for finished floors and ceilings, the steel space frame for long-span structures (supported by concrete in simple compression), masonry for infill and mass, and metal buildings for flexibility. Earthen construction in the form of a berm disperses the sound of a nearby highway.

This kind of analysis and particularization of building systems might seem to be the opposite of integration. Designed-in flexibility does restrict integration to the *connected* or *touching* levels; while the systems are separate and exposed, they combine to achieve a fairly high level of visible integration. The brightly colored ductwork and the degree of detail exposed in the space frame results in a dynamic spatial composition.

3. Visible integration, pp. 381–385, 398–400, 406–407.

Unfinished concrete elements, along with exposed ducts and lighting equipment, are visible in an interior view of the public entry (top). The museum's pavilion-like quality is evident in a view facing west (center). The solid "inner envelope" is barely visible. The play of light on the space frame is striking at night (above).

Structural, envelope, and mechanical elements are exposed in the atrium. Daylighting and plants enhance the semi-outdoor atmosphere of this naturally ventilated space.

Project: Museum of Science and Industry.
Architects: Rowe Holmes Barnett Architects, Inc., Tampa, FL. Design team: H. Dean Rowe, AIA; John L. Tennison, AIA; S. Keith Bailey, AIA; Michael A. Shirley, AIA; Dwight E. Holmes, FAIA.
Structural Engineers: Rast Associates, Inc., Tampa, FL.
Mechanical and Electrical Engineers: OSSI Consulting Engineers, Inc., Tampa, FL.
Landscape Architect: Thomas Balsley, ASLA, New York, NY.
General Contractor: C.M. Constructors Managers, Inc., Houston, TX.
Cost: \$3,987,556; \$58 PSF. Completed February 1980.
Photographs: Gordon H. Schenck, Jr. (courtesy of Rowe Holmes Barnett Architects, Inc.).

Stockton State College
Pomona, New Jersey

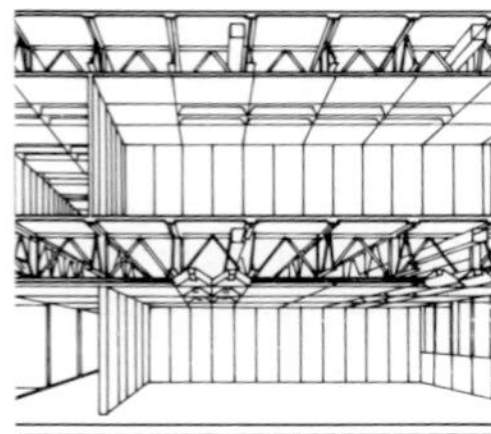

Stockton State College may be the leading example in the United States of "systems building" as that concept emerged as a distinct process in the late 1960's. As such, it serves to illustrate the distinction between systems building and systems integration. Systems building, involving a compatible collection of distinct systems, does not usually result in a high level of physical integration. Stockton State exhibits both greater and lesser degrees of integration, but throughout it exemplifies the thinking that underlies an integrated approach to design.

The architects and their client, an embryonic state college which had just acquired 1600 acres of unimproved land in the Pine Barrens near Atlantic City,[1] began with a set of criteria that included a very tight schedule. Voters had mandated immediate creation of the new college; the state government had fixed an initial enrollment of 1000, and directed that the institution should be under roof, in permanent quarters, in less than a year. Another major criterion was flexibility, since there was not yet a faculty or an academic plan. There was no need, as there was in the case of the Vocational Technical Education Facility at the University of Minnesota,[2] to coordinate the design with existing buildings of a particular historic style.

RESPONSE TO CRITERIA

Economy was also a prime consideration, both in initial cost and life-cycle cost. Thus the program emphasized conservation of construction time and resources. At the same time, the college and the firm of GBQC both recognized that the success of the project, and indeed of the college itself, depended on quality design, and that the ideal of a nonmonumental, responsive campus was bound up with the need to preserve the environmentally sensitive site.

Addressing this complex set of criteria, the architects set out three possible alternatives to conventional construction. These were pre-engineered building (one-source, industrially produced and packaged systems), engineered building (largely conventional construction except for frame and siding), and systems building (compatible but separately produced major subsystems).

The designers concluded that the first two alternatives were insufficiently flexible for Stockton State's program. In addition, they concluded that pre-engineered buildings would exhibit a temporary quality inconsistent with the client's esthetic goals, while engineered buildings would require longer construction time than the other alternatives. Recognizing these limitations, and inspired by California's School Construction Systems Development project, the architects and client decided that the college's needs would best be accommodated by a systems building solution.

The architects defined and set criteria for five major system categories: structure, heating/ventilating/air conditioning, ceiling/lighting, floor covering, and demountable partitions. In later phases, exterior walls were also included, raising from 20 percent to over 45 percent the portion of project cost that was competitively pre-bid by subsystem suppliers.

From an integration perspective, the system categories are related to one another primarily in terms of dimensional compatibility, in response to the larger need for con-

An aerial view of the college looking south emphasizes the environmental sensitivity of the 1600 acre site. Absence of existing buildings as an architectural context allowed considerable design freedom.

1. Visible integration, pp. 381–385, 387.
2. Compare Vocational Technical Education Facility, pp. 98–101.

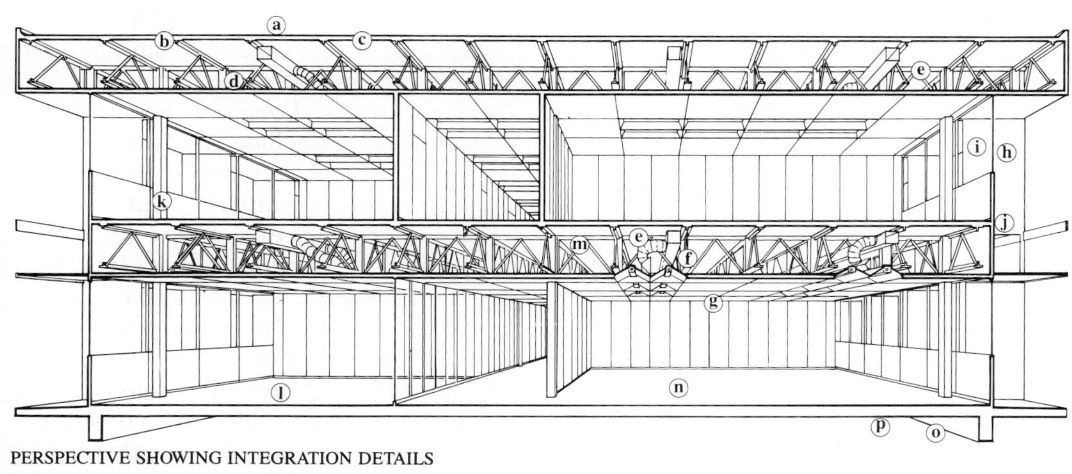

PERSPECTIVE SHOWING INTEGRATION DETAILS

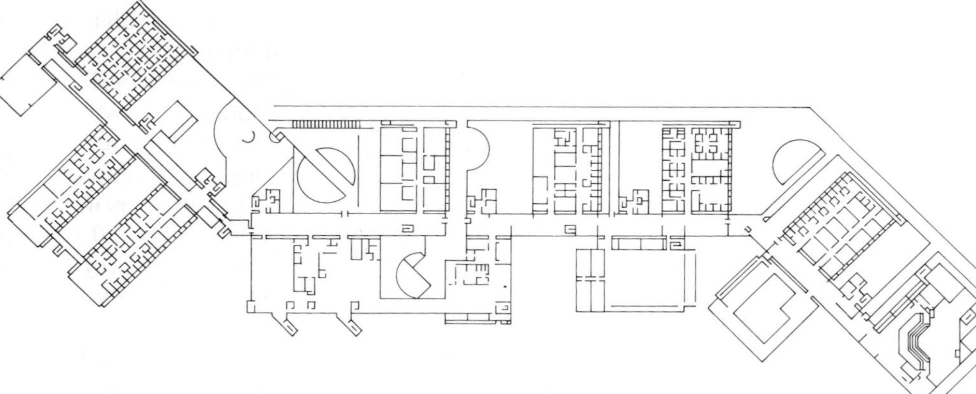

COMPOSITE OF TYPICAL FLOOR PLANS

N

a. *Roofing*
b. *Batt insulation*
c. *Metal roof deck*
d. *Steel bar joists*
e. *Ducts*
f. *Air-handling luminaires*
g. *Lay-in ceiling*
h. *Sunscreens*
i. *Window wall assembly*
j. *Lightweight insulating panels*
k. *Steel frame*
l. *Ceramic tile (in gallery)*
m. *Steel bar joists and metal floor deck*
n. *Floor covering*
o. *Cast-in-place concrete foundations*
p. *Waterproof membrane*

Diagram detail page 369

Photo: Ezra Stoller. ESTO

A meshed *relationship of structure and interior is evident in the section perspective (top). In plan (center), construction phases are clearly marked by angles in the two-story spine. A view of this interior street (left) shows exposed structure and lighting. The mechanical system is also exposed, a treatment extended to the swimming pool (above) and gymnasium spaces.*

struction speed and quality control. The criteria included formal considerations, but the emphasis was on physical fit among the chosen systems. The steel structural frame had to be able to accommodate ducts, support the integrated ceilings[3] and access floors,[4] and accept vertical openings. Ceilings had to accept demountable partitions and possess integral air supply and return capability in the form of air-handling luminaires.[5] Partitions had to attach to the ceiling grid in regular modules and accommodate internal wiring. Structural frame configurations determined duct sizes. Exterior panels[6] were designed to accommodate both ceilings and interior partitions, and to allow for structural deflection. Finally, there was the overriding requirement that all systems be capable of being disassembled and reassembled on weeks' or even days' notice, and at low cost.

PERFORMANCE AND EXPANSION

In terms of these criteria the basic design, revised and expanded but not fundamentally changed up to the present, has performed even better than expected. Phase one broke construction time records; phase two came in under budget despite a more complex program. (Insulating glass[7] was specified for the latter phase.) Changes are easily made, to the extent that office moves are reported to have become all too popular. The project has evolved into a sprawling complex that includes classrooms, laboratories, auditoriums, a library, a 25-meter pool, and a gymnasium, all connected by a two-story spine or interior street. Conservation of space has not been an issue, as it would be on an urban or a suburban campus.

Formally, the coordination of "off-the-rack" elements in terms of dimension, color, and detail is a form of visible integration. In Hartman-Cox's National Permanent Building,[8] the sense of formal amenity in beautifully coordinated systems complements their operation. At Stockton State the effect of dimensional coordination and careful choices is to transform what could otherwise be an apparent makeshift—an industrial loft conversion that ran out of money—into a convincing and elegant environment for higher education.

Photo: Ezra Stoller, ESTO

Dimensional coordination and attention to detail result in an appropriate environment for higher education. Envelope details include outdoor lighting and seating integrated into an extension of the structure (above). Clip-on sunshades are provided for facades exposed to direct sunlight (above right). Panelized construction contributed to construction speed (below right).

More easily recognized kinds of integration are present as well. Structure, envelope, and mechanical elements are exposed to form the interior, for instance. Shades clipped to the envelope augment the natural shading of surrounding trees and help to control solar gain. Overall, however, the project is characterized by integration at the *connected* level, combining flexibility with the visual and intellectual coherence that is one of systems integration's main appeals.

3. Integrated ceilings, pp. 182–184.
4. Access floors, pp. 202–204.
5. Air-handling luminaires, pp. 185–186.
6. Lightweight insulating metal panels, pp. 219–222.
7. Insulating glass, pp. 209–211.
8. Compare National Permanent, pp. 90–91.

Photo: Harvey Krasnegor

Photo: Norman McGrath

Project: Stockton State College.
Architects: Geddes Brecher Qualls Cunningham: Architects, Philadelphia, PA.
Structural Engineers: David Bloom, Inc., Philadelphia, PA.
Mechanical and Electrical Engineers: Vinokur-Pace, Jenkintown, PA.
Consultants: KMK, Inc., White Plains, NY—acoustical; Edward Elliott, New Smyrna Beach, FL—food service.
General Contractor: Costanza Contracting Co., Pennsauken, NJ—Phases I and II; Superior Consolidated Contracting, Inc., Burlington, NJ—Phase III.
Cost: $27,604,000 (1971 estimate of cost of Phases I, II, and III); $70 PSF (estimate based on 390,000 gross academic square feet). Completed October 1974.
Photographs: GBQC unless otherwise noted.

Walter Reed General Hospital
Washington, D.C.

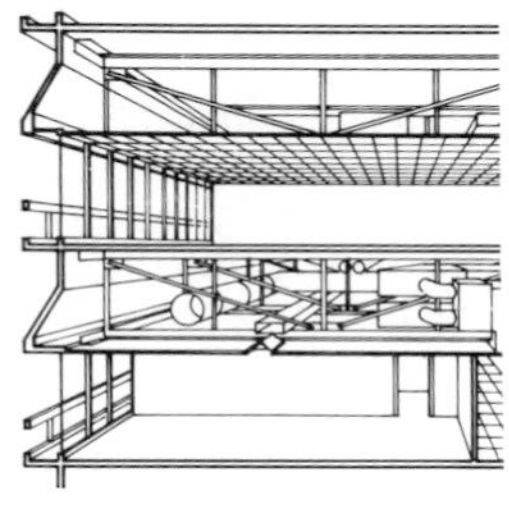

The design of a modern hospital complex tends to be governed by the need for flexibility in an environment that must also be highly sanitized and barrier-free. The program for the Walter Reed General Hospital was further complicated by the requirement that it accommodate a wide range of patient care, laboratory, teaching, and support functions that had previously been housed in 43 smaller buildings scattered around the medical center's 100 acre campus. This multiplicity of demands has been addressed in a highly ordered design of very large scale.

Vertically, this order is expressed in a series of interstitial mechanical floors. The interstitial concept is the clearest instance of systems integration in this 1 million sq ft building. Here the 7 ft depth needed for an economical long-span structure is also used to create a continuously accessible, completely flexible mechanical space. The structurally efficient cantilevering of the interstitial trusses results in sunshading that reduces cooling loads and facilitates air intake into the mechanical system.

INTERIOR FLEXIBILITY

Formally, too, the interstitial floors provide a strong profile that articulates the mass of this enormous low building. In the interior, these trusses help achieve large, flexible 30 x 60 ft bays with relative economy and without interrupting mechanical, materials handling, and communications runs. The floor structure of the occupied floors is a simple reinforced concrete slab, while the interstitial floors have lightweight concrete walking decks.

The interstitial concept is a device for organizing interior spaces that is common to many modern hospitals. In Walter Reed, it is closely related to the design of the building envelope as well. Occupied floors are largely glass-enclosed and recessed, while interstitial floors are cantilevered outward on the steel trusses. Covered in precast concrete panels, they function as window shading, window washing platforms, balconies, and air-intake housings.

Photos: Pflueger Architects

The cantilevered interstitial floors of the hospital create a strong profile and articulate the low building mass (top). Landscaped courtyards penetrate the top three floors (above), introducing natural light and views to the corridors and giving the huge floors a sense of scale.

In plan, the occupied floors are organized on a grid pattern that stresses flexibility and order. The top three floors are penetrated by eight courtyards which introduce natural light and air into the deep mass of the hospital, reducing mechanical loads and diminishing the need for elaborate interior treatments. The courtyard spaces provide visitors with a sense of scale, facilitate clear, separate traffic paths, and arguably create a more therapeutic environment.

The courtyards and the strict rectilinearity of the grid in turn generate order in the mechanical and electrical runs, communications equipment, and materials handling subsystems. The latter include auto-

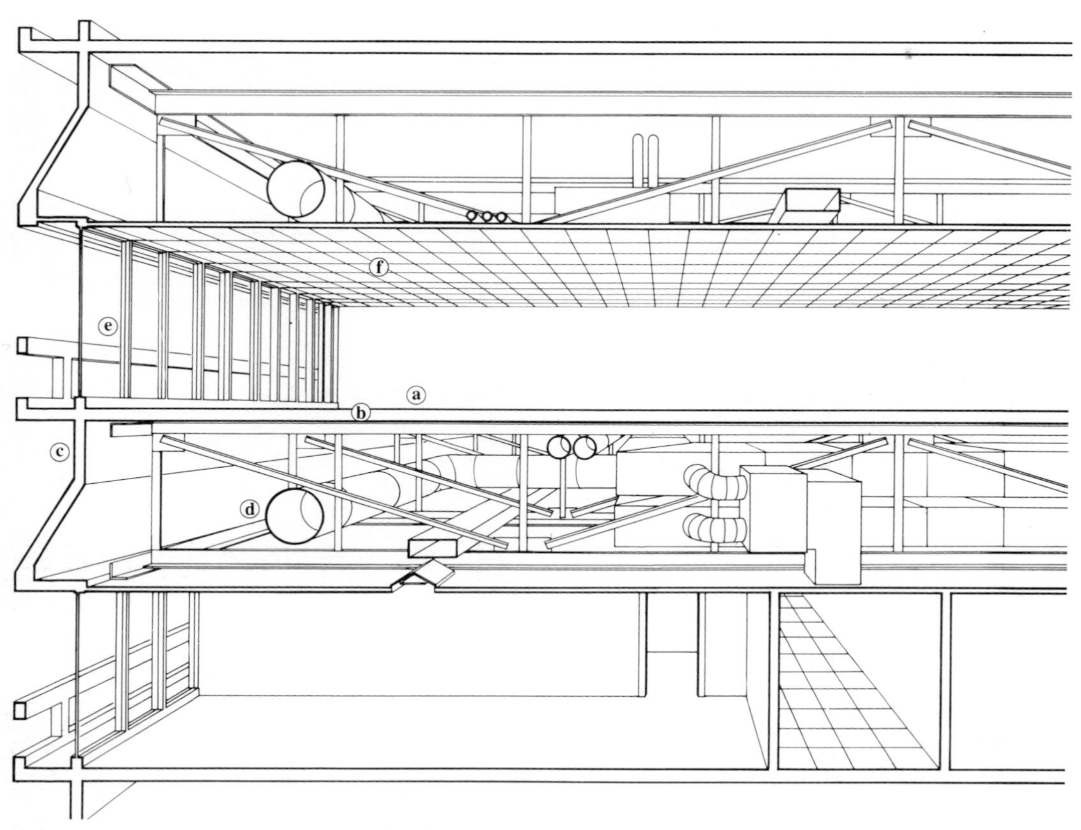

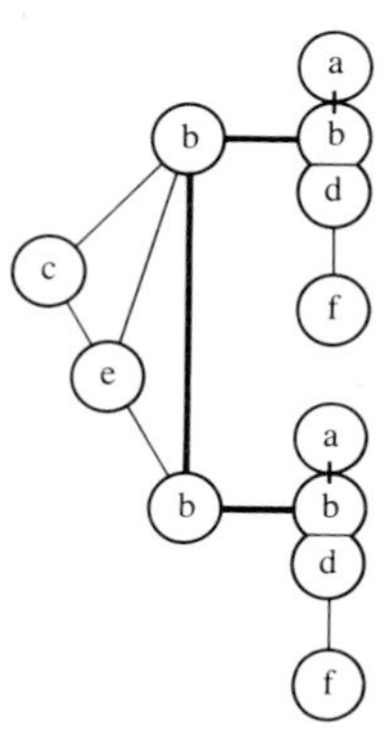

a. *Carpet*
b. *Concrete slab and steel truss*
c. *Precast concrete spandrel panels*
d. *Ducts*
e. *Window assembly*
f. *Suspended ceiling*

Diagram detail page 368

PERSPECTIVE SHOWING INTERSTITIAL FLOORS

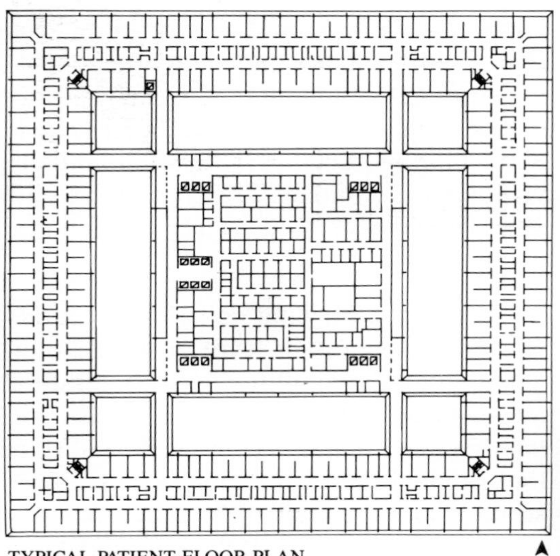

TYPICAL PATIENT FLOOR PLAN

Photos: Pflueger Architects

The section perspective (top) shows how the space defined by the trusses is used to house mechanical equipment. The grid plan of an occupied floor (above) stresses order and flexibility.

Precast concrete panels form the envelope at the interstitial floors (right), which cantilever outward to provide shading, balconies, window-washing platforms, and air-intake housings.

Photos: Pflueger Architects

As emphasized in the model photo (above), the strict grid pattern and courtyard spaces generate order in the mechanical and electrical runs, communications equipment, and materials handling subsystems. A typical operating room (right) shows how many support functions are integrated with the ceiling. A view of an interstitial floor (below right) shows the automated dumbwaiter/monorail carts. The monorail is partly housed within the interstitial spaces.

mated dumbwaiter/monorail carts, a high-speed modular mini-rail network for transporting documents and small objects, pneumatic trash and linen chutes, and central housekeeping vacuuming. Dedicated conveyances include a monorail in the food service department and dumbwaiters serving surgery, central supply, and floor pharmacies. The multiplicity of conveyances allows separation of functions, a benefit in terms of sanitization. These conveyances are accommodated almost entirely within the interstitial floors, where changes and repairs can be made without interrupting activities on the floors above and below.[1]

VERTICAL TRANSPORTATION

Like any large modern hospital, Walter Reed requires considerable redundancy in vertical transportation. A three-elevator bank is located in each building quadrant for patient and staff use, with a six-elevator bank at the main entrance for visitors.[2] A master antenna serves as a co-axial cable system for patient nurse call and television, and integrated bedside units handle medical gases and electrical services. A central reverse osmosis system supplies pure water.

Basic HVAC subsystems are subdivided into individually served quadrants on each floor,[3] with smaller air-handling components on the interstitial floors. Modular distribution anticipates inevitable future changes. Return air and heat are recovered, and environmental controls are computerized;[4] steam heat is generated in an existing central plant.

Overall, the hospital complex is characterized by a *meshed* level of integration, most strongly exemplified in the interstitial mechanical floors, with structure and envelope fixed to allow maximum flexibility in the mechanical and interior systems. This strategy and the vast scale of the building allow considerable isolation of system components. This not only satisfies sanitation, acoustical privacy, thermal, and security criteria, but conserves time when modifications or repairs are needed.

1. Visible integration, pp. 381–385, 401.
2. Elevators, pp. 187–189.
3. Air quality performance, pp. 252–253.
4. Energy management control systems, pp. 158–160.

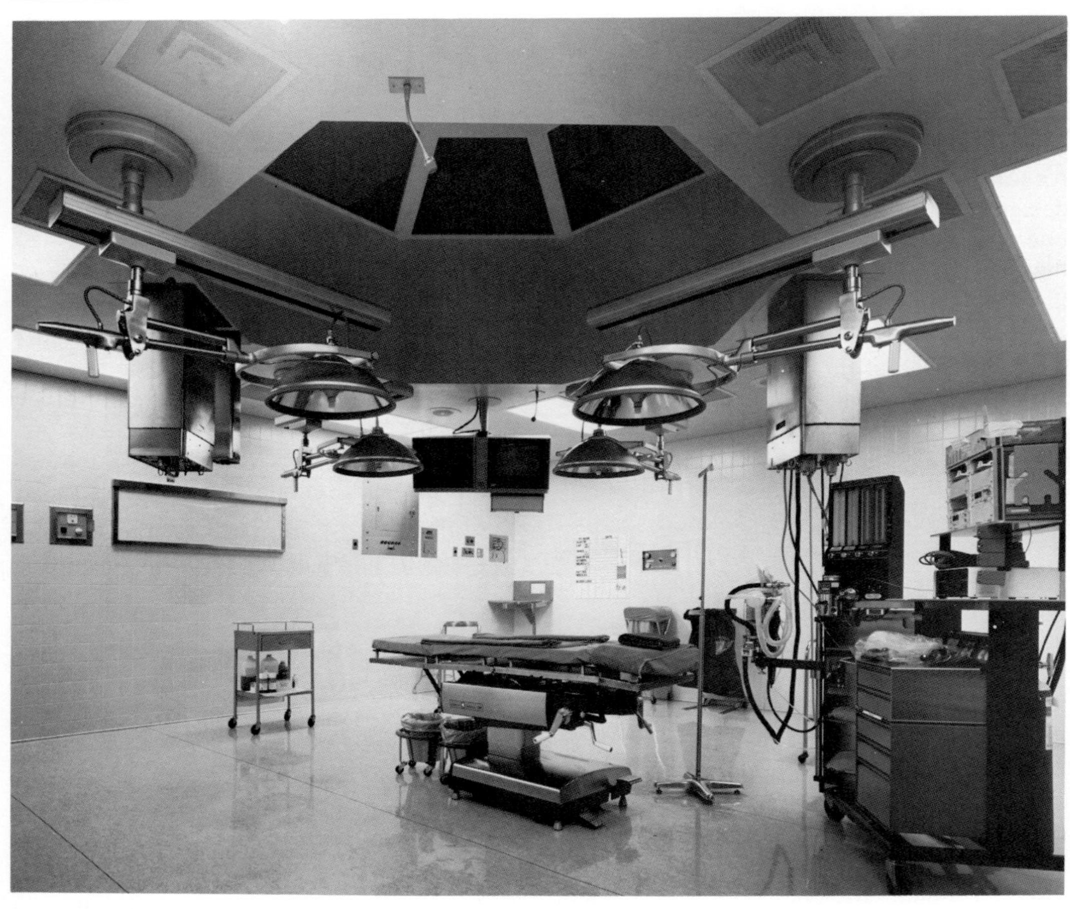

Project: Walter Reed General Hospital.
Architects: Stone, Marraccini and Patterson Architects/ Planners, San Francisco, CA, and Milton T. Pflueger, Architect, San Francisco, CA (a joint venture).
Structural Engineers: I. Thompson and Associates, San Francisco, CA.
Mechanical and Electrical Engineers: Buonaccorsi and Associates, San Francisco, CA.
Consultants: SWA Group, Sausalito, CA—landscape design; TRW, Redondo Beach, CA—facility design integration; Dames and Moore, Washington, DC—soils and geology; Wayne Hackney, Palo Alto, CA—physics; E. H. Hesselberg, San Francisco, CA—elevators; Gage-Babcock and Associates, Inc., Oakland, CA—fire protection; E. L. Toffelmier, Walnut Creek, CA—window wall; Concrete Consulting Corporation, Berkeley, CA—concrete materials and finish; Wilson-Ihrig and Associates, Oakland, CA—acoustical; John D. Porterfield, M.D., Chicago, IL—coordinating medical consultant.
General Contractor: Blake Construction Company, Washington, DC, and U.S. Industries, New York, NY (a joint venture).
Cost: $96,839,000 (bid); $88 PSF (bid).
Completed December 1978.
Photographs: Harlan Hambright unless otherwise noted.

Georgia Power Company Corporate Headquarters
Atlanta, Georgia

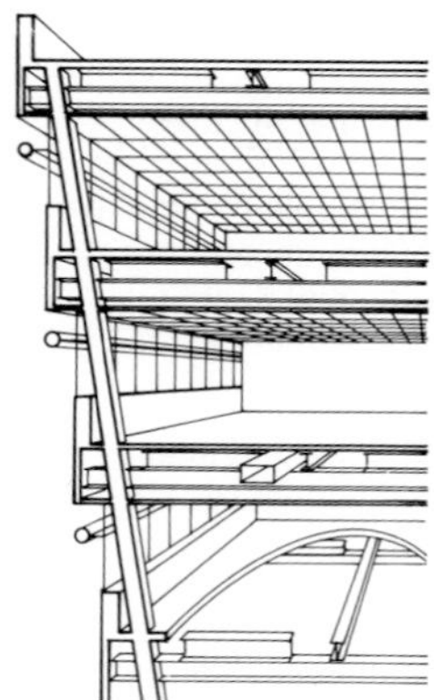

The distinctive, stepped-back facade of the Georgia Power Company Corporate Headquarters calls attention to its major design criterion: low energy use.[1] The client power company, in an effort to set an example for its customers, asked the architects to design a building whose energy use would be one-third to one-half that of a comparable highrise Atlanta office building, at no premium in construction cost.

Shading from the summer sun is provided by the setback of the south wall, a visually striking feature which gives the tower its strong image. Each 15 in. overhang is augmented by a 12 in. diameter aluminum tube hung just above eye level; these plus the overall cantilever of 26 ft provide shading from direct sunlight on this facade for seven months of the year. The resulting lateral load is supported by steel cross bracing concealed in the windowless east and west walls, with only a few moment-resisting connections along the north and south column lines.

The reduction in energy use reflects substantial mechanical system reductions, although some of this can be attributed not to the envelope or other design elements but to the operational efficiency of the mechanical system. Mechanical functions are divided between a 24-story office tower, normally occupied about 10 hours a day, and a 3-story lowrise building containing all 24-hour functions and any unusual mechanical equipment (e.g., a TV studio). An array of parabolic trough-tracking solar collectors, mounted on the roof of the lowrise building, supplies about 15 percent of the complex's energy needs. The tower's energy appetite is further limited through a combination of structural, envelope, mechanical, and interior strategies.

1. Visible integration, pp. 381–385, 391.
2. Open plan office furniture, pp. 196–199.
3. Insulating glass, pp. 209–211.
4. Protected membrane roofing, pp. 167–168.
5. Structure and mechanical *meshed*, p. 325.
6. Conservation of space, p. 236.

NORTH AND SOUTH EXPOSURES

A potentially controversial programmatic decision, but an effective one in terms of energy criteria, was to minimize perimeter office space. East and west walls are devoted to elevator core, conference room, mechanical, and storage spaces, leaving office areas with north and south exposures only. Open plan office furniture[2] with a mix of high and low partitions makes use of these efficiently proportioned spaces while providing limited access to outdoor views. The partitions also incorporate power and communications hookups, so that one hookup from a raceway at the perimeter can serve as many as six work stations. High-pressure sodium lamps in widely spaced direct/indirect pendant fixtures are placed on the line of the open office grid, and provide direct lighting for two offices apiece. In addition, reflectors allow indirect light to cover a square pattern; regular repetition of these patterns creates even ceiling illumination.

The glazed north wall of the tower requires no shading, but uses the same bronze-tinted reflective insulating glass[3] as the south facade. This is an instance of visible integration. Only 50 percent of these walls are vision glass; opaque wall sections incorporate a 6 in. thick metal-lined insulated panel. A single-ply protected membrane roof is used on the tower.[4]

In the lowrise building, a single ribbon window penetrates only about 20 percent of the highly insulated brick and concrete masonry wall, reducing mechanical loads to a minimum. A skylit gallery running between the lowrise building and the tower provides lounge and conference space with minor HVAC impact.

Given the client's desire for open, relatively column-free office areas, a steel-framed structure with stub girders was chosen for the tower. The typical interior spaces resulting from this structural decision are 25 x 43 ft. Floor-to-floor height is reduced by means of a composite steel floor deck and stub girder framing, conserving space for ductwork and other systems components.[5] Thus the building's design successfully integrates structural, interior, and mechanical systems, conserving space and resources.[6] The lowrise building is composed of cast-in-place concrete beams and

An exterior view (top) shows the office tower and the lowrise building that contains all 24-hour mechanical functions. A skylit lounge and conference space (center) connect the two buildings. Parabolic trough-tracking solar collectors (above) occupy the roof of the lowrise building.

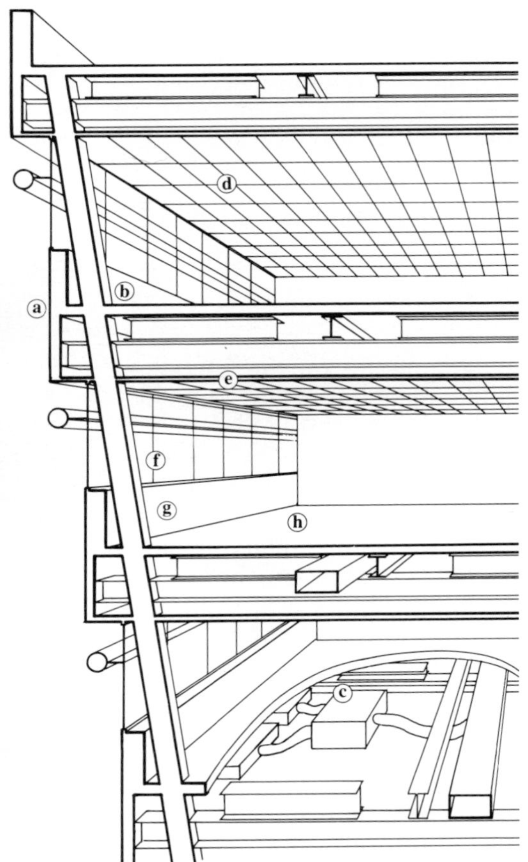

PERSPECTIVE SHOWING STRUCTURAL DETAILS

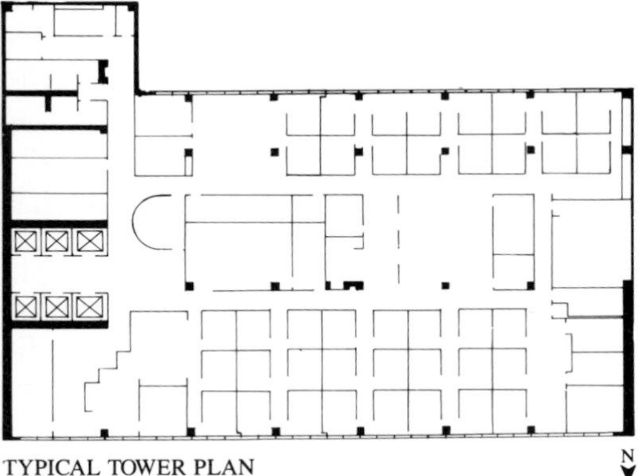

TYPICAL TOWER PLAN

The section perspective (top) depicts the tower's structural system. A composite steel floor deck and stub girder framing save space for ductwork. A typical tower floor plan (above) shows how this structural system helps create the relatively column-free office spaces requested by the client.

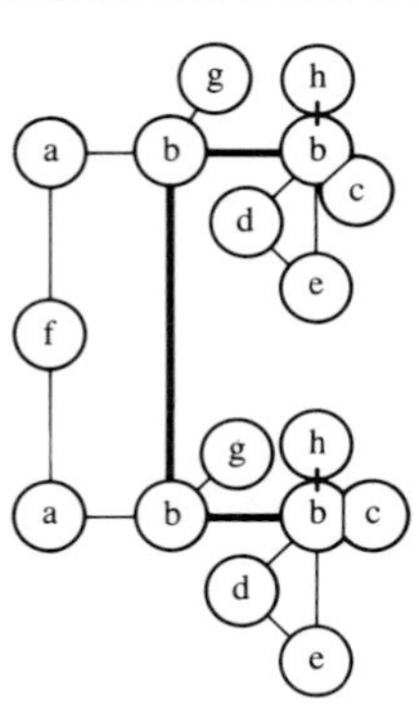

a. *Aluminum and glass curtain wall*
b. *Steel frame; composite steel and concrete deck; stub girders*
c. *Ducts and conduits*
d. *High-pressure sodium lighting*
e. *Suspended ceiling*
f. *Window assembly*
g. *Perimeter heater*
h. *Floor covering*

Diagram detail page 373

The south facade's profile (right) provides shading from the summer sun and gives the tower its distinctive image. Partitions in the office spaces (above) incorporate power and communications hookups for up to six work stations.

slab with precast concrete joists and load-bearing masonry.

ENERGY-SAVING CRITERIA

Mounted on the roof of the lowrise building are Georgia Power's active solar collectors. These activate a 260-ton hot-water-driven absorption refrigeration machine, which augments domestic hot water supplies as well as providing hot water for heating the building. The solar-powered chiller supplements a conventional closed-loop chilled-water system which is fed by two 650-ton centrifugal chillers. One of these chillers includes a double-bundle condenser which can use waste heat for building heating. A variable air volume (VAV) system is used, with one supply air handler on each floor of the tower. There are between 20 and 30 zones per floor, and a VAV induction box is used in the larger interior zones, mixing ceiling plenum air with primary air to equalize temperatures. Exterior zones include a constant fan and electric duct heater; there is also an air side economizer cycle. The lowrise building incorporates both VAV and constant volume air delivery according to area function, and requires almost no active space heating.

In focusing on energy-saving criteria, the client was able to take advantage of an already highly organized and integrated corporate structure. The building program is likewise integrated with regard to issues of energy conservation, construction economy, and functional clarity. The tower envelope is radically modified to achieve energy goals; an open office system and specially designed lighting and air handling techniques complement the floor plan, which also incorporates mechanical runs. Only the active solar elements seem removed from the overall building design, although smoothly incorporated into the mechanical system. With the exception of the solar collectors, the architects approached the design as a "reallocation of component cost" within the $43 million construction cost of a similar conventional building.

Energy concerns dominate physical integration, with energy loads controlled by programmed on/off control of mechanical systems,[7] demand lighting, outdoor air optimization, heating and chiller water control, and the designed response of each facade to its solar orientation. Certain trade-offs have occurred, of course; but the result is a dramatic net gain in energy savings.

7. Energy management control systems, pp. 158–160.

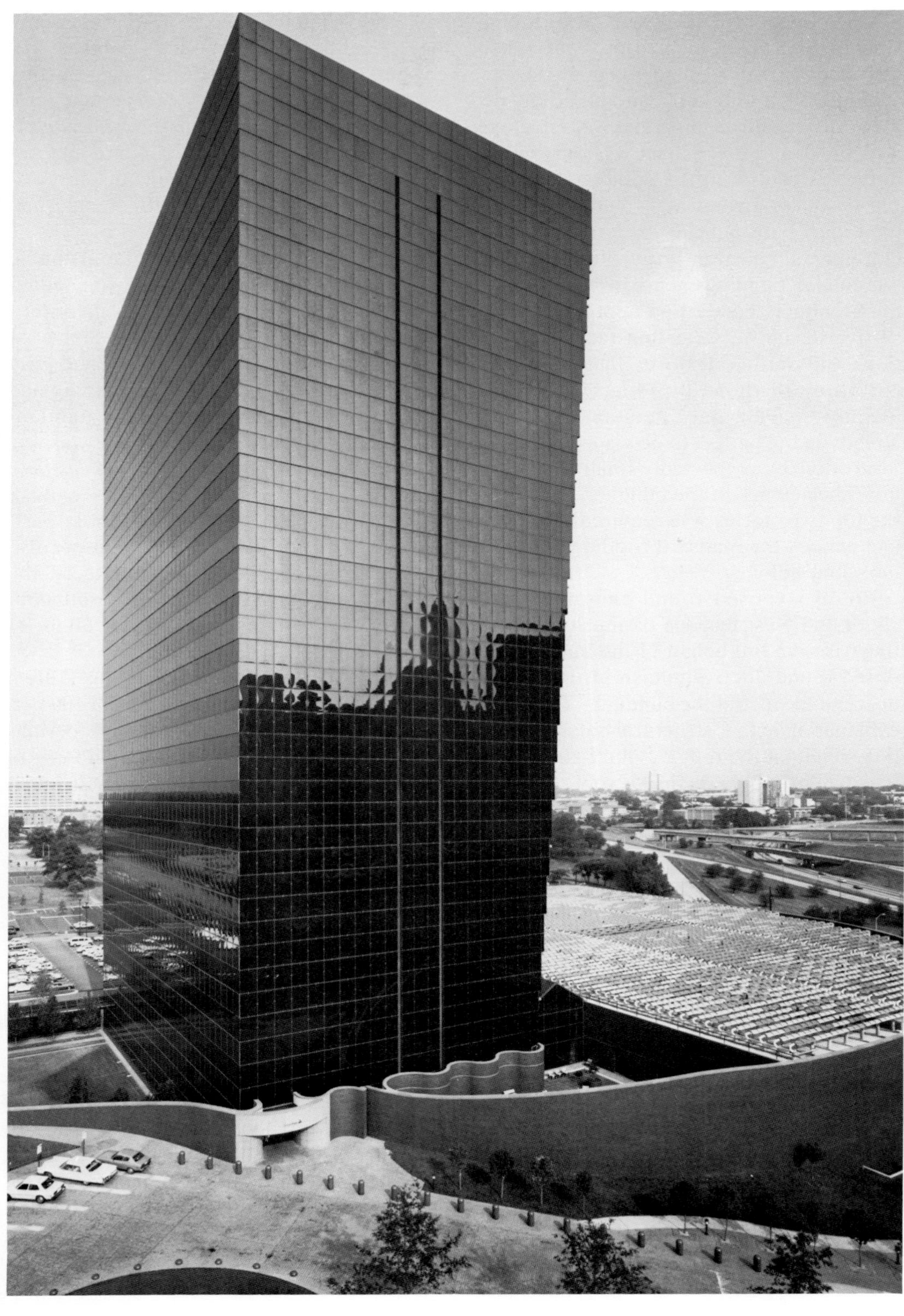

Project: Georgia Power Company Corporate Headquarters Building.
Architects: Heery & Heery, Architects & Engineers, Inc., Atlanta, GA.
Structural, Mechanical, & Electrical Engineers: Heery & Heery, Architects & Engineers, Inc., Atlanta, GA.
Consultants: Gillum-Colaco, Houston, TX—wind frame analysis, structural steel; Eugene O. Tofflemire, Sun Valley, ID—main curtain wall; PPG Industries, Atlanta, GA—skylight/window wall; Soil Systems, Inc., Marietta, GA—foundations; M. David Egan, Anderson, SC—acoustical; Jacobs-Del Solar Systems, Inc., Pasadena, CA—solar energy systems; Joseph R. Loring & Associates, Inc., New York, NY—vertical transportation.
General Contractor: Hardin International, Inc., Atlanta, GA and R.A. Banks & Co., Inc., Atlanta, GA (a joint venture).
Cost: $44,500,000 (bid); $56 PSF. Completed June 1981.
Photographs: Hursley/Lark/Hursley (courtesy of Heery International, Inc.).

National Permanent Building
Washington, D.C.

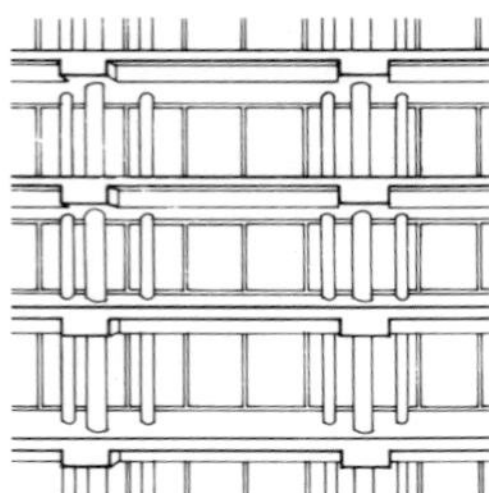

The National Permanent Building in Washington, D.C., located on a prominent three-sided Pennsylvania Avenue site once occupied by a well-known hotel, boldly displays the effective integration of envelope, structural, and mechanical systems which, in fact, is central to the building's success. The design originated as a solution to a combination of formal and programmatic requirements, however. With columned, highly modeled buildings nearby as precedents, the architects created an appropriately assertive design by selecting facade proportions and surface textures that were compatible with those buildings,[1] and then literally "pulling out" functional elements already in the budget to do visual and sculptural duty, for a reportedly small cost premium. The setback of the building envelope at the top two stories was required by zoning, and echoes the mansard roofline of the demolished hotel.

Boldly exposed round columns on the south and west facades diminish in size as they rise the full height of the building; exposed round ducts diminish in size as they descend the face of the building.[2] The logical explanation is that structural columns carry less weight at the top of a multi-story building, while it is here that a rooftop HVAC system handles the most air and needs its biggest ducts. The degree of change from top to bottom is deliberately exaggerated, however. Combined with black anodized aluminum window trim, glass set back 6 ft from the face of the edge beams on the south and west, and a beige latex emulsion finish on the concrete, these two elevations visually integrate mechanical and envelope while isolating structure.

VISIBLE INTEGRATION

In the National Permanent Building, more than any other building discussed in this chapter, the interrelationship between structural, envelope, and mechanical systems is governed by an emphasis on the building's appearance and visual response to its context. Most of the levels of visible integration are achieved in this design: system elements have been exposed to view, painted, reshaped, and relocated for visual reasons rather than for maximum system efficiency.[3] Since the building is speculative, the emphasis on visible integration is a contextual response rather than a programmatic one. Visible integration becomes, in effect, an urban planning issue.

The combination of overhangs and double wall systems results in a significant reduction of cooling loads, another design criterion in this project. On the south and west sides, in addition to the setbacks and gray glass, floor slabs and edge beams are joined by subway grating, which provides additional shading and serves as a window-washing platform. The north elevation, less visible than the south and west ones, is a flush facade with clear glass for the most part, except for the top two stories, which are also set back.[4] According to the architects, the combination of shading devices throughout the building reduces solar gain by about 43 percent overall.

The building's VAV air-handling system allows outside air to be varied from 100 percent to 0 percent of total circulation, permitting natural cooling and pre-conditioning of the office spaces while the building is unoccupied. Return-air ceiling plenums reduce the amount of lighting heat that reaches the office workers. Perimeter offices have adjustable room thermostats, while other spaces are monitored by a local automatic temperature control system;[5] additional heat is provided by an electric baseboard throughout.

RAMIFICATIONS OF DUCT PLACEMENT

One disadvantage of the mechanical design is the location on the exterior of the building of many of the air delivery ducts. This, along with their black-painted finish, requires that they be heavily insulated against heat gain. Like any exterior painted metal, they must also be scrupulously maintained. In addition to their dramatic formal

1. Visible integration, pp. 381–385, 388–389.
2. Exposed ducts, pp. 179–181.
3. Visible integration, pp. 381–385, 397.
4. Visible integration, pp. 381–385, 393.
5. Energy management control systems, pp. 158–160.
6. Protected membrane roofing, pp. 167–168.
7. Flat plate, pp. 130–131.

A view of the building's west facade (above) emphasizes the overhangs, setbacks, and gray glass responsible for a 43 percent reduction in solar heat gain.

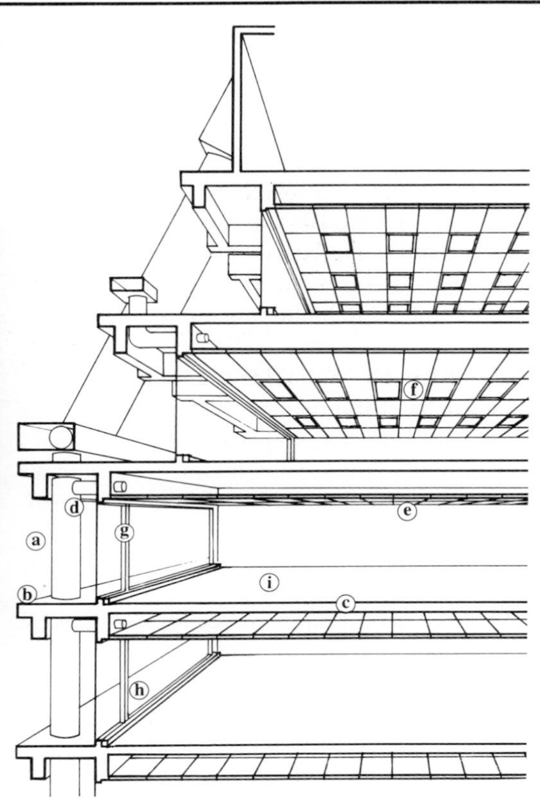

PERSPECTIVE SHOWING SETBACK

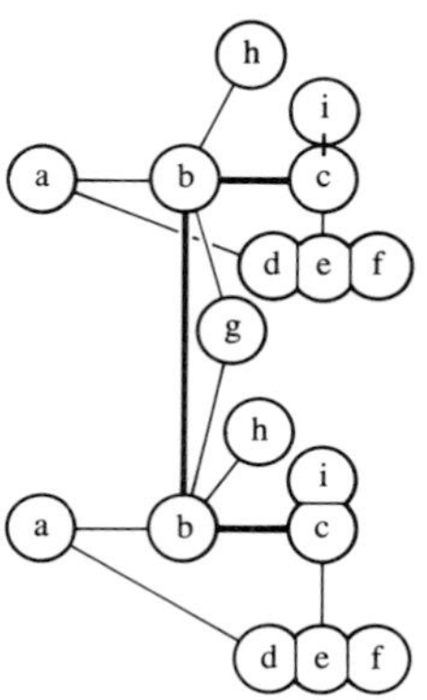

a. *Exterior ducts*
b. *Exposed concrete slab*
c. *Concrete floor slab*
d. *Ducts*
e. *Suspended ceiling*
f. *Fluorescent lighting*
g. *Window assembly*
h. *Baseboard heaters*
i. *Floor covering*

Diagram detail page 374

qualities, however, they also contribute to a small net increase in rentable floor space. The protected membrane roof[6] also requires exterior insulation.

The bulk of the structural system, the anodized aluminum windows, and the tenant spaces are not unusual features of a generic flat-plate concrete mid-rise office building.[7] Because the project was speculative, integration of the interior with other building systems is minimal.

The concept of a deeply recessed building skin behind exposed structural and mechanical systems is a recurring one in modern design, but this example is particularly remarkable for two reasons. The building owner and general contractor are one and the same, which contributed to the low cost per square foot (under $25 in 1977); and the envelope, structural, and mechanical systems are thoroughly integrated in a design that was primarily generated from formal requirements.

Photo: Warren Cox

The setback of the upper stories (top), required by zoning regulations, echoes several surrounding rooflines. This contributes to visible integration, as do exposed round columns and ducts (above). Columns diminish in size as they ascend the facade, and ducts diminish in size as they descend to ground level.

Project: National Permanent Building.
Architects: Hartman-Cox Architects, Washington, DC.
Structural Engineers: KCE Structural Engineers, Washington, DC.
Mechanical and Electrical Engineers: General Engineering Associates, Washington, DC.
General Contractor: The Lenkin Company, Bethesda, MD.
Cost: $6,000,000; $25 PSF. Completed 1977.
Photograph: Robert Lautman unless otherwise noted (courtesy of Hartman-

Pike and Virginia Building
Seattle, Washington

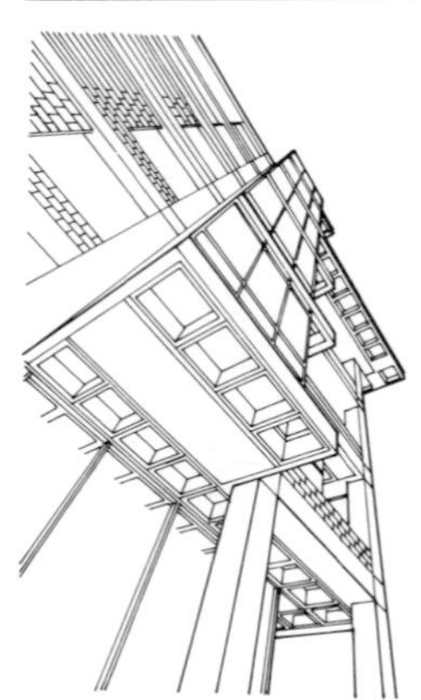

Olson/Walker have created a building that programmatically integrates 14 condominium apartments with commercial and parking facilities, and which in turn is visually integrated with the warehouse buildings in the Pike Place Market Historic District where it is located.[1] And though the mixture of residential and commercial might complicate building security, there is a corresponding advantage in balancing energy demands.

EXPOSED CONCRETE FRAME

The structural system dominates the design, with vertical and horizontal members of the cast-in-place reinforced concrete frame exposed within and without. Concrete waffle slabs serve as subfloors and finish ceilings. Because these elements are on view, their surfaces must be treated with a degree of care appropriate to interiors.[2]

The waffle slab, spanning in two directions, lends itself to square bays. Hence most of the units, which vary in size from 500 to 3000 sq ft, include a 30 ft square, column-free bay, allowing great freedom of plan for both housing and commercial spaces and wide, unobstructed views from deep inside the unit. In planning terms, such flexibility is a conservation issue, a design variation which allows many options within the same framework.

The relatively massive structure readily braces the deep retaining walls and provides the overall horizontal structural integrity needed for seismic and wind bracing on a steep hillside site. It easily and economically accommodates such recessed and extruded elements as roof decks, bay windows, and balconies. As walking surfaces, the roof decks perform what is usually thought of as an interior function while remaining an element of the envelope.

The concrete frame embodies a high degree of systems integration, combining structure, exterior and interior finish, shading, and, in the coffers of the waffle slab, an integral surround for light fixtures and radiant ceiling panels.[3] The care required for the cast surfaces is justified by the result.

A mix of commercial and residential uses balances day and night energy demands. The massive structure and long spans allow flexibility.

ENVELOPE TREATMENT

While small bays thrust out unshaded, most of the metal-framed double-glazed window walls[4] are recessed into the shadow of the concrete frame. Again, the freedom offered by the structure is exploited, and the glass line is pushed in and out to form terraces and balconies. Concrete masonry blends visually with the frame while the glazing stands out, compositionally isolated. Electrical wiring is routed within the topping slab, and radiant heat panels, recessed into the coffers of the waffle slab, supplement the forced-air electrical HVAC system. Ducts for the latter are grouped near the building cores with stairs, elevators, and other vertical elements, freeing the areas formed by the bays.

The highest level of visible integration is seen in the clusters of metal fireplace flues, which are brought together as sculptural elements on the rooftops. Together with pipe railings and the metal window framing, they form a visual contrast and complement to the heavy concrete frame.[5]

In general, the combination of a heavy exposed concrete frame with light infill offers considerable structural redundancy at a reasonable price and a degree of flexibility that is seldom economically justifiable, especially in housing. This translates into a desirable combination of basic permanence with the economically attractive potential for change.

1. Visible integration, pp. 381–385, 388.
2. Visible integration, pp. 381–385, 394, 406.
3. Radiant heat panels, pp. 177–178.
4. Insulating glass, pp. 209–211.
5. Compare National Permanent, pp. 90–91.

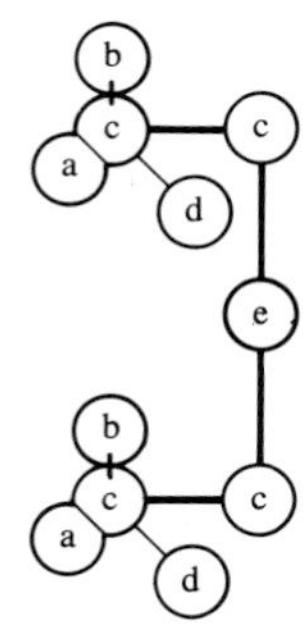

a. *Rigid insulation*
b. *Floor finish varies with occupant*
c. *Exposed waffle slab*
d. *Radiant heat panel*
e. *Window assembly*

Diagram detail page 375

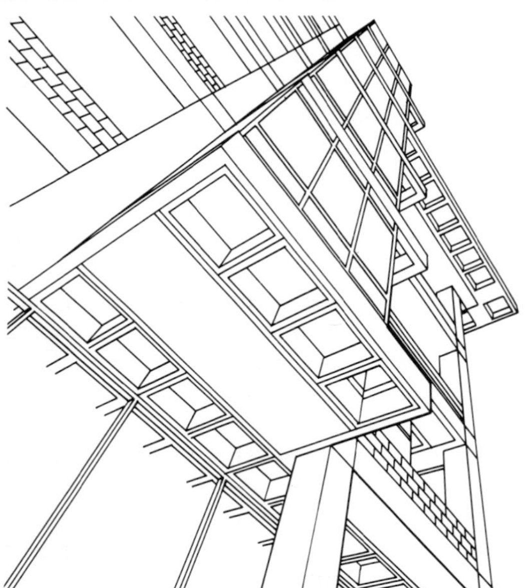

PERSPECTIVE SHOWING WAFFLE SLAB

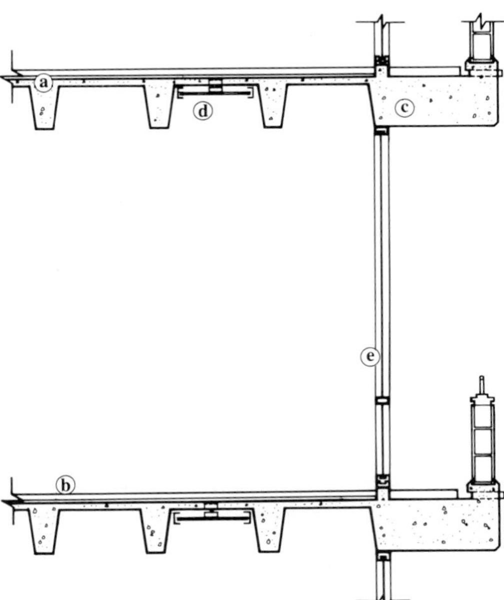

TYPICAL WALL SECTION

Dramatic views of Seattle's Pike Place Market and Puget Sound (top) provide part of the economic justification for the project. Recessed and extruded elements—roof decks, bay windows, and balconies—are easily accommodated (above). As shown in the section (above right), most of the metal-framed, double-glazed window walls are recessed into the shadow of the concrete frame, while light fixtures and radiant heat panels are suspended in the coffers of the waffle slab. Units were sold unfinished, with interiors designed by the various owners. A lower floor plan (right) shows both retail and residential functions of the building.

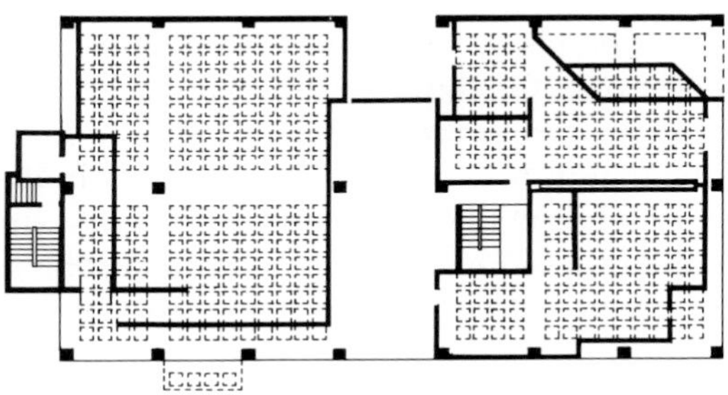

COMPOSITE FLOOR PLAN N➤

Project: Pike and Virginia Building.
Architects: Olson/Walker Architects, Seattle, WA.
Structural Engineers: Ratti/Fossatti Associates, Seattle, WA.
Mechanical Engineers: Richard Stern Consulting Engineers, Seattle, WA.
Electrical Engineers: Sparling & Associates, Inc., Seattle, WA.
General Contractor: Eberharter & Gaunt, Inc., Seattle, WA.
Consultants: Jean Jongeward Interiors, Seattle, WA.
Cost: $1,500,000; $45 PSF. Completed June 1978.
Photographs: Dick Busher (courtesy of Olson/Walker Architects).

Occidental Chemical Company Corporate Office Building
Niagara Falls, New York

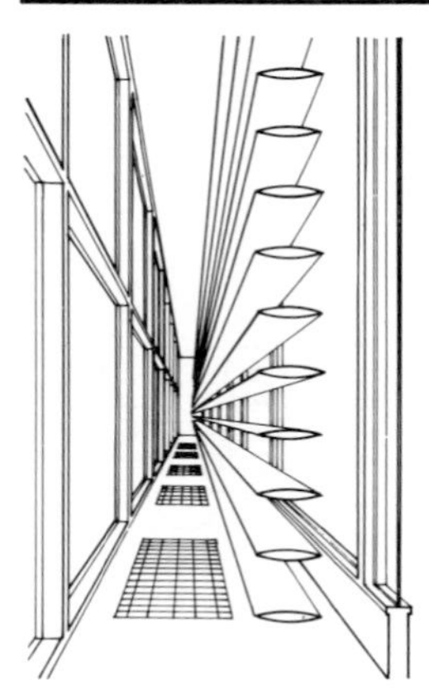

This corporate headquarters reflects one set of circumstances that has seemed to promote integration: a relatively unspecific office program, a client willing to experiment for the sake of a corporate symbol, and a conscious team approach to design, with a full range of disciplines included from the outset. Cannon Design has responded to this situation with a design that combines early modern architecture's elegant simplicity with efficient energy performance. The result is a thorough integration of envelope, mechanical, and interior systems in what is demonstrably one of the most energy-efficient office buildings in its region, if not in the country. Sited at the axis of the Rainbow Bridge, it further serves as a symbol of renewed downtown Niagara Falls.

In this double-skinned building, the air space separating the glass curtain walls[1] of the envelope is enlarged to accommodate operable louvers which respond actively to climate, and effectively integrate envelope and interior at the *meshed* level. These enlarged window blinds function as thermal shutters, adjusting to directional solar and thermodynamic requirements.[2] As applied to all four elevations, this strategy determines the visual and formal qualities of the building envelope while strongly influencing the interior.[3]

EMPHASIS ON ENERGY EFFICIENCY

Occidental's program was developed during the first wave of enthusiasm for energy-efficient design, and the building reflects an unusually well-focused, highly competitive determination to fulfill one criterion: to use less than half the energy of a conventional office building. The design team developed three programmatically realistic alternative schemes, each an incremental response to the goal of maximum energy conservation. The scheme that combined a double skin and louvers was identified as the most energy-efficient, and was the one chosen by the client.

Implicitly at least, the design criteria involved the acceptance of higher maintenance costs and the risk of mechanical failure associated with the envelope. The double envelope also required a sacrifice of floor space; yet the design is an appropriate one, given the resulting savings in mechanical equipment and life-cycle costs.

Sited at the axis of the Rainbow Bridge, the building commands dramatic views of American Falls, Horseshoe Falls, and Goat Island.

The double skin, which is both the principal design element and the main integration idea, is really several ideas at once. Two fully glazed window walls (the outer one of insulating glass[4]) 4 ft apart create an enormous nine-story passive solar collector with automatic venting dampers at the top and bottom. The dampers can create either a sealed, warming "greenhouse" around the entire building or a "chimney" from which warm air is naturally exhausted by convection. The louvers, which were adapted from dampers used in high velocity HVAC ducts, can be controlled automatically by photocells on each of the four elevations. These allow the building to "track" the sun and almost completely block direct sunlight at any time of day. The white-finished louver blades are also designed to reflect indirect sunlight into the building interior; an estimated 50 percent of the usable floor area benefits from this daylighting strategy. Finally, the louvers can be closed completely to help retain heat during periods when the building is empty.

The building is seldom empty, however. Its occupants include a large computer facility operating 24 hours a day, and the attendant increase in the use of artificial

1. Compare Equitable Life, pp. 102–105.
2. Thermal performance, pp. 250–252.
3. Visible integration, pp. 381–385, 386–387.
4. Insulating glass, pp. 209–211.

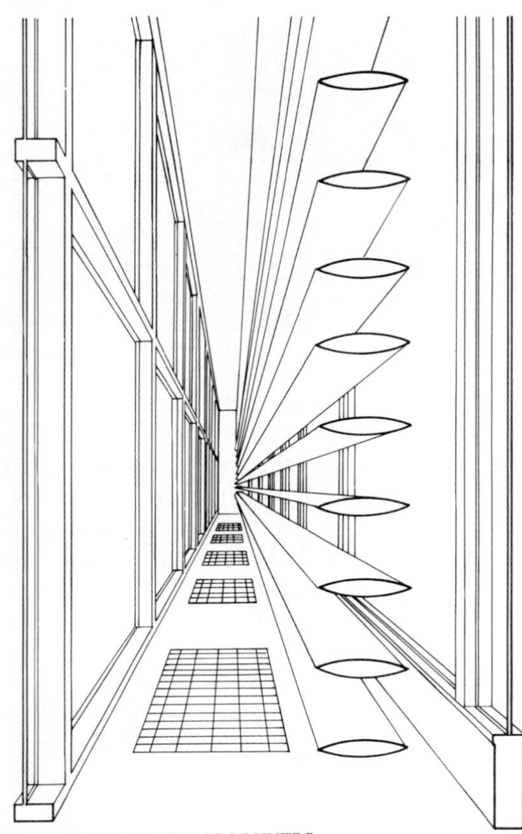
PERSPECTIVE SHOWING LOUVERS

The section perspective (above) shows the air space, louvers, and double-glazed skin that form the principal design and integration concept for the project's nine-story passive solar collector. Venting dampers at top and bottom allow the greenhouse effect and chimney effect to occur. The double envelope insulates the building effectively, putting emphasis on cooling loads while combining passive solar and daylighting. The louvers serve as both thermal and visual shutters. The section (above right) details the louvers and illustrates the operation of the dampers. Photocells mounted on each elevation control the louvers, letting the building "track" the sun and block direct sunlight at any time of day. The white-finished louvers also reflect light into the interior. When closed completely, they retain heat. The floor plan (right) shows the open interior spaces with perimeter columns, made possible by the frame's 45 ft clear spans, which enhance the building's daylighting potential. The structure, a steel frame with metal deck floors, efficiently frames the building's cube shape and integrates envelope, mechanical, and interior systems at the connected *level.*

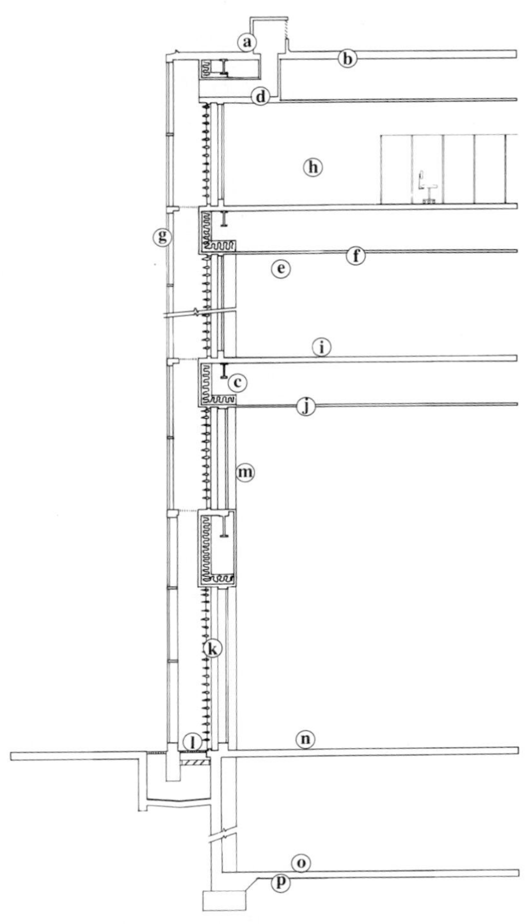

DOUBLE ENVELOPE WALL SECTION

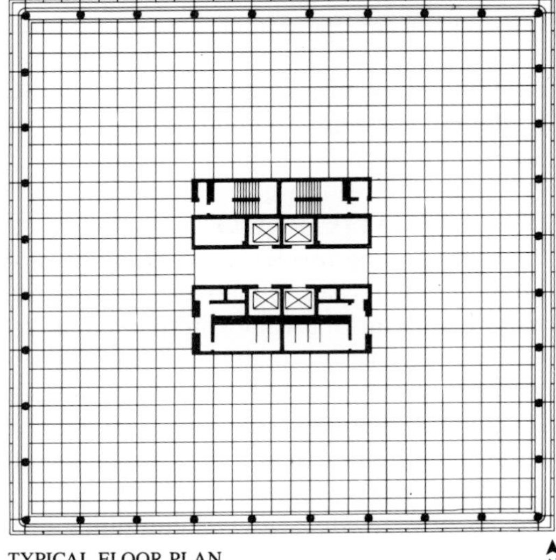
TYPICAL FLOOR PLAN

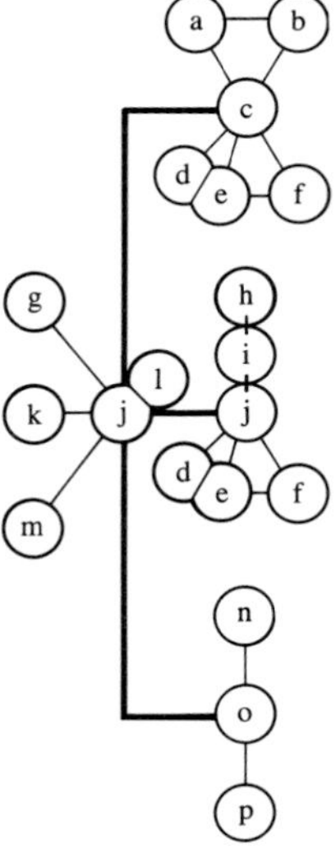

a. *Vents and motorized dampers*
b. *Single-ply roof and rigid insulation*
c. *Steel frame and metal roof deck*
d. *Ducts*
e. *Acoustical tile ceiling*
f. *HID lighting*
g. *Insulating glass wall*
h. *Open office furniture*
i. *Carpet*
j. *Steel frame*
k. *Return air grilles*
l. *Lightweight metal insulating panels*
m. *Resilient tile flooring*
n. *Slab on grade foundations and pinned caissons*
o. *Vapor barrier*

Diagram detail page 371

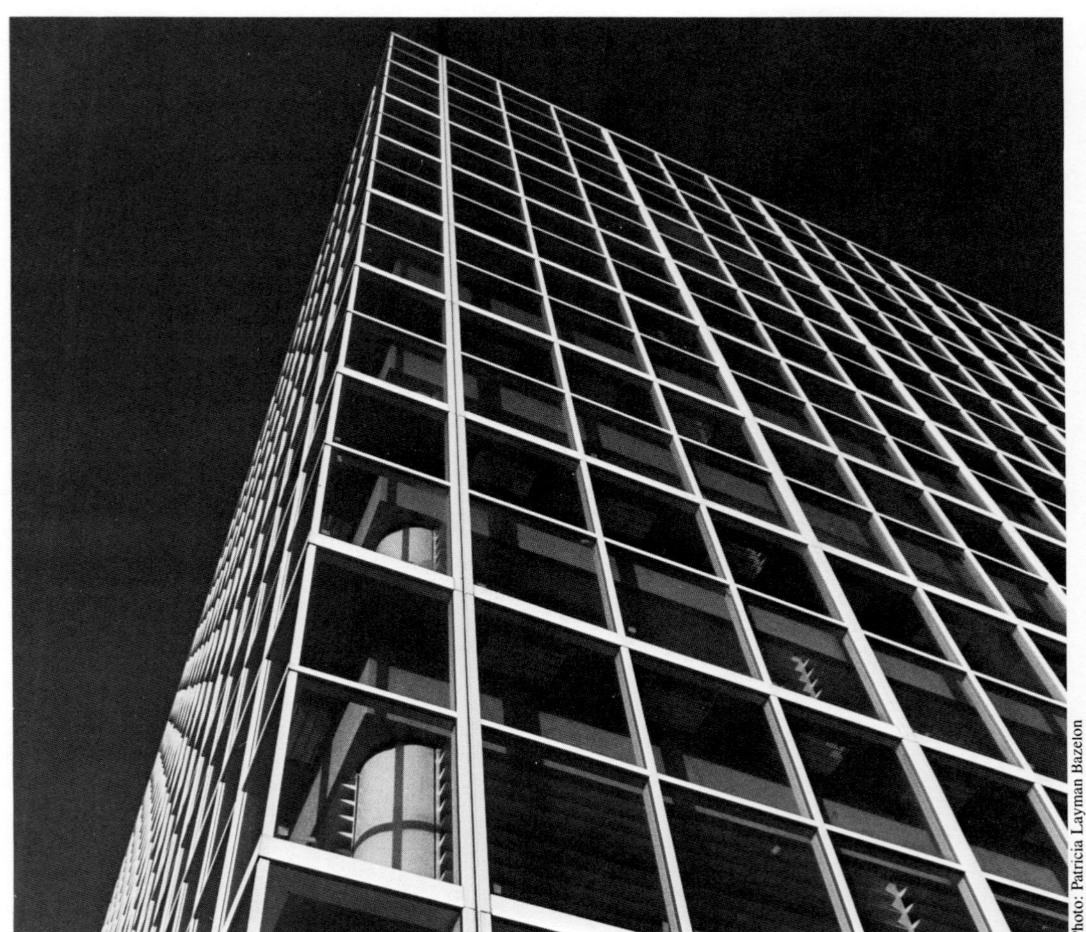

Photo: Patricia Layman Bazelon

The use of double-glazed skin and operable louvers on all four elevations determines the formal and visual qualities of the envelope, and influences interior form as well.

lighting has yielded an unexpected benefit: the added internal gain has reduced the heating load to nothing. At present, the boiler is not being used.

LIMITING INFILTRATION

The insulating properties of the louvered double envelope are enhanced through the use of insulating glass and silicone sealants.[5] The envelope acts as an unconditioned buffer zone, tempering the impact of outside temperatures by limiting infiltration, and putting the emphasis on cooling loads, which are relatively economical to handle in this climate and location. It combines passive solar design and daylighting, and fulfills the design team's basic criterion of substantially reduced energy use. These approaches are further integrated with the building's lighting by means of a 15 ft perimeter zone where two-stage lighting controls can reduce energy use when natural light is plentiful. Nearer the core, task-ambient lighting provides a comparable level and quality of light.

A low pressure variable air volume system allows air handling to respond to the changing relationship between the double envelope and the interior. Active heating and cooling are provided by an oil-fired boiler with complete heat recovery and electrically driven chillers. A computer controls and

5. Silicone sealants, pp. 225–226.

A corner view of the building (above) shows the air space and the louvers. The exterior view (above right) emphasizes the formal consistency of the elevations. A lobby view (right) shows the louvers as seen from the interior.

Project: Occidental Chemical Company Corporate Office Building.
Architects: Cannon Design Inc., Grand Island, NY. Principal in charge: Mark R. Mendell. Design team: Mark R. Mendell, Gautam Shah, Charles Arraiz, Alan Sloan, Jack Foster, Gerald Maslona, Dale Gaff, Douglas Purcell. Consulting architects: Hellmuth, Obata & Kassabaum, New York, NY.
Structural Engineers: Gillum Consulting Engineers, PC (formerly Gillum-Colaco), New York, NY.
Mechanical and Electrical Engineers: Cannon Design Inc., Grand Island, NY.
General Contractor: Sigfried/Scrufari Joint Venture, Buffalo, NY, and Niagara Falls, NY.
Consultants: Prof. John Yellott, Phoenix, AZ; Prof. Richard S. Levine, Lexington, KY; Burt, Hill, Kosar, Rittleman Associates, Butler, PA; Bolt, Beranek & Neuman, Inc., Cambridge, MA.
Cost: $12,500,000; $62 PSF. Completed 1981.
Photographs: Barbara Elliott Martin unless otherwise noted (courtesy of Cannon Design).

monitors all building functions, conserving both time and energy.[6] In addition to maintaining environmental comfort and optimum energy performance (and presumably balancing those sometimes contradictory needs), this energy management control system helps monitor the building for fire safety and security.

The structural system, a conventional steel frame with metal deck floors, achieves a *connected* level of integration with the envelope, mechanical, and interior systems. It proved to be the most economical way to arrive at the building's overall cube shape[7]—a shape which creates a favorable perimeter-to-volume ratio, cutting both the double skin's initial construction cost and its vulnerability to heat loss and gain. The daylighting strategy is aided by the steel frame's 45 ft clear spans, which eliminate the need for interior columns while allowing perimeter column sizes consistent with the desire for a transparent skin.

In these details, as in its integration of envelope, mechanical, and interior elements, the Occidental Chemical Building gives evidence of an integrated design process and a heightened awareness of design criteria and theoretical possibilities. These have contributed decisively to a building in which formal and operating systems are thoroughly integrated.

6. Energy management control systems, pp. 158–160.

7. Conservation of space, p. 236.

Vocational Technical Education Facility
University of Minnesota, St. Paul

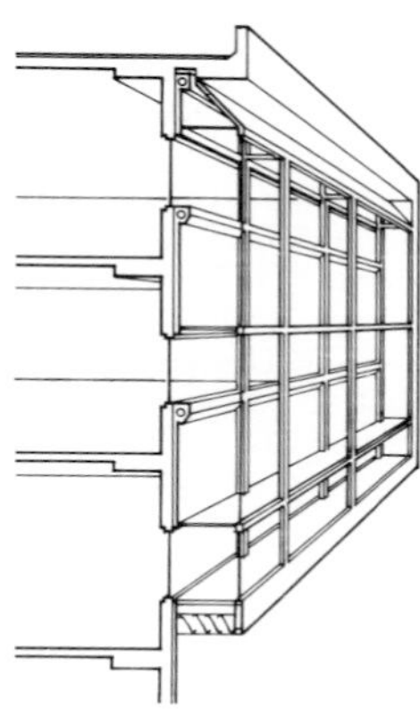

This project, a classic example of adaptive reuse, has its origin in a plan to renovate the University of Minnesota's 1904 livestock pavilion for offices and classrooms. When the old building proved unable to yield the requisite space, the designers chose the south-facing slope behind it as the site for an addition. The topography permitted the new, much larger building to remain a backdrop to the historic red brick pavilion, maintaining the same roofline. The site also provided the opportunity for two especially noteworthy elements of the design: a south-facing Trombe wall and an atrium on the north side adjoining the pavilion.

The atrium is enclosed by a clerestory over the rear wing of the original building and a skylight between its rear facade and the structural steel roof of the addition. It transcends its status as an amenity by incorporating such visible integration issues as exterior preservation of the pavilion and attention to its contextual relationship with the new building.[1] In addition, it has allowed the designers to avoid both a northern exposure for the new wing and the destruction of a historic elevation that would have resulted from butting it directly against the pavilion. The atrium also integrates circulation paths and relates the building to the university skywalk system, which provides sheltered access to nearby classroom and dormitory buildings.

FACADES AS INTERIOR

Two facades of the 1904 building are preserved inside the atrium, where they add dark, ornamented elements to an otherwise light-colored space. Clerestory and skylight apertures are sized and located to provide complete natural illumination of the atrium, to reinforce the focus on the existing building, and to create a multiple and varied exposure which lends a dynamic quality to the space throughout the day and year. The new interior glass block facade admits light into office and classroom spaces, and windows surrounding the lounge area allow natural light to reach the basement level.

Glass block admits daylight from the atrium into an office in the addition. Outline of the pavilion's south doorway is dimly visible at center.

The glass block interior facade *unifies* envelope and interior systems, providing a masonry wall, a light source, and decorative features that affect the interior space. Such translucent masonry offers security and privacy as well.[2]

The complex's most striking energy-saving feature is the unvented Trombe wall on its south side. The Trombe wall is an envelope strategy that makes a major contribution to the mechanical system. The interior, thermal wall is constructed of filled concrete block and structural concrete spandrel beams, and provides the thermal mass storage necessary for temperature stabilization. In its construction, the Trombe facade is consistent with the structure of the new wing itself (as distinct from the atrium), consisting of cast-in-place concrete footings and columns and waffle slab floors. The exterior brick masonry has a core of concrete block and rigid insulation. The exterior glass "moisture" wall is 3 ft from the thermal wall, creating a variation on the double-skin greenhouse space. Walkway grilles within this space shade the windows, and thermostatically controlled insulating shades can be rolled down to shield the thermal wall mass or totally cover wall and window, depending on the time of day and the season of the year. Conventional heating is supplied as needed from the university steam plant.[3]

1. Visible integration, pp. 381–385, 390.
2. Glass block, pp. 216–218.
3. Energy management control systems, pp. 158–160.

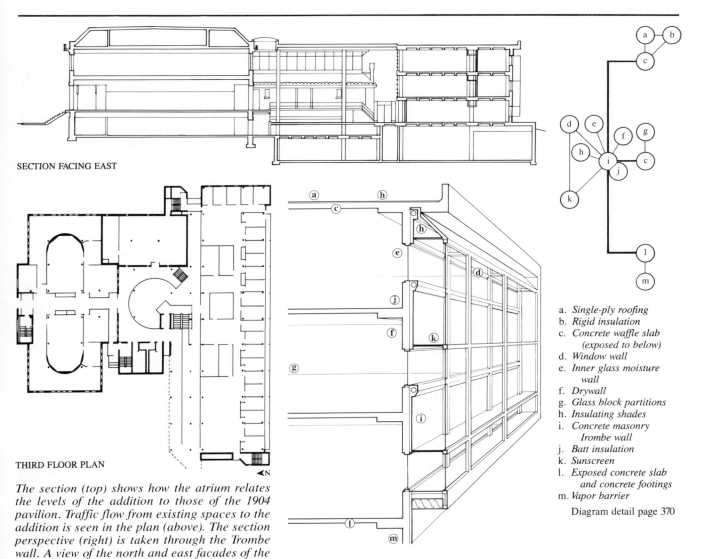

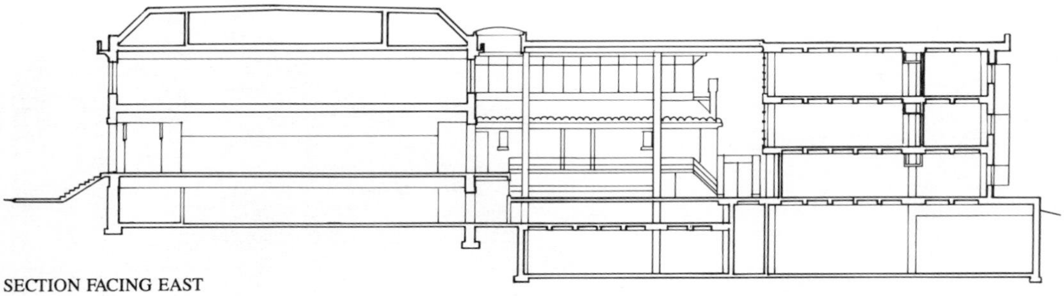

SECTION FACING EAST

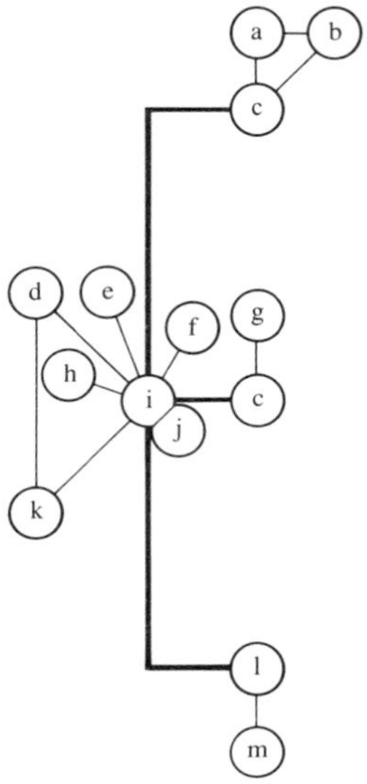

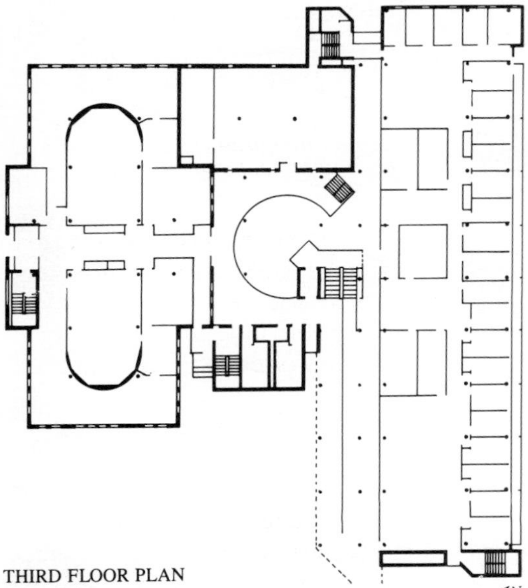

THIRD FLOOR PLAN

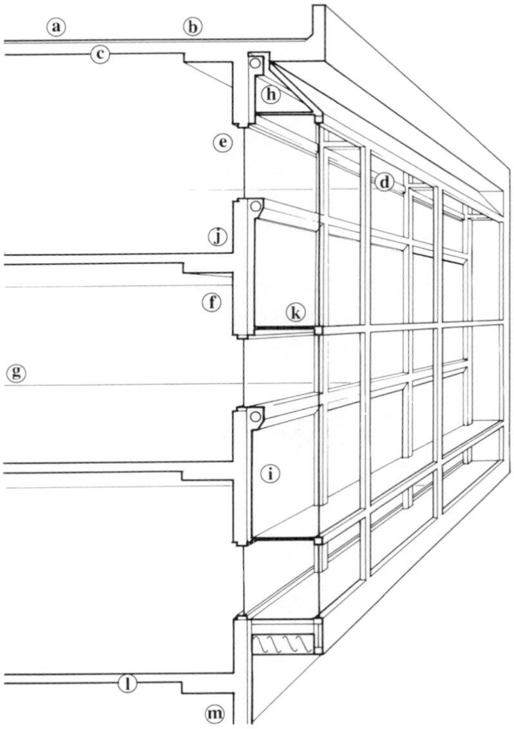

The section (top) shows how the atrium relates the levels of the addition to those of the 1904 pavilion. Traffic flow from existing spaces to the addition is seen in the plan (above). The section perspective (right) is taken through the Trombe wall. A view of the north and east facades of the pavilion (below) shows how the addition maintains the existing roofline.

PERSPECTIVE SHOWING TROMBE WALL

a. *Single-ply roofing*
b. *Rigid insulation*
c. *Concrete waffle slab (exposed to below)*
d. *Window wall*
e. *Inner glass moisture wall*
f. *Drywall*
g. *Glass block partitions*
h. *Insulating shades*
i. *Concrete masonry Trombe wall*
j. *Batt insulation*
k. *Sunscreen*
l. *Exposed concrete slab and concrete footings*
m. *Vapor barrier*

Diagram detail page 370

An atrium view (left) takes in the skylight, east-facing clerestory, and glass block interior wall. Streetlamps suggest continuity with the outdoors. Windows surrounding the lounge admit daylight to the basement level. On the south-facing Trombe wall (top), thermostatically controlled shades are closed. In the detail (above) two of the shades are open.

Project: Vocational Technical Education Facility, University of Minnesota.
Architects: Architectural Alliance, Minneapolis, MN.
Principal in charge: Herbert A. Ketcham, FAIA. Project designer: Thomas J. deAngelo. Project team: Art Yellin, Chris Johnson, Linda McCracken-Hunt, George Stevens, Peter Pfister.
Structural Engineers: Meyer Borgman & Johnson, Minneapolis, MN.
Mechanical and Electrical Engineers: Lundquist, Wilmar, Schultz & Martin, Inc., St. Paul, MN.
General Contractor: Knutson Construction Company, Minneapolis, MN.
Cost: \$5,194,350; \$52 PSF. Completed May 1982.
Photographs: Franz C. Hall (courtesy of Architectural Alliance).

Southern Service Center for the Equitable Life Assurance Society
Charlotte, North Carolina

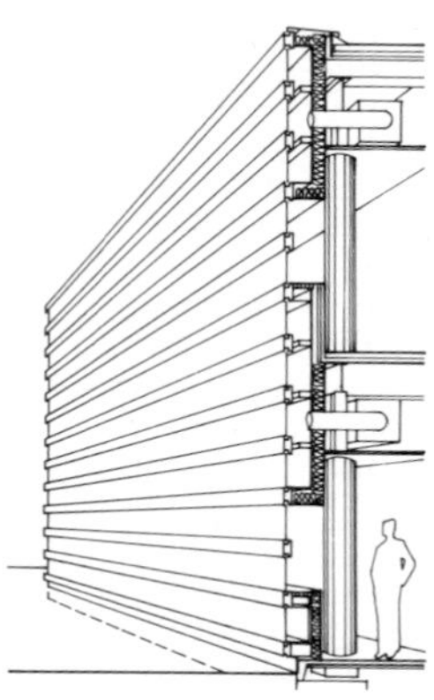

The program for the Equitable Life Assurance Society building provided its design team with several constraints. This speculative office building was to be designed and constructed within six and a half months, with the further requirement that it be energy-efficient. Strict adherence to component development, dimensional unification, and a highly organized decision-making process contributed to the building's completion on time and within budget. The solution addresses conservation issues, both of time and resources. Because the site is so large, conservation of space was not a significant issue.

Juxtaposing standard, separate systems, Equitable Life achieves a remarkably high level of visible and functional integration. Schedule, construction costs, and market dictated the choice of steel frame and independent glass and aluminum curtain wall,[1] systems whose separate constraints allowed them to be developed simultaneously. The second floor slab was designed with the potential for flexible power and communications distribution.

Since this was to be a speculative building, specific interior functions could not be known by the architects. This led to the relatively neutral design which, through abstraction, paradoxically gives the building its strong identity. All elements, including interior column spacing and curtain wall joints, are dimensionally coordinated. The interior stairs echo the striped imagery of the exterior.[2] The use of an open office plan[3] with a perimeter corridor reinforces the concept of layered systems, as does the use of access floors in some areas,[4] although the interior as designed by the client is not fully integrated with the other systems. The suspended ceiling conceals ductwork, exemplifying a visible integration strategy that is fairly commonplace in open plan office construction.

PASSIVE SOLAR STRATEGY

After determining an economical structural bay size of 24 x 32 ft, the architects pursued the ideal of a curtain wall that would project beyond the edge of the structure to help produce the 65,000 gross sq ft required by the program. The resulting thermal or solar belts represent an expansion of the conventional notion of a curtain wall composed of a watertight outer layer, insulation, and an inner finish layer.

Solar belts are created by pulling the curtain wall out from the structure. These air spaces act as passive heat collectors and integrate envelope and mechanical systems.

A unique feature of this building, the solar belts are actually air spaces between the metal-and-glass weather envelope and the insulated drywall interior finish wall, created by cantilevering the curtain wall from horizontal structural mullions three feet beyond the office perimeter. Because the solar belts completely encircle the building, its four sides are virtually identical. This represents a form of visible integration that this building shares with another double-walled structure, the Occidental Chemical Company Building.[5]

1. Glass and aluminum curtain wall, pp. 212–215.
2. Visible integration, pp. 381–385, 393.
3. Open plan office furniture, pp. 196–199.
4. Access floors, pp. 202–204.
5. Compare Occidental Chemical, pp. 94–97.

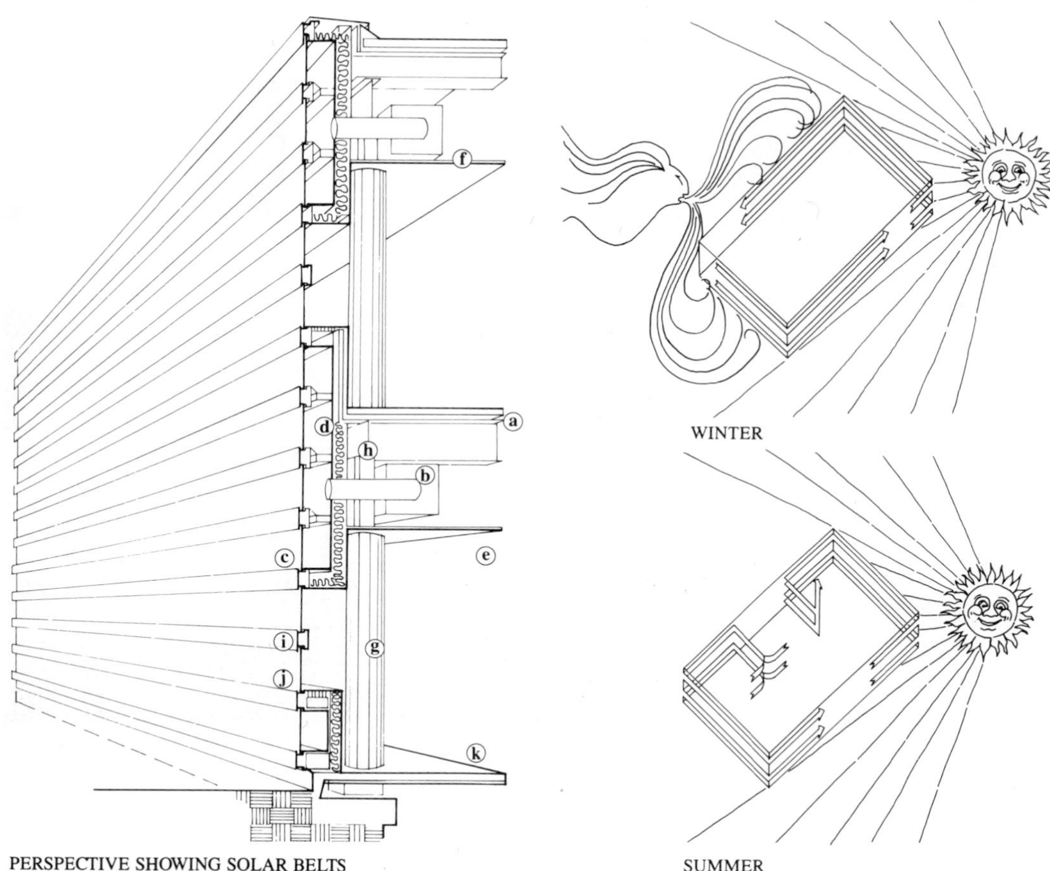

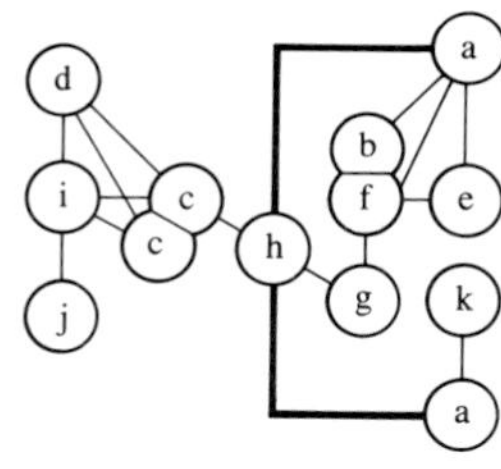

a. *Slab and steel beams*
b. *Ducts*
c. *Sunbelts*
d. *Aluminum panels*
e. *Fluorescent light*
f. *Suspended ceiling*
g. *Column wrapping*
h. *Steel columns*
i. *Curtain-wall mullions*
j. *Glass spandrel panels*
k. *Slate*

Diagram detail page 372

Photo: David Franzen, ESTO

The operation of the solar belts is depicted above. As shown in the section perspective (top left), the belts are continuous air spaces between the metal-and-glass weather envelope and the insulated interior finish wall. Fans move heated air collected in the belts to the cooler side of the building in winter; in summer, cooled exhaust air is circulated to the warmer side (top right). In this way, outer surfaces of occupied spaces are maintained at constant temperatures. A variable air volume mechanical system supports the belts, clearly visible in the distant view (above).

The solar belts encircle the building and create four almost identical elevations. Although floor lines are not discernible from the exterior, a night view (above) of the lighted entrance facade suggests the interior organization. Polished aluminum bands alternating with clear butt glazing create the strong statement desired by the client (right).

The addition of clear spandrel glazing (given the small area of vision glass, single glazing is used throughout) makes the resulting air spaces effective passive heat collectors. Fans move heated air to the cooler side of the building in winter, and exhaust or replace it with cooled exhaust air (waste air from bathrooms) in summer. The solar belts are the major element in Equitable's successful mechanical/envelope integration, circulating heated and cooled air around the building to hold the outer surfaces of the occupied spaces at even temperatures. The belt system is supported by a conventional variable air volume mechanical system, which remains concealed.

CUSTOM-DESIGNED CURTAIN WALL

The building's appearance grew out of the desire for a distinctive identity, coupled with the desire to improve the energy efficiency of the conventional metal and glass curtain wall. The image chosen reflects the way in which the solar belts move air around the building. The building skin, again, is based on two horizontal elements: 9 in. bands of polished aluminum alternating with 18 in. clear butt glazing. The overall height measurement is related to the modular units of the curtain wall. Floor lines are not discernible from the outside (interior organization is more apparent at night, when the building is lighted from within), contributing to a sleek, scaleless quality. A custom-designed image is thus produced with standard, readily available building elements.

Equitable Life was designed and built in less than the required six and a half months, was completed within budget, and according to the architects will pay back the cost of its energy-conserving features in two to five years.

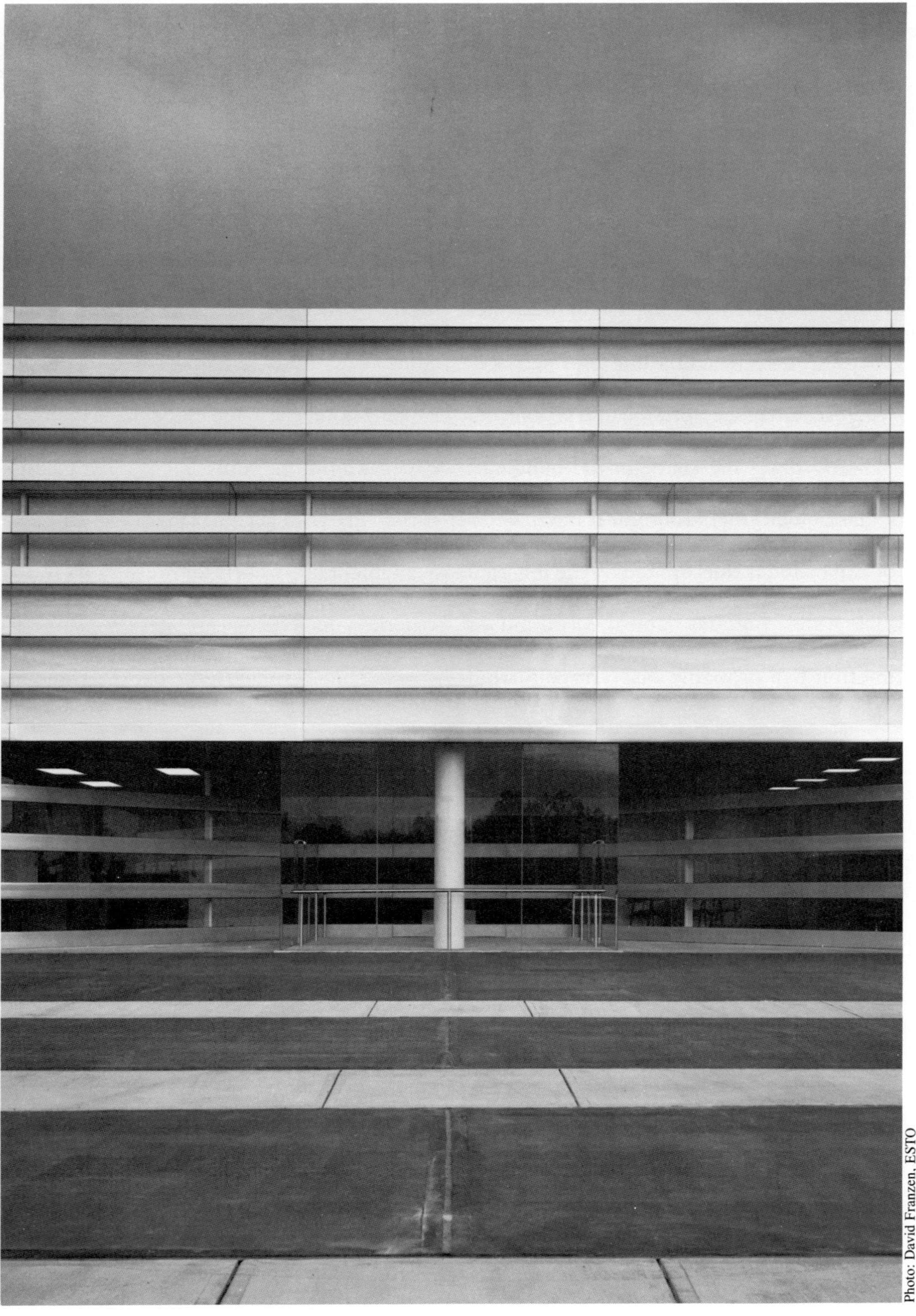

Photo: David Franzen, ESTO

Project: Southern Service Center for the Equitable Life Assurance Society.
Architects: Wolf Associates, Charlotte, NC.
Structural Engineers: King-Hudson Associates, Charlotte, NC.
Mechanical Engineers: James A. Story & Associates, Charlotte, NC.
Electrical Engineers: Bullard Associates, Charlotte, NC.
Consultants: Olive & Associates, Charlotte, NC—specifications and technical; Antoine-Heitmann & Associates, Inc., St. Louis, MO—curtain wall.
General Contractor: F.N. Thompson, Inc., Charlotte, NC.
Cost: $1,621,985; $25 PSF. Completed August 1977.
Photographs: Ezra Stoller, ESTO, unless otherwise noted.

Addition to Submarine Training Facility
Groton, Connecticut

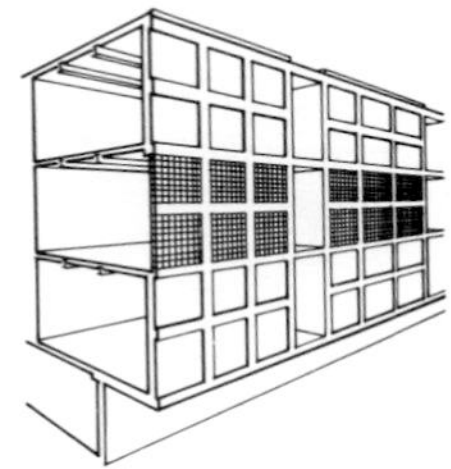

Contained in its smallest component—an 8 in. square glass block[1]—is the basis of successful systems integration in the addition to Building 427 at the Navy's submarine training facility in Groton, Connecticut. The glass block itself involves a *unified* two-system integration; like a window, the block is both envelope and interior.[2] In addition, the bronze metallic-oxide coating on the block's exterior surface helps control natural light and solar heat gain, while the air space within it performs an insulating and indirect mechanical function. Its shape acts as a form generator, the elemental unit of a series of grids which visually integrate the building's structure, envelope, interior, and visible mechanical elements. And ultimately this shape becomes the shape of the building.

Glazed-brick veneer surrounds the panels of glass block; the structural frame is steel with metal decking. The building's capacity for expansion is thus limited by the inherent difficulty of demolishing and adding on to brick walls. But the cubical form and its appropriateness to a relatively permanent function will probably discourage further expansion in any case.

SECURITY REQUIREMENTS

The Navy's major design criterion for this project, and the one which suggested glass block as a means of admitting light, color, and movement to the interior, was the requirement that the addition be largely windowless. The facility houses a simulated undersea attack center, which is protected by maximum security measures. The Navy had originally asked for a blank-walled brick shed on the south side of Building 427, a linear extension of an existing brick building. The architect kept the idea of an economical, secure masonry box, but modified it to meet at least two more criteria: a sense of the outdoors for sailors who had just completed long stretches of submarine duty; and a sense of importance appropriate both to the facility and its site, one of the most dramatic on the naval base. The architect sought a more dynamic relationship with the existing building, taking advantage of the natural site and locating the addition on the steep hillside to the west of the larger building, using it as a backdrop. The simple box, consequently, becomes more of an autonomous object. This strategy also eliminated the need to blast the granite ledge on the south side, which would have disrupted the Navy's computer banks of classified information in the existing building.

The addition required a separate structural system to isolate sensitive equipment from vibrations caused by settling of the existing structure. A separate earth-filled concrete foundation anchored with rock bolts, slipping joints at each floor, an expansion joint at the roof, and rubber insulation between adjoining walls accomplished this physical separation of old and new structures. Program requirements for simple classroom and laboratory spaces adjacent to a double-loaded corridor were met by the plain, three-story box design. With these criteria satisfied, the architect was free to pursue his formal predilection for a box whose shape was reiterated by a three-dimensional grid incorporating all visible building systems.[3]

There are actually two grids in the design. One is the pattern of 8 in. squares established by the dimensions of the glass block and the brown glazed brick which makes up the exterior wall. Superimposed on this grid is a larger one that articulates the building's steel frame. Strips two bricks wide intersect to enclose panels 5 ft 8 in. (or eight blocks) square. The glass blocks project 1½ in. beyond the brick grid. In other places, the infill of this large grid is more of the same brick, with the panel recessed ½ in. behind the grid. Two grid panels equal one floor height, so that in the absence of such scale cues as doors (entrance is from the existing building only) the apparent size of the building is doubled. This serves the architect's purpose of relating the building to the commanding, central site, despite a relatively small program of 12,500 sq ft.

Most classrooms are on the south side of

1. Glass block, pp. 216–218.
2. Envelope and interior *connected*, p. 328.
3. Visible integration, pp. 381–385, 392–393.
4. Access floors, pp. 202–204.

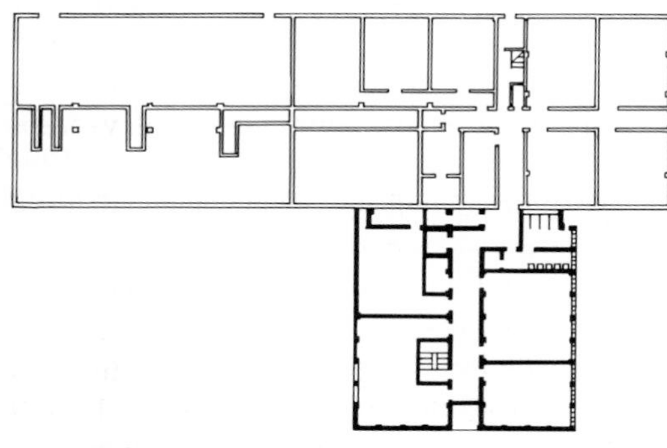

PLAN WITH EXISTING BUILDING ◄N

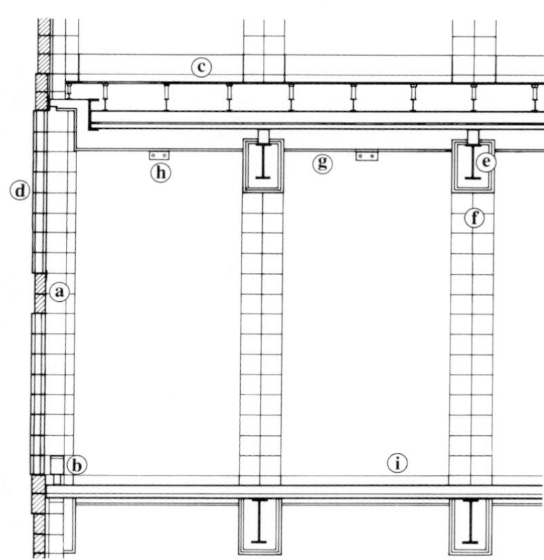

TYPICAL WALL SECTION

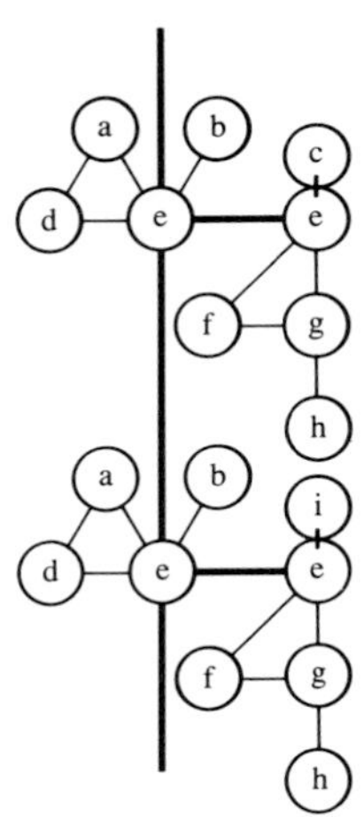

a. *Solid CMU*
b. *Convector*
c. *Access floor*
d. *Glass blocks*
e. *Concrete on metal deck and steel beam*
f. *Drywall*
g. *Suspended acoustical tile ceiling*
h. *Fluorescent light*
i. *Floor covering*

Diagram detail page 377

The building's only transparent windows are at the ends of corridors (top left). The section perspective (above) focuses on the windowless south wall. Glass block panels admit light into windowless classroom and office spaces (center left). The plan (bottom left) shows the addition in relation to the existing building.

the building and take daylight through the glass block infill; brick infill is used on the north side, where the sonar training rooms are located. The result is appropriate both in terms of the daylighting strategy and energy efficiency achieved.

MECHANICAL AND INTERIOR RELATIONSHIPS

The structural grid is expressed in the interior spaces by masonry-protected steel columns supporting a series of one-way steel beams boxed in gypsum. Surface-mounted strip lighting fixtures are centered within the bays, and hot-water baseboard heaters fit between the columns. A VAV air-handling system combines diffusers and ceiling plenums; the latter are used for supply air in classrooms and return air in corridors. The absence of operable windows means that thermal comfort is achieved solely by means of the mechanical system. In addition, the lack of exterior doors raises the issue of fire safety. Sprinkler heads are used throughout the building, and the access floors[4] used for half the building's floor area are protected by a carbon dioxide discharge system.

The constraints imposed by the security issue are many, and there are corresponding costs. The additional weight of the glass blocks neutralizes whatever structural advantage is to be gained by their contribution to the building's rigidity. Within these constraints, however, the building performs well; in daylighting and its use of site, it does far more than its client was prepared to ask of it.

Project: Addition to Building 427, Submarine Training Facility.
Architects: Hartford Design Group, Hartford, CT. Tai Soo Kim, principal.
Structural, Mechanical, & Electrical Engineers: Minges Associates, Avon, CT.
General Contractor: Robert S. Sullivan, Inc., New London, CT.
Cost: $1,600,000; $128 PSF. Completed 1980.
Photographs: Nick Wheeler (courtesy of Hartford Design Group).

Stephen C. O'Connell Activities Center
University of Florida

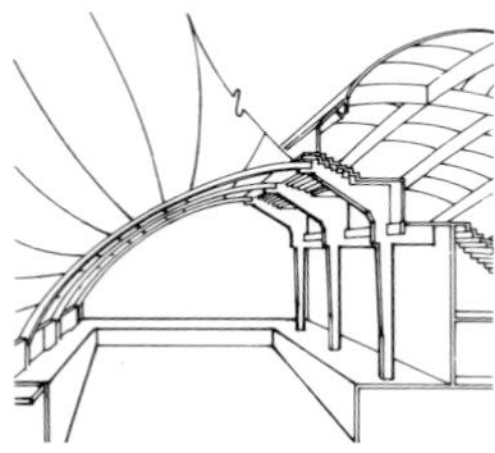

Air-supported and tension fabric structures[1] are by nature highly integrated.[2] Combining conventional and innovative building systems, the O'Connell Center gives evidence throughout of an integrated attitude toward organizing people, functions, and information, from the design process to the orchestration of daily operations.

Probably the decisive reason for the use of an air-supported structure was its ability to deliver a large, flexible, column-free space at low first cost. In addition, an energy analysis concluded that a roof of translucent air-supported fabric, if carefully coordinated with the other systems, could save 13,400 BTU's per square foot per year compared to a conventional opaque shell. The Teflon coating on the fiberglass insures little or no day-to-day maintenance (small quantities of the original fabric are stored nearby in case repairs are needed). The restraining cables offer a considerable factor of safety, since the cables will suspend the deflated fabric roof in the event of a mechanical failure or membrane puncture. Materials and design time were conserved through the use of a cable system patented by the engineering firm of Geiger Berger & Associates; this had been developed in the course of designing several other air-supported structures, including the Pontiac Silverdome. The cable-supported fabric unifies structure (in the main space, the air from four huge fans completes the structure), envelope, and interior.

It should be noted that these advantages were realized at some cost. The problem of building security is complicated by the need to keep vandals off the fabric roof. Artificial lighting for the assembly space could not be closely integrated with the bubble design; it is therefore treated in effect as suspended equipment. This is a visible integration problem, with the lights and speakers and their supporting cables exposed as ductwork might be.[3] Mechanical equipment in general is hard to add to air-supported buildings, a factor that can limit their flexibility; such equipment is often exposed to view in buildings involving fabric structures.

1. Tension fabric structures, pp. 152–153.
2. Structural fabric, pp. 173–176.
3. Structure and interior *unified*, pp. 326–327.

AIR-SUPPORTED AND TENSION FABRIC

The cruciform pattern described by the cables is reflected in the placement of the four large entranceways, which in turn frame the tension fabric "skirts." Earth berms surround the building, contributing the temperature stabilization characteristic of earth sheltering. A concrete compression ring surrounding the arena space holds the cables, which shape and stabilize the air-supported fabric dome. The frame is of precast concrete, chosen for construction speed. The fabric skirts are stretched taut over precast concrete half-arches, whose form is completed by the space under the arena grandstand. The grandstand structure, in turn, is integral with the perimeter concrete structure, as well as with the concrete compression ring of the bubble, and helps create the natatorium and the gymnastic studio.

Concrete structural elements, both painted and unfinished, combine with the fabric envelope to form the interior. The envelope's translucency has a strong impact on the interior as well as on mechanical design. Although the skin's translucency is only four percent, interior spaces are typically bathed in even light during the day, reducing the need for artificial illumination. A disadvantage is the impossibility of darkening the interior in the daytime. At night, interior lighting illuminates the bubble so that it functions as a very large outdoor light.

ENERGY ISSUES

From an environmental conditioning point of view, the translucent envelope raises issues common to all passive solar and daylighting strategies. Even given the envelope's insulating properties, which prevent 75 percent of solar penetration, the potential for energy saving from "free" light and heat had to be balanced against the cooling demands of the Florida climate. The university's central heating and chilled water plant made this consideration less urgent, but there remained the enormous variability

At night the fabric envelope's translucency makes the center a vast outdoor lamp (top left). The frame is precast concrete, as is the compression ring (visible at the top of the photo above left), which stabilizes the fabric dome. The plan (left) shows the arena's seating capacity. Tension fabric "skirts" stretched over precast concrete half-arches shelter the basketball practice area (above) and natatorium, as shown in the section perspective (below).

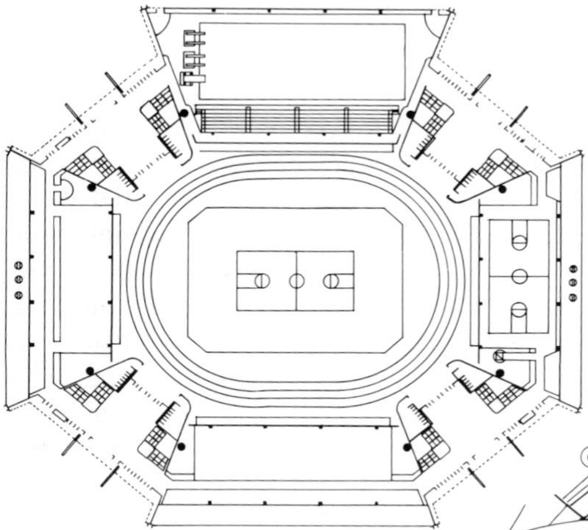

SEATING PLAN N

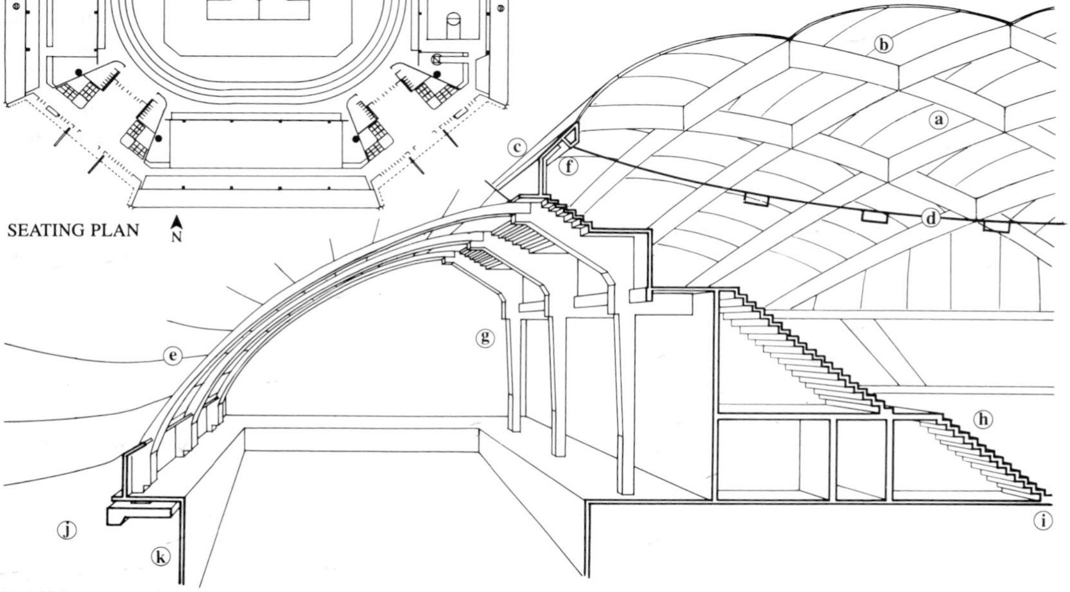

PERSPECTIVE SHOWING PRECAST ARCHES

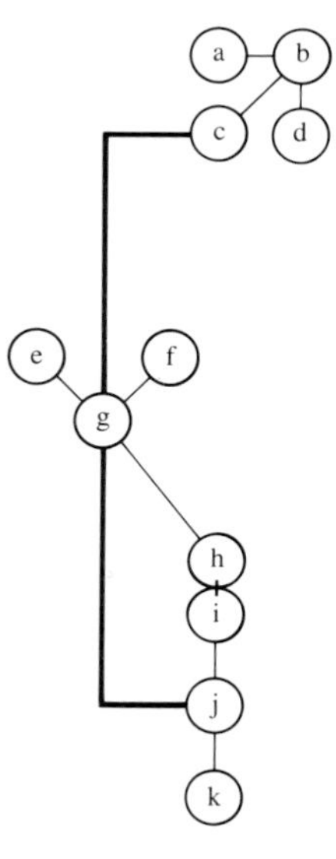

a. *Roof vents*
b. *Air-supported, Teflon coated fiberglass roof*
c. *Concrete compression ring and cables*
d. *Cable-supported lighting*
e. *Cable-supported tension skirts*
f. *Fans/AC system*
g. *Precast concrete frame*
h. *Operable bleachers and partitions*
i. *Wood flooring and resilient tile flooring*
j. *Cast-in-place concrete foundations*
k. *Vapor barrier*

Diagram detail page 365

Banners are used in combination with the fabric dome's inner layer to minimize sound reflection in the arena. Lighting and sound equipment, which could not easily be attached to the fabric, is suspended within the space.

of the solar source. Combined with the multiple and often simultaneous uses of the Center, from commencements and concerts to swim meets and weight lifting, acceptance of these solar changes required adequate building controls and a large, flexible air-handling system.

The Center's four 100-horsepower fans have a combined air conditioning capacity of 750 tons; a separate system with 60 tons capacity cools the south-facing swimming pool area. The cost of this cooling system is justified by its effective role as part of the structural system. There are few precedents for this type of structural-mechanical integration, a dynamic relationship that is both computerized and manually overridden according to weather and occupancy;[4] indoor and outdoor conditions are integrated and further related to occupancy levels. The giant fans are actuated in sequence to meet requirements that range from low pressure (an empty building) to maximum pressure (a capacity crowd leaving during a torrential rainstorm). Roof vents relieve over-pressurization automatically, and doors can be opened to release pressure manually.[5]

One of the design team's most successful strategies was the programmatic and physical integration of the ancillary spaces—the pool, practice basketball courts, gymnastic and dance studios, and entranceways—as simultaneously usable facilities surrounding the main space, which is also designed to accommodate multiple functions. Comparison with a similar, almost twin project in Tampa, built without these skirts, underlines the inclusiveness and utility of this design. The inner layer of the fabric roof controls acoustical reflection. Operable partitions,[6] moving floors, and mechanical bleachers enhance the adaptability of the various spaces.

The roof of the O'Connell Center represents a very complicated and demanding level of integration. In it, conceptual and physical criteria are brought together in a way that is unique among the buildings in this chapter. Structural, lighting, and acoustical needs are all satisfied by the roof, and all are closely interrelated in terms of building performance criteria.

4. Energy management control systems, pp. 158–160.

5. Thermal performance, pp. 250–252.

6. Operable partitions, pp. 193–195.

Ancillary spaces surrounding the arena, such as the natatorium shown here, allow multiple events and activities to take place simultaneously. Note moveable bleachers in the retracted position at right.

Project: Stephen C. O'Connell Activities Center.
Architects: Design architect: CRS/Sirrine, Inc., Caudill Rowlett Scott Division, Houston, TX. Paul Kennon, FAIA, design principal; Suthipan Smitthipong, AIA, project designer. Associate architect: Moore May Graham Brame Poole/Architects, Inc., Gainesville, FL.
Aquatics consultant: R. Jackson Smith, AIA, Stamford, CT.
Structural and Mechanical Engineers: Geiger Berger & Associates, New York, NY.
Electrical Engineers: Flack & Kurtz, New York, NY.
Acoustical Engineer: Coffeen Anderson & Associates, Mission, KS.
Aquatics Engineer: Eggers Group, New York, NY.
General Contractor: Dyson & Co., Pensacola, FL.
Cost: $11,954,418; $48 PSF. Completed December 1980.
Photographs: Balthazar Korab (courtesy of CRS/Sirrine, Inc., Caudill Rowlett Scott Division).

George R. Moscone Convention Center
San Francisco, California

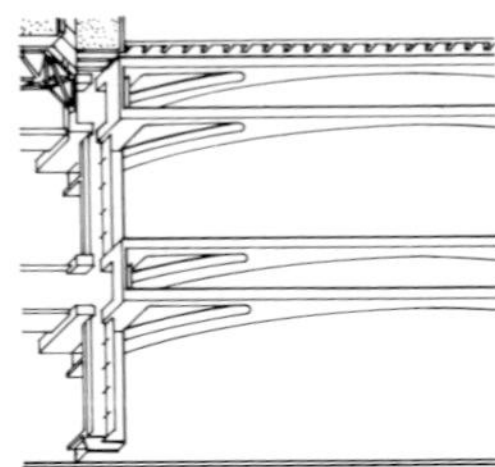

As Horatio Greenough once observed, there is just one main idea here, but it speaks loud. He was speaking of the design for the Washington Monument, but the same could be said of the George R. Moscone Convention Center in San Francisco. Believed to be the world's largest column-free exhibition space, this 650,000 sq ft convention center is located almost entirely underground and includes a 265,000 sq ft exhibition hall, 34 meeting rooms with capacities from 60 to 600, administrative offices on the mezzanine level, and a 30,000 sq ft ballroom. The exhibition hall and ancillary meeting rooms are divisible into multiple configurations through the use of operable partitions,[1] a space-conserving strategy that provides the flexibility needed for simultaneous uses.

It is the exhibition hall that best expresses the building's systems integration potential. Its sixteen 275 ft span, post-tensioned concrete arches, the 60 ft long precast T's which they support, and the surrounding cast-in-place concrete perimeter are at once structure, envelope, and interior, and the underground location that they make possible is decisive in terms of building energy consumption as well.

ENVELOPE AS SITE

Externally, the envelope performs the additional function of a site. The convention center was planned as the centerpiece of the Yerba Buena redevelopment area, and underground development was mandated by the city's planning committee in response to community pressure. Local precedent for underground construction had been set by the BART subway system and the Union Square parking garage. Ultimately, the design for Moscone Center became much more than camouflage: the five-acre roof can support several buildings of lightweight construction or up to 5 ft of soil. At present, the earth topping serves as ballast for the protected membrane roof.[2]

At present, the one pavilion in this rooftop park is the Moscone Center lobby. Its all-glass skin and exposed steel space frame

1. Operable partitions, pp. 193–195.

2. Protected membrane roofing, pp. 167–168.

The envelope of the Moscone Center acts as a site (top). The five acre roof can support light buildings and presently serves as a downtown park. A view from the entrance (center) shows the all-glass skin and exposed steel space frame roof structure of the lobby. Mezzanine lounges (above) provide views of the exhibition floor between paired arches.

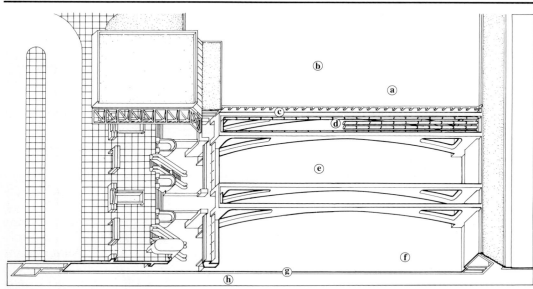

PERSPECTIVE SHOWING PAIRED ARCHES

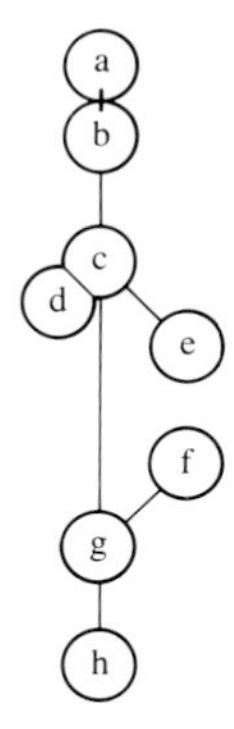

a. *Protected membrane roof*
b. *Poured-in-place concrete roof*
c. *Exposed tees, arches, box girders*
d. *Exposed ducts*
e. *Fluorescent lighting*
f. *Floor covering*
g. *Mat foundations*
h. *Waterproofing*

Diagram detail page 378

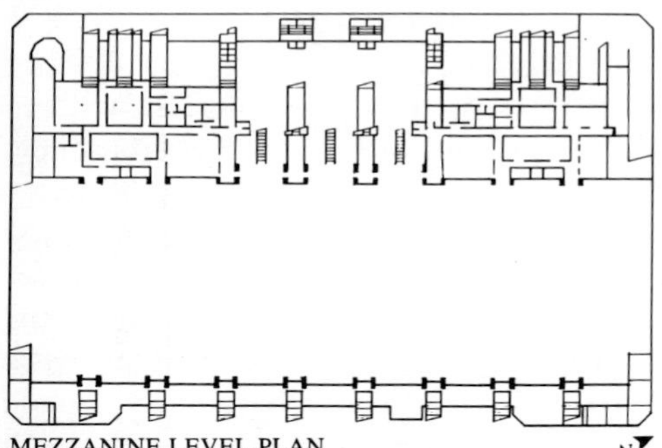

MEZZANINE LEVEL PLAN

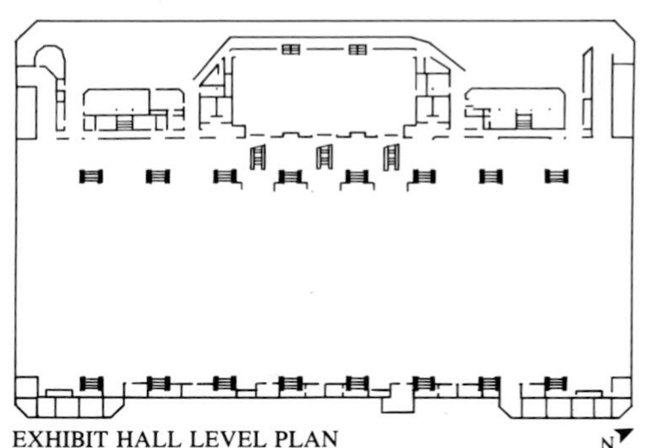

EXHIBIT HALL LEVEL PLAN

The section perspective (top) focuses on two arch pairs as seen from above. Plans show mezzanine and exhibit hall levels (center). A view of the exhibit hall (above) reveals long clear spans created by the 16 post-tensioned concrete arches. Trucks and other equipment can drive directly onto the floor.

roof structure impart a feeling of lightness while allowing natural light to penetrate to the levels below. At the same time, the lobby is a discrete building that serves to announce the scale of the main space below.[3]

ARCHES CREATE INTERIOR IMAGE

In the exhibition hall, the trusses and shorter spans originally proposed were discarded in favor of the maximum flexibility of a long clear span achieved with the sets of paired arches. A complete and satisfying interior image in themselves, the giant arches are practical from the exhibitor's point of view, while the long clear spans obviate the feeling of oppressiveness that can arise in an underground space. In the tradition of masonry construction translated into concrete,[4] structure becomes form and finish.

Underground construction involved more than the usual cost premium in this case ($20 million), as considerable groundwater existed on the site. A mat foundation, 7 ft thick to counteract groundwater pressure, contains the post-tensioning cables for the 275 ft arches. Almost all of the interior surfaces in the main hall are actively structural.

The ballroom, which is also column-free, further integrates structural and interior systems. The room is framed by giant concrete box girders which also serve as supports for the steel trusses of the lobby above, and as exit tunnels from the lower level. These box girders serve as structural support for the roof and, as exposed, further articulate the ballroom ceiling. The design also integrates exhibition hall emergency exits, which are located within the box girders and between the arch pairs, all leading directly to the street.

These elaborate structural needs are counterbalanced by the advantages of earth-sheltered construction. The project's mechanical engineers see heating and cooling costs cut by 25 percent, while the rooftop space, effectively used, can eventually become income-producing for the city of San Francisco.

Given its location in an earthquake region, the building's resistance to seismic loads was a major concern, one that was addressed in part by the decision to build underground. This issue may also have influenced the selection of the firm of T.Y. Lin, known for their work in seismic design, as structural engineers, and ultimately the use of post-tensioning.

FIRE PROTECTION

A related issue is fire protection, particularly since fires often occur in the aftermath of earthquakes. In this regard, underground location can present multiple egress problems similar to those in the addition to the Submarine Training Facility at Groton.[5] The placement of emergency exits, visibly integrated with the arch pairs, serves to alert the occupant to the location of all the exits once he or she has noted the location of one. Double rows of sprinkler heads, which run along the inside edges of the paired arches, are also visibly integrated with structure.

Light fixtures in the exhibition hall and the lobby reflect a sensitivity to the geometry and space around them, both in shape and placement. Partial concealment of the main ductwork in the exhibition hall is made possible by its placement between the arch pairs, exemplifying a *meshed* level of physical integration.

Nine separate, single-zone draw-through systems serve the exhibition hall, each with heating and cooling coils and fans. The ductwork is also part of the smoke-control system. The other spaces are served by their own HVAC systems. The large meeting room has three single-zone, rooftop-mounted air-handling units, with two packaged, single-zone draw-through air conditioning units located under planters adjoining the lobby. Steam and chilled water are supplied by a central plant.

Overall, the Moscone Center achieves a high level of visible and physical integration, with envelope, structural, and interior systems inextricably linked, and the mechanical requirements subordinated to them.

3. Visible integration, pp. 381–385, 394–397.
4. Structure and interior *unified*, pp. 326–327.
5. Compare Addition to Submarine Training Facility, pp. 106–107.

The exhibit hall's 16 paired arches partially conceal the main ductwork while their bases frame the emergency exits. Note placement of sprinkler heads.

Project: George R. Moscone Convention Center.
Architects: Hellmuth, Obata & Kassabaum, Inc., San Francisco, CA. Associate architect: Jack Young & Associates, San Francisco, CA.
Structural Engineers: T.Y. Lin International, San Francisco, CA.
Mechanical Engineers: Hayakawa Associates, San Francisco, CA.
Electrical Engineers: The Engineering Enterprise, Berkeley, CA.
Consultants: Flambert & Flambert, San Francisco, CA; Paul S. Veneklasen & Associates, Santa Monica, CA; Rolf Jensen & Associates, Pleasant Hill, CA; The SWA Group, Sausalito, CA; Dames & Moore, San Francisco, CA; Tudor Engineering, San Francisco, CA; Cygna, San Francisco, CA.
Construction Manager: Turner Construction, San Francisco, CA.
Cost: $126,000,000. Completed December 1981.
Photographs: Peter Aaron—ESTO.

William B. Hartsfield Atlanta International Airport
Atlanta, Georgia

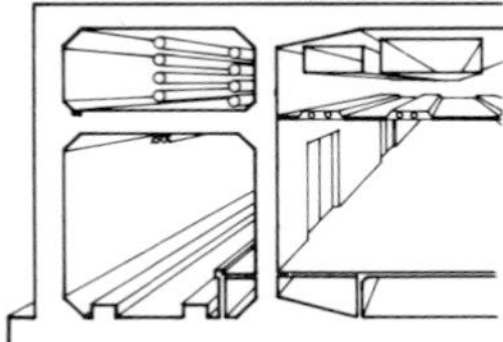

In terms of population and land area, the William B. Hartsfield International Airport in Atlanta is the fourth largest city in Georgia. It represents 13 years of planning, and the design as built is the product of a unique joint venture involving architects, engineers, and planners. Yet for all the superlatives used when speaking of it, Atlanta's airport is a collection of ordinary building forms, systems, and elements that might be found in a project of almost any scale. What distinguishes and energizes these elements is their integration with transportation systems that range from elevators and moving sidewalks to 747's.

Hartsfield's overall design is a straightforward piece of problem-solving. With nearly 75 percent of all passengers coming to Atlanta just to change planes, the designers saw an opportunity to dispense with the dominant, hub-like terminal building form. Instead, they defined a series of four simple, 2200 ft long passenger docks or concourses, spaced 1000 ft apart and connected by an underground spine for convenient airplane access and maneuvering. A fifth concourse for international flights is connected directly to the terminal. The resulting efficiency in airplane movement has led to considerable savings in jet fuel (estimated to cost $17.50 per engine per minute while taxiing) and fewer conflicts for planes entering and leaving the gates.

CIRCULATION REQUIREMENTS

With building shape determined by the circulation requirements of airplanes, enormous distances result, and these in turn require conveyances to assure adequate circulation of passengers. The issue in this case is conservation of time.[1] The principal conveyance is a people-mover that operates along the 6000 ft spine connecting the four domestic concourses with the terminal complex. This horizontal elevator is fully automated, and its 17 rubber-tired vehicles are capable of operating in one-, two-, and three-car trains. In the three-car mode, it can transport 8670 passengers per hour. The trip from one end of the spine to the other takes five minutes.

Moving sidewalks running parallel to the people-mover provide convenient transportation between adjacent concourses, and complete accommodations are provided for the handicapped. The terminal complex combines ticketing and baggage with arriving and departing vehicle access, an international concourse, parking structures, and a Metropolitan Atlanta Rapid Transit System station. Functionally, however, the spine is the essence of the building, even more than the high-ceilinged ticketing concourses of the conventional terminal. The structure, of cast-in-place concrete columns and floor slabs, is a linear, earth-sheltered building that incorporates inbound and outbound ve-

1. Conservation of time, pp. 236–237.

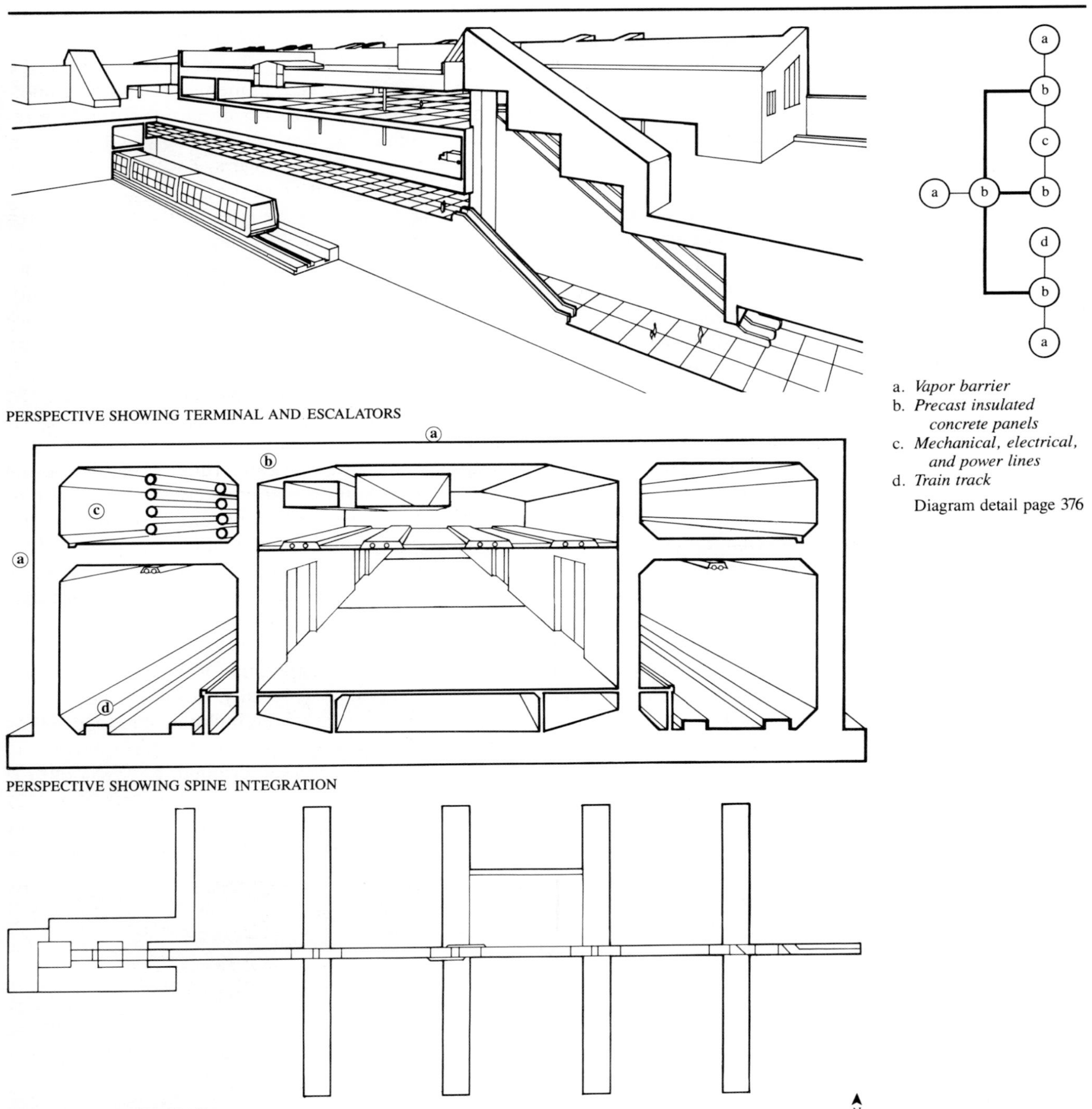

PERSPECTIVE SHOWING TERMINAL AND ESCALATORS

PERSPECTIVE SHOWING SPINE INTEGRATION

NEW TERMINAL SITE PLAN

N

a. *Vapor barrier*
b. *Precast insulated concrete panels*
c. *Mechanical, electrical, and power lines*
d. *Train track*

Diagram detail page 376

The terminal building (left) incorporates an international concourse and a rapid transit station. People-mover and escalators appear in a cutaway view of the terminal complex (top). A section perspective through the spine (center) shows the two people-mover tunnels, with walkway and moving walks between them and mechanical equipment above. The great distances generated by aircraft circulation requirements are evident in plan (above). Horizontal transportation systems make this rectilinear layout possible by conserving time used in traversing the spine.

hicle lanes; a walking mall and moving sidewalks; an automated baggage system compartment; and electrical, mechanical, and telecommunications distribution. Escalators[2] and elevators[3] at the terminal and concourses bring arriving passengers up to the above-ground levels.

Structure, envelope, and interior do not generally display a high level of integration with the transportation systems that dominate this complex. To an extent the isolation of transportation systems is required for reasons of safety. The flexible signage system, however, represents an integration of interior with circulation requirements.[4] The signage system is also integrated with the linear plank metal ceilings, which allow quick and easy access to wiring in the return air ceiling plenums.

NOISE REDUCTION

Noise reduction is an issue, as it is in all airports, and sound transmission is reduced in the concourses through the use of concrete masonry exterior cladding on the ground floor.[5] On the second floor, from which passengers board, a modular exterior wall system of porcelain enameled metal panels is used. The interchangeable door, window, and wall units permit quick changes of aircraft boarding positions.

The airport complex uses about half the energy normally required by airports, partly owing to the energy management control system.[6] Working with the stable temperatures of the below-ground spaces, a central steam system increases its cooling capacity through a turbo-absorption system, recycling steam to drive two turbine-powered chillers. Light levels throughout the public areas are kept relatively low.

The project was successfully fast-tracked by the three-firm joint venture, with four years elapsing between the beginning of the construction documents phase and project completion. An ordinary, available, and flexible range of materials, imaginatively used, resulted in an energy-efficient airport constructed within the allotted budget.

A view of the entrance to the spine (above) shows the airport's flexible signage. The terminal is connected with the spine by escalators (below) and houses all baggage functions (bottom). A view of the spine's walkway shows moving walks and the concrete masonry interior finish (above right). At a people-mover station (below right) the right-of-way is enclosed, reinforcing the similarity to an elevator where only the interior of the cab is visible to the passengers.

2. Escalators, pp. 190–192.
3. Elevators, pp. 187–189.
4. Visible integration, pp. 381–385, 409.
5. Acoustical performance, pp. 254–256.
6. Energy management control systems, pp. 158–160.

Project: William B. Hartsfield Atlanta International Airport.
Architects: Stevens and Wilkinson Architects Engineers Planners Inc., Atlanta, GA; Smith, Hinchman & Grylls Associates, Inc., Detroit, MI; Minority Airport Architects & Planners, Atlanta, GA.
Structural, Mechanical, & Electrical Engineers: Stevens & Wilkinson Architects Engineers Planners Inc., Atlanta, GA; Smith, Hinchman & Grylls Associates, Inc., Detroit, MI.
General Contractors: HOH Construction Co., Atlanta, GA (a joint venture).
Cost: $143,000,000; $65 PSF. Completed October 1980.
Photographs: Balthazar Korab (courtesy of Stevens & Wilkinson; Smith, Hinchman & Grylls; and Minority Airport Architects & Planners).

References

HERMAN MILLER SEATING MANUFACTURING PLANT

Dean, Andrea O. "Streamlined Shapes Enclose a Splendid Workplace." *AIA Journal*, Mid-May 1982, pp. 186-202.

Murphy, James. "Image and Morale." *Progressive Architecture*, February 1982, pp. 110-113.

TRUST PHARMACY

Fisher, Thomas. "Post-Industrial Architecture." *Progressive Architecture*, April 1983, pp. 109-113.

AID ASSOCIATION FOR LUTHERANS HEADQUARTERS

"On the Wisconsin Prairie, A Reposeful Building with Strong Presence." *Architectural Record*, February 1978, pp. 121-128.

KIMBELL ART MUSEUM

"Post-Tensioned Shells Form Museum Roof." *Engineering News Record*, November 11, 1971, pp. 24-25.

Kahn, Louis. *Light Is the Theme: Louis I. Kahn and the Kimbell Art Museum*. Fort Worth, TX: Kimbell Art Foundation, 1975.

Meyers, Marshall D. "Louis I. Kahn: Yale Art Gallery and Kimbell Art Museum." *Global Architecture*, No. 38, 1976, pp. 18-40, 46-47.

Meyers, Marshall D. "Masters of Light: Louis Kahn." *AIA Journal*, September 1979, pp. 60-62.

JOHN C. NUTTING APARTMENTS

Rouse, Roland E. *Passive Solar Design for Multi-Family Buildings*. Commonwealth of Massachusetts, Executive Office of Energy Resources, 1983.

Rush, Richard D. "Barrier-Free and Energy-Conscious." *Progressive Architecture*, April 1982, pp. 150-153.

ILLINOIS REGIONAL LIBRARY

"Stanley Tigerman on Being Just a Little Less Serious." *Architectural Record*, September 1976, pp. 111-117.

Miller, Nory. "Fanciful and Functional." *Progressive Architecture*, April 1978, pp. 76-81.

MUSEUM OF SCIENCE AND INDUSTRY

"How Value Engineering Cut Costs 25%." *Building Design and Construction*, May 1980, pp. 57-61.

"Museum of Science and Industry." *Architecture and Urbanism*, March 1982, pp. 83-88.

Morton, David. "The Elements and Form." *Progressive Architecture*, April 1981, pp. 108-113.

STOCKTON STATE COLLEGE

"Geddes Brecher Qualls Cunningham uses 5 Subsystems and Careful Master Planning for This Experimental College in New Jersey." *Architectural Record*, March 1973, pp. 103-108.

"USA Universitas." *The Architectural Review*, October 1978, pp. 205-207.

Marlin, William. "It's Back to School for the Systems Approach." *Architectural Record*, May 1977, pp. 95-102.

WALTER REED GENERAL HOSPITAL

"A Famous Army Institution Builds a Technological Showcase." *Architectural Record*, August 1981, pp. 100-102.

GEORGIA POWER HEADQUARTERS

"Georgia Power Company." *Architecture and Urbanism*, July 1982, pp. 69-74.

Miller, Michael J. "Energy Savings at No Extra Cost." *Building Design and Construction*, June 1981, pp. 128-133.

Rush, Richard D. "Conclusion: The Future Is Rich." *Progressive Architecture*, April 1979, pp. 144-148.

Slavin, Maeve. "Powerful Design in Atlanta." *Interiors*, April 1981, pp. 80-81.

NATIONAL PERMANENT BUILDING

"Complex, Muscular Facades on Pennsylvania Avenue." *AIA Journal*, Mid-May 1981, pp. 238-239.

"National Permanent Building." *Architecture and Urbanism*, December 1981, pp. 99-102.

Knight, Carleton. "Hanging Out." *Progressive Architecture*, December 1977, pp. 54-57.

PIKE AND VIRGINIA BUILDING

Global Architecture. Special Issue on Houses, February 1984.

"News." *Architectural Record*, February 1981, pp. 104-107.

OCCIDENTAL CHEMICAL BUILDING

Dixon, John Morris. "Glass under Glass." *Progressive Architecture*, April 1983, pp. 82-85.

Murphy, James. "Rainbow's End." *Progressive Architecture*, April 1980, pp. 102-104.

Sloan, Alan M. H. "Dynamic Curtain Wall Integrated with HVAC." *Building Design and Construction*, November 1983, pp. 80-83.

VOCATIONAL TECHNICAL EDUCATION FACILITY

Morton, David. "A North Star." *Progressive Architecture*, April 1982, pp. 128-131.

SOUTHERN SERVICE CENTER FOR THE EQUITABLE LIFE ASSURANCE SOCIETY

"Equitable Life Assurance Company, Southern Service Center." *Architectural Record*, March 1979, pp. 140-143.

Conroy, Sarah Booth. "The Best Buildings of 1980." *Horizon Magazine*, June 1980, p. 54.

ADDITION TO SUBMARINE TRAINING FACILITY

Brenner, Douglas. "The Not-So-Simple Art of the Box: Two Projects by the Hartford Design Group." *Architectural Record*, August 1981, pp. 72-75.

STEPHEN C. O'CONNELL CENTER

"Stadiums Take Cover Under Fabric Roofs." *Building Design and Construction*, December 1981, pp. 118-121.

"Stephen C. O'Connell Center." *Architecture and Urbanism*, January 1982, pp. 117-121.

McDermott, Jeanne. "How to Save Energy." *Interiors*, February 1982, pp. 76-77.

Rush, Richard D. "Mr. Bubble." *Progressive Architecture*, August 1981, pp. 82-87.

MOSCONE CONVENTION CENTER

Dean, Andrea O. "Going Underground to Escape Controversy." *AIA Journal*, January 1983, pp. 62-63.

Keller, Karl P. "Heading Underground for the Wide Open Spaces." *Building Design and Construction*, February 1982, pp. 48-53.

ATLANTA INTERNATIONAL AIRPORT

Ebisch, Robert. "Airport Maximizes Efficiency for Passengers, Planes." *Building Design and Construction*, January 1981, pp. 60-64.

"The Planning of Hartsfield-Atlanta." *Airport Services Management*, November 1980, pp. 40-43.

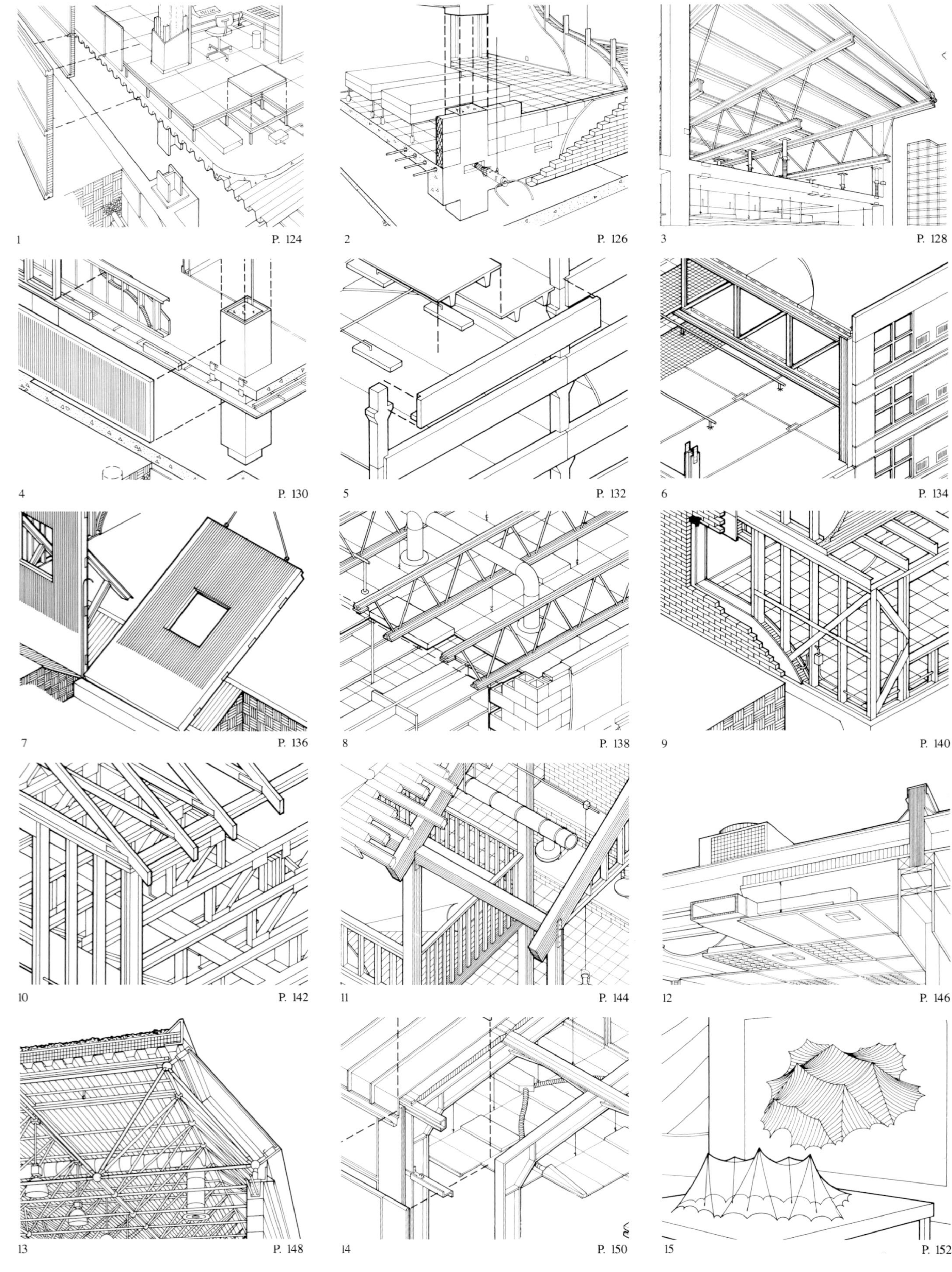
1 P. 124
2 P. 126
3 P. 128
4 P. 130
5 P. 132
6 P. 134
7 P. 136
8 P. 138
9 P. 140
10 P. 142
11 P. 144
12 P. 146
13 P. 148
14 P. 150
15 P. 152

Chapter 4
Generic Examples

Author:
Thomas Vonier, AIA

This chapter illustrates integration issues and opportunities as presented by a range of widely used building technologies. The examples reflect basic approaches to design, construction, and materials usage that are applicable to a variety of occupancy requirements. They embody key integration issues that arise in the process of combining the components and subsystems to produce complete buildings.

Each example includes a description of the unique system features, a characterization of circumstances in which its use is likely to be most appropriate or particularly advantageous, and a discussion of the main opportunities and challenges presented for systems integration. The drawings stress the essential interconnectedness among design decisions; the design process is seen as an effort that integrates the knowledge of many disciplines, each with an understanding of the value and import of the others' contributions.

The examples encompass structural, envelope, mechanical, and interior systems. In most examples one of these systems (usually structure) or a combination of two systems (often structure and envelope) tends to dominate the integration potentials and priorities, setting clearly prescribed limits around what is prudent and possible for introduction of the other systems. Each example also tends to represent a set of internally generated rules about how combinations, connections, and interfaces among systems may occur. For some projects these properties may be sought explicitly; the systems are chosen on the basis of their ability to meet performance requirements set by the intended building functions, or out of a need to respond to constraints of schedule, site, and available technology. In other cases the rules are simply dictates that must be observed if the systems are to be integrated successfully.

These examples do not necessarily represent the only combinations or variations possible within a given building vocabulary, but they are intended to be common and reasonable. The individual subsystems and components shown could be used in alternative ways, or could be replaced entirely by others that would be suitable.

Other chapters of this handbook offer additional insight into related integration issues by way of theoretical considerations, product characteristics, system performance criteria, and further examples of applications. It should be noted that the drawings are not to be interpreted as construction documents. Particular climates, products, loading, and building codes would obviously preclude any one set of systems as being universally applicable.

1. Access Floor and Curtain Wall

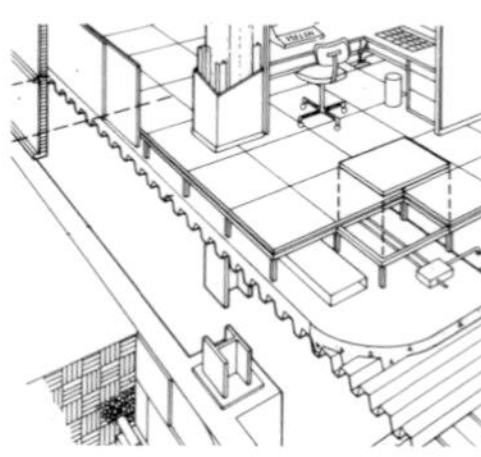

Reviewer:
Jan Kalas, AIA
The Eggers Group
New York, NY

Illustration:
Darrell Downing Rippeteau, Architect
Richard J. Vitullo, designer in charge
Washington, DC

This example employs a structural steel frame, braced for wind resistance by welded and bolted end brackets, enclosed by an exterior curtain wall of preassembled spandrels and heat-reflecting glass. Structural floors are constructed with corrugated light-gauge steel deck, welded to primary frame members, and cast-in-place concrete. A central service core of cast-in-place concrete shear walls adds rigidity to the frame.

The interior access floor system touches, but is independent of, the structural floor system, introducing some redundancy. It rests on the structural deck by means of adjustable pedestals and a grid of metal stringers, to which removeable square floor panels are fastened. The carpeted floor panels can integrate structure and interior finish materials either by means of reinforcing ribs or a structural eggcrate pattern cast on their underside, or through the use of captive retaining screws for fastening to the stringers. Special interchangeable panels are fitted with flush power receptacles and communication jacks.

The space between the top of the concrete topped steel deck and the bottom of the access floor can contain all power, lighting, electronic, and communications distribution systems, as well as ductwork for space conditioning systems.[1]

PRINCIPAL APPLICATIONS AND ADVANTAGES

Steel frame and curtain wall construction allows for off-site fabrication of frame components, easy shipping to the site, and rapid assembly. The corrugated steel deck becomes a working surface as soon as it is placed and provides formwork for the concrete topping, which does not need to be removed or shored. The steel and concrete in the floors can be designed to act as a composite diaphragm, providing a thin, lightweight structural element with or without an access floor.

The access floor shown is advantageous particularly in office environments that need especially flexible interior layouts. The access floor keeps all wires and cables in the space (generally not less than 4 in. deep) below the finish floor and out of wall cavities, easily accessible by removeable floor panels. Work areas can be reconfigured quickly, without need for interior refinishing, and relocation of telephones and electrical outlets is less costly.[2] System selection usually considers reduction of the buildup of static electricity in the floor and the ensuing risks of equipment damage or shocks.

KEY INTEGRATION ISSUES

In this example, spray-on fire-resistant coatings protect structural steel and the corrugated deck. Fire-resistive materials encase columns and beams. Fire-rated suspended ceiling assemblies are an alternative.

Factory preassembled curtain wall units that integrate glazing and spandrel panels must be designed with shipping, storage, and handling in mind, emphasizing protection at all stages. Control of uniformity in color for both glass and spandrel units is also a key concern, as variations in production runs may lead to discernible differences.

Access floor systems are not well suited to applications that involve heavy point loads or shifting of heavy equipment. Stringerless systems are among the most flexible and least costly varieties, but lack the stability of fully gridded systems and depend on perimeter walls for restraint. Although such systems may add to overall floor-to-floor heights, the access floor conceals the most visually obtrusive distribution elements. However, use of the access floor area as an air plenum may defeat advantages gained from being able to run wires, cable, and piping unobstructed. Joints between the floor panels must be as tight and uniform as possible, to assure continuity in the appearance and wear in the floor finish and to prevent dust and dirt from reaching the open space beneath the floor.

1. Access floors, pp. 202–204.
2. Glass and aluminum curtain wall, pp. 212–215.

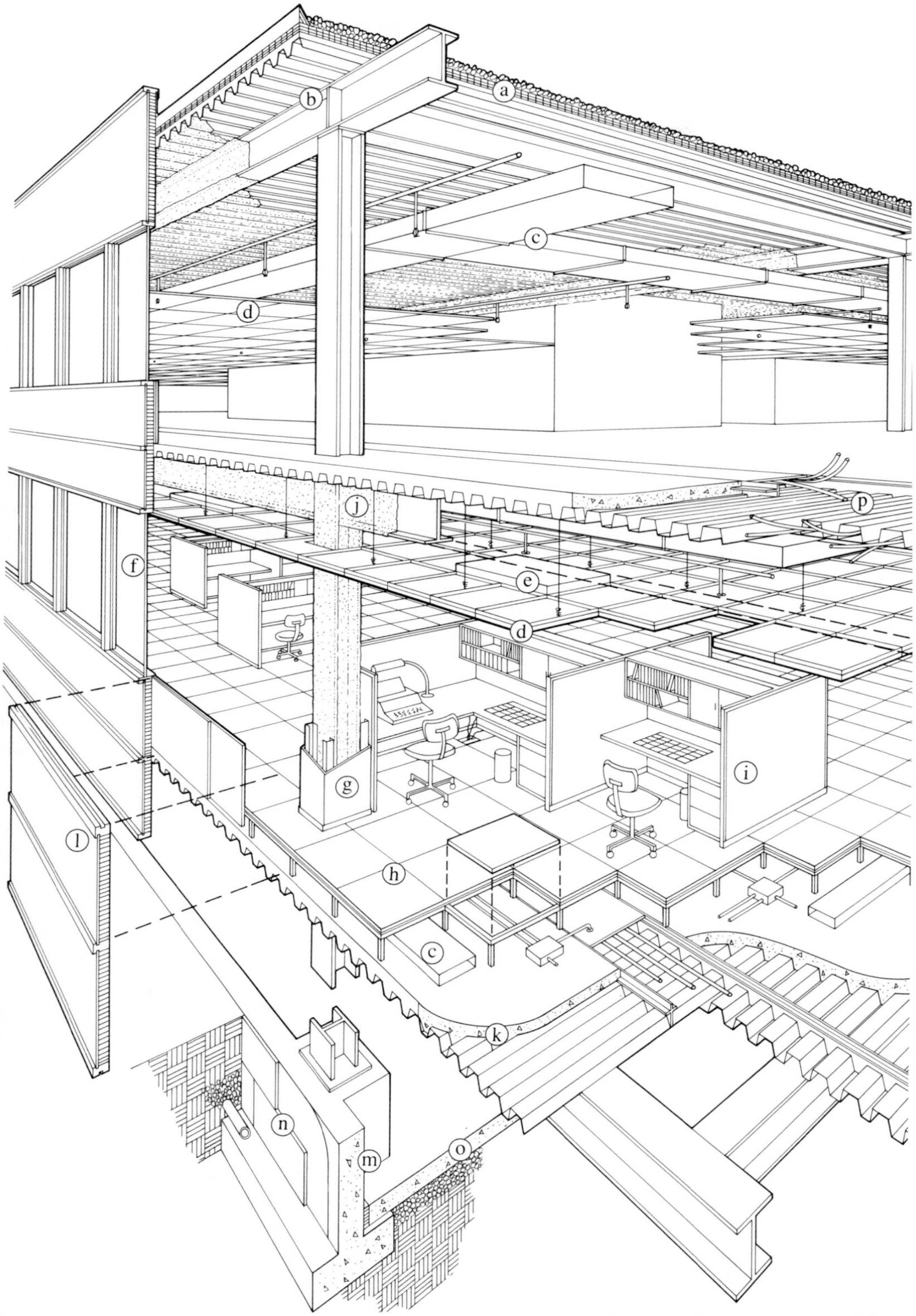

a. *Built-up roofing and rigid insulation*
b. *Steel beams and steel roof deck*
c. *Ducts and diffusers*
d. *Suspended acoustical tile ceiling*
e. *Fluorescent light fixture*
f. *Window assembly*
g. *Drywall*
h. *Carpeted access flooring*
i. *Open office furniture*
j. *Steel beams and columns*
k. *Steel decking with cast-in-place concrete topping*
l. *Insulated spandrel panels*
m. *Slab on grade and concrete foundation*
n. *Waterproofing and protective board*
o. *Vapor barrier*
p. *Structural/electrified floor*

Diagram detail page 348

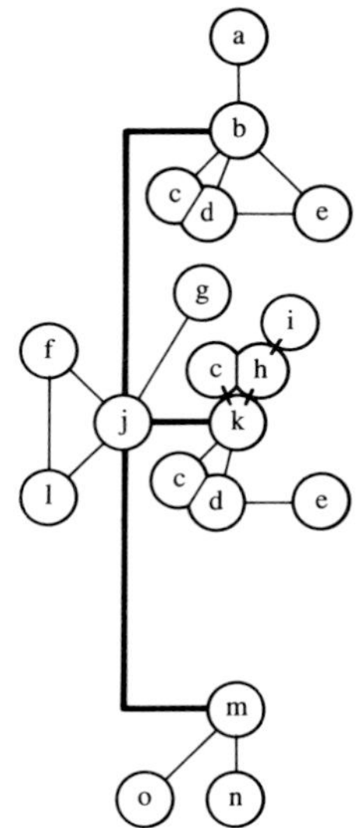

Structural steel framing and a steel and concrete floor diaphragm result in relatively long, uninterrupted clear spans. Structural/electrified floors and access floor systems are both shown as possible solutions for a flexible interior environment. The steel frame is structurally independent of the envelope elements, providing great flexibility in the weight and configuration of envelope systems employed. The access floor is touching *the composite structural slab and actually provides a redundant floor structure. Mechanical systems are* meshed *within the space between structural floor and finished floor. The suspended ceiling also provides space for distribution of internal services, but tends to be used principally for overhead lighting and ductwork, which, if placed in the floor, could block the path of wires for power and signal distribution. Fire protection of steel members is eased by use of the cellular concrete deck, although fire compartments may be interrupted by through-floor penetrations and by light fixtures and air grilles in the ceiling.*

2. Post-Tensioned Concrete

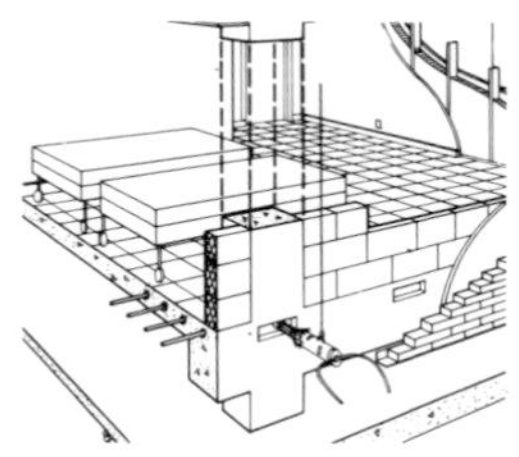

Reviewer:
Donald W. Velsey, AIA
Metcalf and Associates
Washington, DC

Illustration:
Darrell Downing Rippeteau, Architect
Richard J. Vitullo, designer in charge
Washington, DC

Post-tensioning is a technique for concrete prestressing that reduces or eliminates tensile stresses on the concrete under use-loading. Tubes, channels, or conduits are cast in the slab; after curing, high-strength steel tendons are placed in the tubes, anchored, and then jacked into tension from one end.

Tendons may be flexible or solid, and often include multiple wire strands. They need not be sheathed, but can be lubricated and wrapped to reduce friction with the slab. After stresses are applied, the tendon channels may be grouted to bond the tendons to the slab.

For tendon lengths greater than 100 ft, stresses must be applied simultaneously from two ends. This can be accomplished in mid-slab by means of special jacking devices and anchoring details. Concrete slab forms must be blocked out at edges, and in some cases in mid-slab, to provide for the positioning of anchors and the operation of the jacking equipment used to apply stresses. Mechanical devices anchor the post-tensioning strands at the edges of the slab. The devices also restrain the strands after tensioning. The technique strengthens the slab without increasing its thickness or adding the dead loads introduced by additional steel reinforcing rods.

PRINCIPAL APPLICATIONS AND ADVANTAGES

Post-tensioning is useful where the thickness of the floor slab is important to the economical or functional design aspects, or where concentrated live loads are high and the building height must be kept to a minimum. This technique is well suited to unenclosed parking structures; the resulting surfaces are much denser than those obtained from ordinary casting, and are thus less subject to leakage from standing rain or salt-laden slush from vehicles. Post-tensioning is also effective when project conditions require minimal floor-to-floor heights with maximum ceiling heights and generous space above the ceilings.[1] Additions to hospitals and other medical facilities often require that the floor-to-floor heights of the existing structure be matched, yet contemporary standards for servicing and equipment require deeper interstitial spaces than were provided in the original building.

1. Conservation of space, p. 236.

KEY INTEGRATION ISSUES

The post-tensioned structure depends for its strength and overall performance on the integrity of the tendons within the concrete slabs. The location of major through-slab penetrations for vertical risers must be precisely determined and located before forming. Consultation with structural and mechanical engineers at the earliest stages of project development is essential. Later modifications that involve slab penetration may be difficult or even impossible without endangering the prestressed characteristics of post-tensioned slabs. The location of the tendons is often marked during construction so that in future tendons can be avoided if new slab penetrations are required.

It is essential that the structural contractor have experience with post-tensioning to ensure the success and the safety of the technique during construction. The tremendous structural forces involved suggest that more than the ordinary degree of on-site inspection is warranted.

In recent years concerns have developed regarding possible hazards associated with the demolition of post-tensioned structures. Nearly explosive and potentially lethal forces are stored within post-tensioned slabs, and can be released under circumstances where the slab is broken apart during demolition operations. Some experts suggest that post-tensioned buildings and structures be identified by a prominently placed notice. Improper execution of post-tensioning operations in new construction may also present similar hazards.

Post-tensioned construction results in a tight, rigid structure that resists creep and movement. This makes the technique well suited to use of masonry infill envelope construction.

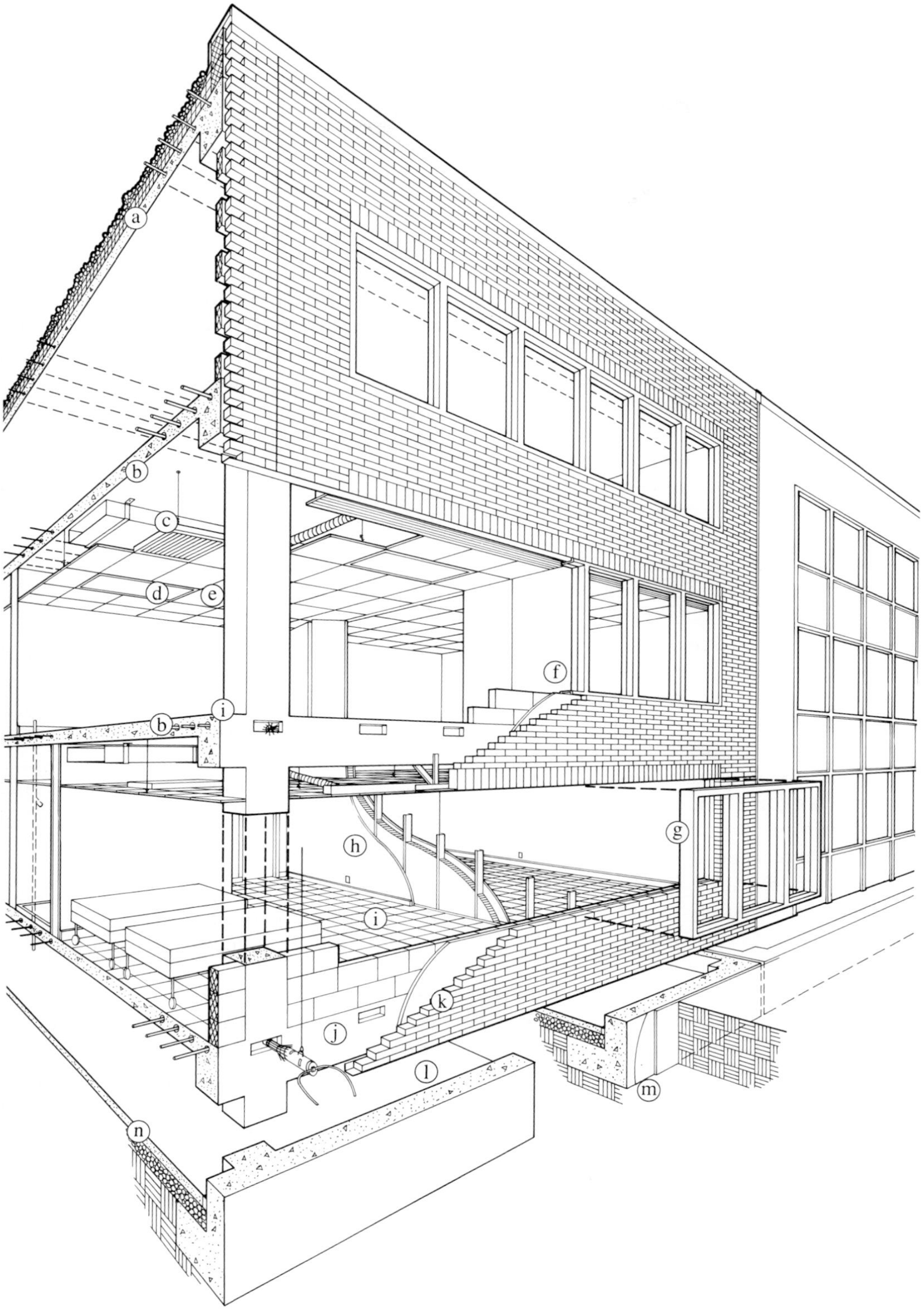

a. *Built-up roofing*
b. *Concrete slab*
c. *Ducts and diffusers*
d. *Fluorescent light fixtures*
e. *Suspended acoustical tile ceiling*
f. *Operable partitions*
g. *Window assembly*
h. *Metal stud and drywall assembly*
i. *Resilient flooring*
j. *Rigid concrete frame*
k. *Brick and concrete masonry and rigid insulation*
l. *Slab on grade and concrete foundation*
m. *Waterproofing and protective board*
n. *Vapor barrier*

Diagram detail page 349

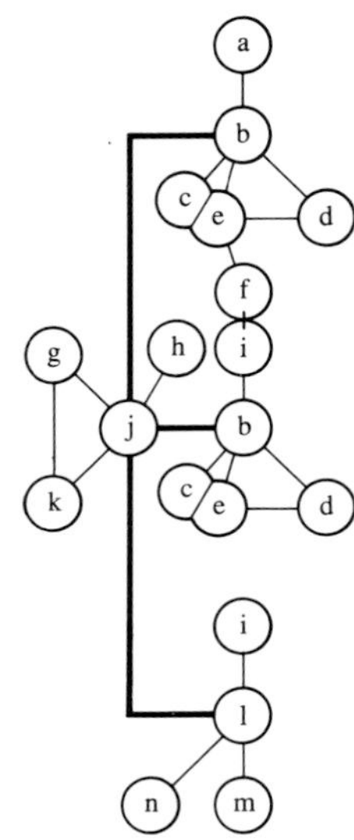

Post-tension construction is a highly sensitive integration of the compressive strength of concrete with the tensile strength of steel. Systems integration is influenced greatly by the positioning of the tendons, because this determines the possible locations for through-slab penetrations. Post-tensioning allows shallower beams and slabs, reducing overall building height and permitting longer spans with thinner structural members. Most systems are integrated at the connected *level, in part due to the need to maintain the structural system as a distinct element. The resultant structure is quite rigid and less subject to movement and creep than other types, making connection of the unit masonry skin appropriate. The potentially dangerous forces involved in post-tensioning require care and experience on the part of the contractor. Alterations can be difficult and must in any case preserve the integrity of the tensioning elements.*

3. Flying Form

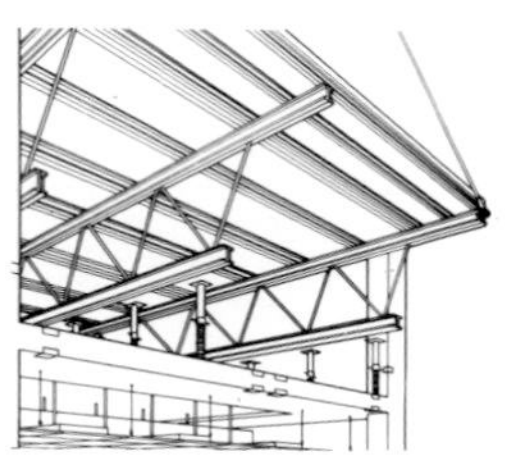

Reviewer:
John Zils, AIA, SE
Skidmore, Owings & Merrill
Chicago, IL

Illustration:
Darrell Downing Rippeteau, Architect
Richard J. Vitullo, designer in charge
Washington, DC

The systems employed with flying form construction do not differ substantially from those found in other types of reinforced concrete construction; the difference lies in the method of forming slabs and spandrels and in the sequencing of pours. Flying form construction requires almost total regularity in structural bay widths. Flying forms can be used to construct flat slabs, pan-joist slabs, waffle slabs, and various types of beams-in-slab. They are also used to form spandrels of varying configuration. Flat plate or flat slab construction is preferred, as this eases movement of the flying form "table" and minimizes special additional forming. For flying forms to be economical, the building structural layout must be uniform, and the beams and spandrels should be very shallow.

There are three principal types of flying forms: adjustable post shoring, manufactured truss forms, and column-supported forms. Adjustable post shoring uses scaffolding that rests on a wood sill and blocking and is raised by jacks. The forms are moved horizontally, usually by means of rollers, and are generally suitable for pours of up to 40 ft in length.

Manufactured truss forms, ranging up to 50 x 100 ft in side dimensions, use 4 to 6 ft deep trusses and are raised by a series of uniformly distributed jacks. The forms are moved by crane from one floor to the next, often in a staggered or stepped sequence. Greater widths in truss forms are made possible by the use of additional longitudinal trusses.

Column-supported forms employ adjustable brackets that "climb" the columns and are shored after initial positioning. This type is better suited to applications involving relatively close column spacings.

Usually the same work crew sets and strips the flying forms; half of the crew works below the deck level that has been cast, while the other half works above the previously cast area, setting the forms that have been removed. Conventional temporary shoring, separated from the surface forms, is set in place after removal of the flying forms. To speed the process of curing and to enable quicker removal of the forms, early high strength concrete is frequently used.

PRINCIPAL APPLICATIONS AND ADVANTAGES

Speed of construction, the economies realized through reuse of the forms,[1] and the high quality of finished surfaces[2] are among the most attractive features of this construction method.

A disadvantage of the flat plate construction system is the relative difficulty of punching through the slab or plate. However, in office applications, the high quality of the slab's finished surface lends itself readily to the use of flat wiring for power, lighting, electronics, and communications.[3] Because they are flat, these wiring systems increase the flexibility of open office planning; they are attached to the slab with steel tape prior to the installation of carpet tiles, with direction changes accomplished by folding the flat cable. Extra fire protection measures are unnecessary, as there are no through-slab penetrations to be sealed.

KEY INTEGRATION ISSUES

An important consideration with the use of flying forms is the regularity of bay spacing and the absence of deep beams or spandrels. Interior and exterior columns must align with the direction of the flying form's movement, to allow removal of the form without obstruction.

Often employed to meet very tight schedule completion demands, the relative speed of the flying form method places pressure on trades to complete related work more quickly than might be the case in conventionally formed concrete construction. At the same time, flat wiring frees the electrical system from restraints imposed by the structure, permitting the furniture layout and power needs to remain variable until very late in the construction process.

1. Conservation of time, pp. 236–237.
2. Visible integration, pp. 381–385.
3. Flat conductor cable, pp. 205–206.

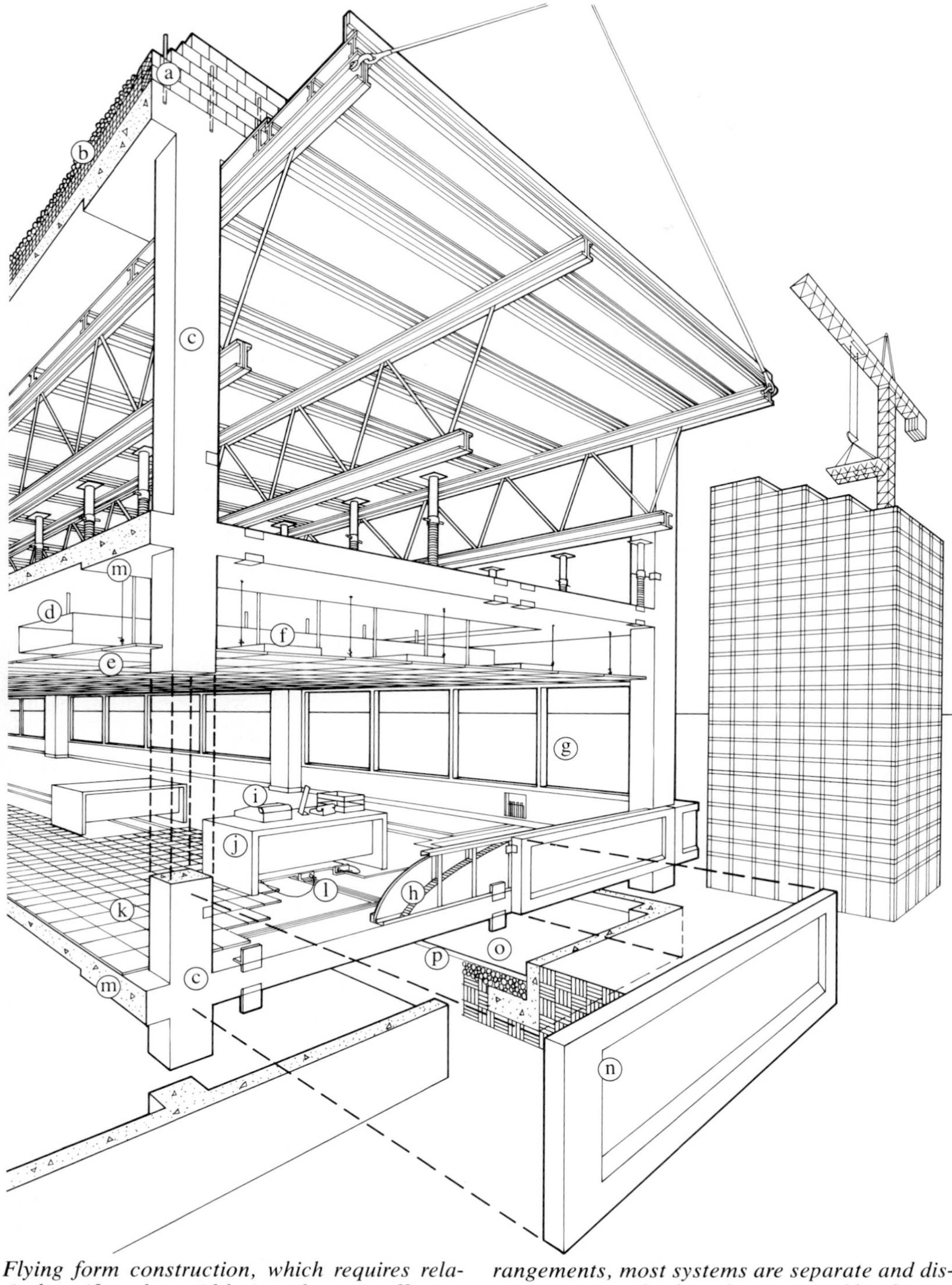

a. *Concrete masonry parapet back-up*
b. *Built-up roofing and rigid insulation*
c. *Rigid concrete frame*
d. *Ducts and diffusers*
e. *Suspended acoustical tile ceiling*
f. *Fluorescent light fixture*
g. *Window assembly*
h. *Metal stud and drywall assembly*
i. *Electrical office equipment*
j. *Office furniture*
k. *Carpet tile*
l. *Under carpet flat cable*
m. *Flat plate*
n. *Precast concrete spandrel panels*
o. *Slab on grade and concrete foundation*
p. *Vapor barrier*

Diagram detail page 350

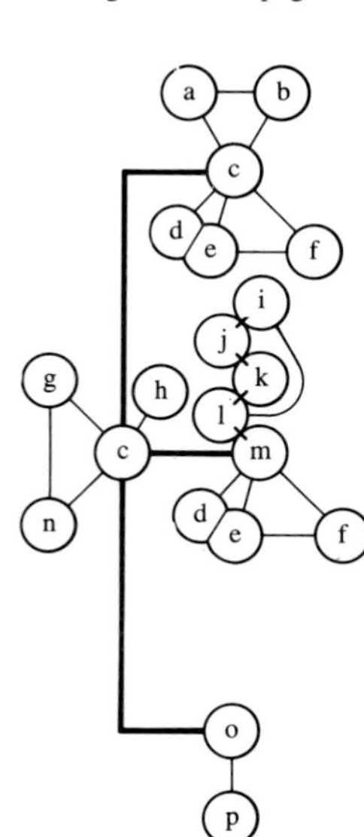

Flying form construction, which requires relatively uniform bay widths, can have an effect on visible integration because it produces a regularity in the rhythm of structural elements. To allow for easy removal and relocation of the forms, and to permit their repeated use, column spacings throughout the structure must not vary, and the depth of spandrel beams must be minimal. During construction the forms are placed and removed in a sequence of related operations, with temporary shoring used after form removal under the slabs until they have cured. The repetitive use of the forms can lead to conservation of both time and, of course, the materials used in forming. As a direct consequence of the need for flexibility in interior layouts and furniture arrangements, most systems are separate and distinct, integrated only at the connected *level. As in the case of conventionally cast-in-place flat plate concrete construction, the structural and mechanical systems are concealed from view, with the precast concrete envelope spandrel and glazing units* connected *to the structural frame. Mechanical and interior systems are* meshed *in the suspended ceiling assembly. The use of flat wiring atop the floor slabs for internal distribution of power, lighting, electronics, and communications dictates the use of removeable carpet tiles and yields a set of requirements for interfaces with furnishings and equipment—a case where the desire for flexibility restricts certain choices with respect to systems integration.*

4. Flat Plate

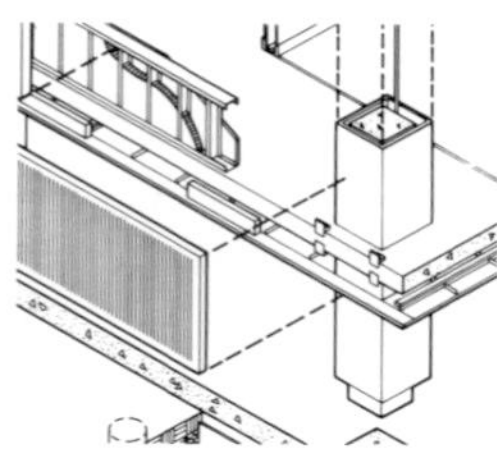

Reviewer:
Darrell Downing Rippeteau, AIA
Charles King, system designer
Washington, DC

Illustration:
Darrell Downing Rippeteau, Architect
Richard J. Vitullo, designer in charge
Washington, DC

This example combines cast-in-place columns and two-way concrete flat slab plates, uniformly thick, with precast concrete spandrel panels. The system usually has a central core for vertical circulation and services, and is typically employed for low-to-medium-rise construction, due to the costs and difficulties associated with placement of materials and labor in higher buildings. The need for interior flexibility in office environments dictates that interior systems be integrated at the *connected* level with structural and envelope elements.[1]

PRINCIPAL APPLICATIONS AND ADVANTAGES

The central core is key to the system. It permits relatively uniform and short horizontal runs for power, communications, plumbing, lighting, and HVAC equipment. Two-way flat plate concrete floors are among the simplest concrete structures for reinforcing, formwork, and detailing. The central core also permits consolidation of vertical service risers, thus increasing fire protection by reducing or eliminating through-floor penetrations in office areas.[2]

Office work stations require daylight exposure and views. Because the central core is farthest removed from perimeter zones, maximum use can be made of exterior zones for usable floor areas. On constrained urban sites the central core may be moved against an unfenestrated wall and still retain this advantage.

KEY INTEGRATION ISSUES

Interior services are generally distributed floor-by-floor horizontally in a drop-ceiling plenum. To maintain the system's fire-containment advantages, avoid floor penetrations outside the core or designated shafts.

Work stations in unpartitioned interior office arrangements can be serviced by ceiling-height power and communications service poles, which are unobtrusive even in completely open office environments. Columns and corridor partition walls often incorporate power and signal receptacles to reduce the number of service poles required. Where interior partitions can be used even on a limited basis, the distribution of services to offices and work stations is eased considerably, because power and signal wiring can be *meshed* into steel stud and drywall partition assemblies.

Exterior precast concrete panels can be attached on lower floors, even with flat plate shoring still in place, while concrete is being poured for upper-floor columns and plates. Likewise, ceiling plenum mechanical and electrical work can proceed while upper-floor structural work is in progress.

Most interior concrete surfaces must be concealed by other finishes; special forms are used when the concrete is to remain exposed. Finished ceilings are most often suspended acoustical tile, and floors are generally finished with acoustical-backed fire-resistant carpeting.

When crane-hoists are used to lift concrete buckets or large equipment, a hole is generally left in a section of each plate to allow for passage of the hoist; this hole is filled later, when large components have been moved and concrete pouring is complete. Elevator shafts are not used for this purpose, as elevators are usually installed before construction work is complete.

In this example, precast concrete or composite spandrel units are welded in place to a series of angle clips fastened into the concrete flat plates at their edges. Window-framing elements and glazing are installed after the spandrels have been set. Tolerances within the system grow progressively tighter, with the cast-in-place concrete requiring least attention, the placement of steel angles for eventual welding of the spandrels requiring greater exactitude, and the positioning of spandrels to accommodate framing and glass requiring greatest care.

1. Structure and envelope *connected*, pp. 323–324.
2. National Permanent Building, pp. 90–91.

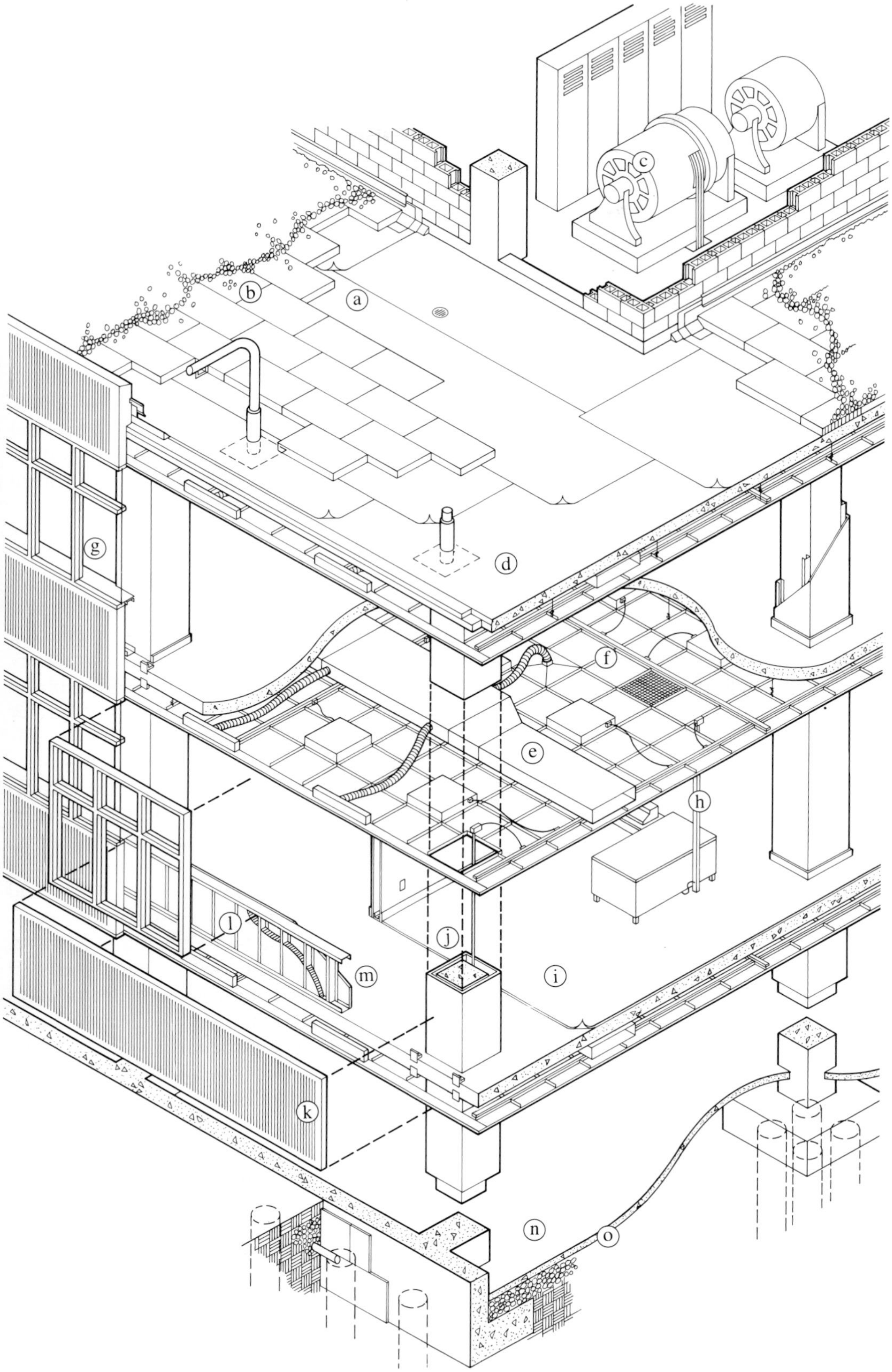

a. *Rigid insulation and ballast*
b. *Protected roof membrane*
c. *Elevator equipment*
d. *Cast-in-place concrete flat plate*
e. *Ducts and diffusers*
f. *Suspended acoustical tile ceiling*
g. *Window assembly*
h. *Power and communications poles*
i. *Carpeting*
j. *Concrete columns*
k. *Precast concrete spandrel panels*
l. *Batt insulation*
m. *Metal stud and drywall assembly*
n. *Slab on grade and concrete pile foundation*
o. *Vapor barrier*

Diagram detail page 351

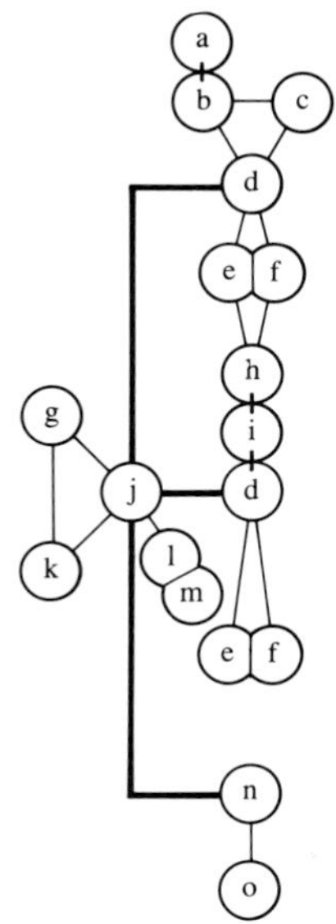

Nearly every element in flat plate construction is integrated at a connected *level, except for the interior walls and the ceiling assemblies, where mechanical and interior elements are* meshed, *and the roof assembly, where elements are* touching *but not* connected. *Precast concrete spandrel panels are* connected *to the structural concrete frame and backed up by a steel-stud and drywall assembly that also allows for a* meshed *level of electrical and mechanical distribution. Window assemblies* connected *to the concrete spandrel units complete the exterior envelope.*

5. Precast Frame

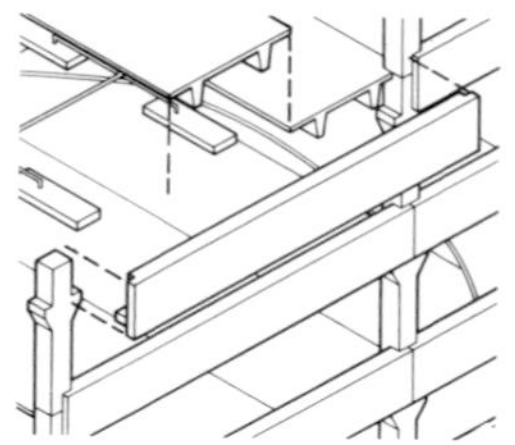

Reviewers:
Professor William R. Phillips
California Polytechnic State University
San Luis Obispo, CA

Richard T. Anderson, AIA
RNL
Denver, CO

Illustration:
Darrell Downing Rippeteau, Architect
Richard J. Vitullo, designer in charge
Washington, DC

Pretensioning is a method of prestressing concrete where steel tendons are stretched prior to placement of concrete and maintained in tension until the concrete is cured. The stresses are then transferred to compress the concrete. This example employs prestressed columns, inverted T-girders, ledger girders, and double-T joists. Once the floor and roof T's are set, the surface is covered with a thin concrete topping that provides the finished weather-exposed surface and a horizontal structural diaphragm.

The precast components are usually fabricated off-site and lifted into place by crane. A variety of finished surfaces is possible, and the unity of materials presents an opportunity for natural visible integration.[1] Thin brick or tile can also be used as a surface material.

PRINCIPAL APPLICATIONS AND ADVANTAGES

Prestressed concrete components are used where a high degree of regularity in structural bays and long, column-free spans are sought, such as in parking garages and office buildings. It is advantageous to use the maximum number of similar elements; floor T's, girders, and columns should all be the same length and design.

Adding final finishes and installation hardware to prestressed components before erection helps reduce on-site construction time.

KEY INTEGRATION ISSUES

Double-T joists are generally 8 or 12 ft wide, at a depth of 18 to 36 in., depending on the spanning requirements. Spans of 60 ft are generally considered maximum, due to the constraints of shipping and lifting the pieces, but longer spans and deeper sections are possible.

Mechanical and structural components are integrated at the *meshed* level.[2] In parking structures the requirements for through-floor penetrations are minimal. Holes can be cast in the stems and flanges of the T's, to allow for passage of conduit and piping or for on-site pouring of concrete where T's rest atop girders. Tying the top of the T with the girder adds to the structure's overall rigidity. The stem of the T is not attached at girders, columns, or bearing walls, but rests on a teflon or neoprene pad so the structure can respond to shrinkage and deflection. Holes and openings cast into the stem of the girder can be as great as one-third the stem's total depth, but must avoid the reinforcing tendons. This suggests openings toward the top of the stem in midspan and toward the bottom at ends. Preplanning of all openings is essential to minimize sitework and to realize the inherent economies of the system. T's may be notched at the ends to permit passage of conduit along girders or bearing walls. More often, a channel is formed by chamfered edges at the mating point of the flanges of adjacent T's; electrical conduit for the floor below is run in this channel and is then covered with a concrete topping.

Contractors should study erection procedures, carefully marking the pieces, their sequence of use, and the number and sequence of crane movements. The architect should specify procedures for delivery and storage of the prestressed components. Temporary shoring and bracing may be required during construction, particularly (if the structure is composite) until the toppings have cured to service strength. Lifting loops are generally embedded in the precast pieces and then covered with the topping or cut off after installation.

In parking garages, the depth of the structural T's and concerns for minimizing floor-to-ceiling height present special challenges for the integration of lighting and signs.

Consultation with precasting representatives should begin early in the job. Manufacturers can provide technical advice, and useful design resources are available from manufacturers' associations.

1. Structure and envelope *unified*, p. 324.

2. Structure and mechanical *meshed*, p. 325.

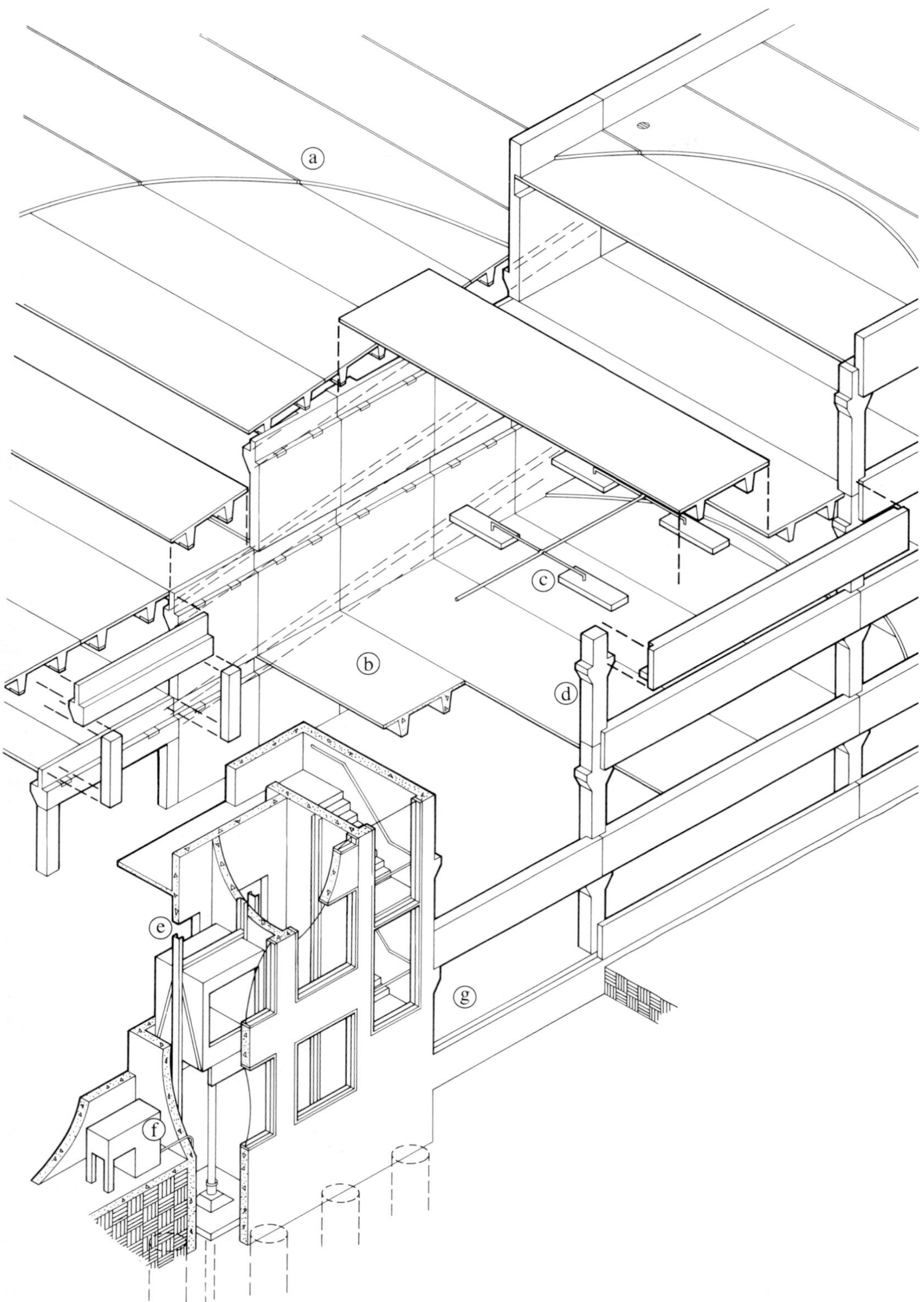

a. *Concrete topping*
b. *Precast prestressed concrete double T's*
c. *Fluorescent light fixtures*
d. *Precast concrete columns and spandrel beams*
e. *Elevator and stair core*
f. *Hydraulic elevator and elevator equipment*
g. *Slab on grade and cast-in-place concrete piles*

Diagram detail page 352

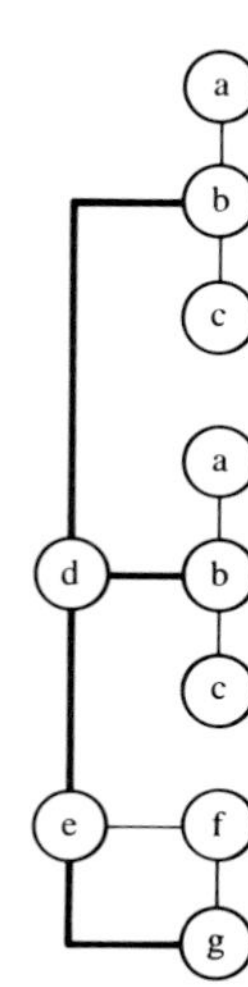

Use of a precast concrete frame for an unenclosed parking facility results in structural, envelope, and interior systems that are unified. *Off-site precasting can conserve time and materials for concrete forming, and on-site erection time is considerably faster in comparison with cast-in-place construction. The visible building materials are of one basic kind, thus also leading to natural visible integration. Some mechanical and interior elements are integrated at the* connected *level (as in the case of curbs, handrails, and signs), but power distribution lines are* meshed *with the upper surface of the precast floor T's and the concrete topping, as are pipes for surface drainage and supply of fire-sprinkler heads. The site-poured concrete floor topping provides a smooth, tightly sealed surface. The adjacent stairway and elevator envelopes integrate security and life safety considerations with requirements for impermeability to weather, by providing transparent insulated glass viewing panels toward the outside. The cast-in-place walls for these circulation elements also provide lateral stability to the frame.*

6. Staggered Truss

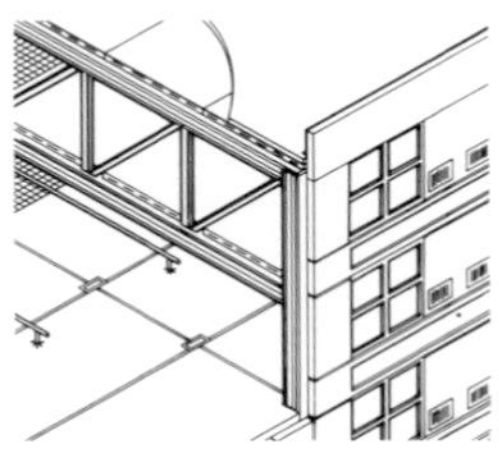

Reviewer:
Eugene A. deMartin, AIA
East Rutherford, NJ

Illustration:
Darrell Downing Rippeteau, Architect
Richard J. Vitullo, designer in charge
Washington, DC

Multifamily residential buildings usually involve highly repetitive floor plans and can benefit from systems that integrate structure, interior unit separations, fire-compartmentalization, and acoustical privacy objectives.[1] The staggered truss system is a construction technique developed by private practitioners and the architecture and engineering departments at the Massachusetts Institute of Technology, under sponsorship of the United States Steel Company. Placement of floor-height Pratt trusses atop every other column in a staggered pattern strengthens the structural system while reducing overall weight. A precast hollow-core concrete plank deck serves as the floor and is often laid without a topping. Lower floor levels rest upon the bottom chord of each truss, while upper floors rest on each top chord.

The first deck is laid parallel to the longer dimension of the building, perpendicular to the spanning direction of the staggered trusses. The floor acts as a structural diaphragm and the length of column-free interior space is increased, reducing the distance that must be spanned by the floor deck.

Exterior walls of precast concrete are erected as the structure rises; they also serve as the external walls and augment the building's rigidity for wind-bracing on its longer dimension.

PRINCIPAL APPLICATIONS AND ADVANTAGES

The staggered truss system is best suited to multiunit residential and hotel or motel buildings of 7 to 30 stories, although higher buildings have been built using the system. The system is not generally considered economical for lower buildings due to the costs of manufacturing the jigs for trusses and the forms for spandrel precasting. The staggered truss system, when used in combination with precast floor planks and wall spandrels, minimizes the need for "wet trades," as there is no concrete pouring and little plastering. Joints between the hollow concrete floor planks are grouted, with the top carpeted or tiled. The underside is painted or covered with acoustical ceiling tile, depending on project needs. Openings in the deck planks for vertical risers and utilities are often precut. The elimination of concrete pouring and unit masonry construction in all but the foundation is an advantage for cold weather construction.

The system easily allows for structural bays of 56 x 64 ft, thus permitting a high degree of flexibility in unit interiors. The ground floor is free of trusses and interior columns, allowing for parking or retail commercial use. The system's light weight reduces foundation size.

KEY INTEGRATION ISSUES

Because the Pratt-type trusses extend floor to ceiling, with openings only for corridors and elevator doors, the horizontal running of pipes, wiring, and ductwork can present difficulties. The use of separate heating and air conditioning systems on a unit-by-unit basis is often preferred for this reason and because unitary HVAC systems offer economic and maintenance advantages in multifamily residential construction. Utilities are typically fed upward through chases and risers placed against outer walls, with service or supply units placed to either side on each floor. End wall stair enclosures are also used for this purpose. Most sprinkler systems are laid out in this fashion as well.

Fire protection for the trusses generally results from the addition of a fire-resistant membrane, such as drywall, to each side of a staggered Pratt truss; these walls also serve to divide individual units. Lower floors in the staggered truss system can be finished and trimmed while upper-level structural members are still being laid. The structure is rigid as soon as precast exterior wall panels and the outer concrete deck elements have been installed.

The staggered truss system can be erected with a single small crane which has a narrow-base column, a great advantage on constrained sites.[2]

1. Noise isolation, pp. 291–292.

2. Conservation of resources, p. 236.

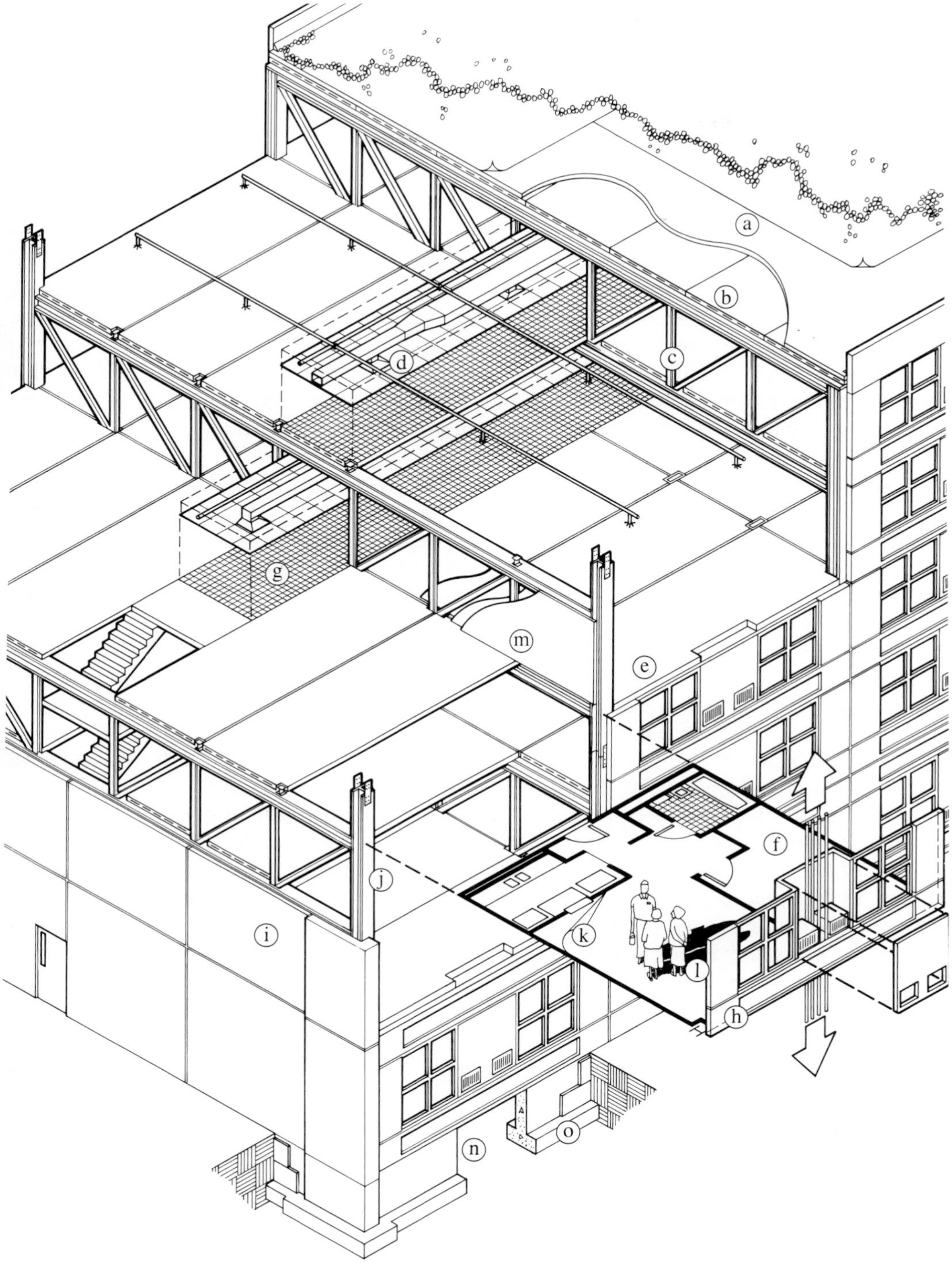

a. *Rigid insulation, elastomeric roofing and ballast*
b. *Precast hollow core concrete plank deck*
c. *Steel truss*
d. *Ducts and sprinkler*
e. *Window assembly*
f. *Utility risers and piping*
g. *Seamless resilient flooring*
h. *Precast stiffener beams*
i. *Precast shear panels*
j. *Steel columns*
k. *Carpet*
l. *Precast concrete fascia panels*
m. *Drywall*
n. *Concrete foundation*
o. *Waterproofing and protective board*

Diagram detail page 353

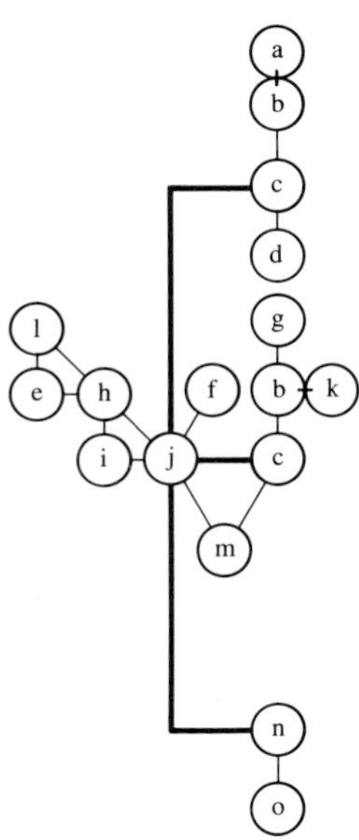

In this example, large floor-to-floor steel trusses serve as load-bearing members for roofs, floors, and ceilings. The layout of the structural trusses, which are staggered in a brick-joint pattern from floor to floor, creates highly regularized compartments or bays and accommodates openings for circulation and mechanical systems. The trusses also serve as the plane for attaching fire-resistive partitioning materials between units or bays, thus integrating structure, envelope, and interior systems within individual spaces. The trusses provide a rigid frame in the direction of the truss axes, while precast floor, roof, and perimeter wall panels stabilize the structure in the direction perpendicular to the trusses and provide the envelope. In this sense, envelope and structure are unified *for a portion of the system. Such construction can proceed very rapidly, with most components manufactured off-site and erected quickly by cranes and hoists. Although interior and mechanical systems are for the most part integrated with the structure only at the* connected *level, the trusses do provide, by means of a special Vierandeel section at the center of a double-loaded corridor layout, an appropriate place for meshing of mechanical and structural systems. Staggered truss construction is most often indicated for double-loaded residential-type occupancies, including hotels, highrise apartments, nursing homes, and hospitals.*

7. Tilt-up Wall

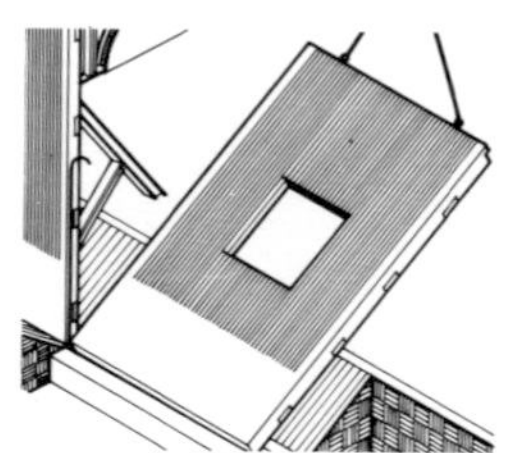

Reviewer:
Kirby Perry, AIA
Austin, TX

Illustration:
Darrell Downing Rippeteau, Architect
Richard J. Vitullo, designer in charge
Washington, DC

Load-bearing tilt-up wall panels provide a *unified* vertical envelope, structure, and interior.[1] The panels are precast on-site, generally using the floor slab or grade as the casting surface, and tilted or lifted into position. The floor slab used as a form must be level, smoothly finished, and treated with a bond-breaking agent to permit easy separation of the cast pieces. The wall panels, usually 6 in. in nominal thickness, may extend from one to several stories in height, and must be designed to withstand the bending loads involved in tilting and lifting, as well as loads that will be encountered once in place. They may be plain, reinforced, or prestressed and are often provided with temporary timber or steel "strongbacks" for tilting, particularly where there are large window openings.

The panels must be braced during construction until all wall and roof structural members are in place. Columns are usually cast in place following installation of the panels. In load-bearing tilt-up wall systems the roof and floor members are bolted or welded to plates and angles cast into a continuous ledger beam. Roofing systems may be steel open-web joists, precast concrete T's, or hollow-core planks. Flashing reglets and other roofing connection details can be cast with the panels.

The clear spans produced by the bar joist roof structure and option for hung ceiling allow interior partitions to be introduced virtually anywhere, with *meshed* interior and mechanical systems[2] provided by a ceiling-mounted radiant heat panel.[3]

PRINCIPAL APPLICATIONS AND ADVANTAGES

Tilt-up walls have been used routinely in a variety of building types and heights, especially for single-story buildings with large, uncomplicated exteriors. The system is also increasingly used for multistory lowrise projects. Significant savings in time and formwork costs can be achieved, and long lead times required for precast or structural steel components are often averted.

The building shell can be erected quickly, permitting interior work to proceed along with final joining and sealing of the envelope panels. Because most of the forming and erection work is done within the floor slab area, tilt-up systems work well in confined construction sites.

KEY INTEGRATION ISSUES

Conservation of time and forming material is realized when there is uniformity in panel design and when the floor surface can be used for forming. Careful planning of the forming, storage, and lifting sequence is essential, and early consultation with manufacturers and contractors is advisable. Because the floor slab on which the panel is cast must be smooth, utility raceways, pipes, and conduits that will penetrate the slabs must be stubbed below the finish slab level, covered during wall panel casting, and then uncovered for final connections.

Regular inspection of casting and lifting operations is essential. Joints between panels should be designed to be concealed; this is easily accomplished where cast-in-place columns are designed to lap the panel edges, or where the panels insert at their edges into a precast column channel. Connections between panels should not be rigid, so caulks and sealants are important.

Mechanical and interior systems are generally combined at a *connected* level to the structure and envelope.[4] The location and installation of angles, channels, weld plates, conduits, connectors, and other hardware should be carefully planned and detailed, with regular and careful inspections before placing the concrete. Lifting forces and special complications due to openings require exacting structural analysis and special erection hardware.

Foundation and slab detailing are key to preventing water infiltration at the panel bases. It is good practice to design the system so that the slab level is slightly above the bottom edge of the vertical tilt-up panel.

1. Structure and envelope *unified*, p. 324.
2. Mechanical and interior *meshed*, p. 330.
3. Radiant heat panels, pp. 177–178.
4. Structure and mechanical *connected*, p. 325.

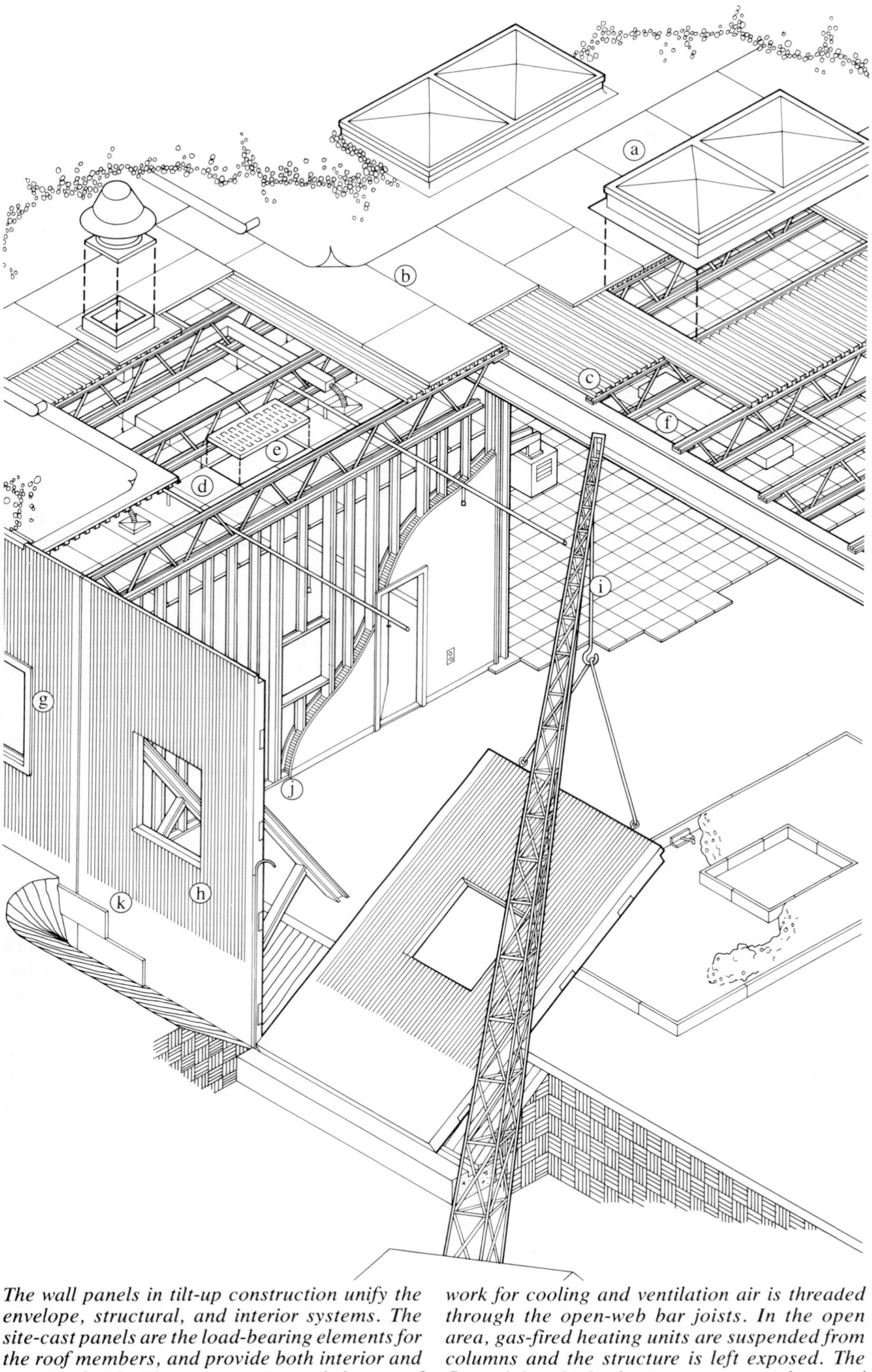

a. *Skylights*
b. *Built-up roofing and rigid insulation*
c. *Steel deck and open web steel joists*
d. *Suspended acoustical tile ceiling*
e. *Radiant heat panels*
f. *Fluorescent lighting*
g. *Window assembly*
h. *Precast concrete panels*
i. *Resilient tile flooring*
j. *Slab on grade and concrete footing*
k. *Dampproofing and protective board*

Diagram detail page 354

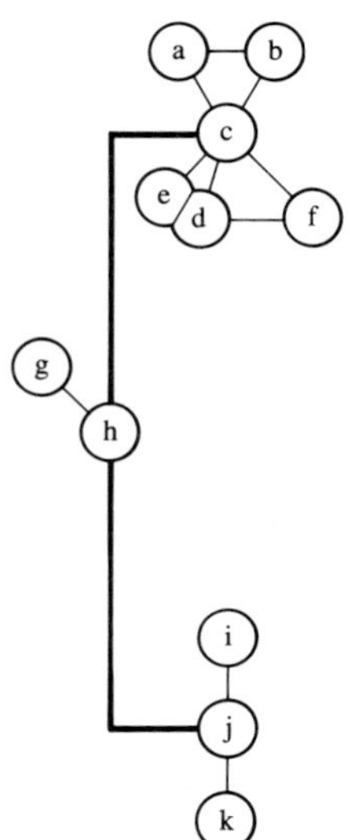

The wall panels in tilt-up construction unify the envelope, structural, and interior systems. The site-cast panels are the load-bearing elements for the roof members, and provide both interior and exterior finish. These properties and the use of repetitive wall modules offer major advantages in the conservation of time and materials. In the enclosed office area, the mechanical and interior systems are meshed. *The suspended ceiling panels incorporate radiant heat panels while ductwork for cooling and ventilation air is threaded through the open-web bar joists. In the open area, gas-fired heating units are suspended from columns and the structure is left exposed. The floor slab, which also integrates envelope and structure at a* unified *level, serves as a casting surface for the tilt-up wall elements. It is held away from the edge of the building to aid in tilting operations and to permit backfilling of earth against the base of the panel below grade.*

8. Bearing Wall and Bar-Joist Roof

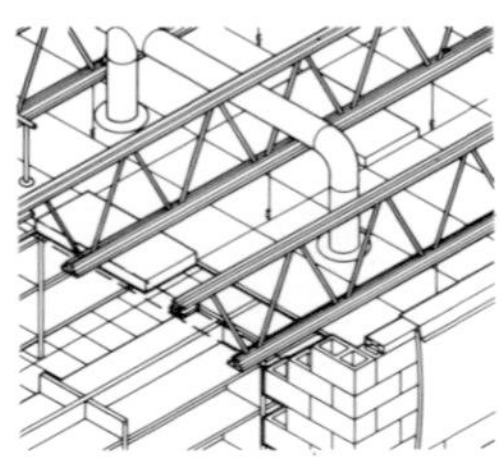

Reviewer:
John Woods, PE
FDE Limited
Alexandria, VA

Illustration:
Darrel Downing Rippeteau, AIA
Richard J. Vitullo, designer in charge
Washington, DC

Retail commercial facilities usually require flexibility in lighting, partitioning, and mechanical systems, while placing space at a premium; the envelope and structural systems chosen often reflect these demands. Bearing wall and bar-joist roof building systems employ masonry walls bearing on a turndown slab-on-grade, or conventional spread footings. The walls support a roof structure of open-web steel bar-joists, through which mechanical distribution systems are threaded. The roof deck may be precast concrete plank, tongue-and-groove wood decking, or steel decking. Small openings in the roof area can be framed between joists by means of special headers designed expressly for that purpose. Exterior and interior finishes are highly variable, depending on the demands of the occupancy; suspended interior ceilings are among the most common.[1]

PRINCIPAL APPLICATIONS AND ADVANTAGES

Masonry bearing walls and joist roofs are among the simplest and easiest to design and build. The relatively low cost of the system makes it attractive for speculative projects, as does speed of construction.[2] The height to which masonry bearing walls can be built without resorting to lateral bracing is limited, however, so they are used most frequently in one-story structures. Spans for J- and H-series open-web joists generally may not exceed more than 20 times the joist depth, or more than 50 to 60 feet. Long-span joists are available, as are a wide variety of special shapes.

By nature, open-web joists spaced at even intervals are best suited to relatively light, uniform loads. Joists may be doubled or tripled to accommodate heavier, concentrated loads, or may be combined with other steel framing for roof openings and rooftop mechanical equipment.

The distances that can be spanned by lightweight steel bar joists make them popular for retail and similar facilities requiring large expanses of column- and wall-free floor area. The spacing and depth of joists is related to the spanning capability of the roof decking material and the requirements for loads on the roof structure.

The simplicity of the system and its components makes it attractive to contractors, as the system is a familiar one and easy to erect.

KEY INTEGRATION ISSUES

If ductwork is to be housed within the depth of the joist, headers or branches must be fed through the joist webs, perpendicular to the spanning direction. It is important that the webs of joists be aligned and bearing walls with projections taken into account.

If the building owners are also tenants, relatively fixed interior lighting and mechanical systems may be planned. Otherwise, overhead and in-floor systems should be laid out for maximum flexibility. In cases where the joist depth is insufficient for the diameter of ductwork to be carried, such equipment is suspended from the bottom chord of the steel joist.

Suspended interior ceilings are nearly always preferred to directly attached interior ceilings. Finished ceilings that are attached directly to the joist bottom chord must be designed to accommodate the high degree of deflection that the roof assembly will experience; these are also more difficult to change. The camber of the joists alone is generally not sufficient for roof drainage, and roof ponding is a frequent problem.

In buildings with masonry bearing walls, each joist should be anchored to the masonry by means of a joist anchor embedded in the masonry, or welded to a bearing plate anchored into the masonry. Steel bar joists can be designed to cantilever beyond the edge of the bearing walls. Continuous horizontal bracing of both top and bottom joist chords is possible with spot-welded connections at each joist, with the ends of the bracing members anchored to a bearing wall at their ends; this type of system is quite well suited to seismic risk zones.

1. Structure and mechanical *meshed*, p. 325.
2. Conservation of time and resources, pp. 236–237.

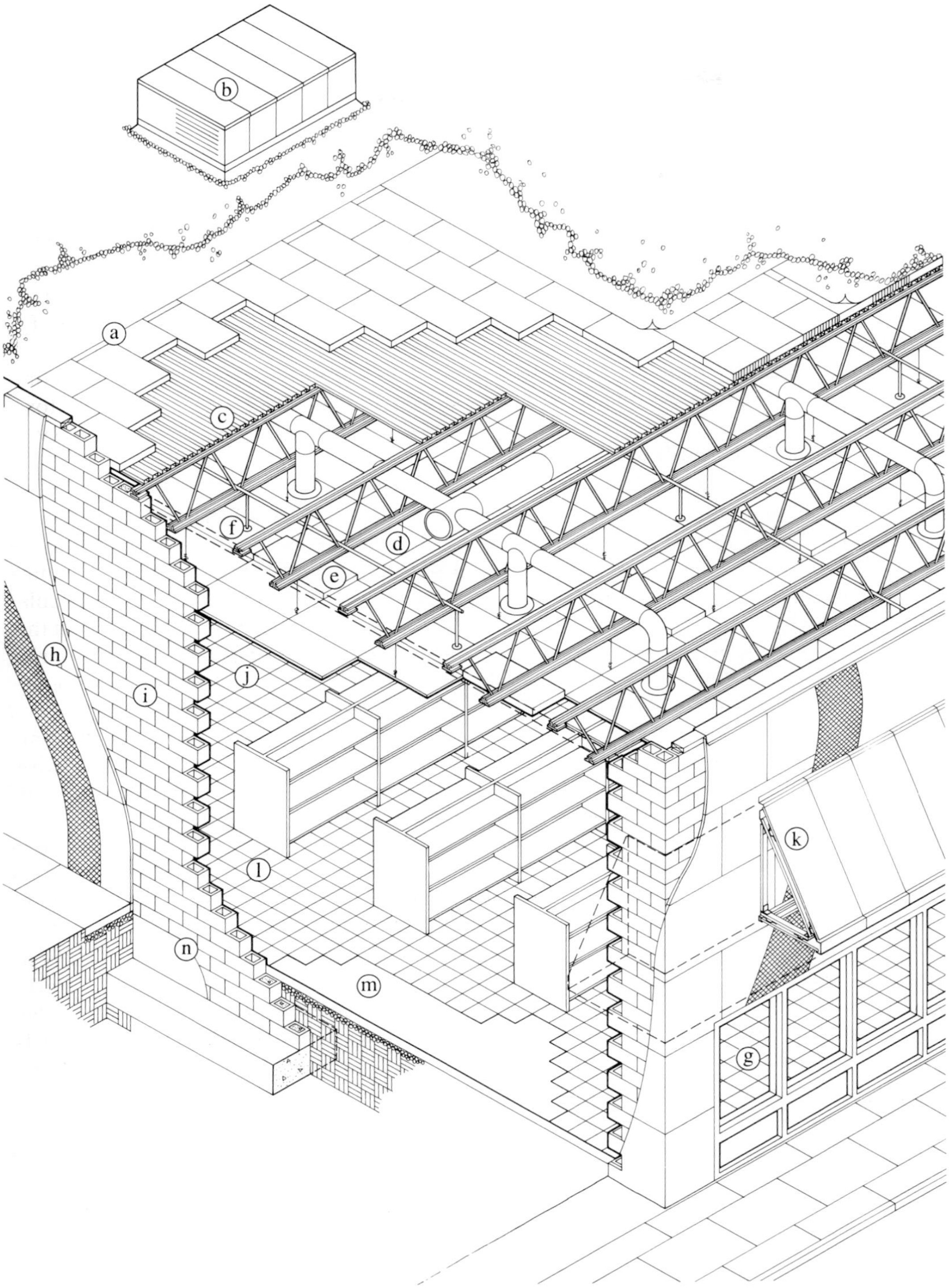

a. *Built-up roofing and rigid insulation*
b. *HVAC unit*
c. *Steel decking and open web steel joists*
d. *Ducts and sprinkler piping*
e. *Fluorescent light fixture*
f. *Suspended acoustical tile ceiling*
g. *Window assembly*
h. *Rigid insulation and veneer coating*
i. *Concrete masonry bearing wall*
j. *Glazed face*
k. *Canopy assembly*
l. *Resilient tile flooring*
m. *Slab on grade and concrete footing*
n. *Vapor barrier and dampproofing*

Diagram detail page 355

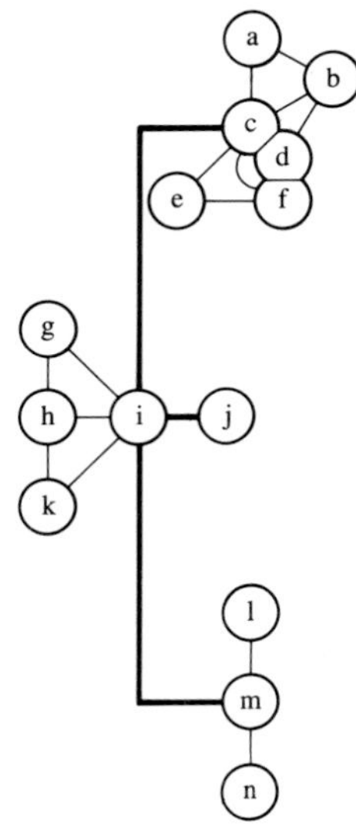

Bearing wall and bar-joist construction yields buildings that have relatively large interior clear-spans and flexible interior layouts. The open webbing of the bar joists provides a lightweight structure that is easily penetrated by mechanical systems. The meshing *of mechanical and structural systems in the roof plane also conserves vertical spaces. The bottom chords of the bar joists are used for suspension of interior finishes, lighting fixtures, and air diffusers in finished areas, or may be left uncovered. In this case, the structural, mechanical, and interior systems would be fully* meshed. *The concrete masonry unit bearing walls are insulated on the exterior to take better advantage of the wall's thermal mass by placing it toward the occupied site. Long-span open-web bar joist roofs can deflect substantially, and the camber of the joists alone is often not sufficient to maintain the necessary slope to roof drains. Beams running in a transverse direction to the joists can block the threading of piping, ductwork, and wiring, and variations in the configuration of perimeter walls should not disrupt the regular pattern of the joist web elements in a manner that will interfere with straight runs for mechanical components.*

9. Lightweight Steel Frame and Brick Veneer

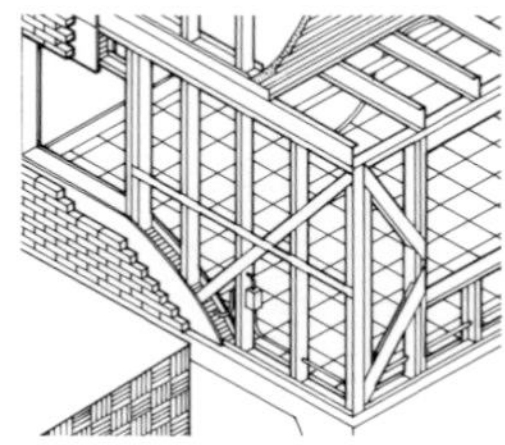

Reviewers:
Dr. Frederick Bentel, FAIA
Bentel & Bentel
Locust Valley, NY
Marvin D. Suer, FAIA
Bartley/Long/Mirenda
Philadelphia, PA

Illustration:
Darrell Downing Rippeteau, Architect
Richard J. Vitullo, designer in charge
Washington, DC

In this example the cold-rolled steel structural frame and single-wythe brick masonry veneer are *connected*,[1] with mechanical and structural systems *meshed*. Framing elements are C-section runners, channels, or Z-sections. In some applications members have an I-section to accommodate nailing or enhance stiffness. Drywall applied to both sides of the steel studs provides additional lateral bracing and an interior finish. Intermediate floors are concrete over a metal deck supported by cold-rolled C-joists or special lightweight steel framing members. The roof deck is similarly supported and may be a metal deck, concrete over metal deck, insulating fill over metal deck, or plywood sheathing attached by self-tapping screws to cold-rolled C-joists.

Lightweight steel-frame bearing-wall construction is being used more often in low-rise commercial and residential buildings. The long-term performance of lightweight steel framing in structures over three stories is a concern. To date, its use in medium- and high-rise buildings has been mainly for exterior partitions or as nonbearing backup for exterior skins.

PRINCIPAL APPLICATIONS AND ADVANTAGES

Speed of construction, noncombustibility, and relative light weight are key advantages of this system.[2] The space between studs eases insulation and accommodates piping and electrical distribution. Because the framing can be completed independent of the masonry veneer, the interior is out of the weather quickly and can be finished while the exterior brick veneer is laid. In nonresidential construction, where fewer bracing walls, longer vertical spans and horizontal runs are likely, added cold-formed bridging or bracing of the frame increases lateral stability. This can also be accomplished by decreasing the stud spacing or increasing the stud gauge.

Prepunched holes in the studs provide easy routing of plumbing and electrical lines. Most codes require the use of electrical conduit or that the prepunched stud opening be sheathed, to avoid stripping the insulation as wires are drawn through. Electrolytic action between framing members and nonferrous plumbing pipes must also be considered, and pipes on exterior walls must be adequately insulated.

KEY INTEGRATION ISSUES

Deflection in lightweight steel frame construction can be several times that of the exterior masonry veneer; these differentials must be accommodated in anchoring details or overcome by adding structural rigidity. Anchoring the veneer to the steel frame should permit free and independent movement of the two materials. Where the veneer depends on the steel frame for lateral stability, anchors should be flexible and not resist shear. Wire ties that allow independent movement are recommended.

Design of framing and fastening of windows and doors should account for the differences in movement. In general, fenestration components should be attached to either the framing or the veneer, but not attached rigidly to both.

Sheathing both sides of the frame provides some lateral stability. Steel studs used for masonry backup should also be x-braced with steel straps. Horizontal and diagonal bracing increases the frame's rigidity. Welded connections are stronger than self-tapping screws. The method of attachment can have substantial cost implications. Care should be taken in specifying the positioning and types of fasteners used for affixing both interior and exterior sheathing, because the techniques employed significantly affect lateral stability.

When filled with batt insulation and fully sheathed, the lightweight steel frame wall is thermally isolated from the single-wythe of masonry. This results in greater differential thermal movement in the veneer than would occur with solid double-wythe masonry construction; the interior heat is not transferred as readily to the exterior masonry.

1. Structure and envelope *connected*, pp. 323–324.
2. Conservation of time and resources, pp. 236–237.

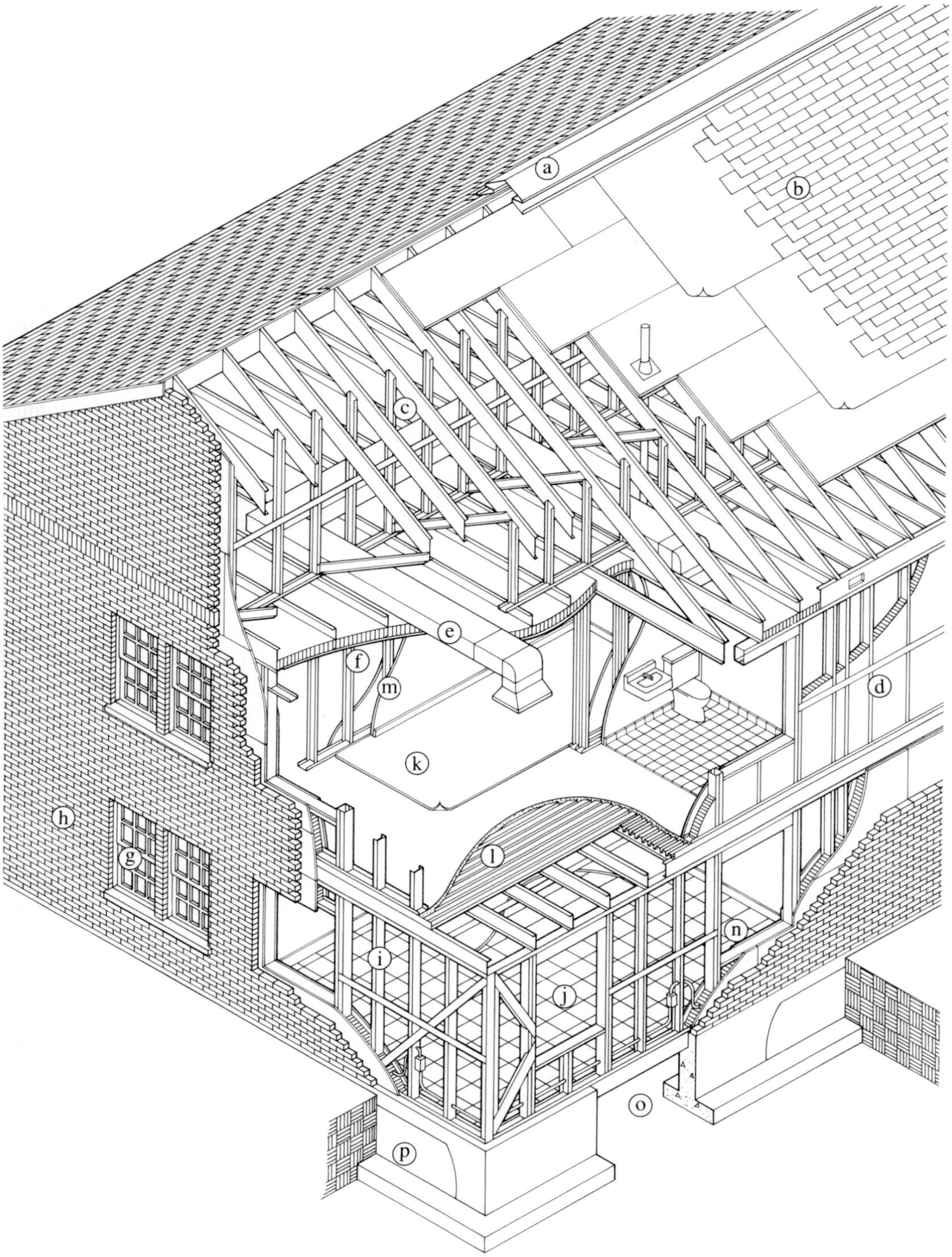

a. *Metal ridge vent*
b. *Roofing*
 • *Roofing felt*
 • *Shingles*
 • *Plywood sheathing*
c. *Metal roof frame*
 • *C-stud brace*
 • *C-rafter*
 • *C-channel*
 • *C-joist*
d. *Batt insulation*
e. *Ducts and diffusers*
f. *Suspended acoustical tile ceiling*
g. *Window assembly*
h. *Brick veneer*
i. *C-stud assembly*
j. *Ceramic floor tile*
k. *Carpet*
l. *Metal floor frame and steel deck and concrete topping*
m. *Drywall*
n. *Resilient tile flooring*
o. *Slab on grade and concrete foundation*
p. *Dampproofing*

Diagram detail page 356

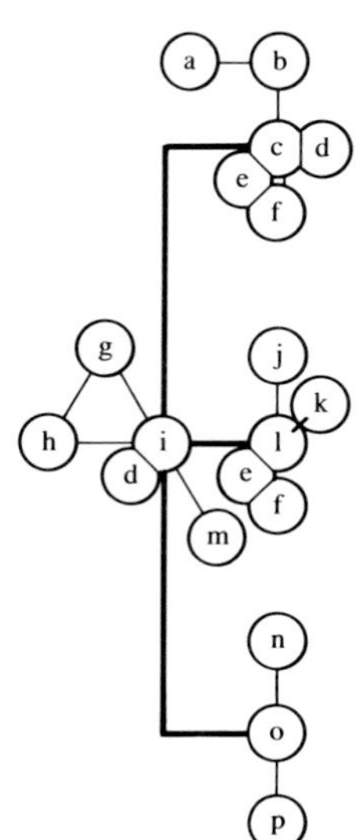

Structural, interior, and envelope systems are connected *in lightweight steel frame and brick veneer construction, while the mechanical systems are* meshed *within the structural walls, floor, and roof. Connections between the brick veneer envelope and the cold-rolled steel structural frame are minimal, to permit nearly independent movement of the two systems, each of which expands and contracts in different ways. Care must be taken in detailing at openings, where sills, jambs, and other pieces span both the frame and veneer. The brick veneer is self-supporting and serves almost exclusively as envelope. The lightweight cold-formed steel members are load-bearing, and beams, columns, channels, headers, and other elements can be built up from standard steel shapes and sections. The rigidity of the frame depends on cross bracing, interior and exterior sheathing, the distance from exterior corner to exterior corner, and on the type and layout of fasteners used. Advantages of cold-formed steel framing include light weight, dimensional stability, speed and ease of assembly, resistance to moisture and decay, and, in some cases, readier availability than wood framing members. Detailing and fastening of the cold-rolled steel frame differs markedly from practices used in wood frame construction, and the technology requires special noncarpentry tools and equipment.*

10. Wood Floor and Roof Truss

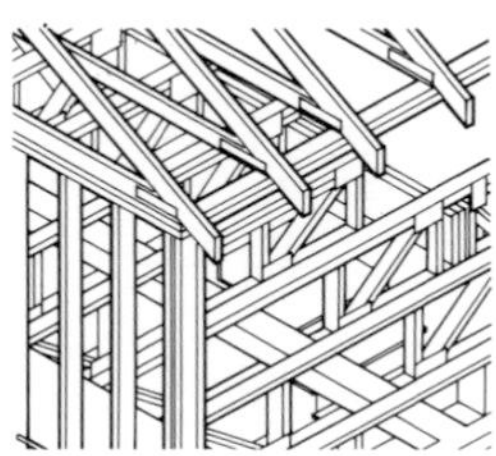

Reviewers:
Cecil Baker
Baker, Rothschild, Hor, Blyth
Philadelphia, PA

Kenneth A. Weinstein, AIA
CHK Architects & Planners
Silver Spring, MD

Illustration:
Darrell Downing Rippeteau, Architect
Richard J. Vitullo, designer in charge
Washington, DC

The wood frame system unifies envelope and structure when the external skin acts as a diaphragm over the studs, joists, and rafters. In this example, a standard wood framing system is employed with prefabricated roof and floor trusses and exterior sheathing. The trusses are factory-built offsite to engineering specifications. The exterior panels act in concert with wall studs as a structural skin and weathering surface. Plywood subfloors are glued and nailed onsite to the top chord of the floor trusses. Heating and cooling are supplied by an air-to-air heat pump[1] and distributed through sheet metal ducts.

The substructure is cast-in-place reinforced concrete foundation walls atop integral spread footings. Basement walls and the basement floor slab are provided with rigid insulation and a field-applied membrane waterproofing.

PRINCIPAL APPLICATIONS AND ADVANTAGES

Prefabricated trusses eliminate much field labor, speed on-site construction, help to assure dimensional stability, and may eliminate the need for intermediate load-bearing partitions.[2] Longer clear spans are possible with floor trusses than with generally available dimensioned lumber, and recent advances in manufacturing techniques make it possible to specify many special features. Open-web trusses are lighter in weight than dimensioned lumber and can be lifted easily in gangs by a small crane or lift.

Trusses are available in standard configurations between 12 and 24 in. deep and allow threading of wiring, piping, and ductwork without resort to on-site drilling or cutting, thus greatly speeding and easing the installation of heating, plumbing, and electrical systems. Often built of 2 x 4 elements, the trusses also provide a nailing edge nominally 4 in. wide along the top and bottom chords for subflooring and decking, an improvement over the thinner edges presented by dimensioned lumber.

Because trusses are made up from components that use the most commonly available dimensioned lumber, there is little chance that projects will be delayed waiting for supplies. Assuming proper factory quality control, there is also little chance for the variations often seen in dimensioned lumber from different mill lots.

KEY INTEGRATION ISSUES

Bridging between floor trusses may be eliminated, depending on the depth of the truss and the application and rigidity of subflooring and ceiling finishes, or may be accomplished by continuous 2 x 4's running perpendicular to the truss chords within the open web and nailed to truss struts. When such bridging is used, it should not block transverse duct runs that may be planned. Most floor truss systems allow for a continuous edge ribbon at the truss ends, in lieu of a header.

Careful planning and specification of truss lengths and configurations is critical, as field-cutting is to be discouraged. While onsite fabrication of trusses is possible, there are significant quality control and cost advantages associated with factory assembly, especially where large quantities of uniform pieces will be needed. Inspection of truss units for uniformity of depth and camber and for general tightness is encouraged prior to lifting into place. If substantial field work is contemplated, it may be desirable to use plywood I-trusses, which can be cut to length and drilled to allow threading of pipes and wires.

Fire retarding treatments of wood components now permit their use in many applications that call for ratings higher than those afforded by untreated wood. Some fire retarding treatments cause discoloration of the material, may accelerate corrosion of metal fasteners, and may alter the structural properties of the wood. All of these considerations should be raised with the truss supplier in the design stage. Most manufacturers provide truss engineering services, and some national firms design products that are made by licensees and are available locally.

1. Heat pumps, pp. 161–163.
2. Conservation of time and resources, pp. 236–237.

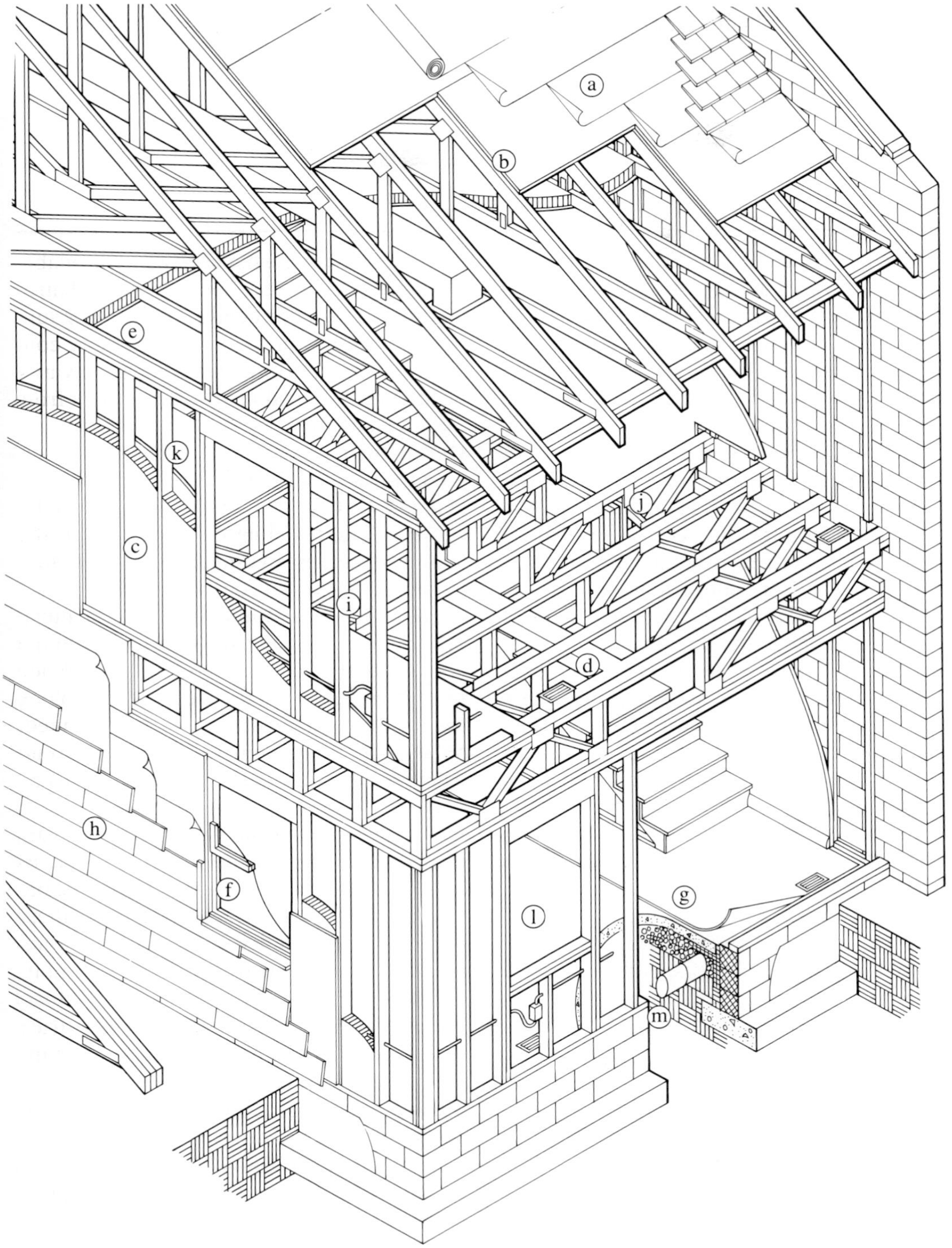

a. *Roofing*
 - *Shingles*
 - *Metal flashing*
 - *Roofing felt*

b. *Wood roof truss and plywood sheathing*
c. *Batt insulation*
d. *Ducts and diffusers*
e. *Acoustical tile ceiling*
f. *Window assembly*
g. *Carpet*
h. *Lapped wood siding*
i. *Wood frame and sheathing*
j. *Wood floor truss and composite plywood subfloor*
k. *Drywall*
l. *Slab on grade and concrete masonry foundation wall*
m. *Perimeter ducts*

Diagram detail page 357

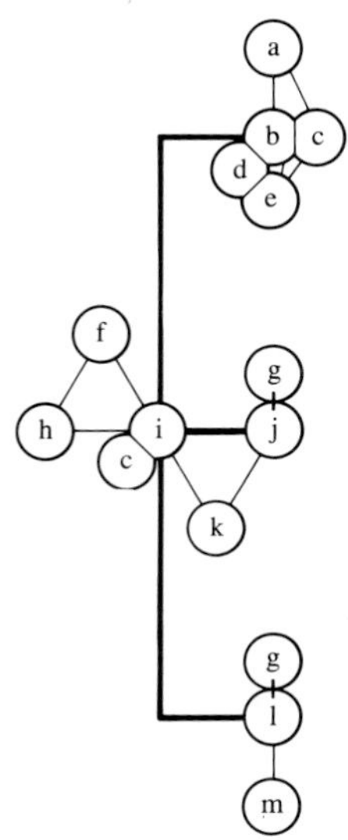

Open-web wood truss and stud frame construction produces natural voids within the structure for placement of mechanical systems. In walls, floors, and ceilings, the structural and mechanical systems are meshed, *although both are ultimately hidden from view by interior finishes. The basement slab unifies structural, envelope, and interior systems, as it is left unfinished. The open-web wood trusses permit longer clear spans than conventional timber framing, leaving greater flexibility in the location of interior partition walls that need not be load-bearing. The open-web wood trusses conserve space and materials; their light weight permits easy penetration by wiring, piping, and ductwork, and achieves a greater degree of dimensional stability than millcut framing lumber. Field-cutting of factory-built open-web wood trusses is difficult, requiring careful and certain sizing before the work. Solid plywood web trusses can be field-cut to length but must also be drilled or cut for passage of mechanical systems. The plywood veneer exterior siding unifies the structural system with the thermal envelope because the sheets act both as structural sheathing for the wood frame and as an integral element of the envelope. In some applications the plywood sheathing can itself become the final exterior envelope. The use of single plywood sheets for interior subfloor and finished floor unifies structural and interior systems.*

11. Laminated Wood Post and Beam

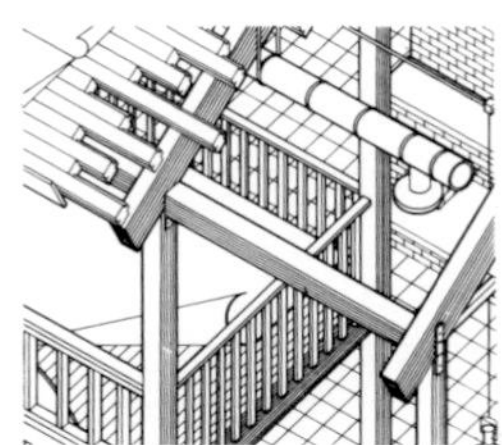

Reviewer:
Thomas C. Moreland, AIA
Moreland/Unrah/Smith
Eugene, OR

Illustration:
Darrell Downing Rippeteau, Architect
Richard J. Vitullo, designer in charge
Washington, DC

Heavy glued and laminated beams and columns, which define the interior of the building, make up the frame in this example. The roof structure is laminated tongue-and-groove decking, nominally 2¼ in. thick, laid over the beams. The underside of the decking is exposed to interior view and should be specified for appearance grade.[1] Lower portions of perimeter walls are framed conventionally with wood studs between main timber columns; a vapor barrier is placed toward the occupied side, and the voids are filled with batt or rigid insulation. Drywall covers interior walls; the exterior is sheathed in plywood and finished with diagonal wood siding. The roof deck is covered with a moisture barrier and insulated on top with rigid insulation board between sleepers. A standing seam metal roof is applied over the sleepers, which also provide diagonal bracing.

Space heating and cooling are provided through a ducted air supply-and-return system. Kitchens, lavatories, and other areas requiring both odor removal equipment and greater amounts of fresh air are separated by walls and covered by suspended or furred ceilings.

PRINCIPAL APPLICATIONS AND ADVANTAGES

Exposed framing and joinery can reduce the amount of interior finishing required. When components have been carefully ordered and weather conditions are favorable, erection of the structural system can proceed quickly. Although used historically for larger buildings, post and beam construction is now generally confined to buildings of three stories or fewer. Its main advantages are simplicity of elements and details, combined with the potential for visible integration[2] and bold structural and architectural forms.

KEY INTEGRATION ISSUES

As in any system with exposed components, cleanliness of details, finishing, and dimensional coordination are of paramount importance. If ductwork cannot be fed through voids in the floor structure into interior and exterior wall voids, layout, finishing, and suspension hardware must be skillfully designed and executed for compatibility, as must interior fire sprinkling systems.[3] Overhead electrical service can be located in rigid conduits that run through the decking. During the application of roofing materials, puncturing these hidden conduits must be avoided.

Considerable flexibility is available in selecting structural modules and bay sizes in heavy timber construction, by varying the depth of beams and increasing the thickness of decking to span between beams. Columns are frequently overdesigned to give an appropriate appearance; if sized only to carry the loads transferred from above, they may appear too spindly in proportion to other framing elements.

Glued laminated beams, columns, and decking are generally preferred over dimensioned sawcut lumber. Appearance is easier to specify and assure; a variety of custom shapes, sizes, and presawn joints can be obtained in glued laminated pieces; and they are drier and more resistant to twisting, checking, and shrinkage. All pieces should remain factory-wrapped until in place and out of the weather, as rain and snow will stain them. If mill-cut lumber is used, it should be cut and dried well in advance and should be specified free of heart centers. Although well suited to pier foundation systems, post and beam framing is often more easily erected atop a perimeter masonry foundation.

Outside air infiltration is increased at endwall joints in tongue-and-groove timber decking and must be controlled through appropriate detailing. Hardware for joinery can be custom fabricated or selected from an attractive range of standard products. It is always important to visualize and specify the desired visible integration of bolts, plates, gussets, or flanges.

1. Structure and interior *unified*, p. 326.
2. Visible integration, pp. 381–385.
3. Exposed ducts, pp. 179–181.

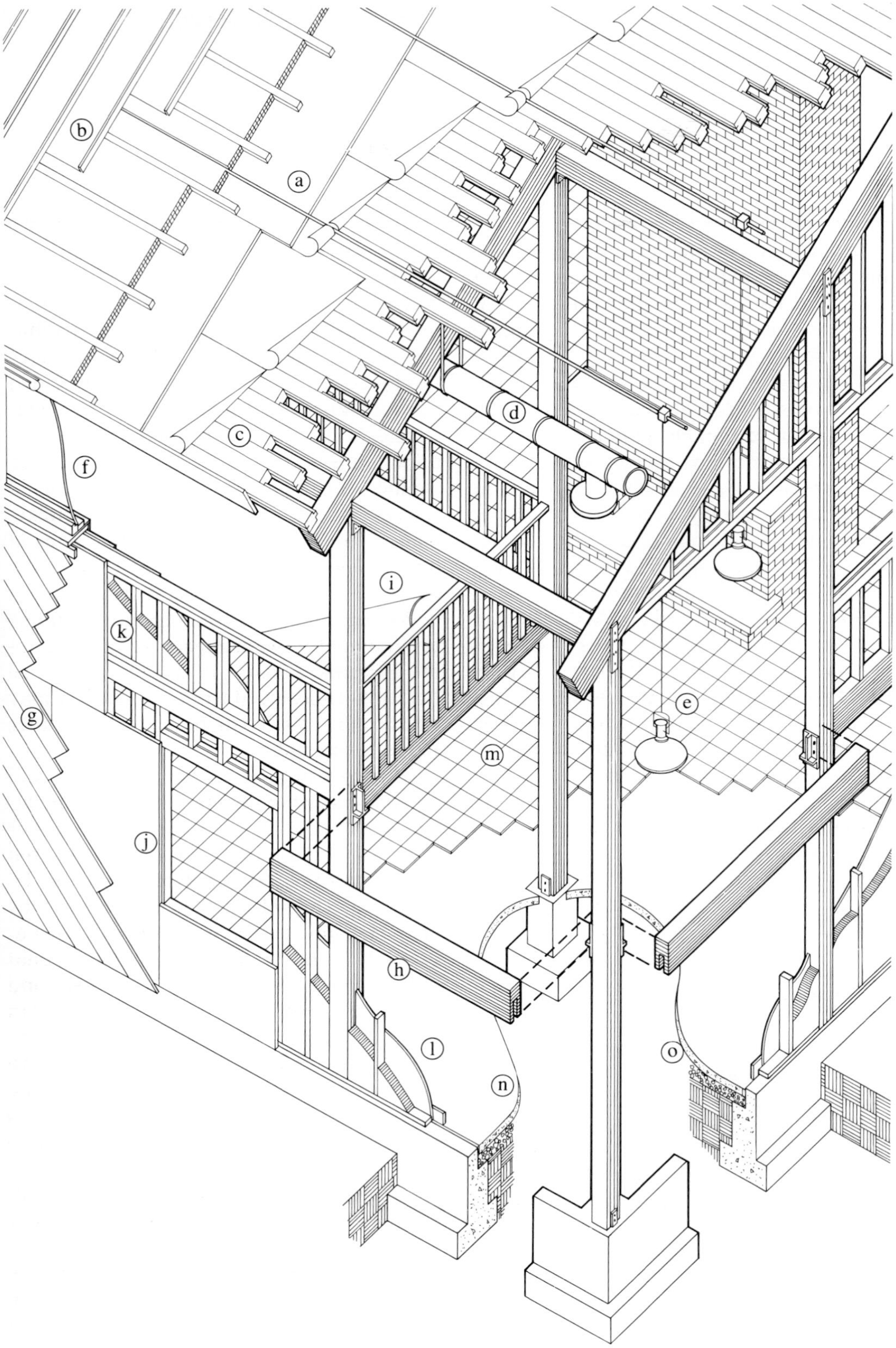

a. *Electrical conduit*
b. *Roofing*
- *Standing seam roof*
- *Roofing felt*
- *Rigid insulation*

c. *Plywood sheathing and wood roof and tongue-and-groove wood decking*
d. *Ducts*
e. *Incandescent light fixture*
f. *Window assembly*
g. *Wood siding*
h. *Glued laminated wood frame*
i. *Carpeting*
j. *Exposed wood frame and plywood sheathing*
k. *Batt insulation*
l. *Drywall*
m. *Clay tile flooring*
n. *Slab on grade and concrete foundation*
o. *Vapor barrier*

Diagram detail page 358

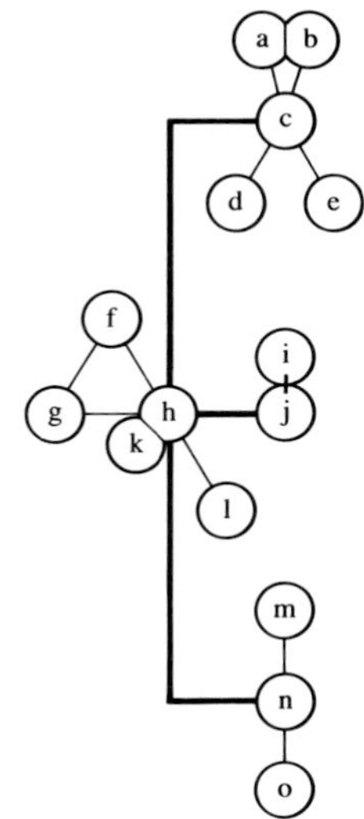

Structure and interior are unified *in post and beam construction. Because the structural elements in this system are exposed to view in the finished building, as are portions of the mechanical system, care is required in the visible integration of these components and in the design and appearance of hardware used for joinery of the wood members. Certain parts of the mechanical system can be* meshed *within interior partitions and exterior walls, leaving them concealed. The sizing of structural members and joinery details may be influenced more by considerations of visual proportion and appearance than strictly by the loading and stress conditions involved.*

12. Lightweight Mobile Modular Buildings

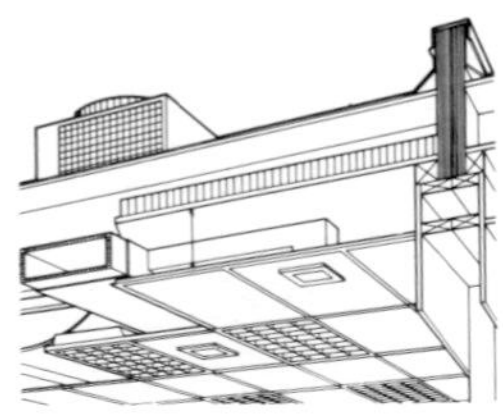

Reviewer:
Kevin J. McKinney
Gelco Space
Bala Cynwood, PA

Illustration:
Darrell Downing Rippeteau, Architect
Richard J. Vitullo, designer in charge
Washington, DC

Lightweight mobile modular buildings consist of factory fabricated wooden structures. Although both smaller and larger dimensions are available, the most common size is 12 ft x 60 ft.

Wiring and plumbing, installed at the factory, are easily hooked up at the destination site. Stud framing, floor joists, and roof rafters are supported on steel I-beam frames until the unit is placed on its foundation. Nearly all system components are installed at the factory, including heating, cooling, and ventilation equipment.[1] In many cases furnishings and such equipment as fire sprinklers and fire and security systems are also factory installed. Claddings, exterior and interior wall finishes, door and window types, floor finishes, and envelope thermal insulation levels can be specified to order. Site grading, foundation work, connection of utilities and services, landscaping, and interconnection of the modular units are the only on-site activities required.

PRINCIPAL APPLICATIONS AND ADVANTAGES

Speed of construction and low initial cost are the main advantages of mobile modules. On-site labor requirements are minimal. Where weather, labor, or site problems affect other options, or for emergency or temporary use, mobile/modulars are often the appropriate solution.[2]

Mobile/modular use has increased significantly in areas of rapid growth and development, especially in areas with large influxes of temporary population. Modules can be easily moved, even when assembled as a complex. In many cases modules are leased to occupants—an attractive aspect of their financing—and therefore the lessor has an interest in assuring that the modules are easily moveable.

KEY INTEGRATION ISSUES

Modular units can almost always be combined. Door openings should not be placed at the mating lines between modules; such placement requires field installation of the doors and may result later in binding of the door due to differential movements between the mated modules.

Ordinarily floor plans are based on the relatively narrow dimension of the module, and require great care in planning for interior layouts, although it is possible to obtain large clear-spanned floor areas. For occupancies that require substantial interior partitioning, HVAC supply and return registers should be planned for high wall or ceiling locations. Electrical interconnections among modules should permit eventual functioning of each module as an independent unit, in the event of relocation.

When planning the complex, the manufacturer should be apprised of the location of utilities and services on the site; any local building code requirements which differ from major codes; and handicapped access needs. Distance of the site from the manufacturing plant is a major cost factor, and any complications in shipping should be investigated.

Modules are tied together through the concealment of joints and mating lines, accomplished by holding the cladding material back from the mating line, and spanning between two units with field-installed components to cover the area left unclad. They are then bolted at the steel frame, in addition to being anchored to the foundation.

Foundations can range from simple masonry piers that are laid dry, on which the units are placed and then earth-anchored, to permanent field-poured footings and block foundations. Skirting at the base of the units is often necessary for appearance and security, with field-set steps required at entrances.

Roof treatment at mating lines can be handled by capping over curbs at the ends of units, or by affixing a strip of sheet aluminum on either side of an uncurbed joint. Plans for roof drainage and water carryoff should be resolved with the manufacturer.

1. Structure and mechanical *connected*, p. 325.

2. Conservation of space, time, and resources, pp. 236–237.

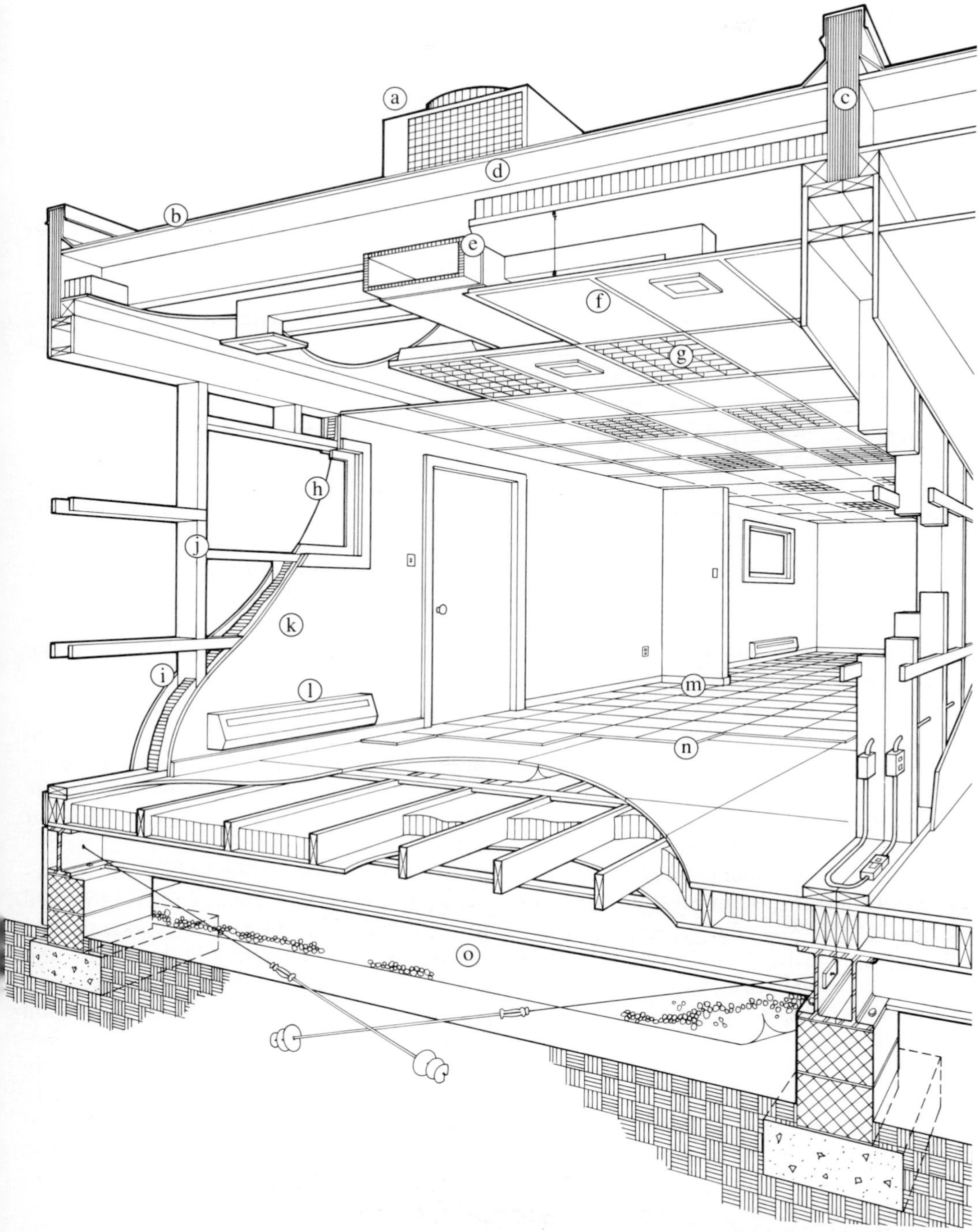

a. *HVAC unit*
b. *Sheet metal roofing and metal cap flashing*
c. *Glued laminated beams and wood deck*
d. *Batt insulation*
e. *Insulated ducts*
f. *Suspended acoustical tile ceiling*
g. *Fluorescent light fixture*
h. *Window assembly*
i. *Aluminum siding*
j. *Wood frame and sheathing*
k. *Drywall*
l. *Electric baseboard heaters*
m. *Resilient flooring*
n. *Plywood subfloor on lateral steel beams*
o. *Vapor barrier*

Diagram detail page 359

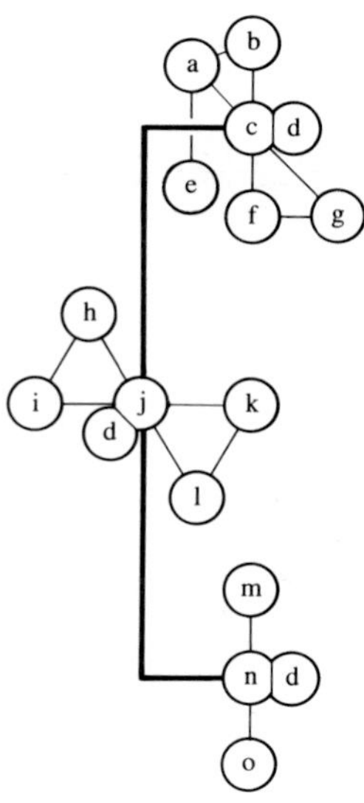

The temporary, low-cost, and "packaged" nature of lightweight mobile modular structures dictates a relatively high degree of integration within each unit. Structure, envelope, and interior systems are connected *with wood framing members interacting with the sheet metal roofing and suspended ceiling to produce structure, weathering skin, and interior finished surfaces. Mechanical systems are* meshed *within voids in the structure and envelope assembly and are basically self-contained within each unit; even when plans call for the linking together of units to form a complex, mechanical and electrical systems for the individual units are allowed to remain independent. Openings in the envelope for doors and windows may present difficulty in mating units, due to differential movement of the units, which are normally placed on separate and less-than-permanent foundations. Entrance doors, for example, should not span between unit mating lines, even when the installation is not considered temporary. Exterior siding can be held back from the mating lines between units and then field-installed to span the joint lines. This technique improves visible integration and also helps to tie units together structurally. At the roof, special curb caps are available or may be field-fabricated to span across low parapets on mated units. If a complex must mate some units at all four sides, mechanical system plants may be roof-mounted. Modular units are normally tied down by cable and earth-embedded anchors.*

13. Space Frames

Reviewers:
Steven Henkelman
Cope Linder Associates
Philadelphia, PA

Wendel Wendel,
President
Space Structures
International
Plainview, NY

Illustration:
Darrell Downing
Rippeteau, Architect
Richard J. Vitullo,
designer in charge
Washington, DC

Space frames serve as both structural and interior systems,[1] while providing a structure for envelope connections and space for meshing of mechanical distribution elements. The space frame shown is covered by a metal deck and built-up roof. Space frames may appear in horizontal, vertical, domed, vaulted, stepped, sloped, or tower configurations. In this example, the edges of the space frame are glazed to permit perimeter clerestory lighting of interior areas. Tubular high-strength extruded aluminum struts are joined by means of solid aluminum hubs, also designed to accommodate the hardware for fastening of clerestory glazing. The frame can also be cantilevered beyond the continuous perimeter masonry wall, which allows for effective plate structural action.

PRINCIPAL APPLICATIONS AND ADVANTAGES

The triangulated space frame network is one of the strongest and most efficient structural configurations, permitting long column-free spans with lightweight, highly repetitive elements. Slender structural members make space frames advantageous in cases where high light permeability is sought, yet significant live structural loading may occur. Typical applications include spans above entries, sports arenas, and convention centers. Space frames are increasingly common as atrium covers and have also been used as structures for entire building envelopes.[2] In perimeter-supported applications, truss depth-to-span ratios of up to 1/30 are practical. Besides their light weight and economy of materials, space frames have the quality control advantages of factory production.

Recent developments in strut and hub technology make space frames highly durable and well engineered. The lightweight frame components are easily shipped, quickly assembled on site, and then lifted into place.[3] Sometimes the frames are factory assembled and shipped whole or in subsections to the site. Careful coordination and assembly instructions are important to keep pieces in sequence for field assembly. Field bolting is almost always preferred to field welding of frame components, because welded space frames are expensive, and quality control can pose problems.

KEY INTEGRATION ISSUES

Because the space frame is a highly regular structure and is exposed to view in most applications, the coordination of service systems with patterns in the frame is essential for visible integration.[4] Piping can be suspended from the hubs of the frame, but should correspond to the patterns of the frame. Utility runs generally follow the orthogonal grid, while the sprinkling apparatus and electrical conduits may be run diagonally. Fireproofing of space frames generally destroys their appearance, so sprinkling is usually a consideration unless the exposed frame is 20 ft or more above floor level.

Column spacing is highly flexible; the selection of a space frame module is governed by the integration of cladding systems, the spanning characteristics of deckings, and the mullion spacing for glazings. A space frame network may be enclosed with metal decking, glass, acrylic, membrane, or insulated paneling. Space frames must usually be engineered and fabricated by a specialty engineer and/or fabricator, although strut sections and hubs generally do not need to be specially designed for each application. Space frame modules are typically 6 to 15 ft, with spans exceeding 100 ft. Fabricators are also able to provide a wide range of colors and painted or anodized finishes for frame components.

Where the space frame will not be supported by a continuous perimeter wall, the design of supporting points is crucial. Certain spanning and rigidity advantages are gained by the design of supports that extend the pattern of the space frame above or below the plane of the main truss.

1. Structure and interior *unified*, p. 326.
2. Museum of Science and Industry, pp. 74–77.
3. Conservation of time, pp. 236–237.
4. Visible integration, pp. 381–385.

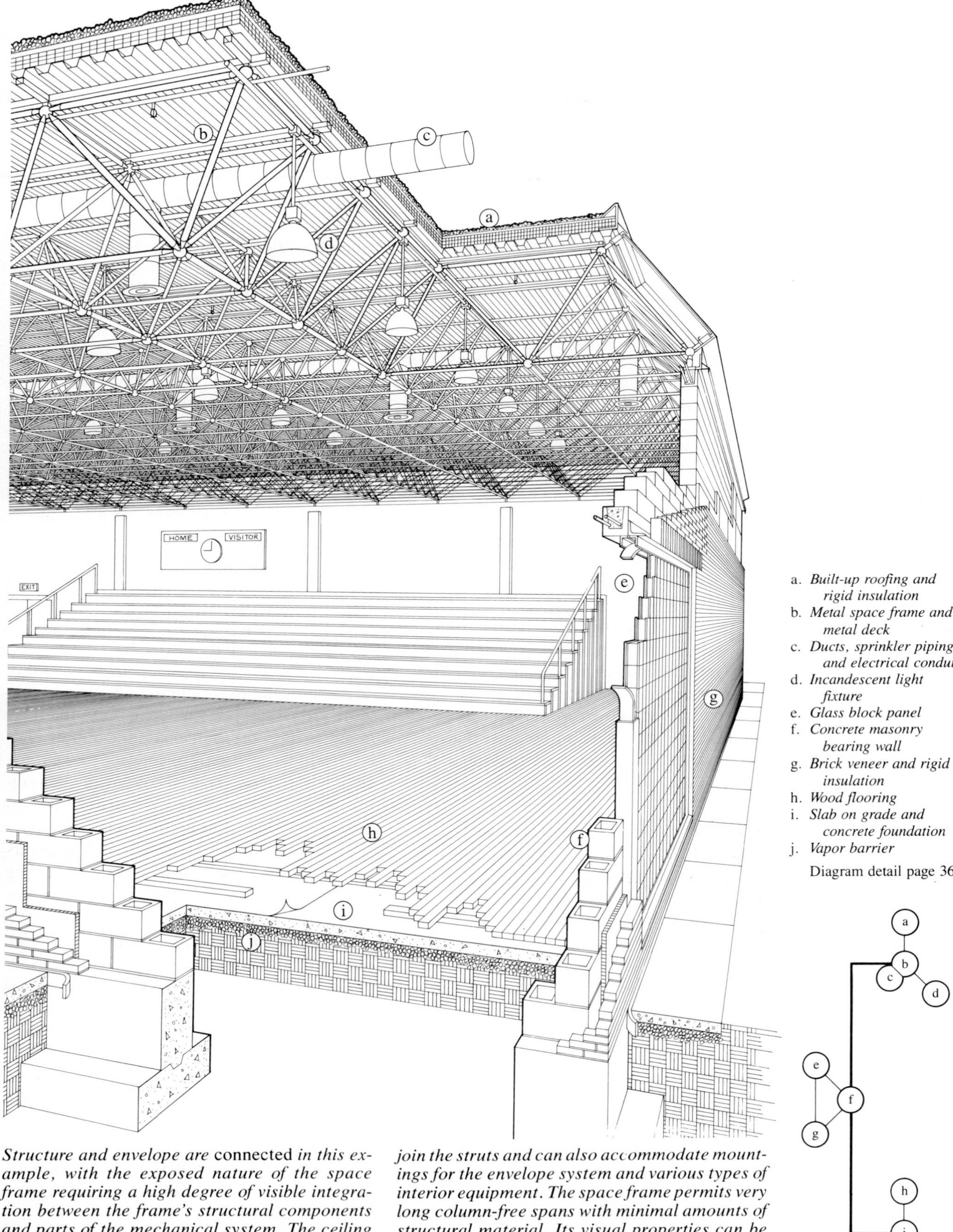

a. *Built-up roofing and rigid insulation*
b. *Metal space frame and metal deck*
c. *Ducts, sprinkler piping and electrical conduit*
d. *Incandescent light fixture*
e. *Glass block panel*
f. *Concrete masonry bearing wall*
g. *Brick veneer and rigid insulation*
h. *Wood flooring*
i. *Slab on grade and concrete foundation*
j. *Vapor barrier*

Diagram detail page 360

Structure and envelope are connected *in this example, with the exposed nature of the space frame requiring a high degree of visible integration between the frame's structural components and parts of the mechanical system. The ceiling unifies interior and structural systems, and meshes them with* unified *mechanical and interior systems. The solid hubs in the frame serve to join the struts and can also accommodate mountings for the envelope system and various types of interior equipment. The space frame permits very long column-free spans with minimal amounts of structural material. Its visual properties can be destroyed if the frame is coated for fire protection; in many cases coating can be forgone if the frame is placed 20 ft or more above floor level.*

14. Metal Building Systems

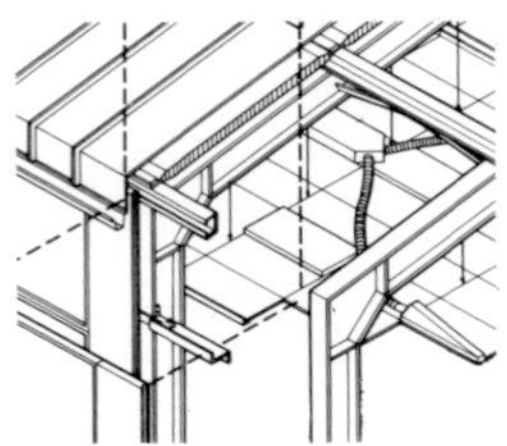

Reviewer:
Melanie Burnette, AIA
Stevens & Wilkinson
Columbia, SC

Illustration:
Darrell Downing Rippeteau, Architect
Richard J. Vitullo, designer in charge
Washington, DC

Metal frame and skin building systems take advantage of factory assembly techniques and quality control. The structural integration of frame components with the building skin, for strength and rigidity, permits major economies in the size and number of steel framing components. Primary and secondary framing members, fasteners, and panels interact to produce a light, stable building shell. All framing and cladding components are designed, engineered, and fabricated in a plant, then shipped to the site for erection. The same company often designs, engineers, and builds the system. Metal structural components are generally sized and deployed according to the exact requirements of an application, permitting economies in materials and speed of construction.[1]

A variety of exterior cladding alternatives is available, ranging from lightweight corrugated metal skins to fully insulated sandwich panels that provide both interior and exterior finishes.[2] Manufacturers also offer door, window, and skylight components that work as integral elements of the envelope and interior systems.

PRINCIPAL APPLICATIONS AND ADVANTAGES

Pre-engineered primary frames and claddings are dominant in warehouse, agricultural, and light industrial buildings. They are also increasingly used for office and retail facilities. Their use is generally confined to one-story construction, but there is growing experience with multistory buildings.

Centralization of responsibility for engineering, fabrication, and construction permits close cost control and early assessment of building costs. Architects working with pre-engineered building systems can rely on technical support from the manufacturer, including the preparation of fabrication and subsystem engineering documents.

This construction approach is particularly advantageous for applications requiring large interior clear-spans, the support of heavy overhead cranes, or substantial expanses of roof. More often associated with "standard" building components and even "standard" buildings, the metal building systems industry is able to respond to highly specialized needs, while still employing standardized structural components and factory fabrication.

The standing seam metal roof system requires less maintenance than other alternatives, and its long-term performance record is excellent. Most standing seam metal roofs provide a free-floating monolithic membrane, connected by a series of slotted clips that allow movement. This method freely accommodates expansion/contraction cycles caused by thermal changes. In addition, a variety of details, colors, and finishes is available.

KEY INTEGRATION ISSUES

Although the structural and envelope systems of metal buildings are usually highly integrated, the mechanical and interior systems are rarely considered in any detail by manufacturers. When insulating metal sandwich panels are used for interior and exterior finishes, special care is required in detailing the power and signal wiring, and in providing for its protection once in place.

The standing seam metal roof presents several items of concern to architects: the modularity of roof panels and seams, important for locating plumbing stacks, skylights, and other roof apertures; proper expansion details at intersections with flashing, especially at upper-roof ridge; and the critical importance of crickets, parapet caps, and other details to avoid buildup of standing water.

Metal systems are very lightweight. In areas subject to high winds, special care should be taken for wind bracing the structural frame and for fastening and design of exterior cladding details. Building corners and edges are particularly subject to wind-induced uplifting and suction.

1. Conservation of time and resources, pp. 236–237.
2. Lightweight insulating metal panels, pp. 219–222.

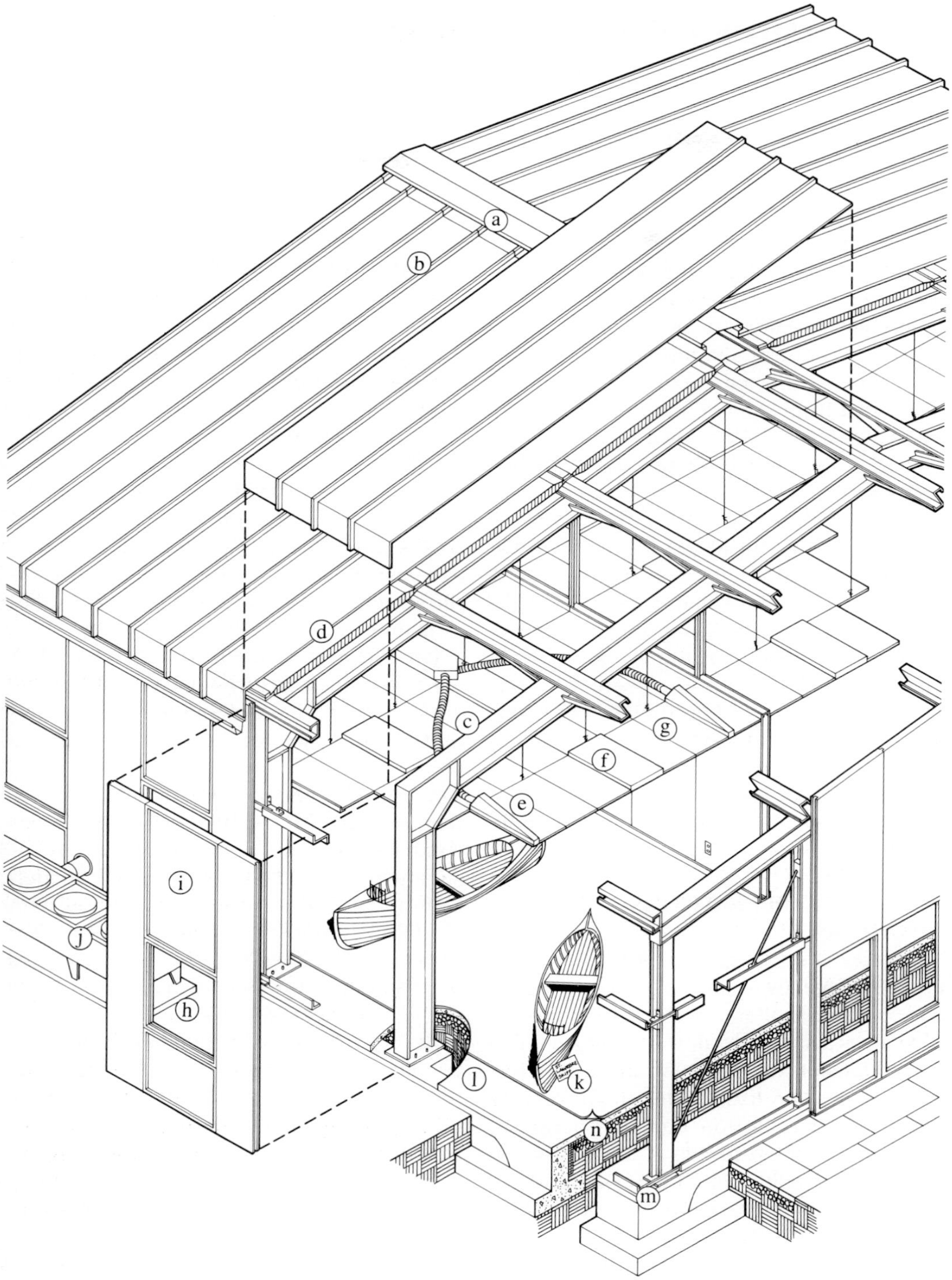

a. *Ridge vent*
b. *Standing seam metal roof*
c. *Rigid steel frame*
d. *Batt insulation*
e. *Ducts and diffusers*
f. *Fluorescent light fixtures*
g. *Suspended acoustical tile ceiling*
h. *Window assembly*
i. *Insulated metal wall panels*
j. *Heat pump*
k. *Carpet*
l. *Slab on grade and concrete foundation*
m. *Dampproofing*
n. *Vapor barrier*

Diagram detail page 361

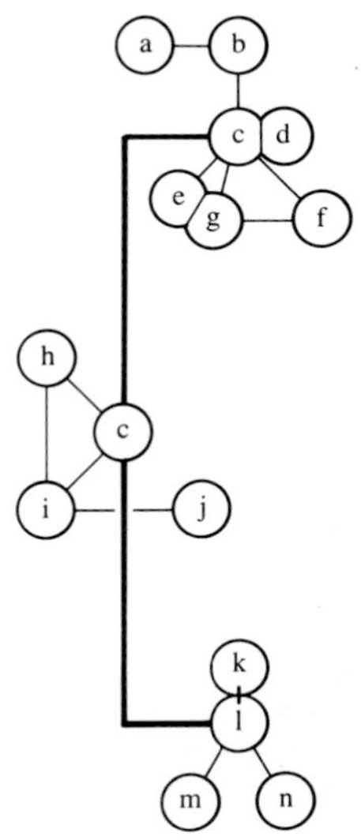

The pre-engineered metal building integrates lightweight structural and envelope components at the connected *level, but the result is a structure and envelope that combine to produce a common structural effect; each component adds strength and rigidity to the overall form. The floor slab, often left uncovered in warehouse and industrial applications, unifies the envelope, structure, and interior systems, and is normally the only major site preparation required for erecting the building. The pre-engineered, cold-formed steel componentry is very flexible and can be used for a wide variety of building shapes and sizes. Such buildings can be rapidly dismantled and moved.*

The rectilinear nature of such systems usually results in buildings that are easily expanded in the longer dimension. Mechanical and interior systems are meshed *in the ceilings, but the mechanical plant (here shown on the ground adjacent to the building, but just as easily roof-mounted) is normally kept on the exterior, sometimes presenting visible integration difficulty. The light weight of the envelope system, which is valuable for shipping, is especially vulnerable to wind uplift and requires great care in design and layout of fastenings. For applications where privacy or sound isolation are issues, the thin sheet steel presents an acoustical problem.*

15. Tension Fabric Structures

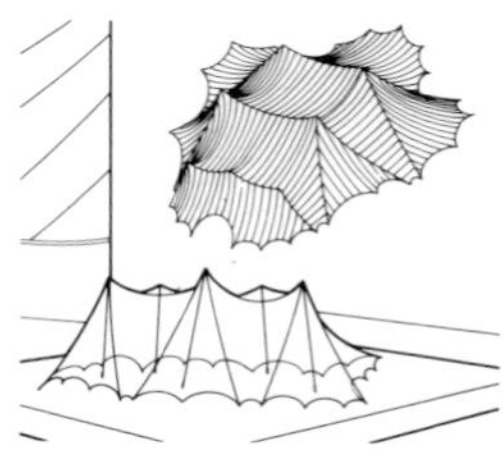

Reviewers:
Nicholas Goldsmith
FTL Associates
New York, NY

Joseph Valerio, AIA
Chrysalis of Wisconsin
Milwaukee, WI

Illustration:
Darrell Downing Rippeteau, Architect
Richard J. Vitullo, designer in charge
Washington, DC

In this example the structural, envelope, and interior systems are *unified*.[1] A fabric membrane, usually configured to follow an optimal structural shape, is anchored by steel cables attached to the fabric and is suspended from steel or aluminum masts to form a roof or total enclosure.

Fabrics for temporary use are typically composed of a polyester substrate with a polyvinyl-chloride-coated outer layer. A more expensive but longer-lasting fabric is either Teflon coated or silicone coated fiberglass. Cables are clamped to the fabric, which is cut and sewn according to patterns for the structural shape employed.[2]

The rules of structural geometry that govern the design of tension structures impart a unique and particular form which does not easily permit deviations. The formal qualities of tension structures are derived from surfaces of revolution and saddle surfaces.

PRINCIPAL APPLICATIONS AND ADVANTAGES

Several features give tension structures an advantage over low-cost wood, metal, and concrete shelters. If a lifetime of around 15 years is acceptable for the facility, a PVC-coated tension structure will suffice at a low initial cost. The usual solution for greater permanence is Teflon coated fiberglass. Clear spans of up to 100 ft are easily obtained with lightweight fabric structures.[3]

Color is an integral element of fabrics and will have an effect on the quality of natural illumination beneath the canopy. Because the fabric provides both interior and exterior finished surfaces for the envelope, the columns and masts are typically the only structural members used for mounting such items as lighting fixtures and power receptacles. Gantries hung from columns or masts provide additional service areas.[4]

Designers can consult with specialists on engineering and shop drawings. Design/build firms will produce complete shop drawings and often fabricate all components or erect the structure on the site.

KEY INTEGRATION ISSUES

Architects unwilling to relinquish control over formal design often begin designing with model studies in cooperation with a consultant or engineer. A computer analysis is frequently included to verify load expectations and to help guide pattern-making for the fabric.

In general the skin and cables of these structures are in tension, while columns and arches are subject to compression. Under dynamic loading conditions, an efficient tensile structure will adjust and allow slight deformation.

Unique aerodynamic properties assist open tension structures in overcoming the difficulties of wind-driven rain; wind conditions subject most of the fabric to negative pressure, "lifting" rain away from the skin. The use of vegetation or architectural barriers at ground-level openings also reduces wind and rain effects under the canopy.

Fabric-covered structures for the performing arts are generally equipped with electrical systems designed for safety in wet conditions. Sealing of the holes at the peaks of tensile structures where masts protrude is not usually necessary.

Several of the major building codes now contain provisions governing tensile structures, but it is advisable to consult local code officials early in the design process. The treatment of electrical wiring within or affixed to rigid columns and masts, which must be designed to permit some movement, may be a concern. Some fabrics are classified as noncombustible, and some are only fire retardant, so it is important to determine early on which fabrics are acceptable in a specific situation.

Careful detailing of steel and cable elements, joints, and attachments is critical to overall appearance, as most will be exposed to view. Steel and wire rope manufacturers can provide assistance with detailing.

1. Three-system integration, p. 318.
2. Structural fabric, pp. 173–176.
3. O'Connell Center, pp. 108–111.
4. Visible integration, pp. 381–385.

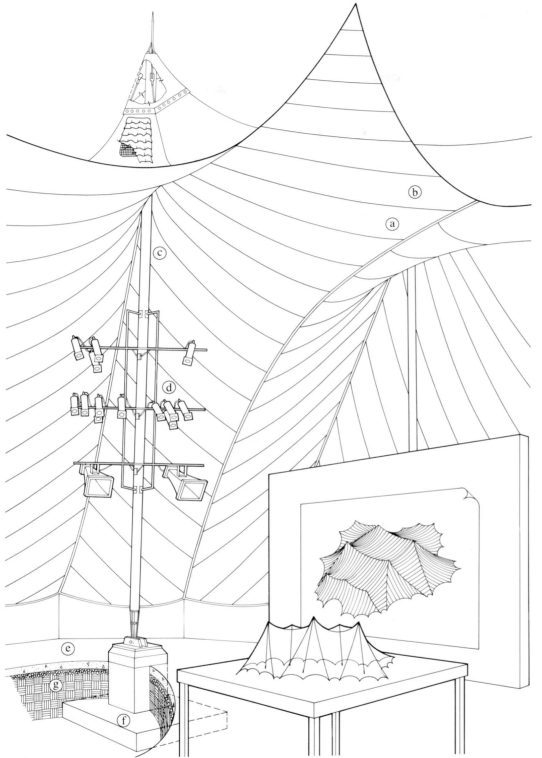

a. *Steel cables in fabric sleeves*
b. *Non-combustible fabric membrane*
c. *Steel masts*
d. *Incandescent light fixtures and sound system speakers*
e. *Slab on grade*
f. *Pivoted mast base plate and concrete footing*
g. *Vapor barrier*

Diagram detail page 362

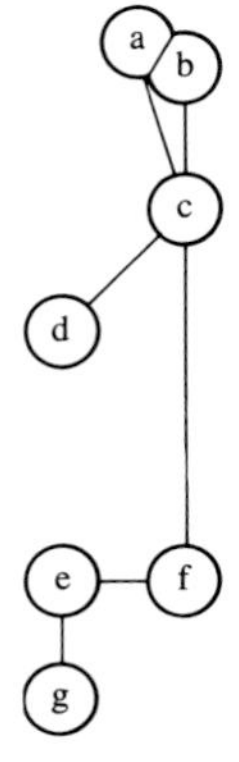

Structure, envelope, and interior systems are unified *in fabric buildings. The fabric provides all three functions and, because it is light-transmitting while blocking direct rays of the sun, also assumes some functions normal to mechanical systems. Electrical lighting and other equipment are difficult to integrate, due to the thinness of the structural envelope membrane, and are nearly always attached to the structural masts or placed on independent, freestanding structures. Tension fabric construction can conserve time and material. Fabrics can range in service life from several years to several decades, but vary accordingly in cost. Acoustical, thermal, and fire-safety considerations are difficult to accommodate in tension structures, although their light weight and dynamic properties under wind loading make them very safe from a structural point of view. If areas of fabric are placed close to the ground or in other easily accessible locations, vandalism becomes a concern, as most materials suitable for tensile structures are easily cut.*

References

ACCESS FLOOR AND CURTAIN WALL

American Institute of Steel Construction. *Manual of Steel Construction*. 8th ed. Chicago: AISC, 1980.

American Iron and Steel Institute. *Specifications for the Design of Cold-Formed Steel Structural Members*. Washington: AISI, 1980.

Construction Specifications Institute. *Technical Aid Series*, Section 05120. Washington: CSI, 1982.

POST-TENSIONED CONCRETE

Prestressed Concrete Institute. *PCI Design Handbook for Precast Prestressed Concrete*. Chicago: 1984.

FLYING FORM

Hurd, M. K. *Formwork for Concrete*. 4th ed. Detroit: American Concrete Institute, 1984.

FLAT PLATE

Hornbostel, Caleb. *Construction Materials: Types, Uses, and Applications*. New York: Wiley, 1978.

Merritt, Frederick S. *Building Construction Handbook*. 3rd ed. New York: McGraw-Hill, 1975.

Palmer, Alvin E., and M. Susan Lewis. *Planning the Office Landscape*. New York: McGraw-Hill, 1977.

PRECAST FRAME

Phillips, William R., and David A. Sheppard. *Plant Cast, Precast and Prestressed Concrete: A Design Guide*. The Prestressed Concrete Manufacturers Association of California, 1980.

Prestressed Concrete Institute. *PCI Design Handbook, Second Edition*. Chicago, 1981.

STAGGERED TRUSS

Bethlehem Steel Corporation. *Building Case Histories 69, 74* and *53*. Bethlehem, PA: BSC, 1981.

Massachusetts Institute of Technology and the United States Steel Corporation. *Staggered Truss Steel Framing Systems*. Cambridge, MA: MIT Departments of Architecture and Civil Engineering, 1966.

TILT-UP WALL

Portland Cement Association. *Architectural Design Aid, 3d-12-81: Tilt-Up Construction*. Chicago: PCA, 1981.

BEARING WALL AND BAR-JOIST ROOF

Steel Joist Institute. *Standard Specifications for Open-Web Steel Joists, J-* and *H- Series*. Arlington, VA: SJI, 1981.

LIGHTWEIGHT STEEL FRAME AND BRICK VENEER

Merritt, Frederick S. *Building Construction Handbook*. 3rd ed. New York: McGraw-Hill, 1975.

Brick Institute of America. *Technical Note 28B: Brick Veneer and Curtain Walls*. McLean, VA: BIA, 1980.

WOOD FLOOR AND ROOF TRUSS

Melaragno, M. *Simplified Truss Design*. New York: Van Nostrand, 1981. Pp. 81-90.

Truss Plate Institute. *Bracing Wood Trusses*. Frederick, MD: TPI, 1976.

Truss Plate Institute. *Design Specifications for Metal Plate Connected Parallel Chord Trusses*. Frederick, MD: TPI, 1980.

Truss Plate Institute. *Design Specifications for Metal Plate Connected Wood Trusses*. Frederick, MD: TPI, 1978.

Truss Plate Institute. *Quality Control Manual for Light Metal Plate Connected Wood Trusses*. Frederick, MD: TPI, 1977.

LAMINATED WOOD POST AND BEAM

American Institute of Timber Construction. *AITC Source Materials*. Washington: 1960.

Breyer, Donald E. *Design of Wood Structures*. New York: McGraw-Hill, 1980.

Oberg, Fred R. *Heavy Timber Construction*. Chicago: American Technical Society, 1963.

LIGHTWEIGHT MOBILE MODULAR BUILDINGS

Bernhardt, Arthur D. *Building Tommorrow: The Mobile/Manufactured Housing Industry*. Cambridge, MA: MIT Press, 1980.

Nutt-Powell, Thomas E. *Manufactured Homes: Making Sense of a Housing Opportunity*. Boston: Auburn House, 1982.

Rabb, Judith, and Bernard Rabb. *Good Shelter: A Guide to Mobile, Modular, and Prefabricated Houses, Including Domes*.New York: Quadrangle/New York Times Book Company, 1975.

SPACE FRAMES

Wendell, Wendel R. *Spaceframe Basics: A Handbook for Spaceframe Design and Engineering*. Plainview, NY: Space Structures International Corporation, 1983.

METAL BUILDING SYSTEMS

American Iron and Steel Institute. *Handbook for the Design of Cold-Rolled Steel Members*. Washington: AISI, 1983.

Metal Building Manufacturers Association. *Metal Building System Design Manual*. Cleveland: MBMA, 1981.

Vonier, Thomas. "Beyond Shade and Shelter." *Progressive Architecture*, March 1982, pp. 129-135.

TENSION FABRIC STRUCTURES

"Tent Structures: Are They Architecture?" *Architectural Record*, May 1980, pp. 127-134.

Beitin, Karl I. "Energy Performance of Fabric Roofs." *The Construction Specifier*, July 1982, pp. 12-15.

Drew, Phillip. *Tensile Architecture*. Boulder, CO: Westview Press, 1979.

Educational Facilities Laboratories. *Four Fabric Structures: A Report*. New York: 1975.

Otto, Frei. *Tensile Structures. Design, Structure, and Calculation of Buildings with Cables, Nets, and Membranes*. Cambridge, MA: MIT 1973.

Rush, Richard D. "The Era of Swoops and Billows." *Progressive Architecture*, June 1980, pp. 110-119.

CONTENTS

Chapter 5
Products

Author:
Barbara Golter Heller, AIA

Contributor:
Doris King

Chapter—1st draft reviewer:
Walter Rosenfeld, AIA, CSI
The Architects Collaborative
Cambridge, MA

Architectural drawings:
Allen Assarsson

The products discussed in this chapter are drawn from the buildings and building types examined in Chapters 3 and 4, and illustrate the integration opportunities presented by a broad range of product types and combinations. The selection here is in no sense exhaustive. Rather, it is intended to form a context for discussion that can apply to products generally.

The mere repetition of a product in a built situation may be thought of as a system. The relationship between the parts may be rigid or flexible, and the parts themselves may be discrete or linked together by a methodology. Drywall, for example, is a system that begins with individual pieces, but these rarely remain identifiable as such in a building.

We have defined all buildings as integrated. All building components are therefore integrated in that they relate to the rest of the building. Generally, the smaller the component is, the simpler the integration will be, and the easier it will be to identify. This facilitates the architect's task where products are concerned, because this task is typically one of analysis: the architect is not called upon to design the product, but to derive its integration characteristics. Once this is done, the product's normal usage (as well as a range of options surrounding that usage) will become clear. The question is to what degree a given product can be integrated in a given building situation. It will be evident, too, that some products that are very highly integrated within themselves (integrated ceilings and open plan office furniture, for example) can be among the most difficult to integrate with other products and systems.

The products in this chapter are grouped together according to their usual location within the building. To the extent that a parallel structure is imposed on our discussion of them, it is intended to break out instances of their use covered in Chapters 3 and 4 (Examples), issues affecting the product and the system of which it is a part (Immediate Considerations), and issues arising out of its relationship to other systems (General Considerations). Cross-references are given in the text to related topics.

The depth of the discussions was limited by the degree of variation within a given product. Generally, the reader will find more detail in the discussions of products such as heat pumps than in that of insulating glass, for example. In all cases, it should be borne in mind that the subject is addressed in the context of integration. References at the end of the chapter direct the reader to more general treatments. As always, exact product information of the kind needed in design must be obtained from the manufacturer.

Energy Management Control Systems

Reviewer:
Alan M.H. Sloan
Cannon Design Inc.
Buffalo, NY

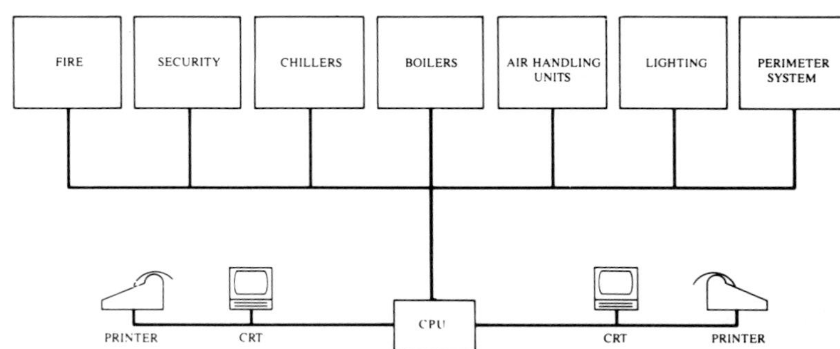

A sophisticated energy management control system monitors and regulates numerous functions in the Occidental Chemical building, including the position of the operable louvers in the building's double envelope.

A computerized control system presents the opportunity to coordinate a vast number of electronically activated products, regardless of size or use. A computer can be programmed to make control decisions automatically, and sometimes simultaneously, for a multitude of discrete systems. It transforms a set of small systems into a single large system. Integration in the context of circuitry becomes the conscious establishment of a relationship between the controls (and the functions that are being controlled) of the different systems. Creativity occurs when the integration of the systems in question actually causes a new control possibility to exist by virtue of the relationship that did not exist before.

On a purely functional level, this creates an efficiency that can be quantified and rationally measured. The desired results may include optimizing conservation of resources or conservation of time and labor for an extraordinary number or complexity of tasks.[1] This discussion will focus on energy management control systems. An energy management control system, or EMCS, is a centralized control system that typically includes a microprocessor or computer to collect and display data concerning the mechanical system and regulate the system accordingly. Every control system has a sensor and a controller; a wall-mounted thermostat is a control system. An EMCS includes a number of remote sensors (also called points) and a central controller. The points are connected to remote panels that communicate with the central processor through a trunk cable.

1. Conservation of resources and time, pp. 236–237.

With over 140 systems available, the variations in system capability are enormous. The distribution of data processing is a critical part of the system. Currently the hardware for distribution of information to points (called field interface devices) is becoming more intelligent, especially with the advent of direct digital control. These devices house the software necessary to control the system (called proportional integral and derivative control loops, or PID loops) in such a way that the devices are virtually self-sufficient.

The decision that is the most difficult with control systems is not what to include, but rather what to leave out. Some manufacturers advocate integration of security features, elevator control, life safety system control, and energy management control in one package.[2] Others argue that separating functions minimizes the chance of a critical system failure with resulting compromise of life safety. Because of the central control capability which usually results, a vertical dependency between functions could result that would disrupt many functions if only one was shut down. Another concern has to do with what happens if the control system needs to

2. Building integrity, p. 258.

be overridden or shut down. When it is not working, everything connected to it may be inoperable, and this may include almost anything that operates by electricity. As with escalators, the difficult part of the design task is not designing the system to work, but designing it so that it fails predictably.[3] Although the controlled products are usually part of the mechanical systems, the elements to be monitored may be located in other systems like structure, interior, or envelope.

EXAMPLES

Eleven of the nineteen buildings in the Chapter 3 case studies use computerized control systems of one kind or another. The O'Connell Center[4] uses a central processing unit as both a central data bank and optimizing controller. A computer control system constantly monitors the air pressure and continuously displays data to the building manager. The system is designed to compensate immediately for over-inflation or under-inflation. Wind gauges on the roof help the mechanism evaluate whether or not to compensate for high winds. It is safe to say that without such sophistication, a large-scale air-supported building would be extremely difficult to maintain.

The computerized system at Occidental Chemical[5] includes security alarm and fire alarm systems as well as energy management. The owner was enthusiastic about using a sophisticated and centralized system and is very interested in getting data about the thermal response of the building. Sensors have even been placed inside concrete slabs at many points around the building perimeter and in other locations so that data about the thermal performance of the building can be monitored and analyzed on a continuing basis. The owner and architect are very satisfied with the system's performance.

The EMCS at the Atlanta/Hartsfield International Airport[6] controls the HVAC system and is used, for example, to adjust the cooling load when peak passenger volumes create a heavy demand for cooling.

3. Escalators, pp. 190–192.
4. O'Connell Center, pp. 108–111.
5. Occidental Chemical, pp. 94–97.
6. Atlanta International Airport, pp. 116–119.

At Walter Reed,[7] the EMCS includes the fire alarm system as well as HVAC. The owner has found the system's ability to diagnose problems useful in reducing maintenance.

At the Vocational Technical Education Facility at the University of Minnesota,[8] the system is used exclusively to adjust the shading devices on the Trombe wall to accommodate solar load.

7. Walter Reed General Hospital, pp. 82–85.
8. Vocational Technical Education Facility, pp. 98–101.

IMMEDIATE CONSIDERATIONS

Size: A small system has 16 to 24 points, while a medium-size system controls up to a million square feet of space and a large system may control a building complex as large as an entire college campus or army base.

Controlled systems: Typically, heating, cooling, ventilating, and lighting are controlled by EMCS, but other functions can be added.

Software: Determining the best software package is very difficult. A tremendous range of software packages is available, and manufacturers will custom-design software programs for special projects. A necessary step in evaluating different systems is to prepare a list of functions required to be performed by the EMCS relative to the standard software offerings of the industry. Many architects write a performance specification based on a sample input-output list and get bids from vendors. The bids can then be evaluated and a vendor selected to complete the design for the EMCS prior to completion of the contract documents. This is done because the building design can be materially altered by EMCS, and because different vendors have different requirements; it is most cost-effective to understand those requirements during the design process.

Input/Output (I/O) requirements commonly include on/off control for fans, air-handling units, radiation pumps, lighting, boilers, chillers, and electric reheat and reset of thermostats or damper positions. Alarms may be included to warn of clogged filters, non-functioning fans, low fuel levels, unusually high or low water temperatures, or loss of water pressure. The I/O points can be digital (on/off) or analog (reset or varying range of response). An analog point typically costs six times as much as a digital point.

Cost effectiveness: Ideally, an EMCS saves money by conserving manpower, energy, and equipment by reducing equipment running time, optimizing temperatures, restricting demand, and minimizing energy consumption. Many conflicting requirements and circumstances make cost-effectiveness hard to evaluate.

While fully centralizing all building systems will yield the lowest operating cost, the initial cost of including each system must be considered. The lowest initial cost would be obtained by purchasing a system with limited capacity and functions. The maximum environmental quality would be achieved by a large number of sensor points, a sophisticated computer program, and, most important, a highly skilled operator. With distributed processing, it is now becoming cost-effective to start with a small system and build up in size and sophistication. However, it is still difficult to mix equipment from different manufacturers.

Console control: The functions performed by the central console may include starting and stopping equipment, monitoring equipment, recording events for management use, determining and implementing proper control values, and determining when maintenance services are needed.

Personnel: The human operator is an essential component of the system. The operator may have a great deal of control, with the EMCS primarily facilitating data collection and providing a centralized control keyboard, or the machinery may be programmed to control most functions while the operator merely observes and maintains the system. The system must be maintained by someone knowledgeable in the manipulation of software programs, the proper functioning of the EMCS system, and the proper functioning of the mechanical system. When operating personnel are confused or uneducated about the proper use of an EMCS, they will bypass it and do the work manually. Full documentation of the functions of the EMCS and complete training of personnel by the vendor should help minimize this problem.

Equipment location: The space designed for the central processing unit must be environmentally controlled for temperature, dust, static, vibration, and noise. Space must also be provided for the wiring and piping runs required to interconnect the system.

Sensor and control points: The number and type of sensors and control points affects system performance and cost.[9] These can range from a temperature sensor and an on/off control to sensors that measure humidity, temperature, supply air temperature, and return air temperature, and provide temperature compensated stop and start. The environmental requirements of a laboratory or a precision manufacturing area would justify the installation of very precise sensors and controls.

9. System performance, p. 232.

Mechanical system integration: When using EMCS, it is best to use components in the mechanical system that lend themselves to proportional control of the environment (analog control) as opposed to components limited to either on or off (digital control).

Wiring: A plethora of wiring designs are used, ranging from those that use 100 wires to those that use only two wires for data transfer.

GENERAL CONSIDERATIONS

Security: Like other computers, the EMCS can be damaged or have its memory erased by magnets. Access to the computer and program discs should be restricted.

Expansion: Expanding or updating a system is costly, but this cost is decreasing with the emergence of distributed data processing. Good instruction of operating personnel may allow them to revise and expand the program as necessary.

Heat Pumps

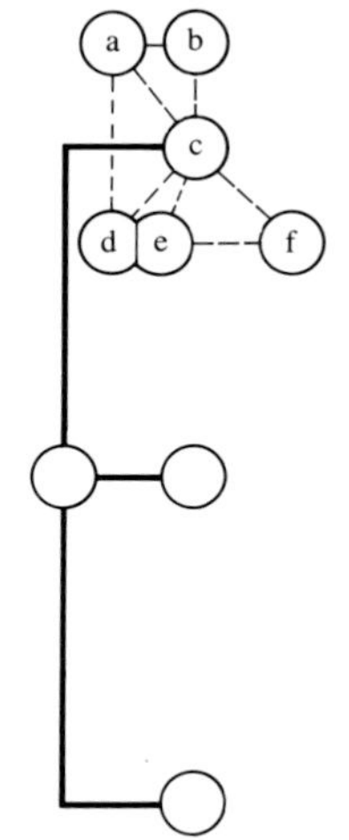

a. *Heat pump*
b. *Roofing*
c. *Roof structure and deck*
d. *Duct*
e. *Suspended Ceiling*
f. *Lighting*

Diagram detail page 336

Reviewer:
Joseph R. Loring, PE
Joseph R. Loring Associates, Inc.
New York, NY

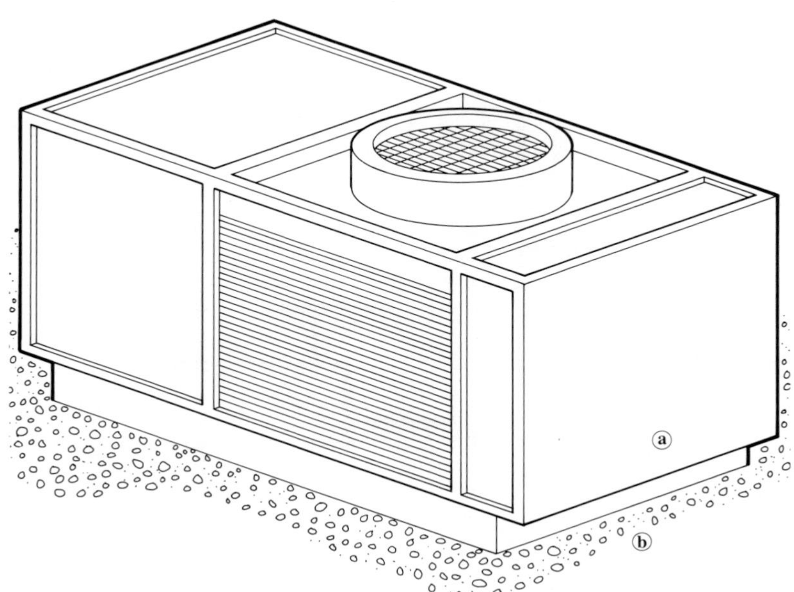

An exterior detail of Generic Example Number 14, Metal Building Systems (below), shows the condenser of the air-to-air heat pump. The condensor above is a rooftop unit. The evaporator is located inside the building.

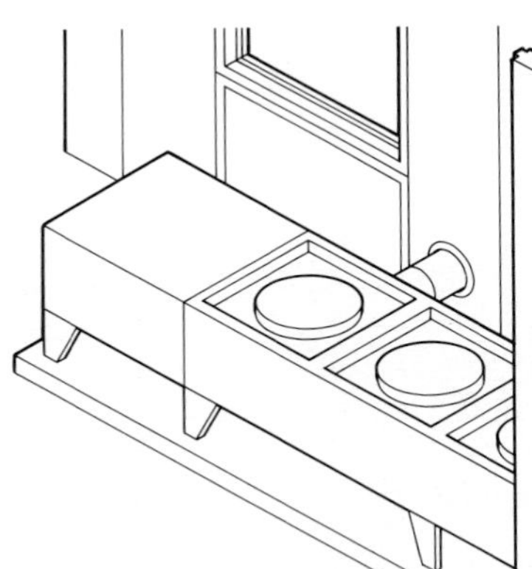

A heat pump is a single mechanical system that integrates heating and cooling functions. In its most basic form it is a continuous refrigerant-filled loop which can be thought of as having two halves, one being the evaporator coil (cold) and the other the condenser coil (hot). A reversing valve is used to switch between heating and cooling functions. Heat pumps have been marketed as cost-saving and energy-saving devices, and under optimal conditions they have an efficiency, measured as coefficient of performance (COP), of over 400 percent. This is based on the principle that a ton of refrigeration, which yields approximately 15,000 BTU/hr of rejected heat, can be generated by 1 kw of electricity, which consumes 3,400 BTU/hr.

Elements of the heat pump system can be located inside or outside the building. The condenser can be placed on the roof or on the ground next to the building; in nearly all cases it is treated like most mechanical equipment and shielded from view.[1] Visible integration is also affected by the type of unit, which may be fed with pipes or ducts. The former are easier to conceal.[2]

The use of a heat pump to heat and cool economically is ideal for moderate climates. In very cold climates where the daily temperature is normally below freezing, a heat pump will not be effective. Like many other specifically integrated systems, the integration works as long as the environment stays within optimal parameters. Occasional exceptionally cold weather can be factored into the design decision and a cost-benefit analysis made.

1. Mechanical system, p. 318.
2. Visible integration levels, pp. 381–385.

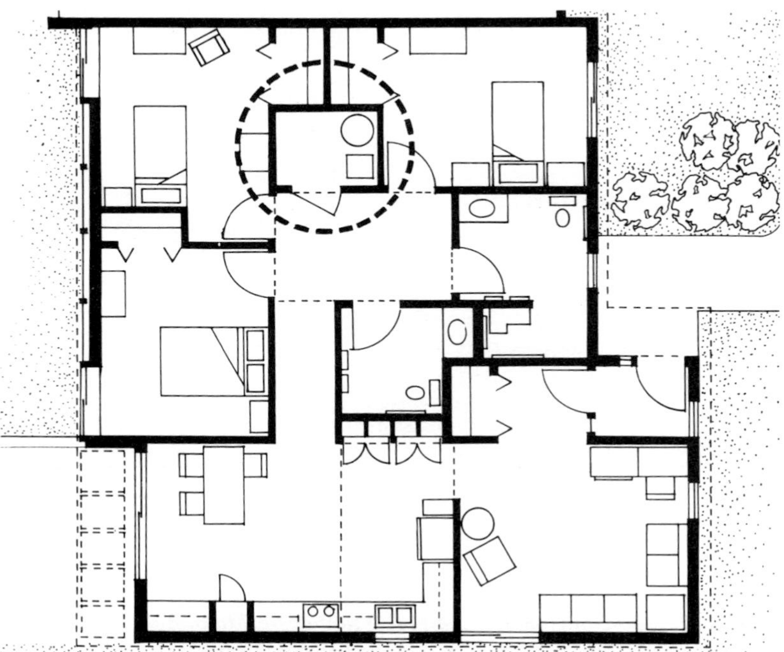

TYPICAL UNIT WITH HEAT PUMP CIRCLED

Photo: D. Randolph Foulds

A plan of a unit in the John Nutting Apartments (top) shows the mechanical room containing the heat pump. A typical condenser is pictured (above).

3. John Nutting Apartments, pp. 68–69.

EXAMPLE

The John Nutting Apartments[3] use air-to-air through-wall units with integral electrical resistance backup heating. The mechanical engineer and architect felt the application was appropriate because the temperature is usually above 40°F; the cooling load was a primary consideration, since the occupants spend much of their time indoors.

IMMEDIATE CONSIDERATIONS

Thermal medium: Heat pumps are usually classified as air-to-air or air-to-water, depending on the thermal medium; air is always the distribution medium. The water can be well water, groundwater, or water that has been preheated in a boiler. A recent innovation is the earth-coupled heat pump, which uses the earth as a heat sink in lieu of air or water.

Single or zoned system: The criteria for deciding between a single or a zoned system are the same as for any HVAC system. A heat pump selected as a central unit would replace a conventional rooftop unit. A through-wall heat pump is effective for heating or cooling small perimeter spaces, which can be individually controlled. Water-to-air units can also effectively control the environment of spaces without exterior walls in zoned systems.

Location: The heat pump typically replaces a standard component of the mechanical system. In a residence, this would be the furnace or boiler. In a commercial structure, the unit replaces the central refrigeration system. No cooling tower is required in an air-to-air heat pump; if water is the thermal medium, a cooling tower is needed to reject heat in the summer. Heat pumps do have the capability of being split, the condenser being located outdoors and the evaporator indoors. It is also possible to design for a use requiring several modular units at various locations; pipes can connect these in an air-to-water system. These units may be located in closets, above the ceiling, or on the floor.

Maintenance: The refrigerant in the coils and the condensate must be drained periodically. Some units are supplied with controlled pan heaters that evaporate the condensation, but these may present maintenance problems in themselves.

Costs: The cost effectiveness of a heat pump depends on the HVAC requirements and the climate where the building is located. All heat pumps should have auxiliary backup heat systems, especially in cold climates. An air-to-air heat pump cannot function effectively at temperatures below 35°F, although some manufacturers claim to have equipment that can function at temperatures as low as 30°F. Each building will have different requirements that must be assessed in determining if a heat pump is cost-effective.

GENERAL CONSIDERATIONS

Controls: Individual consoles are usually regulated by thermostats in the space or in the unit. Controls can be designed to work in coordination with auxiliary heat sources.

Auxiliary heat: Because heat pumps operate on electricity, auxiliary heat is usually provided by electric resistance heaters. Costs and efficiency of auxiliary heat should be determined.

Heat recovery: Although a heat pump can be efficient when used as a component of a conventional HVAC system, it is most effective if it is integrated with a heat recovery system as part of the building design.

Plastic-Domed Skylights

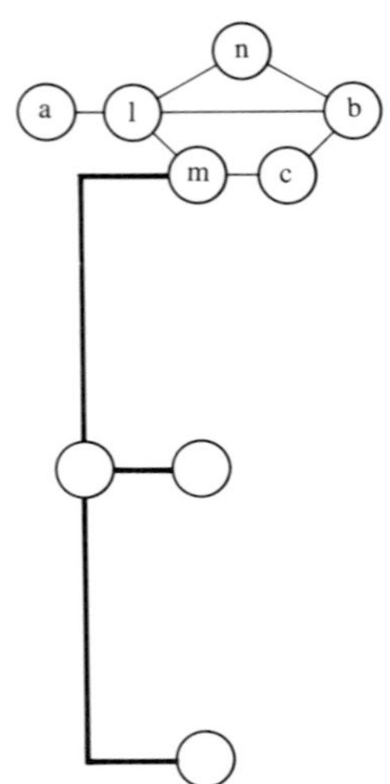

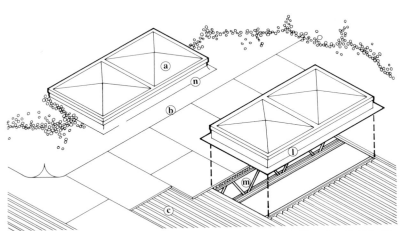

Curb-mounted skylights are shown in Generic Example Number 7, Tilt-Up Wall. Curbs are required for tile, wood shake, and wood shingle roofs to reinforce the roof structure around the opening. They often incorporate thermal breaks.

a. *Skylights*
b. *Built-up roofing and rigid insulation*
c. *Steel deck*
l. *Curb*
m. *Open-web steel joists*
n. *Flashing*

Diagram detail page 337

Reviewer:
Harrison Fraker, Jr., AIA
Professor and Head of the School of Architecture
University of Minnesota
Minneapolis, MN

Skylights, like windows, represent an envelope/interior unification.[1] They are therefore capable of embodying all of the problems and advantages of the interior and exterior of the building. In addition, they may be seen as both wall and roof. View, glare, and privacy can all be issues in skylight design,[2] as well as daylighting, thermal exchange, and acoustical control.[3] These characteristics make skylights a frequent retrofit item, both as individual units and in vaults and clusters.

Skylights bring light and heat gain into spaces that are otherwise mechanically illuminated and heated. They provide an open feeling and protection from the environment at the same time, giving them a strong psychological appeal. As a dramatic "ceiling" they are used in atriums, lobbies, and entrances of commercial buildings. In a broad or deep one-story building with a low ratio of perimeter to interior space, they can be used to introduce daylight in the absence of windows. They are popular in residential construction as a way of providing openness in small spaces and for their potential passive solar properties.

There are as many types of skylights as there are design needs, but the discussion here will be limited to plastic-domed skylights. These are generally off-the-shelf items, but they may also be custom designed. One integration advantage which is characteristic of plastic products in general is the relative ease with which a custom-molded skylight can be fabricated. The only equipment needed is an oven and a form (sometimes a vacuum form). Geometrical integration and dimensional compatibility can be easily accomplished.

EXAMPLES

Pyramid-shaped acrylic skylights are among the off-the-shelf components used in the design of the Herman Miller Seating/Manufacturing Plant.[4] Like windows, they represent a unification of envelope and interior. In combination with clerestories of the same material, the skylights integrate daylighting criteria and solar heat gain to a degree appropriate to the facility's northern location. The skylights are operable and serve the dual function of smoke vents.

IMMEDIATE CONSIDERATIONS

Framing: Skylights are typically framed in aluminum, although galvanized steel, stainless steel, wood, and fiberglass are available for this purpose. Finishes, whether integral

1. Envelope and interior *unified*, p. 329.
2. Visible integration, pp. 381–385.
3. Thermal performance, pp. 250–251; acoustical performance, p. 254; visual performance, p. 256.
4. Herman Miller Seating Plant, pp. 56–59.

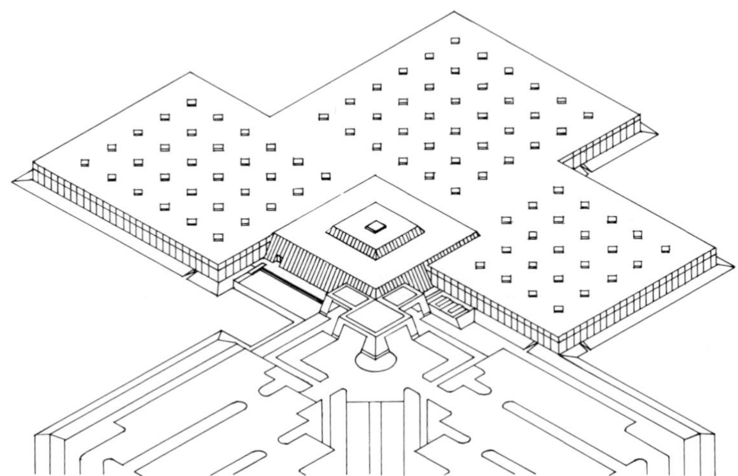

Photo: Balthazar Korab

Skylights are critical to the daylighting strategy of the Herman Miller plant (top). They are also equipped to function as smoke vents (above).

or applied, are a consideration if the frame is exposed to view. Frames are available with thermal breaks for increased thermal efficiency. The skylight may be operable or inoperable as needs dictate. Consideration of internal drainage is critical due to the possibility of condensation.

The number and length of joints affects the thermal efficiency of the skylight and also determines the areas most vulnerable to leaks. The same is true of the curbs on which skylights are frequently mounted. Some manufacturers market curbs that provide extra insulating material to protect against thermal bridging. Curb-mounted skylights may be used on all types of roofs, but are required for tile, wood shake, or wood shingle roofs. Most manufacturers offer self-flashing skylights, which are less vulnerable to leakage.

Materials: The plastic used is either an acrylic or a polycarbonate material, and may be either translucent or transparent. Translucent types are generally available in white or bronze. The plastic may be single-, double-, or triple-glazed, depending on the thermal value required. Unlike glass, double- and triple-glazed plastic skylights are not hermetically sealed units, but are formed with the use of spacers. They are not sealed because of the high rate of water vapor transmission and greater thermal expansion associated with plastic.

Plastic skylights are glazed with neoprene, ethylene propylene diene monomer, or butyl gaskets. One manufacturer offers a product that "welds" the skylight to the fiberglass skirt. While large skylights must be field-glazed, smaller lights may be purchased preassembled and factory-glazed, which provides better quality control and leak protection.

Geometry: The dome may be in the shape of a bubble or a pyramid, while its base may be round, square, rectangular, triangular, hexagonal, or octagonal. The advantage of using acrylics and polycarbonates is that curved shapes such as arches, which are very costly to produce in glass, are easily achieved with plastic. The plastic can be cold-formed in the field or thermo-formed in factory-glazed installations.

Skylights may be single, continuous, or in clusters. A continuous vault or run of domes may be used where a linear space is completely daylighted. Clusters are often used with space frames and geodesic domes, and are sometimes seen on entrance canopies and outdoor shelters where daylighting is desirable. Code requirements may mandate the maximum glazing area allowed, as well as permissible distances between skylights. Curbs may also be required.

Maintenance: Skylights should be accessible from the interior and the exterior to facilitate cleaning and replacement.

GENERAL CONSIDERATIONS

Mechanical: Orientation and the amount of glazed surface are key factors in evaluating the impact of a skylight on the mechanical requirements of a building. A well-designed skylight can provide more heat gain from solar energy than is lost by conduction in winter, and can provide daylighting to reduce the need for electric lighting without unwanted heat gain during summer. Several skylight manufacturers offer a free energy analysis to assist architects in skylight design. Condensation and frost on skylights, and sometimes between glazing layers, can be a problem in certain climates; adequate air flow should be provided.

Lighting: While some skylights are designed primarily for visual appeal on the exterior, most are designed with the needs of the building user foremost. In commercial buildings they are most often used to enhance public areas. In industrial buildings they are most often used to distribute daylight to the work space. Their energy advantages are principally in the area of daylighting, with attendant savings in lighting energy costs.

When skylights are used to admit natural light to work spaces, their location should be coordinated with work stations. Lighting quality will be influenced by the choice of plastic color and type, and glare is of special concern.[5]

Fire protection: Acrylic-glazed skylights can double as heat and smoke vents, and are frequently marketed with this in view.

Security: Since skylights are frequently inaccessible from the interior, outside glazing is desirable to speed construction time and, where glazing is done in the field, to limit costs.[6] Unfortunately, outside glazing can provide access to intruders. Some manufacturers supply a security type glazing bead or gasket to minimize this problem.

Interiors: Certain plants require light from a part of the spectrum which processed plastic will not transmit. Some study is necessary if extensive plant life is expected to be part of the interior design. Modular spacing of the skylights works well with the use of open office systems[7] so that the arrangement remains flexible.

5. Visual performance, p. 256.

6. Conservation of resources and time, pp. 236–237.

7. Open plan office furniture, pp. 196–199.

Protected Membrane Roofing

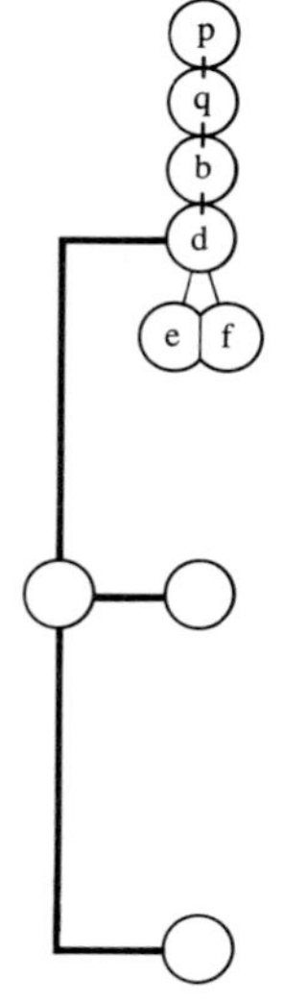

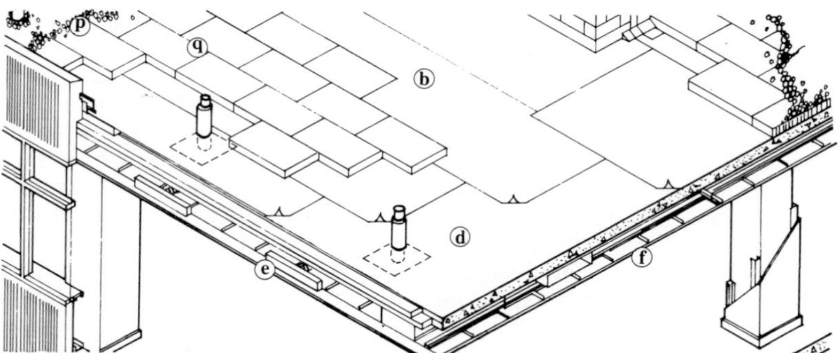

As shown in Generic Example Number 4, Flat Plate, a protected roof membrane is laid directly on the roof deck and topped with insulation and ballast.

b. *Protected roof membrane*
d. *Cast-in-place concrete flat plate*
e. *Ducts and diffusers*
f. *Suspended acoustical tile ceiling*
p. *Ballast*
q. *Rigid insulation*

Diagram detail page 337

Reviewer:
Walter Rosenfeld, AIA, CSI
The Architects Collaborative
Cambridge, MA

Protected membrane roofing, otherwise known as PMR or inverted roofing, differs primarily from a conventional roofing assembly in that the waterproofing membrane is placed beneath the insulation. Ballast is placed above the insulation and serves as protection from ultraviolet light and to prevent uplift of the insulation. Pavers may be used as ballast, and these also provide a walking surface.

The strategy is an attempt to address the chronic problems associated with exposed roof membranes. In some instances, visible integration is involved as well. A flat or nearly level roof is rarely a visible integration issue; the roof is visually integrated by being kept out of sight.[1] But when an aggregate-surfaced flat roof is in view, the best means of achieving a visually acceptable surface is to control the type, size, and color of the aggregate surface. Eliminating the flood coat of the traditional built-up roof means that no bitumen is obvious on the aggregate surface of a protected membrane roof.

The protected membrane roof represents one of the few built conditions that includes integration at the *touching* level.[2] Structure is involved in that it must support the weight of the roof, although there is no direct connection between them. This pays off in faster construction time and lower maintenance. It also enables protected membrane roofing to be used in retrofit situations, provided there is sufficient structural strength to sustain the additional weight of ballast. The only restriction on the structural system is that it be able to carry this weight, typically 10 psf. Careful attention should be paid to drainage as ponding is more likely than with a conventional built-up roof.

Combinations involving this envelope subsystem and systems other than the structure are more limited. There is seldom a relationship between the interior system and a flat roof, although locating the membrane on the warm side of the insulation allows it to act as a vapor barrier, which is ideal for interior spaces with high humidity. It is possible, although not likely, that glare from a roof may distract occupants of adjacent buildings. Mechanical systems, by contrast, frequently penetrate the envelope at the roof level. As with other roof types, edges and penetrations are vulnerable to leaks and require special flashing details. The assembly can have an FM Class 1 or a UL Class A roof classification. The fire rating may be between one and four hours.

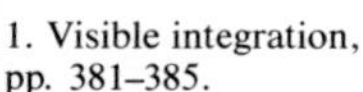

1. Visible integration, pp. 381–385.
2. Structure and envelope *touching*, p. 323.

EXAMPLES

Protected membrane roofs are used on the Georgia Power Company Headquarters[3] and the National Permanent building.[4] This type of roof assembly is also used for the earth-covered roof in the George R. Moscone Center,[5] with the earth acting as ballast. A protected membrane roof is shown in Generic Example Number 1.[6]

3. Georgia Power Company Headquarters, pp. 86–89.
4. National Permanent Building, pp. 90–91.
5. Moscone Center, pp. 112–115.
6. Access floor and curtain wall, pp. 124–125.

IMMEDIATE CONSIDERATIONS

Membrane: Any type of compatible membrane may be used, whether single-ply or built-up. The inorganic felts of a built-up roof membrane are less vulnerable to decay caused by moisture than organic felts. It should be ascertained that the membrane is compatible with the insulation; coal tar pitch, for example, cannot be used with polystyrene insulation.

Insulation: The insulation used is extruded polystyrene; other insulations are not recommended because of their poor moisture resistance and freeze/thaw cycle resistance. Two types of board are available. One has tongue-and-groove edges and latex-modified concrete laminated to the face as ballast and protection; the other is square-edged, with channels around the perimeter for water collection. The amount of insulation depends on the required R value, with a minimum of 2 in. thickness. Ballast and a loose-web, inorganic (usually polyester) fabric must be used with the square-edged board. Ballast may be rock or gravel, or precast pavers, as long as the weight is at least 10 to 15 psf. The fabric prevents individual boards from floating away and also screens ultraviolet radiation.

The insulation may be loose laid or walked into a bitumen. Care should be taken with adhesives to insure that the solvents and the insulation are compatible. When tongue-and-groove insulation boards are used, a perimeter strap attachment is necessary; this keeps the insulation in one piece, even when water accumulation underneath causes it to "float."

Slope: The recommended slope of the deck is ¼ in. /ft, and slopes of up to 2 in./ft are possible. The manufacturer may provide a warranty for a dead level roof, but level roofs have more leakage problems than sloped roofs.

Maintenance: Maintenance recommendations are less rigid than for a conventional roof. There may be required maintenance of the flashing and need for additional caulking. Due to the possible entrapment of water between the insulation and membrane, plant and mold growth has sometimes been a problem. Pavers should be provided for walking, particularly to areas such as mechanical penthouses that require maintenance. An advantage of this system over a conventional roof is that the foot does not come in direct contact with the membrane. For this reason, pavers are also becoming a popular ballast material. Determining the source of a leak may be difficult if the roof is not fully adhered. If the roof is fully and competently adhered, locating leaks should not be a problem.

GENERAL CONSIDERATIONS

Climate: Climatic criteria often limit the use of the protected membrane. In areas with high wind not only is the gravel ballast a potential hazard to adjacent buildings, but also the insulation boards can be blown away, leaving the membrane exposed. In some areas of the country, such as parts of Florida, hurricane codes do not allow gravel ballasted roof assemblies. For the same reason, ballast roofs are not recommended for highrise buildings.

The insulation should be protected from exposure to sunlight and weather during construction, to insure that its R value is not adversely affected. In cold climates perimeter scupper-type drains are not advisable; the expansion that occurs when standing water freezes might displace insulation boards at the perimeter.

EPDM

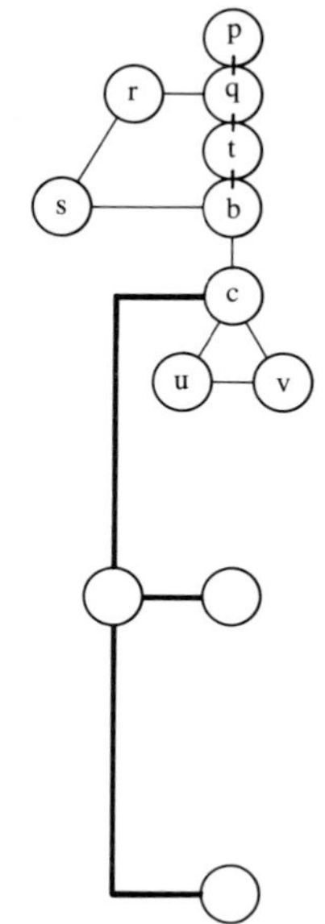

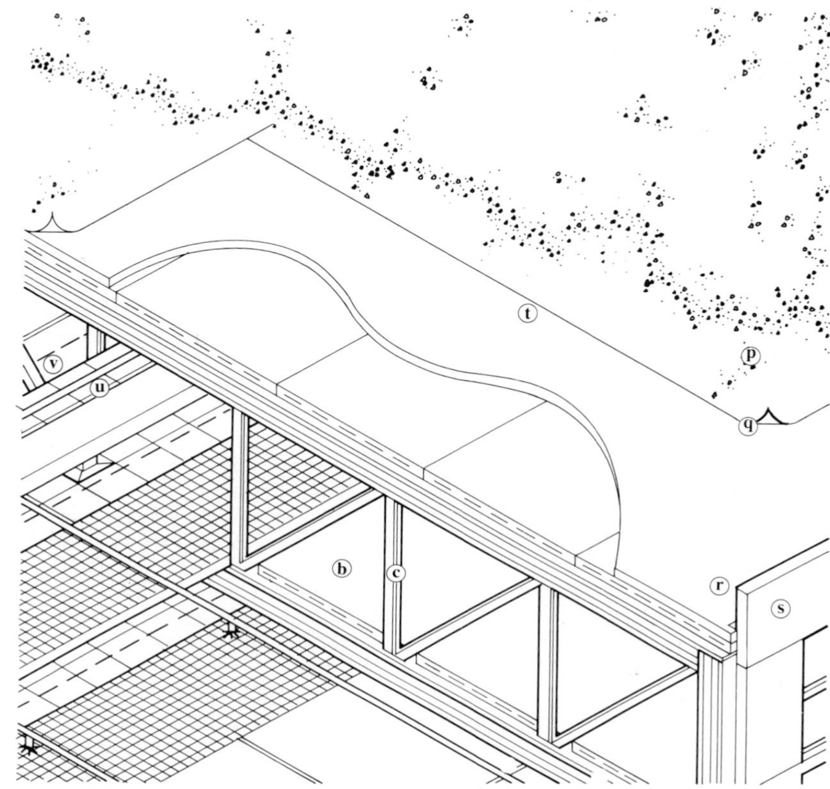

b. *Concrete plank deck*
c. *Steel truss*
p. *Ballast*
q. *EPDM*
r. *Flashing*
s. *Parapet*
t. *Insulation*
u. *Ceiling*
v. *Lighting*

Diagram detail page 337

The EPDM membrane shown in Generic Example Number 6, Staggered Truss, is loose-laid and ballasted to allow for movement in the substrate. Other methods of attachment are fully adhered, mechanically fastened, and partially adhered.

Reviewer:
William T. Lohmann, AIA, FCSI
Murphy/Jahn
Chicago, IL

The acronym EPDM stands for ethylene propylene diene monomer, a thermosetting plastic material originally developed for automobile window gaskets. It is used extensively as a single-ply membrane for roofing. Because of the numerous ways in which it can be used, EPDM single-ply membrane roofing is easily integrated. The fashion of attachment, placement of insulation, roof slope, climate, and weathering conditions do not present restraints that might be encountered in other roofing systems. Because it is a relatively new product, however, roofers may have limited experience with its application. Although ASTM standards are specified for tensile strength and elongation, no specific standards have been developed for EPDM, and documentation of usage is also limited.

Because EPDM does not involve bitumen, the procedures used in asphalt and coal tar application are eliminated. This is a factor not only at the time of installation but also for future repairs and maintenance.[1]

As with any roofing product, penetrations must be carefully designed, and flexibility must be maintained around penetrations for roof stacks, skylights, and drains. Because there is no "backup" layer for the single ply, the detailing and execution are important, especially if a loose-laid ballasted system is selected.

EXAMPLE

An EPDM roof is shown in Generic Example Number 6, Staggered Truss.[2] Sheet-applied membranes, of which EPDM is the most popular, may be loose-laid and ballasted to

1. Conservation of resources and time, pp. 236–237.
2. Staggered truss, pp. 134–135.

accommodate movement in the precast plank substrate. Elimination of asphalt or coal tar application represents an integration of processes with staggered truss construction, which itself minimizes the need for "wet trades."

IMMEDIATE CONSIDERATIONS

Method of attachment: The EPDM membrane may be used as a fully adhered, mechanically fastened, partially adhered, or loose-laid ballasted roof. A fully adhered membrane is costly and requires a solid, smooth substrate, although it may be installed on irregular roof deck surfaces. The partially adhered membrane is mechanically fastened or adhered to a suitable roof deck. This method is useful when a loose-laid roof is not suitable and the membrane must span rooftop expansion joints. The loose-laid ballasted system isolates the membrane from substrate movement and can be installed in almost any weather, but the ballast material imposes a heavier load on the building structure. The EPDM membrane may be used as part of a protected membrane roof assembly.

Color: Membranes are available in white or black. The limited range of colors could restrict EPDM use if a wide range of colors is necessary for coordination and visible integration.[3]

3. Visible integration, pp. 381–385.

Reinforcement: The membrane may be reinforced with fabric or unreinforced.

Rooftop traffic: Like other roof types, EPDM can be punctured, and clearly marked traffic pads should be provided for personnel who need access to the roof.

Flashing: Uncured neoprene is customarily used as a flashing material in conjunction with EPDM membranes. After some exposure to the elements, it cures naturally and becomes less flexible. EPDM flashing is also available.

GENERAL CONSIDERATIONS

Available skilled labor: While single-ply membranes require less labor to install than conventional built-up roofs, roofers must be trained in the proper methods of installation. In addition, EPDM is difficult to field-splice, a process that involves joining two sheets with contact cement. Vulcanized factory-formed seams are much stronger, and these should be used wherever possible.

Building movement: The anticipated movement of the roof deck will determine the desirable elongation properties of the membrane. It should be noted that the elongation of EPDM varies significantly with temperature.

Climate: The climate should influence the choice of roof membrane and roof design. Wind uplift at corners can dislodge ballast or tear an inadequately anchored roof membrane. The amount of exposure to sunlight, and consequently to ultraviolet light and ozone, must also be considered. The expected temperature range is important, although EPDM remains flexible from −75° to +300°F.

Environment: Damage can result from caustic chemicals released nearby or known to be in the environment. The EPDM membrane is not compatible with petroleum oils and gasoline, including asphalt.

Wood Trusses

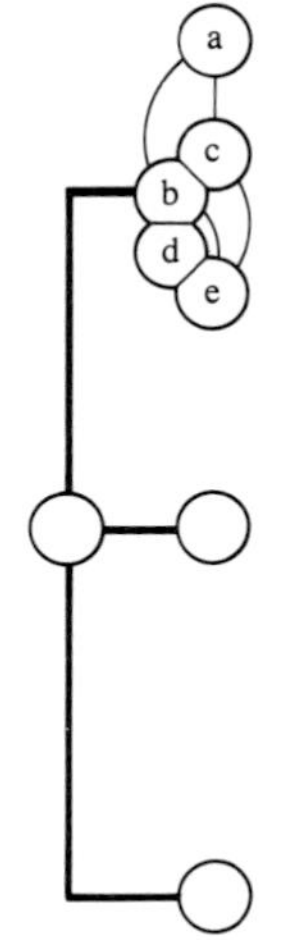

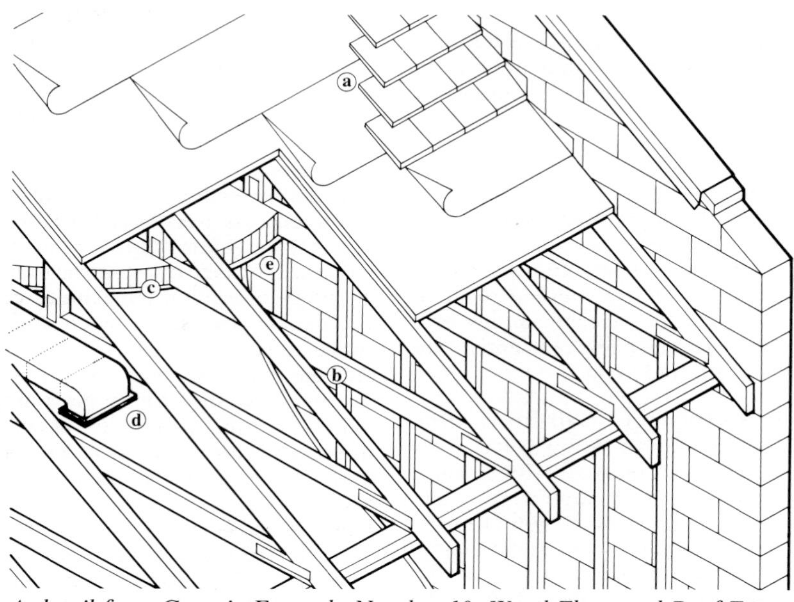

a. *Roofing*
- *Shingles*
- *Metal flashing*
- *Roofing felt*

b. *Wood roof truss and plywood sheathing*
c. *Batt insulation*
d. *Ducts and diffusers*
e. *Acoustical tile ceiling*

Diagram detail page 338

Reviewer:
Kenneth A. Weinstein, AIA
CHK Architects & Planners
Silver Spring, MD

A detail from Generic Example Number 10, Wood Floor and Roof Truss, illustrates the repetition involved in the use of trusses. On larger projects, such as housing developments, this factor can reduce unit cost.

Wood trusses are structural members based on the triangulated composition of smaller members mechanically fastened together. The concept is centuries old. While rules of thumb and trial and error probably determined their design historically, computers help determine the configuration and structural capacity of the trusses used today. Truss design is a very sophisticated procedure, but fortunately it has been systematized to the point where span tables and some advice from the manufacturer make framing design easy.

It has always been more efficient to use a truss but, until recently, it was more expensive at a residential scale to fabricate a truss than to install framing. In less than a decade, volatile lumber prices and rising labor costs engendered a move away from solid floor joists and roof rafters to trusses. Wood trusses are used most often in light commercial and residential construction. In prefabricated residential construction, trusses save construction time, in part because a small crane can lift the roof trusses into place quickly.[1]

1. Conservation of time, pp. 236–237.

Wood trusses are also an economical solution for a long-span structure. Because trusses configure member stresses in terms of either tension or compression, waste material can be minimized in the plane of the truss. Therefore, with the flexible configuration of trusses, it is easy to integrate the space requirements for mechanical systems, which can be threaded through the structure without additional penetrations.[2] The use of trusses in building design requires a great discipline in the dimensioning and positioning of elements coordinating with the trusses. Openings that would routinely be framed in conventional applications must be more judiciously placed, and the possibility of structural weakness from ill-conceived holes in structural members is reduced.

2. Structure and mechanical *meshed*, p. 325.

Trusses conserve time and resources in a variety of ways. The construction process is integrated to the extent that ceiling joists and rafters are set as a unit; the resulting economies of time may be especially important if the weather is a concern. Materials may be further conserved by arranging the trusses at 2 ft centers.[3] Finally, the more trusses used of identical configuration, the greater the savings.

EXAMPLE

Generic Example Number 10[4] shows trusses as they are commonly found in housing. Because the openings between truss members readily accommodate mechanical runs, trusses assume a *meshed* relationship with the mechanical system.[5] They are especially appropriate for use with forced air.

IMMEDIATE CONSIDERATIONS

Configuration: Wood trusses are available in numerous configurations; at a conservative estimate, there are between 70 and 80 variations. The five basic ones now in common use are flat or parallel chord, bowstring, camelback, scissors, and triangular.

Span: Spans of 16 to 200 ft can be accommodated. A 200 ft span is attainable with the bowstring truss.

Fabrication: Wood members may be solid-sawn, glued laminated, or mechanically laminated. The first two methods are the ones most frequently used. The members are either single-leaf, double-leaf, or multiple-leaf. Steel rods may also be used in wood trusses if the structural design requires them.

Connections: Connections at the junctures of web and chord may be made with straps, gussets, split-ring connectors, shear plate connectors, or bolts. Web and chord members are either attached side to side or in the same plane; in the latter case, shear plate connectors are used. A commonly used connector in prefabricated trusses is the truss clip, a type of plate with dozens of nail-like protrusions on one side. When small trusses are field-fabricated, bolted connections are used. Field fabrication of trusses is not recommended without proper supervision.

Shape: A truss can be designed with any pitch required. In a flat chord truss the top chord may be pitched for drainage. Roof shape is related to the span in that some shapes may be best suited to certain spans.

3. Conservation of materials, p. 236.
4. Wood floor and roof truss, pp. 142–143.
5. Structure and mechanical *meshed*, p. 325.

Spacing: In most heavy or long-span trusses, spacing will be 12 to 20 ft apart. When primary members are spaced more than 8 ft apart, secondary framing is necessary to carry the decking. In lighter short-span trusses, spacing will be from 16 in. to 4 ft on center. A spacing of 16 to 24 in. on center is used for light trusses in residential construction.

Structure: Wood trusses can be used in conjunction with most types of vertical supports. Any mechanical connection capable of resisting the load may be used. Joists or purlins run between the trusses and are nailed to the top chords of the trusses and connected to the sides of the chords by ledgers or metal hangers.

Exposed or concealed: Trusses are often left exposed to provide structural expression and for other esthetic reasons.[6] Because conduits and plumbing lines may be easily run through the openings in the truss, a direct hung ceiling is easily installed.

6. Visible integration, pp. 381–385.

Maintenance: Wood trusses require no special maintenance. If exposed, an occasional cleaning may be necessary, or a check for any corrosion of the connectors.

GENERAL CONSIDERATIONS

Fire protection: Wood trusses can be pressure-impregnated with fire-retardant chemicals to obtain a UL rating. Some of these products have been found to increase the moisture absorption properties of the treated wood, resulting in problems with corrosion of the connectors. There are products, however, that will prevent the connectors from corroding in environments having a relative humidity of up to 95 percent. This fire-retardant treatment provides classification as "non-combustible" construction in most building codes, and approximately the same surface burning index as wall board.

Structural Fabric

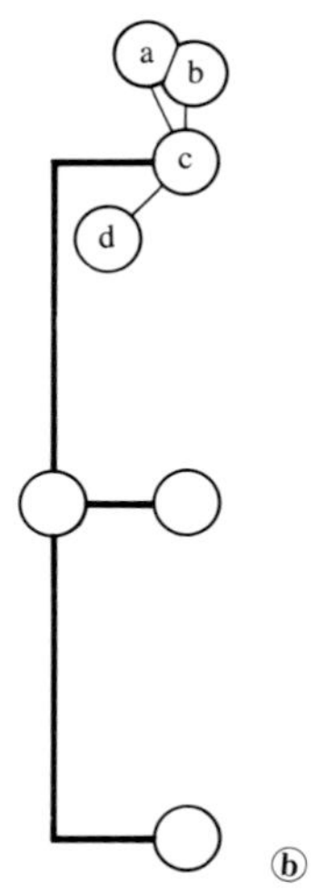

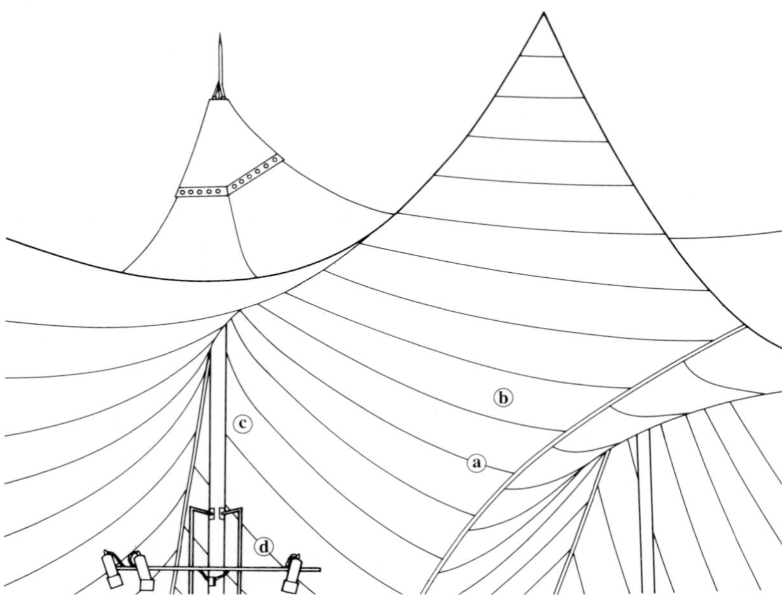

a. *Steel cables in fabric sleeves*
b. *Non-combustible fabric membrane*
c. *Steel masts*
d. *Incandescent light fixtures and sound system speakers*

Diagram detail page 338

Reviewer:
Nicholas Goldsmith
FTL Associates
New York, NY

Generic Example Number 15, Tension Fabric Structure, is mast-supported. Attachments for light fixtures and speakers are visible at lower left. Fabric is cut away near the top of the mast to show details of the cables' attachment.

Structural fabric is coated fabric placed in tension to create a roof or building envelope. This is done either by stretching the fabric over a structural skeleton, by placing it in tension with a cable network, or by air pressure. Developments in the technology of fabric roofs have transformed the industry in recent years. In the past, durability and fire resistance problems restricted fabrics to temporary structures of low fire risk. The trend is now toward structures of as much as thirty-year life expectancy in many fire classifications.

Because they unify structure, envelope, and interior, fabric structures are very demanding on the rest of the systems and on the use of the building as a whole.[1] Fabric is useful as a weight-saving strategy, but it can also be a liability in terms of thermal exchange, security, and acoustical control.[2] As a safety feature, the light weight of fabric is an advantage. Not only do fabric roof failures rarely cause injury, but they are also comparatively quick and economical to repair.[3] Fabric structures are well suited to seismic design because of their relatively greater flexibility and high deflective ability.[4]

Fabric structures in general are extremely precise as to dimensions. They are primarily designed with the aid of computers, with the fabric cut to pattern shapes whose dimensions are determined by computer. Other systems that interface with a fabric roof must reflect the same dimensional accuracy.

EXAMPLE

Teflon coated fiberglass is used in the O'Connell Center,[5] a design that incorporates both air-supported fabric and fabric in simple tension. A single layer of fabric stretched over precast concrete half-arches covers the ancillary spaces; the air-supported dome over the arena space is lined with an inner fabric layer and hanging banners to control sound reflection.

The fabric's four percent translucency allows an acceptable degree of solar gain and daylighting without attendant glare. Little or no day-to-day maintenance is required, although extra fabric is kept on hand

1. Structure and envelope and interior *unified*, pp. 318–320, 333.
2. Thermal performance, pp. 250–251; acoustical performance, p. 254.
3. Conservation of resources and time, pp. 236–237.
4. Performance criteria (seismic), p. 258.
5. O'Connell Center, pp. 108–111.

for repairs. The major problem thus far has been keeping unauthorized persons off the roof.

IMMEDIATE CONSIDERATIONS

Materials: The three types of structural fabric are vinyl coated polyester, fluorocarbon resin (Teflon) coated fiberglass, and silicone coated fiberglass. Vinyl coated fiberglass was initially developed in the 1950's and 1960's for temporary air-supported structures. Teflon coated fiberglass was developed in response to the need for a more durable membrane with lower creep properties. While the glass yarns are more chemically inert than polyester yarns, especially under ultraviolet light, glass yarns do degrade under high moisture. The Teflon coating is inert and resists the effects of most known chemicals and solvents as well as sunlight, moisture, and temperature extremes. The fiberglass is extremely strong in tension and, in combination with the Teflon coating, extremely durable, since the coating protects it from the effects of weather and self-abrasion.

A more recently developed structural fabric, silicone coated fiberglass, combines the properties of the preceding two. The resulting product is more durable than vinyl coated polyester, less fragile in bending than Teflon coated fiberglass, and allows transmission of water vapor. It can be fabricated with translucencies of up to 50 percent, although its fire resistive properties diminish with increased translucency. Another innovation has been the lamination of a Tedlar film on vinyl/polyester fabric, which gives the surface a hard, nonstick quality comparable to Teflon.

Teflon coated and silicone coated fiberglass have a life span of 20 years or more, while the life span for vinyl coated polyester is 8 to 15 years. Teflon coated fiberglass must not be creased in shipping or packing, since it is not flexible in bending. Silicone coated fiberglass has somewhat better handling properties; however, it is not quite as ductile as vinyl coated fiberglass.

Color: Vinyl coated polyester is available in a range of colors, and a selection of colors has been developed for silicone coated fiberglass. Teflon coated fiberglass is oatmeal colored and bleaches to a pure white in the sun.

Structure: In both air-supported and tension structures, form is closely related to structural properties. The curvature produced by the tension of the forms resists design loads. For this reason, design and engineering are completely interdependent processes. While tension structures tend to have high profiles and both positive and negative curves, most air-supported structures have low profiles and double curvature in the same direction, with a ratio of rise to span of .2 or less.

Air-supported structures are inflated by fans that provide constant interior air pressure. Revolving or other air-lock type doors are required to maintain pressure. The inflated fabric must be reinforced with hard structure, such as reinforcing cables, to insure life safety if the air support should fail. In that event, the fabric would remain suspended above the area of occupancy. The edges of the fabric may be secured with clamps. Rope is fused with heat and pressure to the fabric perimeter, providing a continuous anchor, and the edges are then clamped mechanically with lock-nuts.

Air-supported structures generally have low profiles and are minimally affected by wind drag loads, but must contend with wind uplift loads. Rain washes away immediately due to the natural slope of the fabric. Snow loads may be resisted by an increase in air pressure, an increase in the strength of the fabric, or an increase in the amount of heated air on the underside of the fabric to inhibit snow buildup.

In a tension structure, the fabric is stretched in a tent-like fashion from a mast or frame which, together with cables, forms the structure. Compared to tension structures, air-supported structures are designed as a more forgiving stress-release system. Tension structures require

In O'Connell Center, the main arena space is sheltered by an air-supported dome of Teflon coated fiberglass (above). Suspended banners and an inner fiberglass liner are used to control sound reflection. Translucency of the double fabric envelope is four percent. Teflon coated fiberglass is stretched over precast concrete half-arches to form the natatorium and three other ancillary spaces surrounding the arena (right). A detail of the tension roof clamps shows how the two layers of fiberglass are retained by the same clamping devices.

Photos: Balthazar Korab

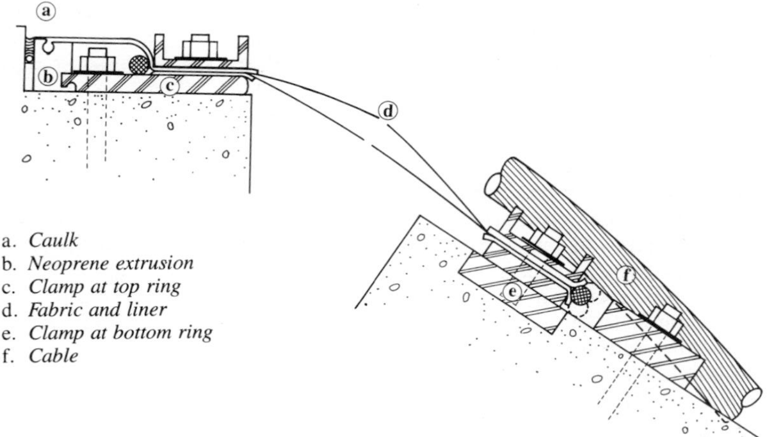

a. *Caulk*
b. *Neoprene extrusion*
c. *Clamp at top ring*
d. *Fabric and liner*
e. *Clamp at bottom ring*
f. *Cable*

DETAIL OF TENSION ROOF CLAMPS

heavier weight fabric to accommodate a higher prestress.

Mechanical: Structural fabrics are integrated with the mechanical system through their daylighting qualities and consequent energy savings.[6] Generally, fabric structures are best utilized where air conditioning loads are high, since high reflectivity (40 to 75 percent) and low to medium translucency are properties of all three fabric types. The U-value of one layer of Teflon coated fiberglass is 1.0, and with two layers it can be reduced to .5. The use of translucent fiberglass insulation between layers of fabric will reduce transmissivity even further and still maintain translucency. In hot weather a fabric structure will transmit overnight more of the heat gained during the day than a conventional structure.

6. Structure and envelope *unified*, p. 324; structure and interior *unified*, p. 326.

Translucency varies with the weave, the thickness of the coating, and the number of layers employed. It can be as low as 4 percent where air conditioning loads are high. Translucency levels as high as 18 percent in Teflon coated fiberglass, 22 percent in vinyl coated polyester, and 80 percent in a single lightweight layer of silicone coated fiberglass can be achieved where the lighting requirements are high. Two layers of silicone coated fiberglass can achieve a minimum translucency of 53 percent. The quality of light is excellent in that there are no heavy shadows, glare is reduced, and natural colors are rendered. The percentage of transmission varies with different wavelengths. Illumination levels with Teflon coated fiberglass vary from 100 to 1,000 footcandles.

Maintenance: Structural fabric is almost self-maintaining. Rain washes dirt and pollution away from the nonstick surface. Tears in vinyl coated polyester can be repaired with a vinyl patch adhered with a compatible adhesive. Silicone coated fiberglass may also be glued, but Teflon coated fiberglass is patched with heat rather than adhesive. Without adequate ventilation, the interior surface of vinyl and Teflon coated fiberglass can develop some plant growth from condensation of interior moisture.

Costs: Fabric structures have a shorter construction time than equivalent conventional buildings. The lighter load means there are savings in the construction costs of the building walls and foundations.[7] Doubling the fabric adds about one-third to the cost per square foot of area covered. Should the fabric wear out, the cost of replacement would probably be one-third of the original cost, since the pattern is predetermined.

GENERAL CONSIDERATIONS

Artificial illumination: The integration of lighting equipment in fabric structures is difficult because it is usually not desirable to attach it to the fabric, if only to avoid penetration of the membrane. Instead, lighting and sound equipment is attached to the structural cables, or to poles or cables installed for the purpose. Fabric roofs reflect light well and spread diffuse, balanced light inside. Therefore, indirect lighting can be used to advantage. In addition, the daylighting potential means that fewer light fixtures are needed.[8]

7. Conservation of materials and time, pp. 236–237.

8. Visual performance, p. 256.

Acoustics: An interior fabric liner is often used to absorb sound under a long-span roof, and this strategy may be applied to an air-supported structure. A domed or conical roof shape focuses sound, and vertical banners or baffles may alleviate this problem.

Fire protection: Teflon coated fiberglass maintains a Class 1 rating in flame spread, with a flame spread of 5 or less and a smoke-developed rating of 5 or less.

Safety: Alarm systems monitor the air pressure in air-supported structures, and trigger supplementary air pressure devices or back-up air systems in case of power failure.

Radiant Heat Panels

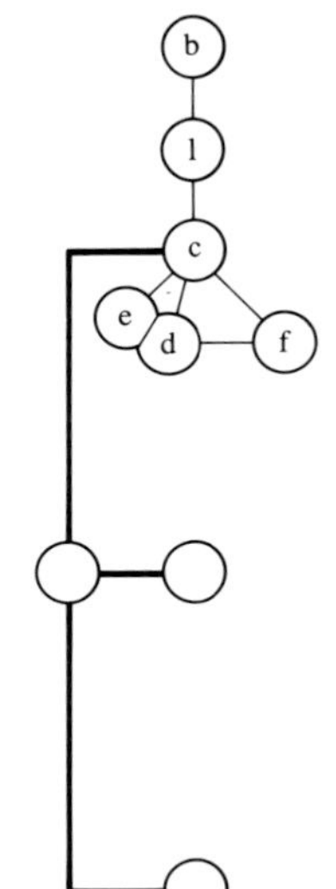

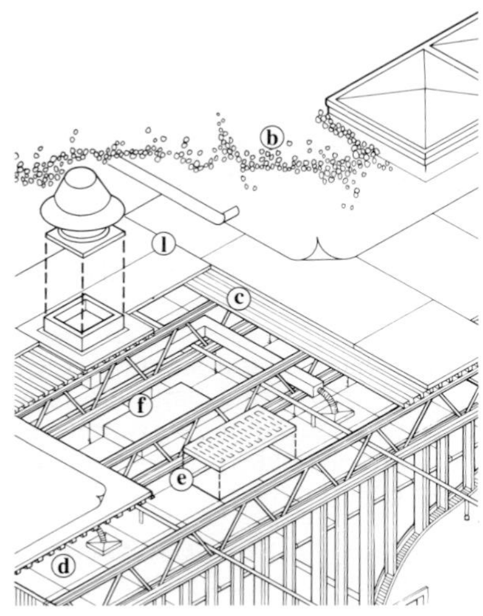

b. *Built-up roofing and rigid insulation*
c. *Roof deck and structure*
d. *Suspended acoustical tile ceiling*
e. *Radiant heat panels*
f. *Fluorescent lighting*
l. *Rigid insulation*

Diagram detail page 338

Reviewers:
Joseph R. Loring, PE
Joseph R. Loring & Associates, Inc.
New York, NY
Harry Misuriello
W.S. Fleming & Associates, Inc.
Washington, DC

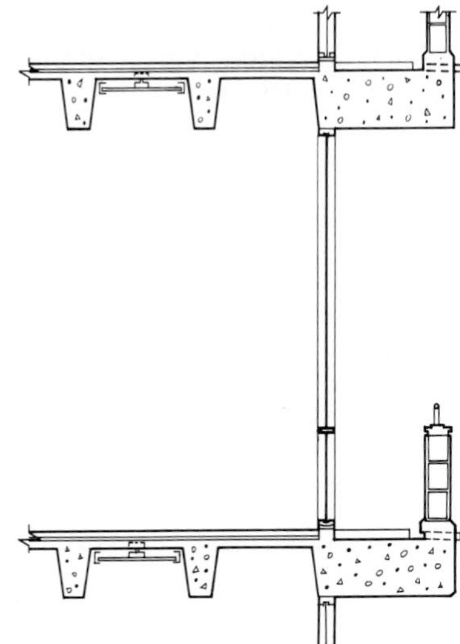

Radiant heat panels are readily integrated with open-web steel joists, as in Generic Example Number 7, Tilt-up Wall (top), and with waffle slabs such as those found in the Pike and Virginia building (above).

Radiant heat panels are electric heating units with no moving parts. They maintain lower temperatures than conventional systems, yet provide good comfort and maintain a higher indoor relative humidity. Using the principle of radiation, the panels heat objects rather than the air.

Radiant heat panels illustrate the principle that overall system efficiency does not always dictate product selection. The high cost of electricity usually means that resistance heating is not the most efficient means of energy conservation for total building thermal exchange. Nevertheless, the choice that arises from the specific function may be different from that suggested by the overall system. For very specific tasks and to satisfy needs of short duration and quick response, radiant heat panels are often the most rational choice.

EXAMPLE

In the Pike and Virginia Building,[1] perimeter forced air is supplemented by radiant heat panels recessed in the coffers of the exposed waffle slab. Radiant panels were selected because, in the absence of a suspended ceiling, they were the least visually obtrusive heat source available.[2]

1. Pike and Virginia Building, pp. 92–93.
2. Visible integration, pp. 381–385.

IMMEDIATE CONSIDERATIONS

Types: Two types of electric heating units are available. In the glass type, the heating element is fused onto specially tempered glass, covered with silicone enamel for protection against corrosion, and then mounted on silicone rubber. A guard covers the unit to protect the glass. In the lightweight type, graphite-based material is laminated between two layers of high dielectric polyester film. The sealed laminate with internal conductors is then bonded to rigid insulation board and the face side oversprayed with a textured finish.

The lightweight panel may only be mounted on the ceiling, either as a drop-in unit integral with the ceiling panels or surface-mounted. Glass panels may be mounted on ceilings, walls, or baseboards. In its ceiling application, the glass panel may be drop-in or surface mounted, and in its wall and baseboard application may either be recessed or surface mounted.

An alternative type of radiant ceiling is composed of aluminum panels clipped to copper pipes through which either hot or chilled water flows. The metal panels are perforated to aid sound absorption and are normally covered with a blanket of insulation, for thermal and acoustical reasons. Two-, three-, and four-pipe systems are available. This system can be cost-effective when both heating and cooling applications are necessary.

Finish: Lightweight panels come with a textured white flame-resistant finish that may be painted with water-based acrylic or latex paints. The glass panel's reflector finish is either stainless steel or polished aluminum.

Size: Lightweight panels range in size from 2 × 2½ ft with 1 in. thickness to 4 × 8 ft; the glass panels are generally smaller, with a maximum dimension of 4 ft. A glass panel unit of 9 × 48 in. will require the same wattage and deliver the same BTUH as a 4 × 4 ft lightweight panel. The 2 × 4 ft lightweight panel is the most popular size.

Installation: Each panel is attached by a connector to supply wiring running directly to the connection box. Surface-mounted panels are mounted with screws, while drop-in panels simply replace the acoustical ceiling tile. The latter require no field assembly or modification. In retrofit situations, radiant heat panels may be more convenient to install than a conventional system.

Controls: Radiant heat panels are extremely useful in a zone-controlled system. The glass panels may be manually or thermostatically controlled, while the lightweight panels, since they are used only in the ceiling, are thermostatically controlled. Options on the thermostatic controls include simple line voltage or low voltage thermostat/contactor combinations, modulating thermostats, or remote sensor/energy management controls.

Radiant heat panels may be used either as the primary heat source or as a supplementary system. When used as a back-up for passive solar heating, they should be sized to provide 100 percent of heat load.

Maintenance and replacement: Lightweight panels require no maintenance. Replacement involves disconnecting and reconnecting the wiring, a matter of 15 to 30 minutes. A five-year warranty is available for most panels.

Appearance: Where visible integration is an issue, the lightweight panels are the obvious choice; their finish more closely matches that of the ceiling material in an office environment. In other applications the panel may become more obvious, and this should be taken into account.[3]

3. Visible integration, pp. 381–385.

GENERAL CONSIDERATIONS

Placement: As a primary heat source, one lightweight panel per average room (assuming dimensions of 10 × 12 ft) is sufficient. The rule of thumb for sizing is 8 to 10 watts/sq ft in a primary unit and 5 to 8 watts/sq ft in a supplemental unit.

In office space, it is wise to locate the panels in the ceiling to facilitate space planning and furniture layout. Panels that provide a supplemental heat source in office space are usually used as perimeter heat. Wall and baseboard mounting results in a 30 to 40 percent loss in radiant efficiency and possible damage to the panel.

Energy use: Radiant heat panels use anywhere from 260 to 1600 watts, depending on their size.

AC system compatibility: Thermostatically controlled panels can be very compatible with zoned or unit air conditioning. Room or zone air conditioning units can be put on the same electrical circuit for first cost savings.

Fire protection: The finish of the lightweight panel has a O flame spread and O smoke generated rating.

Life cycle cost: The lightweight panel manufacturer claims that they are at least 35 percent more cost-effective than electric heat pumps or unit heaters, gas- or oil-fired air/hot water heating, and even zoned baseboard.

Exposed Ducts

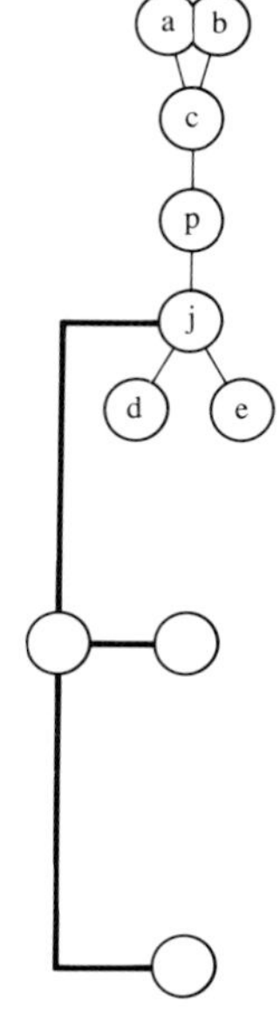

a. *Electrical conduit*
b. *Roofing*
c. *Plywood sheathing*
d. *Exposed ducts*
e. *Incandescent light fixture*
j. *Exposed wood frame*
p. *Exposed wood decking*

Diagram detail page 339

Reviewer:
Joseph R. Loring, PE
Joseph R. Loring & Associates, Inc.
New York, NY

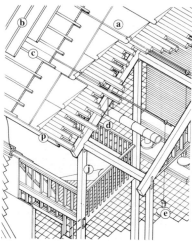

Ducts and structure are exposed in Generic Example Number 11, Laminated Wood Post and Beam.

With the emergence of energy-conscious design, the decision whether to expose ductwork has become an important one. Ducts have become symbolic of energy efficiency in buildings. By eliminating the hung ceiling, exposed ductwork can play an important role in the composition and visible integration of a space.[1]

Other choices follow upon the decision to expose the ducts. Are they to be treated in the same way as concealed ducts, or painted and detailed more carefully? Is their shape appropriate to the existing geometry of the space? Do they turn where the rest of the space would like to see them turn? Normally ducts are round or rectangular and are tapered as the demand for conditioned air decreases with distance (or increases, in the case of return air). Such changes in size and location may easily work counter to the direction intended for movement of occupants in the room.

The highest level of integration ductwork achieves is a *meshed* one with respect to diffusers, air boots on light fixtures, and other diffusing elements. Maintenance and accessibility for dampers and control devices is an issue, as are the installation problems of the various trades involved.

Exposing ducts introduces the opportunity for either heat loss or heat gain, both of which can be controlled with interior duct insulation. Ductwork need not be insulated if it traverses a conditioned space, as long as temperature differentials are accounted for in heat load calculations. When ductwork traverses an unconditioned space, such as a storage room, it must be insulated to prevent condensation which could cause rusting or damage to stored materials.

Exposing the ducts usually means that the structure is also in view, so that it becomes an interior surface definition. Lighting equipment, wiring, and pipes are often exposed as well. The apparent height of the space is therefore not the distance from the floor to the hung ceiling but the distance from the floor to the structural slab. The actual floor-to-floor height may then be reduced, saving space.[2]

Ducts at the floor level are rarely exposed owing to the safety hazard, and because they are not often run in the wall in any case. Few spaces are used so casually as to permit a view of the wiring or pipes outside the walls, and these elements represent a hazard when within the reach of small children.

EXAMPLES

The Museum of Science and Industry[3] has exposed ductwork in some locations. Insulated double-wall round ducts are used, and the duct size is not modified for visual reasons. Special hangers were fabricated for the exposed ducts in this project.

The exposed ducts on the west and south facades of the National Permanent Building[4] represent a major visual statement. Round ducts are painted black and decrease in diameter as they descend, in contrast to the exposed round columns which decrease in diameter as they rise.

IMMEDIATE CONSIDERATIONS

Visible integration: From a functional perspective, the design of exposed ducts need not be any differ-

1. Visible integration levels, pp. 381–385.

2. Conservation of space, p. 236.

3. Museum of Science and Industry, pp. 74–77.

4. National Permanent Building, pp. 90–91.

ent than that of concealed ducts. Detailing, however, is extremely important. For the sake of visual continuity, some designers prefer the ducts to be of a uniform size instead of tapered. Many installers prefer to maintain the same duct size even in concealed locations, and especially when small ducts are used, because it is easier to achieve air balance without tapering. Normal sheet metal accessories such as hangers, clips, and connections do not have a pleasing appearance, and some have sharp edges. For this reason, special accessories could be considered.

Color: Ducts, unlike pipes, are not usually color-coded. If they are painted, color will not confuse maintenance personnel.

Diffuser locations: Essentially, exposed ductwork can be designed in the same way as concealed ducts, with diffuser locations located according to the proposed space plan. Diffusers, like ducts, may not always occur in the most visually desirable place. They can be relocated or redesigned for compatibility, provided proper air distribution is maintained.

Cost effectiveness: Exposing ducts saves money by eliminating the finished ceiling. Nevertheless, the special design problems encountered in providing visual continuity can be costly. The volume of the interior space is also a factor in determining the amount of air to be circulated. Exposed ducts are less obvious in very high spaces. Exposing ducts with a high ceiling that stratifies the air often produces a situation that will require more air circulation than if a lower suspended ceiling were used. In such situations, air distribution devices are often located to heat and cool only the lower portion of the space.

GENERAL CONSIDERATIONS

Fire protection: Exposed ducts have the same fire protection requirements as concealed ducts. The use of fire dampers is the same as it would be for concealed ducts in a given application.

Acoustics: Noise transmission through the ductwork should always be analyzed, especially if the terminal fitting is a short distance from the air handler. Fan noise is usually controlled by sound traps in the fan housing. Additional acoustical control may be achieved by placing an acoustical lining inside the duct, which will increase its size.

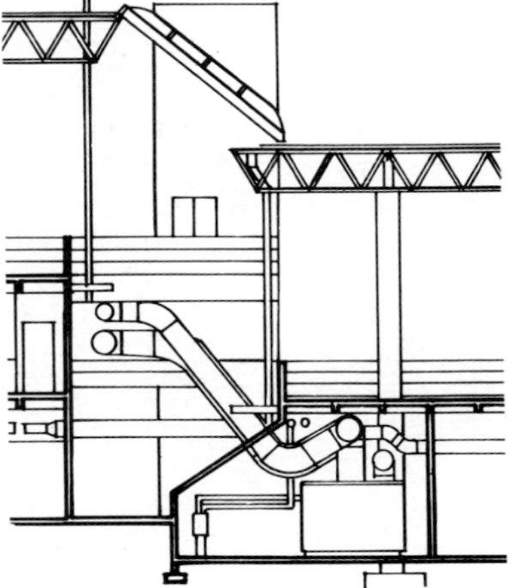

Photo: Gordon H. Schenck, Jr.

Brightly painted and strongly articulated exposed ductwork is used to define semi-outdoor spaces in the Museum of Science and Industry (top and above).

Photo: Howard N. Kaplan

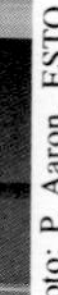

Photo: P. Aaron, ESTO

Photo: Balthazar Korab

Although the deciding factor in the selection of exposed ducts is whether the space will accept them, they are found in a variety of spaces and building types. Set at an oblique angle and painted bright blue, they contribute to the intriguing geometries of the Illinois Regional Library (top left). In Moscone Center, ducts are fully exposed in meeting rooms and hallways and partially concealed between the arches in the exhibit hall (top right). In the Herman Miller plant, brightly painted ducts, electrical and utility lines, and open-web steel joists lend detail to factory and office areas (above).

Integrated Ceilings

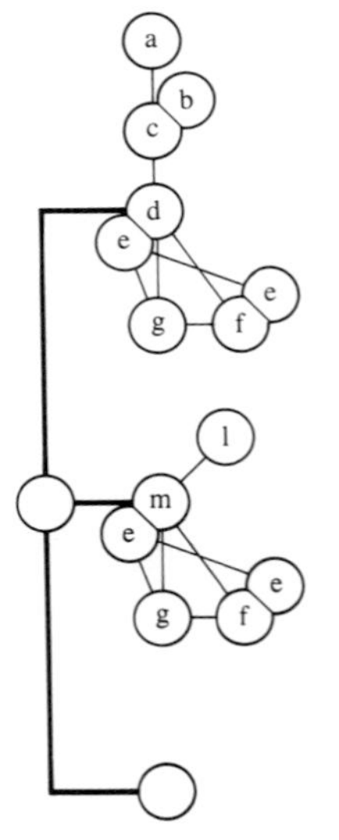

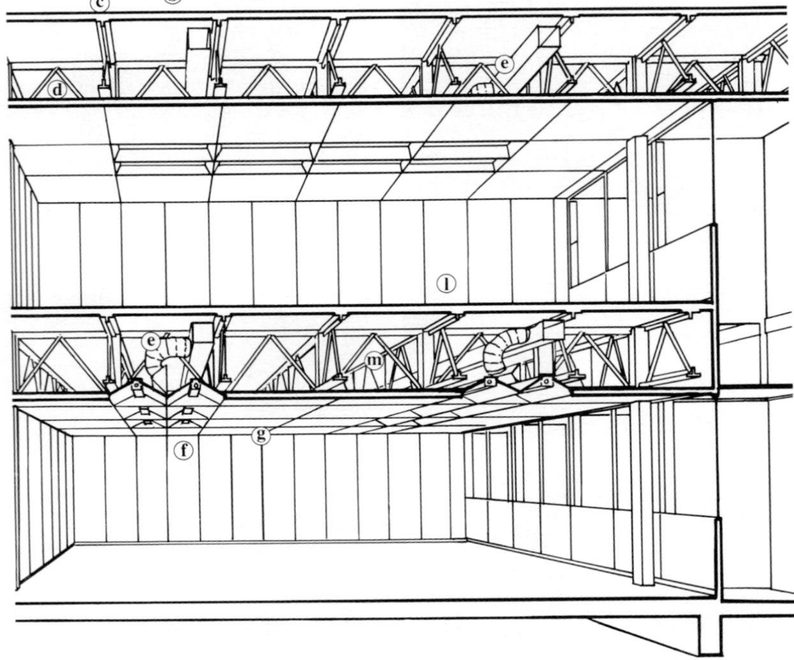

a. *Roofing*
b. *Batt insulation*
c. *Metal roof deck*
d. *Steel bar joists*
e. *Ducts*
f. *Air-handling luminaires*
g. *Lay-in ceiling*
l. *Ceramic tile*
m. *Steel bar joists and metal floor deck*

Diagram detail page 339

Integrated ceilings were among the subsystems chosen for Stockton State College. This design choice was in keeping with the overriding need to conserve time in order to meet this project's unusually tight schedule.

Reviewers:
Gary A. Hall
Hammel, Green & Abrahamson
Minneapolis, MN

Harry Misuriello
W.S. Fleming & Associates, Inc.
Washington, DC

Integrated ceilings are modular systems in which all ceiling components (lighting, diffusers, sound masking, and finish) ideally are supplied by one manufacturer to provide visible integration and functional continuity in the finish ceiling.[1] They are most commonly used in conjunction with an open office plan[2] and in malls, atriums, and other open areas.

There are two types of integrated ceilings available: the grid type with lay-in acoustical panels and the linear type composed of spliced sections of metal pans or planks. Both involve a close relationship between mechanical and interior and require careful coordination of these systems. Integrated ceilings are usually bid as a package, and it is very difficult to delete components in the shop drawing phase. Care must also be taken that esthetics are not emphasized to the detriment of performance. Manufacturers will advise architects on a ceiling design that achieves both a good appearance and good performance.

Although visible integration issues may be paramount for the designer, the major economic motivation for using an integrated ceiling is conservation of time.[3] Because there are fewer components in an integrated ceiling, there are fewer time-consuming decisions to be made in their selection. If a competent, preselected manufacturer advises the architect during the design phase, design time can be saved as well. And because the entire assembly comes from one supplier and can arrive in the same truck, there is no waiting for one component or another to be delivered.

Some architects and engineers who have had good experience with a particular manufacturer find that allowing that manufacturer to design and install a ceiling based on performance specifications can improve results. This approach is useful when design time is limited or

1. Visible integration, pp. 381–385.
2. Open plan office furniture, pp. 196–199.
3. Conservation of time, pp. 236–237.

coordination between members of the design team is difficult.

Problems can arise when the systems that are coordinated must respond to ones that are not. This affects installation when the trades that install the ceiling have strict divisions of labor. Visible integration is affected when the rest of the space must correspond to the esthetic of the ceiling in order to achieve continuity. Breaches of the ceiling due to penetrations unusual to the design of the ceiling can result in fire protection problems.

EXAMPLES

The custom-designed integrated ceiling in the Aid Association for Lutherans Headquarters[4] is one of that building's most distinctive elements. The integrated ceiling used at Stockton State College[5] is a standard manufactured version that incorporates air-handling luminaires[6] and fire and smoke detection devices. Partitions do not penetrate the ceiling except where acoustical privacy is critical. Numerous revisions in the space plan, made necessary by the owner's changing needs, have been accomplished quickly and have proven the flexibility of this integrated ceiling.

4. Aid Association for Lutherans, pp. 62–63.
5. Stockton State College, pp. 78–81.
6. Air-handling luminaires, pp. 185–186.

IMMEDIATE CONSIDERATIONS

Light fixtures: Type and placement should be determined based on the number of watts per square foot required. Most types of light fixtures can be incorporated in an integrated ceiling assembly, but not all manufacturers carry a full range of light fixtures.

Diffusers: Integrated ceilings commonly employ linear diffusers connected to ducts by means of a metal or fiberglass boot or manifold. The unused portion of the diffuser is masked or blocked above the ceiling. In the grid type of ceiling the finished appearance is that of a continuous diffuser in the suspension grid, while the linear ceilings incorporate the diffusers between the metal pans. Some manufacturers offer a wide variety of diffusers, although the differences between them may be largely a matter of appearance.

Panels: The type of acoustical panel chosen for a grid ceiling has a profound effect on its appearance and performance. The panel types vary from traditional flat lay-in panels to vaulted or coffered fiberglass forms and vinyl-faced batt insulation.

Metal spans: These are typically 4 to 6 in. wide. They are available in alu-

Photo: GBQC

Among the criteria governing the selection of the integrated ceiling at Stockton State College was the requirement that it be adaptable to many different types of spaces, including the library shown here.

minum and steel, the latter being less expensive, and come in a wide variety of finishes and colors.

Costs: Integrated ceilings can be very cost-effective and provide excellent service if properly designed and used. They work best when used within open spaces. It should be borne in mind that in order for the ceiling to be most cost-effective, all components should be supplied by one manufacturer. Problems can arise when, for example, the low bidder for the ceiling does not have a diffuser that satisfies the mechanical engineer. Components by different manufacturers can and frequently are used in integrated ceiling systems, but compatibility problems can arise and cost-effectiveness is decreased.

Ceiling type: The configuration and material of the acoustical panels or metal pans have a direct bearing on the acoustical and illumination factors in the space.

The grid type of ceiling can be customized to fit an enclosed office, but the problems of closure when finishing off field-cut metal pans make the linear type difficult to use with partitions. The linear type has three main advantages: it can be easily formed in curves; it is available in a wide range of colors; and it can be used on the exterior if visual continuity is desired at a soffitt. Furthermore, the means of suspension can be reinforced to resist suction or negative pressures. Reinforcement, however, may result in cutting and fitting problems. The ceiling elements can be customized to include both exterior and interior use, but not without difficulty. Penetrations and closure can be problematic, and joints between sections are visible. The linear system is best applied in airport terminals, shopping malls, and other large open spaces that are unlikely to need full-height partitions.

Maintenance: An integrated ceiling is no more difficult to maintain than a conventional suspended ceiling. In the grid type, moisture-resistant or soil-resistant panels should be used the same as they would be in a conventional suspended ceiling. The metal pans used in the linear type dent easily, and should be located out of reach.

GENERAL CONSIDERATIONS

Acoustical performance: In office applications, the panel or pan material should have a high noise reduction coefficient (NRC) to cut down on reflected sound. In spaces with solid partitions, a ceiling material with a low sound transmission coefficient (STC) should be used to prevent sound transfer to adjacent rooms. In open office plans, electronic sound masking is usually desirable.[7]

7. Acoustical performance, p. 254.

A variety of insulating materials are available for use above the ceiling, and are especially useful with metal pans. The most commonly used types are unfaced or black-faced fiberglass batts and semirigid mineral board. Metal pans may also be perforated to enhance acoustical performance.

Fire resistance: While each component of an integrated ceiling may be fire-rated, very few systems are classified as UL fire-rated assemblies. Where a fire-rated assembly is required by code, an integrated ceiling is probably not a good choice since the spacing, size, and degree of penetrations are severely restricted and must be duplicated exactly in a rated assembly. Sprinkler penetrations, if any, must also be part of the system.

Air-Handling Luminaires

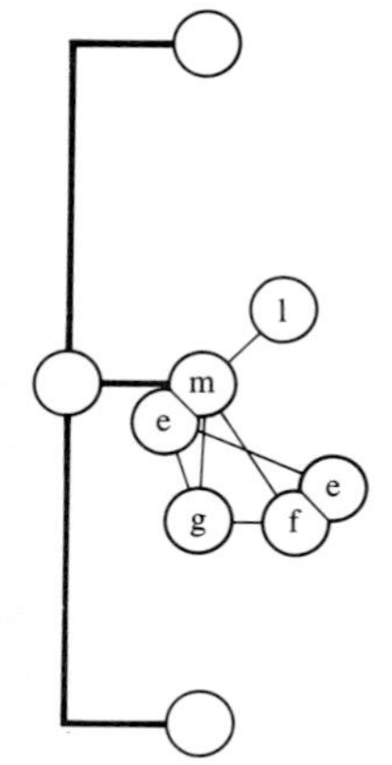

e. *Ducts*
f. *Air-handling luminaires*
g. *Lay-in ceiling*
l. *Ceramic tile*
m. *Steel bar-joists and metal floor deck*

Diagram detail page 339

Reviewers:
Gary A. Hall
Hammel, Green & Abrahamson
Minneapolis, MN

Harry Misuriello
W.S. Fleming & Associates, Inc.
Washington, DC

The integrated ceilings at Stockton State College incorporate air-handling luminaires in many of the public spaces.

Air-handling luminaires are recessed ceiling fixtures that provide either air supply and return or simply air return, depending on the needs of the HVAC system. They have both visual and functional advantages. Visible integration occurs when the mechanical component is not readily visible; in this case the return air grille, with or without the diffuser, is concealed in the light fixture.[1] Functionally, air-handling luminaires allow the heat of the illumination to be drawn away with return air, reducing the amount of heat transmitted to the space and allowing the luminaire to run cooler and more efficiently. Thus, air-handling luminaires conserve resources in office applications, where much of the HVAC load is cooling rather than heating.

Their design conforms to the criteria for conventional light fixtures placed in a suspended ceiling grid. The advantage of accommodating two functions in one ceiling penetration is balanced by the need to relocate both air handling and lighting when revising the space. A single lighting arrangement that applies to most furniture configurations saves time.

If task lighting is used with the system, the frequency of the air supply or return may be less, and additional grilles or diffusers may be required. This is generally not the case where a lighting fixture module for ambient lighting is provided.

1. Visible integration, pp. 381–385.

EXAMPLE

Air-handling luminaires are used in many of the public spaces of Stockton State College.[2]

2. Stockton State College, pp. 78–81.

IMMEDIATE CONSIDERATIONS

Light sources: Available light sources are fluorescent, mercury or metal halide, and incandescent; fluorescent is the most commonly used. Fixtures may use parabolic louvers (open baffle) or photometric diffuser lenses of prismed acrylic.

Air handling: Air supply and return are commonly handled through boots attached to two sides of the luminaire. Air is supplied through recessed air slots, generally one-half inch wide. Air return may either be through slots into the lamp compartment and into the plenum or directly to the plenum.

When air slots are used both for supply and return, about one-third of the slot will be for supply and two-thirds for return. The air can be returned without air slots when parabolic louvers are used. When air slots are not used for return, air may be returned through the lamp compartment and out holes punched in the fixture to the plenum. The return of air through the lamp compartment, or heat extraction, is not used with incandescent lamps since the heat of the lamp cannot be as efficiently extracted. Heat extraction with fluorescent and mercury or metal halide lamps increases their efficiency. Mercury and metal halide lamps are not often used, however, since fewer lamps provide the necessary lighting levels, and the number of fixtures in turn is inadequate for heat extraction.

Dimensions: Fluorescent fixtures are available in 2 × 4 ft, 2 × 2 ft, 1 × 4 ft, 1 × 1 ft, and 4 × 4 ft sizes. The 2 × 4 ft size is used most often.

Rectangular mercury and metal halide fixtures are 2 × 2 ft, with round fixtures available in various dimensions. In general, overall dimensions of the air-handling luminaire are the same as those of the standard light fixture. A fluorescent fixture with air boot and flexible ducting is typically between 7 and 9 in. deep. The bulb size for mercury or metal halide fixtures requires a depth between 20 and 25 in.

Air capacity: Air capacity is a function of the HVAC requirements and the number and placement of the fixtures; a 2 × 4 ft fluorescent luminaire with air supply on two sides has a maximum capacity of 200 cfm. The choice of capacity also depends on the acceptable noise level. A damper control, accessible through the fixture, may be located in the air boot.

Controls: Controls are the same as for standard light fixtures. Dimming may be accomplished manually, through photocells or ultrasonic controls, or with time switches.

Placement and spacing: Placement and spacing are variables of the lighting level and HVAC requirements. Fixtures are usually arranged in a linear pattern to aid connection to the HVAC ducts, but if flexible ducting is used for attachment this is not critical. The function of the space may dictate the location of the luminaires, particularly in office spaces that require a flexible layout. In such cases the light fixtures, whether air-handling or not, must be capable of change. The supply air boots of air-handling luminaires may be relocated.

Lighting levels: In luminaires that draw air through the fixture, the passage of air over the light source increases the light output by as much as 15 percent. This may result in increased lighting levels or a reduction of lamp and wattage requirements. In one application a lighting level of 90 ESI footcandles at task locations was achieved, as compared to 50 ESI footcandles with conventional light fixtures.

Maintenance: Drawing return air through the fixture helps to keep it and the lamp clean. The fixture will therefore require less maintenance. The life of the lamp will not be affected, but that of the ballast may be since it will remain at a cooler temperature than in a standard fixture. The fixture's lens or baffle is usually hinged, with a latch concealed in the half-inch recess at the perimeter. If easy access is required to the plenum without disturbing the ceiling panels, the lamp may be hinged as well. Cleaning is required at five-year intervals in a clean office environment. Adjacent ceiling tiles may need frequent cleaning, since the dirty, smoke-laden return air can soil the area around the grille.

GENERAL CONSIDERATIONS

Ceiling: Increasing the number of runs for the ductwork requires that the length of run be minimized, which in turn requires that the ductwork be *meshed* with the ceiling and the structure from which the ceiling is hung.[3] Bar joist construction or flat plate configurations are less likely to conflict with such mechanical options than concrete beam and slab solutions.[4]

The ceiling configuration itself can be affected by the choice of air-handling luminaires. Coffered ceilings may cause complications in the air-handling function. The placement of sprinkler heads also complicates coordination of the systems.

Flexibility: One advantage of air-handling luminaires is their flexibility for supply air location.The cost of changing and relocating a conventional air supply system should be weighed against that of relocating the supply air boots on luminaires. There is, however, a fixed level of integration inherent in air-handling luminaires, one which demands a high degree of coordination among air supply, lighting esthetics, and acoustics.

Construction coordination: Coordination involves the installation of the fixture by the electrical trade and of the flexible duct by the mechanical trade. The hook-up between the two is usually done by the sheet metal (or mechanical) trade.

3. Structure and mechanical *meshed*, p. 325.
4. Flat-plate or bar-joist systems, pp. 130–131 and pp. 138–139.

Elevators

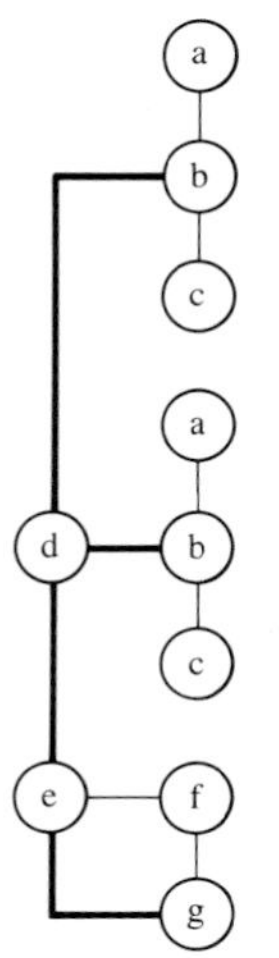

a. *Concrete topping*
b. *Precast prestressed concrete double T's*
c. *Fluorescent light fixtures*
d. *Precast concrete columns and spandrel beams*
e. *Elevator and stair core*
f. *Hydraulic elevator and elevator equipment*
g. *Slab on grade and cast-in-place concrete piles*

Diagram detail page 340

Reviewers:
William S. Lewis
Jaros, Baum & Bolles
New York, NY

George F. Strakosch
Jaros, Baum & Bolles
New York, NY

Harry Misuriello
W.S. Fleming & Associates, Inc.
Washington, DC

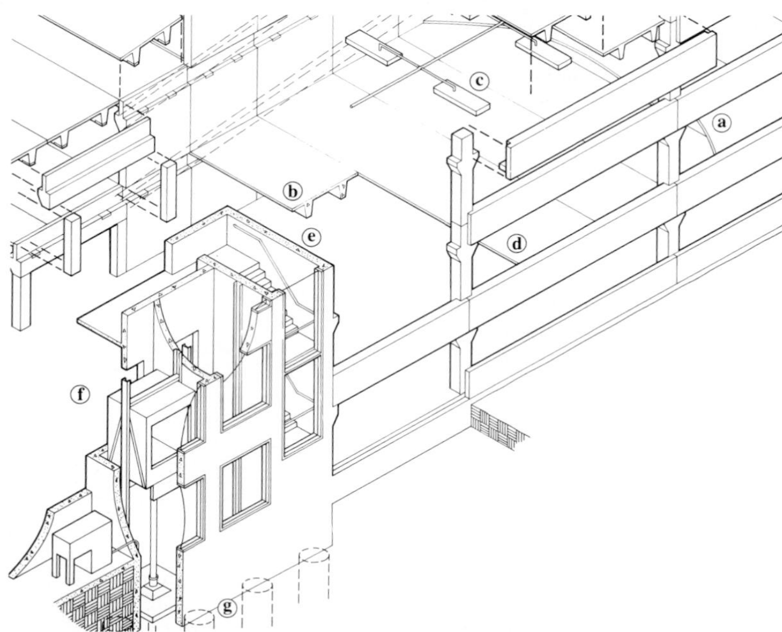

A hydraulic elevator of the kind customarily found in lowrise construction is shown in Generic Example Number 5, Precast Frame. This type of equipment, while slower and less economical to operate than the electric type, is less costly to install for the height shown because it does not require a mechanical penthouse.

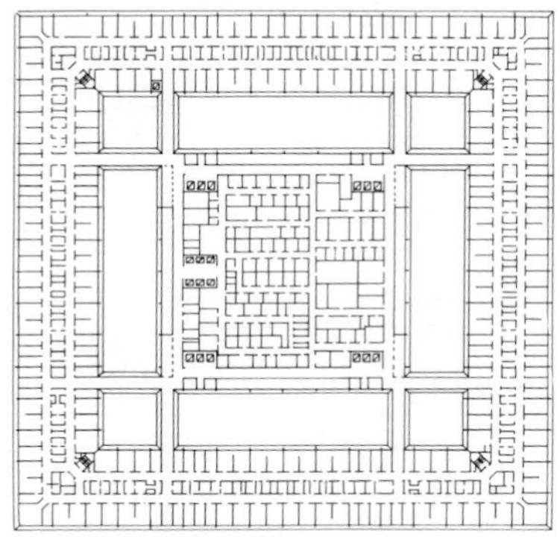

WALTER REED FLOOR PLAN

Elevators are the vertical part of a fully integrated interior circulation system for a multistory building. They complement ramps, stairs, and escalators. In hospitals and office buildings, elevators can be designed in conjunction with other smaller vertical lifts. They save time and space,[1] yet they often represent the most sophisticated mechanical subsystem in a building. An elevator is a highly specialized product engineered to meet specific loading and speed requirements. Because of the extensive variety of elevator sizes, shapes, speeds, and arrangements, it is essential that an elevator consultant or manufacturer's representative be part of the design team.

The major concern in elevator design and procurement is maintenance. A measure of redundancy is required in the design to insure that there will be adequate service when one or more elevators are out of service for repairs. Elevators are also among the least forgiving elements in a building, in that it is extremely difficult to alter or extend them after a building is constructed. Careful initial planning and understanding of horizontal and vertical circulation of pedestrians and materials are essential to the design of a successful vertical transportation system, and consultation with a firm specializing in elevator applications engineering is advisable.

Inadequate elevator service can render an otherwise successful building functionally obsolete in

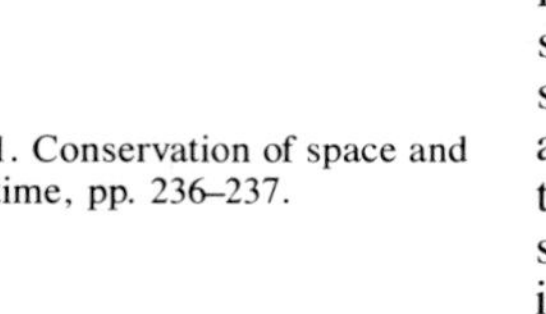

1. Conservation of space and time, pp. 236–237.

two ways. First, a building with units leased to tenants or units sold as condominiums can be difficult to market if elevator service is perceived as inadequate. Second, improperly designed elevators mean extensive waiting times and lead to other traffic congestion problems, all of which waste the productive time of employees.

The opportunity to modernize an elevator and bring it into compliance with current codes usually occurs as part of a building renovation. Custom design is often necessary, and close cooperation with code officials and elevator specialists is required.

EXAMPLES

Walter Reed General Hospital[2] presents a good example of the variety of demands imposed on the vertical transportation system in a hospital, including the need for exclusive use at certain places and times. The elevator system is required to accommodate normal hospital staff and patient traffic in addition to manually wheeled carts, stretchers, and beds. A separate elevator bank for visitors is located near the entrance lobby. A distinction is also made between clean and soiled elevators, the latter handling incoming bulk freight. Dedicated lifts serve the monorail cart system, while small articles are handled by pneumatic tubes and a high-speed modular minirail system.

The Atlanta/Hartsfield International Airport[3] requires vertical transportation between its underground spine and the terminal and concourses. Both hydraulic and electric elevators are used, spanning vertical distances of 65 ft. While escalators handle the greatest volume of people, elevators are included for use by the handicapped and others who prefer not to take the escalators.

The elevator core in the Pike and Virginia Building[4] was purposely placed outside the building perimeter to allow the ductile structural frame within the building to resist seismic loads independently. This electric traction installation uses solid state controls.

The elevator shaft in Generic Example Number 5[5] is used structurally to provide horizontal shear resistance.

IMMEDIATE CONSIDERATIONS

Traction: Hydraulic elevators are slower, limited in rise, and slightly higher in energy consumption than electric traction elevators.

Control options: Solid-state control systems are currently standard for high speed traction elevators, and microprocessors available from manufacturers make it possible to program elevator groups to meet changing demands. Standby power, emergency lighting, handicapped signaling, and earthquake and vibration sensors can be specified. Electrical integration of the elevator with a life safety, fire protection, or building security system is possible, although such designs must address the needs of all occupants, including wheelchair users.

Solid-state power conversion: Solid-state power conversion eliminates the customary motor-generator set. This may require special electrical filtering; however, all vibrating elevator equipment needs acoustical isolation to reduce the harmonics to an acceptable level.[6] Electrical harmonics can be a serious problem in computer or medical facilities if filters are not used.

Quantity, size, speed, and capacity: Preliminary formulas for estimating the number of elevators required are given in *Architectural Graphic Standards* and *Vertical Transportation: Elevators and Escalators*. A wide range of options is available with regard to size, speed, and capacity, but their selection must be specific to the particular installation in order to avoid congestion. Elevator passenger-handling capacity can be increased by the size, number, and speed of cabs. Special options include double-deck cabs that use the same shaft. Operation type will directly influence response time, operating efficiency, energy consumption, and user satisfaction.

Signal equipment: Signals can be designed to match the building's

2. Walter Reed General Hospital, pp. 82–85.
3. Atlanta International Airport, pp. 116–119.
4. Pike and Virginia Building, pp. 92–93.
5. Precast frame, pp. 132–133.
6. Acoustical performance, p. 254.

7. Visible integration, pp. 381–385.

needs. Equipment such as car position indicators, control panels, and call buttons are standard with each manufacturer. Options include braille buttons, digital displays, music, audible signals, and voice synthesizers.

Finishes: One consideration is the visible integration of both the interior and exterior of the elevator cab with the rest of the building,[7] particularly if the lobby or the cab and elevator shaft are exposed to the atrium. In recent years elevators have been used as a focus of attention in large atrium spaces. Many standard finishes are offered which can optimize visual impact and visible integration, and custom finishes are also available.

Considerations of maintenance and durability should enter into their selection as well. Hospitals, for example, routinely scrub down elevators intended for patients. Finishes applied to the face of the hoistway and the elevator cab doors can deteriorate over time.

Emergency services: Even where not required by local codes, the following requirements of the ANSI/ASME A17.1 advisory code should be considered: emergency lights, standby power, two-way communications, and top and side emergency exits. The A17.1 code also requires the fireman's operation feature. With this option, smoke detectors or a fire alarm will cause all elevators to be returned to the main lobby and parked with their doors open. The elevator controls will then be inoperable except by the fire department, which can control the cab operating panel by means of a special key.

GENERAL CONSIDERATIONS

Location: The elevator group should be visible from the building entrance but distant enough to prevent lobby congestion. Care must be taken to locate the shaft properly. When exposed to outside entrances, especially loading docks, the elevator hoistways can provide a channel to pull cold air into a building when the elevator ascends and push warm air out when it descends. Improper sealing of the building or an unbalanced HVAC system can also induce a stack effect in an elevator hoistway.

Security: This can be a significant problem where an elevator provides easy access and egress for intruders, particularly if the areas it serves are difficult to monitor. Key switches or magnetic cards can be used to restrict access when desirable. Security within the elevator cab is more difficult to provide. A convex mirror, mounted in the rear of the cab near the ceiling, allows the user to see everyone in the cab before entering. A closed-circuit TV camera monitored by security personnel is another option, although a more costly one.

Shaft: The elevator shaft can be used structurally to provide horizontal shear resistance for flexible frame buildings.

Shaft enclosure: Codes require that the shaftway and machine room construction be fire-rated. Glass shafts are becoming increasingly popular for certain retail and commercial applications, and these must be custom-designed. The use of transparent shafts on the building exterior presents additional maintenance and security problems.

Escalators

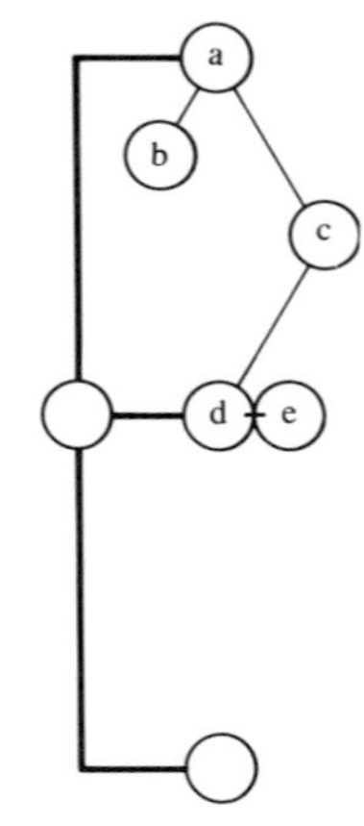

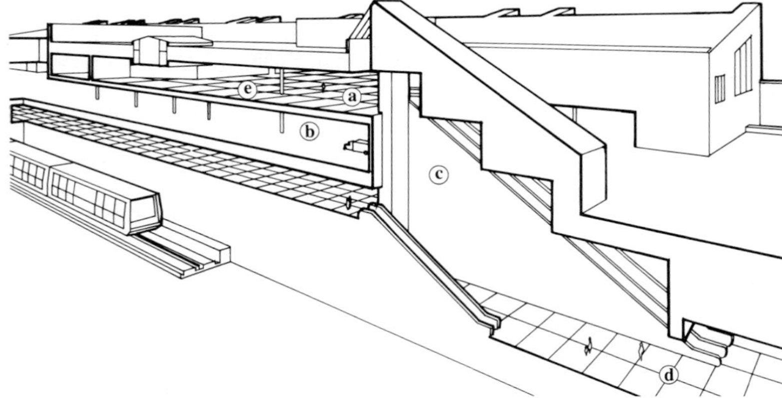

Large-capacity escalators are vital to meeting the circulation requirements of the Hartsfield International Airport in Atlanta. The section perspective shows escalators connecting the terminal and the underground spine.

a. *Upper floor structure*
b. *Ceiling*
c. *Escalator*
d. *Lower floor structure*
e. *Carpet*

Diagram detail page 341

Reviewers:
William S. Lewis
Jaros, Baum & Bolles
New York, NY

George R. Strakosch
Jaros, Baum & Bolles
New York, NY

Harry Misuriello
W.S. Fleming & Associates, Inc.
Washington, DC

Escalators, like elevators, are used in buildings where the vertical rise is too great for pedestrians to climb comfortably without mechanical aid. They are especially useful in situations where speed of movement is important and where there are large numbers of people to be moved. Thus they are well suited to the circulation requirements of hotels and shopping, entertainment and transportation facilities. Subway stations with frequent level changes and massive peak loads depend heavily on escalators to clear platforms so that trains have room to discharge passengers.

Like elevators, escalators represent a specialized form of mechanical/ interior integration.[1] The structural system is involved to the extent that it must be coordinated with slab penetrations. Escalators are difficult to renovate once in place, and it is usually impossible to add more escalators later.

The most difficult aspect of escalator integration into the building is not so much how they integrate when they are working as how they integrate when they are not. More precisely, what alternate means of transportation is available when the equipment is shut down for preventive or corrective maintenance? The distance to be traveled, the number of people involved, and time constraints must all be accommodated. Generally speaking, the fail-safe mode is simply an adjacent stair. The escalator itself becomes an inanimate stair when the power is turned off. An escalator may be part of a chain of mechanisms for moving people; when it stops, others must compensate for the overflow. Overflow points, emergency procedures, and stopping mechanisms have to be carefully thought out and designed. The size and number of escalators must correspond to the capacity of the landings, corridors, doors, and elevators that make up the pedestrian circulation system. In addition, the interior environment of each floor the escalators span must be recognized in the design. When the unit is exposed to weather, exterior materials like stone or concrete can be incorporated into the design.

Escalators have always been somewhat difficult to visibly integrate into a space.[2] Their geometry and mechanical character are difficult to relate to objects that sit on the floor or hang in space, while their function usually requires that they be placed at the focus of pedestrian movements. The growing popularity of atrium spaces has mitigated this problem somewhat by offering a lobby configuration that can be visually enhanced by escalators.

EXAMPLE

The escalators in the Atlanta/ Hartsfield International Airport[3]

1. Mechanical and interior, pp. 329–330.

2. Visible integration, pp. 381–385.

3. Atlanta International Airport, pp. 116–119.

Photo: P. Aaron, ESTO

Visible integration as well as circulation requirements are addressed in Moscone Center, where the escalators serve as a visual link between the above-ground lobby, the mezzanine, and the exhibit hall level.

are a major element of the design. Their ability to handle the large volume of travelers in a continuous flow from level to level is vital to the airport's circulation system and thus to its entire layout. The width of the escalators is the largest available to accommodate suitcases. Signage and the space surrounding the escalators were designed so that adequate movement and back-up flow can be handled. Audio signals for directions are provided as well.

IMMEDIATE CONSIDERATIONS

Width: The standard hip width is 48 in. with a 40 in. stair-tread width. This is barely wide enough to accommodate two people standing side by side or to allow someone to pass. A 32 in. hip width with a 24 in. stair-tread width is the smallest size commonly available.

Length: Given the standard code-required incline of 30°, the length of an escalator is a function of its height. Intermediate supports are usually required when the rise exceeds 18 ft, and very long units are provided with multiple drive machines or extra large exterior drive machines.

Speed: Speeds of 90, 100, and 120 feet per minute are standard. User needs will vary, as speed and tread width are the factors that establish escalator capacity. It should be noted that elderly people prefer slower speeds. Slower speeds reduce the hazard from unexpected stops.

Materials: Solid balustrades can be covered with any decorative material, including bronze, stainless steel, aluminum, plastic laminate, or porcelain enamel. Balustrades can also be constructed of structural tempered glass, either clear or tinted and with or without decorative metal dividers. Decks and skirts are metal finished to complement other exposed metals on the escalator and adjacent wellway railings. Skirts can also be made of laminated glass. Steps are unfinished die-cast metal.

Operation: Reversible operation to accommodate traffic-flow variations is standard.

Safety: This is a primary consideration in any escalator design. Although escalators are not hazardous if properly used, the pedestrian must be attentive in stepping on and off. Wheelchairs, strollers, and other wheeled vehicles cannot negotiate an escalator, so alternative transportation must be provided. Code-required signage is meant to discourage children from playing on escalators, as clothes, fingers, or toes can be caught in the machinery. Emergency stopping in response to automatically actuated safety devices can cause passengers riding down an escalator to be pitched forward unexpectedly.

Safety options: The Safety Code for Elevators and Escalators (ANSI/ASME A17.1) prescribes rules for required escalator safety devices, signage, and stop switch location, as well as structural and mechanical design standards.

Even though some hazards may be depicted graphically or stated in warning signs, escalator safety is not enhanced by providing visual distraction for the passenger at entry and exit points. Circulation congestion at the discharge point should be avoided. Walls should be a minimum of 12 ft from the escalator entry and exit, and doors should not be located in the escalator approach path. Heavy cross-traffic at the head or foot of an escalator should be avoided.

Lighting: Both ambient and task lighting affect escalator safety. Codes require a minimum of 2 footcandles per tread.

Maintenance: As previously emphasized, alternate routing should be available for occasions when escalators are being serviced. Escalators exposed to weather present serious maintenance problems. The consequences of exposure to rain, ice, and melting snow (along with salt and sand) must be addressed. Special features include heaters, special handrails, nonslip treads, drains and gutters within the machine enclosure, and special motor enclosures. Some kind of protective cover over the escalator is most desirable and eliminates the slipping hazard during wet or icy weather. Exposed escalator structure and finishes must be fabricated of corrosion-resistant metal, and structural members must be coated to protect them from corrosion.

GENERAL CONSIDERATIONS

Location: Escalator location is crucial in determining the efficiency and safety of pedestrian circulation within the building.[4] In some building types, such as transportation facilities, considerations of speed are paramount. In others, such as stores or shopping malls, an escalator may be best designed and located to prolong the shopper's view of the merchandise.

4. Performance criteria, p. 232.

Fire safety: Generally, codes do not permit escalators to be used as a required means of egress unless enclosed by fire-resistant walls protected by fire doors. Escalators should be designed to stop if they feed into a smoke- or fire-involved floor.

Security: Controlled access to an escalator is almost impossible to provide except by locked alcoves.

Population served: In general, escalators provide excellent transportation for a large percentage of the population. However, small children, the elderly, and the handicapped experience difficulty in boarding. Codes have recognized this and generally require elevators to supplement the escalators.

Operable Partitions

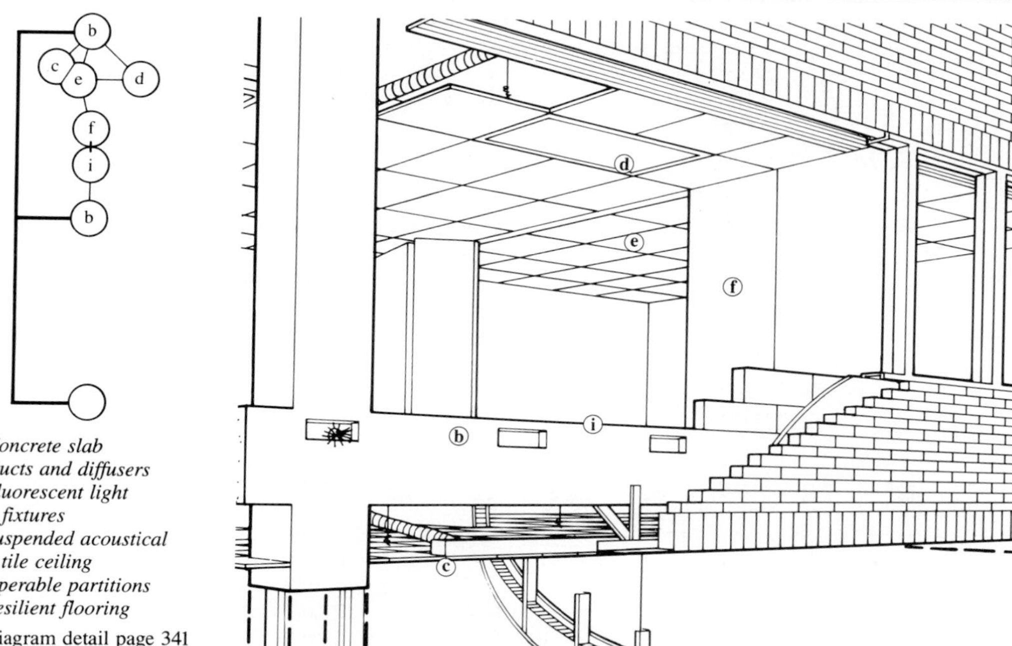

b. *Concrete slab*
c. *Ducts and diffusers*
d. *Fluorescent light fixtures*
e. *Suspended acoustical tile ceiling*
f. *Operable partitions*
i. *Resilient flooring*

Diagram detail page 341

Operable partitions are found in Generic Example Number 2, Post-Tensioned Concrete. Because they allow spaces to be subdivided quickly, operable partitions are well suited to the needs of hospitals and other institutions.

Reviewer:
Marvin D. Suer, FAIA
Bartley/Long/Mirenda
Philadelphia, PA

Operable partitions are composed of moveable flat panels attached to a track. They can be stacked compactly out of the way when not in use. Ease of operation distinguishes operable partitions from the more permanent demountable partitions, and their flat appearance distinguishes them from accordion-type folding partitions. The need for operable partitions is determined by programmatic requirements for flexible sizing of assembly spaces. Operable partitions are commonly used in schools, hotels, and dining facilities to subdivide classrooms, auditoriums, and conference rooms.

Once the decision is made to use operable partitions, the immediate problem is one of visible integration.[1] When they are located in the space, their surface treatment and proportions must visibly integrate with the walls as well as the floor and the ceiling. The operable partitions physically span the distance from ceiling to floor and, frequently, the horizontal distance from wall to wall. The assembly must maintain a physical connection to the structure for support and to the walls for visual and acoustical privacy. The relationship to exterior walls is important if the space is to be daylighted, whether subdivided by the partitions or not. The storage space for the panels should not interfere with natural lighting.

Successful use of operable partitions demands a high level of design integration.[2] The placement of the partition must not compromise the acoustical privacy, fire code ratings, panic exiting flow, programmatic circulation requirements, or thermal comfort of the space. In some buildings, such as schools, vandalism or unauthorized operation may be concerns.

Contact with the floor gives rise to other design constraints. Carpet tile or roll carpet under the partitions may impede automatic opera-

1. Visible integration, pp. 381–385.

2. Spatial performance, pp. 249–250.

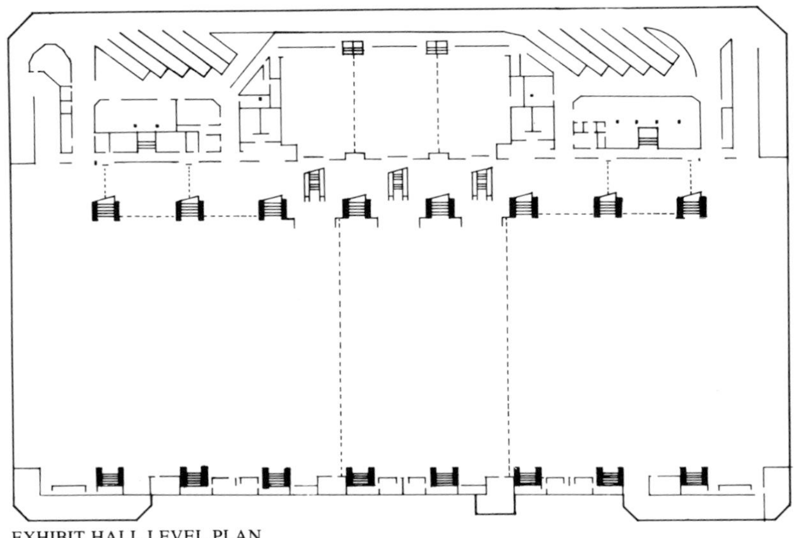

EXHIBIT HALL LEVEL PLAN

Photo: P. Aaron, ESTO

Conference center meeting rooms must respond to very specific spatial performance criteria, including a high degree of finish to prevent these spaces from being perceived as windowless boxes. Operable partitions, indicated by dashed lines in plan (top), allow the exhibit hall and ballroom of Moscone Center to be subdivided, and provide "swing" space at the northeast perimeter of the exhibit hall. This space, framed by the ends of the arch pairs (above), can be partitioned off to form conference rooms.

tion. The complexity of combining an access floor and operable partitions[3] may prove too much for a normal design situation where other options are available.

EXAMPLE

The George R. Moscone Convention Center[4] makes extensive use of operable partitions to create ballrooms, exhibit halls, and meeting rooms of varying size on a daily and sometimes hourly basis. The large exhibit area has three major operable partitions and several minor ones.

IMMEDIATE CONSIDERATIONS

Construction: Operable partitions are usually framed in wood or metal or are of honeycomb construction, with structural faces of sheet metal or plywood.

Panel connection: Partitions may be moved as individual panels, in hinged panel pairs, or as a single large unit. In the latter case, the weight of the partition when all panels are connected may make operation cumbersome.

Tracks: In most assemblies, panels are suspended on overhead tracks, but floor-supported panels with floor tracks are available from some manufacturers.

Suspension system: Most operable partitions for commercial or institutional use have metal ball bearing wheels in metal tracks.

Operation: Operation may be motorized or manual. Motorized operation conserves time, but is usually only economical with very large or heavy panels. Manual operation offers ease of maintenance and lower first cost.[5]

Acoustical seal: Acoustics are a major concern when separate functions take place on either side of an operable partition. Fixed or operable bottom seals enhance acoustical isolation. At the ceiling, the surface to which the track is attached must be level to create an acoustical seal. STC ratings for operable partitions can be as high as 50, but this can be negated if there are no sound barriers above the ceiling, or if the mechanical system runs transverse to the operable partition and penetrates adjacent spaces. In the latter case, the ducts must be modified or sound-trapped. If ducts and structure are exposed, a bulkhead must be built above the track to provide acoustical privacy.[6]

Accessories: Operable partitions are available with pass-through doors, chalkboards and tackboards, chalk trays and other accessories integral with the panels.

GENERAL CONSIDERATIONS

Fire protection: A large installation may include partitions that intersect at right angles or form corridors. It is advisable to check with local fire officials to be sure that such assemblies will not be defined as fire-rated partitions when in place, since no system currently available has such a rating.

Finish: The finish affects the esthetics, acoustics, and durability of operable partitions. Vinyl, fabric, plastic laminate, wood, and carpet finishes are generally available.

Storage area: Most operable partitions are designed to be stacked in a pocket or closet. These storage areas must be large enough to accommodate the fully stacked partitions and have adequate clearance at the side to prevent injury when moving the panels manually.

Mechanical integration: Air supply and return requirements of the spaces created by the operable partitions must be accommodated in the distribution patterns of diffusers and registers, and by the automatic temperature control system. Sound traps should be provided as necessary to minimize sound transmission. Similarly, light fixture patterns and light switch locations must be designed to function in the various spatial configurations.

3. Access floors, pp. 202–204.

4. Moscone Center, pp. 112–115.

5. Conservation of resources and time, pp. 236–237.

6. Acoustical performance, p. 254.

Open Plan Office Furniture

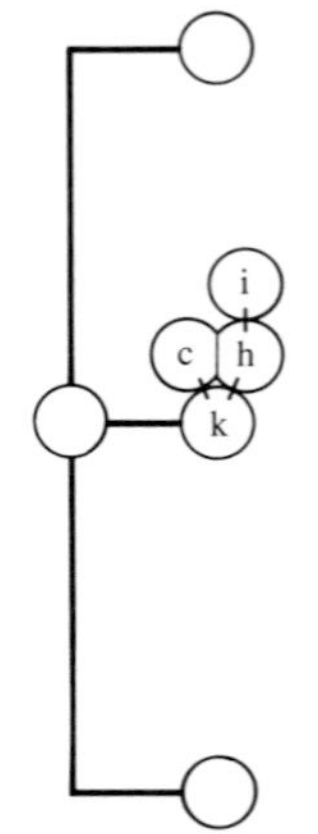

c. *Wiring and ductwork*
h. *Carpeted access flooring*
i. *Open office furniture*
k. *Steel decking with concrete topping*

Diagram detail page 341

Reviewer:
John F. Pile
Pratt Institute
Brooklyn, NY

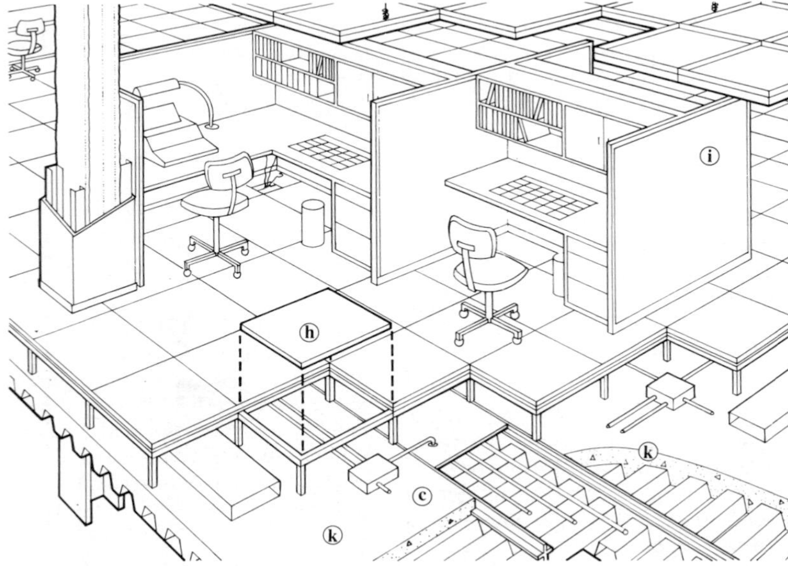

As shown in Generic Example Number 1, Access Floor and Curtain Wall, open office furniture is well suited to use with other products designed to enhance office flexibility, such as access floors.

Open plan office furniture usually consists of a set of work stations, composed of integrated partial height panels, storage units, and work surfaces. Optional elements may include task-ambient lighting, acoustical control, and electrical raceways. Work stations may be defined by freestanding panels or they may be ganged or connected with panels separating adjacent work stations. The intent is to maximize the number of work stations and provide flexibility in areas where a large number of people work. Views, high ceilings, and other amenities may be used to compensate for any crowding that may result.

Open plan office furniture is characterized by a *touching* relationship with structure and interior.[1] Even when the furniture is connected by power lines to the electrical source, it is moveable and therefore has no direct necessary relationship to the other systems. The key to integration in this instance is flexibility,[2] a factor that will become increasingly important as business technology expands.

The prime motivation for using open office furniture is the conservation of space that results from the elimination of full-height walls.[3] This also enables the worker at the smallest work station to appreciate the whole extent of the open space. Conservation of time and materials is involved as well;[4] most open office furniture includes built-in features, which reduce the number of pieces, save time when moving or rearranging,and can be reused.

The decision to use open office furniture has ramifications that affect all of the building systems. The structural bay dimensions and locations of columns in the floor layout are critical to the successful layout of open office furniture. A structural floor type may be chosen for its capacity to provide electrical service to the system, in which case the power supply grid in the floor must relate to the potential placement of the furniture. Electrical lines, task and task-ambient lighting, and even telephone lines can be incorporated into panel and furniture designs.[5] Electrical and lighting systems should be designed with flexibility in mind, as life cycle costs of open office furniture are related to the flexibility of the electrical system.

1. Structure and interior *touching*, p. 326.
2. Flexibility, pp. 237–238.
3. Conservation of space, p. 236.
4. Conservation of materials and time, pp. 236–237.
5. Spatial performance, pp. 249–250.

Photo: Hursley/Lark/Hursley

Photo: Harr, Hedrich-Blessing

Open office furniture lends itself to rectilinear layouts, as in the Georgia Power building (top), and to less formal configurations, suchas those found in the Aid Association for Lutherans Headquarters (above).

The ceiling as a source of lighting and air supply must be similarly coordinated to insure proper light and thermal comfort to the worker at the desk. The choice of air supply can affect the acoustical privacy of the space. In addition, the furniture layout may need to accommodate such issues as the view from the windows at the perimeter and the need for single-position surveillance for security.

Visible integration occurs at a very high level in open office furniture.[6] Because they are designed to complement one another visually, the various elements that define a space can be coordinated in color, geometry, size, shape, and texture. A disadvantage is that other furnishings stand out in disharmony. In addition, most manufacturers acknowledge that between 10 and 15 percent of the office space in a given business must have full-height partitions for privacy and security. These offices must be carefully located to allow for maximum flexibility.

EXAMPLES

The open office systems of both Equitable Life[7] and Herman Miller[8] were chosen and designed for the spaces by the owners. In the case of Herman Miller it was essential to be able to modify the use of space between factory and offices, since the needs are constantly changing. From a lighting standpoint as well the architects felt the open office systems allowed the greatest flexibility when supplemented with task lighting. Even though Equitable Life did their own interiors the architect felt that the open office systems "contributed to the energy efficiency by allowing a broader building" than could be gotten if partitions blocked off light to interior spaces.

6. Visible integration, pp. 381–385.

7. Equitable Life, pp. 102–105.

8. Herman Miller Seating Plant, pp. 56–59.

IMMEDIATE CONSIDERATIONS

Panel size: Panel heights and widths vary greatly, but average 4 to 6 ft high and 3 ft wide.

Panel support: Panels may be attached to other furniture components or freestanding. Freestanding panels can meet other panels at right angles, or can be supported by attached feet or by narrow end panels that act as stabilizing flanges.

Panel color: The choice of color has ramifications that extend over time, and not all of these are purely esthetic. Colors can fade in ultraviolet light, and materials can stain and soil easily through use. In addition, color helps control glare and reflected light.

Acoustical value: Acoustical privacy depends on a number of factors. Partitions should be designed to minimize sound transmission; fabric-covered panels with acoustic material backing offer the best acoustical control. Carpeting is also of value in reducing sound reflection. Ceilings should have a high noise reduction coefficient, and light fixture locations should not be in direct sound paths. Sound-masking speakers are frequently used, but these require careful placement.[9]

Module: Besides providing sufficient work area and storage space, the work station module should be scaled to fit with other units in the space and the general building module.

Ambient lighting: A separate fixture or a combination task-ambient unit can be built into or attached to the panel system.

Task lighting: This important feature should provide proper illumination on the desk surface. Besides helping to focus the worker's attention, task lighting enhances visual privacy. Care should be taken to avoid veiling reflection, the result of mirrored light bouncing off the desk surface.[10] Prismatic lenses are one possible solution to this problem.

Panel height and location: Lower partitions increase communication but decrease privacy. Partitions at the interior of the floor plan should block as little of the perimeter view as possible.

Maintenance: For both esthetic and practical reasons, maintenance is a critical factor in the long-term use of the owner's investment. To minimize wear and tear, fabrics should be durable and treated with a soil-resistant chemical, and work sur-

9. Acoustical performance, p. 254.

10. Visual performance, p. 256.

faces should be covered with replaceable material such as leather or plastic.

GENERAL CONSIDERATIONS

Ceilings: The ceiling has a considerable influence on illumination and acoustics. A light-colored panel with a high noise reduction coefficient is desirable.

Mechanical: Panels should be placed so as not to block the circulation of air, and thermostats should be located within the space rather than in the return air. Supply air should not be warmer than 100°F or cooler than 60°F, even at the perimeter of the open space.

Circulation: Aisles should be arranged to provide the most efficient way of moving people and goods without excessive noise and visual disruption for other workers. Clear orientation is essential.

Building geometry: This unchangeable parameter, with structural columns and mechanical bays, sets the stage for positioning the work stations. A complicated configuration requires special placement and size of work stations.[11]

Facilities management: A primary consideration in the selection of open plan office furniture is the long-range needs of the user. The initial cost can often be justified by an analysis of life cycle costs—a comparison of the initial expense versus the probable expense (and disruption) of remodeling existing space to relocate personnel. Some manufacturers of open plan office furniture provide facilities management studies and projections as an extra service.

Wiring: Connections for light fixtures, computers, and telecommunications equipment must be as flexible as the furniture system itself. A poke-through floor slab may be used, as may a raceway system in combination with receptor panels in the furniture. Flat conductor cable,[12] access floors,[13] and power poles are all compatible with open office furniture.

Illumination: The manufacturers of open plan office furniture systems are enthusiastic about modular lighting. Typically a 4 × 4 ft grid is used, and light fixtures can be relocated along with the furniture to eliminate some of the task lighting. Fixture location should be considered in the initial planning stages.

Security: A serious drawback of open office furniture is the possibility of an intruder gaining access to an open plan area and going undetected behind the low- or medium-height partitions. The only preventives for this are to provide natural surveillance and to design the office layout with a mixture of open and semi-open areas. Aisles should be designed so as not to meander throughout the floor. The designer should also consider providing lockable desks or cabinets for storage of valuables.

Fire protection: The most flammable elements at any work station are usually the fabric covering and acoustical backing of the panels. These can be treated with a fire retardant chemical.

Number of changes per year: In theory, there could be a limitless number of changes of the system during any given year. The disruption of work during any change places a practical limit on this number, however. Generally, alterations will not exceed two per year.

Storage: Storage will be required for components that are not in use. The quantity the user will want to have on hand will depend on the manufacturer's ability to produce and deliver components quickly.

11. Spatial performance, pp. 249–250.
12. Flat conductor cable, pp. 205–206.
13. Access floors, pp. 202–204.

Carpet Tiles

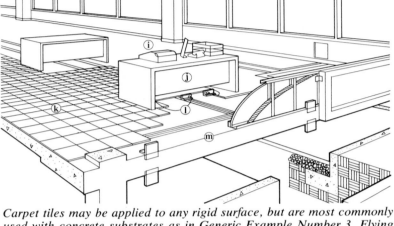

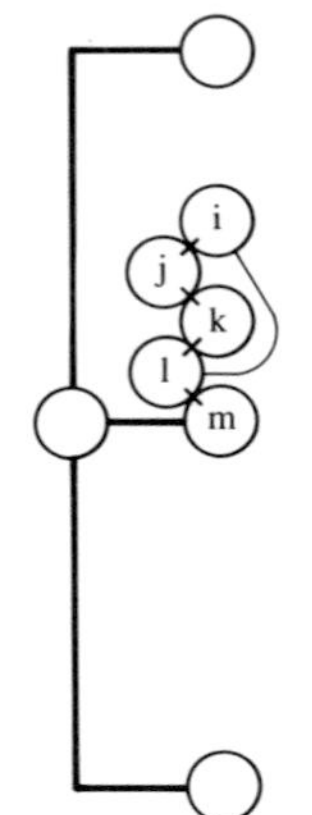

i. *Electrical office equipment*
j. *Office furniture*
k. *Carpet tile*
l. *Under carpet flat cable*
m. *Flat plate*

Diagram detail page 342

Reviewer:
John F. Pile
Pratt Institute
Brooklyn, NY

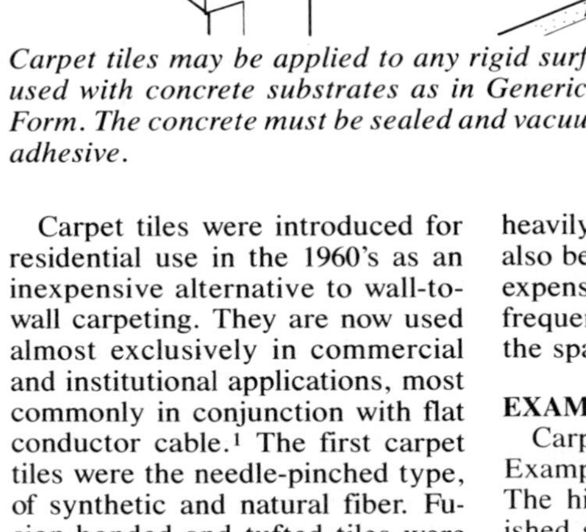

Carpet tiles may be applied to any rigid surface, but are most commonly used with concrete substrates as in Generic Example Number 3, Flying Form. The concrete must be sealed and vacuumed before application of the adhesive.

Carpet tiles were introduced for residential use in the 1960's as an inexpensive alternative to wall-to-wall carpeting. They are now used almost exclusively in commercial and institutional applications, most commonly in conjunction with flat conductor cable.[1] The first carpet tiles were the needle-pinched type, of synthetic and natural fiber. Fusion-bonded and tufted tiles were developed in the early 1970's, and reinforced PVC backings were introduced in the late 1970's. Carpet tile sales have risen from between \$2 and \$3 million in 1972 to over \$22 million, with an annual growth rate of 25 to 30 percent in recent years.

Carpet tile is used in office space primarily because of its inherent flexibility and compatibility with flat conductor cable, open plan office furniture,[2] and raised access flooring,[3] all of which lend flexibility to office design. Carpet tile is inherently more flexible in its installation and size than broadloom carpeting. It offers an opportunity to vary the floor surface not only to meet the taste of the occupant but also to address specific functions of the space. For example, a darker color may be used in heavily trafficked areas to resist discoloration from soiling, with a lighter color in less heavily trafficked areas. A case can also be made for selecting the least expensive carpet tile and replacing it frequently to add to the diversity of the space.

1. Flat conductor cable, pp. 205–206.
2. Open plan office furniture, pp. 196–199.
3. Access floors, pp. 202–204.

EXAMPLE

Carpet tiles are shown in Generic Example Number 3, Flying Form.[4] The high quality of the slab's finished surface makes it suitable for flat cable and carpet tiles, especially in office applications. The speed with which flat cable can be installed may be important to complement the speed of construction achieved with flying forms.

4. Flying form, pp. 128–129.

IMMEDIATE CONSIDERATIONS

Style and color: Carpet tile is available in a variety of styles, all of which are identical to available broadloom styles for easier coordination in the same location. Pile types are the same as broadloom, and face yarn is generally Antron® or Anso®. The selection is only a fraction of the broadloom styles offered, but most carpet tile manufacturers offer custom design services on large jobs.

Backing material: The tile backing is important in that it provides the necessary stability for the carpet. At present, the market is dominated by PVC-backed tile, while a smaller percentage of tiles, about 6 percent, are produced with hot-melt thermoplastic backing. The latter is less expensive to produce than PVC-backed tile and has better results in flammability and smoke generation testing; in addition, it does not fuzz or pill as much as broadloom carpeting because of its stronger tuft bind. In both PVC-backed and hot-melt thermoplastic-backed tiles, the tufts are inserted into a primary backing cloth of reinforced polypropylene. Research is being conducted into other backing materials, including polyurethanes and other forms of hot-melt.

Size: Carpet tiles are available in sizes 18, 24, 30, and 36 in. square. Tiles must be less than 30 in. square if they are to be used with flat conductor cable.

Maintenance: Carpet tile manufacturers usually recommend a dry powder cleaning method, as wet cleaning may cause oversaturation of the tiles. Joints tend to collect dirt and allow moisture to get underneath the tiles. Some carpet tiles are slightly permeable and allow any trapped moisture to escape over time.

Costs: Carpet tiles can cost 20 to 40 percent more than broadloom, primarily because of the backing material. In the absence of flat conductor cable, therefore, they are more likely to be used in custom-built facilities than in speculative ones. Cost advantages occur in terms of life-cycle costs. It is easier to replace stained tiles than to replace broadloom, and carpet tiles can be installed with minimal disturbance during office hours. Nevertheless, manufacturers' claims that heavily soiled areas can be replaced at minimal cost are somewhat misleading. New tiles may be visually distinct from the old carpet surrounding the soiled areas, and therefore the entire carpeted area is likely to require replacement.

Installation: The methods of installation are "free-lay" (without adhesive), spot-glued, and fully adhered. Free-lay carpet tiles are the easiest to remove, and retain their shape when lifted and replaced several times. Adhesives may be used to keep the carpet tile from shifting, and the tile can still be released for repositioning.

GENERAL CONSIDERATIONS

Substrate: Concrete is the most common substrate for carpet tile, but any rigid material is suitable, including most types of raised access flooring. For proper installation, it is critical that the surface be free of bumps, depressions, and loose material of any kind. The only preparation required for concrete is that it be sealed and surface-vacuumed for the application of adhesive.

Fire protection: Both PVC-backed and hot-melt thermoplastic-backed carpet tiles can pass the smoke chamber test, but the hot-melt thermoplastic backing has better results in flammability and smoke generation testing. The PVC-backed tiles cannot get a Class A fire rating for health care facilities and certain other facilities such as nursing homes. There is controversy over the toxic gases released by PVC-backed tiles, but both types give off toxic gases. (There is no standard as yet for measuring toxicity.)

Electrical: Between 20 and 25 percent of carpet tiles are used in conjunction with flat conductor cable. In such applications, the tiles must be less than 30 in. square to permit easy access to the cable. There have been problems with some tile adhesives that chemically interact with the cable sheathing and cause it to melt down; this can be avoided with proper coordination. Also, light-colored tiles may ridge at the cable from dirt and traffic.

Carpet tiles are also well suited for use with access flooring. In these applications it may be desirable to treat the tiles against static buildup. Tile sizes may not match the panel size, in which case it may be necessary to remove several tiles to obtain access to one panel.

Access Floors

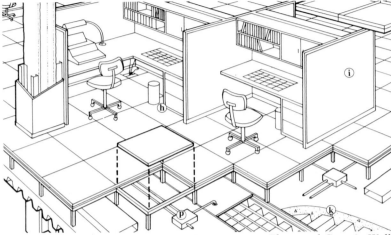

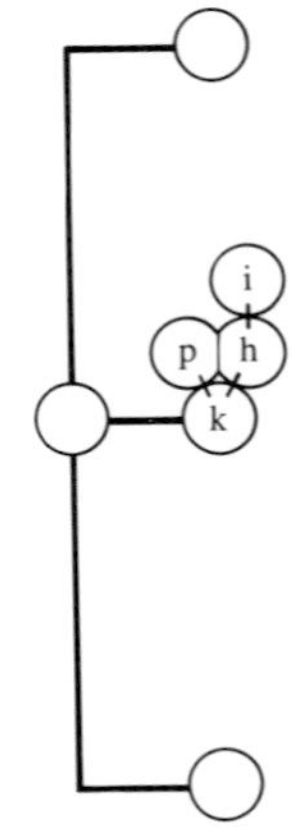

h. *Carpeted access flooring*
i. *Open office furniture*
k. *Steel decking with concrete topping*
p. *Conduit*

Diagram detail page 343

As shown in Generic Example Number 1, Access Floor and Curtain Wall, access flooring may be installed over an existing wiring system (even a structural/electrified floor) to enhance its flexibility.

Reviewers:
Gary A. Hall
Hammel, Green & Abrahamson
Minneapolis, MN
Harry Misuriello
W.S. Fleming & Associates, Inc.
Washington, DC

Access floors, also known as raised flooring, are composed of square floor panels elevated above the slab floor on metal pedestals to provide space for electrical or mechanical equipment or both. The removeable panels provide easy access to the equipment below. These floors are commonly used in computer rooms, which require electrical and mechanical service in excess of typical office space. They represent a *meshed*[1] mechanical/interior combination with a *touching*[2] relationship to the structural floor, and they conserve space by avoiding duplication of the duct space in both the ceiling and the floor.[3]

Access floors are often retrofitted in an existing space to accommodate wiring and air conditioning for a new computer. The decision whether to use an access floor must be made in context with the ceiling decision, perhaps even taking into account the ceiling decision of the floor below. If the floor is used as a plenum or to house ductwork, special dampers may be required to seal off the space in case of fire.

The largest organizational problems with access flooring occur when conventional floor finishes are used adjacent to raised flooring. Floor space is then lost to stairs or ramps leading from normal floor levels to the access floor. A depressed or dropped floor slab can be used to avoid ramps or stairs. To insure flexibility, considerable attention should be given to these decisions, as the expense of redesigning a raised floor at a later time can be considerable.

EXAMPLES

The addition to the Submarine Training Facility at Groton[4] uses access floors in the computer area. They house wiring as well as a carbon dioxide fire extinguishing system. The architect designed a dropped floor slab in the computer area so that stairs and ramps are avoided.

IMMEDIATE CONSIDERATIONS

Panel material: Floor panels can be made of hollow metal, insulated metal, metal pans with lightweight concrete fill, or metal with wood fill. They are rated according to load capacity.

Panel supports: Ordinarily the floor panel is supported at the corners by a pedestal and around the edges by a stringer. The corners can be bolted, friction-fit, or held by gravity to the pedestal. More costly systems eliminate the stringer for maximum accessibility to the equipment below. Pedestals can be bolted to the subfloor, or adhesive-adhered.

1. Mechanical and interior *meshed*, p. 330.
2. Structure and interior *touching*, p. 326. (Note that this relationship can also be *connected*.)
3. Conservation of space, p. 236.
4. Addition to Submarine Training Facility, pp. 106–107.

Panel finish: Panels may be finished in carpet, resilient tile, or high-pressure plastic laminate. Besides being an important visual consideration, panel finishes in a computer room must be non-magnetic, conductive, and grounded to avoid static electricity. Manufacturers' standard finishes are designed for computer rooms, but these requirements must be considered if a custom finish is desired.

The type of finish and its maintenance should be considered with respect to adjacent finishes. A resilient finish similar to an adjacent sheet vinyl floor may prompt a maintenance crew to wet-wash the access floor.

Panel size: A 2 × 2 ft module is typical, but other modular sizes are available.

Panel connections: The use of stringerless panels facilitates access to the underfloor space, but stringers, along with mechanical fasteners (some of which are available with rubber gaskets), decrease panel reverberation.

Floor height: The minimum height of a finished panel above the subfloor is 4 in. Where the underfloor area is used for ductwork as well as electrical distribution, heights of 7 to 18 in. are more common. Floors raised over 1 ft above the subfloor may provide a hiding place and thus pose a potential security problem.

Outlets: Electrical outlets can be flush, concealed, or surface-mounted. These and other protrusions should be located with the traffic pattern in mind.

Costs: The high initial cost of access floors is mitigated somewhat by tax considerations. Because the Internal Revenue Service treats access flooring as furniture, it can be depreciated on an accelerated schedule, unlike other building components. For retrofit use, an access floor may be the only sensible solution in a computer room, despite its high cost, but in new construction the cost trade-offs should be evaluated more carefully. The hidden cost of access flooring is the reduction of floor-to-ceiling height, necessitating higher floor-to-floor dimensions or less head room for the building occupants.

Loading: Concentrated and uniform loads must be within the product's specified tolerances. If rolling and impact loads are significant, such as in areas where frequent heavy moving loads occur, the panel must be able to withstand the added structural load as well as any surface damage that might result.

Accessories: Panel lifters, cut-outs, and perforated panels to facilitate air flow should be specified where appropriate.

GENERAL CONSIDERATIONS

Partitions: Certain operable partition units work well with access floors, but an access floor cannot be used as a foundation for fixed, full-height partitions. Partitions that subdivide computer spaces should be integrated with the fire-resistance requirements and the fire-suppression method used. If inert gas is used for fire suppression, the partitions must provide an airtight seal.

Acoustics: Raised floors can be good acoustical buffers, isolating the computer room from the floor below. Some metal panels vibrate in response to moving or rolling loads and generate a metallic echo. Mechanical fasteners, concrete infill, and other types of insulation help alleviate this problem.

Installation: Access floors pose numerous construction problems. The panels must be precise and dimensionally exact. The finish is installed when the panels are placed, and it has to be protected, even though the construction sequence requires that the floor be installed after wet and dusty work is completed.

Seismic design: Lateral force ratings required to determine earthquake loads should be specified rather than building code compliance, since many building codes do not make specific mention of access flooring.

Electrical performance: Static control can usually be accomplished by maintaining a high relative humidity in the area and by using resistive

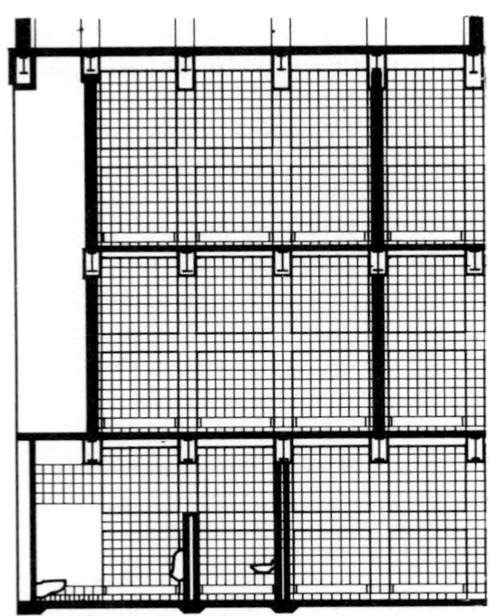

CROSS SECTION

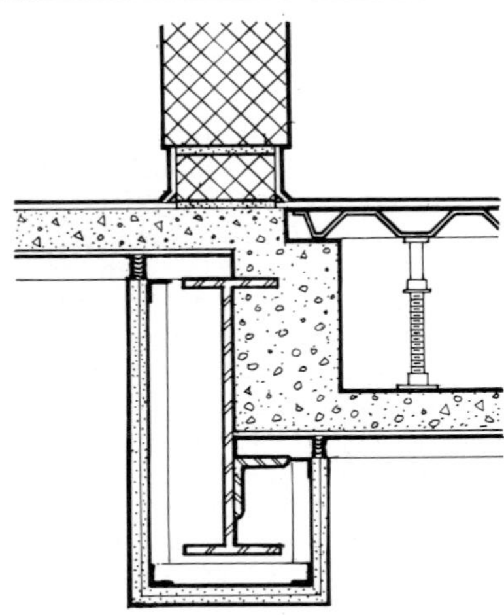

FLOOR DETAIL

Photo: Nick Wheeler

A construction detail from the addition to the Submarine Training Facility at Groton shows the dropped floor slab, a combination of structure and interior that allows transition from the normal floor level to the access floor without steps or ramps.

finish materials. When static control is especially important, conductive floor covering can be used along with other procedures. Electric shock is prevented by properly grounding the understructure components and by providing low resistance between materials used in the assembly.

Adjacent construction: When constructed in the plan interior, a raised floor is surrounded by a partition system, but when it abuts an exterior wall, windowsill heights and the location of perimeter mechanical units must be considered. Non-rectilinear rooms can be accommodated by most access floors, but with some difficulty and expense. Bathrooms and washrooms must use conventional floors, creating another access problem.

In the absence of a dropped floor slab, stairs or ramps must be constructed to provide ingress to a raised floor area. These elements must meet code requirements. They also require substantial space and need to be integrated with the circulation pattern in the rest of the building. Door swings also require attention with respect to code requirements and circulation needs.

Weight: Depending on the type of panel selected, the structural load and connections imposed by the system must be considered in structural design.

Fire protection: Panel materials should be checked to insure that the values for smoke development, heat transfer, and flame spread are sufficient to comply with the required fire rating.

Flat Conductor Cable

i. *Electrical office equipment*
j. *Office furniture*
k. *Carpet tile*
l. *Under carpet flat cable*
m. *Flat plate*

Diagram detail page 343

Reviewers:
Gary A. Hall
Hammell, Green & Abrahamson
Minneapolis, MN

Harry Misuriello
W.S. Fleming & Associates, Inc.
Washington, DC

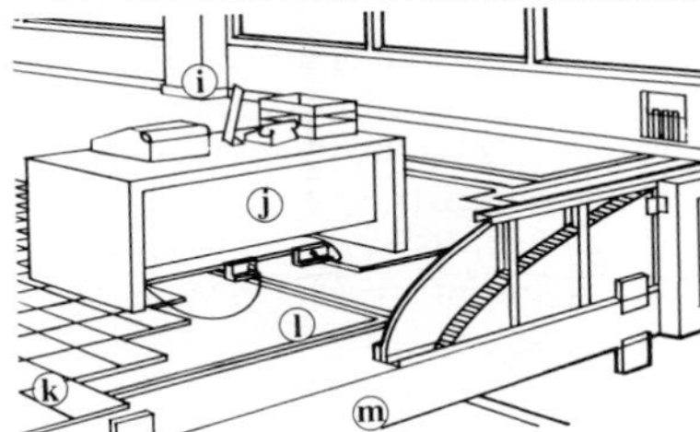

Flat conductor cable is found in Generic Example Number 3, Flying Form. The high-quality finished surface associated with this construction method makes it highly compatible with flat cable.

Flat conductor cable (FCC) as found in buildings today is a refinement of a product that was originally developed by NASA for spacecraft, and is used for branch circuit wiring systems. The FCC system consists of copper wire cable, a plastic bottom shield to protect the wire from abrasion, and a metal top shield that is taped to the substrate. The cable is laid against a solid substrate, usually the floor, taped down, and covered with carpet tiles.[1] It can be folded over itself in order to turn corners.

The appropriateness of flat cable as an integration strategy derives from the conservation of time,[2] both in the construction process and the actual use of the product. Approximate receptacle relocation time is just over two hours. The combination of flat cable and carpet tiles permits changes to be made rapidly. Such a high level of flexibility requires that no *meshed* or *unified* levels be present in the system combinations. Therefore the taped connection of the flat cable to the structural floor slab and the *touching* relationship of the carpet tile to the cable and the floor slab are essential.[3]

The *touching* relationship to the carpeting introduces the possibility of maintenance, security, and safety problems. It should be added that the normal advantages of carpet tile are also present, and that worn pieces or pieces cut in preparation for outlets can be replaced easily without replacing the entire carpet.

1. Carpet tiles, pp. 200–201.
2. Conservation of time, pp. 236–237.
3. Mechanical and interior *touching*, p. 329.

The geometrical freedom of flat cable provides an unlimited range of possibilities, with virtually no restrictions or rigid modular pattern to conform to. Given the close relationship between the arrangement of floor outlets and the desk layout in office applications, and the necessity of coordinating the desk layout with the ceiling and lighting configuration, the entire interrelationship of interior and mechanical elements can be considerably freed of normal orthogonal and modular restraints through the use of flat cable.[4]

EXAMPLE

Flat conductor cable is discussed in the context of total building systems integration in Generic Example Number 3.[5]

IMMEDIATE CONSIDERATIONS

Capacity: Flat conductor cable is typically available in three-, four-, or five-conductor configurations in 10 or 12 AWG, suitable for single-phase 240/120 volt or three-phase 208/120 volt power. Voltage is limited to 300 volts between grounded conductors and 150 volts between ungrounded and grounded conductors. General purpose circuits are limited to a rating of 20 amperes, and individual branch circuits are limited to 30 amperes.

Accessories: Accessories include transition boxes, which connect the flat cable to conventional round wire, and termination boxes, which connect it to receptacles or machinery. Flat cable may be used to transmit power (electricity) or communications (data or telephone).

Flat conductor cable is connected to circular feeder lines by means of a (lift) terminal box, or transition "block." Termination methods vary among manufacturers, and in the case of data cable they are designed to meet the requirements of computer products on the market. Floor or wall receptacles can be used. Besides the conventional duplex type, receptacles are available which combine power, data, and telephone functions in one box.

Costs: The initial cost of flat cable is higher than that of conventional wir-

4. Spatial performance, pp. 249–250.
5. Flying form, pp. 128–129.

ing. As with all products that enhance mobility in the office, however, life cycle costing is a better method for determining actual final costs to the owner. Investment tax credits are available to the owner in some cases, since flat cable can be subject to accelerated depreciation. It is more economical to use flat cable for all three wiring systems (power/data/telephone) in a project than to use it for one with conventional wiring for the other two. Hidden cost savings include earlier tenant occupancy, less need to fireproof slab penetrations, and avoidance of electrified panels for open offices. Renovation or alteration work can be performed during normal working hours with minimal disruption. Considerable lead time is required in ordering, so care must be taken to order all components in sufficient quantities. Hidden costs may include extra installation time due to inexperienced labor.

GENERAL CONSIDERATIONS

Durability: Flat conductor cable has been used for just over ten years in the commercial market. Thus, its long-term durability is not proven. Manufacturers claim that flat cable withstands the pressure of regular office furniture (e.g., a filing cabinet) and will not be affected by normal carpet shampoo. Cuts through the cable have resulted from heavy equipment being wheeled over exposed systems during construction.

Interior finish: Carpet tiles are the only form of carpeting that can be used with flat cable. Many different colors, weaves, and materials are available. The National Electric Code limits the largest dimension of the tile to 30 in. Backings include jute, resin laminates, and vinyl.

Carpet tile must be integrated esthetically and functionally with the rest of the project. Flat cable can telegraph through the tile, especially where cables intersect or turn, but dark-colored loop pile carpet with some tonal variation minimizes this problem. The adhesive used to secure the tiles must be compatible with flat cable; some types can damage the insulating cover. Vinyl-backed carpet requires only spot gluing, while other types of backing require full adhesive coverage. The type of substrate and its condition may limit the types of carpet backing material usable in a particular application.

Safety: Floor receptacles should be located well outside any likely pedestrian traffic. Most flat cable systems have a UL designation and should not pose a fire hazard.

Because of the ease of carpet tile removal and the accessibility of the circuitry, flat cable is not an appropriate design solution where small children have access to the system. The National Electric Code does not permit flat cable in residential, school, or hospital buildings. It is approved for commercial applications only, and its use is prohibited in some locations.

Placement: Flat conductor cable is usually laid under carpet tile. Flat cable may be concealed within partitions if necessary, but with difficulty since it requires a solid substrate. Raceways are required when it is surface-mounted on partitions. Wire and receptacle locations should be assigned with the work station layout in mind. Relocation at a partition may require that a transition box be moved.

Construction coordination: Concrete slabs should be cleaned and sealed prior to the installation of flat cable in order to minimize surface irregularities and enhance the adhesive bond of the steel tape. For very irregular surfaces, a plastic cushion should be used to compensate for the lack of a carpet pad. Power terminations can be made in the field. Telephone and data terminations are either made by the factory or with the aid of field termination kits offered by some manufacturers. Thus, it is necessary to know which equipment requires connection to ensure compatibility.

Structural/Electrified Floors

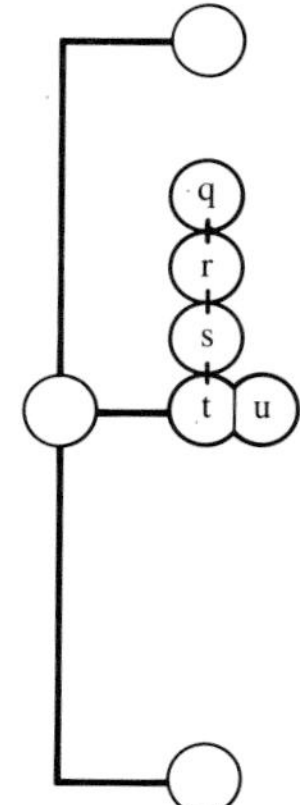

q. *Electrical office equipment*
r. *Office furniture*
s. *Floor covering*
t. *Concrete topping on metal decking*
u. *Conduit*

Diagram detail page 343

Reviewers:
Gary A. Hall
Hammel, Green & Abrahamson
Minneapolis, MN
Harry Misuriello
W.S. Fleming & Associates, Inc.
Washington, DC

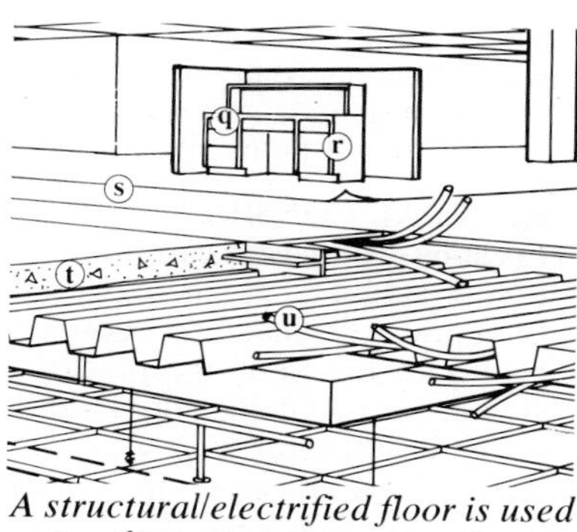

A structural/electrified floor is used as an alternate to an access floor in Generic Example Number 1, Access Floor and Curtain Wall.

The use of steel decking as a raceway for wiring has evolved over 40 years. The system uses discrete deck cells for power and communications wiring, the side wall of the cell being cut to permit easy access. An electrical insert, covering the access space, or a continuous trench cut perpendicular to the active cells can be used. The top of the insert or trench is covered with an easily removeable cover that is flush with the concrete topping. The trench or inserts are usually set in a grid pattern compatible with the proposed furniture layout.

One major advantage of the structural/electrified floor is visible integration.[1] Outlets can be placed near the work stations, and receptacles can be designed to be practically invisible. Visible wires and extension cords are minimized, and wall receptacles can be eliminated. The wires are concealed in the troughs created by the steel floor decking, are accessible at many locations on the floor, and can be reached without disturbing the floor below.

Because they integrate the electrical and telecommunications networks with structure and interior,[2] structural/electrified floors are affected by a diverse set of design constraints. The ceiling must be included in the total integrated concept and the lighting design should complement the seating and desk arrangement. Fire protection, access to spaces, and security are also important issues in an open office design. Acoustics and acoustical privacy affect the placement of the furniture and the choice of the ceiling and lighting systems. The steel pan itself requires fire protection; for this reason the ceiling design can also be influenced by the exposed steel pan above it.

This wiring system must be analyzed and properly designed for its potential to be realized. Careless planning in regard to the outlet placement module and cell capacity can render this system useless. The number and frequency of the preset outlets determines how accurately the services are delivered to the work station.

EXAMPLE

A structural/electrified floor underlies the access floor in Generic Example Number 1, Access Floor and Curtain Wall.[3] This situation is most likely to occur when a building is renovated or when the demands placed on existing wiring (such as by the computer room in certain floor areas as shown in the example) exceed the capacity for change of an electrified floor.

IMMEDIATE CONSIDERATIONS

Decking: The cellular deck is usually galvanized steel to comply with UL requirements. A variety of sizes and profiles are available, with the most common deck depths being 2 and 3 in. The section properties, raceway capacity, and dead load are all related to deck size. The design module of outlet locations must also be compatible with the deck module.

Receptacles: These are flush, concealed, or surface-mounted. The outlet may be completely concealed beneath a hatch lid or access panel. The preset outlets can only be installed at the time of construction; "afterset" inserts can be installed later, but these provide for surface-mounted outlets only.

Color and finish coordination: Outlet covers can be color-coordinated with the finish floor material. Extra lead time and costs should also be considered.

1. Visible integration, pp. 381–385.
2. Structure and interior and mechanical, pp. 318–320.
3. Access floor and curtain wall, pp. 124–125.

Suppliers: Not all deck manufacturers supply outlets, but many types are available. Be sure the outlets chosen are compatible with the deck and perform as specified.

Costs: A structural/electrified floor has a high initial cost, but its flexibility[4] can result in long-term savings. Not all building tenants benefit from the advantages of this type of floor, so a life-cycle cost analysis should be made to determine whether it is economical. This will appeal more to the owner/user than to the speculative developer. Of course, a structural/electrified floor is less expensive in a steel frame building than in a concrete frame building.

4. Flexibility, pp. 237–238.

Capacity: Immediate and future needs must be carefully evaluated to select a deck with sufficient capacity. Abandoned circuits must be removed because the cells will become clogged. Applicable code requirements must be considered, as must the pre-engineered office system if one is selected.

Fire protection: To provide a fire-rated assembly, the electrified deck must be fireproofed, top and bottom, and all components must have proper UL (or similar organization) approval. The deck must be topped with a minimum of two inches of concrete. Spray-on fireproofing can be applied to the underside of the deck, or a UL-rated assembly may be used.

Outlet type: These should be selected for visual order and compatibility with the floor finish, keeping in mind how best to restore it when an outlet is abandoned. Concealed outlets, accessible through a hatch lid or sectional panel, are the most popular. They can be covered with carpet or tile or left with their steel or plastic finish exposed. When a concealed outlet is abandoned, the connection is simply unplugged and the access door closed. With flush outlets, a metal plate can be used to cover a marred finish; patching carpet may also be considered. Anchoring carpet beneath flush fittings can be a problem.

Maintenance: Floor receptacles, even though covered, can be damaged if continuously exposed to water. In areas where floors are frequently washed, surface-mounted outlets should be used.

GENERAL CONSIDERATIONS

Location of outlets: A careful evaluation of actual or potential user stations must be made to coordinate access to the floor receptacles. It should be noted that floor outlets are undesirable for some uses where flexibility is not an issue.[5] Ideally, access should be easily available for a standard 5 ft electrical cord. Several manufacturers recommend a 5 ft module for active cells with outlets spaced on a 2 ft 6 in., 4 ft, or 5 ft module along the active cells. Cost considerations make 5 ft centers the most common. Partitions will not interfere with the system, but should not be located directly above or parallel to a raceway. The choice of preset or afterset floor outlets will affect the amount of electrical work required. Preset outlets require a predesigned furniture layout or module.

5. Spatial performance, pp. 249–250.

Structural system: A structural/electrified floor is usually used with a steel structural frame. Decks can be designed with standard keying features to form composite slabs. When underfloor electrical service is desired in a reinforced concrete structure, it is more economical to use a raceway system set into concrete topping. The trench components and operation are almost identical to those found in the structural/electrified floor.

Hangers: Where a suspended ceiling assembly is attached to the underside of the deck, hanger slots or tabs should be specified. Hangers must have sufficient load capacity for the type of ceiling designed. While most manufacturers include hanger options as part of their deck system, it is important to avoid hanging components such as steam pipes from a deck, as these could subject the deck to vibration and cause it to fail.

Use with other types of electrical service: Supplements to the electrified floor system, using a different distribution system, usually pose no problem.

Insulating Glass

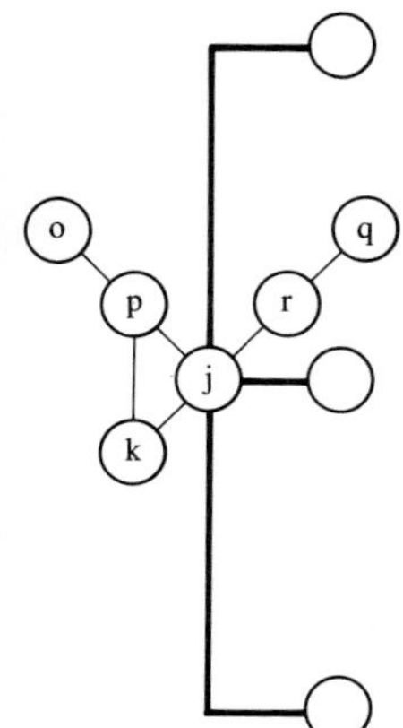

Insulating glass is found in Generic Example Number 2, Post-Tensioned Concrete. When used in a hospital building, as shown, this product helps insure thermal comfort and acoustical privacy for 24-hour occupancy.

j. *Rigid concrete frame*
k. *Brick and concrete masonry and rigid insulation*
o. *Insulating glass*
p. *Window frame*
q. *Interior wall covering*
r. *Drywall*

Diagram detail page 344

Reviewer:
Stephen Selkowitz
Group Leader, Windows and Daylighting Group
Lawrence Berkeley Laboratory
University of California
Berkeley, CA

Strictly defined, insulating glass is a hermetically sealed assembly of two or three lights of glass that are organically sealed to enclose the air space, with a dessicant to control the possibility of cavity condensation. The discussion here will focus on double-glazed rather than triple-glazed units, as the latter are not widely used. This type of glass unit has achieved general popularity since the energy shortages of the 1970's and is used extensively today on building exteriors.

Insulating glass is an energy-saving component whose overriding advantage is additional resistance to heat flow, resulting in improved thermal comfort. Multiplying the number of glazing layers introduces many options and consequences for the designer.

Although double glazing primarily affects the interior and envelope systems of a building, it also affects other systems. In some climates, multiple glazing may reduce the need for condensation removal on windows, and in warm areas it may eliminate the need for perimeter heating at the windows entirely. Because the multiple glazing strategy increases the weight of the window unit, there are structural ramifications as well.

Numerous design criteria must be satisfied by the window surface.[1] In the case of insulating glass, safety, privacy, security, view, and glare reduction are handled by the same product that reduces heat exchange and increases thermal comfort of the area adjacent to an exterior surface. While preserving the acoustical reflectance qualities of single-pane glass, double glazing increases acoustical insulation of the window unit from outside noise.[2] Even the visible integration options increase with double glazing, since the double-glazed openings are more variable than single panes, especially in terms of color and reflectance to light.[3] Planning an interior layout, including desk orientation and task lighting locations, requires consideration of daylight available and the related issues of glare, view, and heat transmission.

The physical connection of the window unit to the envelope or structure is complicated by double glazing. The double-glazed unit is normally thicker and more substantial structurally than the average single-glazed unit. The increased mass affects the operational characteristics and hardware of a double-glazed door or window.

1. Design criteria, p. 232.
2. Acoustical performance, p. 254.
3. Visible integration, pp. 381–385.

EXAMPLES

The built examples provide several illustrations of the use of insulating glass. It is used in virtually all of the buildings where energy conservation is a prime consideration. Insulating glass is vital to the double envelope of the Occidental Chemical Building[4] and the sawtooth roof monitors of Trust Pharmacy.[5] The insulating value of the glass in the clerestories of the John Nutting Apartments[6] helps them retain heat when the sun is not present. Both the fixed and operable insulating units are triple-glazed with clear glass.

Insulating glass is used in the Kimbell Museum[7] to help maintain the precise thermal conditions and relative humidity required for the collection. The window frame is a thermal break type (incorporating a gasket in a metal window to break

4. Occidental Chemical, pp. 94–97.
5. Trust Pharmacy, pp. 60–61.
6. John Nutting Apartments, pp. 68–69.
7. Kimbell Museum, pp. 64–67.

the heat flow), the first to be used on a Kahn building.

Single glazing was used in the first phase of construction at Stockton State College.[8] Insulating glass was chosen for the second phase after studies showed that the resulting energy savings would be sufficient to cover the additional cost. The units used are 1 in. thick with grey-tinted outerlights.

IMMEDIATE CONSIDERATIONS

Thickness: Overall unit thickness is the sum of the thickness of the glass plus the width of the air space. The thinnest standard unit is ⅝ in. thick, and is comprised of two panes of 3/16 in. thick glass and a ¼ in. air space. The thickest standard unit is 1 in., with two panes of ¼ in. thick glass and a ½ in. air space. Unit thickness determines the insulating value; the two glass lights must not differ in thickness by more than ⅛ in.

Framing: The type of framing used strongly affects the insulating value of the wall as well as its appearance. Framing considerations are discussed under glass and aluminum curtain walls.[9]

Glass type and color: These elements are important both for energy control and appearance. Colored or clear glass can have a metallic oxide added to its ingredients to create "heat-absorbing" glass. Colored or clear glass can also serve as a substrate for a coating. Such coatings can strongly influence the heat and light reflective characteristics of the glass. Reflective glass, which has a metallic oxide coating, can present a distorted image (known as "oil-canning") on the exterior. Also, the mirrored surface presented to the exterior during the day becomes a mirrored surface to the interior at night. This may not be desirable for a night-time user who wants to appreciate a view, or in a hotel where guests may not realize that they are easily visible from outside the building. Tinted glass will affect the quality and amount of daylight the windows transmit.

Spandrels: Spandrel panels in a curtain wall should be consistent in appearance and have an insulating value comparable to or better than the other insulating glass units. Spandrel glass is generally formed by fusing ceramic material to heat-strengthened glass to provide an opaque panel. It may also have insulation adhered to it. Spandrel glass typically looks darker than the surrounding translucent glass. In a curtain wall of reflective glass, spandrels will be most obvious at night.[10] Spandrels formed by butting batt insulation to the standard unit have had mixed results.

Installation: The type of sealant and glazing method used should be discussed with the manufacturers of both glass and framing. Insulating glass units frequently require special glazing methods. The glazing sealant must be compatible with the window seal or failures may occur.

GENERAL CONSIDERATIONS

Supplemental shading: The type, color, and location of drapes or blinds used in conjunction with insulating glass will affect its thermal performance. The designer should consider methods of avoiding heat build-up and consequent thermal stress on the glass. Automatic or manually controlled blinds or shutters can create a very flexible solution to this problem.

Noise: If noise is a concern, acoustical properties should be considered in glass selection and unit design. Design criteria are given in AAMA's *Sound Control for Aluminum Curtain Wall and Windows*.

Costs: Glass costs vary widely depending on the type of glass. Cost analysis usually focuses on life cycle comparisons of the cost of the glazing versus the annual energy consumption of the building. The annual cost savings comparison of lower energy consumption should include the cost of the HVAC system required by the glazing.

Warranty: The warranty period for insulating glass units varies widely. The average is five years for the hermetic seal, but it is possible to set a more extensive warranty.

8. Stockton State College, pp. 78–81.

9. Glass and aluminum curtain wall, pp. 212–215.

10. Visible integration, pp. 381–385.

Photo: D. Randolph Foulds

Photo: Mazria/Schiff & Associates

Photo: Marshall D. Meyers

Insulating glass is used in a wide variety of climates and building types. Although the John Nutting Apartments (top) and Trust Pharmacy (center) are quite different building types located in different geographic regions, both include insulating glass as part of their passive solar strategies. It is used in the roof monitors of both buildings, those of Trust Pharmacy being clearly visible in the photograph. In the Kimbell Museum (above), which is located in a hot, dry climate, the need to provide a controlled environment for the preservation of the art collection led to the selection of insulating glass.

Glass and Aluminum Curtain Wall

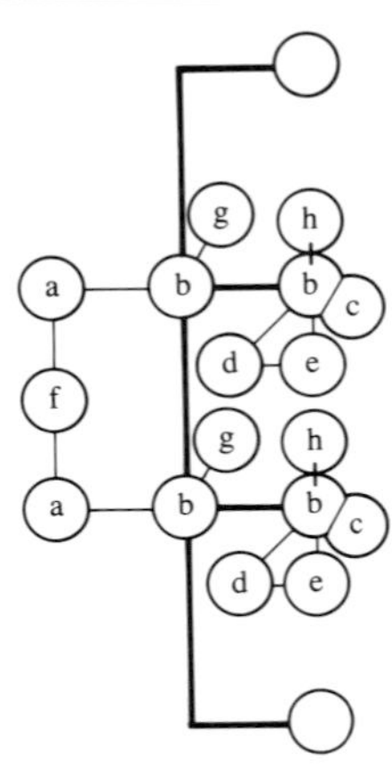

a. *Aluminum and glass curtain wall*
b. *Steel frame; composite steel frame and concrete deck; stub girders*
c. *Ducts and diffusers*
d. *High pressure sodium lighting*
e. *Suspended ceiling*
f. *Window assembly*
g. *Perimeter heater*
h. *Floor covering*

Diagram detail page 345

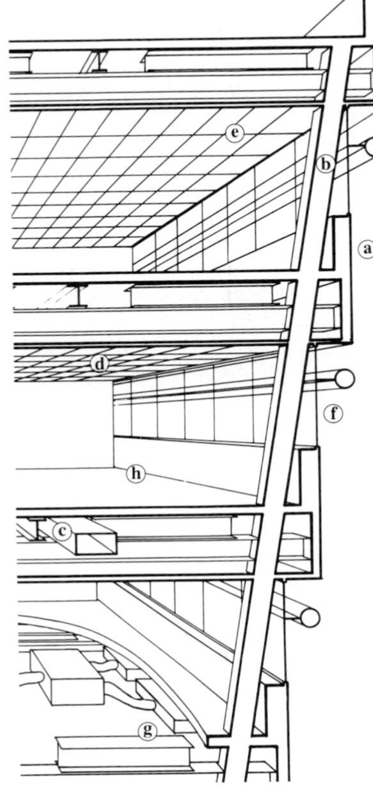

Reviewer:
Stephen Selkowitz
Group Leader, Windows and Daylighting Group
Lawrence Berkeley Laboratory
University of California
Berkeley, CA

Photo: Hursley/Lark/Hursley

The curtain wall on the south side of the Georgia Power building is cantilevered out 15 in. at each floor (top), providing shading from the sun as well as a striking image (above).

The glass and aluminum curtain wall is one of the principal elements of integration in modern highrise construction. It satisfies two important criteria in such construction by providing a lightweight envelope and saving construction time.[1]

This discussion will focus on aluminum framing. Aluminum is popular because it is easily extruded and shaped in fabrication, and a wide variety of mullion extrusions is available. The curtain wall can be flat, sloped, or curved. It usually consists of alternating bands of translucent glass and spandrel glass, and often integrates visibly into the ground-level storefront or entrance design. The curtain wall is primarily an interior/envelope combination.[2] In areas with high winds or seismic problems, or in designs calling for tall or unusually shaped windows, the *connected* relationship between the structure and the curtain wall becomes critical.[3] Design solutions will vary depending on whether the curtain wall is attached to a concrete frame, where creep may be an important factor, or to a more flexible steel frame. The relationship of glass curtain wall to the mechanical system is discussed in this chapter under insulating glass.

Although the exterior appearance of the curtain wall is usually emphasized, there are numerous design criteria that affect its relationship to the interior. The spacing of mullions, for example, will influence the interior partition layout. Glass selection will affect interior light quality; certain finish materials fade quickly if continually exposed to ultraviolet light and some types of glass can filter ultraviolet light. The blinds or drapes used will affect the building's efficiency. The amount of air infiltration will determine the comfort level at the building perimeter and will influence desk locations.

In order to meet code requirements for fire safety, vertically continuous curtain wall will require a fire-resistant material in the space between the panel and floor structure at each floor level.

1. Conservation of time, pp. 236–237.
2. Envelope and interior, pp. 328–329.
3. Structure and envelope *connected*, pp. 323–324.

EXAMPLES

The unique curtain wall used on the Equitable Life building[4] was custom-designed by the architect and manufacturer. Curtain wall was chosen because the project was fast-tracked, and the architect did not have confidence in existing systems for his innovative purposes. The assembly is composed of alternating horizontal bands of clear glass and brushed anodized aluminum held 18 in. away from the inner layer of insulated wall. A thermal break is used, and the glass is butt-jointed to add to the horizontally banded look of the wall.

Two problems that arose required keeping the tolerances in extrusions within acceptable limits and redesigning the fasteners.

The curtain wall design used in the Vocational Technical Education Facility at the University of Minnesota[5] includes an envelope of air between the inner thermal and outer moisture walls. Single glazing was chosen to keep the cost down and the moisture out, and the space between gives a greenhouse effect. The designers initially intended for the faculty offices to have operable windows in the inner wall but these were eliminated to satisfy fire separation requirements.

A custom-designed curtain wall similar to standard stick-type assemblies was chosen for Stockton State College.[6] Leaks developed in the first phase of construction and were attributed to incompatibility between the sealant joint design and the type of sealant used. These problems were resolved in subsequent construction phases.

4. Equitable Life, pp. 102–105.

5. Vocational Technical Education Facility, pp. 98–101.

6. Stockton State College, pp. 78–81.

IMMEDIATE CONSIDERATIONS

Framing: The aluminum sections comprising the frame are characterized as either stick or tube type. Stick framing usually conserves erection time but has lower load capacity than tube framing. The visual effect of stick framing must also be considered, since there will either tend to be more vertical members in order to take the wind load or deeper members than would be necessary in tube framing.[7]

7. Visible integration, pp. 381–385.

Finish: The aluminum frame may be painted or anodized. Compatible paints include fluorocarbon polymer, plastisol, siliconized polymer, and polymethane and are applied either by roller or by electrostatic spraying. Anodized finishes can be clear or colored, the color being either integral or electrolytically deposited. A thorough discussion of finishes for architectural aluminum is found in publications of the Architectural Aluminum Manufacturers Association.

Structural integration: A successful curtain wall must be designed to support structural and wind loads, accommodate cyclical expansion and contraction, and resist water and air infiltration. Framing can be selected or specified according to performance specifications or proprietary preference. In either case, wind-load and seismic requirements, as well as expansion control and internal drainage requirements, should be specified.

The method of attachment is critical to both expansion control and wind-load requirements. Clip angles are usually used to attach the mullions to the structure. These will be fixed against wind loading and may allow for horizontal expansion. The location of attachment and vertical joints with regard to deflection of the structure between columns should also be considered. In addition, sufficient room must be allowed in the horizontal expansion control joint to accommodate differences in loading and deflection from floor to floor.

Glass size and type: The maximum glass size depends on the type of glass selected and the design wind load.

Spandrel: A curtain wall spandrel is a glass or metal panel set into the same aluminum frame as the rest of the curtain wall. In the selection of spandrel materials, the same weather conditions and loading requirements should be considered as in framing design and the selection of translucent glass, with the added concern that a new material will represent another coefficient of expansion to be incorporated into the wall design.

Glazing method: The method of glazing bears directly on the speed of erection and weathertightness of the curtain wall. The two general types are dry glazing, which is done with preformed gaskets, and wet glazing, which is done with sealing compounds. Silicone, polyurethane, and polysulfide are the most frequently used high-performance glazing sealants. Polysulfide is the least expensive, but has the most limited performance characteristics of the three types. Cyclic movement, ultraviolet resistance, water resistance, and strength all affect the choice of glazing method. In addition, a building's orientation and shading may affect glazing performance. Some flexible expansive glazing materials have been found to "snake out" of joints when part of the joint is shaded and part is in direct sunlight for prolonged periods.

Testing: One important decision is whether to rely on wind loads listed in local codes and national standards or to conduct wind tunnel tests of the building. The height and location will be determining factors in this decision. Many cities require a wind analysis on buildings over 20 stories, and such an analysis may be useful for lower buildings in some cases. Recent research indicates that a building's height, shape, and relationship to adjacent structures can have a pronounced influence on the actual wind-load conditions, creating wind loads several times greater than those stipulated in local codes.

A mock-up of part of the actual curtain wall may be laboratory tested for weathertightness. Although such testing is costly, mock-ups can be subjected to an extensive range of tests, and these may prompt design modifications that avoid costly repairs and lawsuits. The ASTM tests for water penetration and wind infiltration are conducted at a test pressure of 25 psf with a sealant or gasket in place. This wind pressure may also differ from actual conditions found at a particular building during a storm.

Maintenance: Accessibility of glass for washing or replacement from both exterior and interior should be considered. Highrise buildings with inoperable windows will often have vertical tracks designed into the curtain wall assembly so that window-washing platforms can be stabilized against the building.

GENERAL CONSIDERATIONS

Occupancy: The phasing of building occupancy can present problems for curtain wall construction. Hypothetically, an interlocking frame type curtain wall installed in a building with an unoccupied floor sandwiched between two occupied floors could experience live load deflection of the floors above and below the unoccupied floor, disengaging the curtain wall above and crushing the curtain wall below.

Leaks: Weeps and gutters for internal drainage are essential to a successful curtain wall installation. It should be noted that adjacent materials may release chemicals or minerals into the runoff that can stain the glass.

The design may also include a thermal break system to reduce thermal transmissivity. A thermal break consists of insulating material separating the interior and exterior sides of the metal or glass. This prevents the exterior temperature from being conducted immediately to the interior.[8]

Privacy: The degree of privacy required by the building's users will influence the decision to use a glass curtain wall, as well as the type of glass selected. Sound transmission between floors and from the exterior may need special attention.

8. Thermal performance, pp. 250–251.

Photo: Warren Cox

Photo: Patricia Layman Bazelon

Curtain wall applications demonstrate a variety of approaches to sunshading and orientation. The north wall of the National Permanent Building (top) is a flush facade, while the west and south walls are set back and shaded by edge beams and subway grating. In the Occidental Chemical building, on the other hand, sunshading is accomplished through the use of operable louvers located between the double curtain walls (above). Each elevation responds independently to the angle of sunlight, permitting four identical elevations.

Glass Block Walls

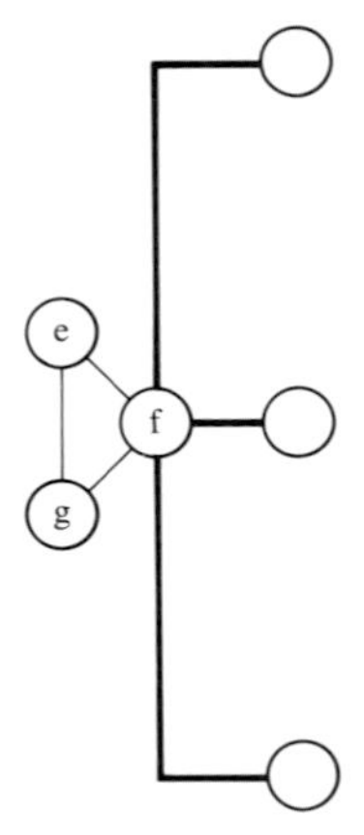

e. *Glass block panels*
f. *Concrete masonry bearing wall*
g. *Brick veneer and rigid insulation*

Diagram detail page 345

Reviewer:
Peter J. Pfister, AIA
Architectural Alliance
Minneapolis, MN

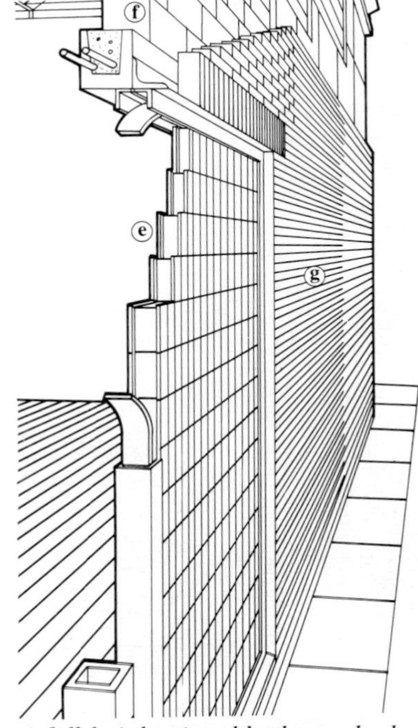

A full-height glass block panel takes the place of a window in Generic Example Number 13, Space Frames.

A very popular building material for institutional and light commercial buildings in the 1950's, glass block has been rediscovered in the 1980's. Pittsburgh-Corning, the last remaining U.S. manufacturer of glass block, was on the verge of halting production when market conditions changed. Now this company is competing with several foreign companies for the newly revived glass block market.

Glass block integrates the rigor of masonry construction and the economy of daylighting in a single unit. It is not loadbearing, however; although its weight greatly exceeds that of a glass panel, it is essentially a double-glazed window with a cement frame. Panels of glass block may be incorporated into non-masonry as well as masonry walls. Since the block cannot be cut, openings must have the proper modular dimension.

Glass block is typically used for reasons of security, insulating value, maintenance, and visible integration and coordination with masonry construction and quality of light. The translucency of the block makes it ideal for applications where shades might present a maintenance problem. At night it appears to be illuminated from the dark side, yet maintains privacy on the light side. The use of glass block is particularly appropriate in shower rooms or swimming facilities, as it is relatively impermeable to water. It may also be used in office areas, although in these it has the potential for casting gridded shadows on work surfaces.

EXAMPLES

At the Vocational Technical Education Facility at the University of Minnesota,[1] 12 × 12 in. clear glass block was chosen to provide a sense of transparency between departmental offices and student circulation spaces in the atrium, and to achieve the necessary fire separation. The glass block wall is broken by niches containing entrances and air transfer grilles.

The addition to the Submarine Training Facility at Groton[2] features panels of 8 × 8 in. glass block in the exterior walls. For security reasons, a bronze metallic-oxide coating is used to further reduce the visibility of the interior. This finish also provides visible integration with the addition of glazed brick masonry.

Glass block is used in the Pike and Virginia Building[3] for decorative purposes only.

IMMEDIATE CONSIDERATIONS

Fabrication: Solid, single cavity, and double cavity blocks are available. In addition, small panels can be prefabricated in preassembled units.

Pattern and color: There are a wide variety of patterned glass blocks on the market. In addition, smooth-faced blocks are available with a special lens-type curvature with unique diffusion and light transmission properties. The glass can be clear, tinted, or have a reflective coating, and the interior rim of the block can be painted to add color and enhance the grid pattern.

1. Vocational Technical Education Facility, pp. 98–101.
2. Addition to Submarine Training Facility, pp. 106–107.
3. Pike and Virginia Building, pp. 92–93.

As an integration option, glass block is especially appropriate for use with masonry infill. A glass block panel facing onto the atrium of the Vocational Technical Education Facility of the University of Minnesota at St. Paul contributes to the building's daylighting strategy (right). Privacy is maintained in the office space, which nevertheless partakes of the "outdoor" quality of the atrium. In the apartments in the Pike and Virginia Building, glass block serves a more purely decorative function (below).

Photo: Franz C. Hall

Photo: Dick Busher

Dimensions: The most commonly used and readily available sizes for glass block are 6×6, 8×8, and 12×12 in. Standard thicknesses are 4 and 6 in. Rectangular block is also available from some manufacturers. Some imported block is only available in metric sizes, and is difficult to incorporate into a building designed with standard American measurements.

Maintenance: Glass block can be cleaned with a hose on the outside or a damp cloth on the inside.

GENERAL CONSIDERATIONS

Location: The light-transmitting ability of glass block is largely determined by its location. If a glass block panel is used as an interior partition, the brightness of the adjacent space and the color of the finishes will influence the light transmitted through the glass block.

Acoustics: The blocks provide better acoustical insulation than normal glazing. When used in interior applications, care must be taken to avoid unwanted acoustical reflection from the glass surfaces.

Insulating properties: The U-value of glass block ranges from approximately .87 for a clear solid block to .44 for a double-cavity patterned block. The latter approximates the

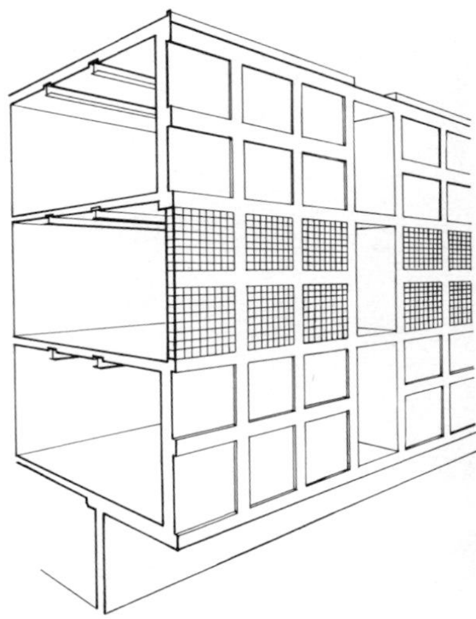

Photos: Nick Wheeler

Security issues were paramount in the program for the addition to the Submarine Training Facility at Groton, where panels of 8 in. square glass block are set into facades of glazed brick (top left). Two panels equal one floor height. This and the commanding site make the building appear much larger than it is (top right). Effective daylighting is achieved without revealing interior details to outside view (above).

value of an insulating glass composition of ¼ in. reflective glass with a ½ in. air space. The mass of the glass block tends to retain its temperature with a flywheel effect much like normal masonry. Close proximity to an exterior glass wall could be a problem for workers during winter.[4]

4. Thermal performance, pp. 250–251.

Security: In addition to its capacity for obscuring interior detail, glass block is difficult to break. It is an excellent substitute for basement windows that might pose security problems.

Installation: The installation of glass block is similar to masonry. Because it is not load-bearing, however, special details must be provided to separate the block from adjacent construction.

Lightweight Insulating Metal Panels

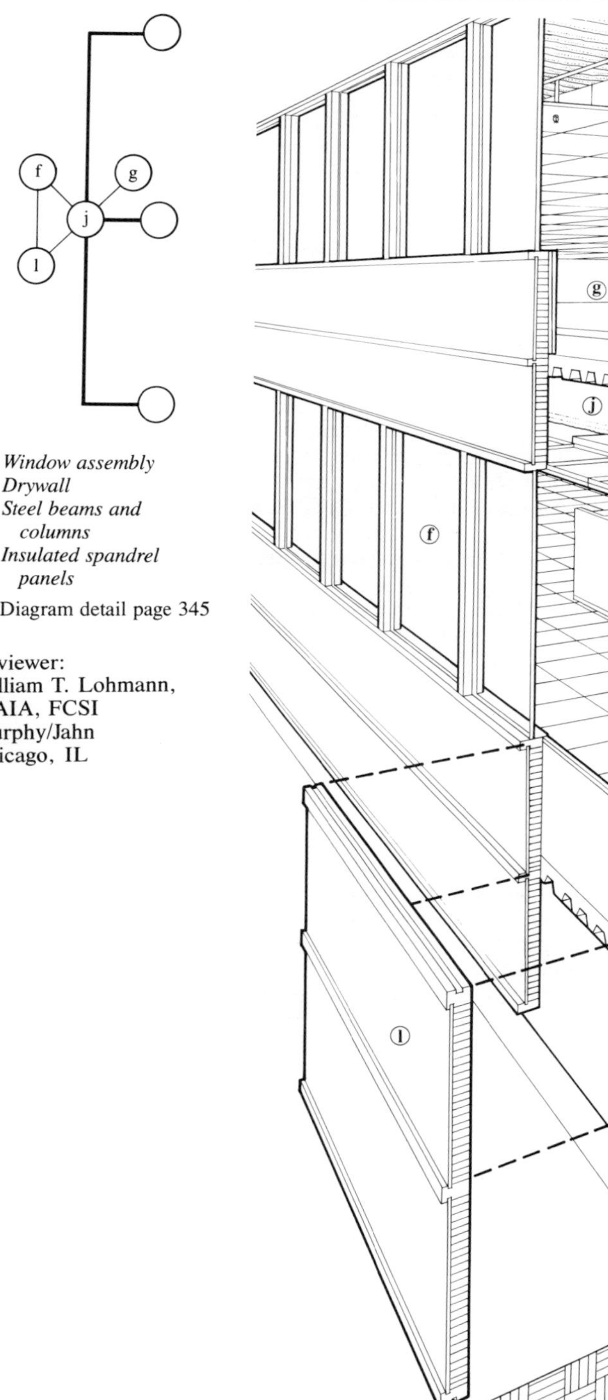

f. *Window assembly*
g. *Drywall*
i. *Steel beams and columns*
k. *Insulated spandrel panels*

Diagram detail page 345

Reviewer:
William T. Lohmann, AIA, FCSI
Murphy/Jahn
Chicago, IL

Lightweight insulating metal panels are used in Generic Example Number 1, Access Floor and Curtain Wall.

Metal panels are generally accepted for use in curtain walls, infill, spandrels, and fascias. The prefabricated, insulated units discussed here differ from metal "sandwich" panels in that the metal encapsulates the insulation and does not require internal fasteners or subgirts.

The metal panel concept represents a unification of envelope and interior.[1] To the extent that their insulating and weather-barrier qualities affect the heating and air conditioning loads, the panels are integrated at a *remote* level with the HVAC system. Ease of installation and removal requires that their relationship to structure be *connected.* The panels' weight is itself minimized to conserve structural material and make the units easier to handle and transport.

In terms of visible integration, the proportioning of the panels and the treatment of the joints combine with panel surface treatment and interior and exterior colors to form both facade and interior space.[2] Curved corner panels are available; these help avoid special joint situations that are prone to leakage.

The integration relationships physically vary from the accommodation of doors and windows to the special design situations presented by the floor plane, roof plane, and ground line. The sculptural option inherent in the panel approach makes it natural to combine panels with other thin sheet materials that permit curves, such as plastic skylights.

Acoustical and thermal properties, light qualities, and maintenance all bear on the choice of panel surface and material. Because the surfaces are finished at the time of manufacture, the individual units must be handled with great care to insure that the panels are not scratched or otherwise damaged.

EXAMPLE

In the Herman Miller Seating Plant,[3] long, narrow panels are laid horizontally to stress the proportions of the long, low building. The panels are suspended between strip

1. Envelope and interior *unified*, p. 329.
2. Visible integration, pp. 381–385.
3. Herman Miller Seating Plant, pp. 56–59.

A section perspective through the Herman Miller plant's wall shows the tubular steel outriggers that connect the panels to the structure.

windows and barrel-vaulted skylights, accentuating their light-reflecting characteristics. The result emphasizes the "assembly character" of the building, visually coordinating its appearance with the actual assembly work accomplished within it.

The panels are clad in brushed stainless steel on the exterior, while interior surfaces are painted. The panels are attached directly to the steel support system via mechanical attachment. One unexpected problem with the panel has arisen. The polluted spray blowing off Lake Michigan causes water to run down the exterior face of the panels, and thus they require more frequent cleaning than anticipated.

IMMEDIATE CONSIDERATIONS

Metal: Metal panels can be made of aluminum, stainless steel, or galvanized or other coated steel. The choice is both economic and esthetic. Stainless steel seems to exhibit the most problems with distortion, or "oil-canning." Metal thickness, alloy, and, in the case of aluminum, temper will all affect the appearance and durability of the panel.

Exterior and interior faces: The faces need not be the same finish or thickness of metal; manufacturers' literature should be consulted for details on available assemblies. Surfaces may be flat, textured, or extruded, have an impressed relief pattern, or be cast to match a custom design. The degree of exposure desired for the interior face will determine whether it receives an applied finish or has a mill finish meant to be concealed. Some manufacturers will assemble a panel with an interior face of plywood or other rigid material.

Connections: A range of proprietary connection methods is usually available with a given manufacturer's panel. The connection detail will depend on loading conditions.

Finishes: Painted, baked enamel, and porcelain enamel finishes are available for steel and steel alloys, while aluminum panels are either painted or anodized. Stainless steel does not usually have an applied finish. Both aluminum and steel may be ordered with factory prime coats for field painting, but this is the least reliable finishing method.

Painted and anodized finishes are available in durable and attractive colors. Anodized finishes are not recommended for applications where they would be exposed to salt water or corrosive pollutants. The patented factory-applied paint finishes have proven very durable, and many come with a five-year warranty. The designer should determine whether the finish coat is applied by the metal manufacturer or the panel fabricator.

Photos: Balthazar Korab

The panels in the Herman Miller plant are attached to the outriggers with clips, and may be demounted and reused (top). The outriggers and structural elements add detail to interior views when the building is lit from within (above).

Size: Limitations in fabrication and transportation restrict panel size. Each manufacturer has a slightly different maximum size.

In a given application, panel size will be determined by design loads and thermal stresses applied to the panel. Finish and color can significantly affect the maximum size of the panel, as dark-colored panels expand more than light-colored ones.

Thickness: The thickness of the panel depends on the type of insulation selected and the insulating value desired. A range of 1 to 8 in. is typical.

Shape: Metal panels may be curved, although the radius desired must be within the standard range of the fabricating plant. Usually, the metal sheet is molded or rolled to the desired radius and then coated with a special epoxy.

Edge treatment: The edge condition of a metal panel is important to its watertightness, durability, and appearance. Each manufacturer has a different type; many are flange-type edges that interlock with adjacent panels but still provide space for expansion and contraction of the adjoining metals. When a moisture-permeable insulation is used, the edge must also allow for venting of the core area.

Joints: Joints are critical in a metal panel assembly. They compensate for thermal expansion, field variations, movement due to lateral loads, misalignment of panels during erection, and differential movements of the panel and supporting frame. In addition, they must be watertight and prevent air infiltration. The connectors provide strength to resist structural loads, and their number and type will be determined by loading conditions. The size of the joints should be determined by the expected differential movement between panels. The sealant protects the assembly against the weather, and should be compatible with the materials used and be able to accommodate the expected movement within the joint.

Windows: The panel system and edge conditions must be carefully detailed to assure compatibility with the type of window selected. Compatibility among sealants is especially important, and material isolation may have to be considered.[4]

4. Silicone sealants, pp. 225–226.

Maintenance: Panels should be accessible for cleaning. The factory-applied finishes have a good record of durability, but painted panels should probably be protected from potential impact damage. There is some risk of deterioration with a field-applied finish, because quality control procedures are not easy to enforce in the field and because the prime and finish coats may not be as compatible as when both coats are factory-applied.

GENERAL CONSIDERATIONS

Fire rating: The type of insulation used determines the fire rating, since insulation is the most flammable part of the assembly.

Acoustical properties: No STC rating is available from metal panel manufacturers. Sound transmitted by resonance of a metal panel may be a factor for a building located near a source of chronic loud noise, such as an airport.

Thermal value: The desired R-value for the wall will determine the insulation selected and the panel thickness.

Future removal of panels: If it is anticipated that the panels will be removed at a future date to accommodate expansion or for another purpose, the fasteners can be designed to facilitate panel removal.

Explosion relief: If an explosion-resistant design is required, special fasteners can be used.

Exterior Insulation Systems

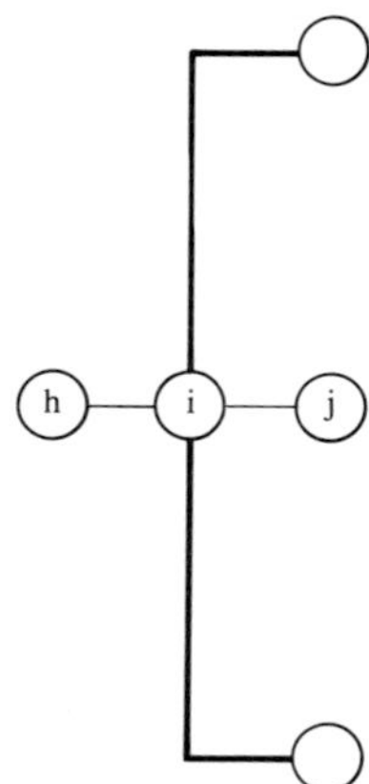

i *Rigid insulation and veneer coating*
j. *Concrete masonry bearing wall*
k. *Glazed face*
Diagram detail page 346

Reviewer:
Richard L. Crowther, FAIA
Energy Concept Architect
Denver, CO

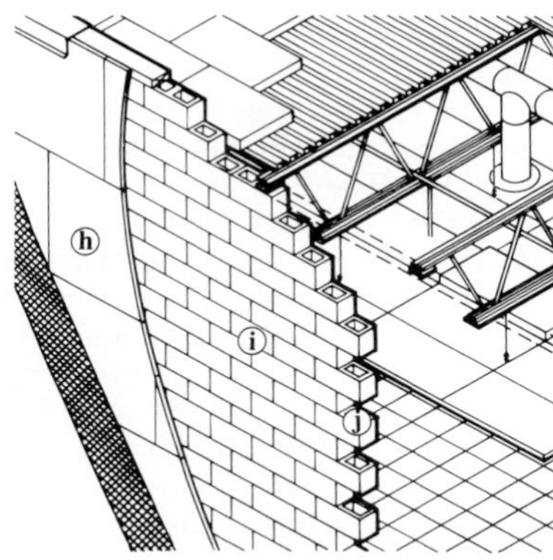

An exterior insulation system is shown in Generic Example Number 8, Bearing Wall and Bar-Joist Roof.

Exterior insulation systems, or EIS, involve placing insulation outside the structural frame to minimize thermal bridging and to protect the structure itself from thermal expansion and contraction. They were introduced to the United States in the late 1960's by Frank Morsilli, founder and now president of Dryvit, Inc. Rising energy costs have contributed to a growing consumer demand for these products.

The major components of an exterior insulation system are the insulation and a protective coating of cementitious or acrylic veneer. The thickness of this coating may be as little as 1/32 in., and can be varied to meet the insulating needs of a building's climatic exposures while maintaining a uniform appearance on all facades. The early exterior insulation systems had problems with impact resistance, installation, and quality control in general. The problem of impact damage to the veneer has been partially solved by reinforcing, but maintenance and security issues must still be addressed in the design process.[1]

1. Design criteria, p. 232.

There are many climates where the placement of insulation on the exterior layer of the envelope does have significant energy conserving qualities, especially in combination with thermal mass. In the Southwest, for example, thick masonry walls are used to retard the entry of heat during the day and delay its departure at night. Insulation placed on the exterior of a high mass wall traps heat leaving the building, enhancing the wall's capacity to act as a heat sink and at the same time reducing infiltration.[2] Colors may be chosen to absorb or reflect heat. In addition, the ease with which the appearance of stucco is achieved contributes to its potential for visible integration.

Veneer coatings are available in a wide range of colors and finishes. Exterior insulation systems can be used over almost any substrate, and are well suited to retrofit work. Their use can greatly simplify detailing; they can meet glass without a frame, do not require expansion members, and can cover dissimilar materials for a uniform appearance. Exterior insulation systems have also been used in historic preservation work to mimic the appearance of carved stone, terra cotta, and other building materials that are no longer available or are difficult to obtain.

Theoretically, the veneer coating can be applied to any shape that the substrate assumes. The continuity of the protective coating can be used as a thermal shield over projecting elements, such as chimneys, as well as on planar surfaces. It can also be used on slopes greater than 45 degrees. The common uses of these systems seem to follow the more traditional profile customarily seen with stucco or precast concrete walls.

EXAMPLE
Exterior insulation is shown in Generic Example Number 8.[3] It is well suited for large expanses of wall area without penetrations.

2. Thermal performance, pp. 250–251.
3. Bearing wall and bar-joist roof, pp. 138–139.

IMMEDIATE CONSIDERATIONS
Coating: There are two general types of veneer coatings available. These are the acrylic polymer-based coatings, or PB, and the polymer-modified portland cement coatings, or PM. Acrylic coatings are very flexible and can be applied in very thin coats. They usually come ready-mixed from the factory, and hence their color consistency is

good. They have less impact resistance than cementitious coatings, however, and usually require reinforcement. Cementitious coatings are more rigid and require a thicker application. While some products use only an acrylic veneer, most are a combination of a cementitious base coat and an acrylic finish coat.

Most manufacturers will mix custom colors in addition to those featured in their color chart. The available hand-troweled or machine-applied finishes include a complete range of standard stucco finishes as well as ones that imitate limestone, corrugated concrete, and exposed aggregate concrete.

Impact resistance: The problem of impact damage to the veneer has been partly solved by reinforcing. The base and veneer coatings can be reinforced with wire mesh, although most manufacturers prefer a glass fiber fabric. Some coatings include chopped glass fibers in the matrix that act as internal reinforcing. Nevertheless, protection from predictable impact sources such as car bumpers and lawnmowers should be considered in the design, as well as the possibility of intentional penetration by intruders.

Insulation: Expanded polystyrene (EPS) or bead board is by far the most commonly used insulation. Other types have been used successfully, but expanded polystyrene is preferred because of its low cost. All types of rigid insulation now used with EIS are flammable. Some fiberglass insulation manufacturers are investigating the possibility of marketing a system that incorporates rigid glass fiber insulation, which would improve the fire safety characteristics.

Maintenance: Exterior insulation systems resist fading, can be readily repaired, and are easily re-applied as future needs dictate. One manufacturer has recently marketed a recoating veneer.

GENERAL CONSIDERATIONS

Installation: Exterior insulation systems may be installed as prefabricated panels, or the veneer may be field-applied. Application of the veneer is relatively economical; the veneer can be applied quickly and the procedure is not technically complex. There is some controversy about the proper method for connecting the insulation to the substrate, especially when gypsum sheathing is used. Some manufacturers use mechanical fasteners while others use a liquid adhesive. The Gypsum Association objects to the use of adhesives alone to attach to a gypsum sheathing substrate; they claim that the sheathing paper face is not structural and is asphalt-impregnated so that delamination can easily occur. Most manufacturers will use mechanical fasteners if required to do so.

Structure: One of the principal advantages of exterior insulation systems is their ability to provide thermal and moisture protection without placing a heavy deadload burden on the structure. When the system is supported by light gauge metal framing, however, the architect must determine the proper allowable deflection of the frame. Most manufacturers recommend L/240 as a proper allowable deflection, but other elements of the building, such as windows where the exterior insulation system is used as a spandrel, should be considered.

Code requirements: All current building codes contain restrictions on exterior insulation systems. New York and Los Angeles prohibit their use, while other cities review it on a case-by-case basis. The principal difficulty is that both the veneer coating and the plastic insulation are flammable and emit toxic gases when burned. To date, however, no fires have occurred in which flame or smoke spread was associated with these materials.

Silicone Sealants

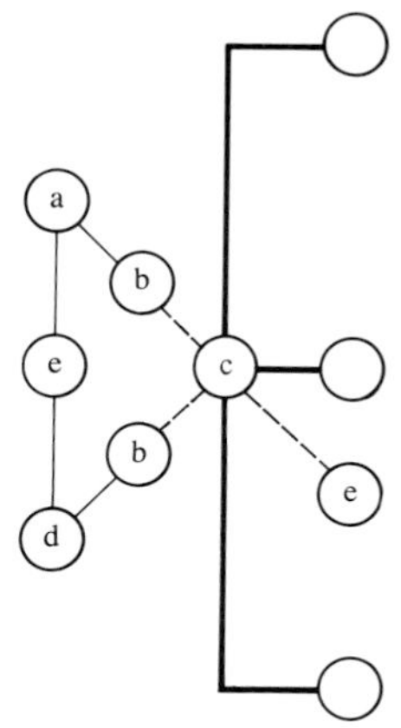

a. *Window assembly*
b. *Sealant*
c. *Structural frame*
d. *Wall panels*
e. *Drywall*
Diagram detail page 346

Reviewer:
William T. Lohmann, AIA, FCSI
Murphy/Jahn
Chicago, IL

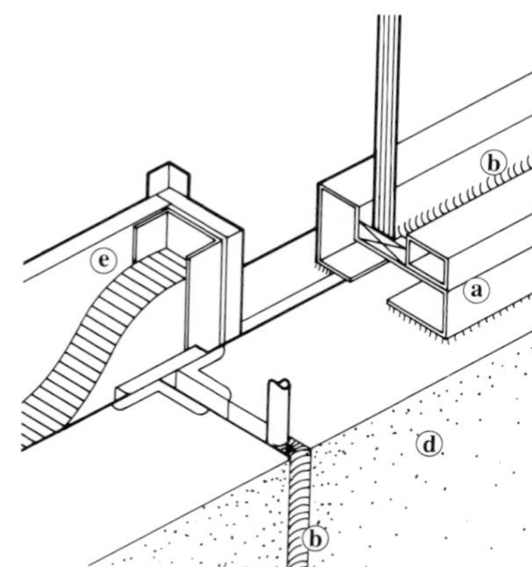

The joint situation shown above indicates the number of materials that can come in contact with a sealant, whether directly or through runoff.

A sealant is a connection between materials, and as such is possibly the most integrated product in a building. Sealants as we know them did not exist forty years ago. Before the emergence of curtain wall construction, oil-based caulking was adequate for wood and masonry joints. New products were needed to accommodate the metal substrates' high coefficient of expansion. This led to the development of high-performance sealants.

While latex polymer sealants with silicone additives are available, this discussion will focus on silicone-based sealants. Silicone is an inorganic compound offering good durability, high strength, ozone resistance, and excellent adhesion to most building materials. It is used for glazing, building joints, and expansion joints. Silicone is the only sealant currently recommended for use in structural glazing applications; that is, where panes of glass are joined edge to edge, eliminating the mullions.

Sealants keep wind, rain, and noise out of the building, accommodate movement, and keep the hot or cold air in the building as required. A good sealant is an energy-conserving product; it also reduces maintenance time and avoids the waste associated with material failure.[1] When the sealant joint succeeds, it simply joins two surfaces and accommodates their differential expansion while it functionally integrates numerous system criteria.

A sealant joint can fail for any of a number of reasons, many of which are remote from the actual joint design. The foundations of the building may settle unexpectedly; material movement due to expansion and contraction or (in the case of concrete) creep may be more than anticipated; the sealant may have been applied in ambient temperatures that were too cold or too hot; the joint surfaces may have been dirty when the sealant was applied; or the sealant may have combined chemically with runoff from adjacent building materials. Clear silicone sealant is transparent to ultraviolet light, which may cause deterioration of the backer rod or other substrate. The sealant can also abrade and take on dirt. Sealant joints exposed to unequal shading conditions—with one part of the joint perpetually shaded and another part occasionally exposed to sunlight—can fail because of differential expansion of the sealant within the joint.

Extremes of wind, rain, or freeze/thaw conditions will cause even the best sealant joints to deteriorate. Oddly enough, one of the most common reasons for sealant joint failure is the designer's emphasis on very thin joints. Such visual priorities can compromise the function of the product.

There are sealants in all of the buildings in the case studies and in the Generic buildings as well. That they exist in every building, regardless of type or size, demonstrates their multipurpose characteristics. Integration is simply the assembly of disparate parts of systems, and this is the designed purpose of sealants as well.

EXAMPLES

Silicone sealants are used in building conditions as diverse as the Occidental Chemical building's double envelope[2] and the Illinois Regional Library's window wall.[3] This product's use in a variety of the ex-

1. Conservation of materials and time, pp. 236–237.
2. Occidental Chemical, pp. 94–97.
3. Illinois Regional Library, pp. 70–73.

amples in Chapter 3 is a measure of its universality of application, comparable only to glass itself.

IMMEDIATE CONSIDERATIONS

Types: There are several types of silicone sealant, and selection depends on the application desired. Distinctive qualities include shelf life, degree of adhesion, type of curing agent, one-part or two-part mixtures, and modulus of elasticity. The low modulus sealant is best for expansion joint applications, while the high modulus is best for glazing. The traditional acid cure requires a carefully cleaned and prepared substrate, and is not suitable for marble or copper substrates. The methanol cure has better adhesion than the acid cure.

Color: Silicone sealants cannot be painted, and are available in transparent form and in standard white, black, neutral, aluminum, bronze, and limestone colors. Custom colors are available when ordered in large quantity.

Surface preparation: Certain substrates require the use of primers before the application of silicone sealant. Concrete in particular requires the use of a barrier coat primer if the sealant extends below grade and is to serve as a weather seal. The lime from the concrete may leach in the presence of continuous moisture and cause the seal to deteriorate.

Location: Silicone sealants are not recommended for traffic-bearing joints, unless the sealant is recessed below the traffic level. It must be protected from umbrella points and spike heels.

Structural requirements: If silicone sealant is to be used as a structural seal as well as a weather seal, calculations must be made to determine proper joint design. The manufacturer should be consulted for sealant strength ratings.

Compatibility with adjacent materials: One difficult task in choosing a sealant is selecting one that will adhere to two very different materials. While it has good adhesive properties with most common building materials, silicone is not compatible with other sealants or with some types of backer materials. The salt residue left on anodized aluminum has been known to create bonding problems with silicone sealant. There are also bonding problems due to imperfect adhesion when the substrate is unclean or contaminated. Most manufacturers will provide test data and guidance to architects regarding compatible materials and will recommend field or laboratory tests if there is any doubt about the suitability of silicone sealant for a given application.

Weathertightness: Silicone sealants are very durable and resist water penetration. Some ceramic tile manufacturers recommend silicone sealant as a structural adhesive and weather seal for ceramic tile panels.

Allowable joint movement: As with any type of sealant, the joint should be designed based on the anticipated joint movement, either in shear or in tension and compression, and the modulus of elasticity of the sealant selected. Silicone sealants are relatively weak in shear. Many types of silicone sealant can expand or contract by a factor of 50 percent of their original width.

Cost: Silicone is more expensive than polysulfide or polyurethane, the two other generic types of high performance sealants. Sealant cost is usually a very small percentage of the total project budget, however, and cost is usually not a factor in a situation appropriate for a silicone sealant.

GENERAL CONSIDERATIONS

Fire protection: Many silicone sealants are fire-resistant, and none are toxic unless ingested.

Life expectancy: Thirty years is considered a realistic life expectancy for silicone sealant.

Compatibility with other sealants: When used with an exterior flush glazing system, the sealant manufacturer should be consulted about the type of insulating glass used if such units are selected. The plasticizers in the glass seal may migrate, resulting in loss of adhesion with the silicone.

References

ENERGY MANAGEMENT CONTROL SYSTEMS

American Society of Heating, Refrigerating and Air Conditioning Engineers. *Handbook & Product Directory*. 1980 Systems, Chapter 34. New York: ASHRAE, 1980.

Haynes, Roger W., PE. "Interfacing an EMCS to an HVAC System." *The Construction Specifier*, August 1982, pp. 109-111.

Vitelli, Jack, and Erling C. Hallanger. "Understanding EMS Software." *The Construction Specifier*, August 1982, pp. 34-39.

HEAT PUMPS

The American Institute of Architects. *Energy in Design: Techniques*. Energy in Architecture Series. Washington: AIA, 1981. Pp. 7.10-7.11.

Schneider, Raymond. *HVAC Control Systems*. New York: Wiley, 1981. Chapter 4.5.

PLASTIC-DOMED SKYLIGHTS

AIA Service Corporation. *MASTERSPEC 2*. Washington: AIA, 1983. Section 07800.

Dietsch, Deborah. "Let There Be Light, Again." *Progressive Architecture*, November 1982, pp. 129-133.

PROTECTED MEMBRANE ROOFING

Fricklas, R. *Nonconventional Roofing Systems*. Englewood, CO: Roofing Industry Educational Institute, 1980.

Griffin, C. W. *Manual of Built-Up Roof Systems*. 2d ed. New York: McGraw-Hill, 1982. Pp. 225-244.

National Roofing Contractors Association. *The NRCA Roofing & Waterproofing Manual*. Chicago: NRCA, 1983.

EPDM

Griffin, C. W. *Manual of Built-Up Roof Systems*. 2d ed. New York: McGraw-Hill, 1982. Chapter 11.

"The 1984 Handbook of Single-Ply Roofing Systems," *Roofing/Siding/Insulations*. New York: Harcourt Brace Jovanovich, 1984.

Kenney, Hugh. "Ethylene Propylene Diene Monomer." *Roofing Spec*, May 1981, p. 130.

WOOD TRUSSES

Melaragno, M. *Simplified Truss Design*. New York: Van Nostrand, 1981. Pp. 81-90.

Truss Plate Institute. *Bracing Wood Trusses*. Frederick, MD: TPI, 1976.

Truss Plate Institute. *Design Specifications for Metal Plate Connected Parallel Chord Trusses*. Frederick, MD: TPI, 1980.

Truss Plate Institute. *Design Specifications for Metal Plate Connected Wood Trusses*. Frederick, MD: TPI, 1978.

Truss Plate Institute. *Quality Control Manual for Light Metal Plate Connected Wood Trusses*. Frederick, MD: TPI, 1977.

STRUCTURAL FABRIC

"Tent Structures: Are They Architecture?" *Architectural Record*, May 1980, pp. 127-134.

Beitin, Karl I. "Energy Performance of Fabric Roofs." *The Construction Specifier*, July 1982, pp. 12-15.

Drew, Phillip. *Tensile Architecture*. Boulder, CO: Westview Press, 1979.

Educational Facilities Laboratories. *Four Fabric Structures: A Report*. New York: 1975.

Otto, Frei. *Tensile Structures: Design, Structure, and Calculation of Buildings with Cables, Nets, and Membranes*. Cambridge, MA: MIT, 1973.

Rush, Richard D. "The Era of Swoops and Billows." *Progressive Architecture*, June 1980, pp. 110-119.

RADIANT HEAT PANELS

"Horizons: A Closer Look at Radiant Heat." *Construction Specifier*, November 1981, pp. 18-20.

American Society of Heating, Refrigerating and Air Conditioning Engineers. *Handbook and Product Directory*. New York: ASHRAE, 1980.

Germer, Jerry. "A Twist for Radiant Heat." *Solar Age*, March 1984, pp. 40-44.

Lewis, Scott. "Radiant Floors." *Solar Age*, May 1982, pp. 42-44.

EXPOSED DUCTS

AIA Service Corporation. *MASTERSPEC 2*. Washington, DC: AIA, 1983. Section 13070.

Carrier Corporation. *Handbook of A/C System Design*. Syracuse, NY: Carrier, 1972.

INTEGRATED CEILINGS

The Construction Specifications Institute. *Acoustical Ceilings*. CSI Monograph 09M510, April 1974.

Harmon, William M. *Engineering Bulletin: Exposed Ductwork*. Westerville, OH: United Sheet Metal [undated].

Rush, Richard D. "The Down Side of Up." *Progressive Architecture*, September 1980, pp. 220-227.

AIR-HANDLING LUMINAIRES

Frieden, H. Richard. "Lighting: Specifying the Benefits." *The Construction Specifier*, March 1983, pp. 62-71.

Henderson, S. T., and A. M. Marsden. *Lamps and Lighting*. New York: Crane, Russak, 1972. Pp. 391-397, 452-460.

The National Lighting Bureau. "Shedding Light on Productivity." *Consulting Engineer*, June 1982, pp. 84-89.

ELEVATORS

American National Standards Institute and American Society of Mechanical Engineers. *ANSI/ASME A17.1: American Standard Safety Code for Elevators, Escalators, and Moving Walks*. New York: ANSI/ASME, 1981.

Lewis, W. S., Ed. "Vertical and Horizontal Transportation." In Council on Tall Buildings and Urban Habitat, *Monograph on Planning and Design of Tall Buildings*, Vol. SC, Ch. SC-4. New York: American Society of Civil Engineers, 1980.

McGuinness, William J., Benjamin Stein, and John S. Reynolds. *Mechanical and Electrical Equipment for Buildings*. 6th ed. New York: Wiley, 1980.

Ramsey, Charles G., AIA, and Harold R. Sleeper, FAIA. *Architectural Graphic Standards*. 7th ed. Robert T. Packard, AIA, Ed. New York: Wiley, 1981.

Strakosch, George R. *Vertical Transportation: Elevators and Escalators*. New York: Wiley, 1983.

ESCALATORS

American National Standards Institute and American Society of Mechanical Engineers. *ANSI/ASME A17.1: American Safety Code for Elevators, Escalators and Moving Walks*. New York: ANSI/ASME, 1981.

Kort, Calvin L. "A Guide to Escalator Planning." *Progressive Architecture*, May 1974, pp. 112-115.

Lewis, W. S., Ed. "Vertical and Horizontal Transportation." In Council on Tall Buildings and Urban Habitat, *Monograph on Planning and Design of Tall Buildings*, Vol. SC, Ch. SC-4. New York: American Society of Civil Engineers, 1980.

McGuinness, William J., Benjamin Stein, and John S. Reynolds. *Mechanical and Electrical Equipment for Buildings*. 6th ed. New York: Wiley, 1980.

Ramsey, Charles G., AIA, and Harold R. Sleeper, FAIA. *Architectural Graphic Standards*. 7th ed. Robert T. Packard, Ed. New York: Wiley, 1981.

Rush, Richard D. "Designing the Moving Experience." *Progressive Architecture*, December 1979, pp. 92-99.

Strakosch, George R. *Vertical Transportation: Elevators and Escalators*. New York: Wiley, 1983.

OPERABLE PARTITIONS

"Changing a Ballroom Into Three Spaces While Still Keeping Acoustical Privacy." *Architectural Record*, January 1968, pp. 171-172.

OPEN PLAN OFFICE FURNITURE SYSTEMS

"Open Office Furniture Systems and How to Design Them." *Facilities Design and Management*, January 1983, pp. 66-75.

"Productivity at Work." *Interiors*, June 1981, pp. 76-81.

Duffy, Francis, Colin Cave, and John Worthington. *Planning Office Space*. London: The Architectural Press Ltd. 1976.

Pile, John. *Interiors 3rd Book of Offices*. New York: Whitney Library of Design, 1976.

CARPET TILES

Della Corte, Evelyn. "Selections: Modular Floor Tile Products." *Interiors*, December 1982, pp. 112-113.

Dietsch, Deborah. "Under the Carpet." *Progressive Architecture*, July 1983, pp. 106-109.

ACCESS FLOORS

Hall, Gary. "Wired for Change." *Architectural Technology*, Spring 1984, pp. 14-23.

FLAT CONDUCTOR CABLE

"Flat Wire: New Alternative for Wiring Office Space." *Architectural Record*, April 1984, pp. 144-151.

Dietsch, Deborah. "Under the Carpet." *Progressive Architecture*, July 1983, pp. 106-109.

National Fire Protection Association. *National Electrical Code*. 1984 Edition. Quincy, MA: NFPA, 1983.

Pearce, Phil. "Streamlining Interiors with Flat Conductor Cable." *The Construction Specifier*, November 1982, pp. 82-84.

Wright, Gordon. "What Cable Pioneers Learned at Four Buildings." *Building Design & Construction*, November 1980, pp. 42-59.

STRUCTURAL/ELECTRIFIED FLOORS

Daryanani, Sital L., and William P. Lull. "Open Office Planning: The Total Environment." *Buildings*, March 1983, pp. 74-78.

Fischer, Robert B., and James B. Gardner. "Modern Wiring Systems: An Innovative and Maturing Technology." *Architectural Record*, October 1982, pp. 134-141.

Hall, Gary. "Wired for Change." *Architectural Technology*, Spring 1984, pp. 14-23.

INSULATING GLASS

Architectural Aluminum Manufacturers Association. *Recommended Glazing Guidelines for Reflective Insulating Glass*. Chicago: AAMA, 1978.

Architectural Aluminum Manufacturers Association. *Sound Control for Aluminum Curtain Wall and Windows*. Chicago: AAMA, 1975.

Architectural Aluminum Manufacturers Association. *Voluntary Test Method for Thermal Transmittance of Windows, Doors, and Glazed Wall Sections*. Chicago: AAMA, 1980.

Flat Glass Marketing Association. *FGMA Glazing Manual*. Topeka, KS: FGMA, 1980.

Thimons, Arnold J. "State-of-the-Art Glass." *Buildings*, July 1983, pp. 64-68.

Rush, Richard D. "Glassoline." *Progressive Architecture*, September 1981, pp. 223-241.

GLASS AND ALUMINUM CURTAIN WALL

Architectural Aluminum Manufacturers Association. *Aluminum Curtain Wall Design Guide Manual*. Chicago: AAMA, 1979.

Architectural Aluminum Manufacturers Association. *Sound Control for Aluminum Curtain Walls and Windows*. Chicago: AAMA, 1975.

Flat Glass Marketing Association. *Sealant Manual*. Topeka: FGMA, 1983.

Rush, Richard D. "A Stain in the Pane." *Progressive Architecture*, August 1979, pp. 94-99.

Skolnik, Alvin D. "Exterior Wall Testing." *Progressive Architecture*, March 1983, p. 157.

Smith, Gordon H. "Design and Testing of Metal/Glass Curtain Walls." *Architectural Record*, April 1981.

Thornton, Dr. Charles H. "Avoiding Wall Problems by Understanding Structural Movement." *Architectural Record*, December 1981, pp. 108-112.

GLASS BLOCK

Glass Block Installation Specifications. Pittsburgh: Pittsburgh-Corning Corp., 1982.

Stubbs, M. Stephanie, and Maureen Cunningham, "Practicality with Pizazz—Glass Block is Back." *Architectural Technology*, Fall 1984, pp. 68-73.

LIGHTWEIGHT INSULATING METAL PANELS

AIA Service Corporation. *MASTERSPEC 2*. Washington, DC: AIA, 1983. Section 07410.

EXTERIOR INSULATION SYSTEMS

Exterior Insulation Manufacturers Association. *Classification of Exterior Insulation Systems*. Washington: EIMA, 1983.

Heller, Barbara. "The Pros and Cons of Prefab Panels." *Architectural Technology*, Fall 1983, pp. 82-87.

SILICONE SEALANTS

Glass Digest. Annual Sealants Issue, December 1981.

"Characteristics of High Performance Sealants, Part II." *The Construction Specifier*, April 1970, pp. 46-50.

"How to Select Sealants, Part III." *The Construction Specifier*, June 1970, pp. 44-43.

Brower, James R., CSI. "Surface Preparation—The Key to Proper Sealant Adhesion." *The Construction Specifier*, July 1976, pp. 46-52.

Cook, John Philip. *Construction Sealants and Adhesives*. New York: Wiley, 1970.

Spatial Performance

1. Design of Indiv. Space and Furnishings
2. Aggregation of Indiv. Spaces
3. Provision of Conveniences and Services
4. Design of Amenities

Thermal Performance

dependent on
1. Air Temperature
2. Radiant Temperature
3. Humidity
4. Air Speed
5. Occupancy Factors & Control

Indoor Air Quality

dependent on
1. "Fresh" Air
2. Fresh Air Movement Distribution
3. Mass Pollutants
4. Energy Pollutants
5. Occupancy Factors Filtration/Controls

Acoustical Performance

1. Sound Source
2. Sound Path
3. Sound Receiver

Visual Performance

1. Ambient & Task Lighting Levels: Illuminance
2. Contrast & Brightness Ratios
3. Color Rendition
4. Occupancy Factors & Controls

Building Integrity

maintaining
1. Mechanical (Structural) Properties
2. Physical Properties (Water, Air, Heat, Light, Sound)
3. Visible Properties (Color, Texture, Finish, Form)

CONTENTS

Chapter 6 Integration for Performance

Authors:
Volker Hartkopf,
Vivian E. Loftness, and
Peter A.D. Mill

Reviewers:
Richard L. Crowther, AIA
Denver, CO

Gerald Davis
Harbinger Group
Toronto

Robert Dean, AIA
Heery International
Atlanta, GA

Fred Dubin
Dubin-Bloome Associates, P.C.
New York, NY

Ben Evans, FAIA
College of Architecture
Virginia Polytechnic Institute and State University
Blacksburg, VA

Hal Levin
Center for Environmental Design Research
University of California, Berkeley, CA

Robert G. Shibley
Chairman, Department of Architecture
School of Architecture and Environmental Design
State University of New York Buffalo, NY

Francis T. Ventre
Professor and Director, Environmental Systems Laboratory
College of Architecture
Virginia Polytechnic Institute and State University
Blacksburg, VA

Ewart A. Wetherill, AIA, MRAIC,
Wilson, Ihrig and Associates, Inc.,
Acoustical Consultants
Oakland, CA

Building criteria that stem from human needs are not specific to particular systems, and are by their nature integrative. For this reason, all buildings in use are defined as integrated. Integration tends to be taken for granted, however, with the result that many criteria, and certainly their interrelationships, remain unstated. To the extent that what is unstated is understood by all concerned, the harm done may only be in missed opportunities for integration. To the extent that it is not generally understood, performance failures can result.

It should be noted in this context that the concept of building performance is a useful fiction. Buildings don't perform; the people who design, build, and use them do. Building "performance," then, is merely a reflection of designer, builder, and user performance. The question is, how do these people perform together?

Communication is the key to this process, and the communication of building performance criteria tends to be verbal. What the owner and other users want from the building, what codes and standards require of it, and what the specifications writer tells the contractor to put into it are all, to a large degree, expressed in words. This fact may partly explain why this chapter is the longest in the book.

There are many ways to define the expectations placed upon a building. Defining them in terms of human comfort, as is done in the following pages, may seem at odds with the technical emphasis of this book. It would be a mistake, however, to suggest even by omission that the user's needs are external to the building process, or that they must pass through some kind of technical filter to become involved in it. They are in fact central to it.

In many respects, this chapter can be approached as a model. Like a model building code, its content could be reorganized with a different emphasis and still be a valid discussion of the same universal set of performance criteria. The essential goal is to provide a format with which these criteria can be presented so that they can be related, compared, consciously coordinated, and evaluated. On a conceptual level this requires the same sort of creative, integrative activity that takes place in the physical universe of building design. A set of criteria such as these underlies the success or failure of every building.—*Ed.*

Six Performance Mandates

Building Performance Mandates

1. Spatial Performance
2. Thermal Performance
3. Air Quality
4. Acoustical Performance
5. Visual Performance
6. Building Integrity

One of the primary motivating forces for systems integration is performance. Such design criteria as energy or resource conservation, functional appropriateness, strength and stability, durability, fire safety, weathertightness, visual comfort, acoustical comfort, and economic efficacy, are only delivered when the entire building performs as an integrated whole. Design for performance demands conscious systems integration, with a heightened understanding of how each two-, three-, and four-system combination affects the delivery of each performance criterion.

Fundamentally, performance is the measurement of achievement against intention. The communicated performance of the ultimately integrated system, or building, is a measure of the satisfaction of the various building clients. This satisfaction might be stated in terms of such goals as comfort, efficiency, and beauty, or in terms of their physiological, psychological, sociological, and economic desires.

To insure that satisfaction, the measure of performance, is indeed given, the designer needs to establish a set of criteria to determine where systems integration is critical or significant, and to recognize the level of integration that will be most capable of delivering the performance desired. These criteria are themselves integrative. Maintaining a common set of building performance criteria, from the design to the use of the integrated systems, depends entirely on communication throughout the building delivery process. In all cases, a building that performs over time provides a suitable, reliable, and flexible built environment for the functions and intentions of the full set of clients.

In order to examine the impact of various types of building systems integration on performance, it is necessary to begin with a manageable definition of the building performance criteria,[1] or mandates, to be met in the design, construction, and operation of a building. To this end, six discrete performance mandates will be outlined—spatial performance, acoustical performance, thermal performance, air quality, visual performance, and building integrity. Each of these performance mandates is defined by physiological, psychological, sociological, and economic[2] needs, or design limits of acceptability. This inherent complexity allows the six discrete performance mandates to encompass otherwise massive lists of building performance criteria[3].

The first five mandates comprise interior occupancy requirements (human, animal, plant, and artifact occupancies) and the elemental parameters of health, safety, and well-being in relation to the spatial quality, thermal quality, air quality, acoustical quality, and visual quality of the spaces being designed. Responsibility for delivering these occupancy performance mandates has been divided largely along disciplinary lines. Architects have taken primary responsibility for spatial quality and delegated responsibility to mechanical engineers for thermal quality and air quality, to lighting engineers for visual quality, and to acoustical engineers for acoustical quality.

Second, there has been a fundamental mandate over the centuries for building integrity—protection of the building's appearance and of its mechanical and physical properties[4] from environmental degradation by moisture, temperature, air movement, radiation, chemical and biological attack, and environmental disasters such as fire, flood, and earthquake. Established by concerns for health, safety, welfare, resource management (energy, time, space, and money), and image, the requirements for building integrity are set by owner/occupancy limits of "acceptable" degradation (of the visual, mechanical, and physical properties). These limits range from slight decay to debilitation in the ability to provide weathertightness or environmental conditioning for the function to total devastation or destruction.

The accompanying outline (Table 1) expands the definitions of these six performance mandates in terms

1. ISO/TC 59 "Performance Standards in Building—Principles for Their Preparation and Factors to Be Considered." International Organization for Standardization, 1982.

2. Blanchere, G. "The Notion of Performance in Building: Building Requirements" and "What are the Natures of Performance and Evaluation for the Three Levels: Building, Components, Materials?" *Performance Concept in Buildings*. Washington: National Bureau of Standards, 1972.

3. CIB Report Publication 64. "Working with the Performance Approach in Buildings." January 1982, pp. 5, 10, 17, 20.

4. Fix, W., and A. Rubben. "A New Approach for Calculating Time Dependent Effects in Polymer Building Materials." *Performance Concept in Buildings*, Third ASTM/CIB/RILEM Symposium, Lisbon, Portugal, 1982.

of the sets of conditions (created by integrated systems) that contribute to delivery in each performance area. Explanations of these six mandates may be found later in this chapter. It should be emphasized that each of these performance mandates must be fulfilled over time through the provision of integrated systems that are immediately suitable, that are reliable[5] over the longer term, and that are flexible enough to adapt to changing functions and occupancies.

5. Lemer, A. C., and F. Moavenzadeh. "Performance of Systems of Constructed Facilities." *Performance Concept in Buildings*. Washington: National Bureau of Standards, 1972.

THE LIMITS OF ACCEPTABLE PERFORMANCE

For all buildings there are physiological, psychological, sociological, and economic limits of performance. These are often dictated by building function. Many theaters, for example, demand heightened levels of acoustical performance, while nursing homes require excellent thermal performance and air quality. Monuments demand unusually good building integrity against degradation in appearance, (e.g., spalling), in structural integrity, and of physical properties such as weathertightness. In order to address all performance mandates capably, however, the designer must establish the priorities of the particular client, regardless of building function (see chart, p. 235).

6. Woods, J. E. "Do Buildings Make You Sick?" Proceedings, Third Canadian Buildings Congress, *Achievements and Challenges in Building 1982*. National Research Council No. 21158.

7. Ibid.

Each performance mandate has what may be described as a "comfort zone" established by the limits of acceptability for the type of occupancy concerned. These limits, often translated into codes and standards as well as budgets and guidelines, arise from the physiological, psychological, sociological, and economic requirements of the occupancy. The limits must correspond to the range of building or space functions and to the full range of occupancy types and factors (age, metabolic rate, clothing, and sensitivities).

With regard to human occupancy (with parallels for animal, plant, and artifact occupancies), physiological requirements are intended to protect the physical health and safety of the building users. This involves

8. "Working With the Performance Approach in Building," International Council for Building Research and Documentation, January 1982.

Table 1: Six Building Performance Mandates

I. SPATIAL PERFORMANCE
- A. Individual Space Layout: size, furniture (surface, storage, seating); ergonomics
- B. Aggregate Space Layout: adjacencies; compartmentalization; usable space; circulation/accessibility/wayfinding/signage; indoor-outdoor relationships
- C. Conveniences and Services: sanitary; electrical; security; telecommunications; circulation/transportation
- D. Amenities
- E. Occupancy Factors and Controls

II. THERMAL PERFORMANCE
- A. Air Temperature
- B. Radiant Temperature
- C. Humidity
- D. Air Speed
- E. Occupancy Factors and Controls

III. INDOOR AIR QUALITY
- A. "Fresh" Air
- B. Fresh Air Movement and Distribution
- C. Mass Pollutants[6]
- D. Energy Pollutants[7]
- E. Occupancy Factors and Controls

IV. ACOUSTICAL PERFORMANCE
- A. Sound Source
- B. Sound Path
- C. Sound Receiver

V. VISUAL PERFORMANCE
- A. Ambient and Task Levels: aritificial light and daylight
- B. Contract and Brightness Ratios (glare)
- C. Color Renditions
- D. View/Visual Information
- E. Occupancy Factors and Controls

VI. BUILDING INTEGRITY (versus visual, mechanical and physical[8] degradation of the structure, envelope, servicing, and interior systems)
- A. Loads; dead loads, live loads, impact, abuse, vandalism, vibration, creep
- B. Moisture: rain, snow, ice, and vapor resulting in erosion, penetration, migration, condensation
- C. Temperature: thermal gradient (insulation effectiveness), thermal bridging, freeze-thaw cycle, differential thermal expansion and contraction
- D. Air Movement: erosion, abrasion, tearing, air infiltration, exfiltration; pressure differential
- E. Radiation and Light: environmental radiation, electromagnetic long wave (solar radiation), visible light spectrum
- F. Chemical Attack
- G. Biological Attack
- H. Fire
- I. Natural Disaster: earthquake, flood, hurricane, tidal waves, volcanic eruptions, etc.
- J. Man-made Disaster

Table 2. Organizing Performance Criteria for Evaluating the Integration of Systems

	PHYSIOLOGICAL NEEDS	PSYCHOLOGICAL NEEDS	SOCIOLOGICAL NEEDS	ECONOMIC NEEDS
	Performance Criteria Specific to Certain Human Senses, in the Integrated System			
1 SPATIAL	Ergonomic Comfort Handicap Access Functional Servicing	Habitability Beauty, Calm, Excitement, View	Wayfinding, Functional Adjacencies	Space Conservation
2 THERMAL	No Numbness, Frost-bite; No Drowsiness, Heat Stroke	Healthy Plants, Sense of Warmth, Individual Control	Flexibility to Dress w/the Custom . . .	Energy Conservation
3 AIR QUALITY	Air Purity; No Lung Problems, No Rashes, Cancers	Healthy Plants, Not Closed in, Stuffy No Synthetics	No Irritation From Neighbors Smoke, Smells	Energy Conservation
4 ACOUSTICAL	No Hearing Damage, Music Enjoyment Speech Clarity	Quiet, Soothing; Activity, Excitement "Alive"	Privacy, Communication	
5 VISUAL	No Glare, Good Task Illumination, Way-finding, No Fatigue	Orientation, Cheer-fulness, Calm, Inti-mate, Spacious, Alive	Status of Window, Daylit Office "Sense of Territory"	Energy Conservation
6 BUILDING INTEGRITY	Fire Safety; Struct. Strength + Stability; Weathertightness, No Outgassing	Durability, Sense of Stability Image	Status/Appearance Quality of Const. "Craftsmanship"	Material/Labor Conservation
	Performance Criteria General to All Human Senses, in the Integrated System			
	Physical Comfort Health Safety Functional Appropriateness	Psych. Comfort Mental Health Psych. Safety Esthetics Delight	Privacy Security Community Image/Status	Space Conservation Material Conservation Time Conservation Energy Conservation Money/Investment Conservation

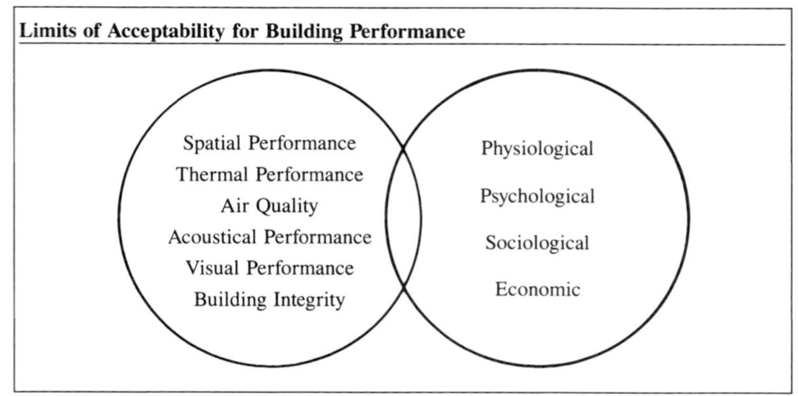

Performance Priorities for Various Building Types

	Spatial	Acoustic	Thermal	Air Qual	Visual	Integrity
Small Office	✓		✓			
Large Office	✓	✓	✓	✓	✓	
Multi Family	✓	✓				✓
Single Family	✓		✓			✓
Stores					✓	
Shopping Centers	✓		✓	✓	✓	
Hotel/Motel	✓	✓	✓			✓
Elementary Schools	✓	✓	✓	✓	✓	✓
Secondary Schools	✓	✓	✓	✓	✓	✓
Warehouses						
Assembly		✓		✓	✓	
Clinics	✓			✓	✓	
Nursing Homes	✓		✓	✓	✓	✓
Hospitals	✓		✓	✓	✓	✓

sheltering basic bodily functions—sight, hearing, breathing, feeling, movement, etc.—from wear or destruction by such conditions as fire, building collapse, poisonous fumes, high and low temperatures, and inadequate or excessive light.

Psychological requirements involve support of individual mental health through appropriate provisions for privacy, interaction, clarity, status, image, and change.

Sociological requirements (also referred to as socio-cultural requirements) pertain to the well-being of the community within which the individual acts, relating the needs of the individual to those of the group. Building esthetics, that intangible quality held uppermost by designers, is also a manifestation of the sociological (and possibly psychological) requirements for building performance.

Finally, economic requirements embody the aim to allocate resources in the most efficient manner to serve user needs within the wider social context.

The interdependencies among the first three limits of acceptability might best be illustrated through an example relating to acoustical performance. Guidelines, codes, and standards have been developed to protect the building occupant against excessive noise. To avoid physiological hearing damage, both noise intensity and duration are considered. To avoid psychological discomfort, noise frequency (even beyond the hearing threshold) is evaluated, in order to eliminate the distraction of low frequency rumbles and high frequency hisses. To avoid hearing discomfort of a sociological kind, consideration is given to speech articulation, in order to help insure privacy in offices or between apartments.

Finally, the availability of resources (financial, technical, and material) superimposes another layer of requirements, establishing limits of feasibility alongside the limits of acceptability. Decisions, however, must be tempered with the full understanding of resources over time, evaluating allocations necessary for initial outlay, operating costs, maintenance costs, eventual replacement or conversion costs, and personnel costs associated with each step in this process.

CONSERVATION OF SPACE, MATERIALS, ENERGY, AND TIME: THE ECONOMIC LIMITS OF ACCEPTABILITY

In exploring the implications of the physiological, psychological, sociological, and economic limits of acceptability with respect to systems integration, it becomes clear

Reprinted, with permission, from Ernst Neufert, *Architect's Data*, Halsted Press, 1980.

that the economic value of conservation plays a major role in promoting deliberate integration. Although conservation can happen within any single system, four major conservation opportunities present themselves in the context of systems integration: conservation of space, of materials, of energy, and of time.

Conservation of space can be achieved through such strategies as optimizing site usage, reducing programmed square footage demand, and establishing dual- or multi-purpose spaces. Conservation of space can also be achieved through the *meshed* or *unified* integration of several building systems, such as by running mechanical pipes or ducts through the structure, floor, ceiling, or wall. Visible integration alternatives[9] can also contribute to the conservation of space, with exposed ductwork enabling room height and width to be used more effectively.

9. Visible integration, pp. 381–385.

Conservation of materials is also significantly affected by systems integration, through such strategies as minimizing envelope surface area, increasing structural efficiency, and unifying building subsystems. Architects as dissimilar as Buckminster Fuller and Antonio Gaudi demonstrated ways to maximize enclosed space while minimizing the material used to enclose it. An even greater contribution to the conservation of materials may be achieved through the *unified* integration of building systems. Generated from the premise that the ultimate structural system does the most work with the least material, and that the unification of structure and envelope furthers this aim, large-scale fabric structures and shell structures exemplify the beauty inherent in the conservation of materials.

Conservation of energy resources also depends on systems integration to minimize demand, make effective use of renewable resources, and allow adaptive reuse of existing facilities and infrastructures. Again, minimizing enclosure while maximizing enclosed space can be important, given the appropriate building type and function. A range of *remote*, *touching*, *connected*, and *meshed* levels of integration of components and systems is then necessary for effective passive solar heating, cooling, and daylighting, and for the optimization of mechanical system sizing and operation. These combinations of building systems, however, must also be flexibly designed so that they can accommodate changing functions and occupancies while conserving the material in existing facilities and infrastructures and the energy embodied in them.

Finally, conservation of time (in design, construction, operation, maintenance, alteration, and even demolition) is also heavily dependent on the level of building systems integration. An integrated design

Varying Space Requirements in Four Projects

	Project 1	Project 2	Project 3	Project 4
enclosed single room	11	8	15	10
work place area	33	22	20	25
adjacent	7	4	5	6
ancillary	8	8	5	6
special area	26	47	21	33
primary circulation	15	11	34	20

Analysis of space use 4 projects showing percentage of space requirements

The Shell Oil Building integrates envelope and mechanical systems to provide effective daylighting and conserve energy. Photograph: Dubin-Bloome Associates.

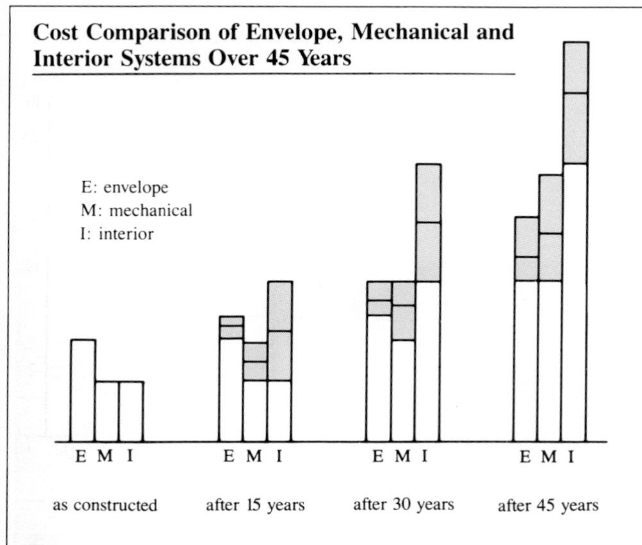

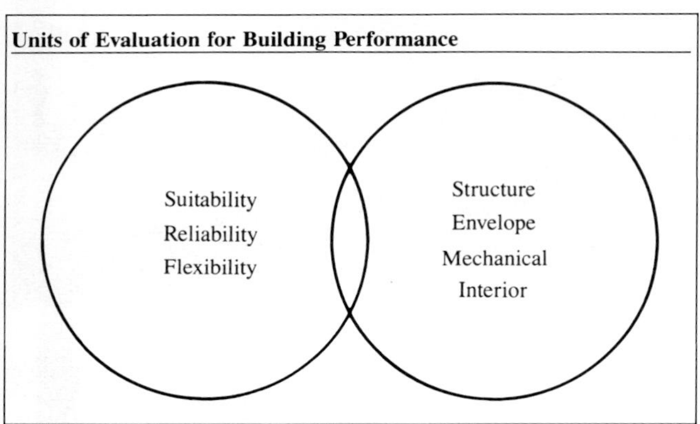

(Top) Reprinted, with permission, from Ernst Neufert, *Architect's Data*, Halstead Press, 1980.

process involving team decision-making, rather than an iterative, linear process, can offer major time savings. Fast-tracking, manufactured components, and improved critical path methods have greatly increased the conservation of time in construction. Mechanization and, more recently, electronics have greatly improved the conservation of time in the operation and maintenance of buildings. However, it is the quality of systems integration embodied in the design (and in the resulting construction) that most affects the time required in maintenance. Indeed, maintenance is one of the major justifications for the conscious integration of building components and systems.

The conservation of these resources—space, materials, energy, and time—forms the basis of building economics, with each contributing to the reduction of first cost and life-cycle costs. The degree to which a designer succeeds in providing cost-effective spatial, thermal, acoustical, and visual performance, as well as air quality and building integrity against degradation, is the major measure of a building's success. Effectiveness is thus a measure of its ability to deliver the required performance over time while using resources efficiently.

THE ELEMENT OF TIME: UNITS OF EVALUATION FOR SYSTEMS INTEGRATION

The materials and components of which buildings are made must be synergistically integrated to fulfill the basic mandates for spatial performance, thermal performance, air quality, acoustical performance, visual performance, and building integrity. Although we may speak of a curtain wall "system," or a fire safety "system," the building itself consists of systems defined at a higher level. Building systems integration encompasses not only the assemblage of materials and components, but also the environmental conditions achieved within the assemblage and the occupancy within those environmental conditions.

The length of time over which this integrated system must perform depends on the intended life of the building and its functions as stated at the outset of design. For this purpose, performance goals can be stated, and alternatives compared, in terms of suitability, reliability,[10] and flexibility.

Suitability is a measure of the degree to which a building and its integrated component parts serve user needs in the present and near future. Reliability is an expression of the probability that the service will continue to be performed as intended throughout the life of the facility, given specified maintenance and use. Flexibility, including adaptability, is a measure of the system's ability to accommodate changing

10. Lemer, A.C., and F. Moavenzadeh. "Performance of Systems of Constructed Facilities," *Performance Concept in Buildings*. Washington: National Bureau of Standards, 1972.

functions and occupancies, and of the continuing effort and resources required during the building's life cycle to maintain suitability.

The level of integration employed has considerable influence on the suitability, reliability, and flexibility of the building assembly in meeting building performance requirements over time. Spaces or buildings that perform suitably in the short term can be created with all levels of systems integration—*remote, touching, connected, meshed*, and *unified*. However, it is critical that these integrations be made deliberately, to suit the needs of the various functions and occupancies.

On the other hand, reliability might be more easily guaranteed with higher levels of integration such as factory-fabricated systems. This may be due to the tolerances required and trades coordination needed on the construction site. Package solar domestic hot water systems are an example of improved reliability achieved through *unified* integration at the factory. *Remote, touching*, or *connected* integrations might be more appropriate for assemblies that are fabricated in the field, since reliability is often dependent on easy access for maintenance and replacement.

Finally, flexibility is often dependent on the relative independence of the four building systems, so that interiors can be changed without structural or envelope implications, for example. At all other levels of integration, the need for flexibility requires that the integration be designed with the intended capacity for change.

Decisions about the level of suitability, reliability, and flexibility required for spatial performance, thermal performance, air quality, acoustical performance, visual performance, and building integrity can often be discussed in terms of the intended life span of the building. Buildings can be commissioned for a temporary time period, for a short time period, for a longer time period with capacity for change, and as permanent edifices or monuments.

Temporary buildings need to be immediately suitable and quickly supplied, with few demands for long-term reliability or flexibility. The speed with which temporary buildings need to be delivered often demands "package" responses which suggest high levels of integration. The ultimate temporary structure is probably a lunar landing module. On the other end of the

Time Units of Evaluation Based on Intent of the Building

	Temporary	Short Life	Long Life	Permanent
Suitability	✓	✓	✓	✓
Reliability		✓ Short Term	✓ Long Term	✓ Long Term
Flexibility			✓	✓

The lunar landing module and barrio housing in Lima both are temporary structures intended for short-term suitability only. Photographs: NASA, Volker Hartkopf.

Monuments like the Lincoln Memorial must be immediately suitable and very reliable over time. Flexibility is sacrificed in favor of permanence. Photograph: National Park Service.

scale, slum structures in the barrios of Lima, Peru, are also temporary (but evolutionary) buildings, using discarded materials, loosely connected, at a much simpler level of integration.

Short-life buildings are designed to serve their particular function as long as that function is needed. Examples would be manufacturing facilities, office buildings, and retail buildings. A drive through any strip development leaving a major city reveals a plethora of short-life buildings—abandoned garages, food franchises, and used car lots.

Long-life buildings, such as museums, schools, and even housing, are designed with a capacity for change to adapt to changing internal organizations or functions. Change is generally accommodated by altering the mechanical or interior systems, though in some cases the structure and envelope are altered as well. Because they require immediate suitability, long-term reliability, and long-term flexibility, long-life buildings present the greatest challenge in the integration of systems for performance.

Permanent buildings such as monuments, religious buildings, and landmark government buildings have a symbolic function and are designed for immediate suitability and long-term reliability; flexibility for spatial or functional change is usually less important. This combination of suitability and long-term reliability may point to *meshed* and *unified* integrations, in contrast to the *remote*, *touching*, and *connected* integrations often found in flexible long-life buildings.

The key, then, is to determine during the design of the building what its intended life span is, and to what degree it will need to accommodate changing occupancies or functions. It is in the middle of the spectrum of permanence that we are likely to negotiate the levels of integration. Generally speaking, the more fixed and permanent a building is conceived to be, the more highly integrated it is likely to be. At the same time, very temporary and portable buildings are also highly integrated. The accommodation of changing occupancies, functions, or technologies (such as automation) over time makes integrating the various systems more challenging and more necessary.

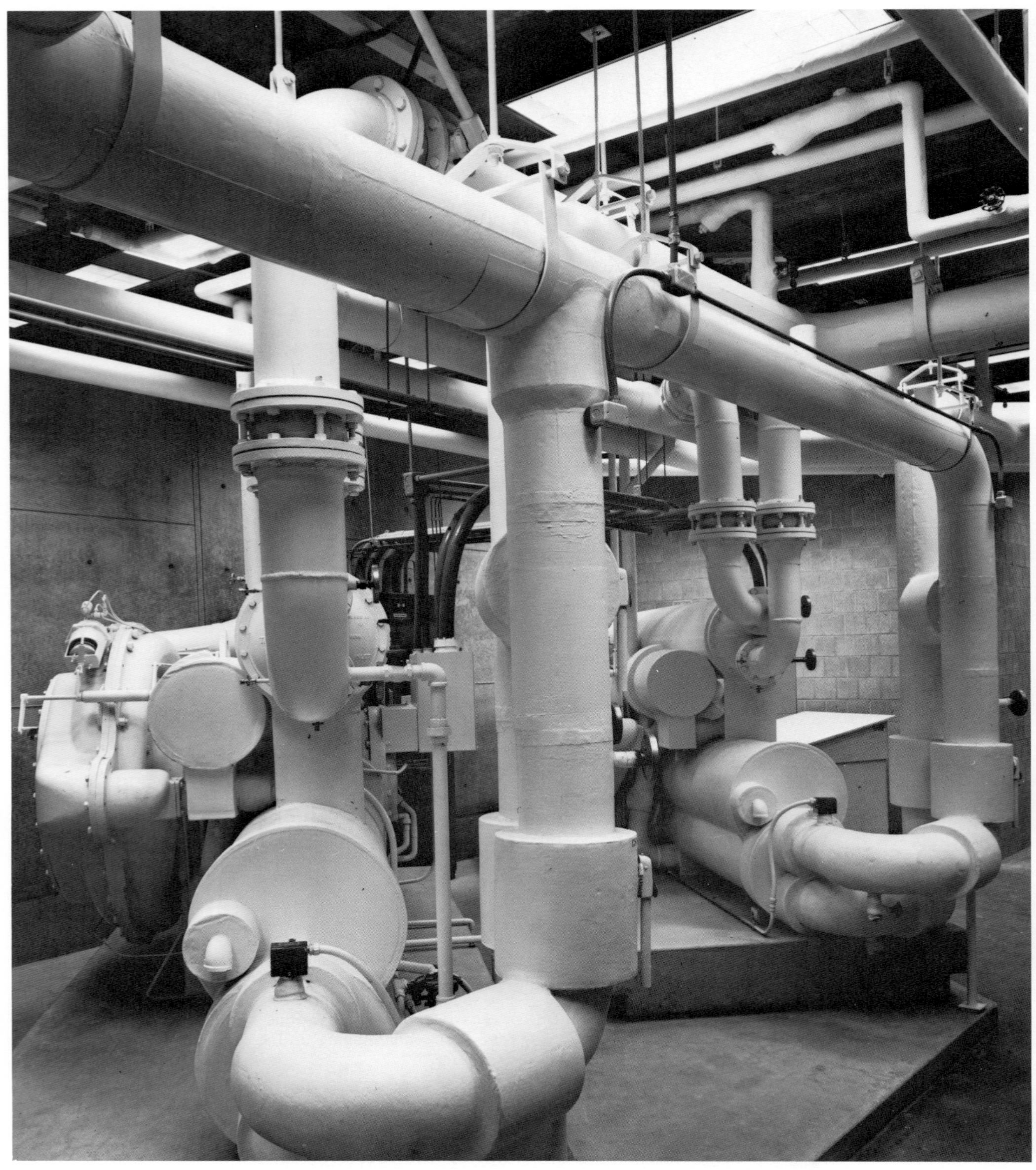

Integration Within Systems and the Delivery of Performance

System Integrations:

Critical To:
1. Spatial Performance
2. Thermal Performance
3. Air Quality
4. Acoustical Performance
5. Visual Performance
6. Building Integrity

The overview of building performance requirements and their limits of acceptability in the preceding pages is intended to initiate discussion about the importance of systems integration to the suitability, reliability, and flexibility of the occupied building. Just as abstractions of system groupings (into structure, envelope, mechanical, and interior) are necessary to initiate thinking about potential component combinations, abstractions of performance criteria (spatial, thermal, air quality, acoustical, visual, and building integrity) are needed in order to discuss their interrelationships and dependencies in terms of building systems integration.

The discussion in this section will focus on the level of component integration within and among systems and the resulting delivery of performance.

First, decisions about component design and integration *within* each of the four systems that are important to building performance will be discussed. The range of physical design decisions made in the assembly of each system is examined with reference to the six performance mandates.

Second, the level of integration *among* the four systems is discussed, reexamining the physical design decisions—highlighted within each of the four component groupings in combination—important to the satisfaction of the six building performance mandates.

The emphasis in both sections is on insuring deliberate or conscious building systems integration for the delivery of total building performance.

EXAMPLE: INTEGRATION WITHIN THE STRUCTURAL SYSTEM AFFECTING PERFORMANCE

The selection of structural system type, and consequent span, bay size, and column spacing, significantly affect spatial performance[11] and the occupants' ability to use spaces flexibly. The structural system's capability for expansion, however, either vertically or horizontally, can relieve some shortcomings in spatial flexibility.

Decisions regarding the structural system also significantly affect building integrity. Integrity versus the degradation of the mechanical properties of the structure (resulting in excessive deflection, cracking, fatigue, and failures) depends heavily on the selection and properties of system materials and on the span, bay size, and column spacing. The selection of system materials and

11. Structural system, p. 318.

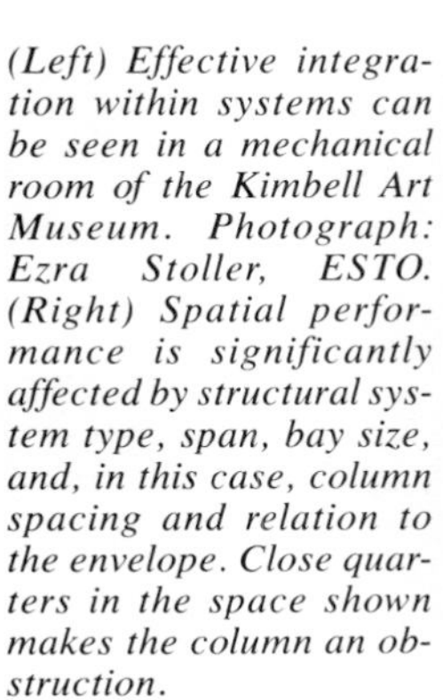

(Left) Effective integration within systems can be seen in a mechanical room of the Kimbell Art Museum. Photograph: Ezra Stoller, ESTO. (Right) Spatial performance is significantly affected by structural system type, span, bay size, and, in this case, column spacing and relation to the envelope. Close quarters in the space shown makes the column an obstruction.

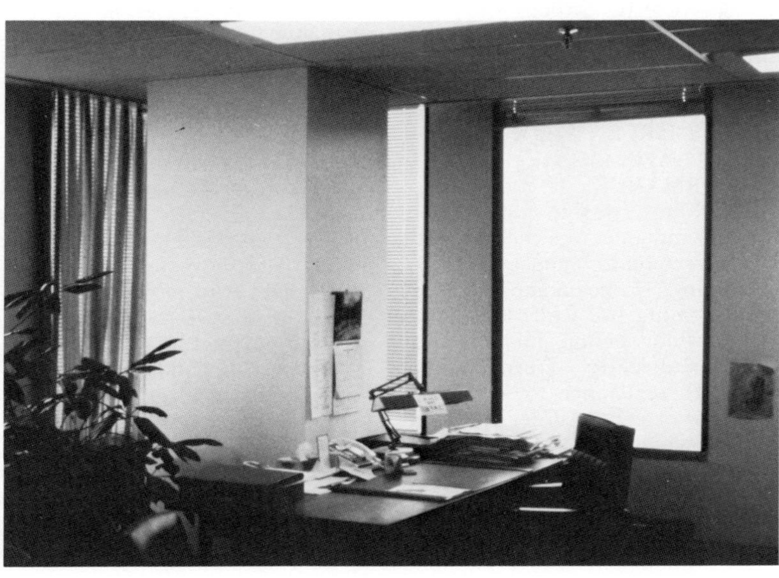

their properties is also important for maintaining the structure's visual integrity.[12]

Decisions in structural system design also will influence thermal, lighting, and acoustical performance. Structural system materials and their properties affect thermal bridging and the potential tightness of joints with envelope materials—conditions important to thermal comfort.

Floor-to-floor height determines the volume of air to be heated and cooled. On the other hand, effective daylighting (and artificial lighting) can necessitate increased floor-to-floor heights and appropriate perimeter bay sizing. Finally, decisions about building form (in plan and in section) often set by the type of structural system selected can greatly affect potential acoustical performance.

Aside from the connections with envelope and mechanical systems, most decisions in structural system design do not significantly influence indoor air quality. However, air quality can be influenced by the choice of structural materials. Treated lumber and concrete admixtures can have adverse outgassing characteristics. The fire-retardant coatings for steel structures can lead to the release of respirable (and therefore harmful) particulates. Concrete aggregates quarried where there are radon deposits can lead to radon pollution in buildings.

EXAMPLE: INTEGRATION WITHIN THE ENVELOPE SYSTEM AFFECTING PERFORMANCE

Envelope design decisions strongly influence the thermal performance (comfort and efficiency) of buildings.[13] The composite materials forming the wall, roof, and exterior floor section and their connections directly determine the building's resistance to unwanted heat loss or gain. All decisions regarding windows (material properties, size, orientation, and control systems) and their connections to wall or roof components are critical to thermal performance.

12. Visible integration, pp. 381-385.

13. Envelope system, p. 318.

Second, lighting performance is affected by decisions regarding the building envelope, and specifically the design of windows or other openings. Material properties (transmission, diffusion, and color) will determine the effectiveness of daylighting and artificial lighting, along with window size, shape, spacing, orientation, and sunshading control systems. The window frame design can also help to reduce contrast and glare. Conscious design for ease of window operation and maintenance will help to insure the cleanliness and working control necessary for effective daylight management.

The third performance area significantly affected by envelope design decisions is building integrity against visual, physical, and mechanical degradation. Exterior surface properties of walls, roofs, and openings will determine the immediate and long-term visual appearance of the building.[14] The physical properties of the entire cross-section, such as transmission, reflection, absorption, expansion, and contraction, will also influence the long-term durability of the building against environmental stress. Such mechanical properties as flexural strength must also be considered for immediate and long-term building integrity.

14. Visible integration, pp. 381–385.

Both acoustical and spatial performance are influenced by the envelope. Interior surface material and the form, slope, and orientation of the enclosing walls, roof, and windows each contribute to the acoustical quality of the enclosed space, as well as to its spatial suitability and flexibility. Spatial performance is also determined by the envelope module and the potential for horizontal and vertical expansion. Window control systems for security, privacy, and light management help influence spatial and acoustical performance as much as interior surface decisions concerning ornament and texture.

Finally, envelope components must be tightly connected to keep out unwanted air pollution. Other air quality problems may result from outgassing and radiation from envelope materials, a process accelerated by ultraviolet light and by heat.

INTEGRATION WITHIN THE MECHANICAL SYSTEM AFFECTING PERFORMANCE

In addition to the obvious relationships between HVAC systems and thermal performance and air quality, between lighting systems and visual performance, and between vertical transportation and spatial performance, there are a number of other important performance considerations in mechanical system design.

Spatial performance, or suitable space layout, accessibility, and flexibility, is critically affected by the planning module and configuration of each of the mechanical systems[15] (HVAC, lighting, telecommunications, plumbing, and vertical transportation), as well as their potential for expansion and relocation. The management or control systems also affect immediate suitability and long-term reliability and flexibility, with options varying from individual manual controls to completely centralized management.[16]

15. Mechanical system, p. 318.
16. Energy management control systems, pp. 158–160.

Acoustical performance is affected by the thickness or volume of HVAC and plumbing conduits, by their configuration and radii of curvature, and by their airtightness and sound insulation levels. The planning module or density of terminal units in mechanical systems (e.g., diffuser spacing that determines speed) and in telecommunication systems (e.g., telephone density) also influence acoustical comfort. The specification of the lighting terminal units or fixtures is important to insure the level of sound absorption in the ceiling plane and to prevent buzzing. Finally, the capacity and configuration of the vertical transportation systems can determine the migration and adjacency of unwanted noise.

In addition to the obvious relationship of visual comfort to lighting system design, visual performance is related to the form and ornamentation of ducts and pipes, as well as to the planning module (space conflict) of the HVAC, plumbing, and fire safety terminal units.[17] At present, the form, material, and ornamentation of telecommunication terminal units such as computer screens is a growing concern in providing visual comfort and health in the workplace.

17. Visible integration, pp. 381–385.

Building integrity versus degradation is affected by several mechanical design decisions. The material properties and the ornament applied to HVAC, lighting, and telecommunication conduits and terminal units influence both visual degradation (appearance) and physical degradation (effectiveness) over time. The number and size of HVAC terminal units is important to their immediate suitability as well as their long-term appearance and effectiveness. Finally, the complexity of control system design and integration is a key integrity (reliability) concern with central, local, or task management systems, whether automatic or manual.

Both thermal performance and air quality depend on all elements of HVAC design. However, air quality also depends on the configuration of vertical transportation (pollution migration); the size/capacity of plumbing conduits; and the material properties of lighting fixtures (radiant pollution and outgassing). Thermal performance may also depend on the configuration of vertical transportation (stack heat losses), the size/capacity and control of lighting fixtures (heat gain), and the size/capacity of computers and other heat-generating terminal units.

INTEGRATION WITHIN THE INTERIOR SYSTEM AFFECTING PERFORMANCE

The performance mandate most significantly affected by interior system design is spatial comfort.[18] All design decisions regarding interior components and their assembly affect the suitability of workstation and workgroup layout for ergonomic comfort, accessibility, wayfinding, and communication. The depth

18. Interior system, p. 318.

Table 3: Examples of System Design Decisions Affecting Performance

STRUCTURAL	spatial	thermal	air quality	acoustical	visual	building integrity
General System Type: Frame, Diaphragm, Tensile, Inflated	●	●		●	○	○
System Materials and Properties: Steel, Concrete, Wood, Plastics	●	●	●	●		●
Span, Bay Sizes, Column Spacing	●	○		○	●	●
Floor to Floor Height	○	●	○	○	●	
Cross-section of Structural Elements (height, width, depth)	○				○	○
Building Form: Plan, Section	○	○		●	○	
Expansion Capabilities (Vert. Horiz.)	●	○	○	○	○	○
Connections to/Accommodation of Other Structural Components	○	●	○	○		●
ENVELOPE						
Wall/Roof/Exterior Floor						
Exterior Surface, Material Prop.		○				●
Composite Materials, Thickness	●	○	○	○		●
Interior Surface	○	○	○	●	●	○
Form: Planar, Curved	●	○		●	○	○
Slope, Orientation	●	○		●	●	○
Module Size, Shape	●	○				●
Connection to Other Envelope Comp.	○	●	○	○		●
Windows/Openings						
Material Properties	●	●		●	●	●
Size, Shape, Spacing	●	●		○	●	
Orientation		●		○	●	○
Control Systems, Sunshading	○	●		○	●	●
Control Systems, Heat Loss		○				○
Control Systems, Security/Privacy	○			●	○	
Frame Connections, Plan/Section	○	○		○	●	●
Access, Visual and Physical		○	○		●	○
Expansion Potential (Vert. Horiz.)	○				○	
Change Potential for Access & Image	○				○	○
Color, Texture, Ornament	○		○		●	●
MECHANICAL						
HVAC (HEATING, VENTILATION, AIR CONDITIONING)						
Service Generators						
Size, Volume	●	●	●	○		
Form, Configuration	●	●	●	○		
Expansion Capability	●	●	●			
Material, Ornament	○					○
Service Conduits						
Thickness, Volume of Service	●	●	●	○		
Form, Shape	○	○		○	○	
Configuration, Distance, rise/run	○	●	○	○		
Interface/Expansion Capability	●	●	●	○		
Material, Ornament	○				○	○
Connection to Other Mechanical	●		○	○	○	○
Access		●	●	○		●
Service Terminals						
Planning Module	●	●	●	●	●	●
Number, Size, Capacity	●	●	●	●	○	●
Form, Material, Ornament	○			●	●	●
Interface/Expansion Capability	●	●	●	○		

KEY

●: Critical implications for the delivery of this performance mandate.

○: Some implication for the delivery of this performance mandate.

(Table 3, continued)

	spatial	thermal	air quality	acoustic	visual	building integrity
Relocation Capability	●	●	●	○	○	
Connection to Other Mechanical	○		○		●	○
Control Systems						
Central Management Systems	●	●	●	○	○	●
Local Management, Automatic/Manual	●	●	●	○	○	●
LIGHTING						
Service Generator—Size, Capacity	○				●	
Service Conduit						
Thickness, Volume of Service	○				●	
Interface, Expansion Capability	●				○	
Material, Ornament						●
Access					●	○
Service Terminals						
Planning Module	●	●		●	●	●
Size, Capacity	○	●			●	●
Form, Material, Ornament	●		●	●	●	●
Interface, Expansion Capability	●				●	
Relocation Capability	●					●
Connection to Other Mechanical	○	●		○		●
Control Systems						
Central Management	●	●		○	●	
Local Management, Automatic, Manual	●	●		○	●	
POWER, TELECOMMUNICATIONS, & SECURITY						
Service Generator—Size, Capacity	●					
Service Conduit						
Thickness, Volume of Service	●					
Interface/Expansion Capability	●					
Material, Ornament	●					●
Access						●
Service Terminals						
Planning Module	●			●		
Number, Size, Capacity	●	●				
Form, Ergonomics, Maneuverability						●
Material, Ornament	○				●	●
Interface/Expansion Capability	●					
Relocation Capability	●					
PLUMBING AND FIRE SAFETY						
Service Generator—Size, Capacity	●					
Service Conduit						
Thickness, Volume	●			○		
Configuration, Distance, rise/run	●			○		●
Interface/Expansion Capability	●					
Access						●
Material, Ornament						
Service Terminals						
Planning Module	●					
Number, Size, Capacity	●		○	○		●
Form, Material, Ornament						●
Interface, Expansion Capability	●					
Relocation Capability	●			○		
VERTICAL TRANSPORT						
Size, Volume of Service	●			●		●
Form, Configuration	●	○	●	○		○
Planning Module	●					
Expansion Capability	●	○	○			
Material, Ornament	○					●

of the ceiling, floor, and wall cross-sectional areas, as well as their planning modules, is important for mechanical and electrical servicing and for spatial flexibility and esthetics.

Building integrity against visual degradation (e.g., staining), physical degradation (e.g., reflectivity), and mechanical degradation (e.g., breakage) also depends heavily on interior component design, specification, and assembly. In all cases, the surface materials and planning modules of ceilings, floors, walls, and furniture determine durability, while access to these component assemblies is necessary for maintenance and change.

Air quality is most significantly affected by interior system design decisions. Surface materials of the wall, ceiling, floor, and furniture components are critical, since outgassing from these materials (and contact) can induce toxic allergic reactions. The tightness of connections between various interior components determines the potential for pollution migration from a room containing chemicals, machinery, or smokers to other rooms, and from floor to floor. The need for appropriate sizing and configuration of the mechanical system makes ceiling, floor, and wall depth critical. Access and planning modules are important for adequate maintenance to insure long-term air quality performance.

Acoustical performance is most strongly influenced by the interior system. Ceiling height, form, and material properties are important, as are the appropriate connections to wall and furniture components. Wall form and surface material, floor surface, and such furnishings as make up a large percentage of the interior volume are all crucial to acoustical performance. Finally, the density and location of equipment or appliances, such as printers or typewriters, will greatly affect acoustical quality.

Daylighting and associated lighting performance in buildings depends on various interior system decisions: ceiling height, shape, and surface materials; wall/partition form, openings, and surface materials; and furniture surface materials. In addition, tall furnishings such as storage cabinets can hamper the distribution of artificial light and daylight.

The relationship of thermal performance and interior component selection and assembly is predominantly concerned with comfort requirements and the spatial distribution of HVAC by mechanical subsystems. Interior system decisions critical to thermal comfort include the volume to be conditioned, the horizontal and vertical distribution plenums created by ceiling, floor, and wall systems, the wall configuration and layout determining thermal zoning, and the introduction of appliances and equipment.

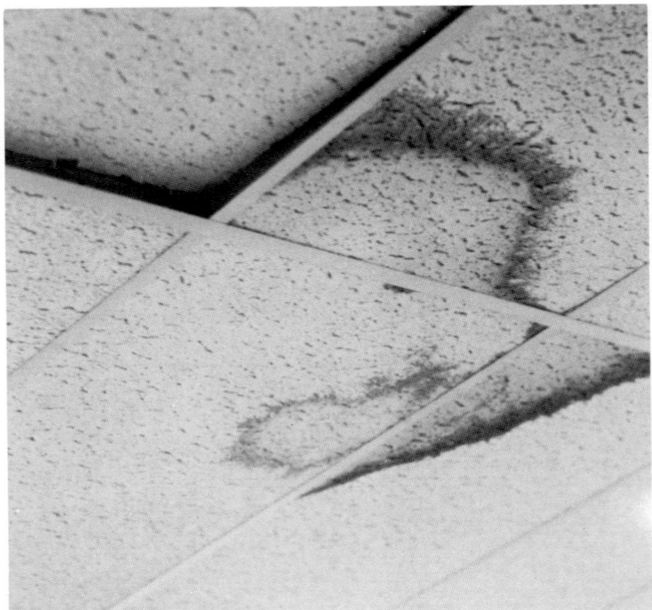

Interior system design, specification, and assembly greatly affect the building's integrity against visual degradation. The stains shown here might have resulted from condensation or leakage. Photograph: Volker Hartkopf.

Table 4: Examples of Interior System Design Decisions Affecting Performance

INTERIOR	spatial	thermal	air quality	acoustical	visual	building integrity
Ceiling						
Height, Shape, Form	○	●	○	●	●	
Depth, Cross-section	●	●	●	○		
Surface, Material Properties			●	●	●	●
Planning Module				○	○	●
Connection to Other Interior Components	●	○	●	●		●
Floor						
Depth, Cross-section	●	●	●	○		
Form, Slope/Steps	●			○	○	○
Surface, Material Properties	●	○	●	●	○	●
Module	●	●	●	○		○
Connection to Other Interior	●	○	●	●		●
Wall						
Form, Depth	●	○		●	●	
Openings (Interior)	●	●	●	●	●	○
Surface, Material Properties		○	●	●	●	●
Planning Module	●				●	●
Connection to Other Interior	●	○	●	●	●	●
Furnishings						
Work Surface: Material, Height, Depth	●	○	○	●	●	●
Sit/Sleep Surface: Material, Ergonomics	○	○	○	●		●
Storage	●		●		●	●
Equipment/Appliances		●	●		○	
Vegetation/Ornamental Objects	○	○	○	○	○	
Connection to Other Interior	●					
Expansion Potential (Vert. Horiz.)	●		○			
Change Potential for Access, Use, Image	●					●
Color, Texture, Ornament	○		○	○	○	●

KEY

●: Critical implications for the delivery of this performance mandate.

○: Some implication for the delivery of this performance mandate.

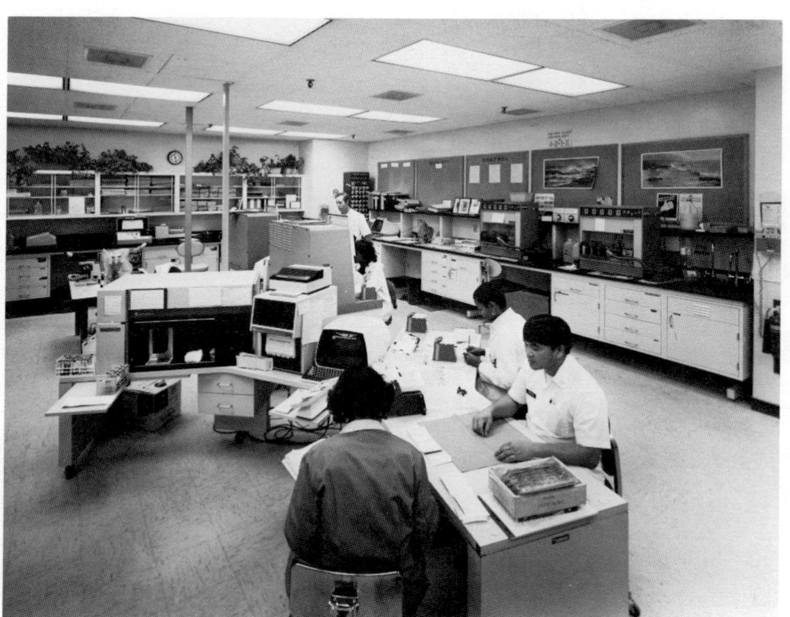

The interaction of people and necessary equipment in this laboratory at Walter Reed General Hospital makes an integrated interior system design complex and demanding. Photograph: Harlan Hambright.

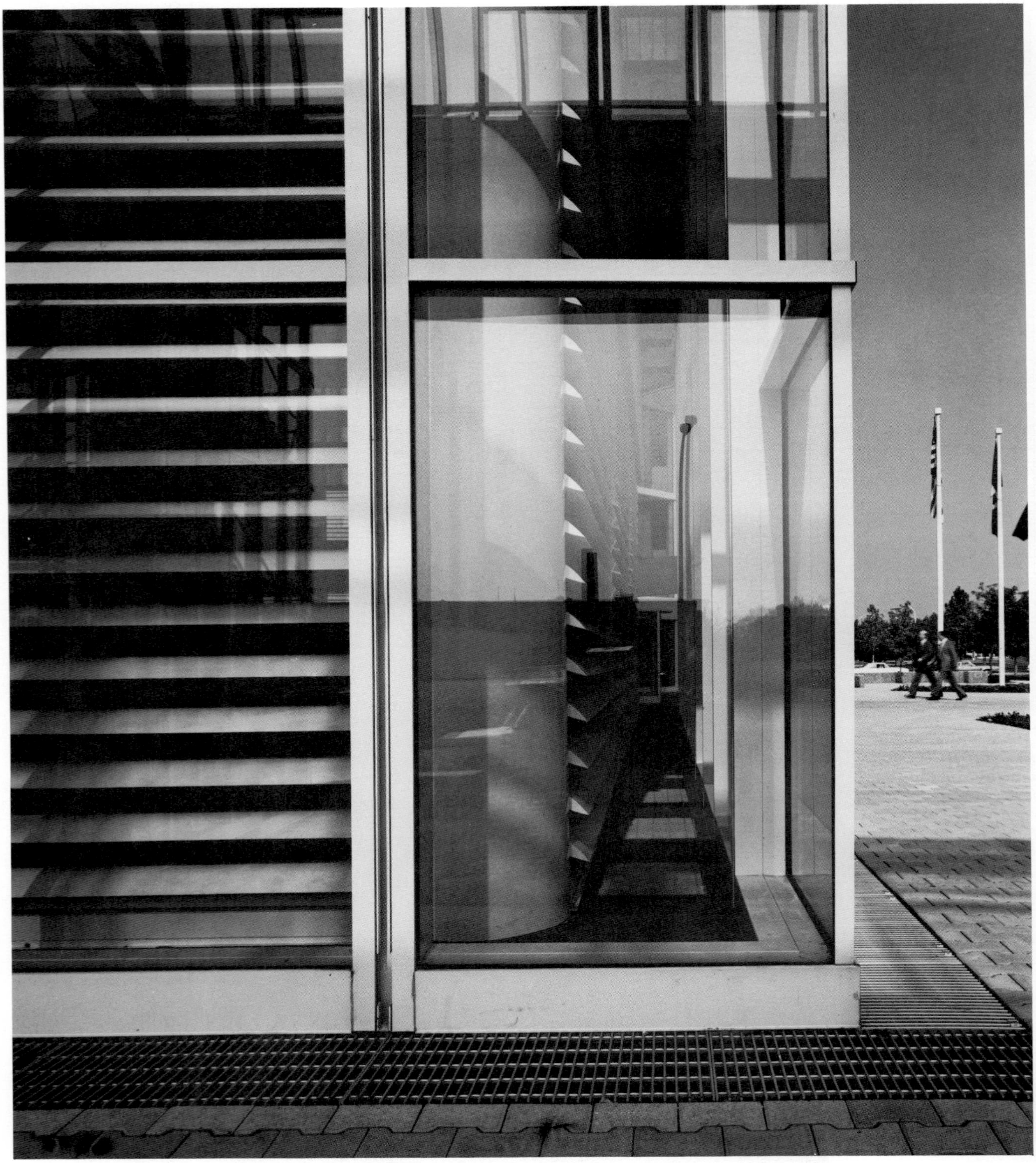

Integration Among Systems and the Delivery of Performance

The foregoing discussions have dealt with the component integrations *within* each of the four systems that are crucial to building performance. On a more demanding level, however, the integration *among* the four systems is even more critical to the delivery of building integrity and of spatial, thermal, air quality, acoustical, and visual performance.

The following pages emphasize the importance and potential of deliberate integrations among the structural, envelope, mechanical, and interior systems in the delivery of the six performance mandates. Performance studies by the National Bureau of Standards and the General Services Administration in the U.S. and by Public Works Canada have indicated that several two-system integrations are necessary for the delivery of certain performance mandates.

The designer can begin to visualize several of the critical system integrations in each performance area by relating the issues highlighted in each of the system discussions. An ongoing debate of these important integrations may illuminate the level of integration[19] that is most appropriate for insuring the performance mandated in each building type and program.

For each performance mandate discussed, illustrations of two- and three-system integrations[20] that effectively contribute to spatial, thermal, air quality, acoustical, and visual performance, as well as building integrity, are drawn from the case studies in Chapter 3.

19. Levels of integration, p. 320.

20. Two- and three-system integrations, pp. 320–321.

SPATIAL PERFORMANCE

Spatial performance criteria can only be met through conscious integration of structural, envelope, mechanical, and interior components. This deliberate decision-making must include all two-system integrations that combine to form three- and four-system integrations, thus forming the whole building. These component integrations are crucial to insuring that the environments created are suitable, accessible, identifiable, useful, ergonomically comfortable, safe, and secure—that they maintain their suitability over time (i.e., are reliable), and that they are flexible.

For example, envelope and interior systems[21] must be consciously integrated to provide an appropriate planning module for compartmentalization and spatial layout flexibility, effective circulation, and indoor-outdoor movement.

The integration of envelope and mechanical systems[22] is important for maximum space utilization, mechanical sizing, and expandability, as well as control over daylighting, passive solar heating, and natural ventilation.

Deliberate integration of interior and mechanical systems[23] is necessary to provide suitable conditioning for flexibility in spatial layout, mechanical streamlining for increased usable space, and space ornamentation and identity.

Structural and mechanical systems[24] must be integrated to insure adequate ceiling height, vertical shaft efficiency, and coordination of volumetric needs. The integration of structural and interior systems[25] determines the planning module, the ratio of moveable to fixed spatial divisions, sight lines, and working ceiling heights.

Finally, structure and envelope integrations[26] determine the image, access, and security of the exterior,

21. Envelope and interior combination, pp. 328–329.

22. Envelope and mechanical combination, pp. 327–328.

23. Mechanical and interior combination, pp. 329–330.

24. Structure and mechanical combination, pp. 324–325.

25. Structure and interior combination, pp. 325–327.

26. Structure and envelope combination, pp. 323–324.

(Left) The relationship of the structural, envelope, mechanical, and interior systems is clearly visible at this corner of the Occidental Chemical building in Niagara Falls, New York. Photograph: Barbara Elliott Martin. (Right) Two-system integrations are critical to the delivery of several performance mandates (dots), with others potentially as important (circles).

Critical Two-System Integrations for Performance

	spatial	thermal	air quality	acoustic	visual	building integrity
Structural & Envelope	●	●	○	○	○	●
Structural & Mechanical	●	○	○	●	●	
Structural & Interior	●			●		
Envelope & Mechanial	●	●	○	○	●	●
Envelope & Interior	●	●	●	●		
Mechanical & Interior	●	●	●	●	●	●

KEY

●: Critical implications for the delivery of this performance mandate.

○: Some implication for the delivery of this performance mandate.

The inventive curvilinear integration of envelope and interior systems in the Illinois Regional Library enlivens the envelope and the spatial performance of the interior. Photograph: Howard N. Kaplan.

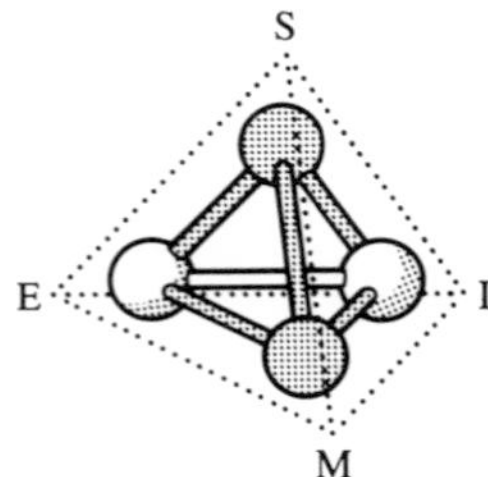

the modules for interior subdivision, and capabilities for expansion or change.

An Illustration of Envelope and Interior Integration for Spatial Performance

The Illinois Regional Library[27] deftly illustrates integration that effectively meets the specific physiological, psychological, and sociological spatial performance needs of the blind and physically handicapped. The organization of spaces, the detailing of interior components and surfaces, and the relationship of envelope to interior systems all work to provide a visually and physically lucid design solution.

The structural columns are rounded to minimize dangerous corners and associated degradation (chipping and scarring) problems. The furniture, also softened and rounded, is built-in and linear to avoid the confusion of rearranged mobile elements. Surface texture is selected to insure safety and wheelchair mobility.

Colors have been selected to delineate the four building systems for the partially sighted and to provide three-dimensional space definition—yellow for structure, blue for mechanical, red for envelope, and white for interior.

Most significant, however, is the logic of the spatial layout created between *remote* envelope and interior systems.[28] From the entrance the blind and handicapped patrons move through a clear linear path (framed by envelope and interior elements) with widenings in the aisle to indicate card catalog, checkout, and meeting and information areas. With the size of the aisle a key to function, the flow through the various areas is clear and unobstructed, allowing the visually handicapped to know where to find staff or reference books. Continuing this "memorable" logic, the audio center is located at one end of the long curved counter. A tipped-up version of the bulging aisle forms the adjacent window wall—a formal demonstration of this simple but effective spatial organization resulting from integrated envelope and interior systems.

27. Illinois Regional Library, pp. 70–73.

28. *Remote* integration, p. 320.

THERMAL PERFORMANCE

The integration of systems for thermal performance also encompasses most two-part combinations. Structure and envelope[29] components must be consciously integrated to avoid thermal bridging, to insure the continuity of the air-vapor barrier, to minimize the volume of air that needs conditioning, and to provide cost-efficient self-shading for windows.

Envelope and mechanical system[30] components must be coordinated so that systems do not fight each other (natural ventilation and air conditioning), are not extravagantly redundant (heating on one side, cooling on the other), do not waste energy, and provide occupancy comfort (avoiding cold mean ra-

29. Structure and envelope combination, pp. 323–324.

30. Envelope and mechanical combination, pp. 327–328.

diant temperatures, unacceptable draft/air patterns).

31. Envelope and interior combination, pp. 328–329.

32. Mechanical and interior combination, pp. 329–330.

Envelope and interior system[31] integrations are necessary for most passive conditioning technologies: reflection, absorption, and capacitance for passive solar heating, heat exchange and capacitance for night air flushing and cooling, and sunshading and night insulation.

Finally, thermal performance depends on the deliberate integration of mechanical and interior systems[32] to insure effective air circulation, appropriate mean radiant temperatures, and reduced conductive losses/gains. Thermal performance also depends on the required length of the mechanical system, its access for maintenance, and its long-term reliability.

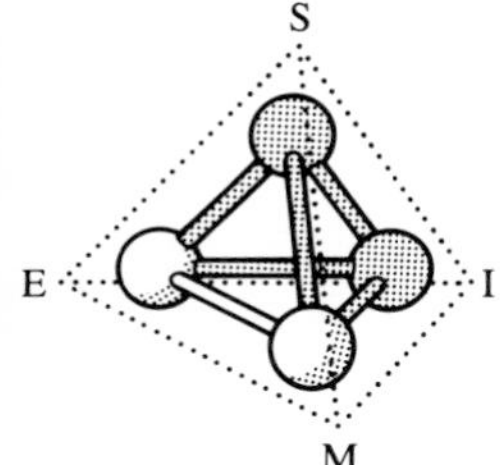

An Illustration of Envelope and Mechanical Integration for Thermal Performance

One of the most common thermal performance failures occurs when architectural decisions regarding the envelope are separated from the mechanical decisions regarding the conditioning systems.

Architects make design decisions about envelope orientation, material, detailing, and control systems that drastically affect the selection and performance of the mechanical systems. In fact, most commercial buildings simultaneously heat and cool, rendering them incapable of achieving thermal comfort or overall energy efficiency in much of the occupied area.

With this common performance failure in mind, it is useful to consider the Occidental Chemical Company Corporate Office Building[33] as a model of integrated decision-making. In this 200,000 sq ft office facility, the double envelope construction—composed of single glazing outside, operable louvers in a 4 ft buffer zone, and double glazing inside—provides a major improvement in both thermal and lighting performance as a result of innovative envelope and mechanical integration.

33. Occidental Chemical, pp. 94–97.

Improved thermal performance results from solar control and venting and from innovative load balancing, both of which are made possible by deliberate envelope and mechanical integration. With direct solar gain, the large louvers—located in the airspace between the glazed envelope "rainscreen" and the interior glazed wall—automatically close to a 45 degree angle, thereby reducing solar transmission and absorption while still permitting other facades to continue to receive indirect sunlight. The 4 ft buffer zone (which may not be as viable in other climates) also acts as a thermal chimney. The zone can be vented in overheated periods to eliminate trapped or non-reflected solar energy. With the interior louvers shut down at night, the double envelope construction provides greater resistance to heat loss and gain than conventional curtain wall construction and significantly reduces infiltration. Because the buffer zone completely wraps the building, heat built up on one facade migrates (laterally and upward in a diagonal loop) to other facades. This unique load balancing (with only a 15° temperature differential north to south versus a typical 50-60°Δ T) minimizes the need for simultaneous heating and cooling and for the design of different mechanical zoning systems and control strategies for each facade.

Lighting performance was also a major generator of this double envelope design. The first 15 ft of the perimeter office area receives effective task-ambient lighting, requiring no artificial lighting during daytime hours. The tracking motion of the horizontal louvers eliminates direct sunshine and glare in the offices since the envelope can be changed from fully transparent to fully opaque. The solar tracking mechanism is augmented by light sensors in the offices that step the artificial lighting levels to maximize the daylight contribution to overall task-ambient lighting.

The result of this *meshed* integration of mechanical and envelope systems[34] is an 80 percent reduction in the cost of annual cooling loads, a 98 percent reduction in annual heating loads, a 50 percent reduction

34. *Meshed* integration, p. 320.

Louvers within the double envelope at Occidental Chemical improve both thermal and lighting performance, as well as affecting the choice of envelope and mechanical systems. Photograph: Patricia Layman Bazelon.

in lighting loads, and a 50 percent reduction in peak loads over conventional office construction. In addition, the Occidental Chemical building offers significant improvements in thermal and visual comfort for the occupants without the loss of environmental contact found in the "minimum window area" energy alternatives.

AIR QUALITY

The most critical integrations between systems in the interest of air quality appear to be envelope-mechanical and envelope-interior.

The conscious integration of envelope and mechanical[35] components is necessary to minimize outdoor pollution intrusion and to assure adequate fresh air from the outside.

Mechanical and interior system[36] integration is important to minimize interior pollution migration and to assure adequate fresh air circulation within the space. Capability for mechanical "flushing" is needed to remove pollution that results from new interior components and from cleaning, smoking, printing, and other sources.

Before these integrations can be successful, however, the specification and use of the interior system must be determined, since major problems with air quality are caused by interior furnishings and finishes and by consumer products and equipment (see expanded definitions, pp. 274–307).

An Illustration of Structural, Mechanical, and Interior Integration for Air Quality

Air quality in buildings has become an important issue in recent years and has led to innovations in mechanical and interior integration. In hospitals, unique functional design problems for spatial flexibility

S

E I

M

35. Envelope and mechanical combination, pp. 327–328.

36. Mechanical and interior combination, pp. 329–330.

Vertical servicing shafts such as this one at Walter Reed General Hospital provide spatial suitability and help solve critical air quality problems. Photograph: Pflueger Architects.

are complicated by absolute demands for air quality and thermal performance. The new Walter Reed General Hospital[37] is a unique example of how performance can be achieved through the *meshed* integration of mechanical and interior[38] systems with the structural systems. Its success stems from the ability to visualize the repetitive horizontal and vertical demands on the mechanical servicing system as a "structure" itself. Repetitive servicing modules similar to structural modules are established. Vertical servicing shafts are established as the equivalent of columns, and horizontal servicing plenums are *meshed* within the structural truss/interstitial floor system.

37. Walter Reed General Hospital, pp. 82–85.

38. *Meshed* integration, p. 320.

Although the major advantages of this *meshed* integration of structural and mechanical systems are the spatial suitability for effective health care and spatial flexibility (with easy access for system modifications), two innovative performance successes resulted from the design. First, the direct mechanical supply to individual rooms, made possible by the interstitial floor system, avoids any short-circuiting or mixing of air from adjacent or stacked patient rooms. The air quality and resulting health advantages of this system cannot be overstressed. Second, the subdivision of mechanical supply and return into quadrants insures that the temperature in each zone is controlled according to its particular needs. Thus, thermal comfort can be promised on an individual basis, despite differences in solar gain, internal heat gains, and occupant temperature preferences. The economics and energy efficiency of this modular mechanical conditioning system also add to the overall thermal and air quality performance of the building.

The innovative interior office ceiling design shown here at the Aid Association for Lutherans Headquarters increases daylighting performance and reduces noise while hiding ductwork. Photograph: Harr, Hedrich-Blessing.

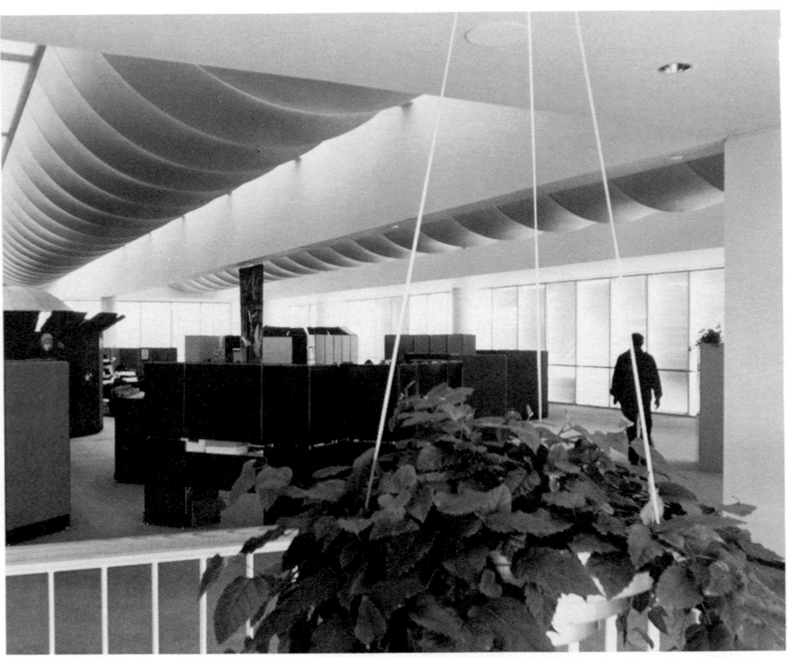

ACOUSTICAL PERFORMANCE

Acoustical performance depends on at least four sets of integrations: structure-interior, envelope-interior, mechanical-interior, and structure-mechanical.

Sound privacy, for instance, depends on the effective integration of interior systems with their structural and envelope[39] interfaces. Envelope systems (such as windows) and interior systems[40] must also be integrated to achieve appropriate sound absorption and reverberation levels.

39. Structure and interior combination, pp. 325–327.

40. Envelope and interior combination, pp. 328–329.

Through deliberate mechanical and interior system integrations,[41] the designer insures the necessary sound pressure levels, background noise, and room absorption that provide the acoustics appropriate to the function of the space. Finally, structural and mechanical system[42] integrations are necessary to eliminate vibration.

41. Mechanical and interior combination, pp. 329–330.

42. Structure and mechanical combination, pp. 324–325.

As with air quality, however, each of these integrations must be preceded by a determination of the specification and use of the interior system. A building's acoustical problems are often determined by interior furnishings and finishes, as well as by the space utilization and equipment in the building.

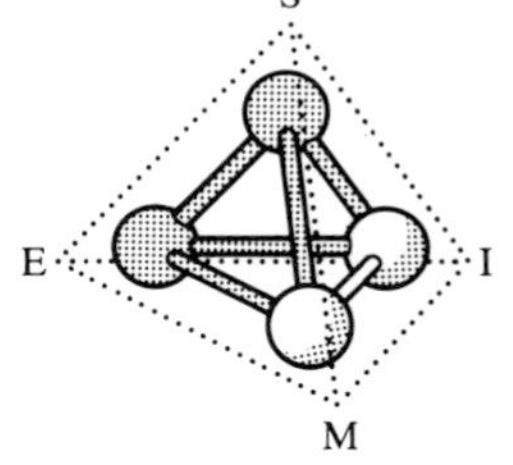

An Illustration of Mechanical and Interior Integration for Acoustical Performance

The flexibility and economy that open office planning seemed to offer in the 1960's led to a surplus of undistinguished acres of columns, fluorescent lights, desks, and acoustical panels in the 1970's. In addition to thermal, air quality, acoustical, and lighting problems, the open "landscaped" office often reveals spatial/egress problems and lack of identity for the individual worker.

In contrast, the Aid Association for Lutherans Headquarters[43] is designed to provide a uniformly high quality of space for all employees, while maintaining the flexibility of open office planning.

The architects designed a *connected* integration of mechanical and interior systems[44] and a *remote* integration of envelope and mechanical systems.[45] These integrations insure not only good daylighting and acoustical performance for all areas but improved thermal and spatial performance as well.

43. Aid Association for Lutherans, pp. 62–63.

44. *Connected* integration, p. 320.

45. *Remote* integration, p. 320.

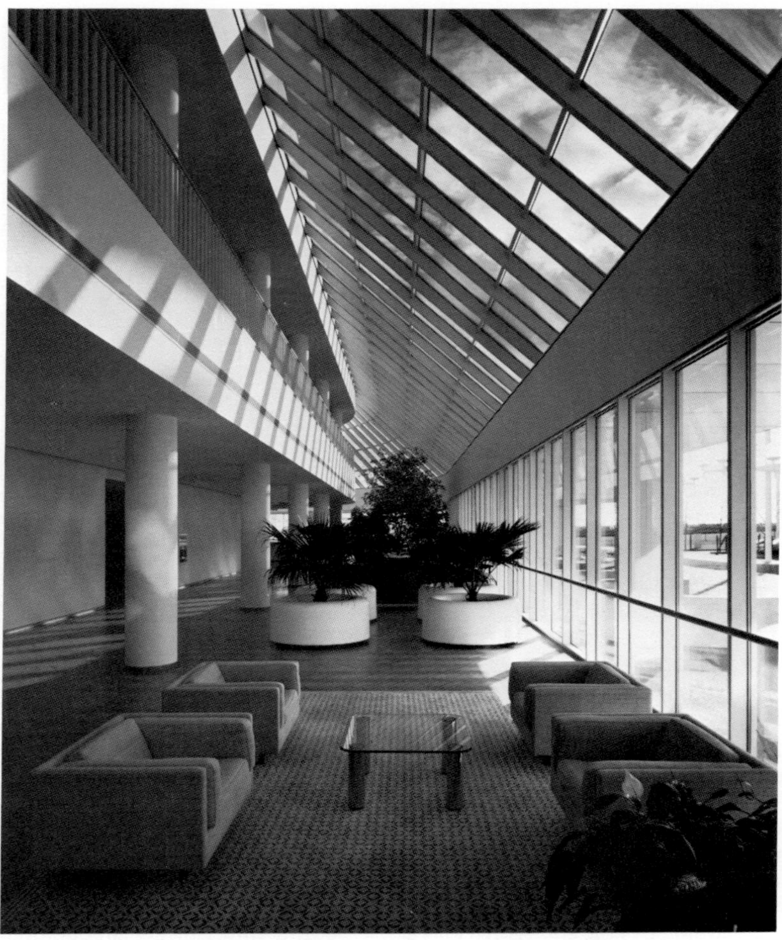

Criteria affecting the acoustical environment for small group discussions provided in the Aid Association for Lutherans Headquarters differ from the individual privacy and sound masking needs of the office work environment. Photograph: Harr, Hedrich-Blessing.

Twelve thousand linear feet of skylight, in repetitive bands, bring daylight into vast open office areas. The light is reflected and diffused by fabric "socks" of fiberglass stretched over metal hoops that house the mechanical systems. The objective was to achieve a quality of light that would suggest the outdoors, and at the same time provide good light to see by. All ceiling elements are employed to this end. Boxed-in girders and socks prevent direct glare, while the socks modulate the brightness of daylight and diffuse it. Cylindrical fluorescent light fixtures emulate daylight when daylight is insufficient to work by.

The displacement of conventional hung ceilings by fiberglass socks and skylights provides acoustical benefits as well as natural lighting. The billowing ceiling plane, created by an acoustically transparent fabric stretched over a metal frame, significantly increases the surface area for acoustical absorption. In addition to a sound-masking system for effective sound privacy in the open plan areas, the fiberglass socks house the mechanical supply and return air components and sprinklers for fire safety.

The thermal performance benefits of this integrated mechanical and interior ceiling system include easy access to the mechanical services for maintenance as well as flexibility to accommodate major changes being brought about by office automation. The mechanical and interior component integration

The integration of interior systems and skylight glazing in the Kimbell Art Museum permits daylighting while avoiding undesirable solar gain and glare. Photograph: Bob Wharton.

for thermal performance is reinforced by the central heat recovery system designed to reclaim heat from lights, skylights, office staff, and equipment.

Finally, the spatial quality of the conventional open office has been improved through the integration of the mechanical and interior ceiling systems. The hooped, double-curved shape of the socks provides a modulated ceiling plane that reinforces the workgroup layouts and lends interesting visual articulation to the space. Without freestanding acoustical screens, open space enhances visual clarity for wayfinding and communication. Easy access for air balancing and mechanical adjustment offers functional flexibility, so often promised in open plan office design.

VISUAL PERFORMANCE

At least three systems integrations are critical to visual performance, each related to the mechanical components for generating and distributing electricity and the terminal units that transform this power into light.

The structural and lighting (mechanical)[46] components must be consciously integrated to insure appropriate bay sizes, to provide distribution space for cabling, and to avoid shadows from the installed fixtures.

Envelope and lighting (mechanical)[47] components must be integrated to avoid glare, to provide effective unilateral, bilateral, or multilateral daylighting, and to provide the appropriate occupancy controls for both the natural and artificial lighting "fixtures."

Interior and lighting (mechanical)[48] components must be consciously integrated to avoid glare and contrast within the space, to insure that acceptable illuminance and control is provided at the task (given surface reflectances).

An Illustration of Structure, Envelope, and Interior Integration for Visual Performance

The Kimbell Art Museum,[49] designed by Louis Kahn, is often mentioned as one of the best examples of effective daylighting in museums. Through a *unified* integration of structure, interior,[50] and envelope components, Kahn's design has resolved the tensions between daylight and glare (lighting performance failure), between daylight and heat

46. Structure and mechanical combination, pp. 324–325.

47. Envelope and mechanical combination, pp. 327–328.

48. Mechanical and interior combination, pp. 329–330.

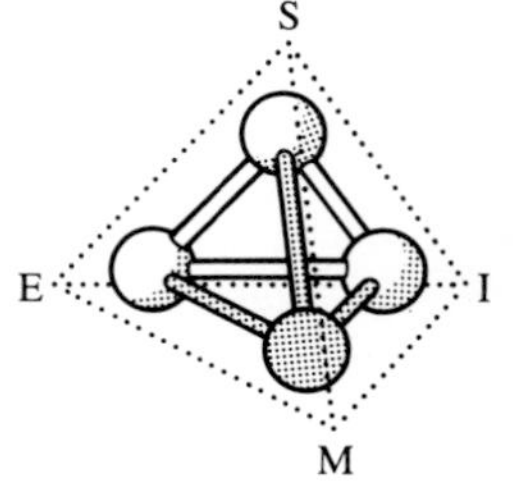

49. Kimbell Art Museum, pp. 64–67.

50. *Unified* integration, p. 320.

The Kimbell Art Museum illustrates how a unified integration of structure, envelope, and interior resolves the tensions between daylight and glare (lighting performance failure), between daylight and heat gain (thermal performance failure), and between daylight and artifact degradation (artifact integrity/visual performance failure). Photograph: Bob Wharton.

gain (thermal performance failure), and between daylight and artifact degradation (artifact integrity/visual performance failure).

Through the innovative integration of these systems, the building demonstrates a delightful use of natural light as a substitute for an ambient lighting system. The decision to use daylight for ambient lighting rather than task-ambient lighting (which would light the paintings and artifacts as well as the space) was the key to success in visual performance. The glazed area could be kept small because ambient lighting needs are very low, and lighting could be kept indirect, eliminating direct and reflected glare for the viewers.

A narrow strip of skylight provides abundant footcandles for visitor orientation and for giving a sense of time and place. It also protects the museum, located in Texas, from excessive solar gain that would result in thermal discomfort and high cooling loads. The punctured aluminum reflector suspended below the skylight reflects and diffuses light onto the vaulted ceiling while allowing some light penetration to reduce contrast at the ceiling plane.

The punctured reflector also protects the paintings and artifacts from direct ultraviolet light, which would cause fading, degradation, and other damage. The reduction and diffusion of daylight provided by the envelope (windows), the structure (concrete vaults), and the interior system (reflectors) are critical to the preservation of artifacts in museums. The use of the concrete vaults as the exposed interior system also guarantees the long-term durability of the building's interior surfaces.

Innovative structure, envelope, and interior integration for lighting performance captures and secures the reputation of this design by providing a sense of orientation and time, the qualities of changing light, and the clear economic and psychological advantages of managed daylight over artificial lighting.

The integration of structure, envelope and interior inherent in fabric structures provides long-term building integrity for the Stephen C. O'Connell Activities Center at the University of Florida in Gainesville, as well as improved visual, thermal, and spatial performance. Photograph: Balthazar Korab.

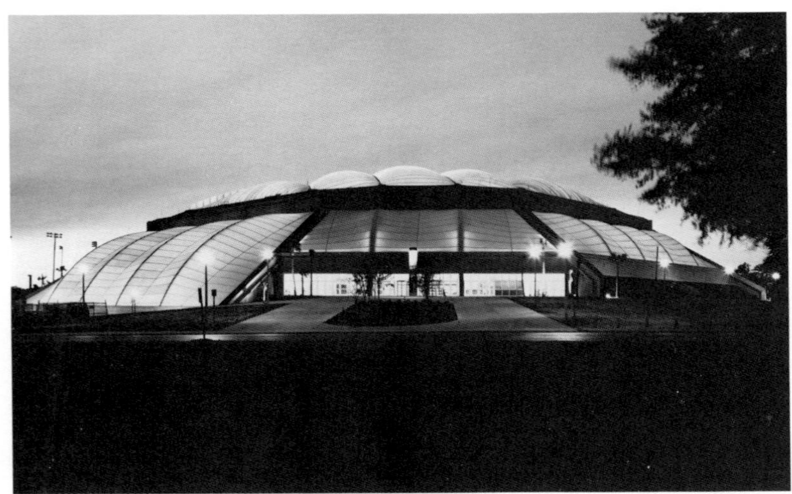

BUILDING INTEGRITY

Although building integrity is highly dependent on decisions concerning component design and specification *within* the four systems, at least three integrations *between* systems are also crucial.

The integration of structure and envelope[51] is critical to structural strength and stability. It is also important for insuring safety (mechanical integrity) and appearance (visual integrity) through seasonal thermal expansion and contraction cycles, through changes in dead and live loads, and in the face of natural disasters.

Envelope and mechanical[52] integrations determine such fundamental shelter conditions as weathertightness and the provision of fresh air. Envelope and mechanical component integrations also influence how much staining and dirt buildup will occur.

Conscious mechanical and interior[53] component integrations ultimately determine fire safety, access for maintenance and change, and such visible degradation conditions as staining, discoloration, and abuse.

51. Structure and envelope combination, pp. 323–324.

52. Envelope and mechanical combination, pp. 327–328.

53. Mechanical and interior combination, pp. 329–330.

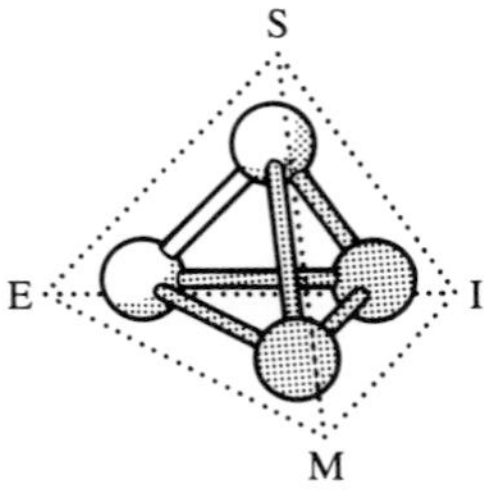

An Illustration of Structure and Envelope Integration for Building Integrity

An example of innovation in systems integration for building integrity is clearly seen in the Stephen C. O'Connell Activities Center.[54] The hurricane wind conditions common in Florida could have dictated a high mass structure, possibly resulting in both excessive costs and restrictive spatial compartmentalization. The architects turned instead to an air-supported and tension fabric structure, unifying structure and envelope. The arched frame tension structure, the concrete compression ring supporting a lightweight, air-inflated arena dome, and the responsive pressurization equipment are capable of withstanding hurricane forces and providing the flexible column-free space desirable in an athletic facility. As a result, the building satisfies the mandate for structural building integrity and spatial flexibility in a cost-effective manner.

Several other building integrity issues have been addressed through the careful detailing of this *unified* structure/envelope[55] system. Four fans in series allow the pressurization to be increased, providing "shock absorption" in the event of hurricane winds and eliminating "ponding" in rainstorms (a problem for all roof types). The fabric's Teflon coating is chemically inert to resist sunlight and aging. The translucent fabric is also treated to insure a low coefficient of friction, thus preventing dirt and dust buildup and allowing rain to wash the surface continuously.

54. O'Connell Center, pp. 108–111.

55. *Unified* integration, p. 320.

A Teflon coated fiberglass skin on the Stephen C. O'Connell Activities Center reflects 75 percent of the solar heat gain while still admitting enough daylight to eliminate the need for artificial lighting during the day. Photograph: Balthazar Korab.

Lighting and thermal performance are also carefully considered in the selection of a *unified* level of integration. The independent mechanical and interior systems are *remote*. Computer simulation comparing daylight gain (lighting advantage) with heat gain (thermal disadvantage) led to the selection of a 4 percent transmission Teflon coated fiberglass fabric for the skin instead of 8 percent or 16 percent. This reflects 75 percent of the solar heat gain (some is absorbed), to cut cooling loads by one-half while still admitting daylight. Because no artificial lighting is needed in the facility during the day, lighting electricity consumption is reduced to 1 W/sq ft and the associated cooling-for-lights consumption is likewise reduced. The double-layer fabric envelope with air space results in an R-11 effective construction, reducing overall heat gain as well.

Finally, acoustical and air quality performance were also significant in the integration of systems in this building. Due to the volume, assembly resiliency, and hanging banners (to reduce sound focusing potential), the facility is reputed to have excellent acoustics, allowing commencement exercises to occur simultaneously with basketball games and swim meets. In addition, the continuous air exchange reduces relative humidity buildup and dissipates the chlorine odor in the swimming pool area.

Table 5: System Decisions and Their Integration, with Critical Implications for Spatial Performance

SPATIAL PERFORMANCE

To Achieve Appropriate:
1. Individual Spaces & Furnishings
2. Aggregation of Spaces
3. Convenience & Services
4. Amenities

*To improve spatial performance and to foster design innovation, examine any two **bold-faced** systems decisions.*

PHYSICAL DECISIONS IN MECHANICAL SYSTEM DESIGN

• HVAC
Service Generators
Size, Volume
Form, Configuration
Expansion Capability
Material, Ornament
Service Conduits
Thickness, Volume of Service
Form, Shape
Configuration, Distance, rise/run
Interface/Expansion Capability
Material, Ornament
Connection to Other Systems
Access Mechanical
Service Terminals
Planning Module
Number, Size, Capacity
Form, Material, Ornament
Interface/Expansion Capability
Relocation Capability
Connection to Other Systems
Control Systems
Central Management Systems
Local Management—Automatic/Manual

• Lighting
Service Generator—Size, Capacity
Service Conduit
Thickness, Volume of Service
Interface, Expansion Capability
Material, Ornament
Access
Service Terminals
Planning Module
Size, Capacity
Form, Material, Ornament
Interface, Expansion—Capability
Relocation Capability
Connection to Other Systems
Control Systems
Central Management
Local Management, Automatic/Manual

• Telecommunications, Power, and Security
Service Generator—Size, Capacity
Service Conduit
Thickness, Volume of Service
Interface/Expansion Capability
Material, Ornament
Access
Service Terminals
Planning Module
Number, Size, Capacity
Form, Material, Ornament
Interface/Expansion Capability
Relocation Capability

• Plumbing and Fire Safety
Service Generator—Size, Capacity
Service Conduit
Thickness, Volume of Service
Configuration, Distance, rise/run
Interface/Expansion Capability
Access
Service Terminals
Planning Module
Number, Size, Capacity
Form, Material, Ornament
Interface/Expansion Capability
Relocation, Capability

• Vertical Transport
Size, Volume of Service
Form, Configuration
Planning Module
Expansion Capability
Material, Ornament

PHYSICAL DECISIONS IN STRUCTURAL SYSTEM DESIGN

General System Type:
Frame, Diaphragm, Tensile, Inflated
System Materials and Properties:
Steel, Concrete, Wood, Plastics
Span, Bay Sizes, Column Spacing
Floor to Floor Height
Cross Section of Structural Elements (Height, Width, Depth)
Building Form: Plan, Section
Expansion Capabilities (Vert., Horiz.)
Connections to Other Structural Components

PHYSICAL DECISIONS IN ENVELOPE SYSTEM DESIGN

Exterior Wall/Roof/Floor
Exterior Surface, Material Properties
Composite Materials, Thickness
Interior Surface
Form: Planar, Curved
Slope, Orientation
Module Size, Shape
Connection of Envelope Components
Windows/Openings
Material Properties
Size, Shape, Spacing
Orientation
Control Systems, Sunshading
Control Systems, Heat Loss
Control Systems, Security/Privacy
Frame Connections, Plan/Sec/Elev.
Access, Visual and Physical
Expansion Potential, Horiz. & Vert
Change Potential for Access & Image
Color, Texture, Ornament

PHYSICAL DECISIONS IN INTERIOR SYSTEM DESIGN

Ceiling
Ceiling Height, Shape, Form
Ceiling Depth
Ceiling Surface, Material Properties
Planning Module
Connection to Other Interior Systems
Floor
Floor Depth
Floor Form/Slope/Steps
Floor Surface, Material Properties
Floor Module
Connection to/Accommodation of Other Systems and Subsystems
Wall
Wall Form, Depth
Openings (Interior)
Wall Surface, Material Properties
Planning Module
Connection to Other Interior Systems
Furnishings
Work Surface: Material, Height, Depth
Sit/Sleep Surface: Material, Ergonomics
Storage
Vegetation/Ornamental Objects
Connection to Other Interior Systems
Office Equipment and Appliances
Access/Circulation
Security Configuration
Expansion Potential, Horiz. & Vertical
Change Potential for Access & Image
Color, Texture, Ornament

Table 6: System Decisions and Their Integration, with Critical Implications for Thermal Performance

PHYSICAL DECISIONS IN MECHANICAL SYSTEM DESIGN

- HVAC

Service Generators
  Size, Volume
  Form, Configuration
  Expansion Capability
  Material, Ornament
Service Conduits
  Thickness, Volume of Service
  Form, Shape
  Configuration, Distance, rise/run
  Interface/Expansion Capability
  Material, Ornament
  Connection to Other Systems
  Access
Service Terminals
  Planning Module
  Number, Size, Capacity
  Form, Material, Ornament
  Interface/Expansion Capability
  Relocation Capability
  Connection to Other Mechanical Systems
Control Systems
  Central Management Systems
  Local Management—Automatic/ Manual

- Lighting

Service Generator—Size, Capacity
Service Conduit
  Thickness, Volume of Service
  Interface, Expansion—Capability
  Material, Ornament
  Access
Service Terminals
  Planning Module
  Size, Capacity
  Form, Material, Ornament
  Interface, Expansion Capability
  Relocation Capability
  Connection to Other Mechanical Systems
Control Systems
  Central Management
  Local Management, Automatic/Manual

- Telecommunications, Power, and Security

Service Generator—Size, Capacity
Service Conduit
  Thickness, Volume of Service
  Interface/Expansion Capability
  Material, Ornament
  Access
Service Terminals
  Planning Module
  Number, Size, Capacity
  Form, Material, Ornament
  Interface/Expansion Capability
  Relocation Capability

PHYSICAL DECISIONS IN STRUCTURAL SYSTEM DESIGN

General System Type:
  Frame, Diaphragm, Tensile, Inflated
System Materials and Properties:
  Steel, Concrete, Wood, Plastics
Span, Bay Sizes, Column Spacing
Floor to Floor Height
Cross Section of Structural Elements (Height, Width, Depth)
Building Form: Plan, Section
Expansion Capabilities (Vert., Horiz.)
Connections to Other Systems

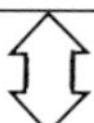

PHYSICAL DECISIONS IN ENVELOPE SYSTEM DESIGN

Exterior Wall/Roof/Floor
  Exterior Surface, Material Properties
  Composite Materials, Thickness
  Interior Surface
  Form: Planar, Curved
  Slope, Orientation
  Module Size, Shape
  Connection of Envelope Components
Windows/Openings
  Material Properties
  Size, Shape, Spacing
  Orientation
  Control Systems, Sunshading
  Control Systems, Heat Loss
  Control Systems, Security/Privacy
  Frame, Connections, Plan/Sec/Elev.
Access, Visual and Physical
Expansion Potential, Horiz. & Vert
Change Potential for Access & Image
Color, Texture, Ornament

THERMAL PERFORMANCE

To Achieve Appropriate:
1. Air Temperature
2. Air Movement
3. Relative Humidity
4. Median Radiant Temperature
5. Occupancy Factors

To improve thermal performance and to foster design innovation, examine any two ***bold-faced*** *systems decisions.*

PHYSICAL DECISIONS IN INTERIOR SYSTEM DESIGN

Ceiling
  Ceiling Height, Shape, Form
  Ceiling Depth
  Ceiling Surface, Material Properties
  Planning Module
  Connection to Other Interior Systems
Floor
  Floor Depth
  Floor Form/Slope/Steps
  Floor Surface, Material Properties
  Floor Module
  Connection to Other Interior Systems
Wall
  Wall Form, Depth
  Openings (Interior)
  Wall Surface, Material Properties
  Planning Module
  Connection to Other Interior Systems
Furnishings
  Work Surface: Material, Height, Depth
  Sit/Sleep Surface: Material, Ergonomics
  Storage
  Vegetation/Ornamental Objects
  Connection to Other Interior Systems
Office Equipment and Appliances
Access/Circulation
Security Configuration
Expansion Potential, Horiz. & Vertical
Change Potential for Access & Image
Color, Texture, Ornament

Table 7: System Decisions and Their Integration, with Critical Implications for Air Quality

AIR QUALITY

To Achieve Appropriate:
1. Fresh Air
2. Mass Pollutants
3. Energy Pollutants
4. Occupancy Factors

To improve air quality and to foster design innovation, examine any two ***bold-faced*** *systems decisions.*

PHYSICAL DECISIONS IN MECHANICAL SYSTEM DESIGN

• HVAC
Service Generators
Size, Volume
Form, Configuration
Expansion Capability
Material, Ornament
Service Conduits
Thickness, Volume of Service
Form, Shape
Configuration, Distance, rise/run
Interface/Expansion Capability
Material, Ornament
Connection to Other Systems
Access
Service Terminals
Planning Module
Number, Size, Capacity
Form, Material, Ornament
Interface/Expansion Capability
Relocation Capability
Connection to Other Systems
Control Systems
Central Management Systems
Local Management—Automatic/Manual

• Lighting
Service Generator—Size, Capacity
Service Conduit
Thickness, Volume of Service
Interface, Expansion Capability
Material, Ornament
Access
Service Terminals
Planning Module
Size, Capacity
Form, Material, Ornament
Interface, Expansion Capability
Relocation Capability
Connection to Other Systems
Control Sysems
Central Management
Local Management, Automatic/Manual

• Telecommunications, Power, and Security
Service Generator—Size, Capacity
Service Conduit
Thickness, Volume of Service
Interface/Expansion Capability
Material, Ornament
Access
Service Terminals
Planning Module
Number, Size, Capacity
Form, Material, Ornament
Interface/Expansion Capability
Relocation Capability

• Plumbing and Fire Safety
Service Generator—Size, Capacity
Service Conduit
Thickness, Volume of Service
Configuration, Distance, rise/run
Interface/Expansion Capability
Access
Service Terminals
Planning Module
Number, Size, Capacity
Form, Material, Ornament
Interface/Expansion Capability
Relocation Capability

• Vertical Transport
Size, Volume of Service
Form, Configuration
Planning Module
Expansion Capability
Material, Ornament

PHYSICAL DECISIONS IN ENVELOPE SYSTEM DESIGN

Exterior Wall/Roof/Floor
Exterior Surface, Material Properties
Composite Materials, Thickness
Interior Surface
Form: Planar, Curved
Slope, Orientation
Module Size, Shape
Connection of Envelope Components
Windows/Openings
Material Properties
Size, Shape, Spacing
Orientation
Control Systems, Sunshading
Control Systems, Heat Loss
Control Systems, Security/Privacy
Frame, Connections, Plan/Sec/Elev.
Access, Visual and Physical
Expansion Potential, Horiz. & Vert.
Change Potential for Access & Image
Color, Texture, Ornament

PHYSICAL DECISIONS IN INTERIOR SYSTEM DESIGN

Ceiling
Ceiling Height, Shape, Form
Ceiling Depth
Ceiling Surface, Material Properties
Planning Module
Connection to Other Interior Systems
Floor
Floor Depth
Floor Form/Slope/Steps
Floor Surface, Material Properties
Floor Module
Connection to Other Interior Systems
Wall
Wall Form, Depth
Openings (Interior)
Wall Surface, Material Properties
Planning Module
Connection to Other Interior Systems
Furnishings
Work Surface: Material, Height, Depth
Sit/Sleep Surface: Material, Ergonomics
Storage
Vegetation/Ornamental Objects
Connection to Other Interior Systems
Office Equipment and Appliances
Access/Circulation
Security Configuration
Expansion Potential, Horiz. & Vertical
Change Potential for Access & Image
Color, Texture, Ornament

Table 8: System Decisions and Their Integration, with Critical Implications for Acoustical Performance

PHYSICAL DECISIONS IN MECHANICAL SYSTEM DESIGN

- HVAC

Service Generators
Size, Volume
Form, Configuration
Expansion Capability
Material, Ornament
Service Conduits
Thickness, Volume of Service
Form, Shape
Configuration, Distance, rise/run
Interface/Expansion Capability
Material, Ornament
Connection to Other Systems
Access
Service Terminals
Planning Module
Number, Size, Capacity
Form, Material, Ornament
Interface/Expansion Capability
Relocation Capability
Connection to Other Systems
Control Systems
Central Management Systems
Local Management—Automatic/Manual

- Lighting

Service Generator—Size, Capacity
Service Conduit
Thickness, Volume of Service
Interface, Expansion Capability
Material, Ornament
Access
Service Terminals
Planning Module
Size, Capacity
Form, Material, Ornament
Interface, Expansion Capability
Relocation Capability
Connection to Other Systems
Control Systems
Central Management
Local Management, Automatic/Manual

- Telecommunications, Power, and Security

Service Genererator—Size, Capacity
Service Conduit
Thickness, Volume of Service
Interface/Expansion Capability
Material, Ornament
Access
Service Terminals
Planning Module
Number, Size, Capacity
Form, Material, Ornament
Interface/Expansion Capability
Selection Capability

- Plumbing and Fire Safety

Service Generator—Size, Capacity
Service Conduit
Thickness, Volume of Service
Configuration, Distance, rise/run
Interface/Expansion Capability
Access
Service Terminals
Planning Module
Number, Size, Capacity
Form, Material, Ornament
Interface/Expansion Capability
Relocation Capability

- Vertical Transport

Size, Volume of Service
Form, Configuration
Planning Module
Expansion Capability
Material, Ornament

ACOUSTICAL PERFORMANCE

To Achieve Appropriate:
1. Sound Pressure Levels
2. Reverberation/Absorption
3. Speech Privacy
4. Vibration
5. Occupancy Factors

*To improve acoustical performance and to foster design innovation, examine any two **bold-faced** systems decisions.*

PHYSICAL DECISIONS IN STRUCTURAL SYSTEM DESIGN

General System Type:
Frame, Diaphragm, Tensile, Inflated
System Materials and Properties:
Steel, Concrete, Wood, Plastics
Span, Bay Sizes, Column Spacing
Floor to Floor Height
Cross Section of Structural Elements (Height, Width, Depth)
Building Form: Plan, Section
Expansion Capabilities (Vert., Horiz.)
Connections to Other Systems

PHYSICAL DECISIONS IN ENVELOPE SYSTEM DESIGN

Exterior Wall/Roof/Floor
Exterior Surface, Material Properties
Composite Materials, Thickness
Interior Surface
Form: Planar, Curved
Slope, Orientation
Module Size, Shape
Connection of Envelope Components
Windows/Openings
Material Properties
Size, Shape, Spacing
Orientation
Control Systems, Sunshading
Control Systems, Heat Loss
Control Systems, Security/Privacy
Frame, Connections, Plan/Sec/Elev.
Access, Visual and Physical
Expansion Potential, Horiz. & Vert.
Change Potential for Access & Image
Color, Texture, Ornament

PHYSICAL DECISIONS IN INTERIOR SYSTEM DESIGN

Ceiling
Ceiling Height, Shape, Form
Ceiling Depth
Ceiling Surface, Material Properties
Planning Module
Connection to Other Interior Systems
Floor
Floor Depth
Floor Form/Slope/Steps
Floor Surface, Material Properties
Floor Module
Connection to Other Interior Systems
Wall
Wall Form, Depth
Openings (Interior)
Wall Surface, Material Properties
Planning Module
Connection to Other Interior Systems
Furnishings
Work Surface: Material, Height, Depth
Sit/Sleep Surface: Material, Ergonomics
Storage
Vegetation/Ornamental Objects
Connection to Other Interior Systems
Office Equipment and Appliances
Access/Circulation
Security Configuration
Expansion Potential, Horiz. & Vertical
Change Potential for Access & Image
Color, Texture, Ornament

Table 9: System Decisions and Their Integration, with Critical Implications for Visual Performance

PHYSICAL DECISIONS IN MECHANICAL SYSTEM DESIGN

- HVAC

Service Generators
- Size, Volume
- Form, Configuration
- Expansion Capability
- Material, Ornament

Service Conduits
- Thickness, Volume of Service
- Form, Shape
- Configuration, Distance, rise/run
- Interface/Expansion Capability
- Material, Ornament
- Connection to Other Systems
- Access

Service Terminals
- **Planning Module**
- Number, Size, Capacity
- **Form, Material, Ornament**
- Interface/Expansion Capability
- Relocation Capability
- **Connection to Other Systems**

Control Systems
- Central Management Systems
- Local Management—Automatic/Manual

- Lighting

Service Generator—Size, Capacity

Service Conduit
- **Thickness, Volume of Service**
- Interface, Expansion Capability
- Material, Ornament
- **Access**

Service Terminals
- **Planning Module**
- **Size, Capacity**
- **Form, Material, Ornament**
- **Interface, Expansion Capability**
- **Relocation Capability**
- Connection to Other Systems

Control Systems
- **Central Management**
- **Local Management, Automatic/Manual**

- Telecommunications, Power, and Security

Service Generator—Size, Capacity

Service Conduit
- Thickness, Volume of Service
- Interface/Expansion Capability
- Material, Ornament
- Access

Service Terminals
- Planning Module
- Number, Size, Capacity
- **Form, Material, Ornament**
- Interface/Expansion Capability
- Relocation Capability

PHYSICAL DECISIONS IN STRUCTURAL SYSTEM DESIGN

General System Type:
- Frame, Diaphragm, Tensile, Inflated

System Materials and Properties:
- Steel, Concrete, Wood, Plastics

Span, Bay Sizes, Column Spacing

Floor to Floor Height

Cross Section of Structural Elements
- (Height, Width, Depth)

Building Form: Plan, Section

Expansion Capabilities (Vert., Horiz.)

Connections to Other Systems

PHYSICAL DECISIONS IN ENVELOPE SYSTEM DESIGN

Exterior Wall/Roof/Floor
- Exterior Surface, Material Properties
- Composite Materials, Thickness
- **Interior Surface**
- Form: Planar, Curved
- **Slope, Orientation**
- Module Size, Shape
- Connection of Envelope Components

Windows/Openings
- **Material Properties**
- **Size, Shape, Spacing**
- **Orientation**
- **Control Systems, Sunshading**
- Control Systems, Heat Loss
- Control Systems, Security/Privacy
- **Frame, Connections, Plan/Sec/Elev.**

Access, Visual and Physical

Expansion Potential, Horiz. & Vert.

Change Potential for Access & Image

Color, Texture, Ornament

VISUAL PERFORMANCE

To Achieve Appropriate:
1. Illuminance: Ambient & Task Ltg.
2. Contrast & Brightness Ratios
3. Color Rendition
4. Occupancy Factors

*To improve visual performance and to foster design innovation, examine any two **bold-faced** systems decisions.*

PHYSICAL DECISIONS IN INTERIOR SYSTEM DESIGN

Ceiling
- **Ceiling Height, Shape, Form**
- Ceiling Depth
- **Ceiling Surface, Material Properties**
- Planning Module
- Connection to Other Interior Systems

Floor
- Floor Depth
- Floor Form/Slope/Steps
- Floor Surface, Material Properties
- Floor Module
- Connection to Other Interior Systems

Wall
- **Wall Form, Depth**
- **Openings (Interior)**
- **Wall Surface, Material Properties**
- **Planning Module**
- **Connection to Other Interior Systems**

Furnishings
- **Work Surface: Material, Height, Depth**
- Sit/Sleep Surface: Material, Ergonomics
- **Storage**
- Vegetation/Ornamental Objects
- Connection to Other Interior Systems

Office Equipment and Appliances

Access/Circulation

Security Configuration

Expansion Potential, Horiz. & Vertical

Change Potential for Access & Image

Color, Texture, Ornament

Table 10: System Decisions and Their Integration, with Critical Implications for Building Integrity

BUILDING INTEGRITY

To Achieve Appropriate:
1. Mechanical Properties
2. Physical Properties
3. Visible Properties

*To improve building integrity and to foster design innovation, examine any two **bold-faced** systems decisions.*

PHYSICAL DECISIONS IN MECHANICAL SYSTEM DESIGN

• HVAC
Service Generators
Size, Volume
Form, Configuration
Expansion Capability
Material, Ornament
Service Conduits
Thickness, Volume of Service
Form, Shape
Configuration, Distance, rise/run
Interface/Expansion Capability
Material, Ornament
Connection to Other Systems
Access
Service Terminals
Planning Module
Number, Size, Capacity
Form, Material, Ornament
Interface/Expansion Capability
Relocation Capability
Connection to Other Systems
Control Systems
Central Management Systems
Local Management—Automatic/Manual

• Lighting
Service Generator—Size, Capacity
Service Conduit
Thickness, Volume of Service
Interface, Expansion Capability
Material, Ornament
Access
Service Terminals
Planning Module
Size, Capacity
Form, Material, Ornament
Interface, Expansion Capability
Relocation Capability
Connection to Other Systems
Control Systems
Central Management
Local Management, Automatic/Manual

• Telecommunications, Power, and Security
Service Generator—Size, Capacity
Service Conduit
Thickness, Volume of Service
Interface/Expansion Capability
Material, Ornament
Access
Service Terminals
Planning Module
Number, Size, Capacity
Form, Material, Ornament
Interface/Expansion Capability
Selection Capability

• Plumbing and Fire Safety
Service Generator—Size, Capacity
Service Conduit
Thickness, Volume of Service
Configuration, Distance, rise/run
Interface/Expansion Capability
Access
Service Terminals
Planning Module
Number, Size, Capacity
Form, Material, Ornament
Interface/Expansion Capability
Relocation, Capability

• Vertical Transport
Size, Volume of Service
Form, Configuration
Planning Module
Expansion Capability
Material, Ornament

PHYSICAL DECISIONS IN STRUCTURAL SYSTEM DESIGN

General Systems Type:
Frame, Diaphragm, Tensile, Inflated
System Materials and Properties:
Steel, Concrete, Wood, Plastics
Span, Bay Sizes, Column Spacing
Floor to Floor Height
Cross Section of Structural Elements (Height, Width, Depth)
Building Form: Plan, Section
Expansion Capabilities (Vert., Horiz.)
Connections to Other Systems

PHYSICAL DECISIONS IN ENVELOPE SYSTEM DESIGN

Exterior Wall/Roof/Floor
Exterior Surface, Material Properties
Composite Materials, Thickness
Interior Surface
Form: Planar, Curved
Slope, Orientation
Module Size, Shape
Connection of Envelope Components
Windows/Openings
Material Properties
Size, Shape, Spacing
Orientation
Control Systems, Sunshading
Control Systems, Heat Loss
Control Systems, Security/Privacy
Frame, Connections, Plan/Sec/Elev.
Access, Visual and Physical
Expansion Potential, Horiz. & Vert
Change Potential for Access & Image
Color, Texture, Ornament

PHYSICAL DECISIONS IN INTERIOR SYSTEM DESIGN

Ceiling
Ceiling Height, Shape, Form
Ceiling Depth
Ceiling Surface, Material Properties
Planning Module
Connection to Other Interior Systems
Floor
Floor Depth
Floor Form/Slope/Steps
Floor Surface, Material Properties
Floor Module
Connection to Other Interior Systems
Wall
Wall Form, Depth
Openings (Interior)
Wall Surface, Material Properties
Planning Module
Connection to Other Interior Systems
Furnishings
Work Surface: Material, Height, Depth
Sit/Sleep Surface: Material, Ergonomics
Storage
Vegetation/Ornamental Objects
Connection to Other Interior Systems
Office Equipment and Appliances
Access/Circulation
Security Configuration
Expansion Potential, Horiz. & Vertical
Change Potential for Access & Image
Color, Texture, Ornament

Failure to Integrate

If the interrelationships between the integration of various building systems and the provision of performance seem logical, then why do buildings fail to perform?

Field evaluations continue to show that most buildings that perform poorly do so as a result of the subdivision of responsibility and accountability by time and by professional discipline. Indeed, it is becoming increasingly clear that individual competence does not lead to collective competence.

S.G.M. Attar of Alberta Public Works in Canada has ascribed poor building performance to the gaps in the building process, taken from conception to commissioning, and the gaps in responsibility between experts in various disciplines. Mattar concludes that "when the building process discontinuities are superimposed on the responsibility gaps, the result is the formation of operational islands (see chart below). This appears to be a reasonable visualization of the traditional organizational form in building projects. The diagram emphasizes and exaggerates the problems of communications and management which can lead to problems of buildability."

Poor performance in buildings might be ascribed to gaps in the building process combined with gaps in responsibility between disciplines.

GAPS IN THE BUILDING DELIVERY PROCESS: THE CONCEPT OF STRESS FACTORS

Performance failure can result from decisions made at any step in the building delivery process, decisions that reduce the alternatives for each succeeding step, so that the final product has less chance for success. The concept might be called "accumulative stress factors" leading to building performance failure.

A client may dictate in conception that money should be allocated to facades, lobbies, or other parts of the building that "show," resulting in tremendous restraints on roof and foundation budgets. The feasibility study and program may dictate that skylit spaces are highly desirable. The architect may present a preliminary design in which flat roofs are an important component, with the skylights dotted across the expanse. In working drawings the specifier may produce a detail that requires construction precision without the assurance of a matching investment in quality materials. Meanwhile the contractor has been asked to fast-track, again with the client's emphasis that "work that shows must be impeccable." Finally, the building manager is conscientiously dealing

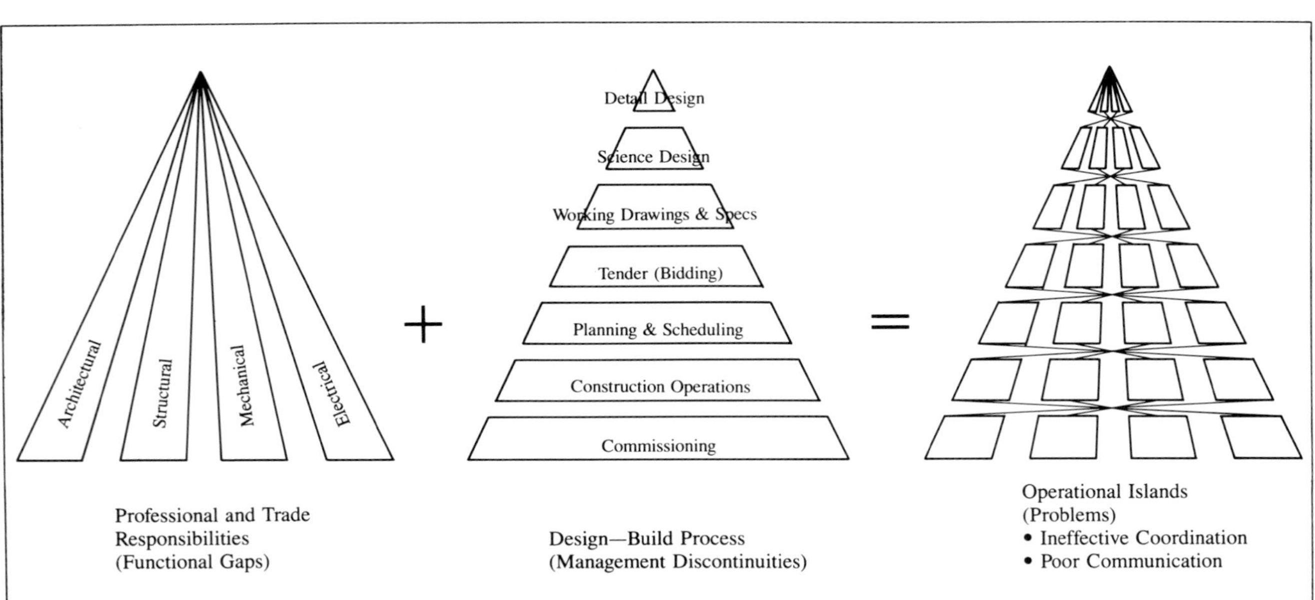

Credit: S.G.M. Attar, PWC Alberta

with problems as they arise, while preventive maintenance of drainage channels and flashing valleys on the roof are left to less hectic times. The result? A massive roof leak. No one decision-maker is at fault, though lawsuits are intended to prove the contrary. The performance failure is a result of stress factors that began at the conception of the project, making it increasingly difficult for each succeeding decision-maker to insure performance. The solution may be a level of comprehension of building science and building performance that spans the entire building delivery process, and a commitment to relieving stress factors at each stage of decision-making.

GAPS BETWEEN PROFESSIONAL DESIGN DISCIPLINES

In the evaluation of performance within the integrated system or building, one can look at these gaps in responsibility in another way. If one lists the design professions or disciplines involved in system design and integration and assigns their traditional performance responsibilities, it quickly becomes clear that there are foreseeable gaps in production.

Only one professional, the acoustical engineer, is assigned primary responsibility and accountability for acoustics in buildings. But acousticians traditionally are involved only in special-purpose buildings, where communication with speech or music is essential. There are some design decision-makers who take some secondary responsibility (without accountability), but they are often not well versed in the fundamentals of acoustics. This may explain the poor acoustical performance of many open office areas, restaurants, athletic facilities, and classrooms.

Air quality performance also has few advocate decision-makers in the design process. Responsibility for good air quality in buildings is assigned to the mechanical engineer and later to the building manager/operator. However, this responsibility is assigned without authority over the realm of design decisions that affect air quality: selection of materials, space layout affecting air distribution, processes and equipment to be housed, and the detailing and construction of vertical shafts and plenums that affect pollution migration.

If it were not for the development of a new design profession—the energy consultant—visual (lighting) performance would have only one advocate in the design process, the electrical/lighting consultant. Again, many integration decisions critical to lighting performance, such as the determination of height and depth of spaces, window size and control systems, and surface colors, are not often relinquished to team decision-making except in such buildings as museums.

Although energy consultants have not become advocates for air quality, they have altered the design process to some extent by strengthening team decision-making processes regarding systems integration, originally for the provision of thermal comfort. As a result of this new design consultant's expertise, decisions regarding structural system type and its integration with envelope, envelope materials and detailing, and interior layouts and furnishings have been added to the traditional "thermal comfort" discussions of the isolated mechanical system design.

Both spatial performance and building integrity have the greatest chance of success, given the number of decision-makers taking responsibility. The design and financing of functional layouts for spatial comfort and the selection of materials and details for building integrity often go through a collective and iterative decision-making process in order to insure performance suitability, reliability, and, as programmed, flexibility.

In considering today's large open office areas, widely used and heavily occupied for long hours, it is crucial to understand the balance and competence needed to insure all building performance mandates: thermal comfort, acoustical com-

Communication plays an important part in classrooms at Stockton State College. Photograph: Graphics Office, Stockton State College.

fort, visual comfort, air quality and health, spatial quality, and building integrity. No specification, installation, operation, or retrofit should be undertaken in the absence of an understanding of the implications it will have for the delivery of total building performance.

Communication: The Key to Integration for Performance

Because the product delivered in each stage of the building process, such as a program or working drawings, is both the result of communication and a means of communication to the next step, there are possible unknowns between the stages in the building delivery that may ultimately lead to failure. This is a function of the perceived gap between the expected environment created for a particular use and the physical quantity and quality actually produced. Although the expectation comes either from previous experience or identification with the experience of others, the communication or comprehension of that expectation is not a simple process. It is often easier to educate the user of the building to close the gap in expectation than it is to alter the building or the design to meet the expectation of the user.[56]

Consequently, building performance not only depends on the quality of the individual products in the building delivery process and the minimization of performance "stress," but also on successful communication between the individual decision-makers. This chapter is based on the assumption that high-performance buildings result from high levels of communication throughout the entire building process. If unconscious needs are not communicated, flaws may be built-in. On the other hand, if conscious needs have never been given the opportunity for expression, the building cannot address them. One way to improve the performance of a building, then, is to increase the knowledge base and experience of the individual decision-makers and to increase the communication throughout the delivery process.

The following six tables illustrate how poor spatial, thermal, air quality, acoustical, visual, and building integrity performance result from the separations between professional disciplines and their ability to participate in the selection and integration of other system components. The tables highlight some of the transdisciplinary failures that can occur in office spaces.

56. Roundtable discussion, p. 38.

It is critical that clear communication exist between the various decision-makers, supported by a fundamental comprehension of each discipline and its terminology. In an effort to improve the basis for communication, this chapter ends with two explorations. First, expanded definitions are given of the six performance mandates, their current limits of acceptability, and the terms (units) for communicating and evaluating each performance mandate throughout the building delivery process. Second, tables showing some of the performance implications of the six two-system integrations are presented[57] which are intended to foster a deliberate team decision-making process, and to improve performance through deliberate systems integration.

57. Two-system integrations, p. 318.

Traditional Accountabilities for Building Performance

	spatial	thermal	air quality	acoustic	visual	bldg. integrity
Architectural	●			○	○	●
Mechanical		●	●			
Electrical	●				○	
Lighting	○				●	
Acoustical				●		
Structural	○					●
Interior	●			○	○	●
Energy Consultant		●	○		●	
Owner/Financer	●					●
Contractor			○			●
Manager/Operator		●	●		○	●
Occupant	○				○	

KEY
● : Primary Responsibility/ Accountability Taken for Building Performance
○ : Secondary Responsibility/ Accountability

Necessary Accountabilities for Building Performance

	spatial	thermal	air quality	acoustic	visual	bldg. integrity
Architectural	●	●	●	●	●	●
Mechanical	○	●	●	○	○	●
Electrical	●				●	●
Lighting	●	●	○	○	●	●
Acoustical	●			●		○
Structural	●	○		○	○	●
Interior	●	●	●	●	●	●
Energy Consultant	○	●	●		○	●

Sample Performance Failures* From Thermal Performance Decisions

Decisions made for:	Leading to failures in:
Thermal Performance	**Visual Performance**
reduced glass area	reduced daylight, increased contrast
increased use of glass on south exposure (reduced glass on other exposures)	glare potential, no bilateral lighting
direct sunshine for occupancy comfort	restricted use possible, e.g., glare and overheating with visual display terminals
dark surfaces for solar absorption	low reflectivity, reduced daylight penetration and lighting effectiveness
reduced usage of incandescent/task lighting due to heat gain	reduced lighting control by individual, poorer color rendition
Thermal Performance	**Acoustical Performance**
high velocity air supply	hiss
cycling constant volume or VAV system	intermittent sound
continuous return air plenum above hung ceiling	flanking sound paths over walls
continuous convector casings at window line	continuous sound paths through convectors, and incomplete acoustical seal between wall and window line
steam or water perimeter heating	chugging, hissing, or clanging with age
local air conditioning units or local heating units (such as heat pumps)	mechanical hum and cycling, vibration potential
Thermal Performance	**Air Quality**
reduced infiltration	fresh air must be mechanically supplied
maximum/minimum settings in air distribution systems determined by thermal needs	inadequate fresh air in smoking areas or copy rooms
sealed, smaller windows to reduce heat loss	inability to get fresh air, ventilation by individual
materials selected for insulation	potential outgassing
minimization of outside air intake	fewer fresh air exchanges per hour
humidification systems	potential bacterial growth
Thermal Performance	**Building Integrity**
increased envelope insulation	greater stress due to increased surface temperature differentials; cracks, dry rot, delamination
increased but discontinuous insulation	potential for condensation on cold, isolated surfaces (thermal bridges)
use of high transmission acrylics for solar gain	yellowing, cracking, warping
passive solar heating	fading, brittleness of interior materials
overhangs, exterior sunshading devices and night insulation	easily damaged by wind, sun, freeze-thaw
interior sunshading and night insulation devices	cracks, breakage due to temperature differentials, wear
increased thermal resistance without continuous vapor barrier	condensation, corrosion, rot due to vapor transmission
unitary heat pumps' or air conditioners	potential for air leakage, rain or moisture penetration
mechanical components penetrating the enclosure	
small return air intake	soot buildup, increased maintenance
increased mass capacitance for heat storage	increased dead loads
radiant heating components (ceiling, floor, wall)	potential fire or short (electrical system) leakage or damage (water system)
increased humidity for comfort	increased potential for condensation
Thermal Performance	**Spatial Performance**
single mechanical plant for ease of control, management	difficulty in meeting various local loads simultaneously
fewer, shorter distribution runs with high velocity supply for greater depth penetration in open office areas	subdivision of spaces difficult, poorer spatial flexibility
bulky perimeter units to cope with heating load	diminshed net usable space

*Examples drawn from five years of occupied office building evaluations in U.S., Canada, and England.

Sample Performance Failures* From Spatial Performance Decisions

Decisions made for:	Leading to failures in:
Spatial Performance	**Thermal Performance**
large open plan, unzoned spaces for complete flexibility	lack of individual control, local discomfort
integration of printers, computers, microfiche throughout workplace	local overheating
individually controlled compartmentalization for privacy (screens)	potential for inadequate supply air and associated heating and cooling supply
open vertical integration of different levels, atria, light wells, circulation	thermal stratification
multi-purpose spaces	potential inadequacy in thermal conditioning for some functions
Spatial Performance	**Visual Performance**
locally managed walls, partitions, bookcases, file cabinets	obstruct and absorb light, cast shadows
complete flexibility in determining space use	inappropriate or inadequate lighting for some functions, overabundance for others
use of perimeter areas for private offices	loss of daylighting for interior spaces
Spatial Performance	**Acoustical Performance**
large, open plan, unzoned spaces for complete flexibility	poor isolation of noise, poor speech privacy
centralized machinery/typists for supervision	intense sound generators, unacceptable occupancy conditions
low density enclosed management spaces, and high-density open spaces, as indication of rank and salary	no speech privacy, high noise levels for large percentage of work stations
operable partitions not penetrating hung ceiling to floor slab	greater speech, noise transmission through flankng paths
building-wide fire alarm/public address system	possible sputtering, distraction from coninuous background music
building servicing equipment: elevators, toilet rooms, conveyors	possible rumbling, clicking, hissing distraction
Spatial Performance	**Air Quality**
including garages, food services, printing facilities, loading docks within building envelope for convenience	potential pollution migration
open vertical and horizontal connections between spaces	potential pollution migration
integration of pollution, emitting equipment (printing equipment, for example) within occupied spaces	pollution buildup
using mechanical rooms as convenient storage for chemicals, cleaning fluids	potential pollution buildup and migration
unrestricted smoking	possible pollution buildup due to inadequate ventilation
Spatial Performance	**Building Integrity**
maximize usable floor area, with thin unarticulated enclosures	potential rain/air penetration
large-span structures for flexibility	possible vibration, movement, deflection; open expansion joints with air, water penetration

Sample Performance Failures* From Building Integrity

Decisions made for:	Leading to failures in:
Building Integrity	**Thermal Performance**
non-operable windows to minimize leakage	no individual control for natural ventilation
vapor-tight enclosure to avoid condensation	high interior humidity buildup
minimized exterior articulation (balconies, awnings, overhangs) for fewer degradation problems (detachment, soot, corrosion, pigeons)	potential local overheating without sunshading
durable metal and concrete furniture instead of fabric and wood	conductive and radiative losses from the human body
more central control systems versus local control systems that require more maintenance	loss of individual control
shutdown of humidification systems due to maintenance required	poor humidity control
Building Integrity	**Visual Performance**
minimized exterior articulation and control systems	unrestricted light/glare

internalized, non-integrated structural components	possible unacceptable brightness ratios
Building Integrity	**Acoustical Performance**
selection of hard surfaces for durability and ease of maintenance	increased noise levels
Building Integrity	**Air Quality**
treatment of wood for preservation (against termites, fungus)	possible outgassing and toxic effects
regular cleaning/maintenance of interior finishes	possible outgassing and toxic effects
introduction of more synthetic materials over natural materials for ease of maintenance and durability	possible outgassing and toxic sweating
elimination of venting of air polluting machines through outside walls for image and weathertightness	pollution buildup in interior spaces
Building Integrity	**Spatial Performance**
fixed, built-in interior scenery	lack of flexibility, adaptability, expansion
hard, durable interior surfaces (chairs, floors)	physical discomfort, ergonomic deficiencies

Sample Performance Failures* From Visual Performance Decisions

Decisions made for:	Leading to failures in:
Visual Performance	**Thermal Performance**
increased floor-to-ceiling height	increased thermal stratification and conditioning needs
reflective glass to reduce glare	reduced potential for solar heating during underheated periods
increased use of glass for daylighting	excessive gains during overheated periods
increased number of light fixtures	excessive heat gain from lights, especially with poor lumens/watt
Visual Performance	**Acoustical Performance**
fluorescent lighting	buzzing, depending on quality, maintenance and age
sea of evenly spaced fixtures for flexibility	increased potential for sound reflection
venetian blinds for light control instead of fabric curtains	increased sound reflectivity
Visual Performance	**Spatial Performance**
ambient lighting only in circulation areas	loss of full spatial flexibility
open plan offices to maximize daylight penetration and artificial light distribution	loss of privacy and hierarchy
central light management systems	loss of individual control, poor energy performance
undifferentiated task-ambient lighting	loss of wayfinding, workplace definition
Visual Performance	**Air Quality**
artificial lighting alone for control and efficiency	without sunlight, potential psychological dissatisfaction; dying plants; germ and mold build-up
use of fluorescent light fixtures	poor spectral distribution; possible radiant and particulate pollution
Visual Performance	**Building Integrity**
reflective film retrofit to reduce glare	fissure cracks, visual degradation
poor selection of light diffusers/lenses on fixtures	dust buildup, yellowing, increased maintenance
highly reflective, light-colored furnishings for light distribution	marring, discoloring, staining; high maintenance
daylighting	fading, discoloring, brittleness, cracking

*Examples drawn from five years of occupied office building evaluations in U.S., Canada, and England.

Sample Performance Failures* From Air Quality

Decisions made for:	Leading to failures in:
Air Quality	**Thermal Performance**
increased ventilation rate	potential drafts, excessive energy costs
reduced humidity to slow outgassing and bacterial growth	inadequate humidity levels
Air Quality	**Acoustical Performance**
intermittent air supply	intermittent sound perceived as noise
elimination of many synthetic materials	reduction of available sound-absorbing materials
Air Quality	**Spatial Performance**
isolation of polluting machinery—printers, copiers, ovens	reduced flexibility, less convenient adjacencies
isolation of polluters, smokers	reduced communciation, proximity, increased social pressures
isolation of polluting chemicals, cleaning fluids	less convenient to equipment
reduced vertical paths/connections between floors (stairs, light wells)	reduced communication, sense of openness, flexibility
reduced screening in open plan offices to ensure air distribution	loss of visual privacy, workspace definition
Air Quality	**Visual Performance**
decreased usage of fluorescent fixtures to avoid poor spectral distribution	decreased lighting efficiency
Air Quality	**Building Integrity**
increased humidity for health	increased condensation potential, corrosion, fungus

Sample Performance Failures* From Acoustical Performance Decisions

Decisions made for:	Leading to failures in:
Acoustical Performance	**Thermal Performance**
freestanding acoustical partitions flush to the floor	poor air circulation at the working plane
soft, sound-absorbing surfaces on floor, walls, ceiling	rapid heating-up with sunshine or running equipment, due to poor thermal capacitance
isolation of noise-generating equipment	large heat buildup, unexpected air conditioning needs
drywall partitioning into grid in ceiling plane	possible cutoff of supply air diffuser
operating supply air or fans continuously as masking sound	possible thermal discomfort, draftiness
subdivision for security, space definition, and privacy	possible misplaced thermostats, control in adjacent spaces
Acoustical Performance	**Visual Performance**
freestanding acoustical panels, especially if dark colored	poor light levels at the working plane
high density freestanding partitions	often askew with lighting grid in ceiling plane, inadequate light supply within workstation
subdivision for security, space definition, and privacy	possible misplaced light switches, control in adjacent spaces
Acoustical Performance	**Spatial Performance**
partitions from floor to ceiling slab for acoustical privacy	poor flexibility for rapid change
isolation of noise-generating equipment	poor accessibility
acoustically isolated typing stations	poor supervision
Acoustical Performance	**Air Quality**
isolation of noise-generating equipment	concentration of potentially polluting equipment
increased use of sound-absorbing materials	possible outgassing of binders, release of particulates
Acoustical Performance	**Building Integrity**
soft, open-pore interior surfaces for acoustical absorption	easily damaged, torn, punctured, and soiled

Expanded Definitions of the Six Performance Mandates: Spatial Performance

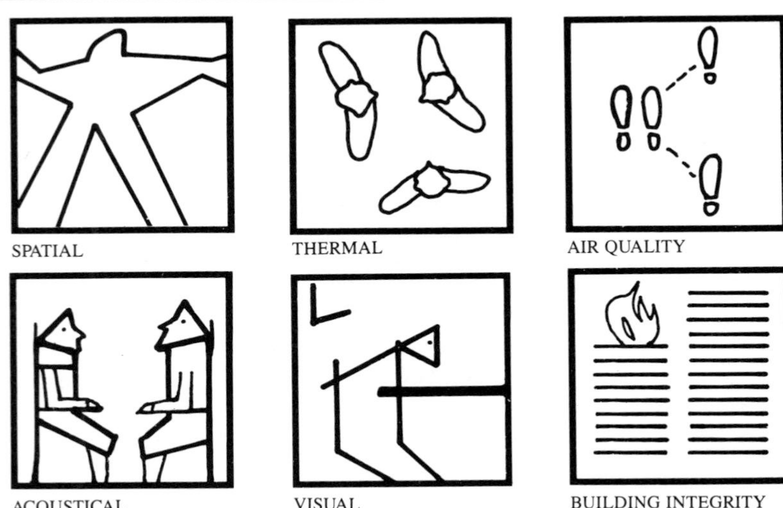

Based on the assumption that satisfactory building performance is highly dependent on integrated decision-making, both between disciplines and throughout the building delivery process, somewhat expanded definitions of the six performance mandates are given here.

These expanded definitions are not intended to replace or even fully define the level of building science comprehension that is available in each discipline. Rather, they are intended to put each of the six performance areas on a comparable basis for discussion, to demystify the communication between disciplines and reduce the isolation of decision-making territories.

The definitions are also intended to improve the designer's empirical processes for evaluating and recording (including visually recording) the levels of integration of structural, envelope, mechanical, and interior systems in the delivery of performance. When a new museum is designed, for example, the "walk-through" of existing museums should not be restricted to an evaluation of their spatial quality (comfort, efficiency, and beauty), but should aggregate information concerning the integration of systems toward insuring overall building performance—building integrity, visual quality, and thermal, acoustical, and air quality for each of the various building occupancies, including artifacts.

SPATIAL PERFORMANCE

Definition

The architectural profession has traditionally concerned itself with design for the provision of spatial performance, with all of its physiological, psychological, sociological, and economic demands. This task includes the design of individual spaces and their furnishings to provide the best support for the individual activity; the aggregation of these spaces, to best support the needs of the activities as a whole; and the provision of conveniences or functional services such as circulation/transportation, electricity, security, and telecommunications.

The challenge of laying out individual spaces successfully, so that they perform within the communicated needs of the client, involves decisions about area, volume, capacity, and furniture, measured in anthropometric and ergonomic terms. Physiological needs for safety and spatial comfort are defined for all user groups with special provisions for the elderly, the very young, and the handicapped. Psychological needs for spatial definition are often expressed in such terms as openness, privacy, intimacy, awesomeness, surprise, and calm, frequently in the form of se-

Spatial Performance

1. Design of Individual Space and Furnishings
2. Aggregation of Individual Spaces
3. Provision of Conveniences and Services
4. Design of Amenities

mantic scales (such as the Osgood scale). Sociological needs are often set by the building community to preserve equity in carrying out all the activities housed in the building. Economic needs are then set by a concern for resources: the conservation of space, materials, energy, and time.

The aggregation of these individual spaces, often the focus of design programming, involves such decisions as the determination of adjacencies needed and acceptable distances; the level of compartmentalization, centralization, or dispersion; indoor-outdoor relationships; the ratio of circulation to usable space; and the design of circulation for accessibility, wayfinding (including signage), and safety.

The functional services or conveniences needed to accomplish particular tasks (in contrast to services that provide individual thermal, acoustical, and visual comfort), include such design elements as stairways, elevators, and escalators for vertical transportation; electricity and telecommunications networks for power and communication; sanitary services; security; and shared services such as cafeterias, lounges, and coffee areas.

Finally, there are amenities, such as color, texture, and ornament, as well as the provision of any of the design qualities described above that may not have been called for in the original program. For example, amenities might include designing for the element of surprise in the creation of an individual space, to meet an uncommunicated psychological need or to express a corporate identity.

Ergonomic Guidelines

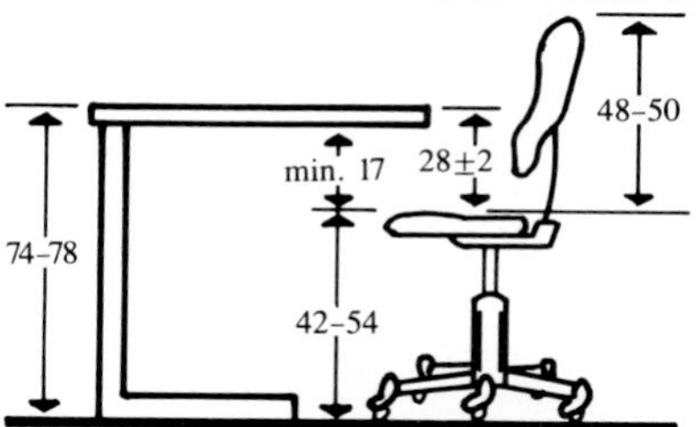

Credit: *NRC Video Displays, Work and Vision.*

For each of these design topics, the question of occupancy control inevitably surfaces. The ultimate satisfaction of the individual using the space, the aggregation of spaces, or the services and amenities in question depends largely on the ability of occupants to personalize, interact, and control their spatial environments. To what degree this interaction is necessary becomes one of the early requirements for communication among the designer, the client, and the building users.

Known Limits of Acceptability

The codes, standards, and guidelines stimulating improved design for spatial performance have expanded significantly in recent years. The introduction of spatial performance standards began with rudimentary safety standards for such decisions as tread heights and egress distances. Minimum property standards were developed to insure that basic physiological and sociological needs would be met in the size of spaces and the provision of conveniences and services to those spaces. Most recently, codes for handicapped accessibility have been added, providing incentives for improving ergonomics, accessibility, and signage. These design improvements have benefitted all building users.

The development of standards and guidelines should not be seen as an annoyance in the design of spaces, but rather as a growing understanding of the needs of various occupancies performing various functions and their minimum limits of acceptability. As a parallel, the early understanding of thermal comfort was bounded only by frostbite and heat stroke, assuming that the 70°F temperature range that lies between is of equal acceptability to the occupants, regardless of function. Only the increased understanding of human comfort, resulting from in-depth research in several countries, has enabled designers to recognize that the comfort "zone" depends on occupancy and function. Design to these more refined zones not only insures better physiological perfor-

Common design faults

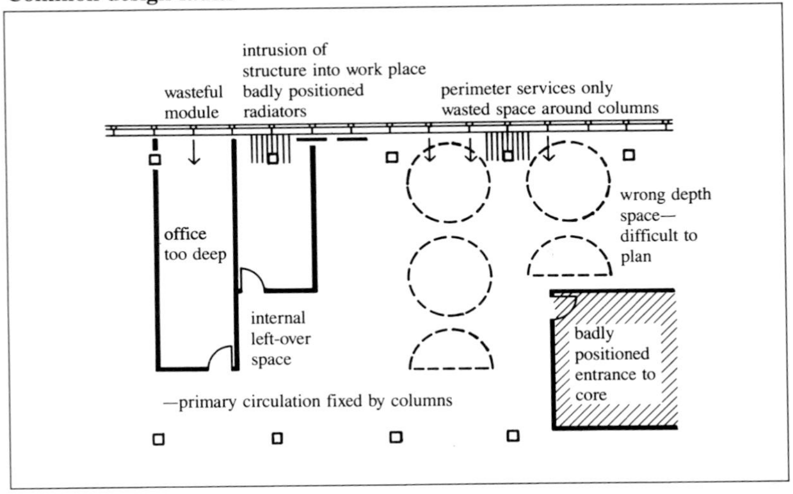

Reprinted, with permission, from Ernst Neufert, *Architect's Data*, Halstead Press, 1980.

mance but also provides a catalyst for creating spaces in which subtle differences can be appreciated.

Typical Units of Evaluation

When designing and specifying for materials, components, and assemblies, specific units are used to express and compare the long-term spatial performance of products. Although these specification units become much more technical in other areas of performance, the suitability of a component or system to provide spatial performance can be evaluated in such terms as surface material, size, position, distance, and identification. The reliability of the product is evaluated in terms of the length of time that these will remain as designed, or the level of effort (maintenance) necessary to retain suitability. The flexibility of the product is evaluated by the ability of that surface, size, position, distance, or identification to change over time or to accommodate change from the outside.

Evaluating spatial performance in an office building requires the assessment of workspace definition, workgroup adjacencies and accessibility, and conveniences and services, as well as the necessary psychological or sociological amenities. The following checklist can be used to evaluate spatial quality in an office building.

REFERENCES

Diffrient, Niels, Alvin R. Tilley, and Joan C. Bardagjy. *Humanscale 1/2/3; 4/5/6; 7/8/9*. Designed by Henry Dreyfuss Associates. Cambridge: MIT Press, 1974.

Environmental Design Research Association (EDRA). *Conference 1–8 Proceedings*. Champaign-Urbana, IL: 1970–1984.

Fisher, Bell, and Baum. *Environmental Psychology*. 2d ed. New York: Holt, Rinehart and Winston, 1984.

Neufert, Ernst. *Architect's Data*. New York: Halsted Press, 1980.

Osgood, C., Suci, and Tannenbaum. *The Measurement of Meaning*. Univ. of Illinois Press, 1957.

Panero, Julius. *Human Dimension and Interior Space: A Source Book of Design Reference Standards*. New York: Whitney Library of Design, 1979.

Ramsey, Charles G., AIA, and Harold R. Sleeper, FAIA. *Architectural Graphic Standards*. 7th ed. Robert T. Packard, Ed. New York: Wiley, 1981.

Spatial Performance: Signs of Stress in Offices

Given an Acceptable Office Space Norm: Internal Space, With View of Window, Medium Density
Adequate Work Surfaces for Function
Adequate Definition for Territoriality, Personalization, Wayfinding
Conventional Services & Conveniences

In a Walk-through, These Signs of Spatial Stress May Be Seen *(circle as noted):*

Weak Definition of Workspace

Ergonomics Poor for Continuous Tasks

Inadequate Space/Furniture for Task

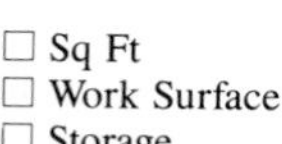

check inadequacy { ☐ Sq Ft ☐ Work Surface ☐ Storage

☐ Task Space
☐ Mtg/Interview Space
☐ Other:

Poor Accessibility

Special Needs

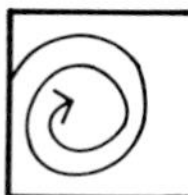

Wayfinding Poor

Poor Privacy/Identity

High Density No Breaks

In Circulation Path

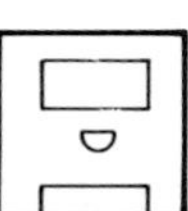

No Edge, Screen, Wall, Task Space

No Separation Between Workgroups

Missing Services

Inconvenient/Hazardous Cabinet/Outlets

Inadequate Telecommunication

Inadequate Copy Services

Inadequate Security

Missing Amenities

No Visual Relief, No View

No Social/Lounge Area

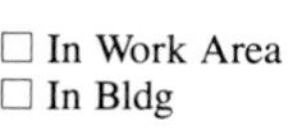

check inadequacy { ☐ In Work Area ☐ In Bldg

No Individual Control of space definition

Also, Look for Any of These User Modifications To the Original Design:

☐ Rearranged Furniture
☐ Rearranged Screens
☐ Brought in Personal Objects

☐ Additional Screens
☐ Additional Furniture
☐

Thermal Performance

Thermal Performance
dependent on
1. Air Temperature
2. Radiant Temperature
3. Humidity
4. Air Speed
5. Occupancy Factors & Control

Definition

Thermal comfort in buildings depends on four design factors: air temperature, air movement, relative humidity, and the radiant temperatures of surfaces.

Most occupants and building managers judge the thermal performance of a space by what registers on the thermostat, that is, by dry bulb air temperature alone. Individuals with arthritis, sinus problems, or dry skin might broaden this definition of thermal comfort to include relative humidity. However, few designers, occupants, or building managers realize that all four of these elements constituting our thermal environment contribute significantly to our sense of comfort.

Even when air temperature and humidity levels are adequate, increased air speeds coming from the mechanical supply or a leaky window can quickly decrease the occupants' sense of thermal comfort in winter. When mechanical air supply is nearby or cooler than the ambient air temperature, this reduction of thermal comfort can be even more drastic.

The radiant temperatures of interior spaces also contribute to thermal comfort or discomfort, and are the primary responsibility of the building designer, although this may not be acknowledged. Even with ideal air temperatures, relative humidities, and air movements, a building occupant may be forced to sit with feet planted firmly on a cold floor or adjacent to a cold window. Alternatively, the mean radiant conditions may be drastically higher than air temperatures (and thermostat readings) due to sunshine or proximity to appliances and equipment that give off heat. In fact, an occupant may be subject to radiant temperature differentials of 50-60°F in one day, while the thermostat may continue to register a perfect 72°F.

The only indication that either of these two thermal discomfort conditions exists—high or low mean radiant surface temperatures or unacceptable air movement—might come from the occupants themselves, in the form of complaints of

A Thermal Comfort Zone Based on Temperature and Humidity Alone

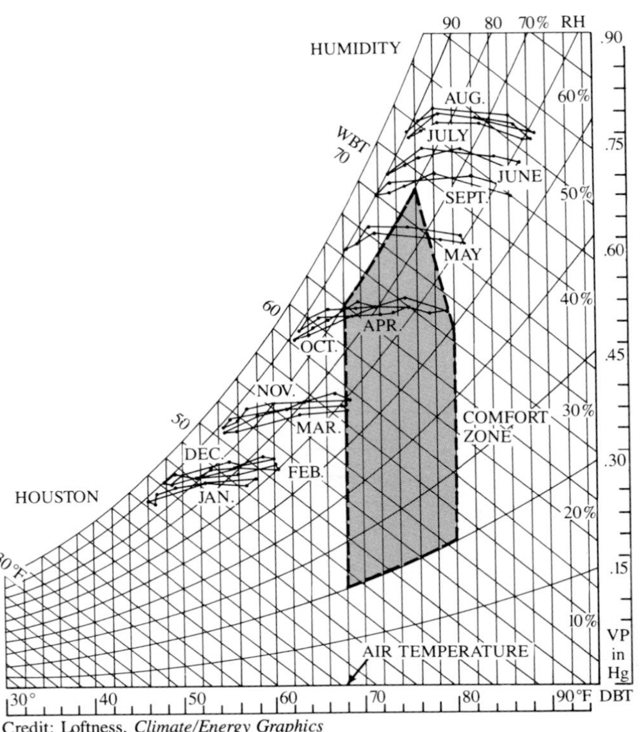

Credit: Loftness, *Climate/Energy Graphics*

stiff necks, cold feet, arthritis, or rheumatism. Design for thermal performance, then, is the provision of adequate air temperature, air motion, humidity, and mean radiant temperature to insure the comfort of the occupants, whether humans, animals, plants, or artifacts.

These four external factors determining the thermal comfort of building occupants are weighed against "internalized" factors regarding the health, activity, and clothing of the occupants. For example, the higher the clothing value the occupant is wearing (called CLO value), the more comfortable he or she will be at cooler temperatures (and the less comfortable at warmer temperatures), shifting the typical comfort zone (see p. 280). The more active the occupant is, referred to by metabolic rate or MET value, the more comfortable he or she will be at cooler temperatures (and the less comfortable at warmer tempera-

The Shifting Comfort Zone With More Activity

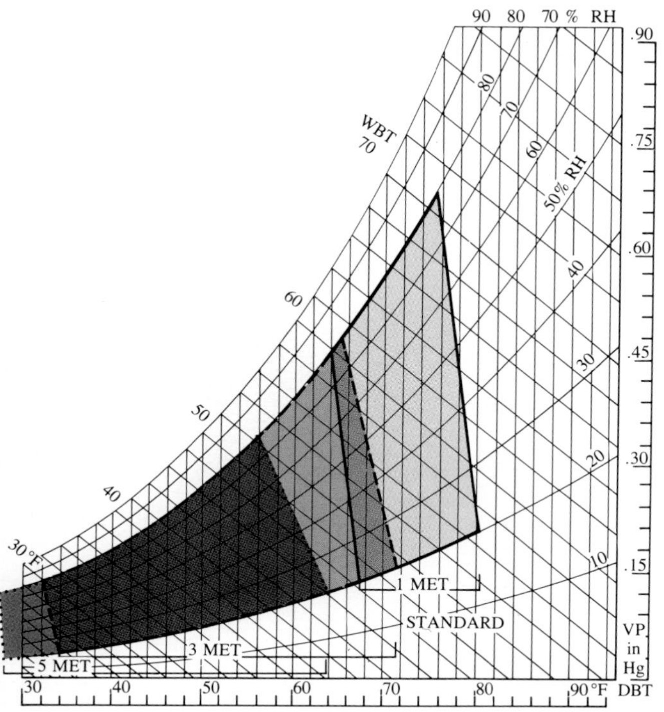

Activity	Metabolic Rate met
Sleeping	0.71
Reclining	0.81
Sitting	1.00
Standing, relaxed	1.21
Walking, level, at 3.2 km/h	2.00
Walking, level, at 4.9 km/h	2.60
Walking, level, at 6.4 km/h	3.81
Walking, 15° upward at 3.2 km/h	4.60
House cleaning	2.00–3.41
Typing	1.21–1.40
Gymnastics	3.02–4.02
Dancing	2.41–4.41
Sawing by hand	4.00–4.83
Heavy machine work (e.g., steel forming)	3.52–4.52

Engaging in vigorous activity also shifts the thermal comfort zone significantly, requiring cooler temperatures for comfort. Credit: Derived from Markus and Morris, The ASHRAE Handbook.

tures). The occupants' health can also have a bearing on their thermal comfort, affecting their metabolic rate or heightening their sensitivities to varying temperatures, humidities, and to increased air movement, as well as low mean radiant surface temperatures.

Finally, there is the question of the occupants' control over their thermal environment. Individual controls are often critical both for insuring the physiological and psychological limits of thermal comfort and for improving economic performance or energy conservation.

Limits of Acceptability

The physiological limits of acceptable thermal performance for human occupancy in buildings have been well established, and are documented in ASHRAE (American Society of Heating, Refrigerating and Air-Conditioning Engineers) Standard 55-1981, *Thermal Environmental Conditions for Human Occupancy*. This standard, in turn, has been adopted by BOCA (the Building Officials and Code Administrators International), by state and local codes, and by numerous international codes. It establishes the high and low limits of air and radiant temperatures, humidity levels, and air speeds within spaces in accordance with metabolic rates (activity levels) and clothing values, set by function and occupancy type. If well understood and followed by the building designer, it should insure acceptable thermal conditions for 80 percent of the building occupants.

The psychological limits of acceptable thermal performance in buildings are less well understood, even though significant research in both the physiological and psychological definition of comfort has been undertaken by P. O. Fanger in Denmark, at Yale University's J. B. Pierce Foundation, at Kansas State University, and at the National Bureau of Standards. Occupancy control over temperature, humidity, and even air speed insures a far greater level of satisfaction by permitting an expanded comfort zone within which designers and building managers can operate. Materials, such as wood instead of metal, and colors, such as reds and warm pinks instead of blues and grays, also have a psychological "warming" effect, often with physical explanations.

The sociological limits of acceptable thermal performance in buildings depend upon how the occupants interact. Thermal discomfort can be quickly amplified when the control for one's comfort lies in another's office or with a central manager.

Discomfort can occur when societal norms suggest that men should wear three-piece business suits in summer, while women wear thin, sleeveless dresses. Within such conditions, buildings must still "perform" thermally, and so constitute a tremendous challenge for building designers and managers.

Economic limits in the design for thermal performance are becoming more and more a dominant factor. This is a result of limited up-front investment available for such hidden components as mechanical systems; limited or nonexistent funding for building retrofit once the occupants have settled in; limited resources such as energy for the operation of buildings; and limited manpower for preventive maintenance or responsive management.

The Units of Evaluation

The units for evaluating the thermal performance of integrated systems and their components are numerous and complex.

The suitability of an integrated system and its component parts for providing thermal performance can be evaluated in the following terms: U-value (BTU/ft^2 °F) and R-value (1/U) for enclosures; percentage of transmission, reflectivity, and emissivity, shading coefficients (S.C.), and air changes per hour for openings; thermal capacity (BTU/ft^2 °F) and conductivity for interior systems; and the ratio of input to output (generation efficiency), temperature cycling, and drifting for mechanical systems. Building designers should be familiar with these thermal performance units. They should also know about the range of products available and the units of evaluation from other building performance mandates that apply to the purchase of these products as well.

The reliability of components and systems related to thermal comfort can be evaluated by the length of time that the conditions necessary for thermal comfort will remain or

The Shifting Comfort Zone With More or Less Clothing

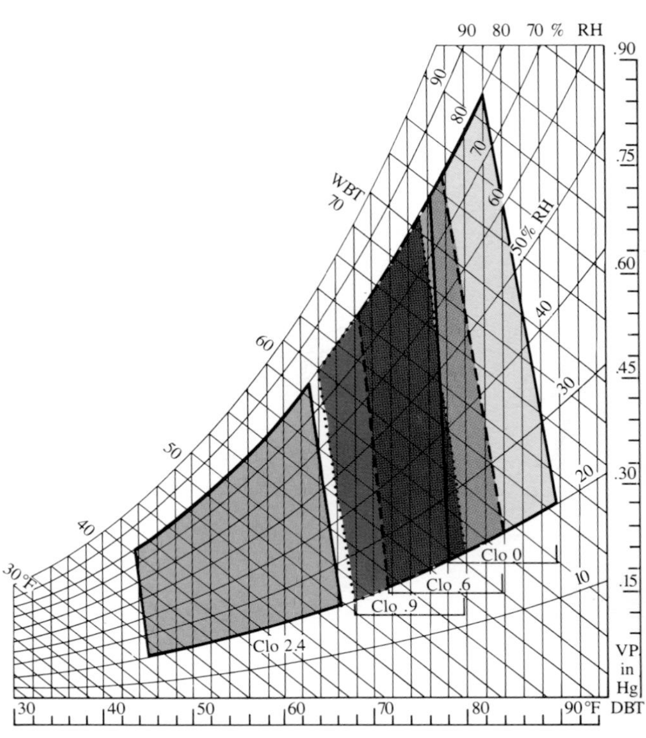

Clothing Ensemble	Insulation CLO Value
Nude	0
Shorts	0.1
Tropical ensemble (shorts, open-necked short-sleeved shirt, socks, sandals)	0.3–0.4
Men's light summer clothing (long lightweight trousers, open-neck short-sleeved shirt)	0.5
Typical men's business suit (plus cotton underwear, long-sleeved shirt, tie, woolen socks)	1.0
Women's indoor ensemble (skirt, long-sleeved blouse and jumper, normal underwear, stockings)	0.7–0.9
Men's heavy suit as above plus woolen overcoat	2.0–2.5

Wearing more or less clothing shifts the thermal comfort zone and has an effect on the perception of thermal performance. Derived from Markus and Morris, The ASHRAE Handbook.

Minimum Recommended R-Values for Various Regions of The United States

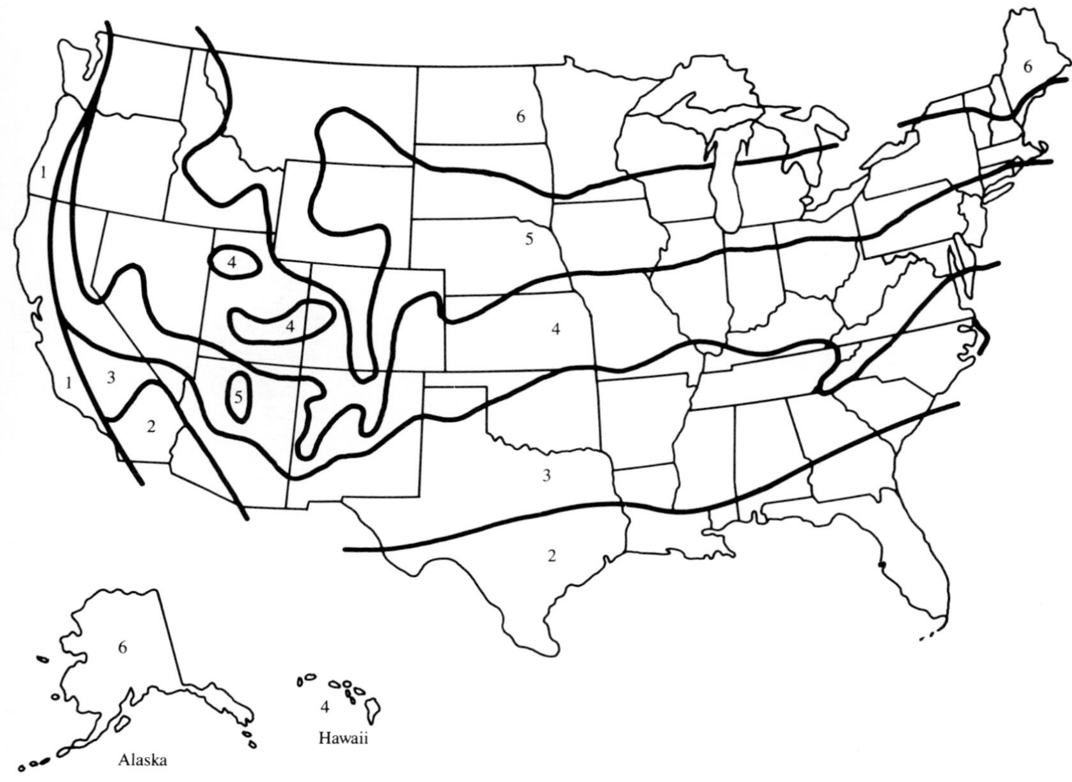

Credit: David F. Hill, Burt Hill Kosar Rittlemann Associates, Butler, Penn.; Donald Bosserman, AIA; Saunders, Cheng & Appleton, Alexandria, Va.

Recommended Minimum Thermal Resistances (R) of Insulation

ZONE	CEILING	WALL	FLOOR
1	19	11	11
2	26	13	11
3	26	19	13
4	30	19	19
5	33	19	22
6	38	19	22

by the level of effort (maintenance) necessary to sustain comfortable conditions.

Flexibility is evaluated in terms of the ability of the thermal conditioning system (the integration of building components and the occupants) to change over time or to accommodate change, so that thermal comfort will be insured given changing occupancies and functions.

Energy conservation has led to the development of units or indices for describing the thermal performance of buildings and the performance of systems in their fully integrated state. These units include: BTU/sq ft per year and BTU/sq ft per degree day; peak power demand; balance point tempera-

Simulated Consumption of Six Well-Known Buildings

Credit: Bazjanac, Vladimir, 1980–1982, *Progressive Architecture*

ture; surface/volume ratio; percent glass; and solar savings fraction, as well as watts/sq ft. The more these indices are discussed in construction literature and at board meetings, the more pressure will be put on those who commission, program, design, construct, and operate buildings to insure thermal comfort and efficiency through the conscious *and* effective integration of building systems.

Systems integration for thermal comfort, therefore, must provide acceptable air temperature, air movement, relative humidity, and radiant temperature for building occupants. As an introduction to the demands of thermal comfort, a checklist has been added for a walk-through evaluation of the thermal performance in an existing office building.

REFERENCES

American National Standards Institute and American Society of Heating, Refrigerating and Air-Conditioning Engineers. Standard 55-1981, *Thermal Environmental Conditions for Human Occupancy*. Atlanta: ANSI/ASHRAE, 1981.

American Society of Heating, Refrigerating and Air-Conditioning Engineers. *Handbook of Fundamentals*. New York: ASHRAE, 1981.

Egan, David M. *Concepts in Thermal Comfort*. New Jersey: Prentice Hall, 1975.

Markus, T.A., and E. N. Morris. *Buildings, Climate and Energy*. London: Pitman, 1980.

Thermal Performance Signs of Stress in Offices

Given an Acceptable Office Space Norm: Internal Space, No Internal Heat Generator
No External Surfaces, No Solar Gain
Approximately in Diffuser Field
Humidified in Winter, Dehumidified in Summer

In a Walk-though, These Signs of Thermal Stress May Be Seen:

Air Temperature (DBT)

Heat Generator (Machinery >1000W in Space)

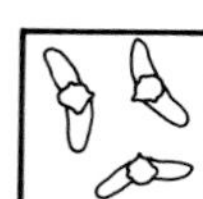

High Occupancy, High Level of Activity

Radiant Temperature (MRT)

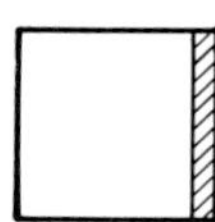

1 Exterior Surface

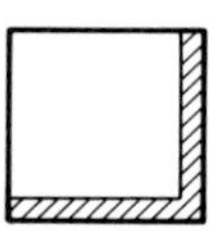

2 Exterior Surfaces

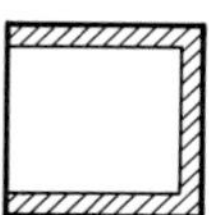

3 Exterior Surfaces

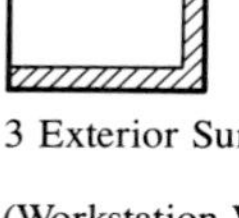

(Workstation with an Immediate External Wall, Floor), Implies Perimeter System

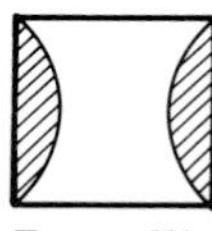

East or West Windows

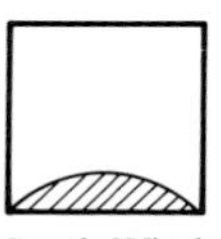

South Windows

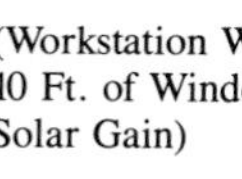

(Workstation Within 10 Ft. of Window & Solar Gain)

Sunshading Available

None or Ineffective

Air Movement

Directly Below Diffuser Thrust

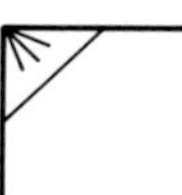

Too Far Away/ Blocked Diffuser

Leaky Wall Humboldt's Current

Humidity (RH)

Mold; Dust Buildup; Cracking, Dried Furniture, Hands

Also, Look for Any of These User Modifications to the Original Design:

- ☐ Taped Over Diffuser
- ☐ Space Heater
- ☐ Special Clothes (Sweaters)
- ☐ Blanket
- ☐ Added Floor/Wall/Window Covering
- ☐ Taped Over Cracks
- ☐ Fan
- ☐ Shading Device
- ☐ Humidifier (Kettle, Plants)
- ☐ Ionizer/Air Freshener
- ☐ Temporary Partitions Blocking Window or Air Supply
- ☐ Moved Workstation Away From Window/Wall, or From Heat Generator

Air Quality in Buildings

Indoor Air Quality
dependent on
1. "Fresh" Air
2. Fresh Air Movement/ Distribution
3. Mass Pollutants
4. Energy Pollutants
5. Occupancy Factors Filtration/Controls

Recent findings indicate that built environments can be more hazardous to human health than previously understood. This is especially true for the very young, the elderly, and the infirm. With the recent emphasis on energy conservation, fan energy savings, and tighter buildings, occupants' concern about indoor air quality has been rising. The reduced number of air changes and the limitation of the practice of flushing out a building containing new materials before people move in have led to higher air contaminant levels or heightened sensitivity. Since people spend 80 to 90 percent of their time inside, indoor air contamination at any significant level is bound to create health problems. The growing concern of occupants and health professionals about air quality in buildings demands, in turn, increasing attention to detail from those who design, construct, occupy, and operate buildings.

Definition

Building design, construction, and management for acceptable air quality require adequate fresh air and fresh air distribution as well as protection from both mass and energy pollutants.

The provision of "fresh" air to the building from the outside is the first major problem. It involves the quality of the outside air, the proximity of possible pollution sources, and the avoidance of possible short-circuiting with the building exhaust. These will determine the location of the air intakes.

Once external "fresh" air has been introduced into the building, there remains the task of distributing it.This task must not only be addressed by the performance of the air-handling system, but by the effective performance of the mechanical system within its integrated environment. The relationship of supply registers to return registers, to the enclosed volume to be ventilated, and to the position of interior and structural systems determines the effectiveness of the interior distribution of external air.

The selection and integration of building materials and processes is the third, equally significant determinant of indoor air quality. Designers must be sensitive in stipulating structural materials, insulations, adhesives, paints, finishes, wallpapers, and even fuels, searching for products with little or no toxic or odoriferous pollutants. Managers and users must be careful to avoid introducing pollutant concentrations in the form of materials, processes, and occupancy behavior.

Protection from mass pollution includes concern for airborne substances, gases, and vapors, as well as viable and nonviable particulate substances. Viable particulates are biological organisms such as viruses, spores, fungi, and bacteria, whereas nonviable particulates include mists, aerosols, fogs, fumes, dusts, and smokes.

Protection from energy pollution includes protection from ultraviolet, visible, and infrared radiation. These lie within the electromagnetic spectrum, which also includes ionizing, microwave, and radio frequency radiation.

Designed protection also involves a very complex and rapidly emerging field of knowledge. Many of these mass and energy pollutants create stressors that are interrelated in complex ways, and their combined effects are poorly understood. It is not always clear whether unacceptable air quality is a result of components introduced into the building, the level of integration of these components, or the total ecological system that is created in the occupied building. Some sources of air pollution, however, have been identified:

1) Outgassing from materials, such as formaldehyde from insulation or glues in particle boards, plywoods, and adhesives;
2) Chemicals and chemical processes such as cleaning fluids, rug shampoos, or printing/copying processes;
3) Infiltration of outdoor pollutants such as industrial emissions, auto exhausts, heating plant gases, pesticides, and particulates (including dusts and pollens);

Ten Components That Can Originate Pollutant Sources:

1. Flues, Chimneys, Exhausts, Duct
2. Copying Equipment
3. Gas Oil/Kerosene Fired Equipment
4. Wood Stoves, Fireplaces
5. Synthetic Furnishings
6. Plywood, Drywall
7. Paints, Glues
8. Cleaning, Deodorizing Chemicals
9. Humidifiers
10. Insulation

Comparison of Methods For Reducing Indoor Air Pollution

Method	Advantages	Possible Disadvantages
1. Flush Pollutant From Building	— need not alter sources — often only moderately expensive	— lose energy — affected individuals still exposed to low levels — polluted outside air contaminates intake
2. Exteriorize Pollutant	— need not alter sources — reduces air infiltration and energy loss — reduces air exfiltration and condensation	— barriers not perfect — seal may deteriorate
3. Scrub Indoor Air	— need not alter sources — reduces ventilation needs and saves energy	— expensive — affected individuals still exposed to low levels
4. Substitute Materials/ Systems	— affected individuals no longer exposed — reduces ventilation needs and saves energy	— sometimes expensive — substitutes often difficult to obtain
5. Seal Pollutant	— reduces or eliminates exposure to affected persons — reduces ventilation needs and saves energy — often relatively inexpensive	— may introduce alternate pollutants — barriers not perfect — seal may deteriorate
6. Treat Pollutant	— reduces or eliminates exposure to affected persons — reduces ventilation needs and saves energy	— may introduce alternate pollutants — not always possible — not always 100% effective
7. Separate People From Pollutant or Remove Pollutant	— reduces or eliminates exposure to affected persons — can sometimes be inexpensive (eg. put volatiles in shed)	— not always possible — can sometimes be expensive (eg. remove UFFI)
8. Isolate Affected People	— reduces or eliminates exposure to affected persons — can be relatively inexpensive	— not always possible — creates social isolation and restricts affected persons

Reprinted, with permission, from *Indoor Air Pollution and Housing Technology: Research Report*, Canada Mortgage and Housing Council, 1983.

4) Release of outdoor pollutants incorporated in the building from soils, materials, or water (for example, radon from the ground upon which the building is built, or from construction materials such as gypsum, concrete, and brick that have been produced from radioactive soils);

5) Release of occupant-generated pollutants, such as tobacco smoke (which is known to generate about 3,800 pollutants) as well as other compounds such as perfumes, air fresheners, and pesticides that can be carcinogenic;

6) The growth and spread of biological irritants or viable particulates such as viruses, spores and bacteria, often through poorly maintained mechanical systems (for example, humidifiers facilitating the growth of legionella, with ducted air spreading the viable particulates);

7) A deficiency in negative or positive ions, where there is convincing evidence that both negative and positive ions inhibit the growth of bacteria and fungi on solid media, exert a lethal effect on vegetative forms of bacteria suspended in water, and cause a reduction in the viable count of bacterial aerosols.[58]

Many of these indoor air pollutants can be minimized through various building design and management strategies: the elimination of the pollutant source and concentrations; the reduction or dilution of the pollutant source; the isolation or the shielding of the pollutant source; and filtration. Of these strategies, the elimination of the indoor air pollutant is most effective and can be achieved by: product/material substitution; behavioral modification; or product modification. Ventilation is the next most effective step when dealing with most mass pollutants, while isolation is critical for energy pollutants.

Although each of these steps may deal with the physiological limits for acceptable air quality, individual control may be the only way of meeting psychological and sociological limits. This strategy not only calls for occupancy control over the quantity and temperature of air supplied, but also the ability on the part of the occupant to isolate himself or herself from unacceptable materials, components, equipment, processes, and even people.

Limits of Acceptability

Although comparatively few standards have been set for indoor air quality, several organizations are working to establish new guidelines, standards, and codes, including the

58. Kureger and Reed. "Biological Impact of Small Air Ions." *Science*, September 1976, pp. 1209–1213.

1. Carbon Monoxide
2. Radon and Radon Decay Products
3. Nitrogen Oxides
4. Sulphur Dioxide
5. Ozone
6. Asbestos
7. Tobacco Smoke
8. Formaldehyde
9. Carbon Dioxide
10. House Dust and Dust Mites
11. Fungi (Mould and Mildew)
12. Bacteria and Viruses
13. Consumer Product Aerosols
14. Other Suspended Particulates
15. Pesticides
16. Ammonia
17. Chlorine
18. Various Organic Vapours

The substances listed above are all possible contributors to poor air quality. Appropriate building standards are being developed for their effective control.

National Institute for Occupational Safety and Health (NIOSH), the American Conference of Governmental Industrial Hygienists (ACGIH), the Occupational Safety and Health Administration (OSHA), and the American Society of Heating, Refrigerating and Air-Conditioning Engineers (ASHRAE). ASHRAE has taken the lead in putting forward its Standard 62-1981, *Ventilation for Acceptable Indoor Air Quality*. Nevertheless, it is now well documented that occupants of large office complexes, for example, consistently complain of poor air quality, stuffiness, odors, eye irritation, headaches, dizziness, skin irritations, and nausea as well as coughs, colds, and inflamed sinuses, all associated with the "sick building" syndrome. Given these conditions, it will continue to be within the mandate of the building designer to investigate their causes and their possible cure.

In the absence of standards, the physiological limits of acceptability for indoor air quality have been set by researchers and practitioners based on the level set for outdoor air quality and industrial standards. This approach has serious limitations for the elderly, the very young, and the infirm. As building evaluation proceeds in conjunction with occupancy medical evaluation, guidelines may eventually be developed that will limit exposure to all environmental stressors that can increase or contribute to respiratory, neurological, and infectious diseases, as well as eye and skin irritations.

Psychological limits of acceptability for indoor air quality will require different criteria because they are often associated with the sense of smell. Building occupants often associate poor air quality with bad smells, even if those smells contain no measurable harmful pollutant. Since research has indicated that many ailments develop in the individual's psyche, it is also critical to limit these perceived indicators of pollution. Complaints of stuffiness, which may be the physiological reaction to inadequate fresh air supply, may also be the psychological reaction to overheated spaces, indicating the interrelated nature of air quality and thermal comfort. On the other hand, healthy plants in clean, naturally ventilated, daylighted spaces can act as a positive reinforcement of the occupants' perception of a healthy surrounding (as well as producing oxygen, increasing relative humidity, and acting as organic filters).

Sociological limits of acceptability for indoor air quality focus on the issues of individuals not making decisions for the group, and on such social taboos as uncontained toilet smells and human sweat. Nonsmokers find it increasingly unacceptable to share the same air with smokers, even if the contamination is well below the legally acceptable limit. Consequently, spaces inhabited by groups of people often require control of the adverse effects of individual decisions, such as smoking, on the larger community.

The larger community is also represented in the economic limits for acceptable indoor air quality. The cost of continuous ventilation associated with certain materials, components, and processes that pollute, or with a population that smokes heavily, may not be acceptable without isolation or containment of those pollutants.

The Units of Evaluation

Since the field of air quality in buildings is still developing, the units for evaluating the suitability of building components and component integrations are not yet well established. Most gaseous and particulate pollutions are measured as concentrations in parts per million (ppm) or in micrograms per meters cubed ($\mu g/m^3$), with acceptable ranges for human health specific to each pollutant. Fresh air supply is measured in cubic feet per minute (cfm) or in air changes per hour, with standards set by space function and occupancy type. Units for evaluating the outgassing of new materials have been developed, but no standards have been established. The potential of new materials for causing allergies and rashes must be considered, and acceptable limits of energy pollution from equipment such as microwaves and computers also need to be established.

Regardless of the standards set for the suitability of individual components, it is usually the integration of components (for which the building designer and contractor are responsible) and the protection of the

Pollutant Sources: Summary Table for Housing

Section/Pollutant Source	Summary
Improper Chimney Construction	Improperly lined chimneys may corrode from the exhaust of a natural gas furnace, leading to blocking and potentially fatal carbon monoxide accumulation in a home.
Gas Stoves	Gas stoves are major producers of carbon monoxide and nitrogen dioxide at rates which are harmful to health.
Kerosene Heaters	Portable unvented kerosene heaters produce carbon monoxide and other gases at levels considerably above outdoor standards, under normal operation.
Fossil Fuel Furnaces	Improperly installed or maintained fossil fuel furnaces can contribute to indoor air pollution, sometimes at dangerous levels. Chemically susceptible persons are more quickly affected by small leaks than others.
Wood Stoves	Burning wood can lead to high indoor pollutant levels if stoves are not well sealed or carefully operated. Infiltration of second-hand wood smoke from neighboring chimneys can also increase indoor pollution significantly.
Furnishings	Many furnishings and decorative materials in the home are responsible for the presence of different organic contaminants in indoor air. While each individual source may appear innocuous, the total pollutant load may be significant for many people, and can definitely cause harm to those who are already chemically susceptible. Alternative products are needed.
Outdoor Pollution	Infiltration of various outdoor pollutants, especially car exhaust from adjacent roads and radon gas from soil beneath a home may present long-term health problems.
Household Chemicals	Many household products (e.g. cleaners) contribute significant quantities of organic chemicals to indoor air, and have been reported to trigger adverse symptoms in susceptible persons. The total load is important.
Appliances	Numerous small household electrical appliances give off a variety of organic chemicals and odors. Some may be significant sources of indoor pollution and are known to affect susceptible persons.
Humidifiers	Household humidifiers which either recycle their water or which include an open water reservoir which can stagnate can become sources of micro-organisms that will contaminate indoor air and could affect health.
Paints	Paint and sealers may release various organic gases, lead, and mercury. Some sensitive individuals can detect paint fumes for three months or more after application. Neurotoxic effects during painting may also increase risk of accidents.
Insulation	Various types of insulation in addition to Ureaformaldehyde foam have been reported to cause some problems particularly for already susceptible persons. Styrofoam, cellulose, and fiberglass are cited.
Activities	Normal processes of living and respiration by people and their pets generate a number of gases and particles. Very few daily activities do not involve addition of pollutants to indoor air in some form. Hobby activities often involve highly toxic materials.

Reprinted, with permission, from *Indoor Air Pollution and Housing Technology: Research Report*, Canada Mortgage and Housing Council, 1983.

CFM of Fresh Air Per Person Based on Function/Activity	
Office	7 cfm
Museum	7 cfm
School	10 cfm
Disco	30 cfm

Credit: Data from BOCA Codes

integrated system (for which the building manager and occupant are responsible) that have the greatest impact on indoor air quality. At the outset, procedures for "outgassing" buildings before occupancy, through natural and forced ventilation and filtration, need to be instituted.

The reliability of the building system over time can be evaluated by the length of time that the conditions necessary for acceptable air quality will remain or by the level of effort or maintenance necessary to retain that acceptability. In this regard, reducing the use of toxic products in building maintenance and containing polluting processes and habits will be critical. It is becoming increasingly apparent, however, that if an air quality problem already exists, retrofit may not be able to diminish the problem *or* the perception of the problem.

The flexibility of the building system is evaluated by the ability of the integrated environmental conditioning "system" (HVAC in its contexts) to change over time or to accommodate change, so that air quality will be insured given changing occupancies, furnishings, equipment, and functions.

The evaluation of air quality in buildings, then, requires the assessment of mass and energy pollution conditions; fresh air supply, filtration, and distribution; and occupancy control. However, "a tremendous amount of investigation, research and observation of the *synergistic* aspects of the indoor (and outdoor) environment is still needed," according to Denver architect Richard Crowther. The following checklist can be used to evaluate quickly the actual and perceived air quality in an existing office building.

REFERENCES

Indoor Pollution: The Architect's Response. Syllabus from a symposium, November 1984, American Institute of Architects, Washington, DC.

American Society of Heating, Refrigerating and Air-Conditioning Engineers. *Standard 62-1981, Ventilation for Acceptable Indoor Air Quality*. Atlanta: ASHRAE, 1981.

Berglund, B., et al. *Proceedings of the Third International Conference on Indoor Air Quality and Climate*. Stockholm, August 1984. Five volumes.

Levin, Hal. "A Report on Indoor Pollution Research and Its Potential and Actual Applications in Architectural Practice." *Research and Design: General Proceedings*. March 1985, American Institute of Architects Foundation, Washington, DC.

Levin, Hal. "Building Ecology." *Progessive Architecture*, April 1981, pp. 173–175.

Levin Hal. "Pentachlorophenol in Indoor Air: Sealing Exposed Pressure-Treated Wood and Improving Ventilation to Reduce Airborne Concentrations." *Research and Design*.

Levin, Hal. "Pentachlorophenol in Indoor Air: Sealing Exposed Pressure-Treated Wood and Improving Ventilation to Reduce Airborne Concentrations." *Research and Design*.

Small, Bruce. *Indoor Air Pollution and Housing Technology: Research Report*. Ottawa: Canadian Mortgage and Housing Corporation, August 1983.

Woods, James E. "Do Buildings Make You Sick?" *Proceedings, Third Canadian Buildings Congress 1982*. National Research Council No. 21158.

Air Quality Signs of Stress in Offices

Given an Acceptable Office Space Norm: Internal Space, Not High Density
No Machinery
Adjacent to No Vertical Shafts (Elev, Mech, Stair) or Mechanical Rooms
In Air Supply Field, No Malfunctions
Non-Humidified

In a Walk-through, These Signs of Air Quality Stress May Be Seen:

Machinery

Heat/Fume/Radiation Generator

Circle: Copier, Printer, Terminal, Other______ Within 20 Ft. of Workstation

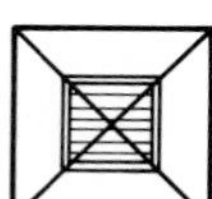

No Ventilation or Exhaust to Outside

Horizontal Migration of Pollutants

Leaky Wall or "Humboldt's Current"

Vertical Migration of Pollutants

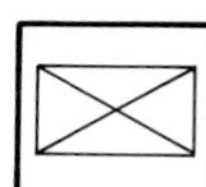

Vertical Shaft Directly Adjacent (Stack Effect)

Mechanical, Migration of Pollutants

Directly Below Diffuser (Bad Air)

Too Far Away/ Blocked Diffuser (No Air)

Humidified Zone (Bad Air) Mold, Fungus. Dried Furniture, Hands. Dirt Buildup, Cracking.

People

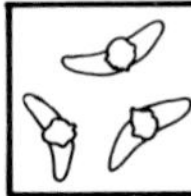

High Density (e.g., Waiting Rooms)

High Activity (Met >3)

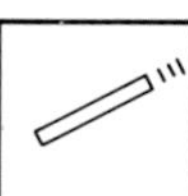

Heavy Smoker in Space or Directly Adjacent

Materials

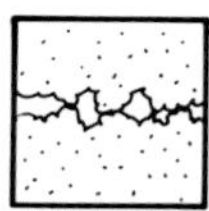

New/Bad

Recent Cleaning

Ceiling, Wall, Floor or Furniture Materials

Also Look for Any of These User Modifications To the Original Design:

- ☐ Fan
- ☐ Ionizer/Air Cleaner
- ☐ Deodorizer
- ☐ Natural Ventilation
- ☐ Electrostatic Precipitator
- ☐ Humidifier/Dehumidifier
- ☐ Taped Over Diffuser
- ☐ No Smoking Sign
- ☐ Barriers for Isolation
- ☐ Air Movement Indicators (Paper, Streamers)

Acoustical Performance

Acoustical Performance

1. Sound Source
   a. signal sound pressure levels
   b. background noise, quiet
   c. signal to noise ratio
2. Sound Path
   a. noise isolation, airborne and structure-borne paths
   b. sound distribution absorption, reflection uniformity, reverberation
3. Sound Receiver
   a. occupancy sensitivities
   b. occupancy controls

It is difficult to give adequate coverage to the field of acoustics in a few pages, since it is one of the most developed building performance areas. The following description is intended to put the acoustic performance mandate on a similar footing with the other five performance mandates. It is suggested that readers carefully consult the pertinent reference texts, or rely upon acoustical consultants when designing building systems for acoustical performance.

Designing for acoustical performance begins with a thorough understanding of a building's occupants, their functions, and their relative sensitivities. The acoustical quality appropriate for a bus terminal, for example, varies significantly from that of a library or a music hall. In any building program, the designer is faced with the need to balance demands for communication with those for privacy and quiet. While a satisfactory acoustical environment in an office usually requires privacy for conversation and relative quiet for concentrated thought, an acoustically satisfying concert hall demands an environment in which music or speech is transmitted to all locations as uniformly as possible.

Programming, designing, constructing, and operating buildings for acoustical quality depends on control of three factors: (1) sound sources, which include the sound pressure levels of various sound generators that contribute to communication and background noise; (2) sound paths, which include designs for both noise isolation (airborne and structure-borne paths) and sound distribution; and (3) sound receivers, which include occupants' sensitivities and controls over sound sources and paths. The strength of the source can be increased or reduced; the sound path can be attenuated to reduce sound transmission; and the receiver can be made more tolerant of noise or more attentive to communication.

Sound Pressure Levels (Loudness) in Decibels (db)

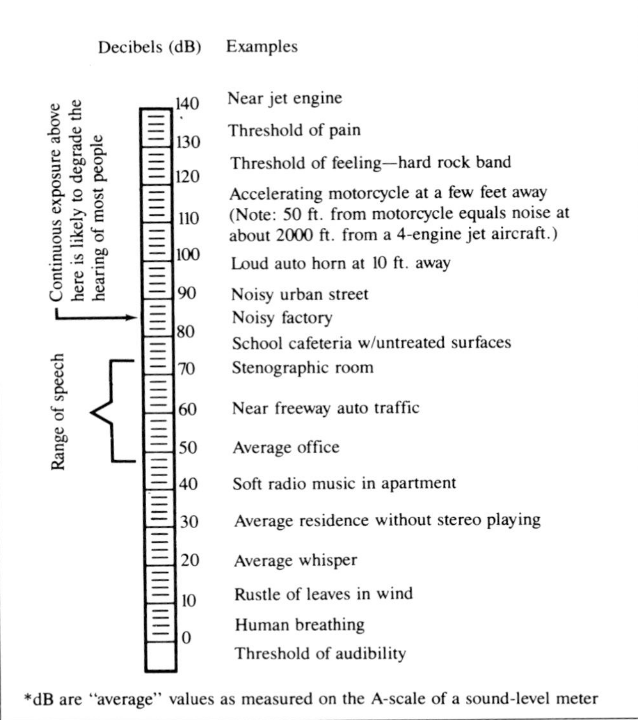

Reprinted, with permission, from M. David Egan, *Concepts in Architectural Acoustics*, McGraw-Hill, 1972.

THE SOUND SOURCE

The intensity of sound in buildings is measured in sound pressure levels on a decibel (dB) scale, as shown in the figure above. The dB scale is logarithmic, comparing the ratios between measured values and a reference value. A drop from 100dB to 90dB, for instance, equals a 90 percent reduction in energy. Both the sound pressure level and the duration of exposure are critical to the health, comfort, and productivity of occupants. Excessive sound pressure levels (in dB) are serious concerns in factories, near airports and major traffic arteries, and in mechanical rooms and printing facilities. The length of exposure to sound (noise) is also critical; continuous noise is far more serious to human health than noise levels that exceed the nominal maximum for short periods.

Sound pressure levels are measured at varying frequencies, from a low of 60 hertz to a high of 8000 hertz. Because the human ear is more sensitive to sound in certain frequencies than others, 30 dB at a

Examples of Maximum Desirable Background Noise (NC Levels) for Various Space Functions

Function	Max. NC Level Background Noise
Sports Arena (w/Amplification)	55
Open Office Areas	50–55
Closed Offices	45
Conference Rm. for 20	35
Conference Rm. for 50	30
Assembly Halls (No Amplification)	30
School Rooms	30
Concert Halls (No Amplification)	25

Sound Pressure Levels at the Range of Frequencies

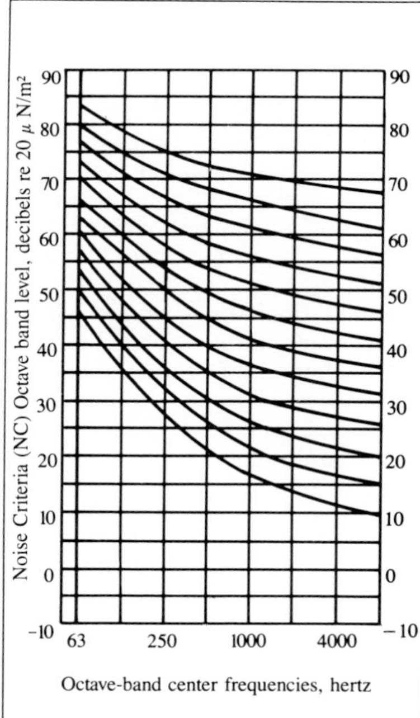

Reprinted, with permission, from Leo Beranek, *Music, Acoustics and Architecture*, Krieger, 1979.

high frequency of 4000 hertz may seem as loud as 50 dB at the low frequency of 125 hertz. Noise criteria (NC) curves have therefore been developed to measure the perceived mix of sound sources (exterior and building noise) at their various frequencies as shown in the chart above.

The appropriateness of various NC levels as background noise or "working quiet" is determined by the function of the space and the ratio of the signal (wanted sound source) to background noise levels. A concert hall requires very low background noise levels; restaurants or offices, where the source of wanted sound is usually near and relatively loud, can have somewhat higher background levels. Background noise, however, must in either setting consist of unobtrusive, broad-band sounds without intermittent sounds or pure tones. Sound masking systems are designed to achieve this goal by capturing the benefits of continuous broad-band sound (in an open plan office, for example), allowing for close communication while "masking" these sounds for nearby occupancies.

Controlling the sound source begins with the selection of the building site (avoiding noisy locations such as airports or thruways), and continues with the layout of interior spaces (isolating noisemakers) and the selection and integration of noise-generating equipment.

THE SOUND PATH: NOISE ISOLATION

The designer must also decide the level of isolation or the level of distribution needed from the wanted sound source to the other occupants and functions of the building. If noise isolation is desired, both the airborne paths and the structure-borne paths of sound must be cut off.

To reduce airborne noise transmission, separation must be assured by the configuration, massing, and layout of the building, the design of the envelope and its openings, the design and construction of interior walls, ceiling and floors, and their integration with mechanical, structural, and envelope systems.

For each component and each on-site component integration situation, sound transmission losses (TL) can be measured at various frequencies to assess whether the construction adequately isolates airborne sounds from one space to another. An overall rating for the sound isolation provided by a particular construction, for the range of frequencies heard by the human ear, is identified as its sound transmission class, or STC rating.

STC ratings, however, must be used with care as they only apply to the audible range and do not extend below 125 hertz to annoying low frequency sounds. Moreover, STC ratings for building products are usually produced in laboratory settings, and on-site results can easily be off from the laboratory results by 5 to 15 STC points. High performance components must therefore be integrated into a detailed design, avoiding "flanking paths" under doors and through interconnecting ductwork, continuous ceiling plenums, pipe and duct penetrations, and electrical boxes. STC ratings should be established on-site to determine whether flanking paths have undermined expensive, high-performance components.

Design for noise isolation also requires that structure-borne sound paths be effectively cut off. Both noise and vibration can be conveyed through a building structure and radiated as audible sound in adjacent or distant spaces. The Impact Insulation Class (IIC) rating has been adopted for many building codes to rate structure-borne noise transmission from impact sources. The location, selection, and mounting of mechanical components and other equipment, the relationship of such equipment to structural and envelope components, and the design of the distribution network are all critical to reducing noise and vibration. Structural system type and bay size (which influence the amount of deflection and resonance) are also critical, especially for reducing the impact noise transmission from such "live" loads as exercise classes or kindergartens.

Sound Path: Sound Distribution

As often as isolation from unwanted noise is demanded in building design, distribution of desirable sounds is also required. Sound radiates spherically and uniformly from its source until it strikes a surface and is absorbed, reflected, or transmitted. The selection and location of absorbing and reflecting materials determines the direction, distance, and clarity with which the desired sound will travel. The materials specified for the defining spaces can be hard, sound-reflective materials or porous materials that absorb sound efficiently over a wide frequency range. The designer must effectively place these absorbing and reflecting surfaces to control sound intelligibility, uniformity, and reverberation.

In the past, design for acoustical quality has focused on theaters and lecture halls where good communication of speech and music is important. However, the steady increase in the noise level of our mechanized surroundings and the increasing mix of functions housed in a single building complex have made the design for acoustical performance more critical in all building types. In the design of open offices or restaurants, where intimate communication is required, more sound-absorbing surfaces are needed, and sound sources should be isolated as much as possible. Sound-absorbing surfaces must be strategically placed around the sound "sphere," taking into account that hard wall surfaces (including window walls), hard ceiling surfaces (including integrated lighting systems), and hard floor surfaces contribute to the unwanted reflection of sound.

In the design of sports arenas or large atrium spaces, where the enclosing walls are far enough away to create long-delayed reflections, or echoes, it is also necessary to make surfaces sound-absorbing. In theaters and lecture halls, uniform distribution of the sound source is accomplished through the use of hard, reflective materials in direct line-of-sight. For speech, it is important that reflected sound reach the listener within roughly 30 milliseconds after the initial, direct sound to enhance loudness and clarity. For music, later arriving sounds will lessen clarity or articulation but will improve the reverberance and fullness of the sound. The ceiling and wall surfaces nearest the stage provide the best short reflection paths necessary for speech, so

Occupational Safety and Health Administration's Permissible Noise Exposures

Duration per day, h	Sound Level, dBA
8	90
6	92
4	95
3	97
2	100
1½	102
1	105
½	110
¼ or less	115

Note: dB levels given are based on the A scale.

Credit: *Federal Register,* 1971

changeability of these surface materials can best accommodate both speech and music communication needs.

Reverberation is defined as the prolongation of sound through the sequence of reflections of sound energy from the surfaces enclosing it. Length of reverberation depends on the relationship of room volume to the amount of sound absorption within the room. Reverberation time is defined as the time required for the intensity of the sound to decrease to one millionth of its original level. Increasing the volume tends to lengthen the reverberation time, while increasing the amount of sound absorption tends to reduce it.

THE SOUND RECEIVER

Hearing acuity varies significantly from person to person, between young and old, male and female, and between those who have spent many years in noisy environments or listening to highly amplified music and those who have lived in quiet settings.

To complicate the physiological condition of hearing acuity, psychological hearing sensitivities also arise. The occupants' functions, experiences, and personalities (empathetic, curious) may greatly affect their sensitivity to noise in their environments.[59]

59. Fletcher, H. *Speech and Hearing in Communication.* New York: Van Nostrand Reinhold, 1953.

Finally, control over the sounds within the environment affects one's threshold of comfort or satisfaction. The ability to move away from a noise source, to create a sound-masking system, or to control noise-makers will greatly affect the individual limits of acceptability.

Limits of Acceptability

Most of the standards defining acoustical performance center on the physiological limits or thresholds in order to minimize hearing damage. Following OSHA standards, *continuous* exposure to decibel levels over 85 has been declared unacceptable in almost all federal, state, and local codes. Based on a more refined comfort zone for concentration and communication, sound absorption guidelines for components and component assemblies (NRC's and STC's) have been established within the industry manufacturing ceilings, floors, and acoustical screens.

Where extreme privacy or excellent sound quality is required, many of these guidelines have become program requirements to meet the physiological limits of acoustical performance.

The psychological limits for acoustical quality usually center on the need to concentrate without distraction. Although continuous sounds below acceptable sound levels are usually not distracting, intermittent sounds (telephones ringing, motorcycles passing, mechanical equipment) and sounds that carry identifiable information (conversations, toilets flushing, faucets dripping) can be very annoying and detrimental to the occupants' performance.

The ability to communicate effectively in large or small gatherings while maintaining privacy of information forms the basis of the sociological limits for acoustical performance.

For speaking, an articulation index that measures the effectiveness of oral communication in offices, restaurants, and lecture halls can be used.

Cost is often the final arbiter of design for acoustical performance. Although programming and early design decisions improve acoustical quality at no added cost, the final selection of envelope materials and integration details must be anticipated in the project budget. Many apartment buildings, motels, restaurants, and open office environments (in which you can hear every word of conversation in the next space) are witness to the economic limit of acceptability. In meeting this limit of acceptability, it is imperative that the client and designer define their acoustical quality needs, that they reduce the performance "stress factors" in each design stage, and then match the investment to the acoustical quality desired.

Units of Evaluation

The units for evaluating the suitability of building components, component integrations, and entire systems for acoustical performance have been introduced, including dB, NC, TL, STC, and IIC. The reliability of the component integrations should be evaluated in light of the length of time that the conditions necessary for acceptable acoustical comfort will remain, and the level of maintenance necessary to sustain that comfort. The flexibility of the building system must be evaluated in terms of the ability of the integrated building "system" to change over time so that acoustical performance will be insured even as occupants and functions change.

The evaluation of acoustical quality will measure and assess the control of sound sources as they contribute to communication or quiet background noise; sound paths, including the design for noise isolation and sound distribution; and sound receivers, including provision for occupants' sensitivities and individual control.

As an introduction to these considerations and the design decisions that lead to them, an occupancy and use assessment should be made, as in the following checklist.

Some Factors That Influence the Annoyance Quality of Noise

Acoustical factors	Sound level
	Frequency
	Duration
	Spectral complexity
	Fluctuations in sound level
	Fluctuations in frequency
	Rise-time of the noise
Nonacoustical factors	Past experience with the noise
	Listener's activity
	Predictability of noise occurrence
	Necessity of the noise
	Listener's personality
	Attitudes toward the source of the noise
	Time of the year
	Time of the day
	Type of locale

Human Factors in Engineering and Design

Reprinted, with permission, from McCormick and Sanders, *Human Factors in Engineering and Design*, McGraw-Hill, 1982.

Incidence of Hearing Impairment in the General Population

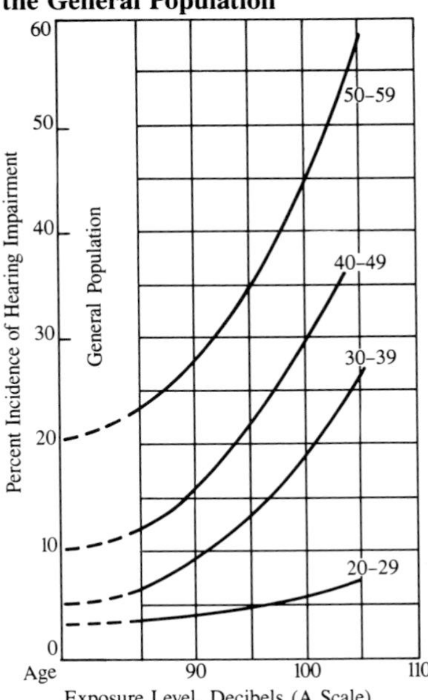

Reprinted, with permission, from *Industrial Noise Manual*, American Industrial Hygiene Assoc., 1966.

REFERENCES

Allen and Rainer. "Floor Vibration." *Canadian Building Digest*, Vol. 173, 1975.

Beranek, Leo. *Music, Acoustics and Architecture*. New York: Krieger Publishing, 1979.

Egan, M. David. *Concepts in Architectural Acoustics*. New York: McGraw-Hill, 1980.

Jones, Robert S. *Noise and Vibration Control in Buildings*. New York: McGraw-Hill, 1984.

McCormick and Sanders. *Human Factors in Engineering and Design*. New York: McGraw-Hill, 1982.

Newman, Robert B., BBN. "Acoustics." *Time Saver Standards*. New York: McGraw-Hill, 1980.

Sulewsky, James E. "Overdesigned Open Plan Acoustics Cancel Natural Masking Noise." *Contract*, July 1983, pp. 112–115.

Wetherill, Ewart A., BBN. "Acoustics and Noise Control." *Proceedings, The Northern Community: A Search for a Quality Environment*. New York: American Society of Civil Engineers, 1981.

Wetherill, Ewart A., BBN. "Noise Control in Buildings." *Sound and Vibration*, July 1975.

Acoustical Performance Signs of Stress in Offices

The Norm: Open Plan
No Internal Noise Generation
Random Acoustical Panels
Acoustic Ceiling
Carpeted Floor in Standard Diffuser Field
Central System

In a Walk-through, These Signs of Acoustic Stress May Be Seen:

Special Needs

Private Conversation

Working Quiet (Freedom From Distraction)

For Function

Noise (Non-Mech.)

Noise Generator: List

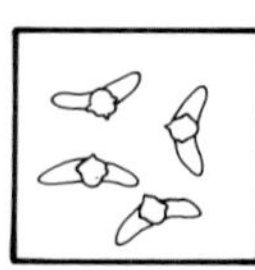

High-Density (5 Workstations 200 sq ft)

Outside:

Mechanical

Quiet: Too Far Away/ Blocked Diffuser

Directly Below Diffuser (Faulty); Adjacent to Perimeter Supply (Faulty)

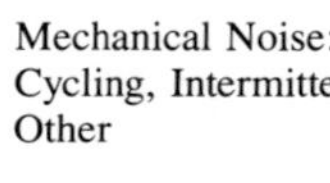

Mechanical Noise: Cycling, Intermittent, Other

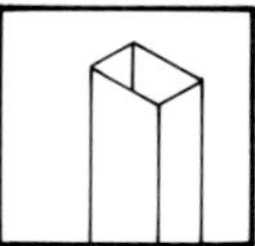

Vertical Shafts; Transport Noise

Poor Absorption

No Acoustical Ceiling

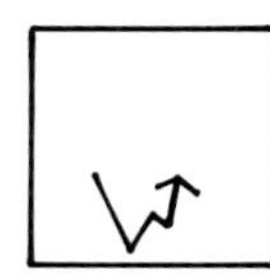

Hard Floor

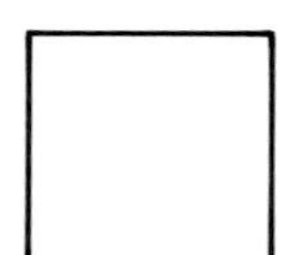

No Acoustical Panels

Open Office

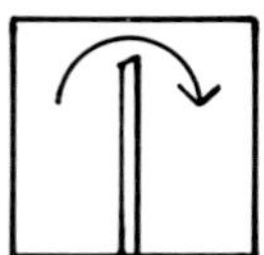

Flanking Paths

Closed Office:

Wall to Hung Ceiling Only; Convector/Duct Path, Other

User Modifications:

☐ Fan
☐ Added Wall Covering
☐ Added Acoustical Screen, Bookshelves, "Plants"
☐ Turned Desk Away From Noise Source
☐ Streamers Attached to Diffusers to Create "Masking Sound"
☐ Other:

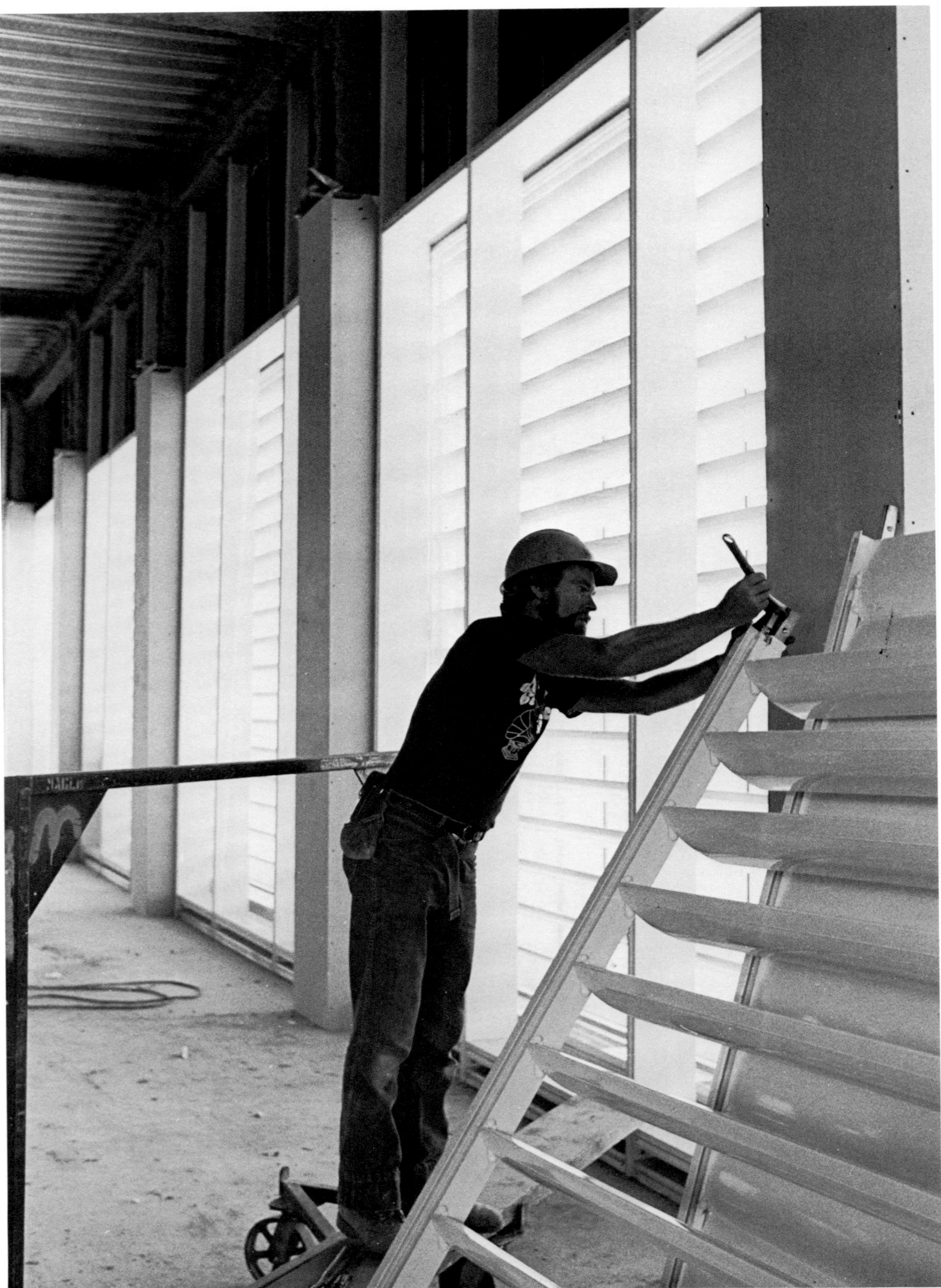

Visual Performance

Visual Performance

1. Ambient & Task Lighting Levels Illuminance
2. Contrast & Brightness Ratios
3. Color Rendition
4. Occupancy Factors & Controls

Louvers at Occidental Chemical Company Corporate Office Building are used to reduce glare and overheating, while allowing for natural diffused lighting. Photograph: Patricia Layman Bazelon.

The four lighting factors that most affect visual performance are illuminance (lighting levels and distribution), luminance ratios (brightness, contrast, glare), color rendition, and occupancy factors and controls.

The illuminance (E) in a space is created by the interplay of artificial light (both ambient and task) and daylight within an integrated set of components and their resultant geometry, texture, and color. Measured in footcandles (fc) or lumens/sq ft (lm/ft^2), the quantity of light or illumination level can vary from 1 fc to over 1000 fc for artificial light, and from 500 fc (overcast sky) to 10,000 fc (direct sunshine) for daylight. Measured on a spherical surface this quantity is known as a candela, equal to a lumen divided by 4 pi or 12.57 (the surface area of a sphere). In metric units, the quantity of light per square meter of surface, one meter away from the source, is known as a lux, or 0.09 fc.

Although it has been shown that the more light available, the better the visual conditions, there is a point of diminishing returns. The standards for lighting quality define the illuminance levels required by various activities, with the lower limits dependent on the physiological needs established by the function or task and the upper limits established by economic needs, as shown in the table. The field method for testing levels and distribution of light is known as the equivalent sphere illumination (ESI) method, which compares the actual lighting situation with the effectiveness of a reference sphere lighting. Design for acceptable illuminance depends mostly on: the location of the light fixtures, the design of the reflectors and diffusers surrounding the lamp in the light fixture, as well as the design of the geometry and surface reflectances defining the space intended to be illuminated below the light fixture.

Reflected and transmitted light, known as luminance or brightness, is measured in footlamberts (fL), and is detectable by the human eye from .0001 fL to 450 million fL (a range of 10^{12}). The ability of the eye to respond to the ratios of two brightness levels, known as the contrast of the task, is only 1000 to 1, setting the second critical factor for visual performance. The contrast ratios, or brightness differences, are not only measured comparing the letters on a page and the page, but also comparing the page and the desk and the desk and the space. The human eye can only clearly perceive if contrast ratios are at least 2 to 1, and cannot adapt quickly enough if the contrast ratios are greater than 40 to 1. The necessary contrast depends on the color and reflectance of the task within its surrounding, given the lighting level.

Excessive contrast occurs when the luminance or brightness ratios are too high, resulting in discomfort or disability glare. Unlike disability glare, discomfort glare does not reduce the ability to perform visual tasks. Direct glare from the sun or a

Physiological and Economic Lighting Limits

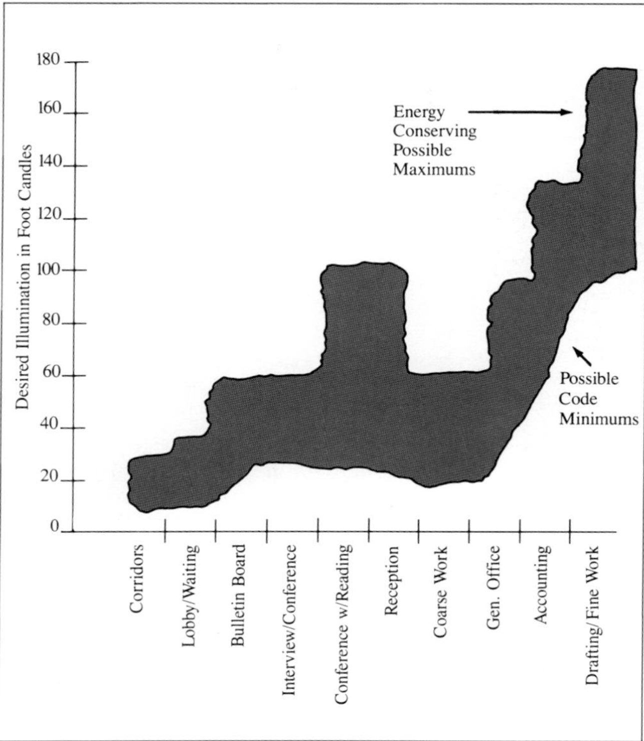

Credit: Minimums from *IES Lighting Handbook*

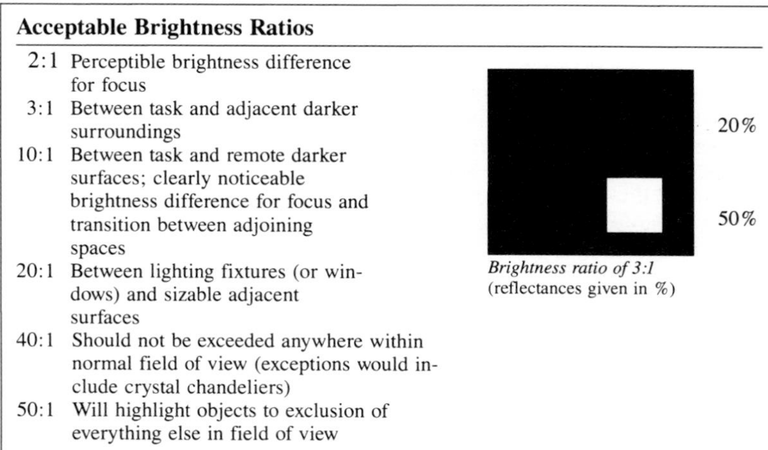

Acceptable Brightness Ratios

2:1	Perceptible brightness difference for focus
3:1	Between task and adjacent darker surroundings
10:1	Between task and remote darker surfaces; clearly noticeable brightness difference for focus and transition between adjoining spaces
20:1	Between lighting fixtures (or windows) and sizable adjacent surfaces
40:1	Should not be exceeded anywhere within normal field of view (exceptions would include crystal chandeliers)
50:1	Will highlight objects to exclusion of everything else in field of view

Brightness ratio of 3:1
(reflectances given in %)

Reprinted, with permission, from M. David Egan, *Concepts in Architectural Lighting*, McGraw-Hill, 1983.

light fixture and reflected glare from a glossy or polished surface can result in either discomfort or disability glare. Veiling reflections occur when small areas of the visual task, such as a magazine page, reflect light, reducing contrast between the task and its immediate surroundings. Design for appropriate brightness contrasts depends on the location of the light source, the shielding of the lamps in the light fixture (or of sunlight, in the case of daylighting), and the selection of appropriate work surface and wall surface reflections.

The third factor for visual performance is color rendition, a critical factor in museum, fashion store, and advertising office design. A color rendering index (CRI) measures how well a light source renders color; a CRI of 100 indicates perfect color match, and a CRI of 50 means very poor color rendition. While fixture location and configuration are critical for illuminance design and insuring appropriate contrast ratios, lamp type becomes critical for color rendition. While daylight by definition provides perfect color rendition, only a few lamps can provide contrast rendering indexes over 85.

Variation in limits of acceptability for visual comfort are a result of such occupancy factors as age, marginal visual impairment (need for magnification), visual disability (need for glasses), and blindness, and of such functional factors as the size and contrast of the tasks to be performed. Some tasks require very coarse manual dexterity or visual discrimination, such as storing materials, walking, and sorting mail, while others such as drawing and engraving require very fine visual discrimination. In addition, some task materials provide a high contrast (black on white), while others place greater demands on visual acuity (off-white on white). Given this range of occupancy and functional requirements, and the unknowns resulting from interior space modification that are critical to visual performance, lighting controls would appear to be mandatory. They are needed to manage both the daylight fixture (the window) and the artificial lighting fixture; they can vary from manual on/off switches to automatic continuous dimming controls. The interrelated design and control of daylighting, ambient (general overhead) lighting, and task lighting are fundamental to visual performance.

Limits of Acceptability

The physiological limits of acceptability and the codes for lighting design are determined by the capability and adaptability of the human eye, given tasks of specific size and contrast. The fact that visual acuity improves with increased levels of illuminance has led to baseline standards for lighting levels. Because the eye can only adapt to contrast ratios of 40:1 (an ability that decreases with age), and because direct and reflected glare can cause visual disability (such as night blindness), individual standards have been set for space, task, contrast, and reflectivity. Variations in the visual capability of various occupancies set up restricted visual comfort zones that must be achieved in the integration of lighting (mechanical), interior, and envelope systems.

The psychological needs guiding design for visual performance go beyond considerations for reducing eye strain and fatigue to include the need for orientation and identifiable "territory." Often dependent on space function, there may be psychological needs for a sense of calm or excitement, a sense of spaciousness or intimacy, for avoiding confusion or dull uniformity, and for a sense of cheerfulness instead of gloom. Light often becomes the final paintbrush in the definition of space function and mood, with the ability to be dynamic or changing with time. The element of time and contact with nature is a fundamental psychological limit of acceptability, demanding that daylight and dynamic lighting, or change, be incorporated in the design for visual performance.

The sociological limits of acceptability for visual performance include such factors as definition of personal territory, privacy, and sense of security on the one hand, and lighting for visual communication and human contact on the other. In addition, many esthetic values become sociological needs, and guidelines for the design of spaces, windows, light fixtures, and controls are set to fulfill current definitions of visual performance.

The economic limits of acceptability for visual performance are often the dominant criteria in lighting design. First costs, in total dollars or dollars/lumen, have always been important. Only recently, as lighting and electricity have become the greatest demand for energy in buildings, have operating costs—in the form of lumens/watt, watts/m^2, and number of operating hours—become significant. Previously, the additional costs of appropriately providing daylighting, task lighting, and lighting controls were often considered "unaffordable." Instead, expanses of internal offices were lit by vast areas of task-ambient fluorescent light fixtures (for maximum spatial flexibility) and controlled on a floor-by-floor basis by master switches. Current studies of productivity and of the physiological, psychological, and sociological conditions most conducive to productivity have begun to put economic value on daylighting, on the separation of ambient lighting (for circulation) from task lighting, and on the provision of individual or group lighting controls.

Units of Evaluation

Many of the units of evaluation for visual performance have already been discussed. Suitability of illumination levels (E) are measured in lumens (lm), candelas (cd), footcandles (fc), and lux against an equivalent sphere index (ESI) measured within the occupied space (and its specific integration of components). The economic suitability of light fixture design is evaluated according to a coefficient of utilization (CU = ratio of lumens on the work surface to lumens emitted by the lamp), lumens output per watt input (lm/w), and watts/m^2. The light fixture is also evaluated for its color rendering index (CRI) and shielding angles (for protecting the occupant from direct glare), factors which are also measured in the visual comfort probability index (VCP).

The reliability of the lighting system in providing visual performance over time can be measured by a luminaire dirt depreciation factor (LDD) and by a lamp aging factor called lamp lumen depreciation (LLD). These multiply into a percentage maintenance factor (MF) that is the ratio of illumination on a given area after a period of time to the initial illumination on that area. A measure of the reliability of daylighting contribution must account for reduced illumination due to dirt accumulation on the window.

Reprinted, with permission, from M. David Egan, *Concepts in Architectural Lighting*, McGraw-Hill, 1983.

The Necessary Shielding Angle

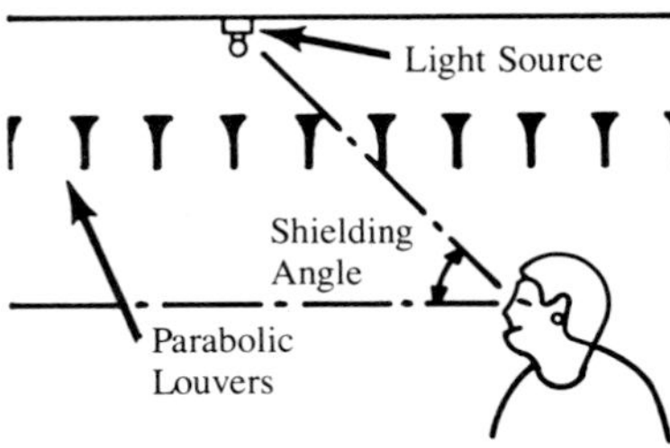

Lighting Control Options

Manual On-Off
Manual Dimming (Continuous)
Manual 3-Way Switching
Automatic On-Off
(By Timers, Occupancy Sensors, Daylight Sensors)
Automatic Step-Dimming
Automatic Continuous Dimming

Given changing functions, layouts, and climatic conditions, the flexibility of the integrated system enabling it to maintain visual performance is most often determined by the controls. Window controls (such as blinds and curtains) are evaluated in terms of transmission (%t) and reflection (%r), as well as by a brightness factor (footlambert) that measures the diffusion/dispersion capabilities of the component. To provide appropriate illumination levels for changing functions and daylight conditions, light fixture controls can range from manual on/off, manual three-way switching, and manual continuous dimming to automatic on/off (triggered by timers, occupancy sensors, and daylight sensors), automatic step dimming, and automatic continuous dimming. When considering these control systems, differentiations should be made between requirements for ambient lighting (for circulation) such as that provided by luminous ceilings, illuminated ceilings, and wall washers; requirements for task lighting such as that provided by individual lamps and luminous ceilings; security lighting requirements; and accent lighting requirements.

The evaluation of visual quality requires the assessment of illumination levels for the function in question, brightness or contrast ratios to minimize discomfort and disability glare, color rendition, and occupancy factors and controls. The following checklist can be used to evaluate the visual quality in existing office spaces for input into retrofit as well as for new space design.

REFERENCES

Egan, M. David. *Concepts in Lighting for Architecture*. New York: McGraw-Hill, 1983.

Evans, Benjamin H. *Daylight in Architecture*. New York: McGraw-Hill, 1981.

Kaufman, J. *IES Lighting Handbook*. New York: Illuminating Engineering Society, 1981.

Lam, William. *Perception and Lighting as Form-Givers for Architecture*. New York: McGraw-Hill, 1977.

Visual Performance Signs of Stress in Offices

Given an Acceptable Office Space Norm: Internal Space, No Windows
Centered Between 2 Light Fixtures, No Partitions
Surrounded by Light-Colored Surfaces

In a Walk-through, These Signs of Visual Stress May Be Seen:

Special Needs

Fine Work

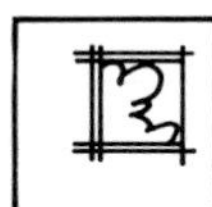
True Color or Modelling Needed

Sunlight

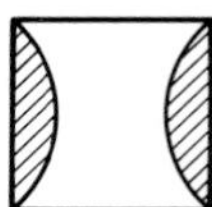
E/W Unilateral Lighting

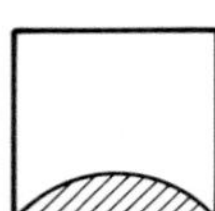
South Unilateral Lighting

Bilateral Lighting

Window Within 15 ft.

W/No Shading

Ineffective/Broken Shading

Contrast

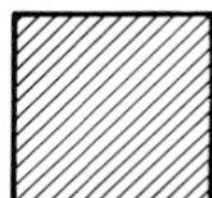
Dark Walls/Partitions, or Work Surface

Reflective Glass/Plastic Work—Surface, Partitions, or Equipment

Screening

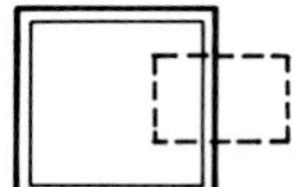
Badly Partitioned, or High Screen, Blocking Fixtures. Not Even One Full Fixture in Space

Also Look for Any of These User Modifications to the Original Design:

☐ Brought in Lamp
☐ Removed Light Bulbs
☐ Added Light Desk Surface
☐ Replaced, Modified Light Diffuser
☐ Turned Desk Away From Window
☐ Covered Window
☐ Added Curtains/Blinds

Building Integrity Against Degradation

Building Integrity

A. Maintaining:
1. Mechanical (Structural) Properties
2. Physical Properties (Water, Air, Heat, Light, Sound)
3. Visible Properties (Color, Texture, Finish, Form)

B. Maintaining properties against:
1. Loads
2. Moisture/Wear
3. Temperature
4. Air Movement
5. Radiation (below)
6. Chemical Attack
7. Biological Attack
8. Fire
9. Man-made & Natural Disater

New facades often degrade before their time because inappropriate integrations between envelope and structure result in air leakage and eventual condensation. Photograph: Peter A. D. Mill, PWC.

Definition

Sustaining building integrity against degradation is crucial for the comfort, health, safety, and welfare of building occupants, and for an appropriate culmination of the mandates for spatial, thermal, air quality, acoustical, and visual performance. In the provision of shelter, building integrity can be defined as sustaining the material, component, and assembly properties to withstand external and internal forces over time. Critical properties that must be sustained include:

1) the mechanical properties of overall geometric stability (component parts and joints), including structural strength and stability (such as compression, tension, and shear) with levels of degradation varying from marking, denting, and stretching to buckling and collapse;

2) the physical properties of watertightness and airtightness, with levels of degradation ranging from staining to flooding; the physical properties of transmission, reflection and absorption of heat, light, and sound, as necessary for the occupancy function;

3) the visible properties of color, texture, and surface finish, with levels of degradation varying from slight discoloration and soiling to a complete change in overall visual appearance. The degradation of visible properties is often a clear (not necessarily early) indication of the degradation of mechanical and physical properties.

Degradation of these properties of building integrity can vary from an entirely superficial stage, with no implications for health, safety, or welfare, to a debilitating stage, endangering both comfort and welfare, to a devastation stage imperiling human safety and health.

In the face of local environmental conditions, aging is a natural and desirable process. However, when the mechanical, physical, or visual properties of the integrated system no longer meet the design requirements, the unacceptable degradation becomes a design failure. The building delivery process must not only produce a building that is immediately suitable, but one that is reliable over time in the presence of environmental forces and abuse.

The forces and mechanisms that

Protect Building Integrity From Electro-Magnetic Radiation

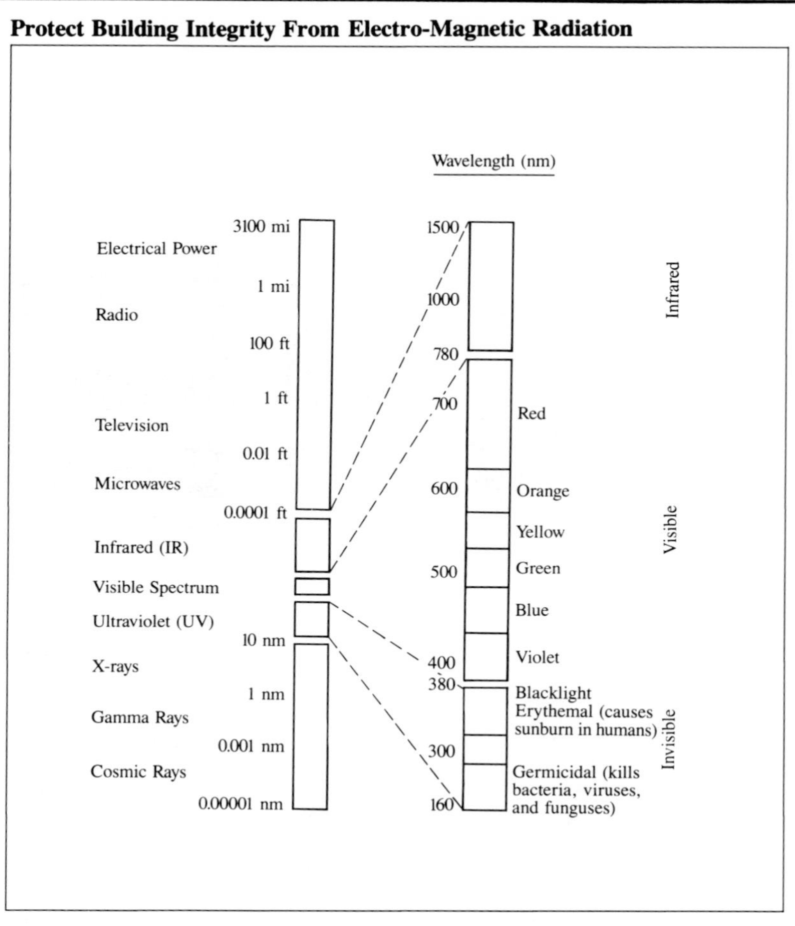

Ultraviolet light or sunlight is not the only cause of building and artifact degradation. Credit: Egan, Concepts in Architectural Lighting.

lead to the degradation of these basic integrity/shelter requirements have been outlined. They include: loads, moisture, temperature, air movement, long-wave radiation and light, chemical attack, biological attack, fire, and natural and manmade disasters. Any of these forces could lead to a degradation of structural strength and stability, resulting in superficial cracking or denting, debilitating crumbling (e.g., chipping of stair treads), or a devastating structural collapse. These forces could also degrade the physical properties of watertightness and airtightness, leading for instance to roof leaks and pollution infiltration. The thermal and acoustical properties of materials that depend on the containment of air, such as resistance to heat loss or absorption of sound, could be seriously impaired by loads (compression of batt insulation), moisture (saturation of batt insulation), or biological attack (batt insulation destroyed by squirrels). The light transmission properties of glass and the reflection properties of interior finishes, both of which are critical to an effective daylighting strategy, could be seriously degraded by radiation, chemical attack, or even loads (excessive denting or warping). Finally, visual properties such as color, surface texture, shape, and finish can also be degraded by environmental forces and mechanisms.

Limits of Acceptability

The physiological limits of acceptability for the degradation of building integrity are well defined in safety and health standards, especially regarding structural strength

The inability of the envelope and mechanical systems integration to withstand environmental forces led to this building integrity failure.

and stability. Building integrity must be designed at levels that will prevent loss of compressive, tensile, and flexural strength, maintaining the design load-bearing capacity. Certain spatial comfort conditions must be maintained so that occupants will not trip, fall, or hit their heads. However, the building integrity necessary to provide thermal, acoustical, air quality, and visual performance over time (maintaining the transmission, reflection, and absorption properties) is less well defined; operational guidelines and OSHA standards are the only written limits describing acceptable degradation. Recently, some limits have been set on the use of materials that can lead to outgassing and toxic radiation.

The psychological limits of acceptability for the degradation of buildings, though unwritten, play an important role in designing for building integrity. Slight degradations in the mechanical properties of building components in terms of shape, dimension, and location may be unacceptable to building users fearing injury from structural failure. Although a dripping window or a strong draft (degradation of physical properties) may not be debilitating to occupancy functions, the psychological impact (feeling of neglect) may be debilitating. Clear-cut limits between acceptable and unacceptable levels of visible degradation, or degradation in appearance, may be difficult to adopt generally. However, users are often the most vocal about the unacceptable appearance of buildings. Clear delineations of unacceptable performance often depend on cultural, economic, and social expectations.

The economic limits of acceptable loss in building integrity often outweigh all other limits except those mandated by codes and standards. Emphasis on first costs in material, labor, and time can result in the substitution of systems and systems integrations with poorer assurance of building integrity. Decisions made for short-term suitability in system selection often result in far greater future expenses.

Units of Evaluation

The units for evaluating the suitability of building systems and systems integrations regarding building integrity are numerous because they must quantify diverse mechanical, physical, and visible properties. Each of these units, when taken over time, will also provide a basis for evaluating the reliability of the integrated system, either in terms of the length of time that the conditions necessary for acceptable building integrity will remain, or in terms of the level of effort (maintenance) necessary to retain suitability. The flexibility of a particular building is evaluated in terms of the ability of the integrated building system to change over time, or to accommodate change from the outside, so that building integrity will still be insured given changing occupancies and functions.

Most of the units of evaluation for building integrity have been developed by the American Society for Testing and Materials (ASTM), the American National Standards Institute (ANSI), Underwriters Laboratory (UL), and trade associations representing various manufactured products (for example, the American Steel Institute). In all cases the units must be comparable, so that the specifier can compare one product with another for suitability, reliability, and flexibility.

The units used to describe the integrity of mechanical properties usually focus on strength in pounds per square inch (psi), be it compressive, tensile, shear, flexural, bonding, or impact strength. Occupancy safety also depends on any possible change of shape and location, measured in inches per inch of weight or temperature applied. For example, the coefficient of thermal expansion, often critical to pedestrian safety on sidewalks, is measured in in./in.°F. In addition, some dimensionless units of evaluation are based on a scale that describes hardness (1 to 100 on the ASTM BARCOL scale), impact resistance, abrasion resistance, resilience, and ease of maintenance or durability ratings.

Mechanical, Physical & Visible Properties of Epoxy Adhesive & Grout

Density	115 lbs./cu. ft. (1842 Kg./M³)
Water Absorption	<4.0%
Compressive Strength	>3,500 psi (246 Kg./cm³)
Bond Strength	<750 psi (53 Kg./cm²)

Chemical Resistance

	R	NR
Acids-Oxidizing		●
Mineral & Petro. Oils	●	
Cooking Oils	●	
Fruit Juices	●	
Milk	●	
Acetone & Ketones		●
Sugar	●	
Brine	●	
Urine	●	
Food Waste	●	

R = Recommended NR = Not Recommended

Physical (absorption), mechanical (strength), and visible properties of a flooring grout should be specified as shown at left. Chemical resistance is very important in certain common building conditions. Reprinted, with permission, from Sweet's Catalog File, *McGraw-Hill, 1985.*

Fire ratings for the mechanical properties of materials and integrated systems include flame spread ratings and hours before collapse, while fire ratings for the physical properties of materials include fuel and smoke contribution factors.

Most of the units used to evaluate the long-term integrity of the *physical properties* of materials and integrated systems have been discussed: thermal transmission (R- and U-values), thermal reflection and emission, and thermal absorption (BTU/ft^2 °F); light transmission (t), light reflection (r), and light absorption (a); sound transmission (STC, IIC), sound absorption (NRC), and sound reflection. Units for evaluating watertightness include permeability and porosity ratings and water repellence and absorption percentiles. Airtightness is measured in terms either of cubic feet per minute (cfm) per linear foot of crack or air changes per hour for the whole or part of the building.

Units for evaluating the integrity

of the visual properties of materials and integrated systems have also been developed and, to some extent, standardized. Color retention and gloss can be rated on a scale from poor to excellent. Surface finish and texture integrity can be rated for resistance to fumes, salt air, sun, fresh and salt water, oxidizing agents, alkalis, mineral acids, and various foods and cleaning products. Resistance to soiling and abrasion can be rated from poor to excellent. The integrity of the shape of materials that make up integrated systems can be evaluated, for example, in terms of maximum resistance to wet and dry heat (in °F) against warping.

The evaluation of building integrity requires the assessment of visual, mechanical, and physical properties over time, accounting for the stresses of loading, moisture, temperature, radiation and light, chemical attack, biological attack, fire, and man-made or natural disasters. As an introduction to these factors and the design decisions that address them, a building walk-through assessment could be made to evaluate the building integrity conditions demonstrated in existing office spaces.

REFERENCES

Sweet's Catalog File: Products for General Building and Renovation. New York: McGraw-Hill, 1985.

American National Standards Institute, 1430 Broadway, New York, NY 10018.

American Society for Testing and Materials, 1961 Race Street, Philadelphia, PA 19103.

Dietz, Albert G.H. *Dwelling House Construction.* 4th ed. Cambridge: MIT, 1980.

Solar Transmission Through Three Glass Types

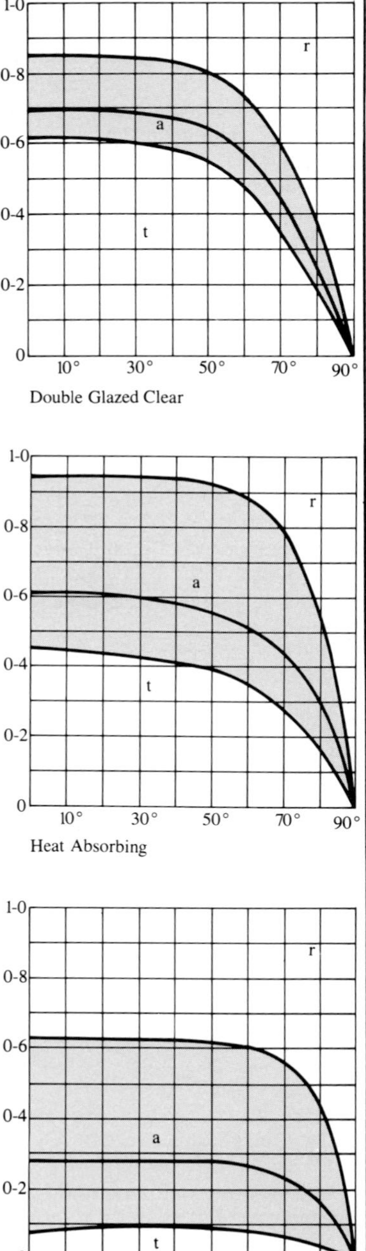

Thermal expansion and contraction in glazing can be a function of the amount of short wave radiation that is absorbed—a specification that varies widely among glazings. Reprinted, with permission, from Otto H. Koenigsberger, Manual of Tropical Housing and Building, *Longman, 1973.*

Building Integrity Signs of Stress in Offices

Given an Acceptable Office Space Norm: Structure Not Shifted, Cracked or Heavily Marred
Envelope Weathertight, Held Fast to Structure, New Appearance
Interior Tight With Structure & Envelope as Designed, Not Worn
Mechanical Still in Place, Functioning, Clean

In a Walk-through, These Signs of Building Integrity Stress May Be Seen:

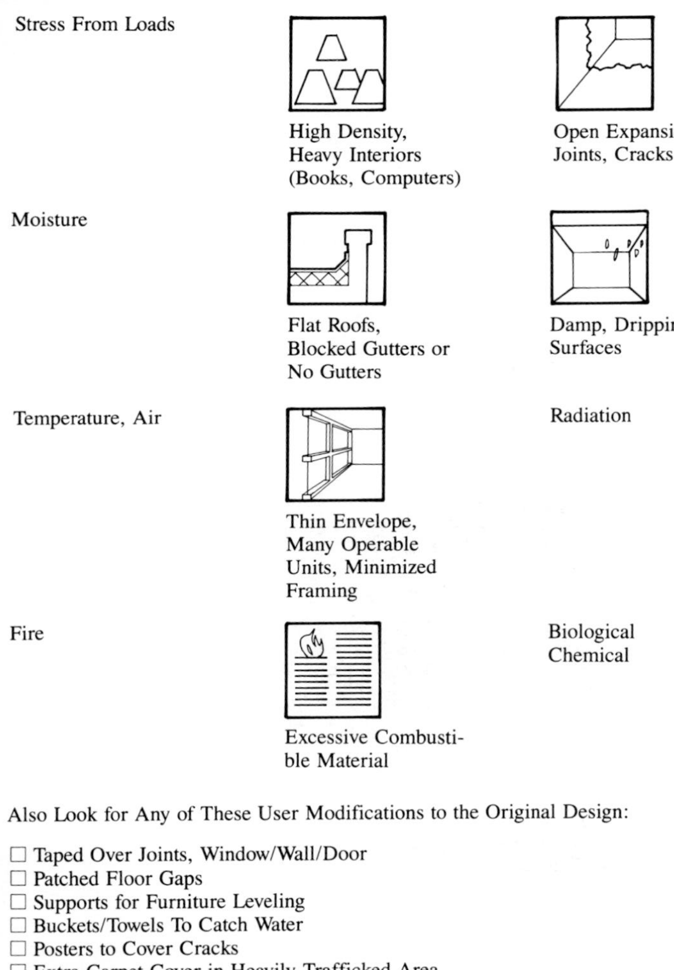

Stress From Loads

High Density, Heavy Interiors (Books, Computers)

Open Expansion Joints, Cracks

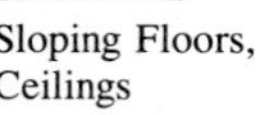

Sloping Floors, Ceilings

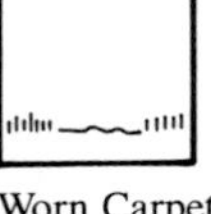

Worn Carpets, Dented Columns

Moisture

Flat Roofs, Blocked Gutters or No Gutters

Damp, Dripping Surfaces

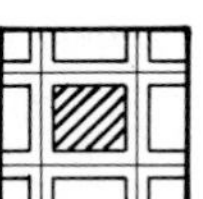

Missing Fascia Panels

Temperature, Air

Thin Envelope, Many Operable Units, Minimized Framing

Radiation

Fading, Yellowing Surfaces

Fire

Excessive Combustible Material

Biological
Chemical

Rusting Metals

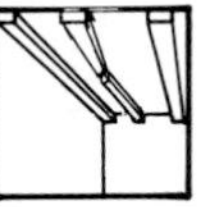

Rotting Woods

Also Look for Any of These User Modifications to the Original Design:

- ☐ Taped Over Joints, Window/Wall/Door
- ☐ Patched Floor Gaps
- ☐ Supports for Furniture Leveling
- ☐ Buckets/Towels To Catch Water
- ☐ Posters to Cover Cracks
- ☐ Extra Carpet Cover in Heavily Trafficked Area
- ☐ Fabrics Turned Around To Even Out Fading, Wear

Setting Performance Priorities

Levels of Integration

1. Remote
2. Touching
3. Connected
4. Meshed
5. Unified

Formal/Apparent Levels of Integration

1. Hidden
2. Clearly Visible
3. Surface Change Only
4. Size or Shape Change
5. Placement Change (Dislocation)

The six performance mandates cannot be understood in isolation from each other. They are related through the multiple effects of building component choice and building systems integration. They are related by their physiological (e.g., comfort), psychological (e.g., privacy), sociological (e.g., beauty), and economic limits of acceptability. To deliver a project that is acceptable in all performance areas, conflicts and opportunities must be resolved between performance mandates, and priorities must be set based on the function of the building or space. The method shown here for setting priorities and integrating multiple performance requirements was developed by a committee of the Conseil International du Batiment.

TEAM DECISION-MAKING

In traditional design processes there has often existed a clear delineation of responsibility and accountability for selecting structural, envelope, mechanical, and interior system components. This division of responsibility often leaves one primary decision-maker for each major set of components, suggesting minimum conflict in the building delivery process, with clear role definitions.

The problem with this division of responsibility and decision-making power is that the provision of spatial, thermal, acoustical, air quality, and visual performance, as well as building integrity, depends entirely on all four systems *and their integration*. For this reason, design for building performance is dependent on a "systems integration" design process, which in turn requires transdisciplinary, team decision-making.[60]

This transdisciplinary process would be based on establishing a full design team, at the time of conception, capable of making collaborative, informed decisions. During the early design stages, each team member would enunciate and champion the building performance criteria for which he or she is responsible, so that the *choice* of the level of integration can be clearly understood, and so that all team members can successfully participate.

The team decision-making process can also successfully isolate or highlight the performance criteria of specific importance to each component or integration under consideration. The following six tables describe some of the performance implications of each two-system integration that call for transdisciplinary decision-making.

In the resolution of integrations for each performance area, building designers have a rich set of alternatives. On a physical level, the systems may be *remote, touching, connected, meshed*, or *unified*. Until proven otherwise, the assumption is that the six performance mandates can be achieved at *each level of integration* through a deliberate team decision-making process. In visual terms, physical integration can be clearly visible, visible with a surface change (color, texture, pattern, and accentuation), visible with a size or shape change, visible with a placement change (dislocation), or completely hidden.

A deliberate team decision-making process can help to insure that the systems integration options described in this book not only occur in such a manner that performance criteria will be met, but also that they will occur in such a way that major innovations can be achieved.

60. Roundtable discussion, p. 28.

Team decision-making requires a rethinking of the typical no-conflict division of responsibility in component selection and system integration.

No Conflict Division of Responsibility for System Selection

	Structural	Envelope	Mechanical	Interior
Architectural (overall)	○	●	○	○
Mechanical			●	
Electrical			●	
Lighting		○	○	○
Acoustical				○
Structural	●			
Interior Planner				●
Energy Consultant		○	○	

Example: Comparing Performance Profiles

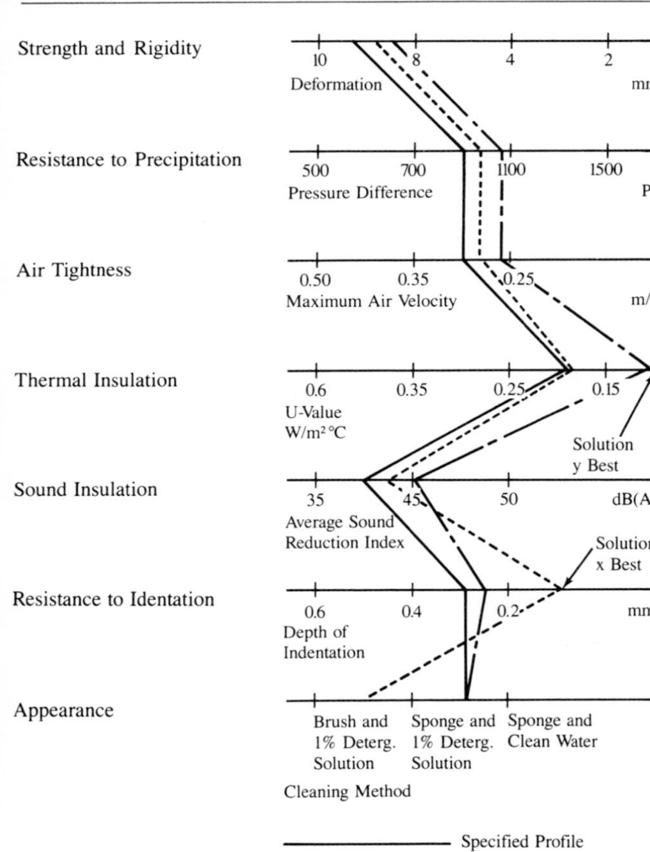

Comparison and weighting of attributes

Whenever several attributes are considered, the comparison of products or solutions against a performance specification requires a measure of judgement. It can, however, be helpful to use numerical methods to combine the separate performances into a *single index* of overall worth or quality. Such methods involve factoring or 'weighting' the individual performances and converting their combined 'score' to a figure on a simple scale. The methods need not be rigid, and can incorporate preferences about weighting expressed by individual clients or users for buildings on particular sites. There are a number of national appraisal systems of this type, especially for evaluating housing designs and components, but so far no method has been endorsed internationally.

An alternative technique is illustrated here which shows the possibility of combining banded scales for different attributes of an item into a single diagram, sometimes termed a *performance profile.*

This technique can be used to visualize the overall worth of different products or solutions, both to compare them against requirements and to choose between them. It reflects the flexible approach to criteria advocated above, since failure to achieve a particular banded level for one or two attributes may be offset by superior performance for other attributes. Where numerical methods for combining the performance for several attributes into overall indices of quality are not available, a performance profile can provide a 'feel' for the best value for money among competing solutions.

Reprinted, with permission, from "Working With the Performance Approach in Building," International Council for Building Research and Documentation, January 1982.

Examples of Integrated Decision-Making Critical to Performance

	S E I M Integrate Envelope and Interior Systems for:
Spatial	• planning module—individual placemaking, usable space • compartmentalization potential • circulation, wayfinding, accessibility • indoor-outdoor access • flexibility of layout, space aggregation potential • occupancy input to change
Thermal	• volume to be heated, compartmentalization & zoning potential • mean radiant temperature balance; passive solar storage • air flow patterns, heating and natural ventilation • individual control/compartmentalization
Air Quality	• air tightness of envelope • effective compartmentalization vs. pollution migration • outgassing prevention through material selection • air flow patterns, adequate fresh air • individual control/compartmentalization
Acoustical	• effective compartmentalization for privacy • surfaces, sound absorption or reverberation for function • stability versus vibration • effective zoning of interior noise generating equipment • individual control of privacy versus communication
Visual	• daylight distribution, minimization of glare • relationship/distance to window—status, daylighting, indoor-outdoor movement, satisfaction • space function/identity • daylighting for task, for ambient, for "display" • individual control/compartmentalization
Building Integrity	• connection to cope with settling • interior surface to reduce wear/abuse of envelope system • envelope/interior design to reduce fading

Examples of Integrated Decision Making Critical to Performance

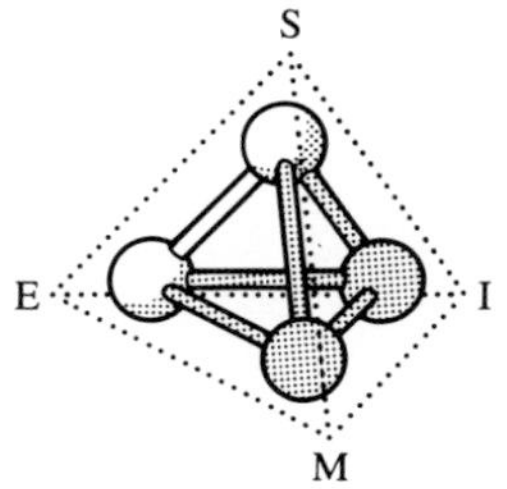

	Integrate Structure and Envelope Systems for:
Spatial	• thickness & connection—placemaking and servicing • connection—security • form—placemaking and usable surfaces • module and span—aggregate spaces, compartmentalization • variations in module—identity, wayfinding, servicing • expansion/change capabilities
Thermal	• volume—to be heated and usable space • continuity of insulation vs. thermal bridging • continuity of air barrier vs. infiltration • window frame—solar access (winter) and shading (summer) • vertical section—stratification • horizontal plan & orientation—cross vent. and infilt.
Air Quality	• elimination of vertical pollution migration paths and structure • envelope tightness against air leakage • space allocation for local mechanical air distribution
Acoustical	• elimination of vertical acoustical migration paths • volume and form—avoiding concentrations, flutter, echo • envelope tightness against outdoor noise (airport, highway)
Visual	• appropriate sunshading with S & E integration each facade • reduction of contrast at window; light diffusion • volume and form for effective daylighting
Building Integrity	• detailing—chemical compatibility • detailing—rain protection • connection—air leakage, continuous air-vapor barrier • building form and wind pressure, tear, load • connection strength vs. loads and disasters • access to biological (termite), organic (rot), & man-made attack

Examples of Integrated Decision-Making Critical to Performance

	S E I M Integrate Structure and Interior Systems for:
Spatial	• module/grid—individual space layout • structure as usable space, space divider • adequate ceiling height for raised floor, dropped ceiling • adequate support for flexibility in loading • vertical shafts for servicing coordinated with structure • sight lines around structure
Thermal	• connection tightness for thermal zoning • adequate mass for passive solar storage • volume, form—reinforce warm air distribution, natural ventilation
Air Quality	• connection tightness to stop pollution migration • protection against potentially polluting building materials • adequate ceiling plenum space for air distribution
Acoustical	• potential tightness of connection for privacy • adequate % distribution of soft and hard surfaces for desired sound reverberation, absorption • appropriate volume/form for sound distribution
Visual	• reduction of contrast, shadow; daylight distribution • structure as light shelf
Building Integrity	• protection of structure versus wear/abuse • S & I connection to cope with settling, loads, expansion

Examples of Integrated Decision-Making Critical to Performance

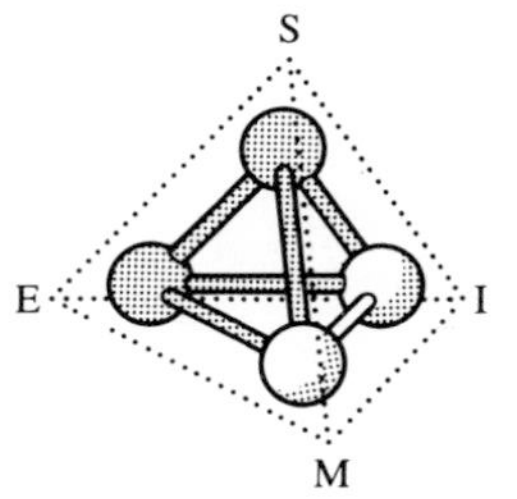

	S E I M Integrate Mechanical and Interior Systems for:
Spatial	• service module for present use and flexibility • space volume and ceiling height, functional identity • individual space layout, compartmentalization & flexibility • suitable servicing to individual space and aggregated space • expansion and change potential • individual control/space management
Thermal	• balanced mean radiant temperatures • air distribution, heating and cooling effectiveness, comfort • humidity impact on interior components • volume to be heated, stratification • mechanical efficiency from source to task
Air Quality	• fresh air distribution effectiveness • flushing vs. outgassing • protection from radiant pollution • individual control, compartmentalization vs. pollution migration
Acoustical	• background noise coordinated with appropriate room absorption • minimization of mechanical noise disturbance • minimization of vibration disturbance • effective acoustical compartmentalization around mechanical components
Visual	• adequate lighting distribution, balance • mechanical components for lighting dispersion, reflection • integration for space/function identity • lighting efficiency from source to task (lens) • flexibility potential • individual control, compartmentalization
Building Integrity	• humidity and temperature compartmentalization for artifact/machine/human "comfort" • staining and dirt buildup from mechanical on interior • vibration disturbance/destruction • mechanical accessibility, maintenance and repair • fire safety

Examples of Integrated Decision-Making Critical to Performance

	S E I M Integrate Envelope and Mechanical Systems for:
Spatial	• integration dimension—placemaking and usable spaces • integration module—compartmentalization and servicing • mechanical size, number—flexibility or expansion • variations in module—space identity • coordinated management—status, flexibility • mechanical core relationship to envelope—spatial flexibility
Thermal	• material and detail—load balancing, acceptable mean radiant temperatures and air flow patterns • natural ventilation, fan and stratification assisted • passive solar, mechanically assisted or distributed • evaporative cooling, time-lag cooling, radiant cooling • coordinated management—comfort, efficiency, flexibility
Air Quality	• adequate fresh air intake; no short circuit with exhaust • mechanically introduced air versus air infiltration • coordinated management for natural ventilation
Acoustical	• enclosure/isolation to reduce mechanical room/rooftop noise • E & M connections, seals against outdoor noise
Visual	• daylight and artificial lighting coordination • mechanical system for shading or daylight distribution • coordinated management (window and lighting)—comfort, efficiency, flexibility • dimension of connection—artificial lighting location, distribution, functional identity
Building Integrity	• weathertightness at junction • staining and dirt buildup on envelope from mechanical • loading of mechanical on envelope, sag, vibration • expansion/contraction stresses on interior (mechanically conditioned) and exterior environment • mechanical humidification impact on envelope

Examples of Integrated Decision-Making Critical to Performance

	S E I M Integrate Structure and Mechanical Systems for:
Spatial	• service module for present use and flexibility • adequate ceiling height • vertical shaft efficiency • adequate shaft space for future servicing • identity and compartmentalization defined • space shape, volume definition
Thermal	• coordination of vertical elements • volume, form—adequate mechanical distribution flexibility • no blockage of mechanical distribution by structural elements
Air Quality	• volume, form for effective air distribution and flexibility • no blockage of mechanical distribution by structural elements • air tightness of S & M verticals versus pollution migration
Acoustical	• vibration from mechanial eqmt. through structure • vertical shafts, distribution of noise • ability to seal from slab to slab for acoustical privacy • sound reverberation from mechanical against structure
Visual	• casting light shadows due to structure • structure to provide glare protection, shading • structure to distribute daylight and artificial light • visual task identified with structure and light integration • adequate ceiling height • service module for present use and flexibility
Building Integrity	• loading of mechanical on structure • staining and dirt buildup on structure from mechanical • reduction of vibration, associated mechanical/visible damage

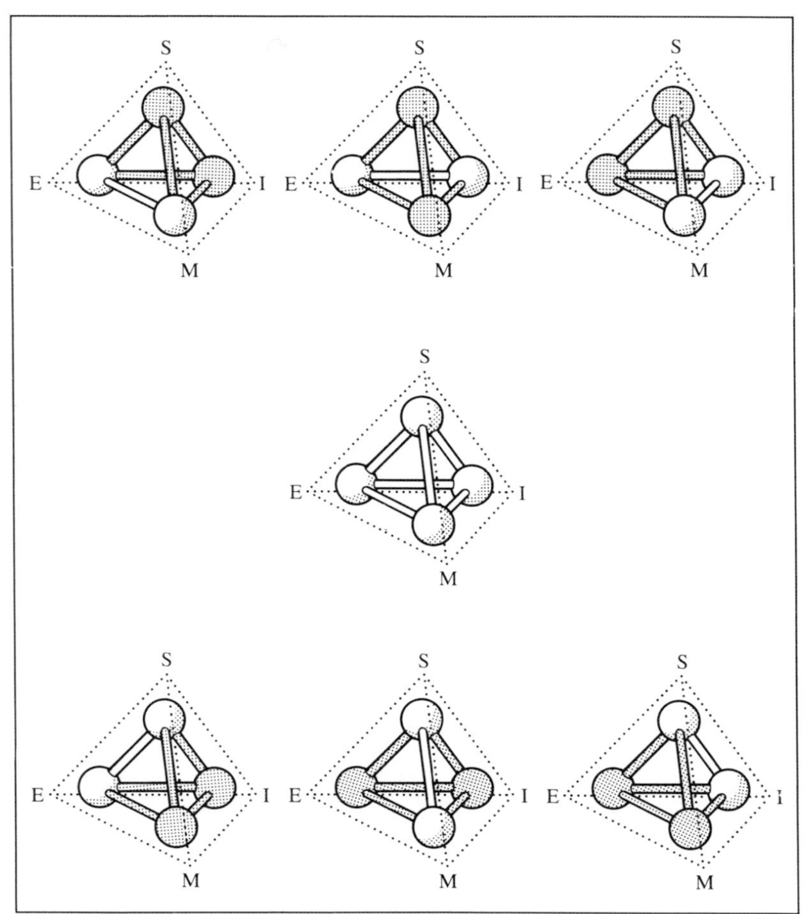

INTEGRATION DIAGRAMING

PP. 318–380

VISIBLE INTEGRATION

PP. 381–409

Chapter 7
Integration Theory

Author:
Richard D. Rush, AIA, and M. Stephanie Stubbs

Reviewers:
Joseph Deringer
The Deringer Group

Robert Shibley
Chairman, Department of Architecture
School of Architecture and Environmental Design
State University of New York
Buffalo, NY

Francis T. Ventre
Professor and Director, Environmental Systems Laboratory
College of Architecture
Virginia Polytechnic Institute and State University
Blacksburg, VA

William Wright
Lecturer, Department of Architecture
Massachusetts Institute of Architecture
Cambridge, MA

Architectural drawings:
Allen Assarsson

Unconscious integration always occurs in the design of buildings. The question raised by this book is, what happens to the design process when integration becomes a conscious act? Conscious thought about integration allows us to recognize and choose our own patterns or change them.

Integration exists as a tangible presence in the materials and machines making up the building. The integration of criteria is evident in the activities possible within the building. Each design decision not only defines the physical combinations and levels of interaction materially, but also determines how easily the intended activities can be accomplished. The building represents either potential resistance or support, and may either deter or enhance an activity.

One goal of integration, therefore, is to reduce the amount of time, material, and space[1] employed in a building while increasing the number of activities that can take place within it. The result is a balance. The task is to abstract the notion of building systems integration with the purpose of achieving the goal. The intent of this chapter is to create a theory and symbolic vocabulary that will allow designers to discuss integration strategies before and after choosing the specific physical systems.

The theory postulates that four systems are sufficient to completely describe a building. The geometrical expansion of this idea generates 11 possible two-, three-, and four-system combinations. The simple two-system combinations are of particular interest. In discussing the combinations, the word *system* is used in a restricted sense, referring only to structure, envelope, mechanical, and interior. To avoid confusion, elements of these systems are referred to as *subsystems*. The theory also postulates five levels of combination: remote, touching, connected, meshed, and unified. By attaching a diagrammatical significance to each combination, it is possible to describe each integration situation both in terms of the systems involved and in terms of the levels at which they combine. Finally, a separate nomenclature is put forward to describe the visible integration of systems.

The mere construction of a two-system diagram is evidence that there are, in fact, two other systems to consider and four other levels of combination. Since consciousness of integration only requires an awareness of the interrelated nature of the choices or decisions involved, the construction of the diagram or even the use of the terminology accomplishes the task of creating an insight. When the distinction among subsystems is made about a specific portion of the building, the function of that portion is defined. Every time the level of combination is designated, the relationship between the subsystems is defined. To define buildings and systems in this fashion is to integrate one's awareness of them.

1. Conservation of space, materials, and time, pp. 236–237.

Defining Integration

DESCRIPTION OF BUILDING SYSTEMS

For the purpose of diagramming the integration strategy of a building situation, each portion of the building must be described. We define four main systems: structure, envelope, mechanical, and interior. This terminology clearly signifies that the major building functions are being addressed by the integration in question. It is postulated that these definitions are valid for describing the total building. This is not to say that they represent the only way in which the total building function can be described, but simply that this breakdown of systems is one that works.

Structure

The structure of a building must continually balance a range of forces. There are natural loads such as gravity, wind, and seismic, as well as programmatic loads based on the way a building is to be used. These forces are distributed to the structural members in such a way that the result is equilibrium. The most desirable state of equilibrium is one in which all structural members are stressed to an allowable capacity. A space frame is an example of an optimal structural form which has all members equally stressed.[2] Other typical structural forms include the truss,[3] post and beam,[4] shell,[5] and fabric structure.[6]

Envelope

The envelope has to respond to both natural forces and human values. The natural forces include rain, snow, wind, and sun. Human concerns include safety, security, and task success. The envelope provides protection by enclosure and by balancing internal and external environmental forces. To achieve protection, it allows for careful control of penetrations. A symbol of the envelope might be a large bubble that would keep the weather out and the interior climate in. The architectural expressions of the envelope are roofing and siding.

2. Space frames, pp. 148–149.
3. Wood floor and roof truss, pp. 142–143.
4. Laminated wood post and beam, pp. 144–145.
5. Kimbell Art Museum, pp. 64–67.
6. Tension fabric structures, pp. 152–153.

Mechanical

The mechanical system works with the envelope to resolve the specific task needs as well as the thermal, acoustical, lighting, and security needs common to all buildings. Mechanical subsystems provide energy and water supply, waste disposal, and material and human conveyance. The mechanical system supplements the static building in the provision of environmental control, and could be characterized as an efficiently operating engine complete with fuel input and service output. Our definition of the mechanical system includes HVAC, electrical subsystems, plumbing subsystems, elevators[7] and escalators,[8] security equipment, and fire safety subsystems. Output is delivered through ducts,[9] conduit, and pipes. The most demanding elements from the point of view of integration are ducts.

7. Elevators, pp. 187–189.
8. Escalators, pp. 190–192.
9. Exposed ducts, pp. 179–181.

Interior

The interior system must resolve the direct demands that people make on the building and provide comfort in supporting human activity. All of the criteria discussed in Chapter 6 apply to the interior: spatial performance, thermal performance, air quality, acoustical performance, visual performance, and building integrity.[10] In its most basic form, the interior system consists of a room that supports the prescribed activity. Interior subsystems consist of ceilings, walls, finishes, furniture, and equipment.

10. Six performance mandates, pp. 232–233.

THE SYSTEM TETRAHEDRON

By placing each of the four systems at a point of a tetrahedron, it is possible to describe geometrically their theoretical potential for equal influence on one another. It is also possible to see clearly the set of six two-system combinations that comprises a four-system integration.

Similarly, there are four three-system combinations available and only one possible four-system combination.

Before designing a building, it is useful to speak of the four systems of a building in the abstract. At preliminary stages of design, the four systems and their integration potential can be discussed without actually specifying the systems. When

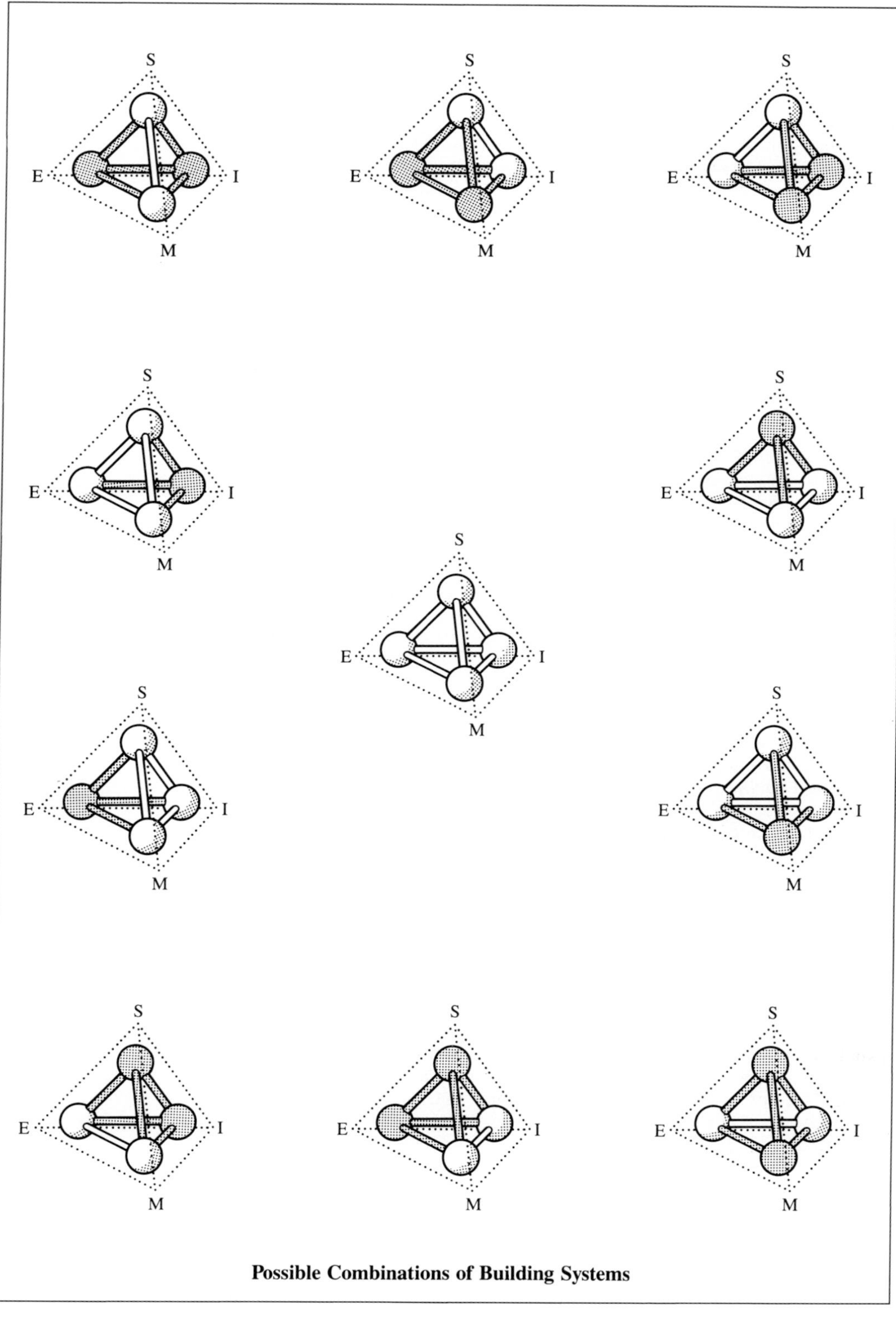

Possible Combinations of Building Systems

describing real buildings, however, there are many more than four systems, and duplication within the same system is common.

LEVELS OF INTEGRATION

Building systems may combine in many ways. The five levels of integration we have defined—remote, touching, connected, meshed, and unified—establish a range of system interaction and serve as a conceptual model for understanding the way integration takes place.

Remote is the first level of integration. At this level, the systems are physically separate from each other yet are still coordinated functionally. The next level is called *touching*. At this level, one system rests on top of another and is held in place by gravity. *Connected* is the third level, and includes systems physically connected by clips, nails, bolts, hangers, or permanent adhesives. At the *meshed* level, systems occupy the same space. The final level of integration is called *unified*; systems are integrated to the point that each shares the physical form of the other and is no longer distinct from it.

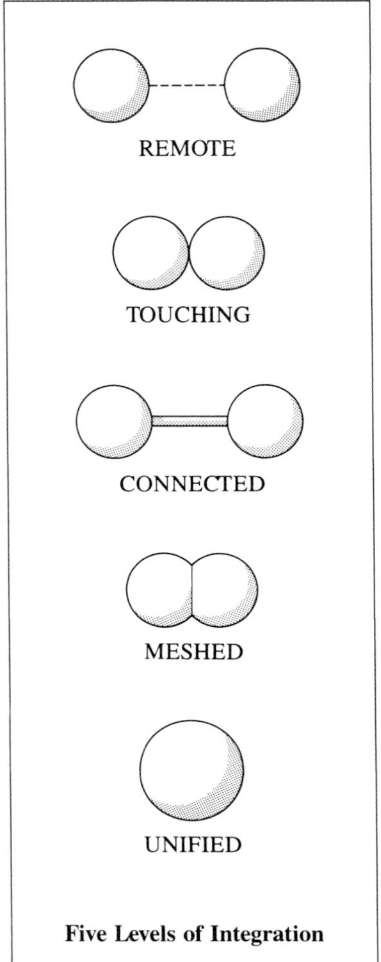

Five Levels of Integration

DERIVATION OF THREE-SYSTEM AND FOUR-SYSTEM COMBINATIONS

There are two fundamental decisions to make about systems integration—what systems are being considered for integration, and what level of integration will exist between or among the systems chosen. Whether a combination is conceived of as a two-system, three-system, or four-system combination, it can be reduced to a single two-system combination or a series of such combinations. There are six two-system combinations. There are four sets of three two-system combinations. There is only one four-system combination.

The conventional building can be designed in pieces or, more accurately, by separate systems. Each system can be created independently of the others, with integration occurring when all of them are assembled for the first time. By the time the systems are considered together, so many restrictions have been put on each one that it may be impossible to reconsider options that might better lend themselves to an appropriate level of integration. In fact, it is probably better to work in the opposite direction; that is, to start with the level of integration desired and then proceed to the combination.

The BSIH Matrix represents the most probable levels of integration between two systems. They are based upon four assumptions:

1. Only the envelope and interior systems are consistently remote from each other in conventional buildings.
2. The touching relationship is

Two-system combinations	Three-system combinations
1. S+E 2. S+M 3. S+I 4. E+M 5. E+I 6. M+I	1. S+E+M or S+E S+M E+M
Four-system combinations S+E+M+I or 1. S+E 2. S+M 3. S+I 4. E+M 5. E+I 6. M+I	2. S+E+I or S+E S+I E+I 3. E+M+I or E+M E+I M+I 4. S+M+I or S+M S+I M+I

Two-System Versions of All Combinations

based upon gravity and most often pertains to roofs, carpets, or other furnishings.

3. The meshed relationship always involves mechanical.
4. The structure and envelope are rarely unified with the mechanical system.

THE BSIH MATRIX

The distinction between or among systems (structural, envelope, mechanical, interior) is very useful in defining the four major tasks that a building must accomplish physically. In the broadest sense, these distinct categories are clear. When the integration levels come into play, the systems need to be more clearly defined. The distinctions among systems must be made with still greater precision when the diagrams for the specific built solutions are drawn. For example, the description "structural system" at the outset of conceptualizing a building means any and all of the subsystems that compose the total system. In the actual building, it may be useful to begin by examining the relationships between various subsystems rather than those between the major systems.

The matrix presented here, referred to as the BSIH Matrix, is conceived of as applying to the overall concept of major systems. It is not possible to conceive of a habitable building, for example, in which the mechanical system does not penetrate from the outside to the inside of the building, since most modern buildings involve water, electricity, and waste disposal. In a particular section of a specific building, however, there may in fact be no mechanical system at all.

The matrix, then, is both a destination and a point of departure. It is an analytical tool for discussing system relationships in general and it can also be used as a tool in the design process. In this regard, the matrix can be compared to the analysis of proximity relationships in the early stages of programming a building. It is a simplification of the kind necessary in order to begin any design process.

By way of a caveat, it should be noted that the application of the matrix in this chapter reflects the belief that the value of being able to begin from a single integrated concept of systems outweighs any confusion or perceived inaccuracy that may result from its application to both the general and the specific. Accuracy in diagraming a specific situation in a building is much less important than having a useful tool for initiating a systems design process that is integrated from the start.

Deductions From the Matrix

1. There are 17 common relationships among all of the two-system combinations.
2. The most common relationship between systems is the connected one. Any two systems can be connected.
3. The least common relationship between systems is remote. In general, it only applies to the relationship between envelope and interior.
4. Touching relationships are gravity ones and are limited to envelope + structure and interior + structure and mechanical + interior.
5. Meshed relationships always include the mechanical systems; this can combine with any of the other systems in that context.
6. The level choices for S + E and S + I are identical.
7. The level choices for S + M and E + M are identical.
8. Eliminating envelope or interior from a four-system combination eliminates only the remote level.
9. Eliminating mechanical from a four-system combination eliminates the meshed category from the three-system combination that remains.
10. Every system can be unified with at least one other system.

BSIH Matrix

	remote	touching	connected	meshed	unified
S+E		●	●		●
S+M			●	●	
S+I		●	●		●
E+M			●	●	
E+I	●		●		●
M+I		●	●	●	●

BSIH Matrix Combinations

All three- and four-system combinations can be reduced to sets of two-system combinations. A three-system combination can be thought of as three two-system combinations. A four-system combination consists of six two-system combinations. By reducing the more complicated combinations to two-system combinations, a simple matrix can be constructed that is useful in illuminating all levels of complexity for 17 common situations.

The following discussion addresses each intersection on the BSIH Matrix that connotes a probable level of combination between two systems. It attempts to clarify what is true generally for systems integration.

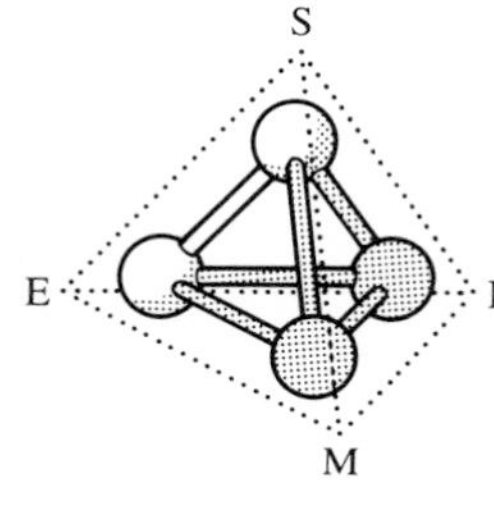

STRUCTURE + ENVELOPE

Structure and envelope combine equilibrium and distribution of loads with enclosure. These two systems have a high propensity for integration. The major concern of this combination of systems is their interdependence. The components of the envelope depend on structure for support, and the structure may depend on the envelope for protection.

When the structure is unified with the envelope, the structural material must be capable of providing protection and building integrity as well as distributing structural loads. Structure must resolve the forces of gravity, dead and live loads, and wind and seismic loads, while the envelope must resolve the forces of climate, air flow, temperature, and moisture.

The integration of structure and envelope may take the form of walls, slabs, domes, shells, tensile structures, or a structural frame enclosed by a skin or membrane. The motivations for the integration of structure and envelope include improved building performance,[11] design expression through visible integration,[12] and simplification of construction processes.[13]

11. Integration for performance, pp. 232–233.

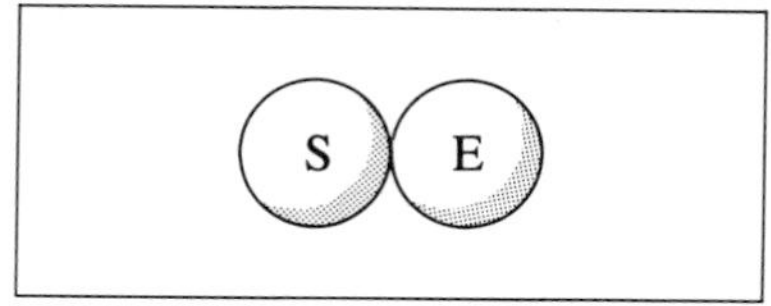

Structure + Envelope: Touching

Description: The envelope rests on the structure and is held in place largely by gravity. Each system is separate and maintains its independence of function, material, and physical characteristics. The envelope generally must be flexible enough to conform to the structure. This level of integration would normally occur between horizontal surfaces.

The construction methods involved are very simple: one system is laid over the other. Changes and repairs are easily made, and expansion and contraction are readily accommodated. Because this integration depends on gravity, it is vulnerable (on the exterior) to weather conditions, such as high winds, that would cause separation or movement. The application is limited to a few conventional structure and envelope assemblies.

Examples: The following product discussions, generic examples, and case studies contain specific instances of structure and envelope touching. Refer to their ball diagrams for details.

Protected Membrane Roofing, p. 337.
Flat Plate, p. 351.
Herman Miller, p. 366.
Moscone Center, p. 378.

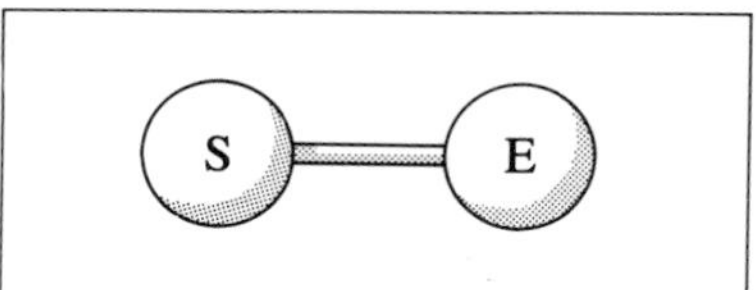

Structure + Envelope: Connected

Description: The envelope is attached to the structure by clips, bolts, nails, or permanent adhe-

12. Visible integration, pp. 381–385.
13. Conservation of resources, p. 236.

sives. The envelope may begin to share some of the other functional requirements of the structure, such as distribution of the wind load, yet it still must provide enclosure. The two systems remain distinct, and the envelope relies on the structure for support.

This level of integration can simplify construction on certain large-scale buildings. The structure can be erected first and the envelope connected later. Each system can be designed independently, but the implications of connection must be considered.

This is one of the most commonly used levels of integration. It makes minor demands on each system and responds to the need to build the structure first.

Examples: The most common situation occurs when exterior panels are attached to a structural frame. The envelope may include glass, masonry, building panels, and other skin materials and can be connected to steel, masonry, concrete, or wood structural systems. There are several examples in this book; for details, refer to the following ball diagrams.

Access Floor and Curtain Wall, p. 348.
Flying Form, p. 350.
Flat Plate, p. 351.
Staggered Truss, p. 353.
Steel Frame and Brick Veneer, p. 356.
Herman Miller, p. 366.
Walter Reed, p. 368.
Pike and Virginia, p. 375.
Atlanta Airport, p. 376.
Submarine Training Facility, p. 377.

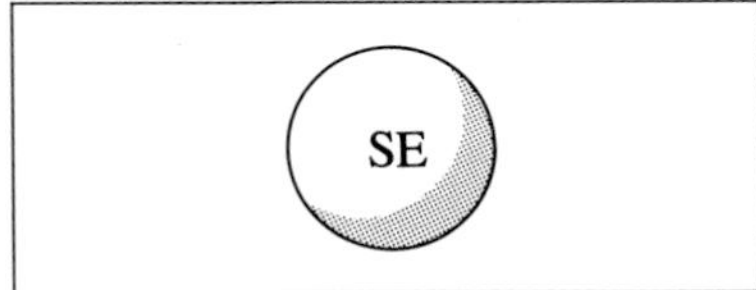

Structure + Envelope: Unified

Description: Structure and envelope share one material and are indistinguishable at this level. The systems completely share function and material as well as physical characteristics and spatial requirements and satisfy both structural and enclosure requirements. Using one material to accomplish two tasks results in conservation of material.

A result may be reduced flexibility for each system. Some structural materials do not perform as well as envelopes and need coatings or other protection. For envelope materials to function as support, such structural details as thickness, reinforcement, and connections to other structural members must be considered.

Examples: Masonry and concrete bearing walls and shell and tensile structures are examples. Ball diagrams depicting these situations are listed below.

Precast Frame, p. 352.
Tilt-up Wall, p. 354.
Tension Fabric, p. 362.

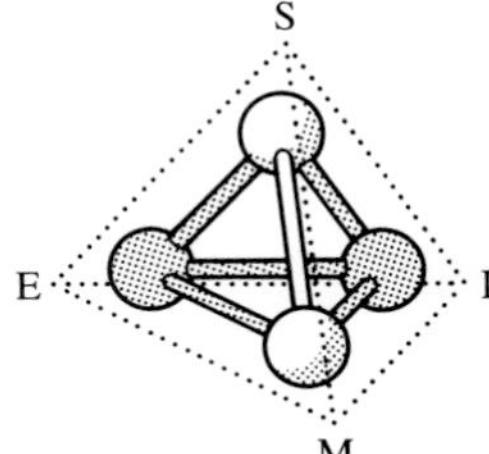

STRUCTURE + MECHANICAL

Structural and mechanical systems combine equilibrium and the distribution of loads with service and environmental control. The problem involved in integrating these two systems is one of accommodation, as they often compete with each other to occupy the same or contiguous space. Both systems serve a technical, utilitarian function, yet each does a different job. Their functions do not overlap; they simply coexist.

Structural and mechanical integration can occur when existing structural voids are used to accommodate ducts, pipes, or wires. This occurs in joists and trusses where the mechanical subsystems are threaded through the voids,[14] and in floor slabs where they are recessed or embedded in the slab. Mechanical subsystems can run vertically through columns or simply be suspended from the structure.

14. Wood floor and roof truss, pp. 142–143.

When structure and mechanical are meshed, the gain is usually a more effective use of space. The integration may also yield a particular design expression such as the concealment of mechanical systems. Exposing ducts or structural members is a major visible integration decision.[15]

15. Visible integration, pp. 381–385.

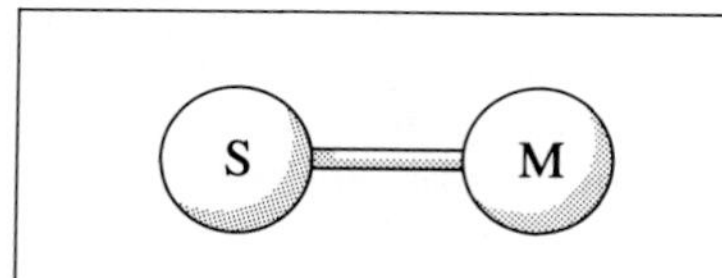

Structure + Mechanical: Connected

Description: Since structure and mechanical systems are made of separate materials and have separate functions, they do not easily achieve unification. Instead, the structure provides support for the mechanical delivery subsystems, which are connected to the structure by hangers, straps, or collars. Without interpenetration, this level of integration makes few demands on the physical structure. The systems may share characteristics but do not share materials or spatial requirements. The connections between structure and mechanical are simple to make and allow for ease of movement, change, and repair. The mechanical system needs to be dimensionally coordinated with the structural system.

Examples: There are several situations shown in this book. Refer to the following ball diagrams for details.

Access Floor and Curtain Wall, p. 348.
Post-Tensioned Concrete, p. 349.
Flying Form, p. 350.
Flat Plate, p. 351.
Tilt-up Wall, p. 354.
Lightweight Mobile Modular Buildings, p. 359.
Metal Building Systems, p. 361.
Occidental Chemical, p. 371.
National Permanent, p. 374.
Atlanta Airport, p. 376.

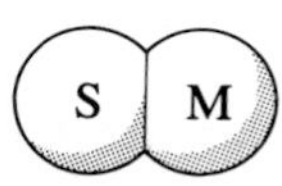

Structure + Mechanical: Meshed

Description: At this level, the structural and mechanical systems maintain their own functions but share the same space. The mechanical subsystems are threaded through, embedded in, or recessed into the structure. The materials and physical characteristics of structure and mechanical may overlap. The meshing of the systems allows the two systems to occupy less space. Recessed mechanical subsystems can be concealed.

Coordination between the two systems can be a major problem. In meshing with one another, the systems lose flexibility and can be more difficult to move, repair, or maintain. Mechanical subsystems may require extra support from the structural system.

Examples: A trench duct and an electrified cellular floor are examples of mechanical subsystems embedded in the structure. Other examples are pipes and ducts threaded through bar joists, castellated beams, or stub girders. Details are given in the following ball diagrams.

Bearing Wall and Bar-Joist Roof, p. 355.
Steel Frame and Brick Veneer, p. 356.
Wood Floor and Roof Truss, p. 357.
Space Frames, p. 360.
Herman Miller, p. 366.
Walter Reed, p. 368.
Stockton State College, p. 369.
Georgia Power, p. 373.
Moscone Center, p. 378.

STRUCTURE + INTERIOR

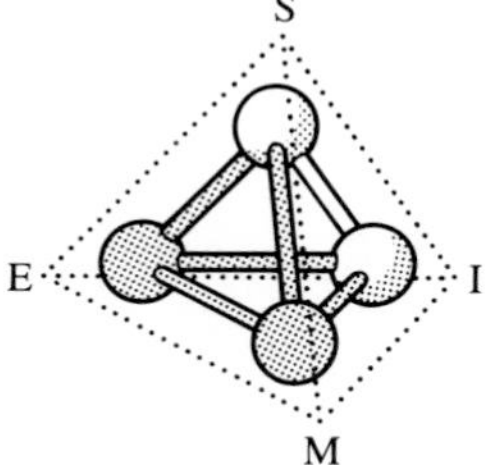

Structure and interior combine physical equilibrium with the support of the activities taking place in the building. Each system is a strong determinant in the design of the building, and therefore each has a constraining effect on the other. Certain human activities demand a corresponding load-bearing capacity of the structure. Others may suggest a particular physical form that can have accompanying structural constraints. An assembly building, for example, requires appropriate sight lines and sound transmission characteristics. The structure usually accommodates this requirement through an increase in span. The structure can also determine the limits of activity that may take place in the building, particularly when the existing structure constrains activities and functions during renovation.

The forces generated by the interior are resolved architecturally by walls, ceilings, floors, equipment, and furnishings integrated with such structural components as bearing walls, structural slabs, structural frames, shells, domes, and tension structures.

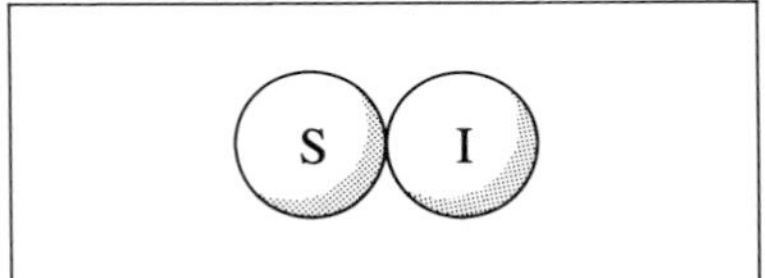

Structure + Interior: Touching

Description: At this level of integration, the interior system simply rests on the structure and is held in place by gravity. The structure is usually the floor slab, and the interior consists of equipment, furnishings, or finishes. The interior subsystems are dependent upon the load-bearing capacity of the structure and provide valuable flexibility for maintenance, growth, and change. Problems can arise, however, in connection with relocating mechanical services that eventually affect the structure.

Examples: Moveable panels that rest on the structural slab, open office equipment, furnishings, and carpeting are examples of this relationship between structure and interior. Several ball diagrams include these situations.

Occidental Chemical, p. 371.
Georgia Power, p. 373.
Illinois Regional Library, p. 378.

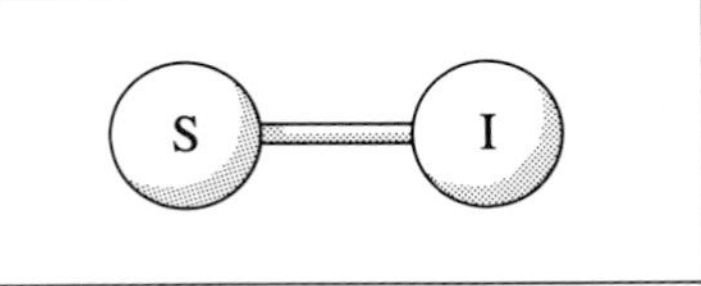

Structure + Interior: Connected

Description: The interior subsystems are connected to the structure by screws, bolts, nails, hangers, or permanent adhesives, with the structure providing support. The interior can depend on the structural properties and the configuration of the structural system. Consequently, the interior is flexible and can adapt to the structural system. The subsystems maintain their own functions, materials, and spatial requirements while sharing physical characteristics. The connections between the systems offer ease of assembly and stability. At the same time, the attachments simplify disassembly and renovation.

Examples: Examples include some types of floor covering such as glued-down tiles, furred walls, and ceilings. Refer to the following ball diagrams for details.

Staggered Truss, p. 353.
Walter Reed, p. 368.
Stockton State College, p. 369.
Vocational Technical Educational Facility, p. 370.

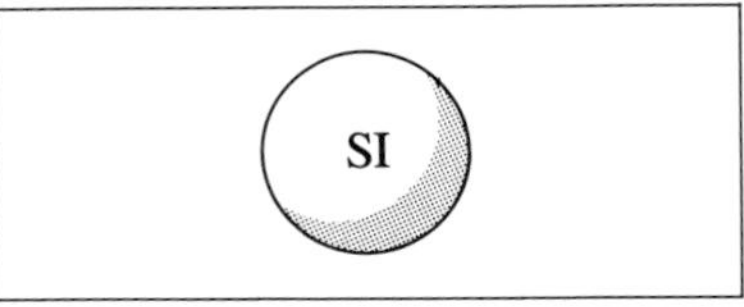

Structure + Interior: Unified

Description: The structure and interior share function, material, physical characteristics, and spatial requirements. At this level, one element must provide both structural support and support for human activities. One surface of the structural system becomes the interior, and the structural system can be expressed architecturally as the interior.

Although material efficiency is usually an attribute, the interior loses its flexibility. In some cases, the formal characteristics or acoustical properties[16] of the interior finish provided by the structure can hinder the intended activities in the building.

16. Acoustical performance, p. 254.

Examples: Concrete or unit masonry bearing walls are typical examples, as are shell and tensile structures. Details are given in the following ball diagrams.

Precast Frame, p. 352.
Post and Beam, p. 358.
Space Frames, p. 360.
Kimbell Museum, p. 364.
O'Connell Center, p. 365.
Herman Miller, p. 366.
Museum of Science and Industry, p. 367.
Pike and Virginia, p. 375.
Moscone Center, p. 378.
Trust Pharmacy, p. 379.

ENVELOPE + MECHANICAL

Envelope and mechanical combine environmental protection and the enclosure with control of natural forces and delivery of environmental comfort. Envelope and mechanical are complementary systems in that the envelope provides physical protection from external forces while the mechanical completes the task with service for the internal demands. The envelope is a barrier, a filter, and a container keeping the outside out and the inside in, or bringing the outside in and letting the inside out.

The need for exterior access to air, water, and power means that the envelope is usually penetrated by the mechanical system. Integration takes place when mechanical subsystems such as wires, pipes, or a through-wall HVAC unit pass through the envelope. Mechanical subsystems such as perimeter HVAC or electrical supply may also run along the side of the envelope.

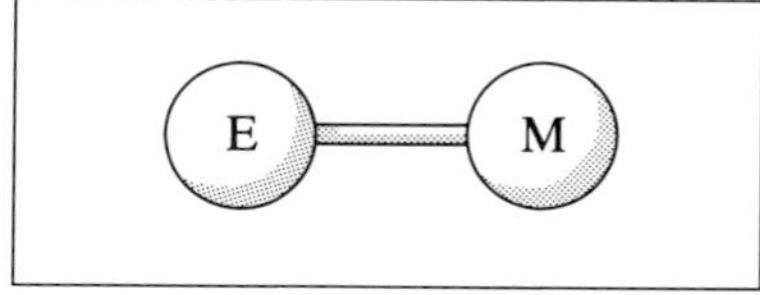

Envelope + Mechanical: Connected

Description: The envelope and mechanical systems are connected by bolts, ties, clips, or seals. The functions of both the envelope and mechanical systems at this level would not overlap, nor would their materials or spatial requirements. Both mechanical and envelope systems depend on the structural system for support. If the mechanical system is exposed to the weather, it is normally fitted with an enclosure that can be removed to allow maintenance or replacement.

Examples: Rooftop HVAC units and heat pumps are exposed to the weather, and their mechanical parts are usually protected by an envelope that comes with the machinery. The entire unit penetrates the roofing membrane and is sealed; the seal is a non-structural connection. Ball diagram examples depicting these conditions are listed below.

Flat Plate, p. 351.
Bearing Wall and Bar-Joist Roof, p. 355.
Metal Building Systems, p. 361.
Equitable Life, p. 372.

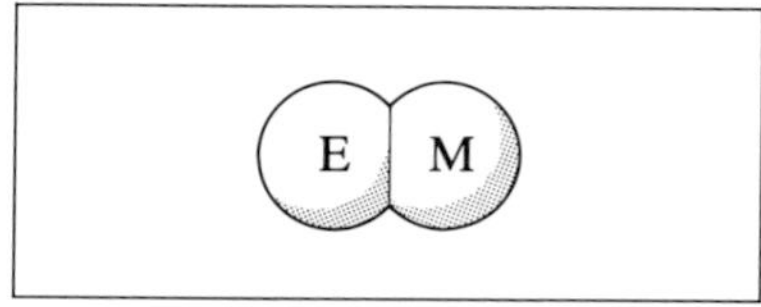

Envelope + Mechanical: Meshed

Description: The mechanical subsystems fit into the envelope. Although the systems share spatial requirements, each is responsible for its own function and there is no sharing of materials. The envelope must be modified to accommodate exterior access for the mechanical system, typically for air intake or exhaust. Because the envelope must

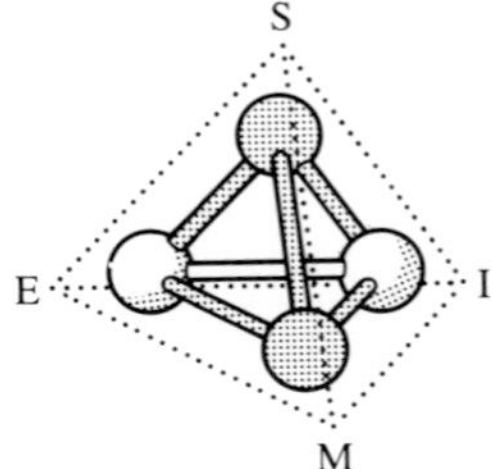

be penetrated and the penetrations sealed, maintenance can be a continual problem.

ENVELOPE + INTERIOR

The combination of envelope and interior involves the integration of protection with the support of human activity; envelope and interior combine to moderate the effects of external natural forces and enhance the activities in the building. The point where they come in contact is where the envelope must directly accommodate the functions of the interior. Complex levels of integration take place as the envelope is modified for light, ventilation, or human access. The envelope must control the natural forces of climate. The interior must control temperature, illumination, access and movement, as well as furnishings and equipment. The physical integration of these systems combines exterior walls with interior walls, and openings for activities of the interior with openings in the walls or roof of the envelope.

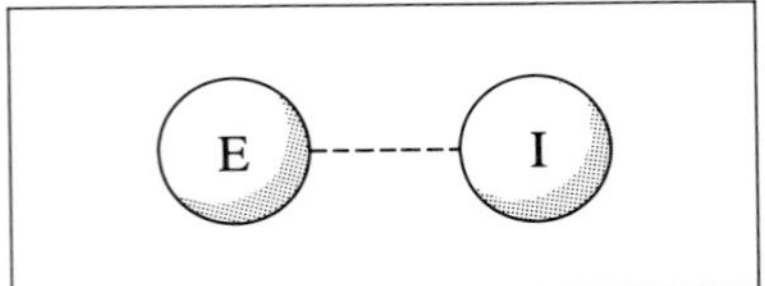

Envelope + Interior: Remote

Description: The interior subsystems are separate from the envelope. Functions, materials, and the space each system occupies are also separate.

Examples: An example is a situation where the exterior wall is physically separate from interior finishes and furnishings. Ceilings, floors, furniture, and equipment are independent from and may have little direct relationship to the envelope. Interior and envelope systems are often dimensionally related. Ball diagrams depicting this situation are as follows.

Access Floor and Curtain Wall, p. 348.
Post-Tensioned Concrete, p. 349.
Flying Form, p. 350.
Flat Plate, p. 351.
Bearing Wall and Bar-Joist Roof, p. 355.
Steel Frame and Brick Veneer, p. 356.
Wood Floor and Roof Truss, p. 357.
Post and Beam, p. 358.
Lightweight Mobile Modular Buildings, p. 359.
Moscone Center, p. 378
John Nutting Apartments, p. 380.

Note that the dashed lines designating the remote level have been eliminated in the complex ball diagrams.

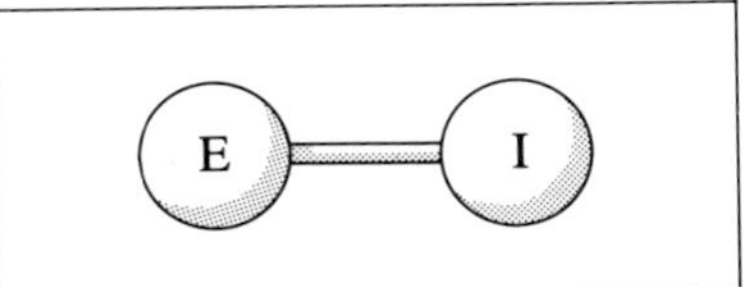

Envelope + Interior: Connected

Description: The envelope and interior are connected to each other by bolts, ties, clips, or permanent adhesives. The functions of each system are separate, and there is no overlap of materials or of spatial requirements. Physical characteristics are shared. This level of integration combines an interior finish with exterior enclosure. Interior and envelope are easily connected, and the assembly may also occupy less space.

Examples: Examples include wall assemblies such as wood or metal stud clad with siding and drywall or with masonry and drywall. Refer to the following diagrams for details.

Metal Building Systems, p. 361.
Walter Reed, p. 368.
Submarine Training Facility, p. 377.
Aid Association for Lutherans, p. 379.

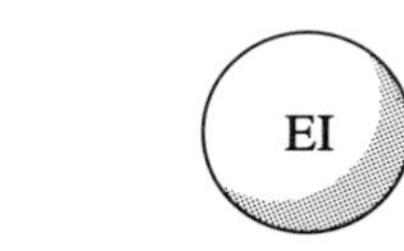

Envelope + Interior: Unified

Description: The envelope and interior systems share the same materials, functions, and space. One assembly or one material provides both enclosure and activity support. Consequently, the materials used at this level are characterized primarily either by their translucency or opacity. If there is a problem with the material, both systems have a problem.

Examples: Examples are doors, windows, and glazing[17] that are parts of ceilings, roofs, and walls and provide access, circulation, ventilation, light, and views. Other examples include non-structural masonry or concrete walls. All buildings studied in this book contain examples of unification of envelope and interior.

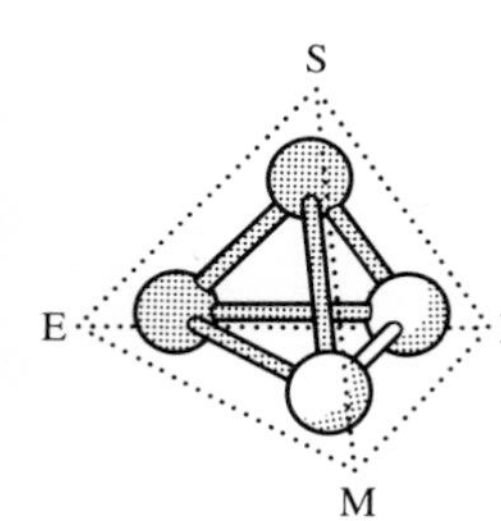

MECHANICAL + INTERIOR

The mechanical system typically serves the interior. It must provide service to support the activities of the interior and must be responsive to changes in those activities. The interior usually makes accommodations for the service of the mechanical system.

The mechanical subsystems provide temperature control, electrical power, water, security, and conveyance, all of which serve the thermal comfort,[18] illumination, activity, and movement needs of the interior. Integration occurs as pipes, ducts, wires, or, in the case of conveyances, pieces of machinery are connected to the walls, ceilings, or floors of the interior. The pipes, wires, or ducts connect to interior subsystems such as lights, outlets, faucets, drains, grilles, or security devices. The primary benefits of integration are operational efficiencies that conserve time.[19]

17. Insulating glass, pp. 209–211.

18. Thermal performance, pp. 250–251.

19. Conservation of time, pp. 236–237.

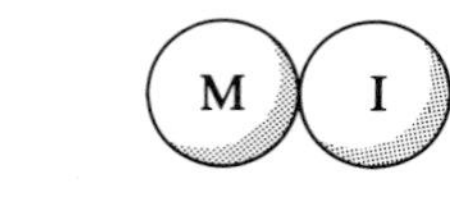

Mechanical + Interior: Touching

Description: In this situation, the interior system rests on the mechanical. This integration occurs in the horizontal plane, typically at the floor. The mechanical and interior are held in place by gravity. The spatial requirements of the two systems overlap, but there is no sharing of materials or functions at this level. The main considerations are the physical characteristics of the materials, since they are in contact with one another. Both systems need to be flat where they meet.

Examples: Flat cable as used under carpeting in office buildings is an example of this form of integration. For greater detail, the ball diagram for Flat Conductor Cable can be found on p. 343. The diagram for Flying Form on p. 350 is also useful as it includes flat cable.

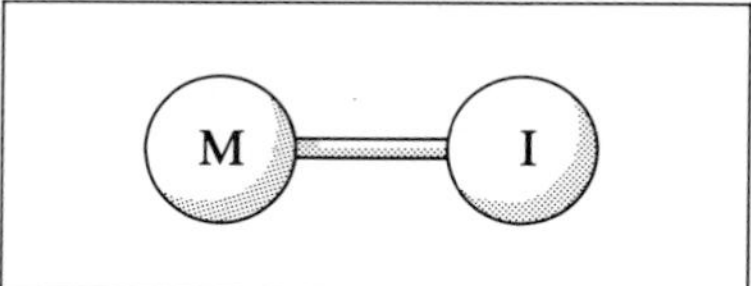

Mechanical + Interior: Connected

Description: The mechanical and interior systems are connected to each other by bolts, screws, ties, clips, or permanent adhesives. The functions of the two systems do not overlap, and they share no common materials or spatial requirements. Both the mechanical system and the interior system depend on the structure for support. A connected relationship between mechanical and interior does not commonly occur in isolation. If the mechanical system is concealed by the interior, it usually has a meshed relationship with it even though it might also be connected. If the mechanical system is visible, it is immediately unified with the interior (e.g., in a light fixture). The relationship of the M + I unification to the interior system (e.g., of the ceiling) is usually connected. Both the M and the I in the unification are connected to the interior system.

Examples: Light fixtures, sprinkler heads, and audio systems are all commonly connected as described above. Numerous examples of these conditions may be found in both the case studies and the generic examples.

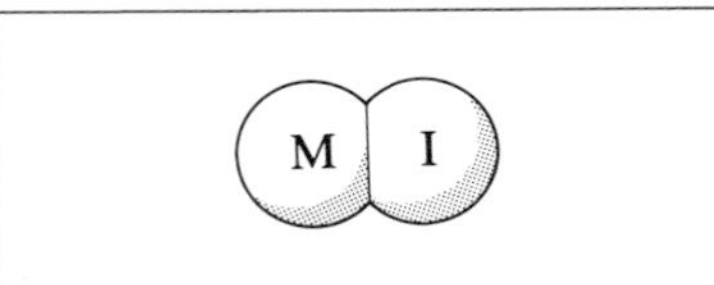

Mechanical + Interior: Meshed

Description: The mechanical system shares the same space with the interior system. The systems rarely share materials or functions, but they do share spatial requirements and have related physical characteristics. Usually the interior subsystems, particularly walls, floors, and ceiling, will make provisions for the meshing of the mechanical subsystems. These provisions include dimensional coordination, manufacturing coordination, and material compatibility. The systems can remain functionally separate, but integrate easily to perform their closely related tasks of providing service and comfort. The systems must be coordinated, and access must be provided for maintaining the mechanical equipment.

Examples: Examples include integrated ceilings, air-handling luminaires, supply and return grilles, vents and electrical outlets. There are numerous ball diagrams illustrating the meshed relationship of mechanical and interior.

Access Floor and Curtain Wall, p. 348.
Post-Tensioned Concrete, p. 349.
Flying Form, p. 350.
Flat Plate, p. 351.
Tilt-up Wall, p. 354.
Bearing Wall and Bar-Joist Roof, p. 355.
Steel Frame and Brick Veneer, p. 356.
Wood Floor and Roof Truss, p. 357.
Metal Building Systems, p. 361.
Kimbell Museum, p. 364.
Stockton State College, p. 369.
Equitable Life, p. 372.
National Permanent, p. 374.

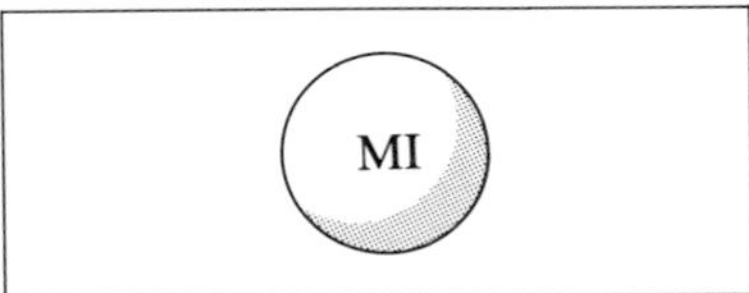

Mechanical + Interior: Unified

Description: The mechanical and interior are unified to the point where they share function, material, spatial requirements, and physical characteristics. One material, assembly, or product provides both service and comfort. Many parts of the interior system, particularly furnishings and equipment, require the mechanical to provide power, water, or service for lighting security, fire safety, or plumbing. The mechanical subsystems can be concealed in, or expressed as, an interior system. There is also an efficient use of material and space, but if one system fails, the other fails.

Examples: Interior ducts, lights, plumbing fixtures, security equipment, and fire safety equipment are examples of this form of integration. Other examples are radiant heat panels and passive solar spaces. Details may be found in the following diagrams.

Tilt-up Wall, p. 354.
Pike and Virginia, p. 375.
Trust Pharmacy, p. 379.
John Nutting Apartments, p. 380.

Diagraming Integration of Any Building Design

The purpose of an integration diagram is to allow the designer to investigate and record the level of connection between any two building components or subsystems. The act of recording opens up the opportunity to investigate other levels of integration to conserve space, materials, or time more efficiently.

The task requires definition of each building component as part of one of the four major systems (structure, envelope, mechanical, or interior) and definition of the relationship between the systems as remote, touching, connected, meshed, or unified. Through analysis of the case studies in Chapter 3 and the generic examples in Chapter 4, we have found that the components and subsystems common to most buildings that should be analyzed for integration potential are the ones listed below.

Typical Building Section Diagram

Roof assembly:

- roof structure and structural deck (S)
- roofing (E)
- ceiling (I)
- lighting (MI)

Wall assembly:

- wall structure (the support plus any lateral bracing, shear panels, or sheathing) (S)
- exterior wall covering (E)
- windows and doors (EI)
- interior wall covering (I)

Interior floor assembly

- interior floor structure and floor deck (S)
- floor covering (I)
- furniture and interior partitions (I)
- ceiling below (I)
- lighting below (MI)

On-grade floor assembly:

- floor structure (S)
- floor covering (I)
- membrane, vapor barrier (E)
- mechanical subsystems (M) (electricity, piping, and wiring), wherever they occur

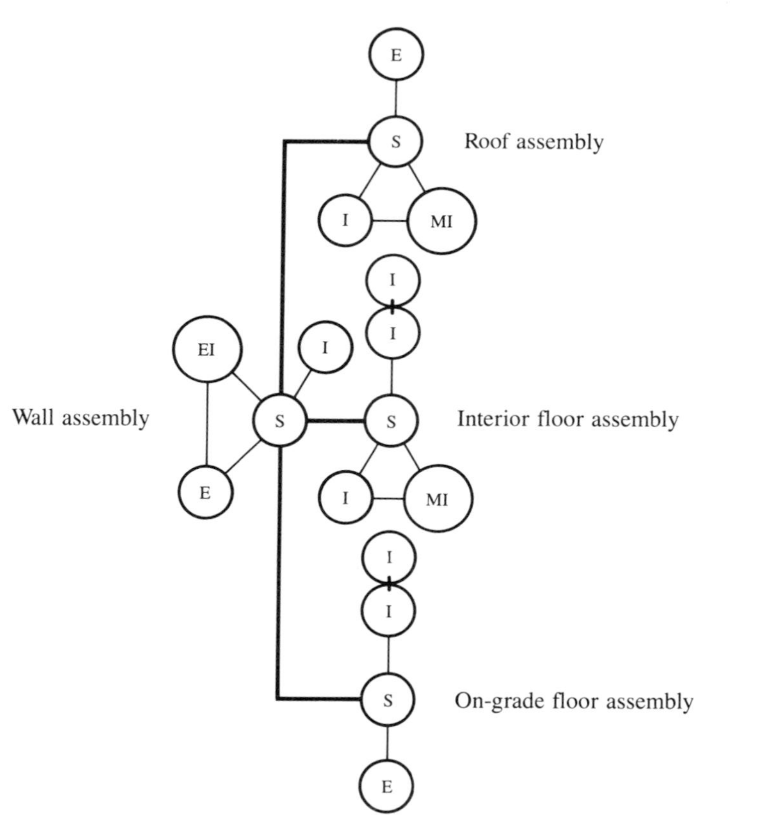

For the sake of simplicity, the components are grouped around four structural subsystems: roof, wall, interior floor, and grade floor. These components may be arranged into the diagram opposite.

To create a similar diagram mapping the integration of any given building, it is useful to follow this procedure:

A. Diagram the structural subsystem connections.
B. Diagram the envelope and interior subsystem connections in terms of roof, wall, interior floor, or subgrade. Particular attention should be focused on unified relationships.
C. Diagram the mechanical subsystem connections wherever they fit in the building. Particular attention should be given to meshed relationships.

Although the process is described step-by-step, it is not necessarily linear. Several iterations may be necessary before a particular diagram can be completed. The following steps represent one method of constructing an integration diagram:

1. **Diagram the structure in four conditions:** roof, wall, interior floor (if more than one story), and grade floor. At what level are the following connections made?

   roof structure to wall structure

   wall structure to interior floor structure

   wall structure to foundation

The example above shows all of the structural components connected. Special cases of more highly integrated structure to structure combinations are unified. An example is a poured concrete frame.

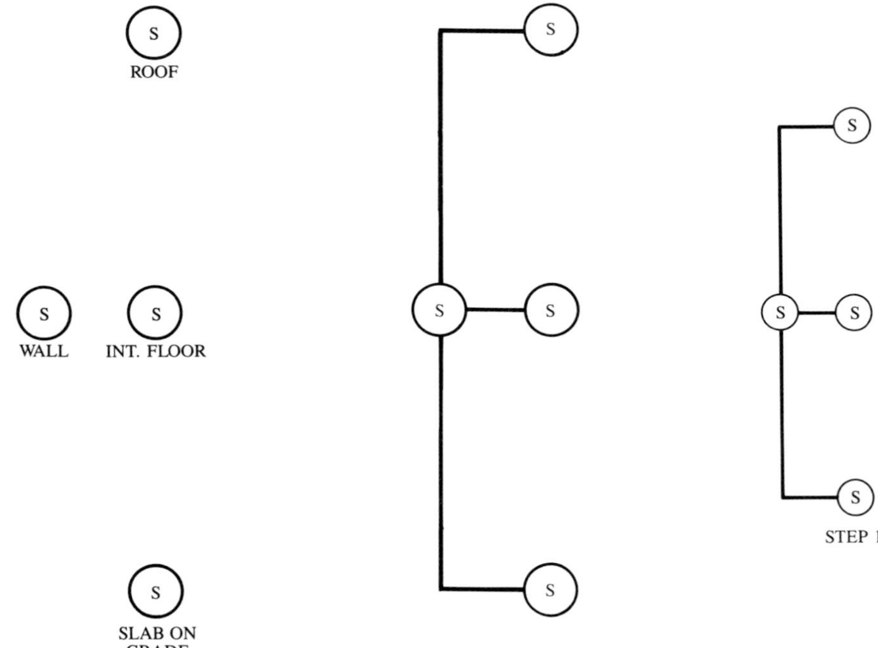

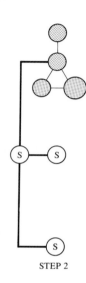

STEP 2

2. **Diagram the roof assembly around the structure.** Consider the relationship of the following connections:
   a. roof envelope to structure
   b. ceiling to structure
   c. lighting to structure
   d. ceiling to lighting

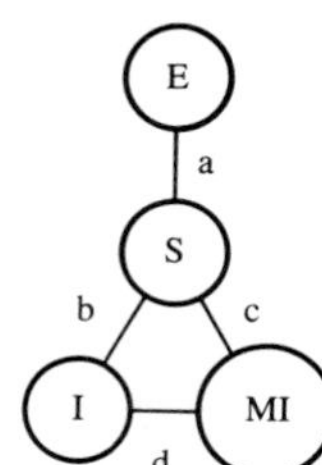

Possible ways to unify roof elements are:

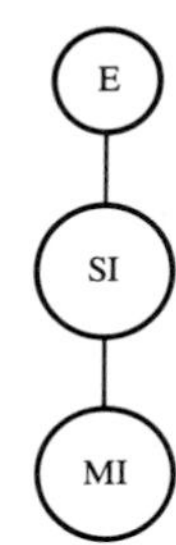

Expose structure to the interior (S + I = u).

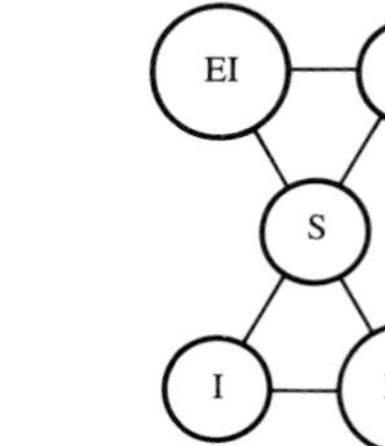

Add skylights or clerestories (E + I = u).

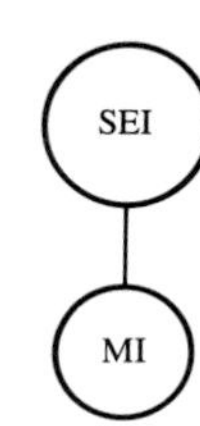

Use fabric structures (S + E + I = u).

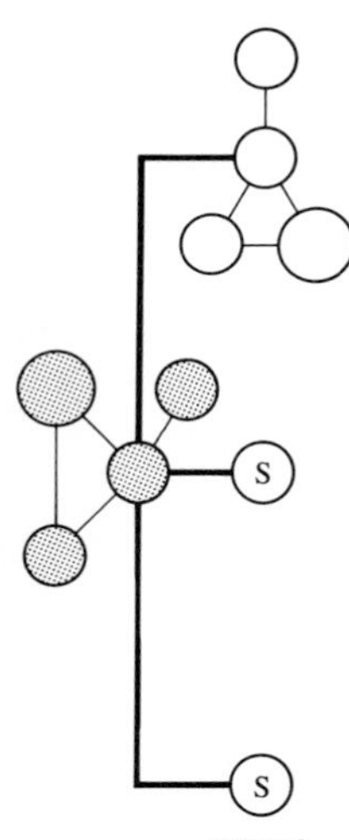

STEP 3

3. **Diagram the wall assembly around the structure.** Consider the following connections:
   e. envelope to wall structure
   f. windows to wall structure
   g. interior wall covering to wall structure
   h. envelope to windows

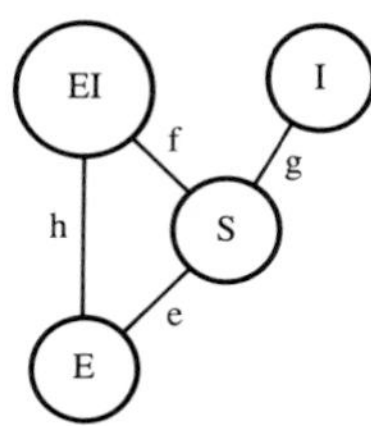

The wall assembly can be unified in the following ways:

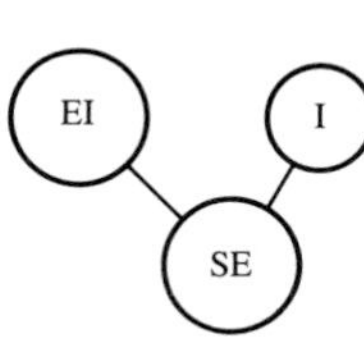

Have the structure serve as envelope (S + E = u).

Expose the structure to the interior (S + I = u).

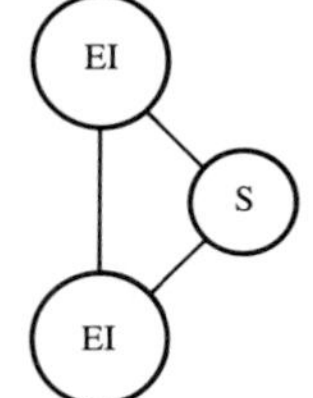

Unify the envelope and interior functions (e.g., lightweight metal insulating panels) (E + I = u).

Expose the bearing wall to interior and exterior (S + E + I = u).

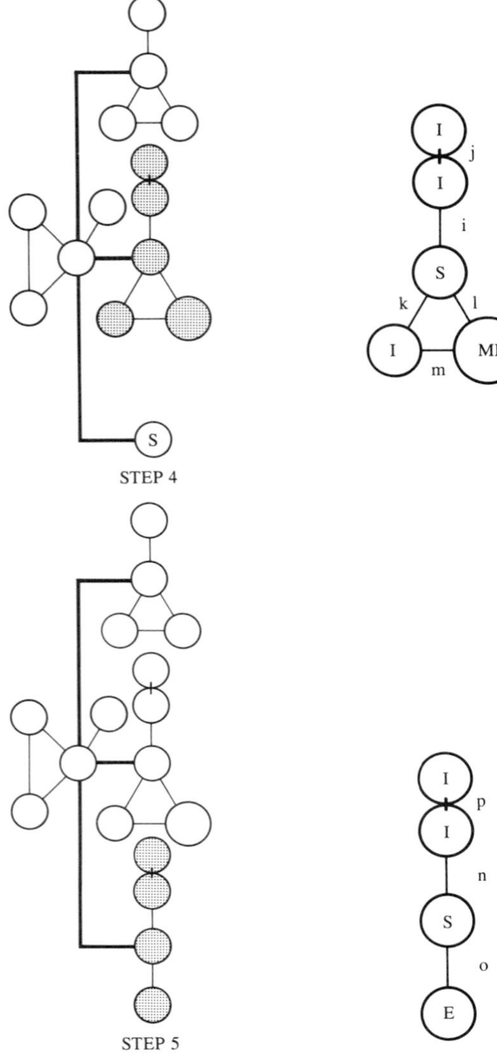

4. **Diagram the interior floor assembly around the structure.** Consider the following connections:
   i. floor covering to floor structure
   j. furniture to floor covering
   k. ceiling to floor structure
   l. lighting to floor structure
   m. ceiling to lighting

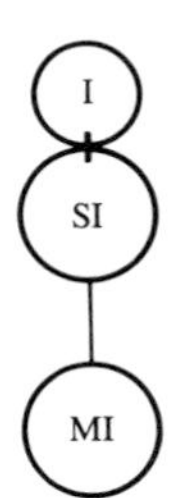

There is little opportunity for unification in this assembly. Structure can be exposed as a floor slab or as ceiling below: (S + I = u)

5. **Diagram the on-grade floor assembly around the structure.** Consider the following connections:
   n. floor covering to slab on grade
   o. envelope to slab on grade
   p. furniture to floor covering

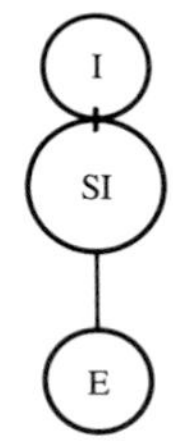

The opportunities for integration include exposing the slab on grade to the interior (S + I = u).

6. **Consider placement of the mechanical subsystems.** With which structural assembly are they integrated? Mechanical subsystems introduce the meshed level of integration and the following combinations:

   S + M = m

   E + M = m

   I + M = m

Mechanical subsystems can also be unified with interior subsystems, which introduces a new level:

M + I = u

At each of the four structural conditions (roof, wall, interior floor, and grade level slab), consider the level of attachment of the mechanical system. Some examples of meshed and unified mechanical subsystems include:

Roof level:

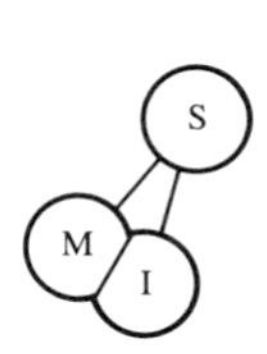

Ducts to suspended ceilings (M + I = m)

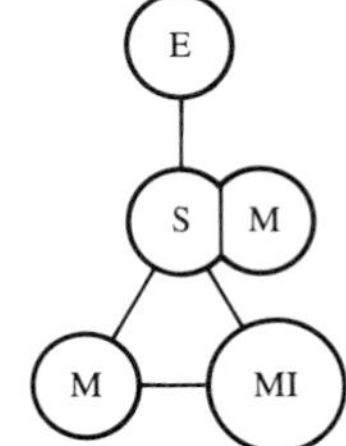

Batt insulation to wood trusses or steel frame (S + M = m)

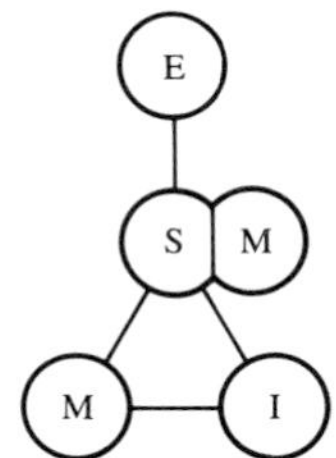

Ducts to wood trusses or steel frame (S + M = m)

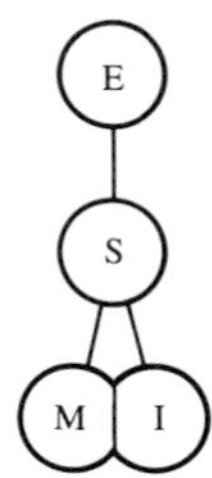

Integrated ceilings (M + I = m)

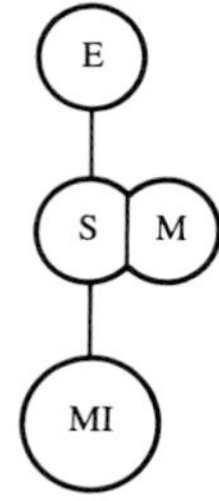

Batt insulation to wood frame, steel frame (S + M = m)

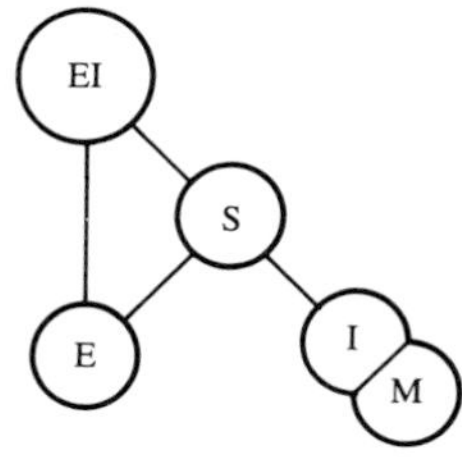

Batt insulation to drywall and metal stud (M + I = m)

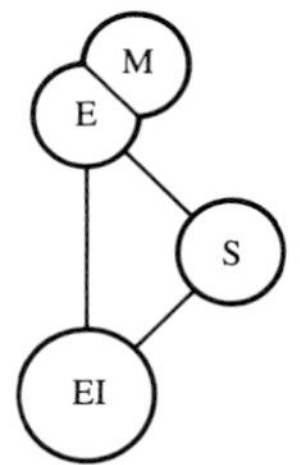

Batt insulation to panels (E + M = m)

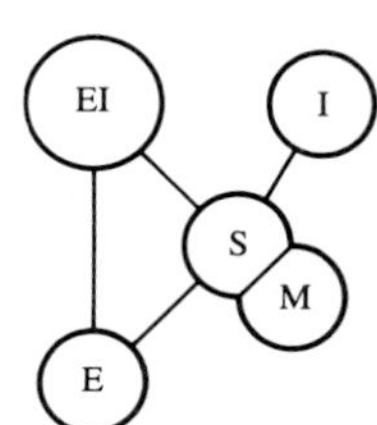

Pipes to wall chase (M + I = m)

Interior floor level:

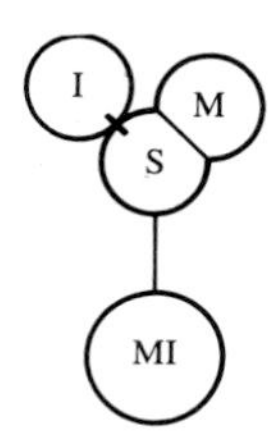

floor decking to wiring (S + M = m) or batt insulation to floor joists (S + M = m)

Slab on grade:

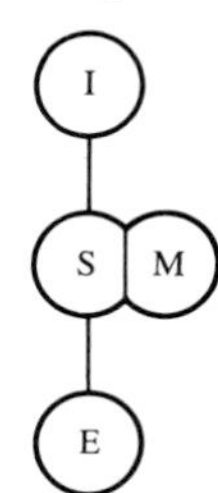

Perimeter ducts to foundation (S + M = m)

NOTE: Exposed light fixtures and exposed ducts are examples of M + I = u

Rules

Creating the diagrams according to the BSIH Matrix requires adherence to the following rules:

A. If a structural or mechanical subsystem is exposed to the interior, the level of integration of that system with the interior is considered unified.

B. Lighting and components such as radiant heat panels[20] are considered to incorporate mechanical and interior functions, and are a (MI) unified component.

C. Glass, doors, skylight infill material, and clerestories are considered (EI) unified components.

D. Ducts and diffusers are considered together as a mechanical (M) subsystem. They are integrated with the ceiling at the meshed level.[21]

E. Rigid insulation is considered part of the envelope system and is connected to other subsystems. Batt, fill, and loose insulation are considered part of the mechanical system. Therefore, they are meshed with other subsystems. It has been found that this distinction adds clarity to ball diagrams.

F. A subsystem penetrating another subsystem, such as a pipe penetrating a wall, represents a connected relationship. A sealant between two such subsystems is connected to both of them.[22]

20. Radiant heat panels, pp. 177–178.

21. Integrated ceilings, pp. 182–184.

22. Silicone sealants, pp. 225–226.

Product Integration: Roof and Ceiling Diagrams

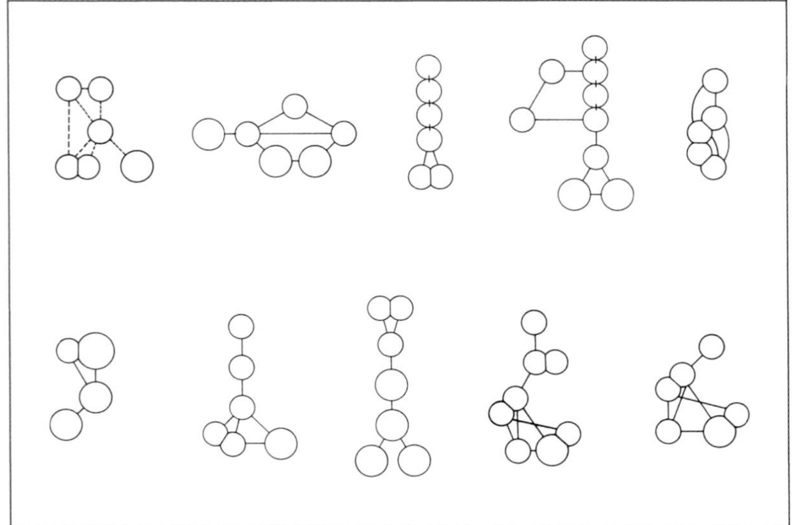

None of the roof conditions represented in this book include the possibility of roof traffic except for maintenance purposes. The main task of those depicted is to protect the occupants of the building from the additional weight or other undesirable consequences of an adverse climate. The principal question has to do with the connections chosen between envelope and structure and interior and structure. The interior connection is one exclusively related to the particular use of the building. A speculative use or one that must accommodate frequent change would most appropriately consider a *connected* level which would easily permit removal. The envelope decision is just the opposite. The owner does not wish to replace the roof no matter what goes on inside the building. The reason that a ballasted system and a *touching* relationship is considered (a seeming contradiction to the permanence suggested) is the overriding advantage of minimal penetration for the avoidance of leaks. The roofing is easily accessible for repair.

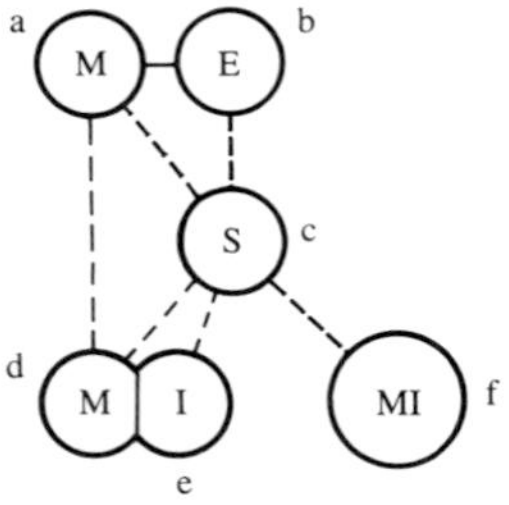

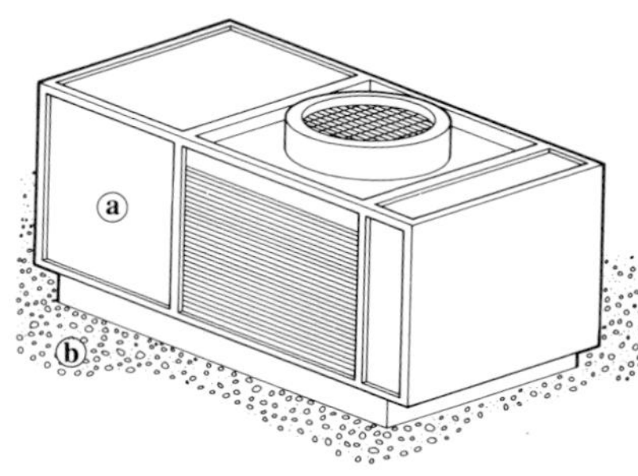

HEAT PUMPS

The integration of a heat pump is similar to that of any packaged mechanical unit found on the roof or the side of a building. Rooftop heat pumps are *connected* to the roofing that they penetrate. They must also be *connected* to the roof deck, and to the roof structure for support. They are *connected* to ducts on the interior of the structure.

Heat pumps are a mechanical system product, and as such can be placed in various locations in the building. They must be adjacent to a fresh air source, so at some point they must penetrate the building envelope. Equipment located outside the building may not have a connection to the structure.

a. *Heat Pump*
b. *Roofing*
c. *Roof structure and deck*
d. *Ducts*
e. *Suspended ceiling*
f. *Lighting*

Note: dashed lines in this example indicate subsystems that are not in view.

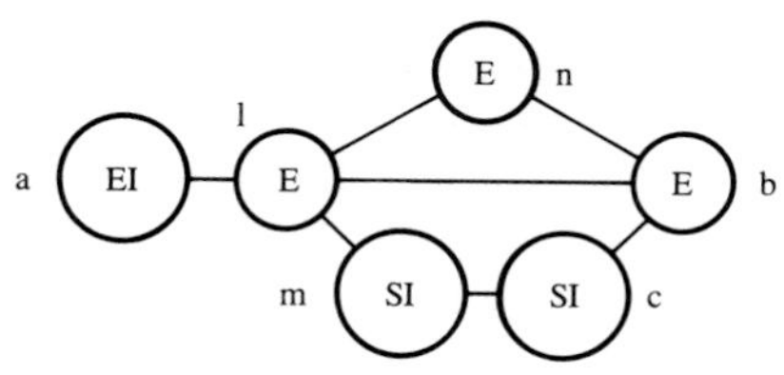

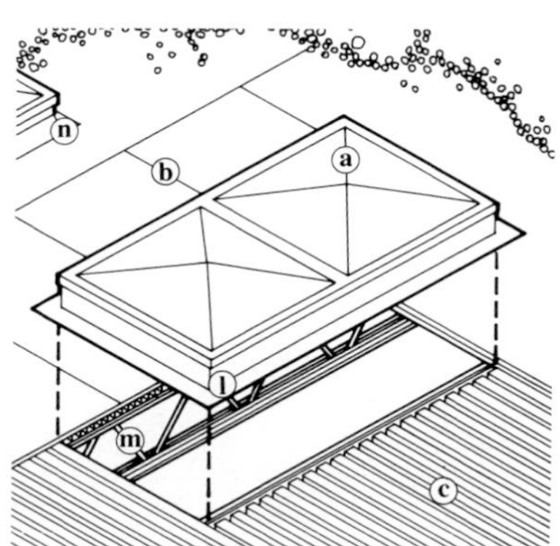

a. *Skylights*
b. *Built-up roofing and rigid insulation*
c. *Steel deck*
l. *Curb*
m. *Open-web steel joists*
n. *Flashing*

PLASTIC-DOMED SKYLIGHTS

Skylights are similar to heat pumps in that they are *connected* to the roofing system; an important point of difference is that they penetrate it, usually with a curb that is part of the roof envelope. They also penetrate the roof deck and must be supported by the roof structure.

Skylights are *unified* envelope and interior products, serving as part of the roof covering as well as a source of light to the interior. Skylights can also be important to the visible integration of a space.

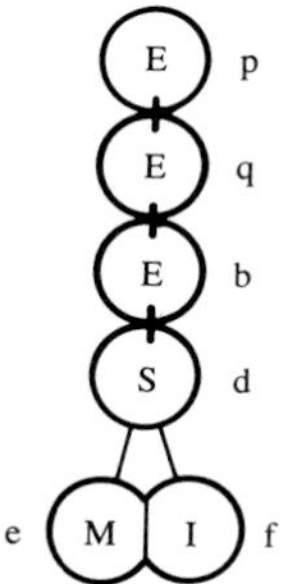

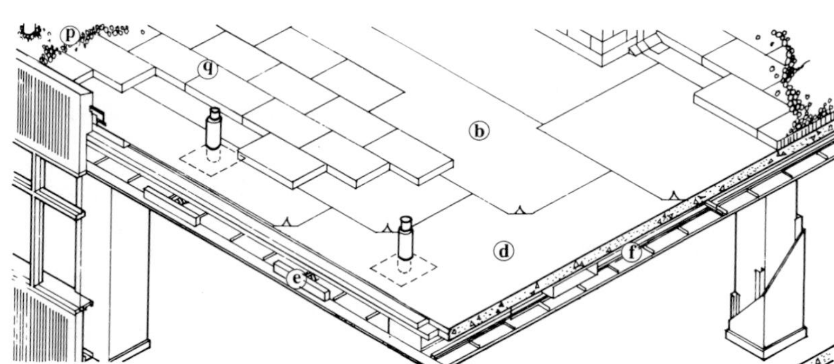

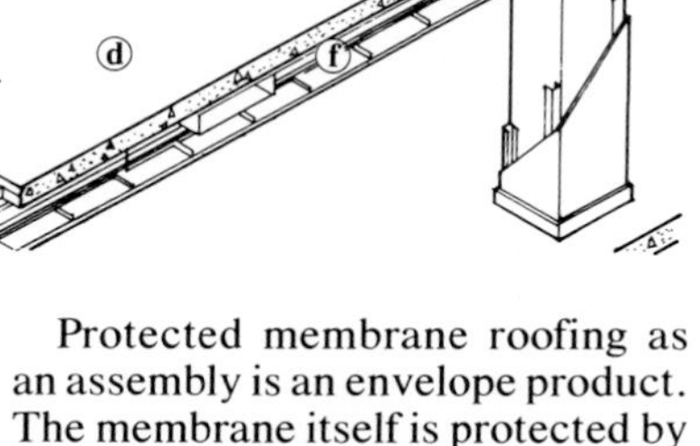

b. *Protected roof membrane*
d. *Cast-in-place concrete flat plate*
e. *Ducts and diffusers*
f. *Suspended acoustical tile ceiling*
p. *Ballast*
q. *Rigid installation*

PROTECTED MEMBRANE ROOFING

Protected membrane roofing can be *connected* to the roof deck or simply *touching* it. In the latter case, additional weight is added to the roof in the form of ballast.

Protected membrane roofing as an assembly is an envelope product. The membrane itself is protected by insulation, which is then covered by pavers or ballast. Each of these layers separately is also considered part of the envelope.

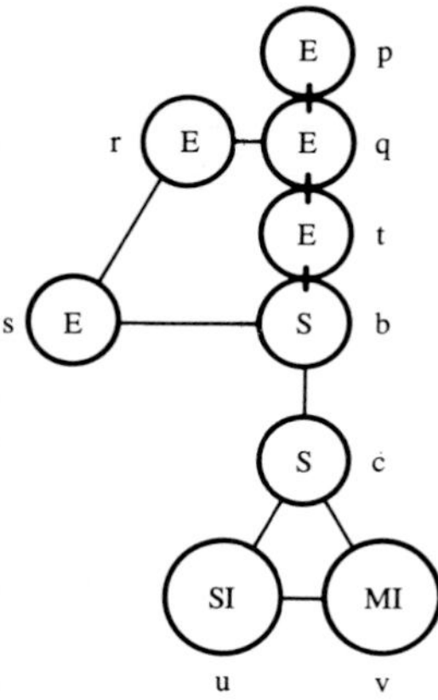

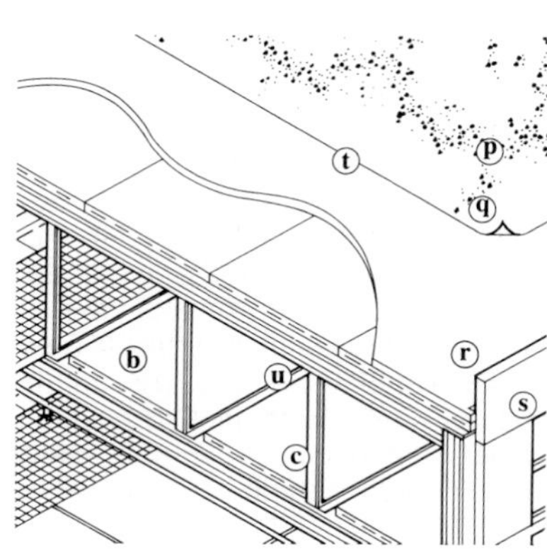

b. *Concrete plank deck*
c. *Steel truss*
p. *Ballast*
q. *EPDM*
r. *Flashing*
s. *Parapet*
t. *Insulation*
u. *Ceiling*
v. *Lighting*

EPDM

EPDM can have either a *connected* or a *touching* relationship with the insulation and roof structure below it. When the relationship is a *touching* one, ballast must be used to secure the membrane. The membrane is *connected* to flashing and to the roof parapet, if one exists.

EPDM, like all roofing, is an envelope product. The single-ply roofing material is consistent with the prefabricated nature of the building shown.

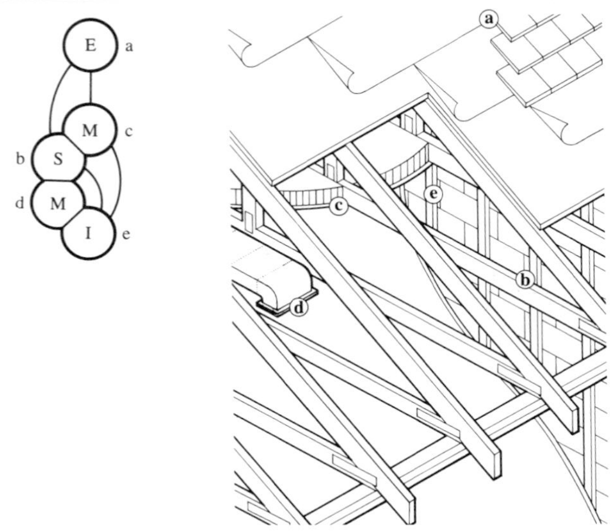

WOOD TRUSSES

Wood trusses are *connected* to the sheathing that serves as a roof deck. They are *meshed* with the batt insulation that runs between them.

Wood trusses are a structural product and serve to support lighting and the ceiling below, as well as the roof deck and envelope. The trusses can also be exposed to the interior below, in which case they will be a *unified* structure and interior product. When exposed, they are important to the visible integration of the space, and encourage exposure of other elements, such as ducts. The structural efficiency of trusses is consistent with the spatial efficiency realized by *meshing* the ducts with them.

a. *Roofing*
- *Shingles*
- *Metal flashing*
- *Roofing felt*

b. *Wood roof truss and plywood sheathing*
c. *Batt insulation*
d. *Ducts and diffusers*
e. *Acoustical tile ceiling*

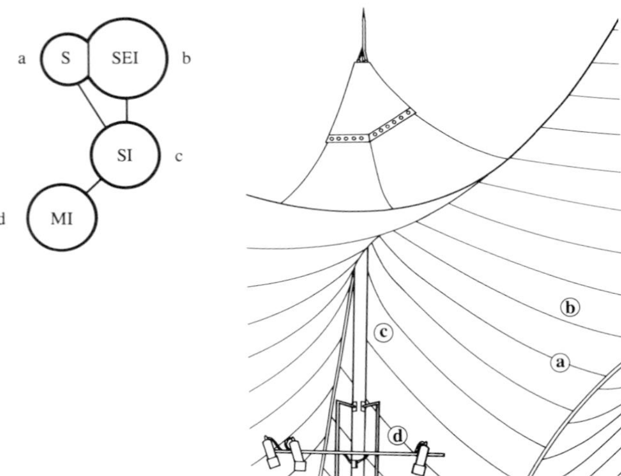

STRUCTURAL FABRIC

Structural fabric is a unique product in that it is a *unified* combination of structural, envelope, and interior systems. This high level of integration may result in low levels of integration elsewhere, such as suspended light fixtures. Structural fabric is *connected* to a secondary structure, such as steel masts, which are exposed to view from the interior.

Structural fabric is often the main expression of visible integration, on the interior as well as the exterior of the building. It allows diffused light into the space and determines the overall form of the building.

a. *Steel cables in fabric sleeves*
b. *Non-combustible fabric membrane*
c. *Steel masts*
d. *Incandescent light fixtures and sound system speakers*

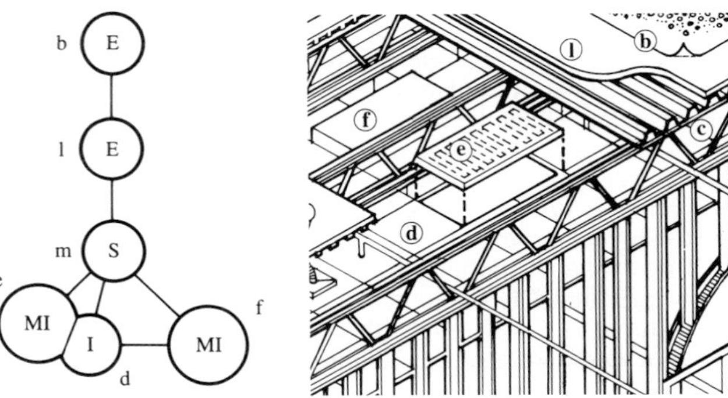

RADIANT HEAT PANELS

Because radiant heat panels perform a mechanical function and are exposed to the interior space, they are represented by a *unified* mechanical and interior combination. This dual-purpose product is the result of conscious integration and responds to both sets of criteria. In this particular example, the radiant panels are dropped into the ceiling grid and *meshed* with the suspended ceiling.

b. *Built-up roof*
c. *Roof deck and structure*
d. *Ceiling*
e. *Radiant heat panels*
f. *Fluorescent lighting*
l. *Rigid insulation*

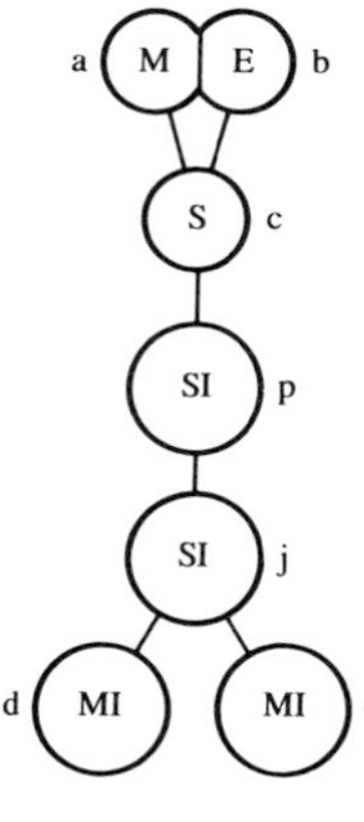

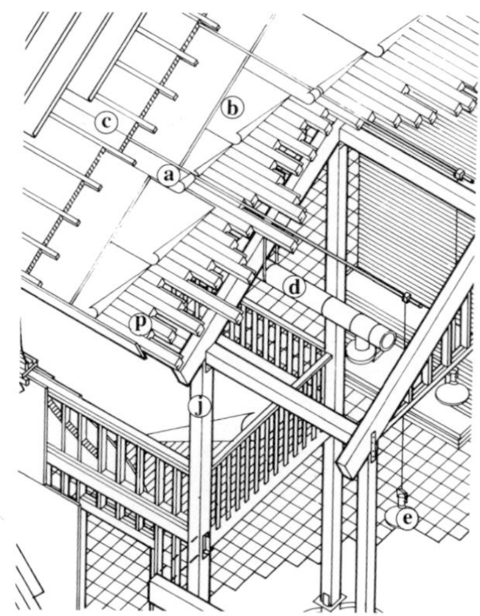

EXPOSED DUCTS

Exposed ducts perform a mechanical function and are exposed to the interior, and are therefore represented by a *unified* mechanical and interior combination. They probably represent the most important single decision with respect to the visible integration of the interior space. Ducts are *connected* to the structure, in this case the exposed wood frame. Exposing the ducts in a building usually involves eliminating a ceiling and exposing the structure and structural deck, which is an important element of visible integration. Exposed ducts are also *meshed* with some other types of structural systems, such as trusses and bar joists.

a. *Electrical conduit*
b. *Roofing*
c. *Plywood sheathing*
d. *Exposed ducts*
e. *Incandescent lighting fixture*
j. *Exposed wood frame*
p. *Exposed wood decking*

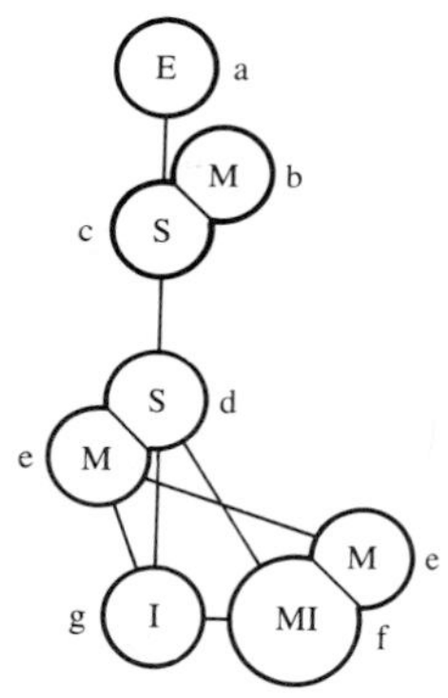

INTEGRATED CEILINGS

Integrated ceilings incorporate many of the components normally supplied by different manufacturers into one "package," and are represented by a *meshed* combination of mechanical and interior, with the same two systems *unified* in the light fixture. Having all the ceiling components provided by a single manufacturer does not fundamentally change the level of integration between them. In this example, air-handling luminaires are *connected* to the ceiling grid. Ducts are *meshed* with the structure (bar joists) and *connected* to the mechanical (return air) portion of the luminaires.

a. *Roofing*
b. *Batt insulation*
c. *Metal roof deck*
d. *Steel bar joists*
e. *Ducts*
f. *Air-handling luminaires*
g. *Lay-in ceiling*
l. *Ceramic tile*
m. *Steel bar joists and metal floor deck*

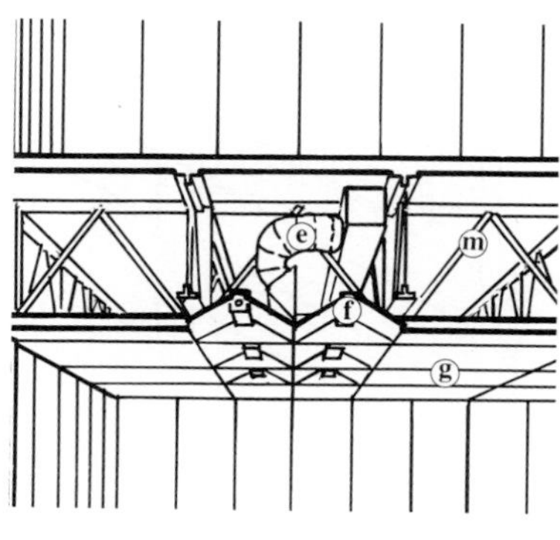

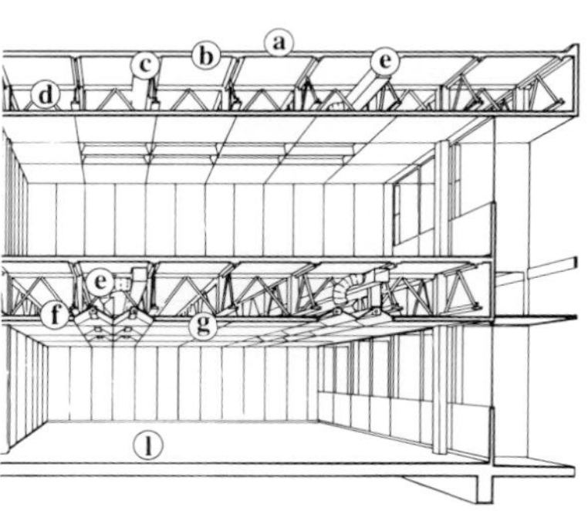

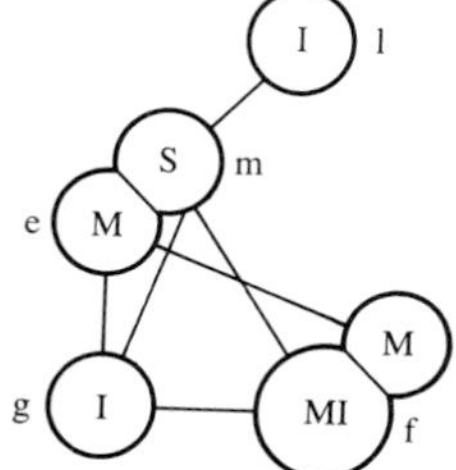

AIR-HANDLING LUMINAIRES

The luminaire itself is a *unified* combination of mechanical and interior and is *connected* to the ductwork. Luminaires are *connected* to the structure, as is the ceiling. Ducts, which are *meshed* with the joists, are *connected* to the air supply/return (mechanical) part of the luminaires. The normally visible ceiling air grille is hidden within the luminaire itself. The level of integration does not differ from that found in an ordinary light fixture, but component relationships are different.

e. *Ducts*
f. *Air-handling luminaires*
g. *Lay-in ceiling*
l. *Ceramic tile*
m. *Steel bar joists and metal floor deck*

Diagrams Between the Ceiling and Floor

The diagrams shown below depict the smaller domain of influence of the various products that follow. Elevators and escalators have an impact on the main structure and circulatory pattern of the entire building, while operable partitions are more likely to affect the choices for a particular floor or large room. Open plan office furniture systems have an influence on the spatial performance of a whole floor, but connection decisions associated with them are quite immediate.

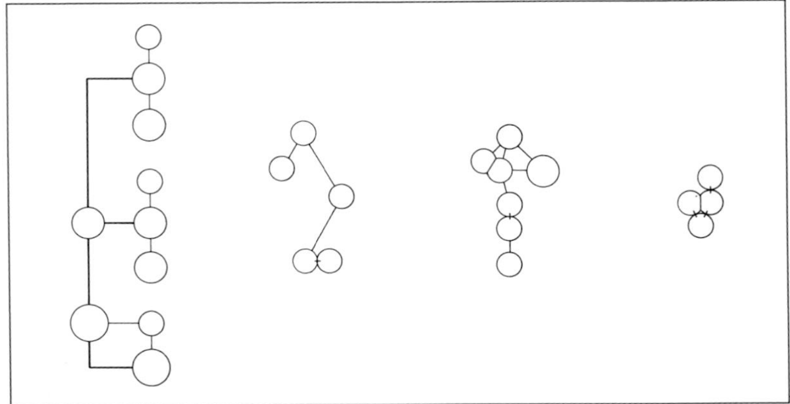

ELEVATORS

Both the elevator car and its hydraulic means of propulsion serve mechanical functions and are *connected* to each other. The elevator car is *connected* to the elevator core, which in this example is constructed of reinforced concrete exposed to the exterior and interior. The car interior relates to the building interior, while the shaft relates mechanically to the rest of the building. In this case, the elevator car is visible from the street; it therefore becomes visibly integrated with the rest of the elevation.

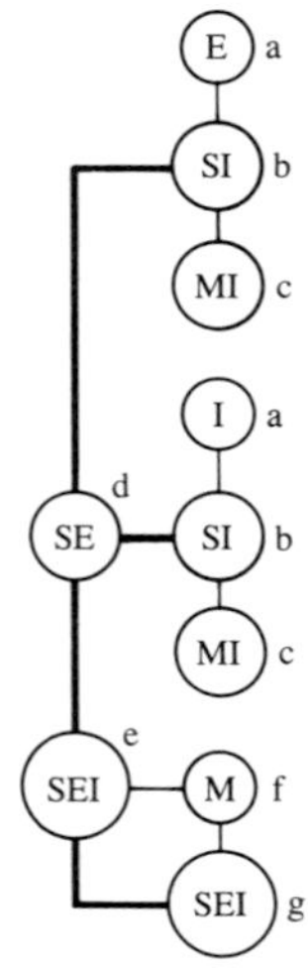

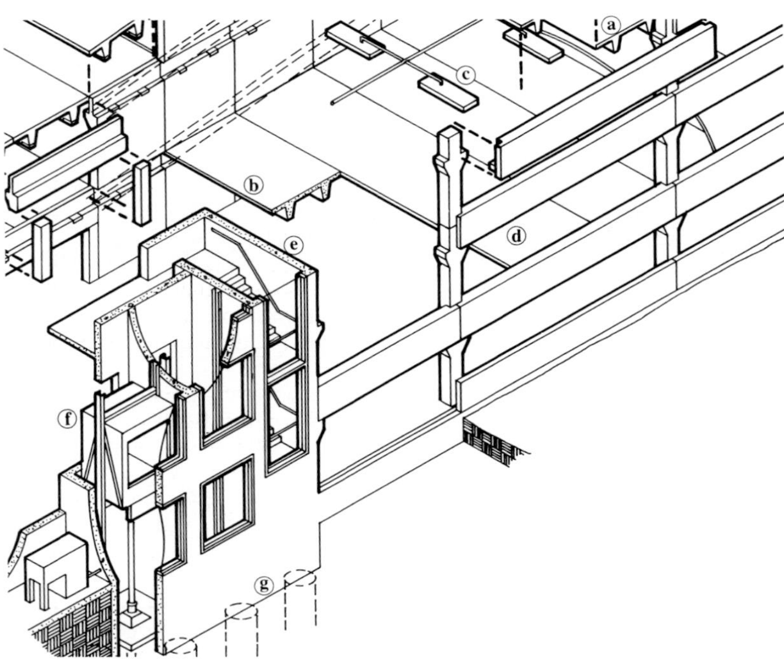

a. *Concrete topping*
b. *Precast prestressed concrete double T's*
c. *Fluorescent light fixtures*
d. *Precast concrete columns and spandrel beams*
e. *Elevator stair and core*
f. *Hydraulic elevator and elevator equipment*
g. *Slab on grade and cast-in-place concrete piles*

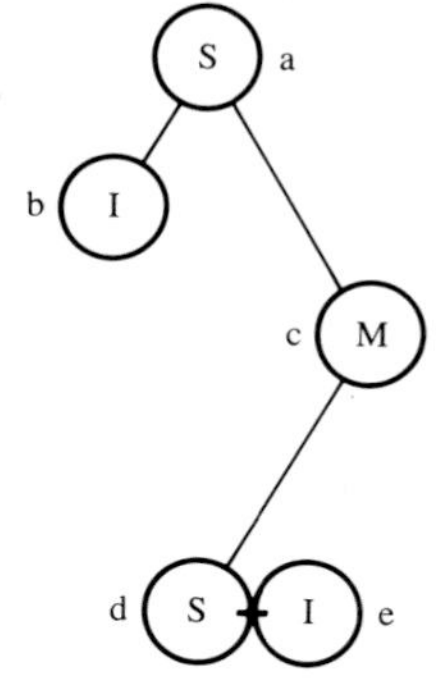

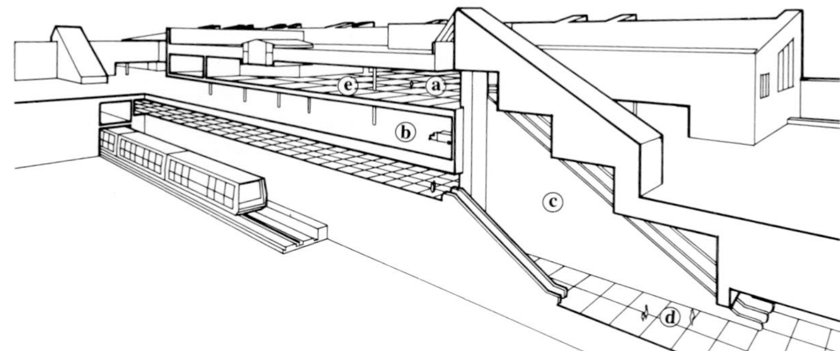

a. *Upper floor structure*
b. *Ceiling*
c. *Escalator*
d. *Lower floor structure*
e. *Floor covering*

ESCALATORS

Escalators are components of the mechanical system *connected* to the structural floors above and below them. The equipment itself is rarely visible, but there remains the challenge of visibly integrating the encasement of the equipment with its surroundings at the wall, floor, and ceiling.

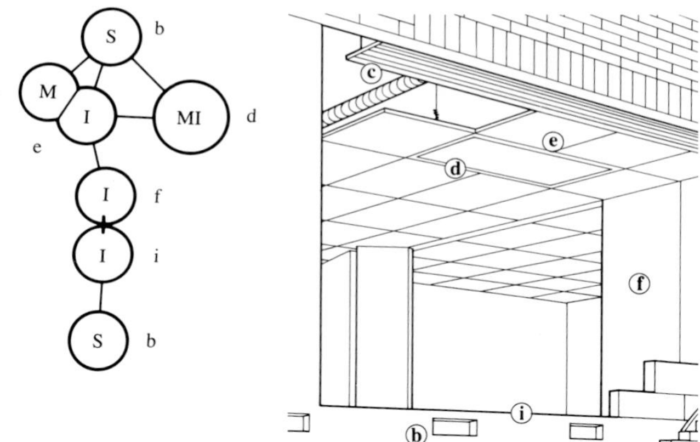

OPERABLE PARTITIONS

Operable partitions are interior components that rest on the floor below them in a *touching* relationship. They are *connected* to the ceiling above. In cases where the partitions are attached to the floor, a *connected* relationship exists at both top and bottom.

Operable partitions are a dual-purpose product, designed to be present in the space or not at the user's option. As an interior element, they offer an opportunity to manipulate the visible integration of a space quite easily by using it as a large, open space or dividing it into smaller spaces.

b. *Concrete slab*
c. *Ducts and diffusers*
d. *Lighting*
e. *Ceiling*
f. *Operable partitions*
i. *Resilient flooring*

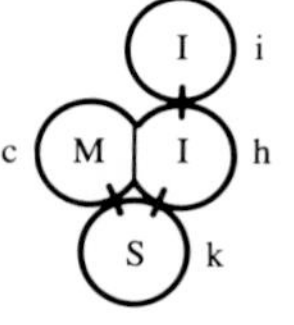

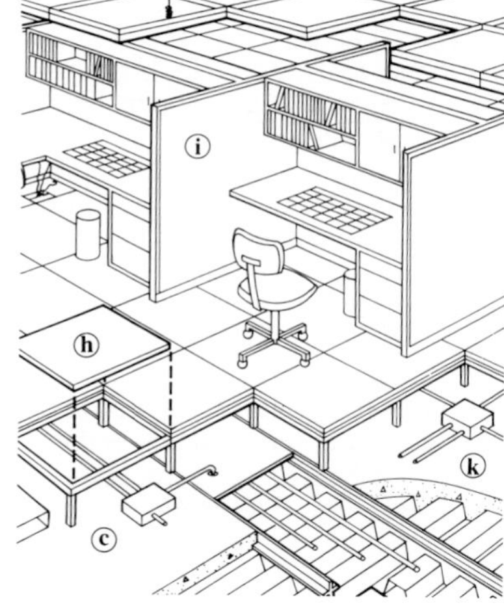

OPEN PLAN OFFICE FURNITURE

Open plan office furniture is an interior system that has a *touching* relationship with the floor surface beneath it, in this case a carpeted access floor.

As an interior element, open plan office furniture affects the visible integration of a space. A number of criteria are embodied in any given open office system, and these must proceed into the use of the units. Panels in particular are often a major part of an office worker's personal environment, and should be integrated visibly as well as functionally.

c. *Wiring and ductwork*
h. *Carpeted access flooring*
i. *Open office furniture*
k. *Steel decking with concrete topping*

Floor Diagrams

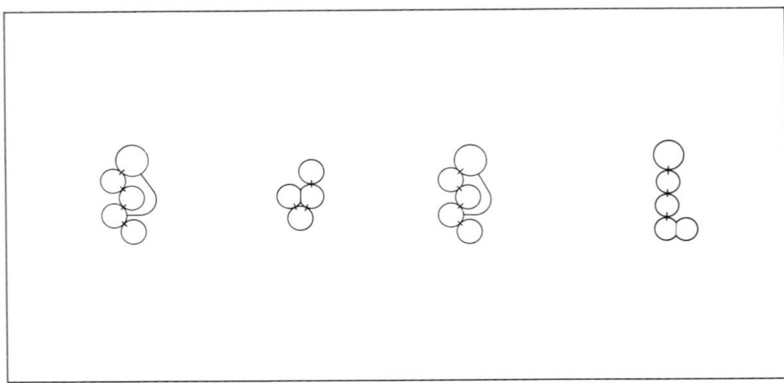

All of the examples chosen for this section originate in Chapter 4. They represent a solid cross-section of use in the contemporary buildings we have assembled. The temporary nature of the innermost surfaces of a building suggests connections that can be easily changed (for alterations and maintenance), but there are situations where considerations of human safety might be at odds with the temporary qualities. All of the situations depicted are appropriate to office useage. For other commercial or residential uses, the number of connection possibilities is very much more limited. The issue of connections only starts to become significant as a design issue when the possibility arises of heavy mechanical interaction with the interior system. For example, the wiring can be located beneath the carpet or beneath the structural floor itself. The impact of the choice of ceiling on the floor below is depicted in the structural/electrified floor example. A complete diagram would contain the ceiling connection below the floor. An advantage of drawing the diagram is that it forces consideration of the relationship of floor covering and the ceiling below, a relationship that is often ignored in deference to the surfaces on view from the room itself.

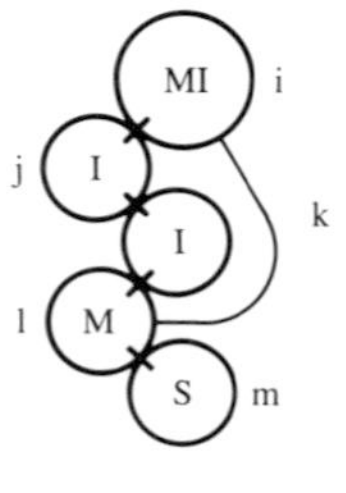

CARPET TILES

Carpet tiles are an element of the interior system whose strength lies in the recognition of the inherent weakness of carpeting: the need for patching. This weakness finds its own solution in a product consisting entirely of patches.

Carpet tiles have a *touching* relationship with the office furniture above them. When applied without adhesives, as is commonly done over flat cable as shown, they have a *touching* relationship with the flat cable and the structure below (in this case, flat plate). In other applications, carpet tiles can be mechanically attached to the structure, in which case the relationship between the carpet tiles and the structure would be *connected*.

i. *Electrical equipment*
j. *Office furniture*
k. *Carpet tile*
l. *Under carpet flat cable*
m. *Flat plate*

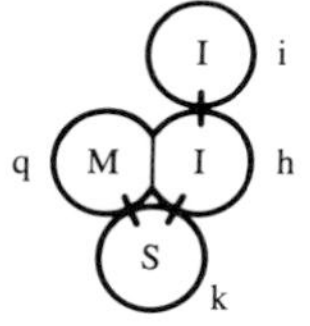

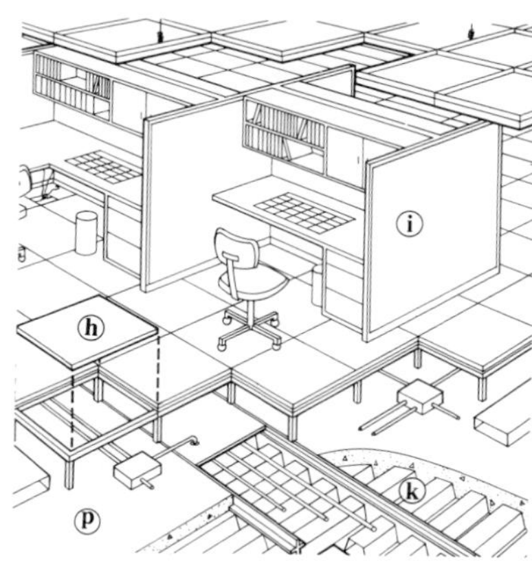

ACCESS FLOORS

Access floors combine the functions of structural, mechanical, and interior systems. The mechanical components, such as wiring, are *meshed* within the space created by the access floor's leg supports and floor topping. In one sense, access floors work like carpet tiles on a larger scale; in another, they resemble the interstitial floors used in hospitals such as Walter Reed.

Mechanical and interior components both have a *touching* relationship with the structural floor below, in this case steel decking with cast-in-place concrete topping. The example also shows a *touching* relationship between the carpeted access floor and the open office furniture above it.

h. *Carpeted access flooring*
i. *Open office furniture*
k. *Steel decking with concrete topping*
q. *Conduit*

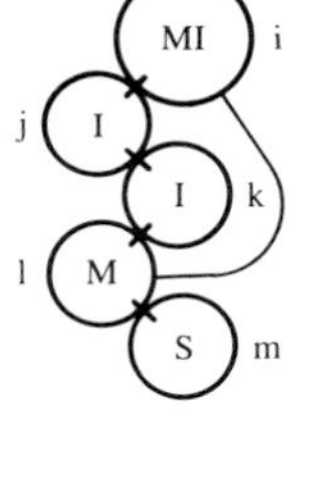

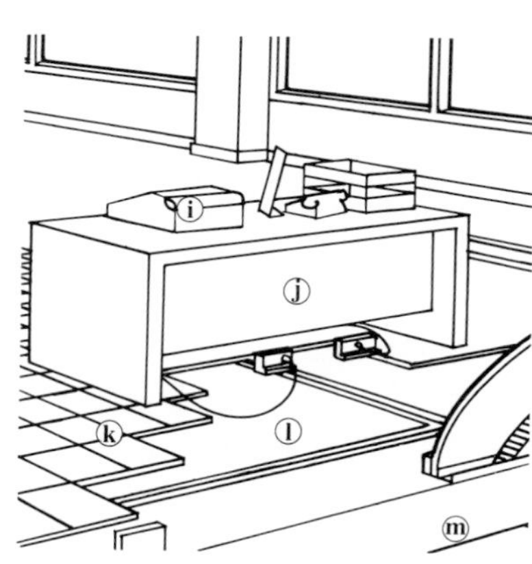

FLAT CONDUCTOR CABLE

Flat cable is a mechanical system component *connected* to the mechanical equipment it serves. Its shape is the key to its integrative character; its flexibility depends heavily on carpet tiles. Flat cable has a *touching* relationship with the carpet tiles that cover it and is *connected* to the structural floor with tape. It is usually left in place and passed over when room layout changes.

i. *Electrical equipment*
j. *Office furniture*
k. *Carpet tile*
l. *Under carpet flat cable*
m. *Flat plate*

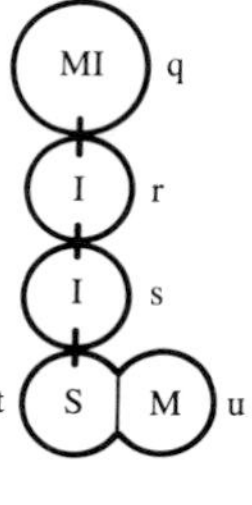

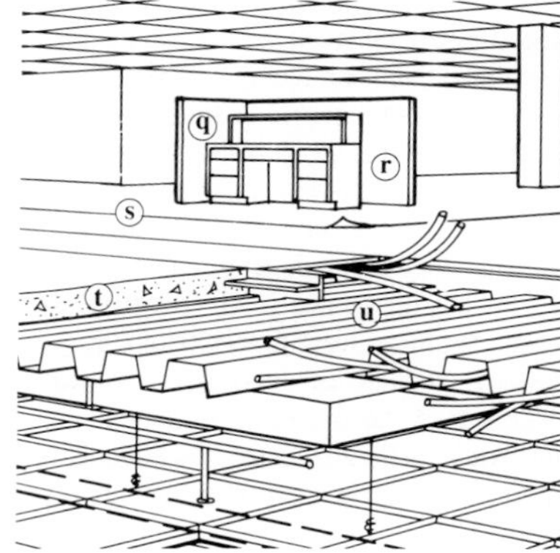

STRUCTURAL/ELECTRIFIED FLOORS

Floor decking that accommodates wiring represents a combination of structural and mechanical systems. It is a uniquely geometrical solution from a visible integration standpoint. The structural subfloor is *meshed* with the electrical conduit and outlet boxes, which are *connected* to each other and are in turn *connected* to the electrical equipment in the room. The structural subfloor has a *touching* relationship with the floor covering above it.

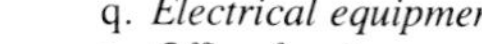

q. *Electrical equipment*
r. *Office furniture*
s. *Floor covering*
t. *Concrete topping on metal decking*
u. *Outlet boxes*
v. *Conduit*

Wall Diagrams

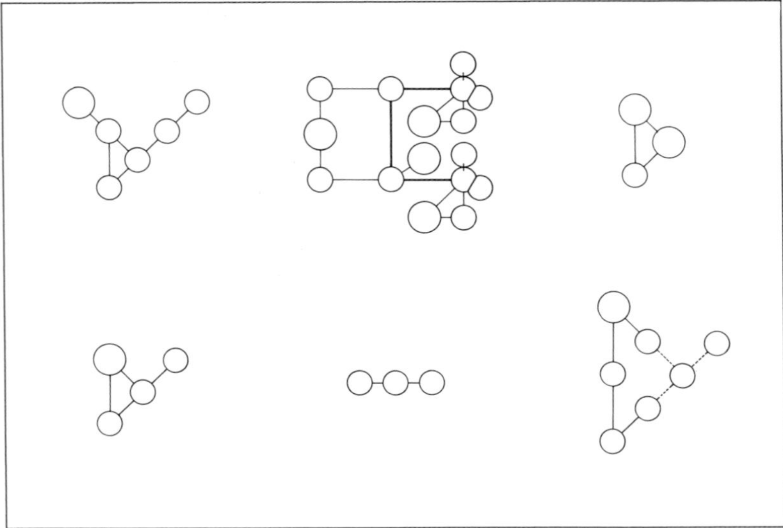

The diagrams above include not only the wall assembly but sealants. It is an appropriate addition due to the frequent use of sealants in glazing and in panel construction. As the diagrams show, the wall condition can be as simple or as complex as desired. Adding passive solar qualities includes mechanical systems integration. The weight and transparency of the products chosen distinctly influence the particular choice of materials and connections in the situations shown. The taller the facade, the more weight is added to the building by the selection of the envelope for its exterior. Like the roof of a building, one does not often intend to change the exterior of the building, while an interior variation is quite likely no matter what the use. The wall is clearly the element of the building where the most dramatic innovation occurs in the buildings selected for this book. Daylighting, glare, view, security, heat gain, and privacy all influence the integration.

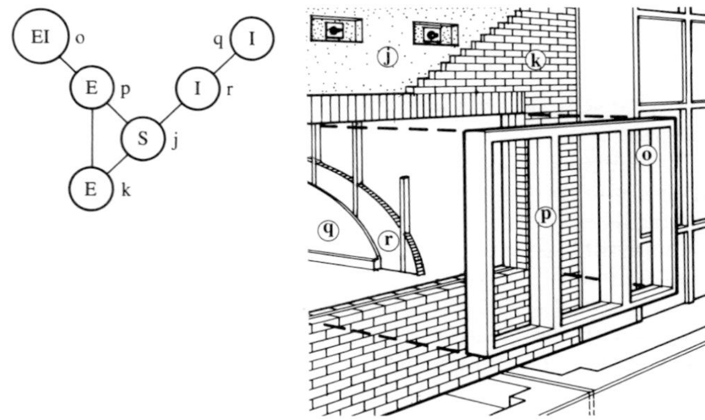

INSULATING GLASS

Insulating glass is a *unified* combination of envelope and interior functions. It is *connected* to a window frame, which is in turn *connected* to the structure, in this case a rigid concrete frame. The window frame and the structural frame are *connected* to the envelope, which is constructed of brick and concrete masonry and rigid insulation.

Insulating glass is distinguished from single-pane glass in that it has a *remote* relationship with the mechanical system. It is a dual-purpose product, allowing the window to perform thermodynamically in the manner of an opaque wall.

j. *Rigid concrete frame*
k. *Brick and concrete masonry and rigid insulation*
o. *Insulating glass*
p. *Window frame*
q. *Interior wall covering*
r. *Drywall*

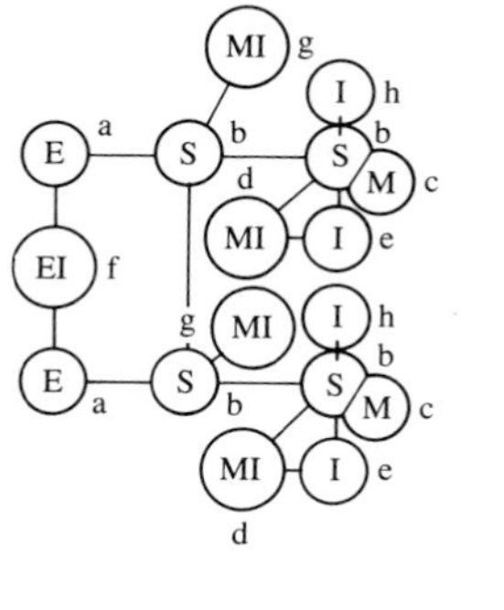

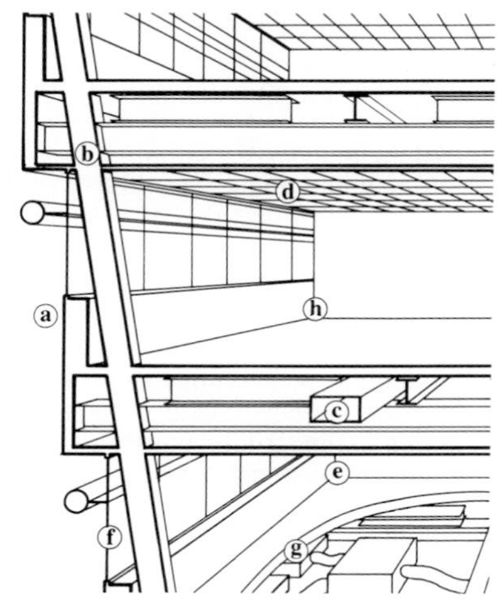

GLASS AND ALUMINUM CURTAIN WALL

The glass in the window assembly of the aluminum curtain wall in this example is a *unified* envelope and interior combination. It is *connected* to lightweight insulating panels and to the structural steel frame. The whole represents the integration of the envelope surface, in this case of the Georgia Power Corporate Headquarters. Its unusual profile represents a detailing challenge in curtain wall design.

a. *Aluminum and glass curtain wall*
b. *Steel frame; composite steel frame and concrete deck; stub girders*
c. *Ducts and diffusers*
d. *High pressure sodium lighting*
e. *Suspended ceiling*
f. *Window assembly*
g. *Perimeter heater*
h. *Floor covering*

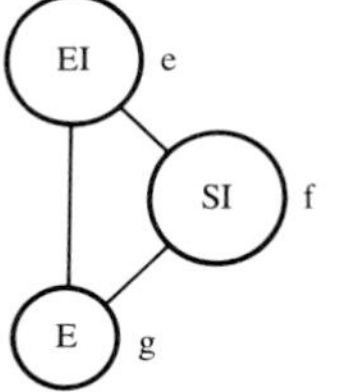

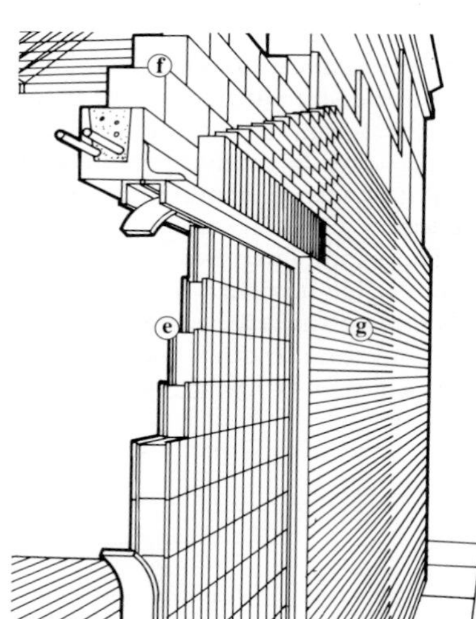

GLASS BLOCK WALLS

Exterior glass block, like other forms of exterior glass, is a *unified* envelope and interior type of wall construction. In this example, the glass block is laid into panels *connected* to the other envelope materials, brick veneer and rigid insulation. Glass block is a dual-purpose product in that it performs both as glass and as a masonry unit.

The envelope materials, including the glass block, are *connected* to the structure, in this case a concrete masonry bearing wall which is exposed to the interior, and is therefore represented by a *unified* structure and interior combination.

e. *Glass block panel*
f. *Concrete masonry bearing wall*
g. *Brick veneer and rigid insulation*

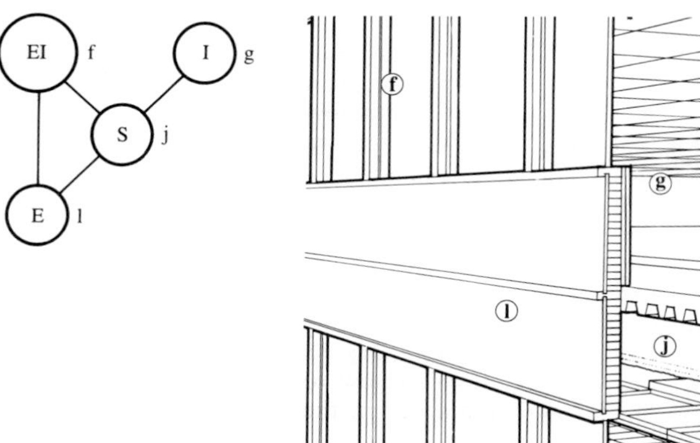

LIGHTWEIGHT INSULATING METAL PANELS

Lightweight insulating metal panels are an example of an envelope element *connected* to the structure and window assembly. Their insulating qualities give the panels a *remote* relationship with the mechanical system. Detailing and color are largely visible integration issues. Because they are prefabricated, panels offer good quality control; their disadvantage is in the large number of joints required.

f. *Window assembly*
g. *Drywall*
j. *Steel beams and columns*
i. *Insulated spandrel panels*

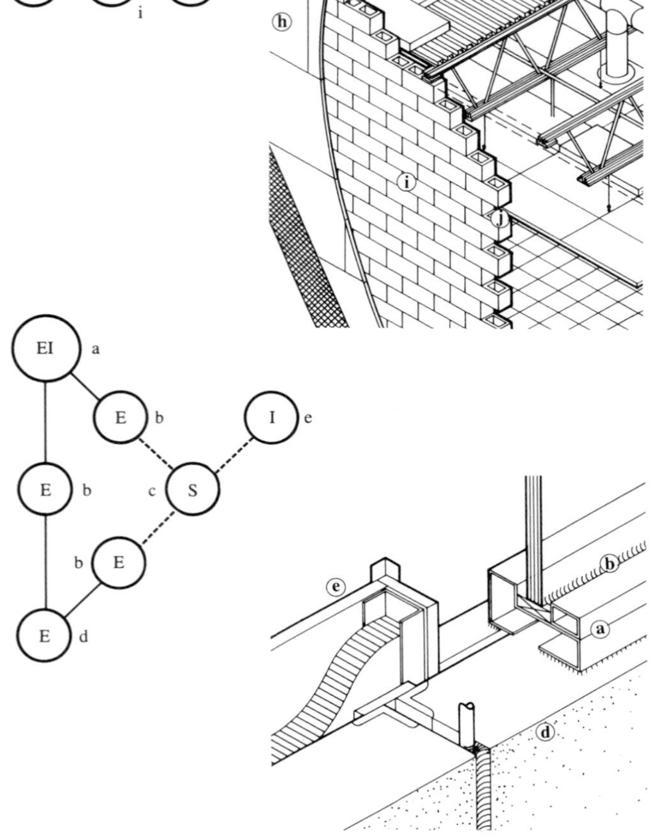

EXTERIOR INSULATION SYSTEMS

In a sense, an exterior insulation system (EIS) is the opposite of insulating panels. Its on-site application provides material integrity but requires simplicity of the surface plane. The example shown is composed of two parts, rigid insulation and a veneer coating; both are part of the envelope system. The EIS is *connected* to the canopy assembly. All these subsystems are then *connected* to the structure, in this case a concrete masonry bearing wall.

h. *Rigid insulation and veneer coating*
i. *Concrete masonry bearing wall*
j. *Glazed face*

SILICONE SEALANTS

Sealants embody one of integration's most important functions, that of coordinating and compensating for variation among systems. They occur in many parts of the building, from roofs to walls to floors.

The example shown is a wall assembly. The sealant is a flexible *connection* between the window assembly and the structure and between the wall panels and the structure.

a. *Window assembly*
b. *Sealant*
c. *Structural frame*
d. *Wall panels*
e. *Drywall and metal stud wall*

Note: dashed lines in this example indicate subsystems that are not in view.

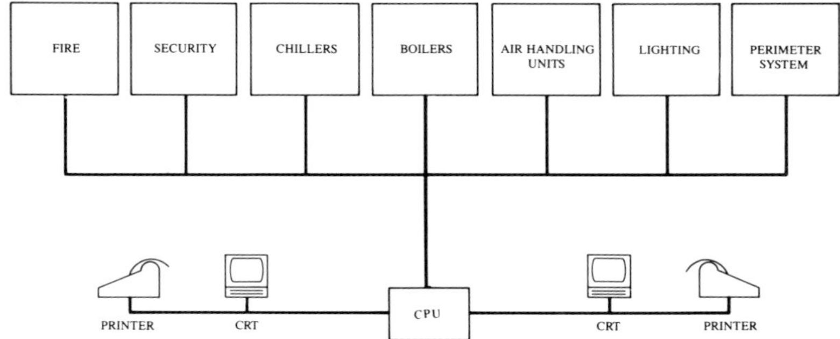

a. *Roof structure*
b. *HVAC equipment*
c. *Lighting*
d. *EMCS*
e. *Floor covering*
f. *Floor structure*

ENERGY MANAGEMENT CONTROL SYSTEMS

The idea of integration as a series of distinct choices is illustrated by energy management control systems. These might be considered mechanical system components, but they perform a unique role in integrating the functions of a number of mechanical systems to control energy use in a building. In this example, the EMCS is *connected* to HVAC equipment and to the lighting.

Chapter Four Ball Diagrams

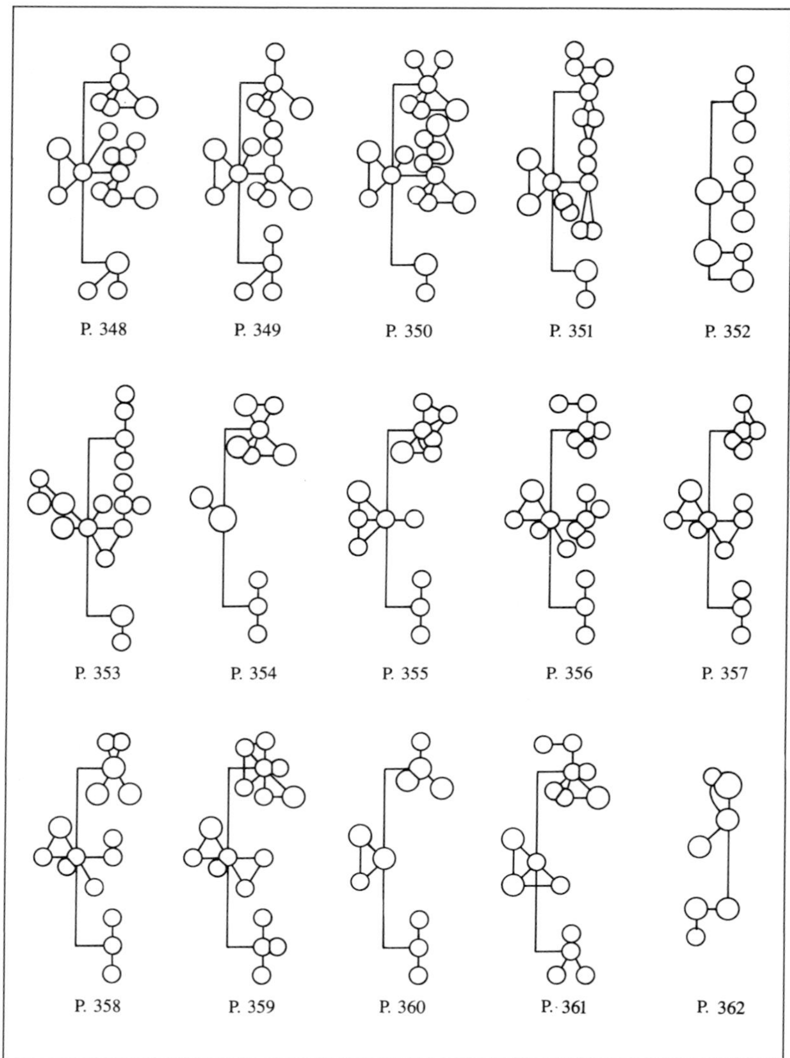

By carefully sifting through the Chapter Four diagrams above, it is possible to derive the diagram used to typify buildings earlier in the chapter (see p. 331). There are many similar patterns between buildings of quite different materials. These building systems are predominant simply because they work; they are economical to design and build. They should be compared with the diagrams of the buildings in the Chapter Three case studies (see p. 363). There is no particular merit in a simple ball diagram or a simple integration. Conversely, a complex and tedious diagram could hide a very direct solution in the physical building. This selection can also be used to compare different combinations of many of the available subsystems as they appear in building section drawings. Most of the conditions that commonly occur as integration possibilities are represented in the generic examples.

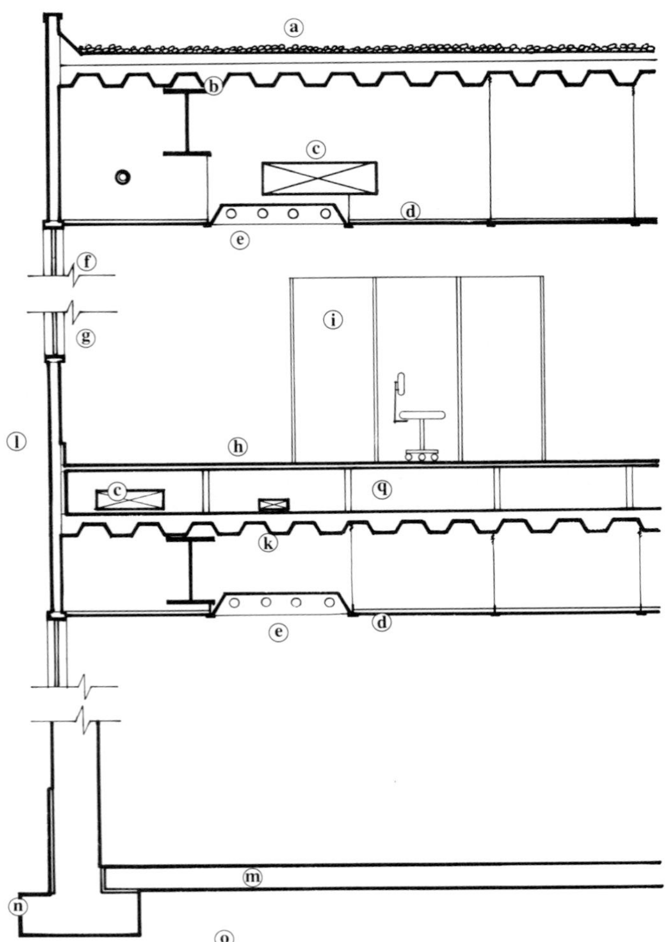

Access Floor and Curtain Wall

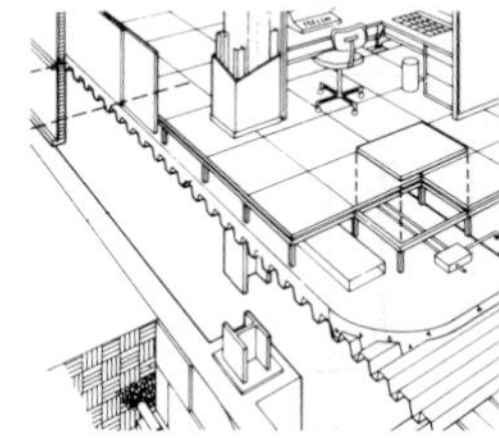

Access floor and curtain wall construction tends to result in a building that forms a gridded fabric with infill. The design process, in turn, is one of selecting or creating connection details. The glazed component of the wall, or window assembly, is a *unified* envelope and interior combination *connected* to the insulated spandrel panels. These panels are the other major envelope component, and are *connected* to the structural steel beams and columns. Conservation of time is a major advantage of this form of construction.

At the interior floor level, the structural floor, which is steel decking with a cast-in-place concrete topping, has a *touching* relationship with the carpeted access floor above it. The access floor itself is represented by a *meshed* mechanical and interior combination.

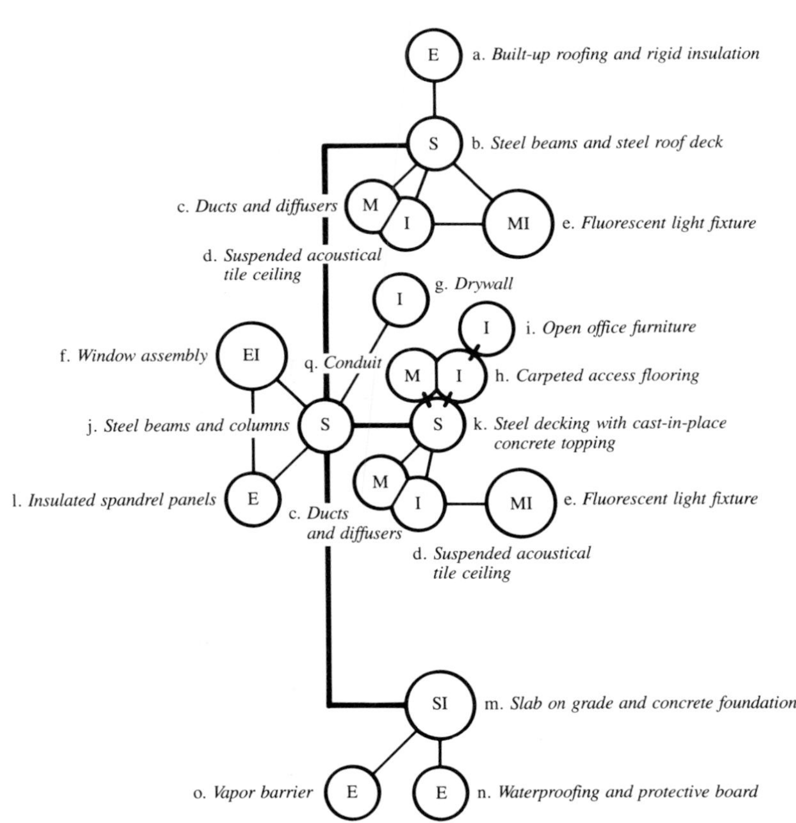

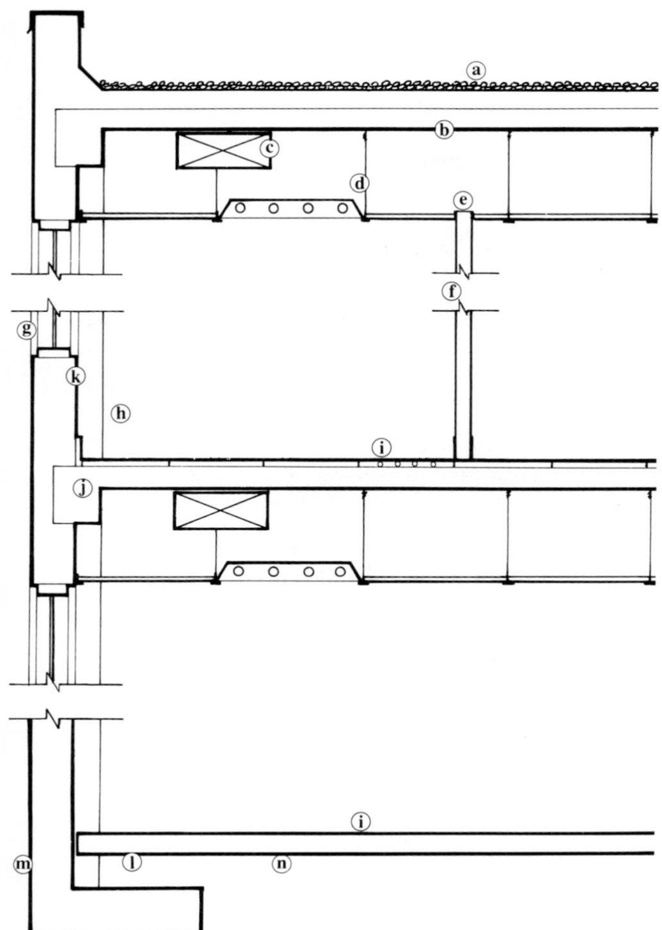

Post-Tensioned Concrete

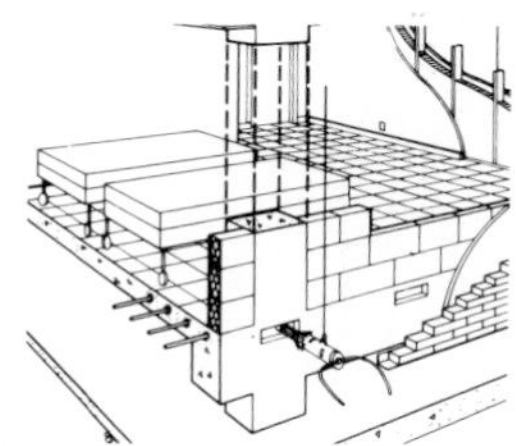

In spite of the difference in materials and construction technology, this building is similar to the curtain wall building; the integration characteristics are independent of the materials. Conservation of space is a motivation in both cases. Post-tensioning has ramifications on slab thickness and therefore on the overall cubage of the building. This spatial efficiency is not reflected in the diagrams.

The structural concrete slab is *connected* to a resilient floor, which in turn is in a *touching* relationship with the operable partitions above it. Fluorescent lighting, a suspended acoustical tile ceiling, and ducts and diffusers are *connected* to the floor slab from below. Lighting is *connected* to the ceiling; ducts and diffusers are *meshed* with it.

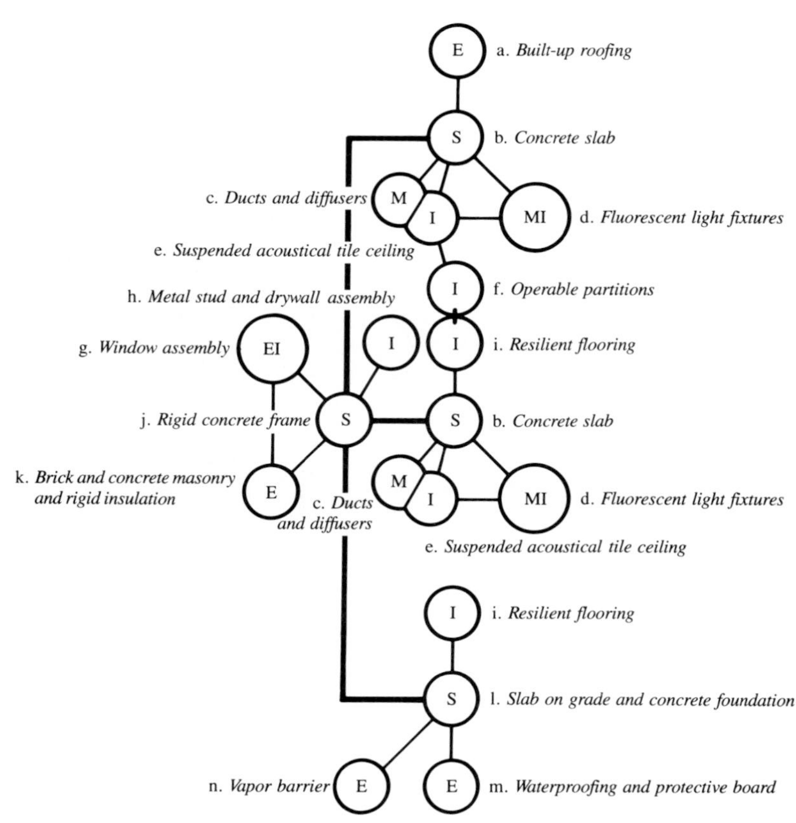

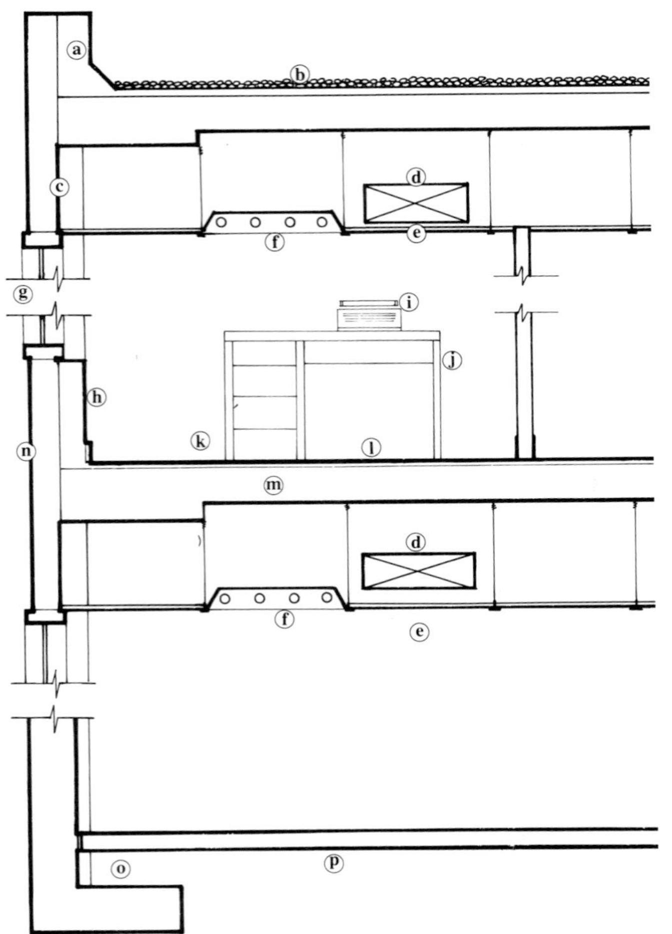

Flying Form

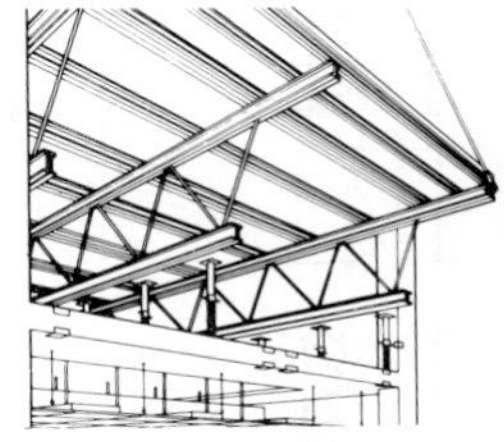

Flying form construction has relatively little impact on the nature of the integration achieved. It does produce a high quality finished slab, however, which allows the structural flat plate to be *connected* to the flat cable directly above it. This further contributes to speed of construction while allowing tenant options to remain open.

The flat plate and flat cable have a *touching* relationship with the carpet tile that rests on them. The structural flat plate is also *connected* to the light fixtures, HVAC ducts and diffusers, and suspended acoustical tile ceiling. The ceiling is *connected* to the light fixtures and *meshed* with the ducts and diffusers.

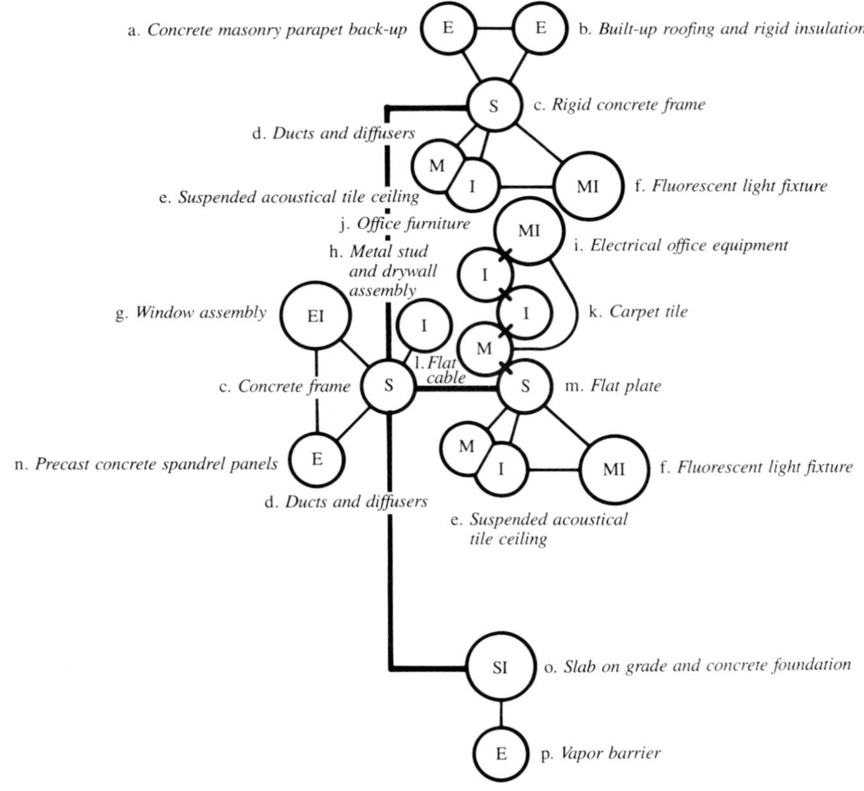

Flat Plate

In the example shown of flat plate construction, power poles provide electrical access through the integrated ceiling. Penetrations of the floor plane are thus avoided, freeing structure and interior from a range of electrical demands.

The power poles have a *touching* relationship with the carpeting beneath them. The elevator equipment is *connected* to the roofing component of the envelope and to the cast-in-place concrete flat plate structure. Batt insulation is *meshed* with the metal stud and drywall assembly on the interior, while the integrated ceiling is a *meshed* mechanical and interior combination. The integrated ceiling is in turn *connected* to the structure above and to the power poles below.

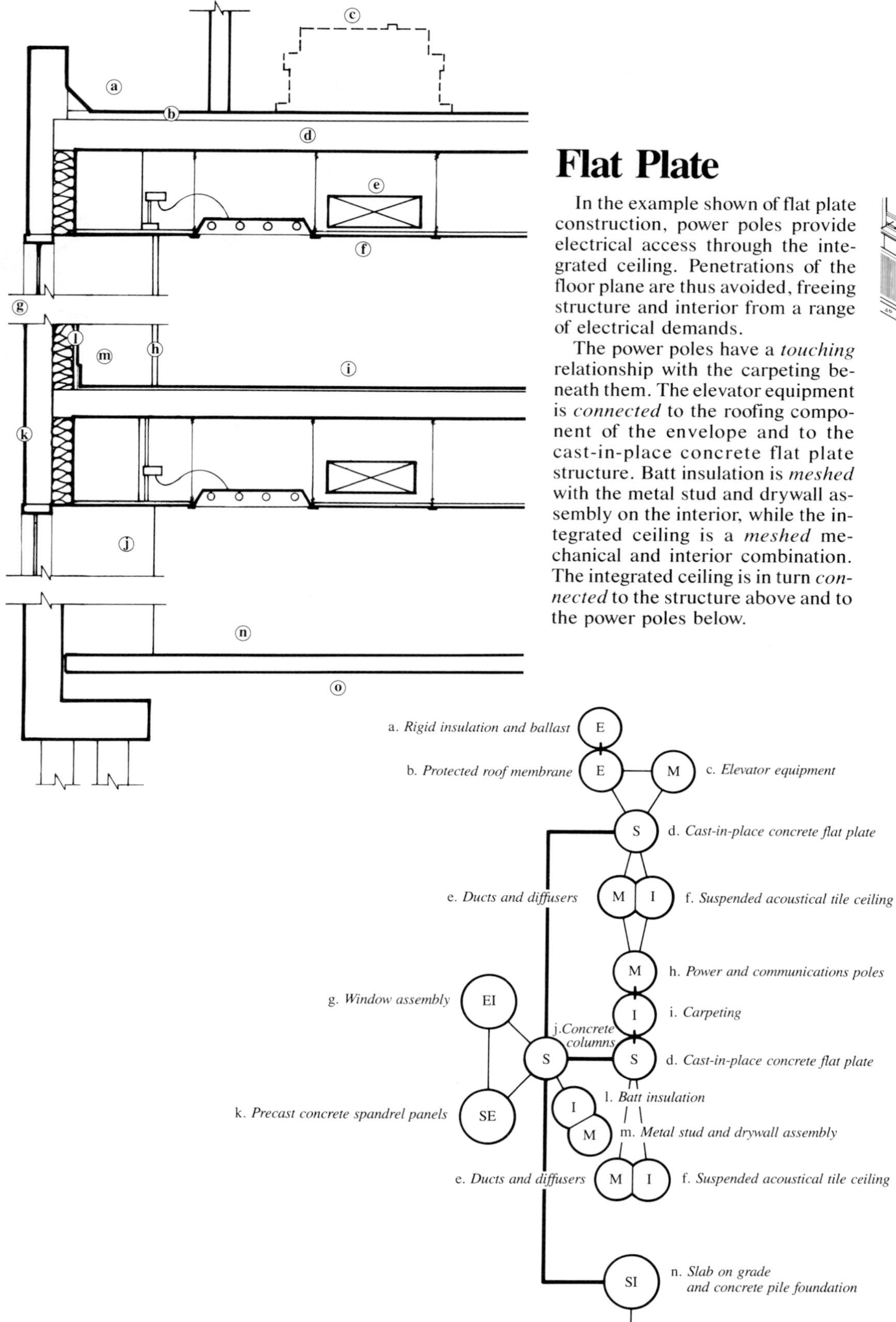

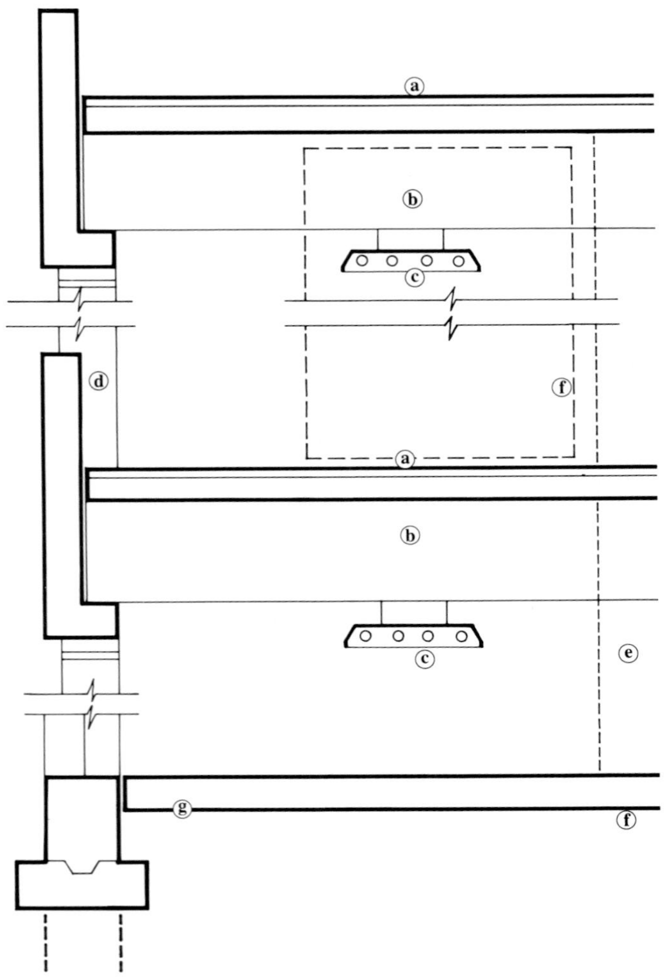

Precast Frame

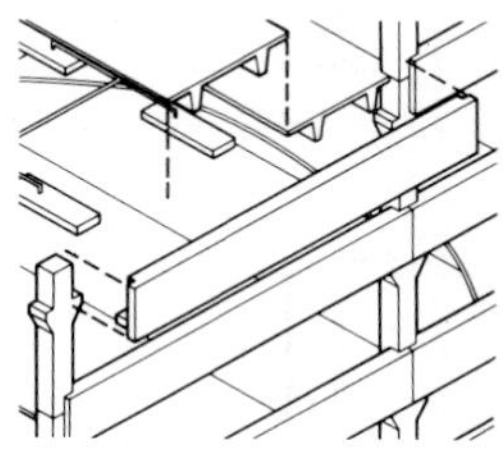

The use of a precast frame introduces a number of integration options, many of which are depicted in the example. One result is a radically simplified ball diagram.

High quality finishes allow the structure to assume a *unified* relationship with interior, envelope, or both. The precast prestressed concrete double T's help form the floors and roof of the building and are exposed to the interior, producing a *unified* structure and interior combination. The structural concrete wall frame and the elevator-and-stair core are exposed to the interior and exterior, and thus are represented as a *unified* structure, envelope, and interior combination. Exposure of the structure in this manner eliminates the need for additional envelope skin materials, interior ceilings, and floor finishes. Buildings of this kind can be constructed quickly and economically.

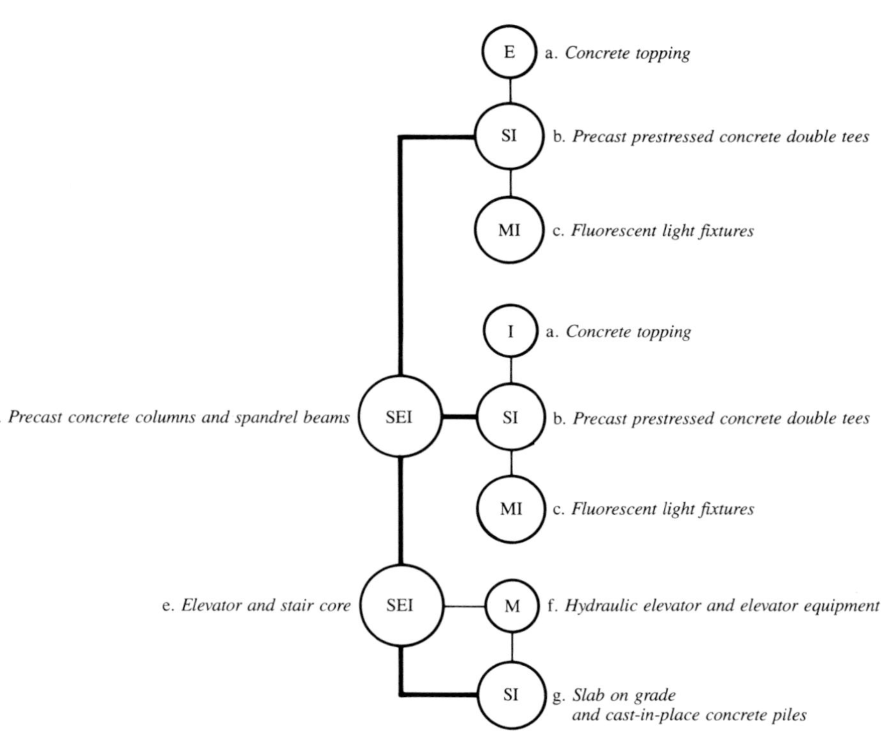

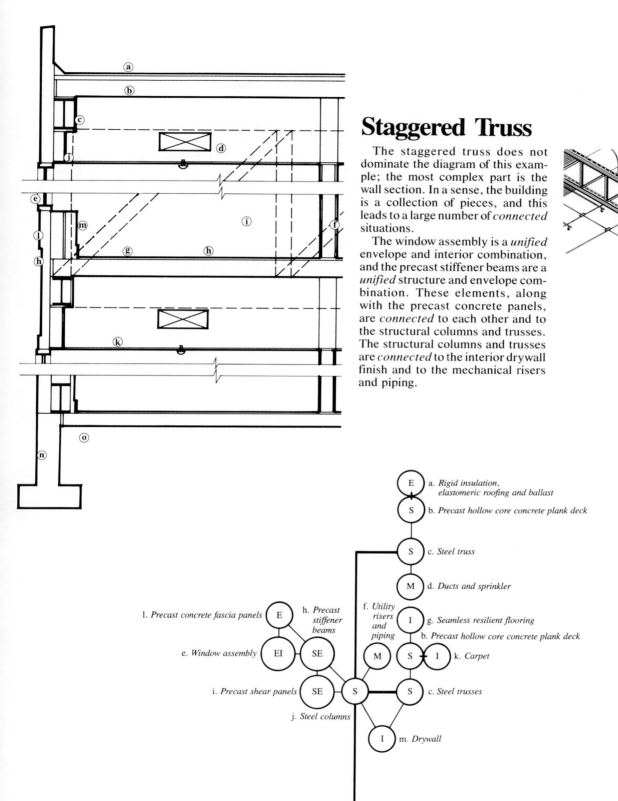

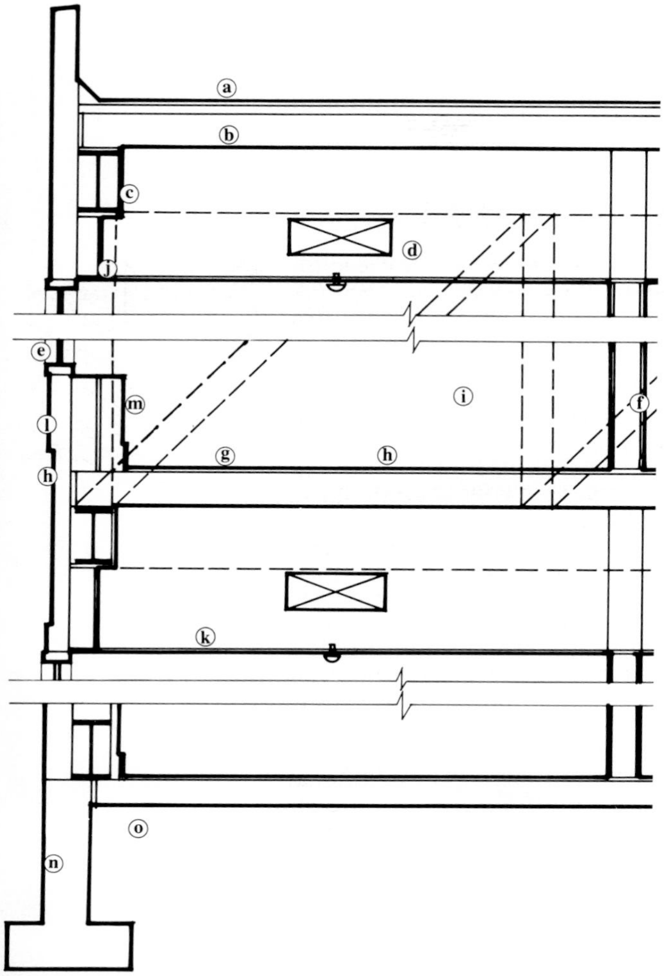

Staggered Truss

The staggered truss does not dominate the diagram of this example; the most complex part is the wall section. In a sense, the building is a collection of pieces, and this leads to a large number of *connected* situations.

The window assembly is a *unified* envelope and interior combination, and the precast stiffener beams are a *unified* structure and envelope combination. These elements, along with the precast concrete panels, are *connected* to each other and to the structural columns and trusses. The structural columns and trusses are *connected* to the interior drywall finish and to the mechanical risers and piping.

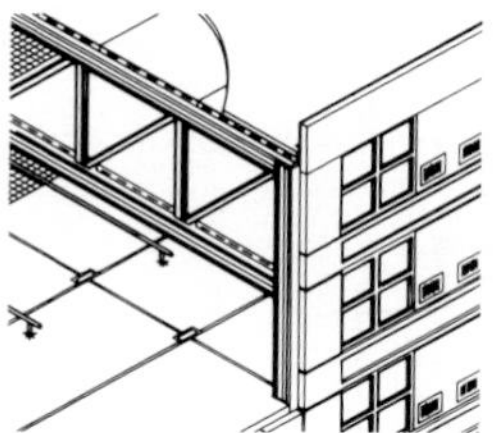

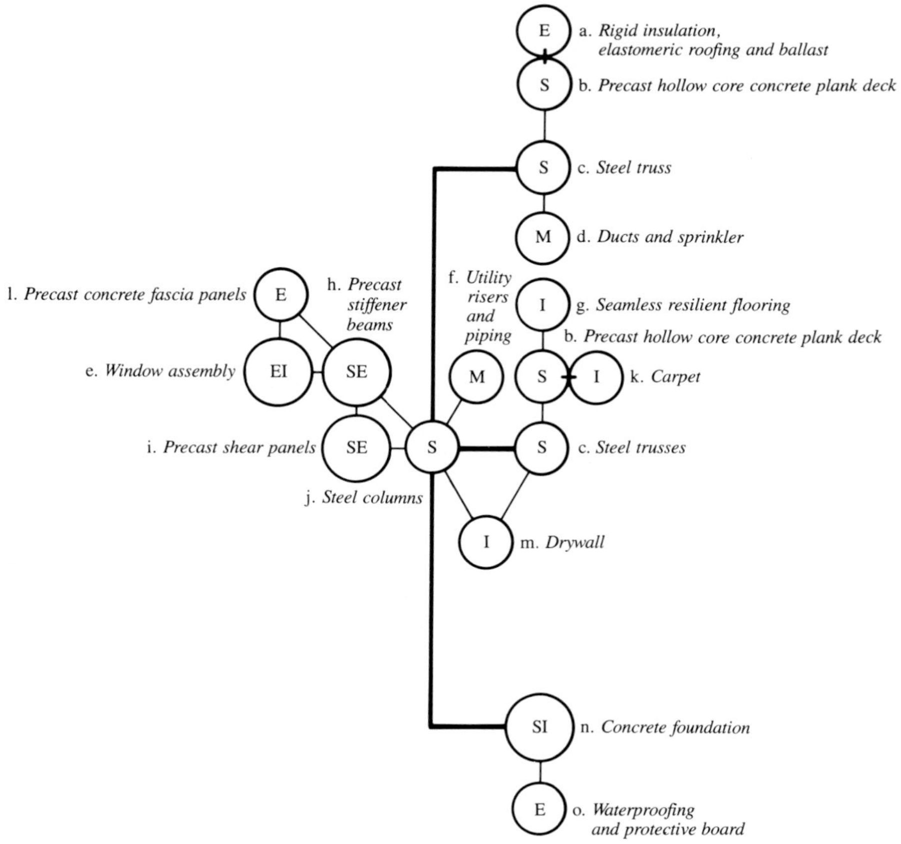

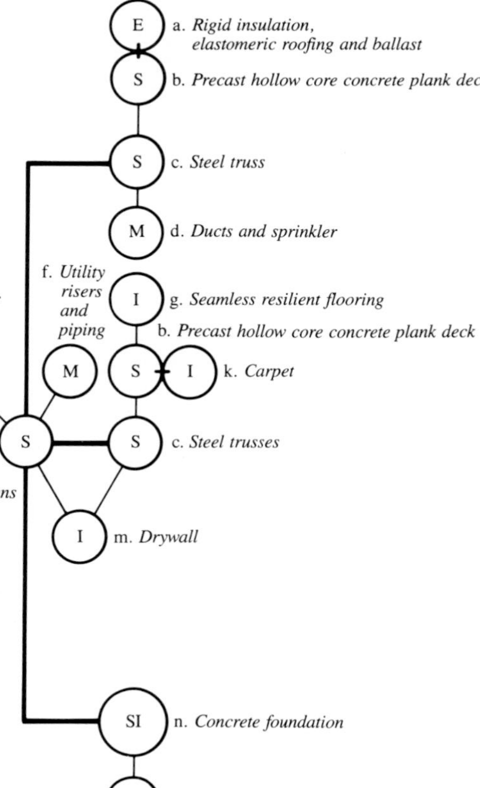

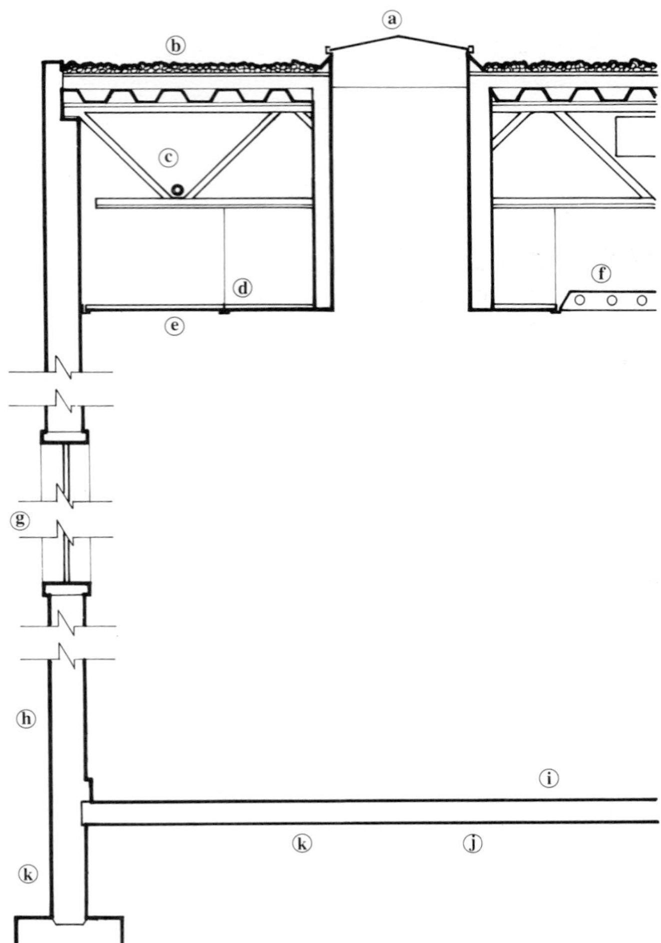

Tilt-up Wall

The load-bearing precast concrete tilt-up walls of this building *unify* structure, envelope, and interior. The resulting ball diagram is much simpler than the previous one with its numerous *connected* relationships. Both ease and speed of construction can be achieved with this method, particularly where a high quality interior finish is not required.

The roof and ceiling involve both *connected* and *unified* levels of integration. Radiant heat panels, which are *connected* to the structural steel bar joists, are an example of a *unified* mechanical and interior product. Skylights in the roof are a *unified* envelope and interior product. The roof and lighting are both *connected* to the roof structure.

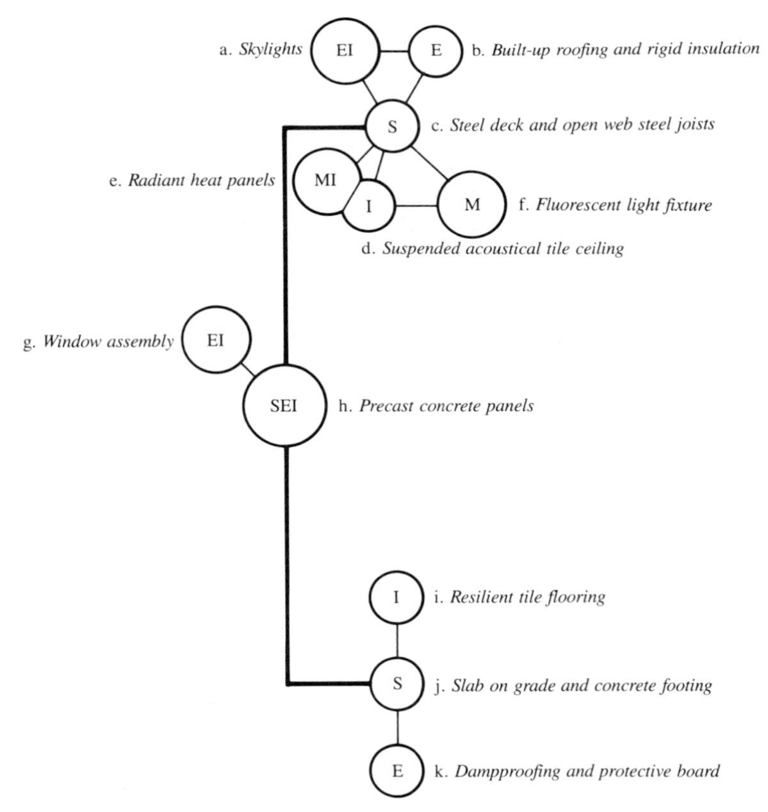

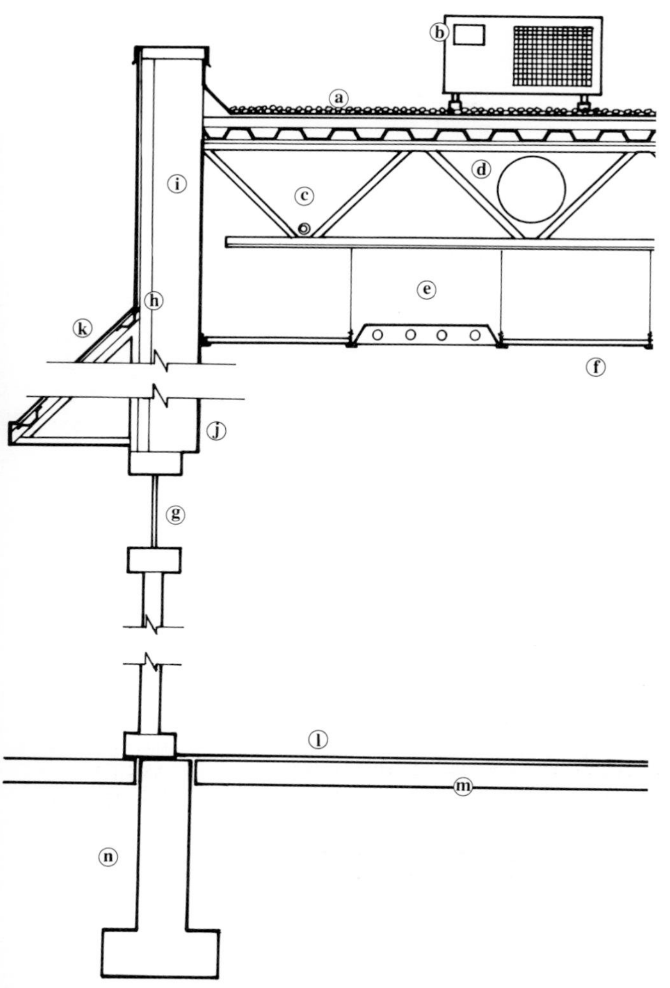

Bearing Wall and Bar-Joist Roof

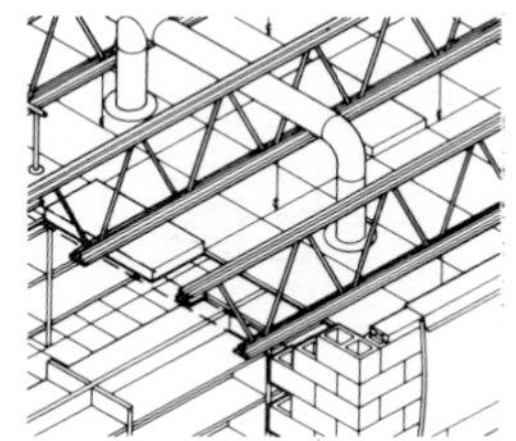

Bearing wall and bar-joist roof is a form of construction often used on speculative jobs, where the flexibility of its *connected* relationships is a distinct advantage. Another advantage is the acoustical isolation provided by the bearing walls.

In the example the exterior insulation *connected* to the concrete masonry wall is diagramed in the same way as face block or shingles would be. The structure of steel decking and open web steel joists is *connected* to the built-up roofing and the HVAC unit above it. In the space below, light fixtures and the acoustical tile ceiling are *connected* to the bar joists while HVAC ducts and sprinkler piping are *meshed* with them. The ducts are also *meshed* with the ceiling and *connected* to the rooftop HVAC unit.

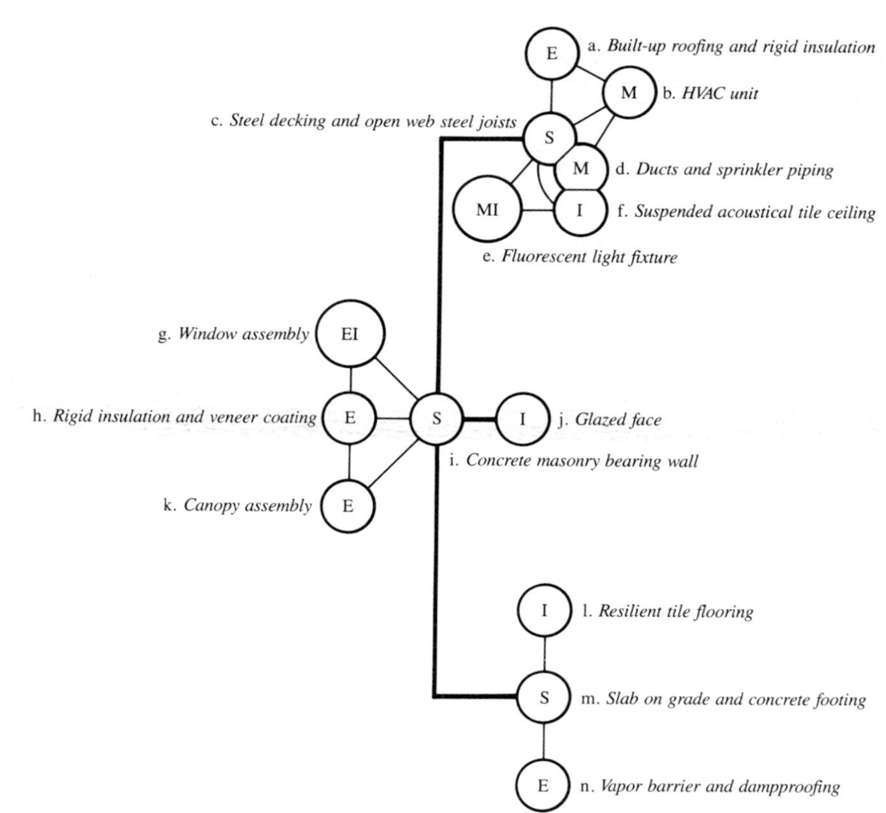

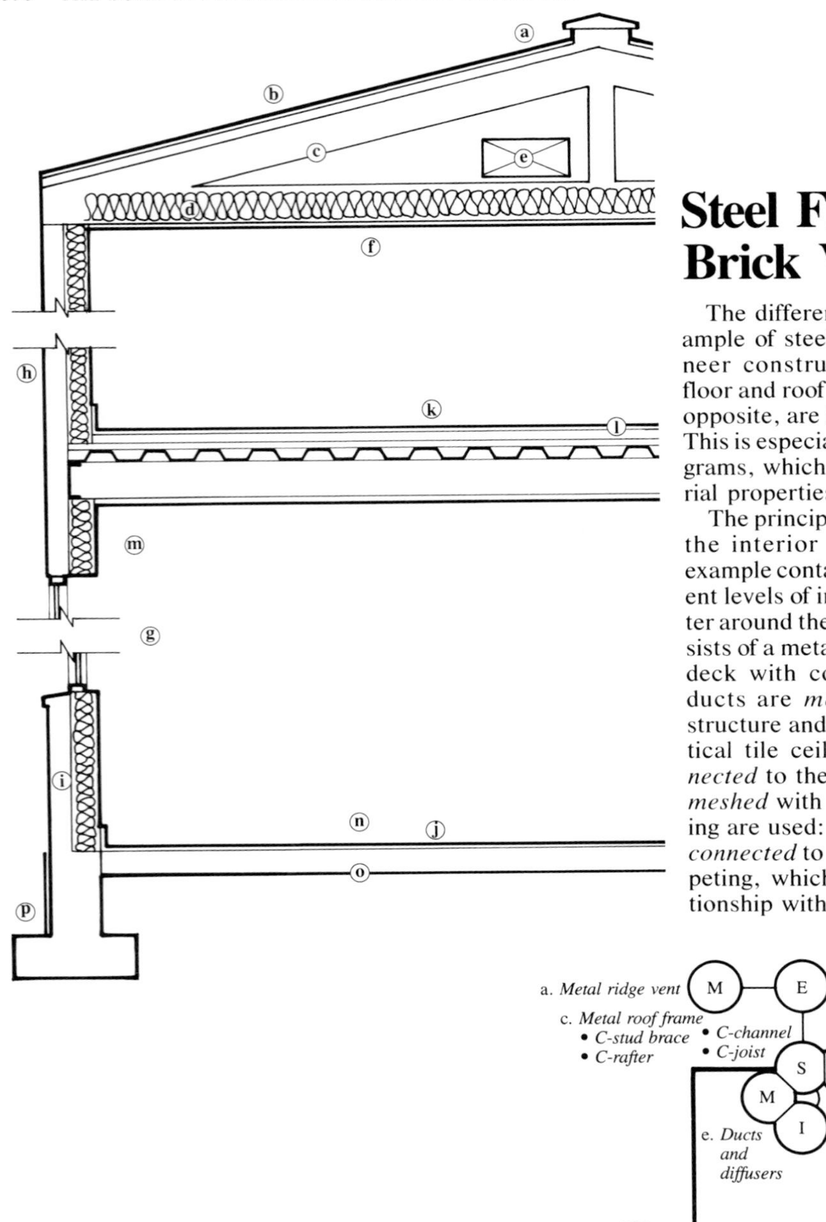

Steel Frame and Brick Veneer

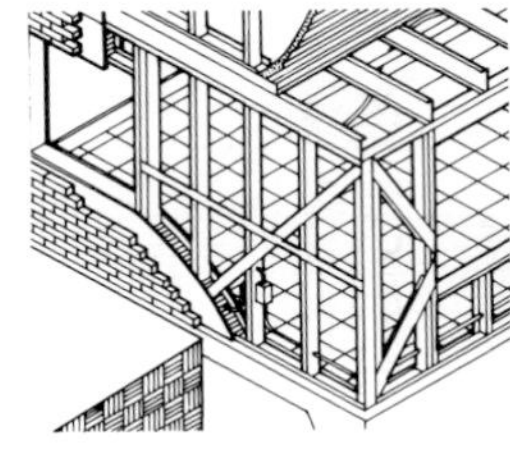

The differences between this example of steel frame and brick veneer construction and the wood floor and roof truss example, shown opposite, are few and rather subtle. This is especially true of the ball diagrams, which do not express material properties.

The principal differences occur in the interior floor, which in this example contains a number of different levels of integration. These center around the structure, which consists of a metal floor frame and steel deck with concrete topping. The ducts are *meshed* with the floor structure and the suspended acoustical tile ceiling. Lighting is *connected* to the ceiling and ducts are *meshed* with it. Two types of flooring are used: ceramic tile, which is *connected* to the structure, and carpeting, which has a *touching* relationship with the structure.

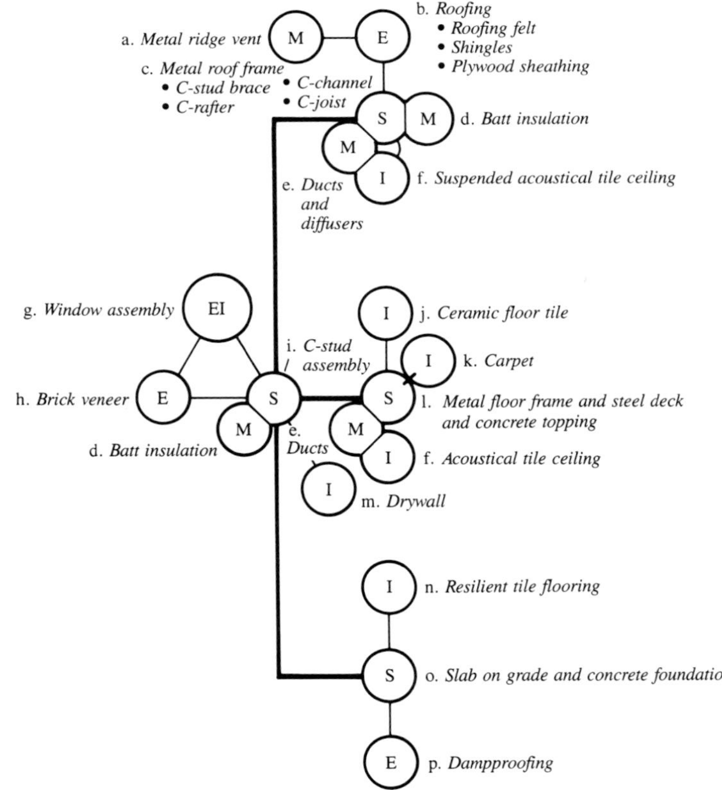

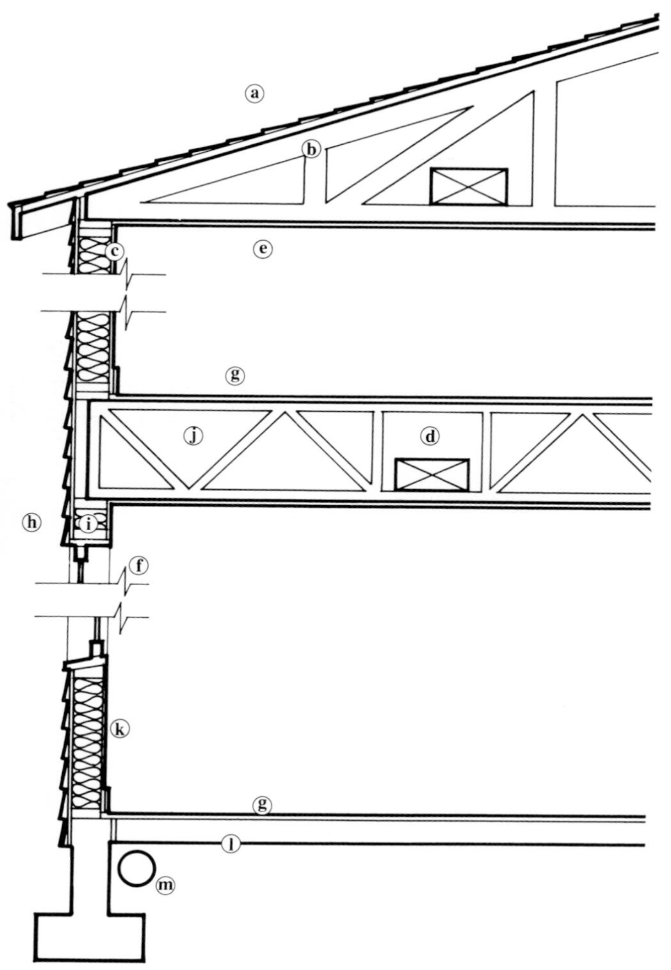

Wood Floor and Roof Truss

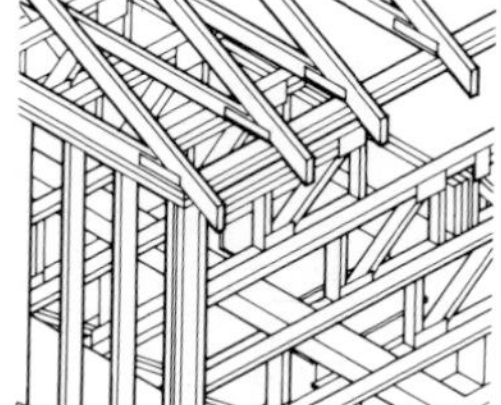

Wood floor and roof trusses are a modern adaptation of what has become a classic form of housing construction in the United States. Advantages include structural efficiency, the ease with which ducts can be threaded between truss members, and speed of construction.

Mechanical elements *mesh* well with wood floor and roof trusses, a relationship that is promoted by the ease of maintenance associated with drywall. The wood truss and sheathing roof structure are connected to the roof and envelope system. Batt insulation and HVAC ducts and diffusers are *meshed* with the joists. A suspended ceiling *connected* to the joists has ducts and diffusers meshed with it.

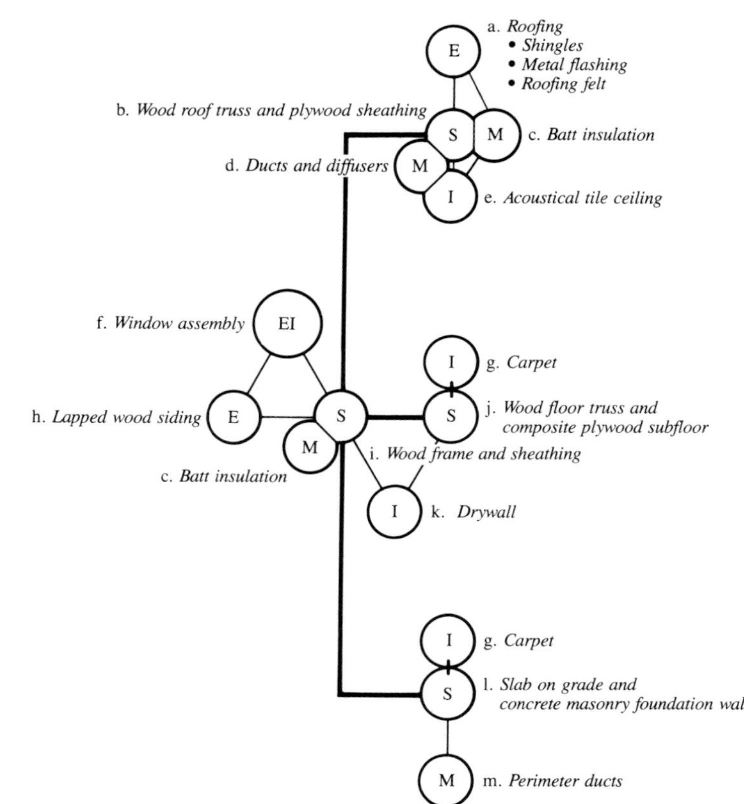

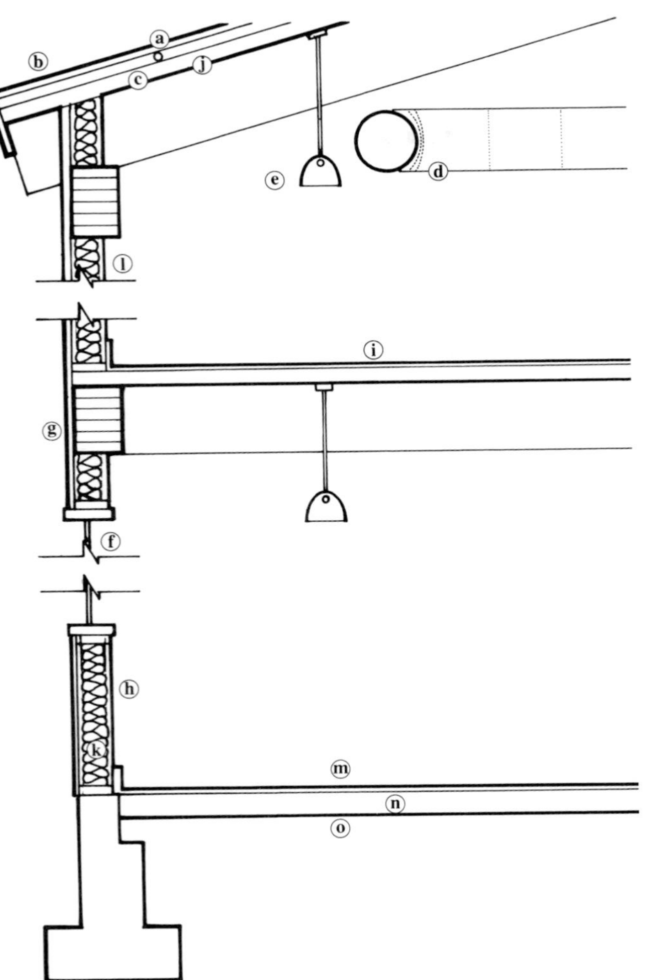

Post and Beam

Laminated wood post and beam construction lends itself to *unified* combinations, and like precast frame produces a simple ball diagram. A point of difference is that wood in its finished state is much more vulnerable to scratching. Connections with other systems, when exposed, require careful detailing.

The exposed wood frame and tongue-and-groove decking *unify* the interior with structure and envelope. HVAC ducts are *unified* with the interior as well; these and the light fixtures are in turn *connected* to the roof structure. On the exterior of the building, the roof structure is *connected* to the electrical conduit and the roofing, which are *meshed* with each other.

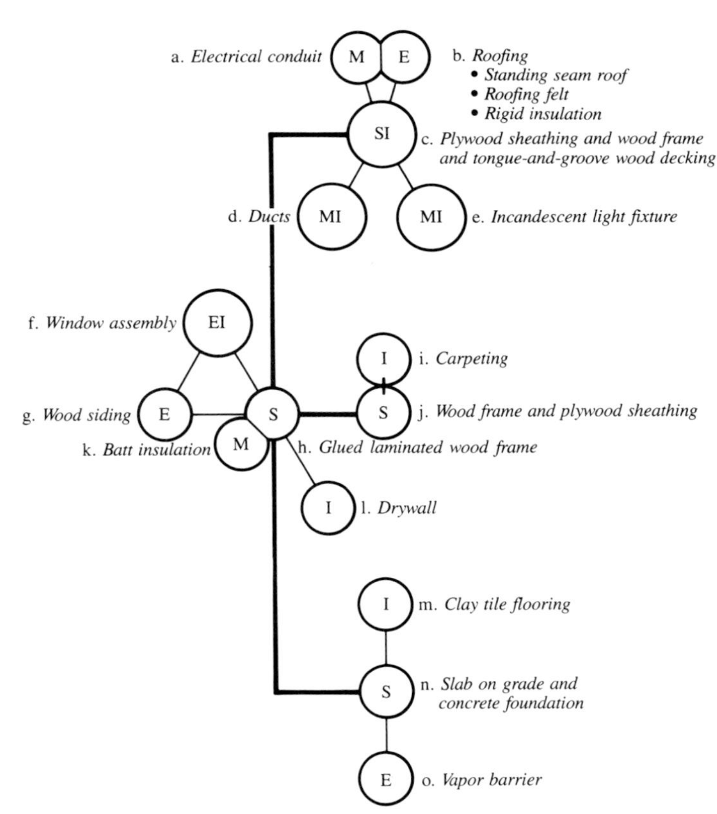

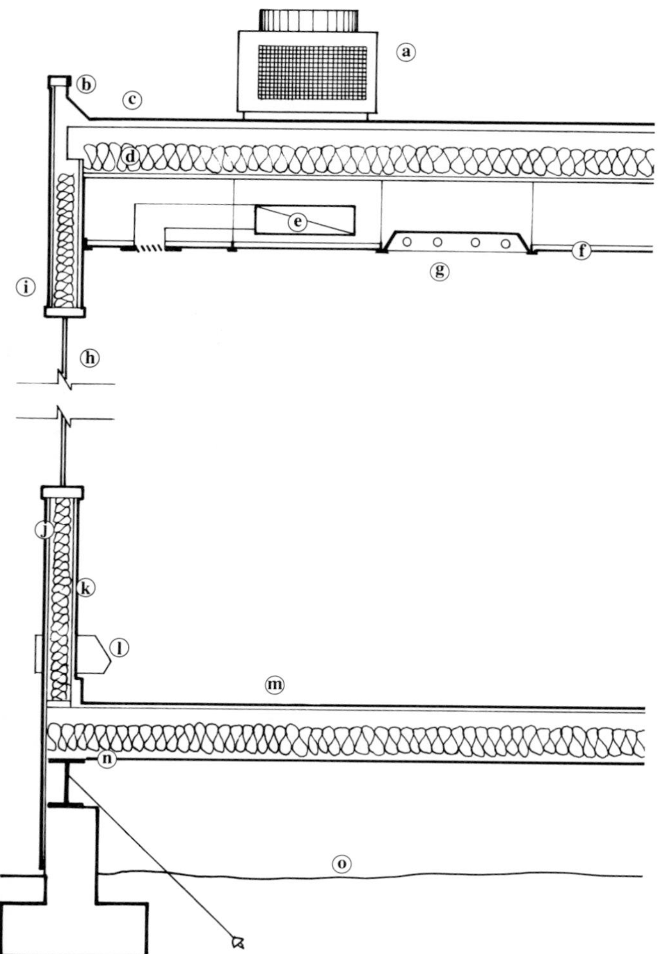

Lightweight Mobile Modular Buildings

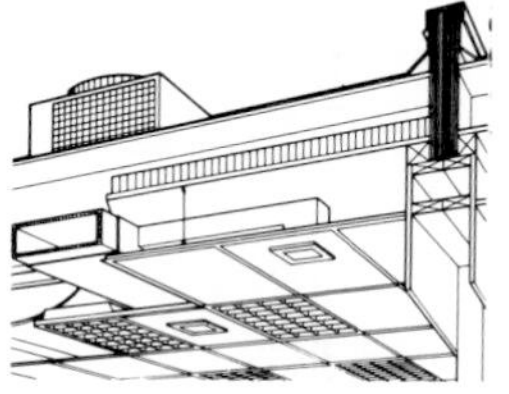

An interesting aspect of these low-cost buildings is that except for baseboard-mounted electric heat panels, there are no exposed structural or mechanical elements. The result, therefore, is maximum interior flexibility.

Batt insulation is *meshed* with the structural wood frame, which has the window assembly *connected* to it; the latter is also *connected* to the aluminum siding. On the interior, the drywall is *connected* to the structure. These connections are made under factory conditions; only mechanical and electrical hookups and connections at foundations and between units need to be made on-site.

Shipping subjects the modules to vibration and impact; criteria arising from these demands may impinge on integration conditions.

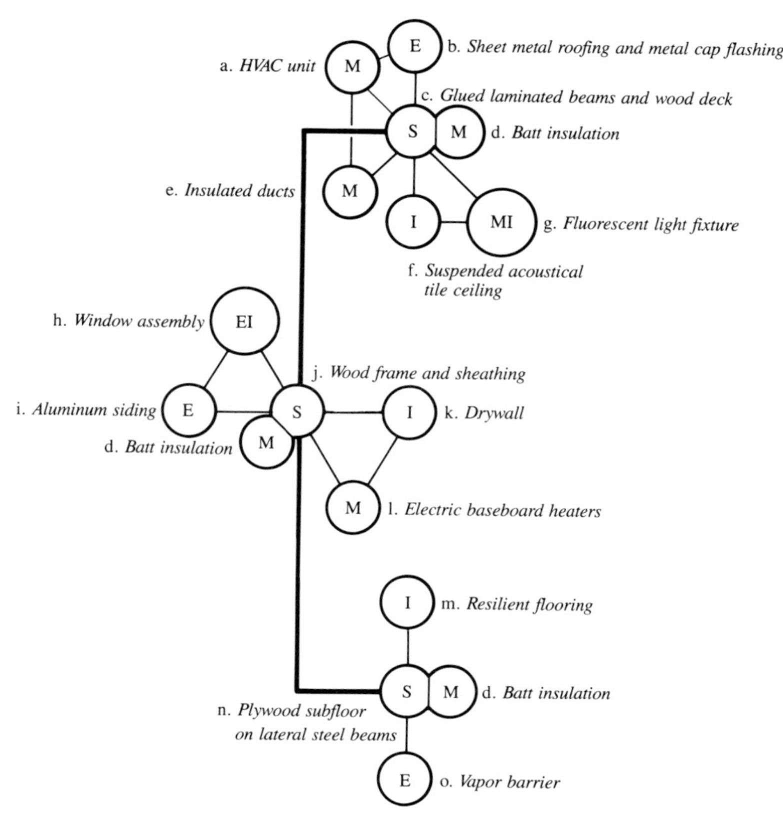

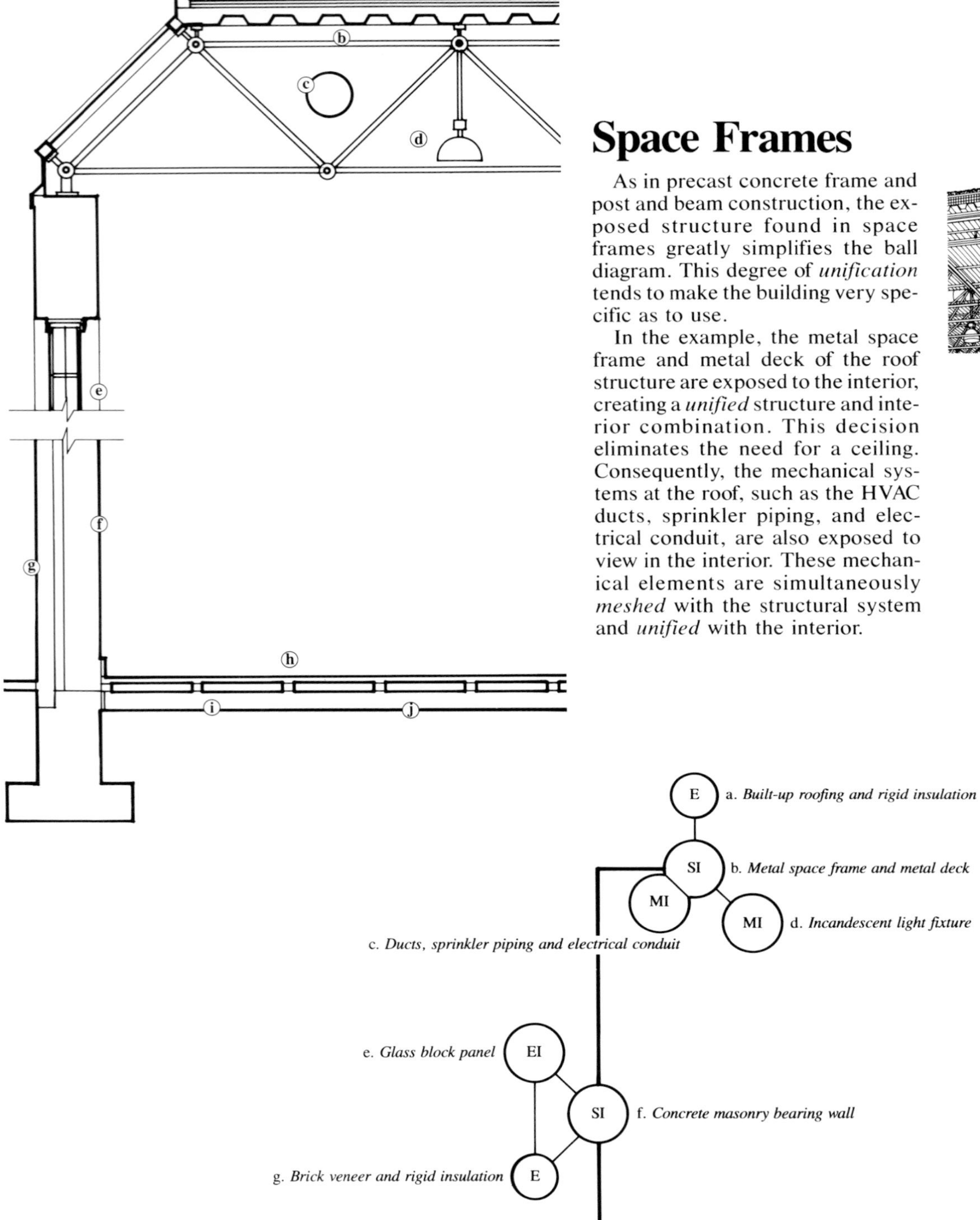

Space Frames

As in precast concrete frame and post and beam construction, the exposed structure found in space frames greatly simplifies the ball diagram. This degree of *unification* tends to make the building very specific as to use.

In the example, the metal space frame and metal deck of the roof structure are exposed to the interior, creating a *unified* structure and interior combination. This decision eliminates the need for a ceiling. Consequently, the mechanical systems at the roof, such as the HVAC ducts, sprinkler piping, and electrical conduit, are also exposed to view in the interior. These mechanical elements are simultaneously *meshed* with the structural system and *unified* with the interior.

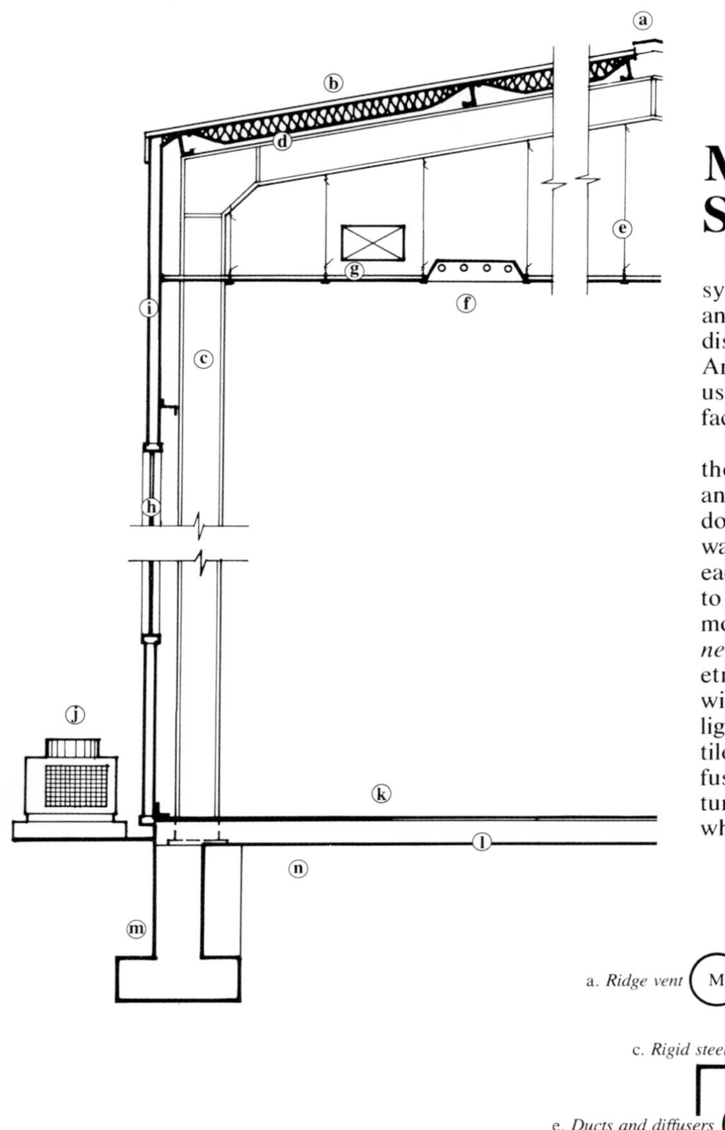

Metal Building Systems

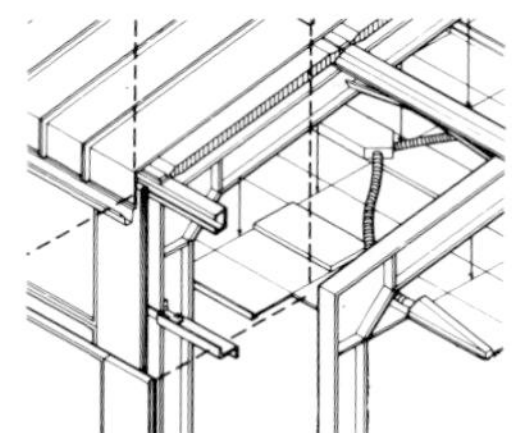

The advantage of metal building systems is in the ability to assemble and disassemble them rapidly. A disadvantage is lack of flexibility. An individual building's identity usually arises from color and surface options.

The two main wall components in the example are *unified* envelope and interior combinations: the window assembly and insulated metal wall panels. They are *connected* to each other, and both are *connected* to the steel frame. The heat pump mounted beside the building is *connected* to the wall panels that it penetrates. Batt insulation is *meshed* with the structural steel roof frame; light fixtures, suspended acoustical tile ceiling, and HVAC ducts and diffusers are *connected* to it. Light fixtures are *connected* to the ceiling, while ducts are *meshed* with it.

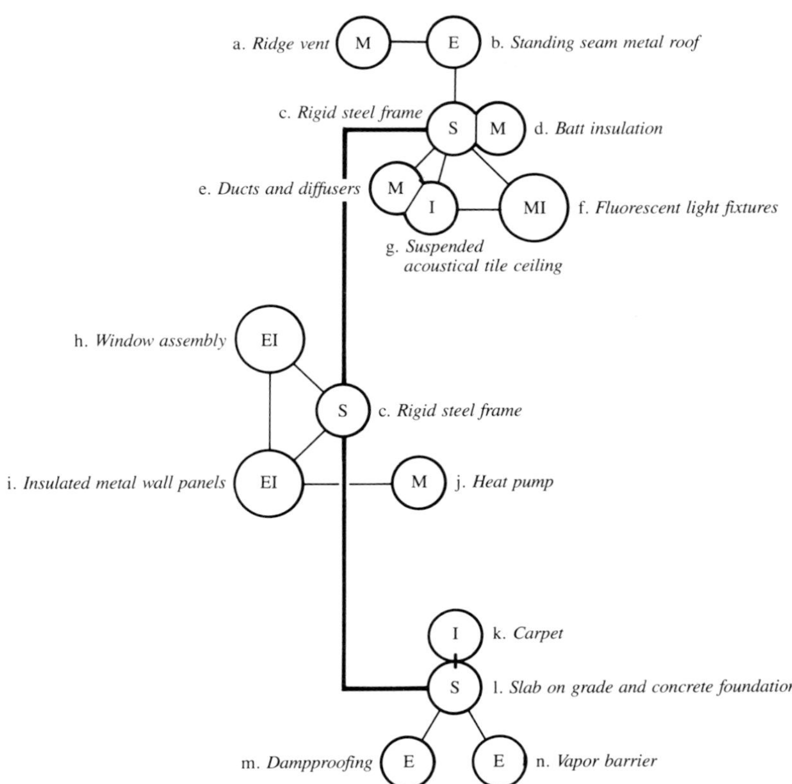

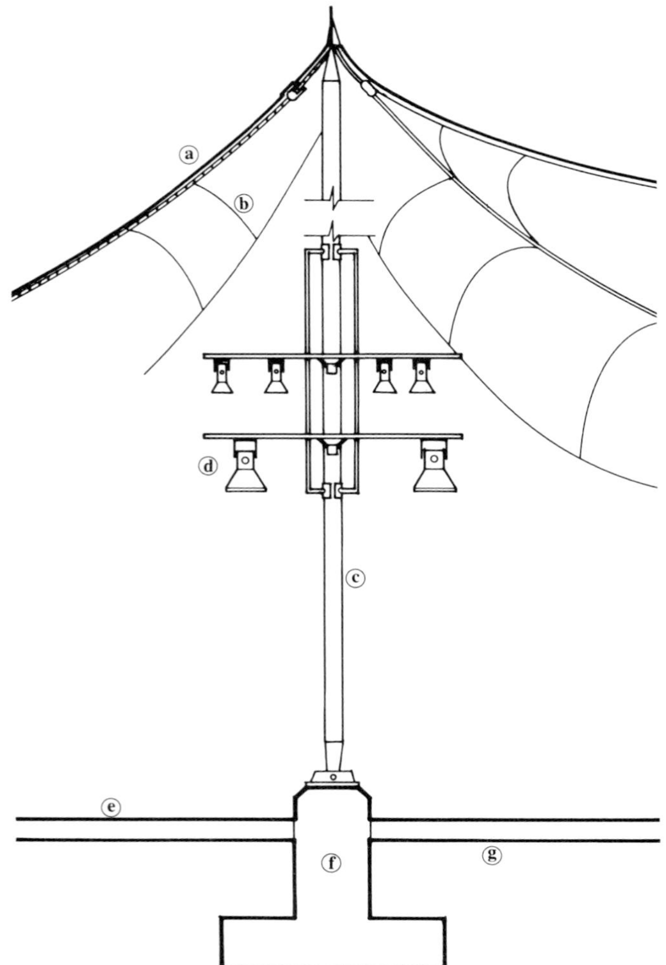

Tension Fabric Structures

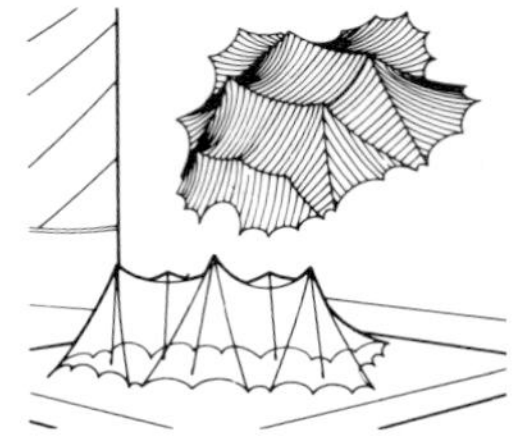

The level of integration achieved in tension fabric structures is elegantly expressed in the simplicity of the ball diagram. A condition that does not find expression in the ball diagram is the physical flexibility of the structure and its ability to accept movement. All systems are exposed to view in a type of construction that offers great construction speed but little opportunity for subsequent alteration.

Structure, envelope, and interior are unified in the non-combustible fabric membrane roof. Structural steel cables, located in sleeves of the fabric to provide extra support, are *meshed* with the roof. Fabric and cables are *connected* to the masts, as are the light fixtures and speakers. The masts, in turn, are *connected* to the floor structure.

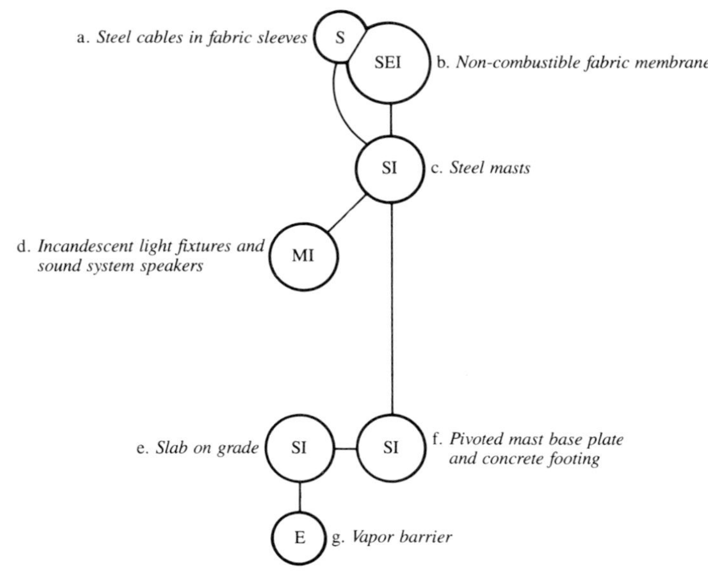

Chapter Three Ball Diagrams

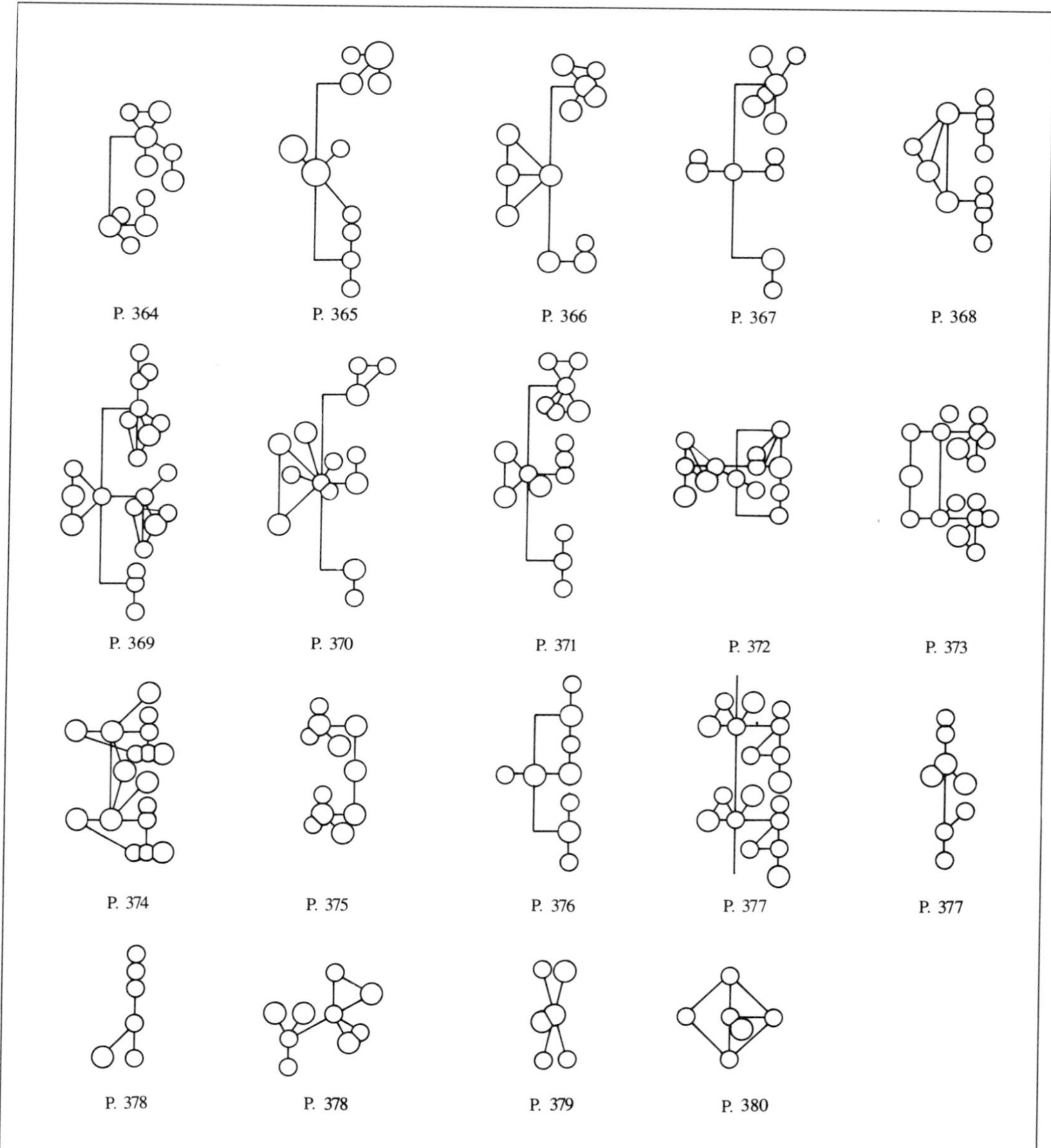

The diagrams shown above represent actual built conditions from the buildings analyzed in Chapter Three. They are interesting in their diversity, non-conformity, and complexity; buildings that are unique produce integration diagrams that are unique. It is impossible to say at this point what would have resulted if these diagrams had been used to generate the design from the inception. The diagrams also suggest a number of interesting exercises. One would be to diagram all of the recent buildings of a single architect; another would be to diagram several buildings of the same type designed by different architects.

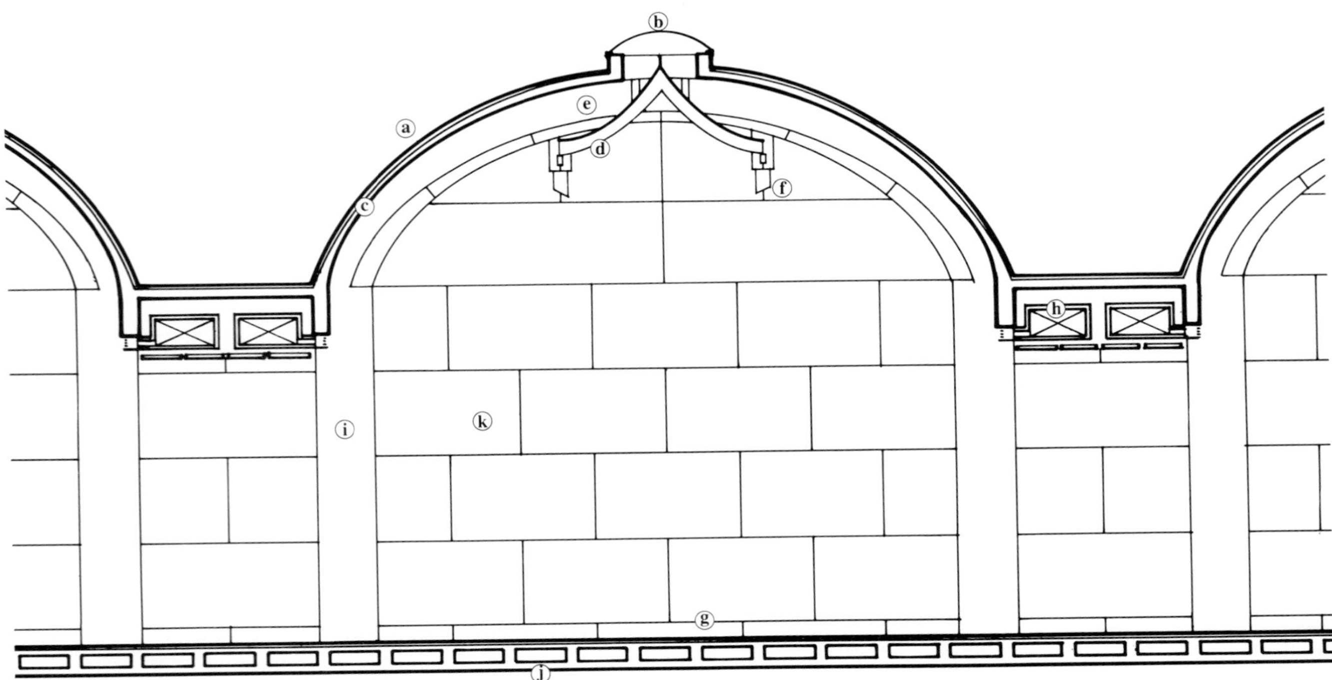

Kimbell Museum

Visual and functional integration are the hallmarks of Louis Kahn's work, and nowhere are they more apparent than in the roof and ceiling composition of the Kimbell Art Museum. Vaulted concrete shells form the roof structure and are exposed to the interior and *unified* with it. The shells, covered with a sheet lead envelope, are split in the middle to accommodate double-glazed acrylic skylights that provide natural light to the gallery spaces. Aluminum "gull-wing" reflectors reflect the natural light up to the shell as well as downward. Incandescent track lighting is *connected* to these reflectors instead of the structure to preserve the geometric lines of the shells. Supply ductwork is incorporated into the roof system between the vault forms.

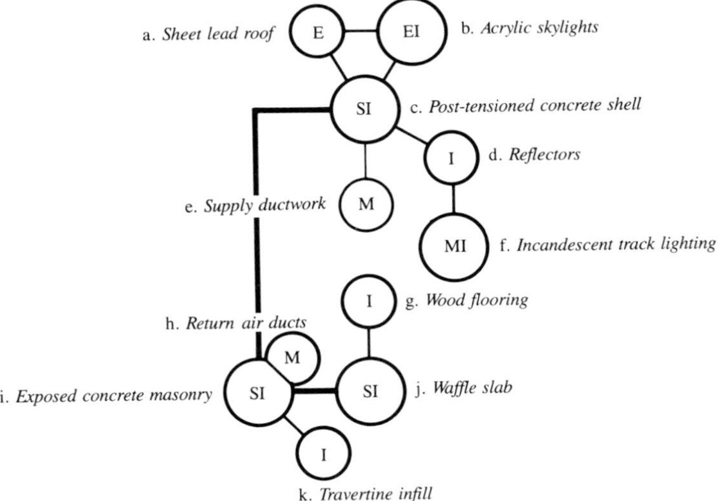

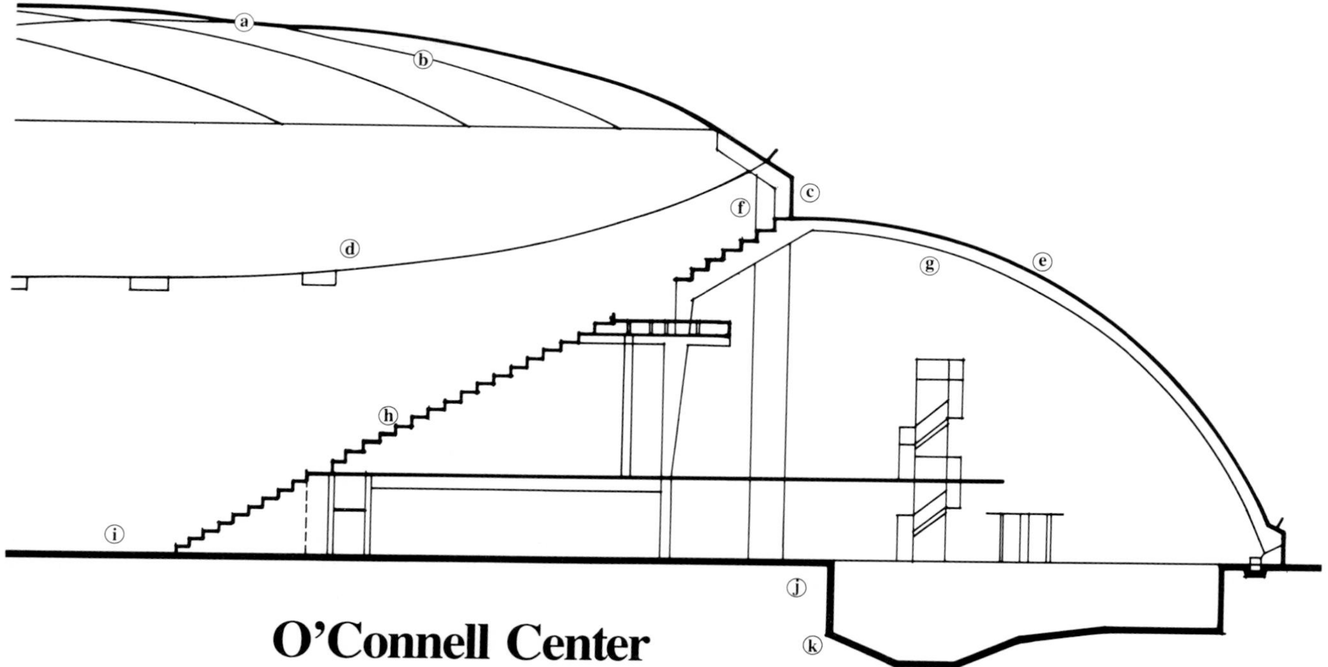

O'Connell Center

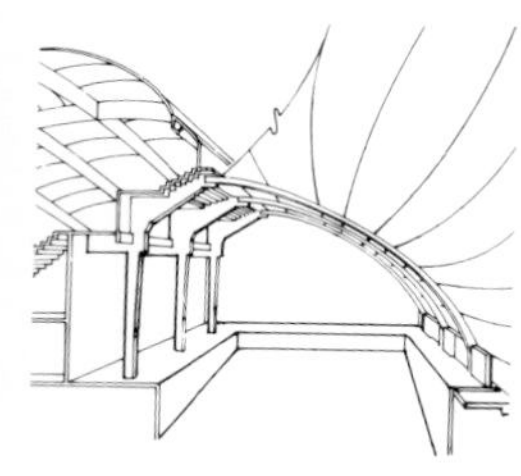

The roof of the Stephen C. O'Connell Activities Center is highly integrated, as structural, envelope, and interior functions are all *unified* by the air-supported, translucent, Teflon coated fiberglass roof over the arena space. The structural advantage of light weight is closely related to its translucence, which permits daylighting and reduces demand on the mechanical system. Roof vents serve to automatically relieve overpressurization, which can result if the building's four 100-horsepower fans overcompensate for exiting characteristics or high winds. The compression ring holding the cables that stabilize the air-supported dome is exposed to view. Lighting for the arena space is supported by cables.

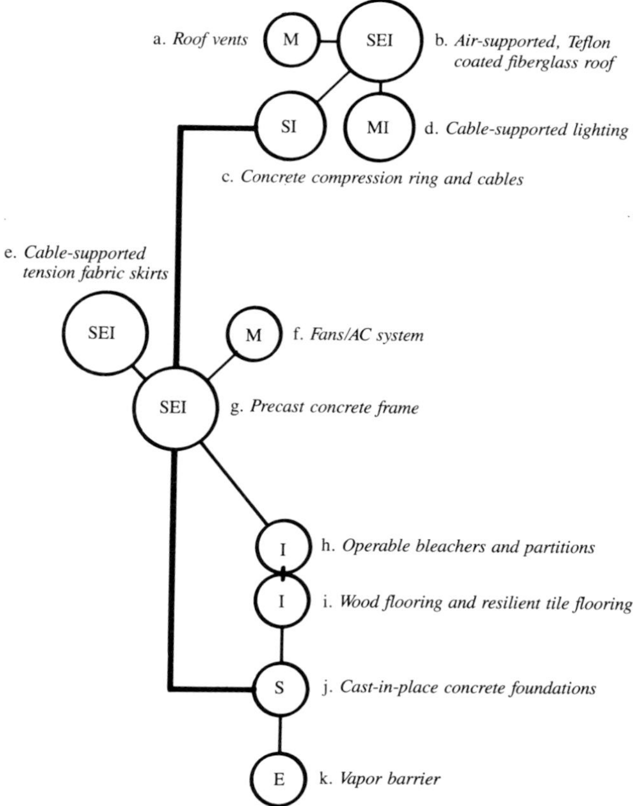

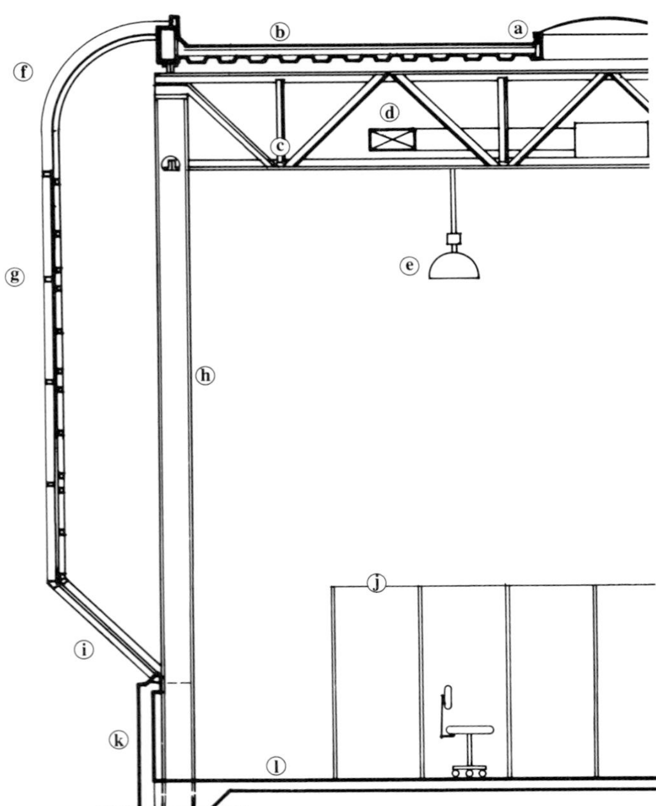

Herman Miller

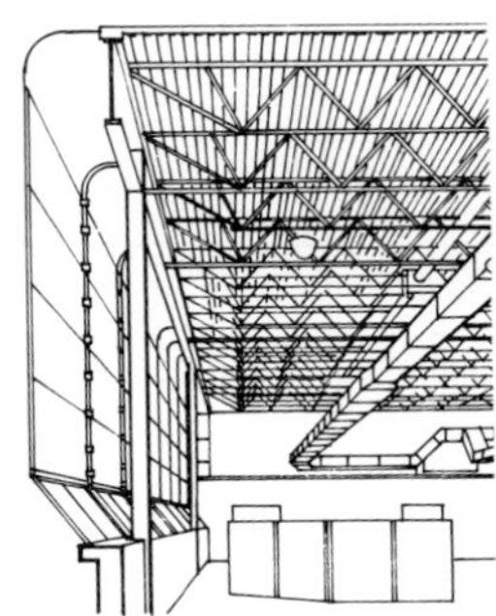

The wall section of the Herman Miller Seating Manufacturing Plant is composed of everyday building products with multiple uses; these combine to form a highly integrated system. The three major envelope components are a curved acrylic clerestory, lightweight insulating metal panels, and operable windows, all of which are *unified* with the interior. The steel curtain wall frame, to which the panels are *connected,* and steel columns are exposed to the interior as well. The base of the wall, of exposed concrete, serves as a retaining wall for an earth berm and is integral with the floor slab.

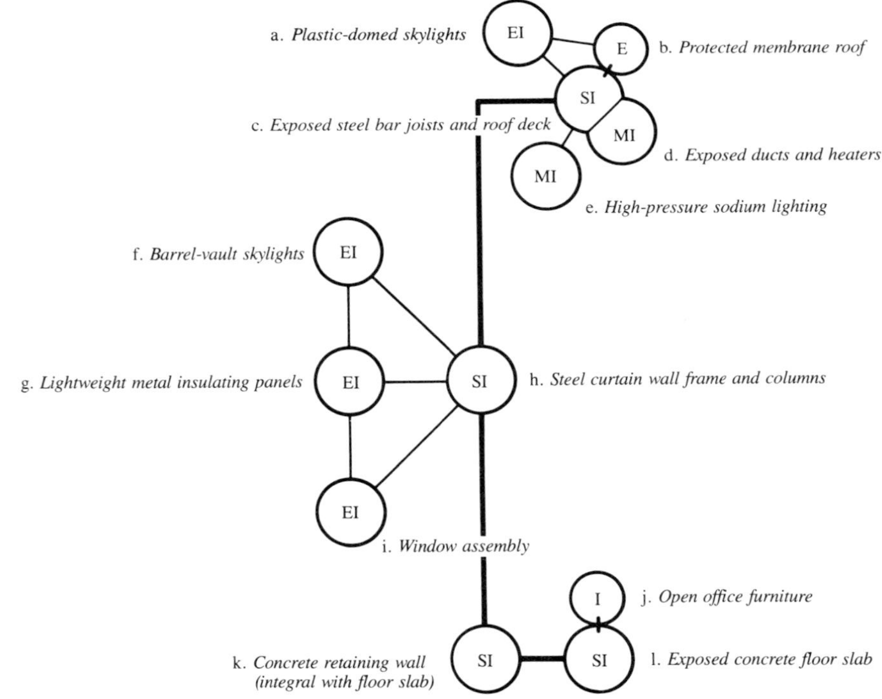

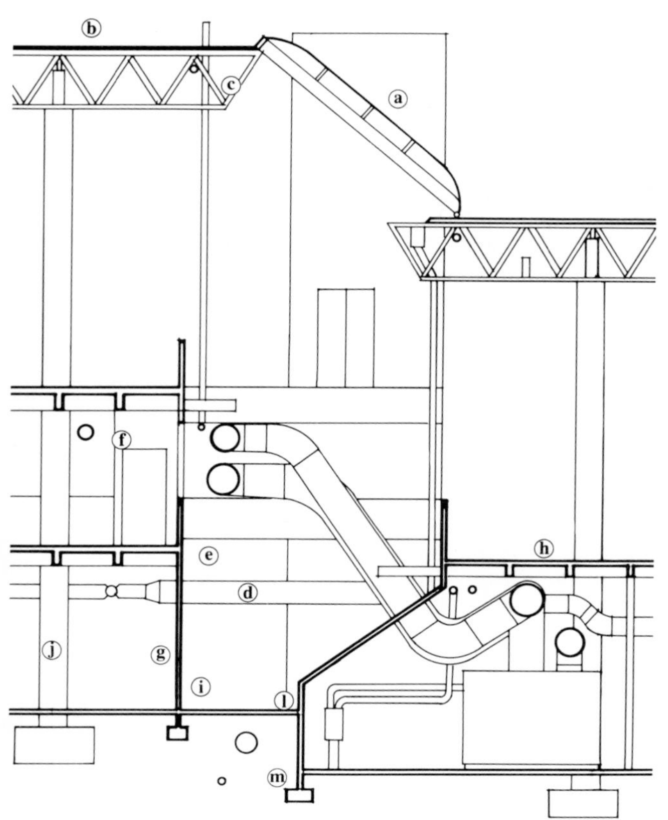

Museum of Science and Industry

The space frame roof canopy is the focal point of integration in the Museum of Science and Industry. Shading provided by this structural solution permits a vast reduction in mechanical system loads. The structural space frame is exposed to the interior and allows visual display of brightly-colored ducts and pipes that are *meshed* through its struts. Exhibit boards and fluorescent and incandescent lighting are hung from the structure. The space frame is covered by an exposed metal deck which in turn is topped with rigid insulation and a built-up roof. Skylights form the north slope of the roof and allow daylight into the spaces below.

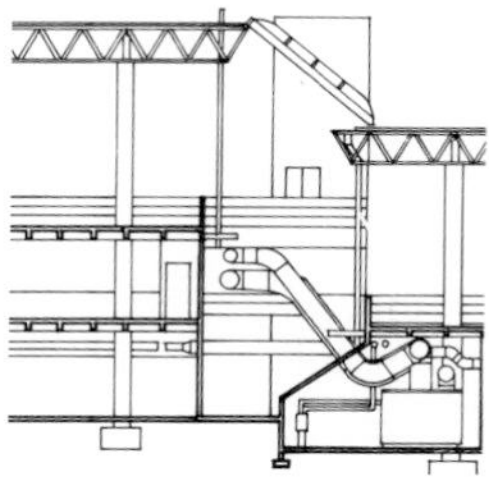

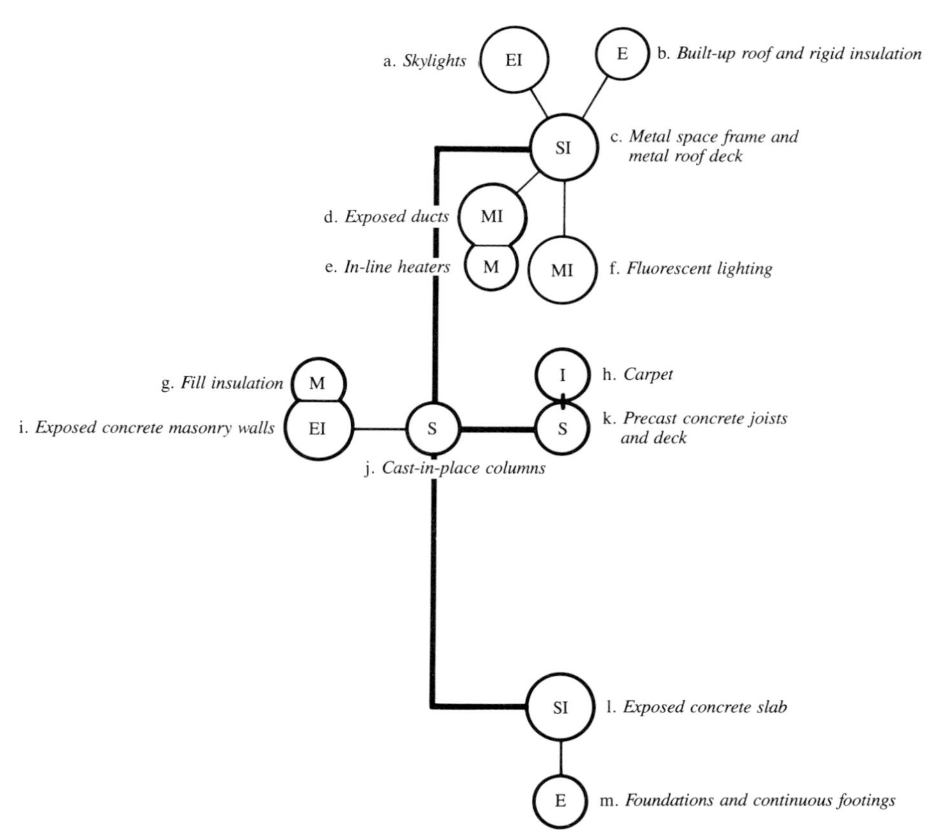

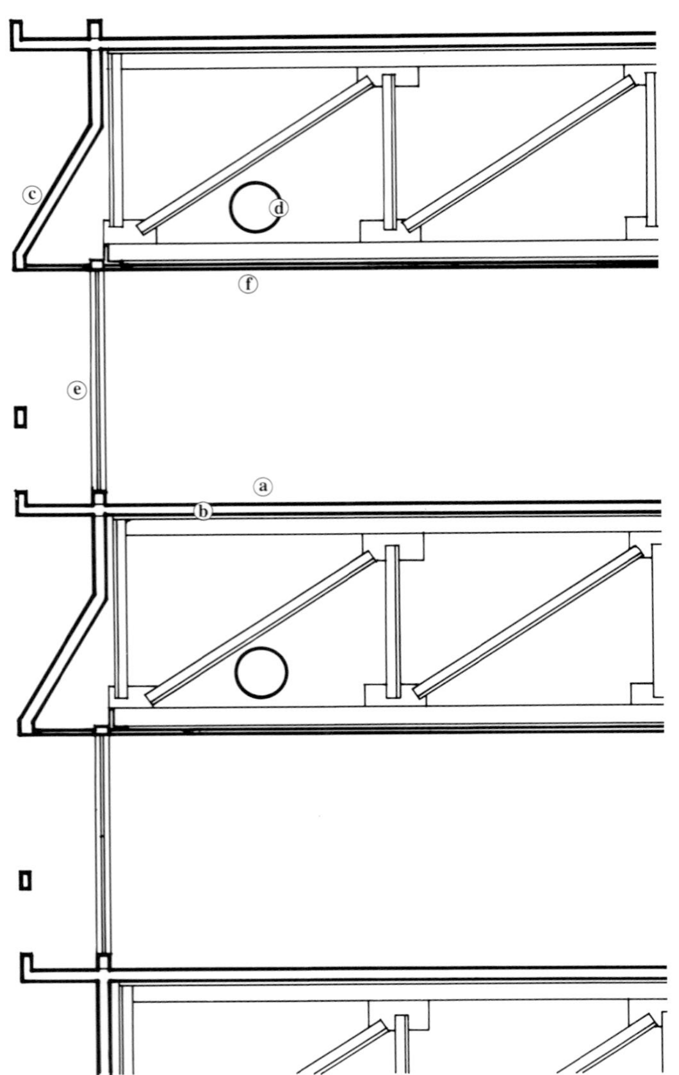

Walter Reed

The need for flexible, easily accessible mechanical spaces led to the design of the 7 ft high interstitial floors of Walter Reed General Hospital. Huge steel floor joists create these spaces and are *meshed* with communications, materials handling, and HVAC equipment away from patient services. This arrangement provides for ease of maintenance and alteration and helps meet sanitation requirements. It also allows for pinpoint alterations of laboratory and operating rooms. The additional cubage is not as critical as the effectiveness of service.

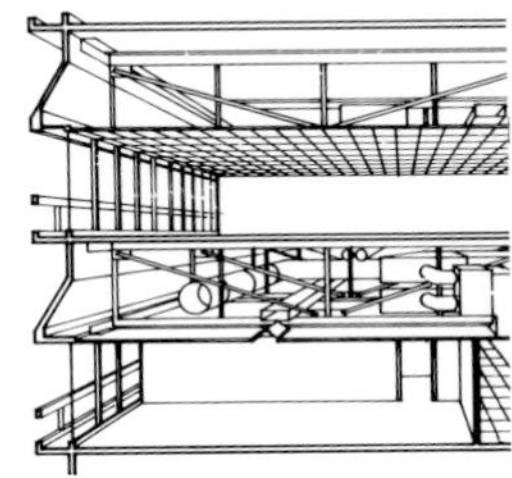

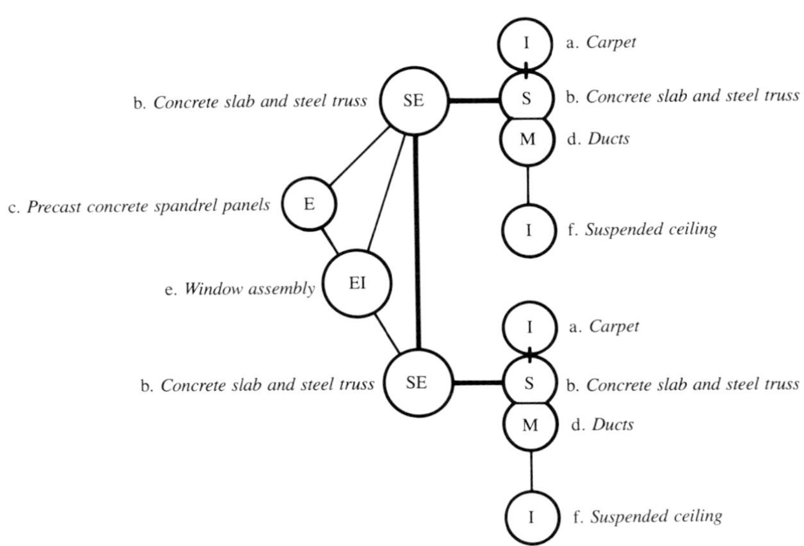

Stockton State College

The roof and ceiling system of Stockton State College uses standard building components to achieve a moderate level of integration. The steel bar joists *mesh* with ductwork and batt insulation and are topped with a metal roof deck and built-up roofing. The joists also support the air-handling luminaires which *mesh* mechanical and interior functions in the lay-in ceiling.

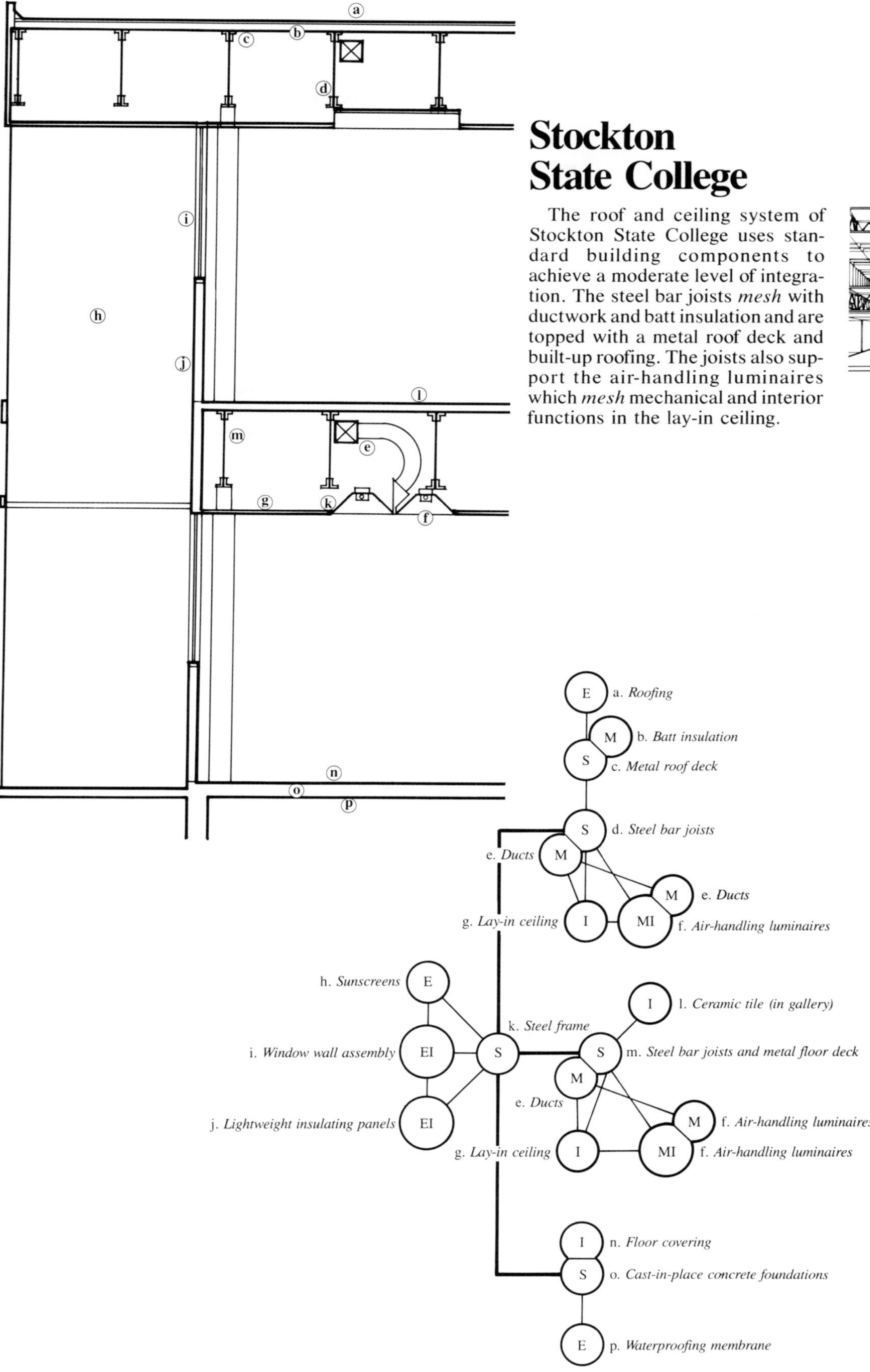

Vocational Technical Education Facility

The Trombe wall construction of the Vocational Technical Education Facility at the University of Minnesota is a good example of double wall construction for energy conservation. Such passive solar combinations are difficult to diagram because inert building materials take on mechanical properties. In this case, the storage wall is structural, consisting of filled concrete block backed with drywall. The exterior "moisture wall" is glass and is placed 3 ft from the mass wall, creating a narrow greenhouse space. Insulating shades and sunscreens within the space shade the wall when solar gain is not wanted.

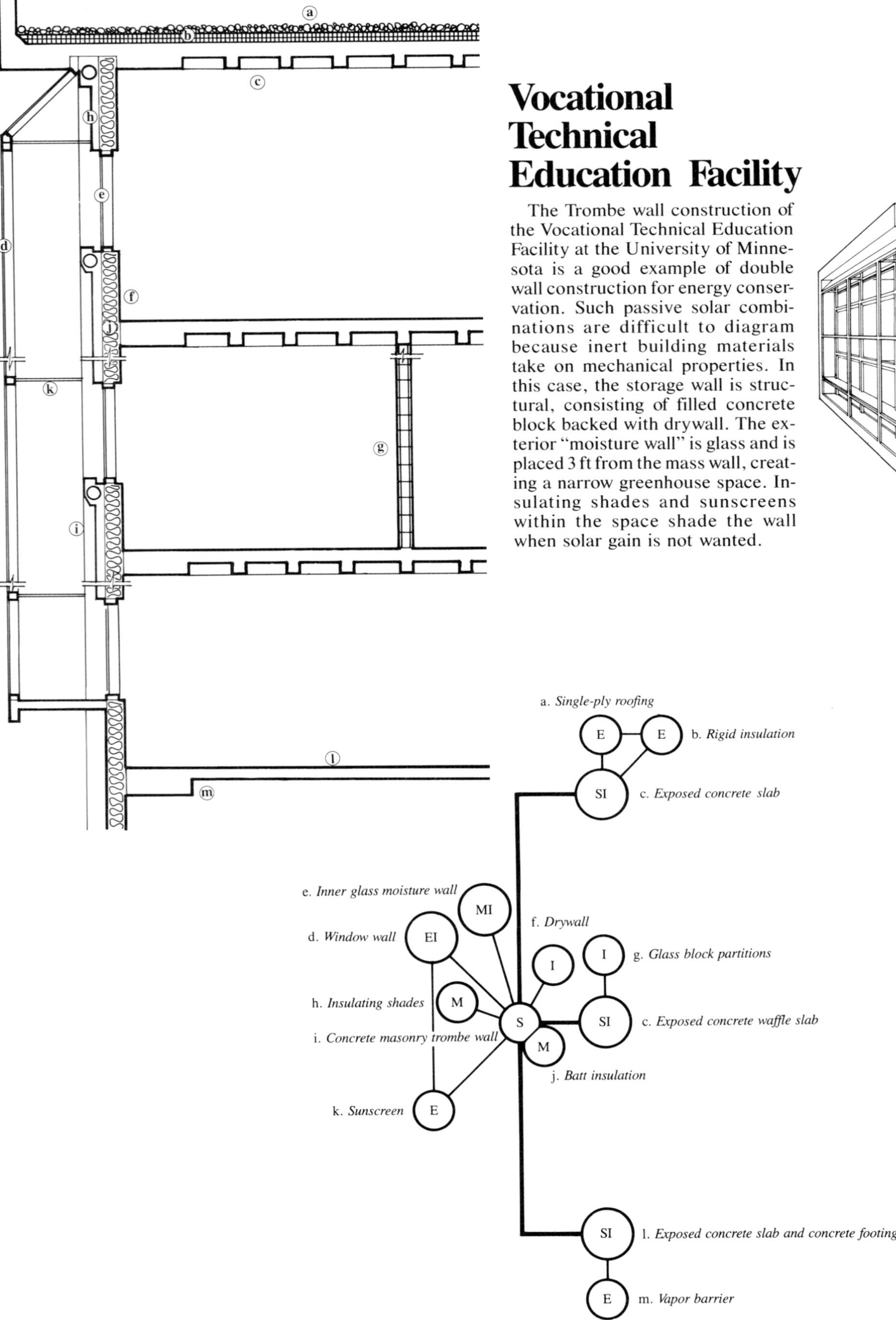

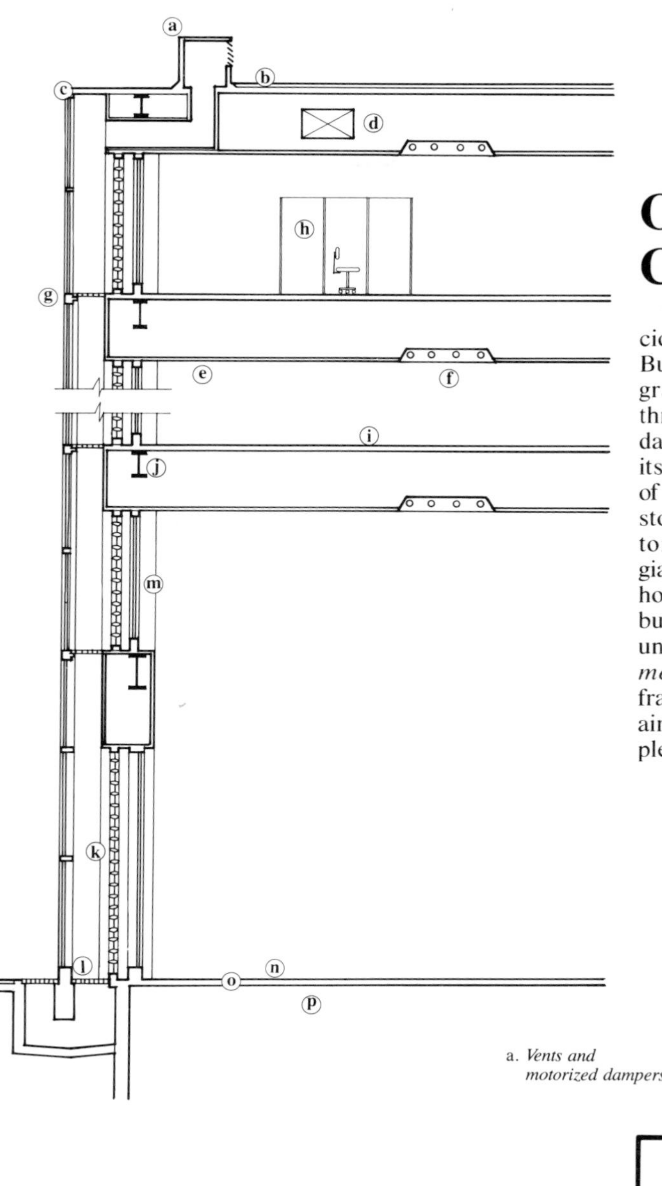

Occidental Chemical

The double curtain wall of the Occidental Chemical Company Office Building is a clear example of integration for energy conservation through control of heat transfer and daylighting. The air space between its inner and outer walls, the former of insulating glass, forms a nine-story air plenum. Controlled by automatic vents and dampers, this giant plenum acts either as a greenhouse to warm the air around the building or as a chimney to exhaust unwanted heat. Return air grilles *meshed* with the steel structural frame's metal deck floors take the air from the office space into the plenum.

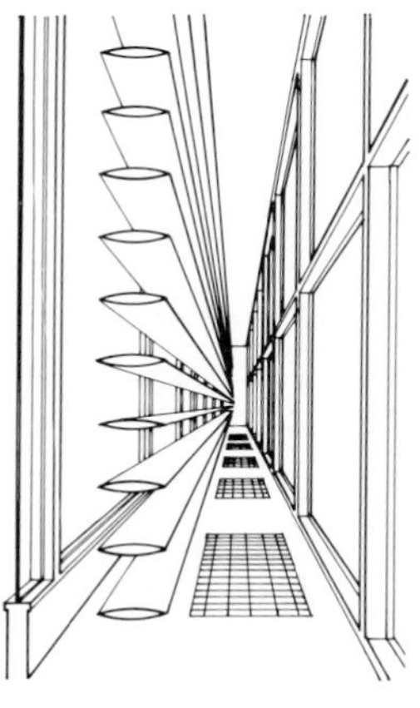

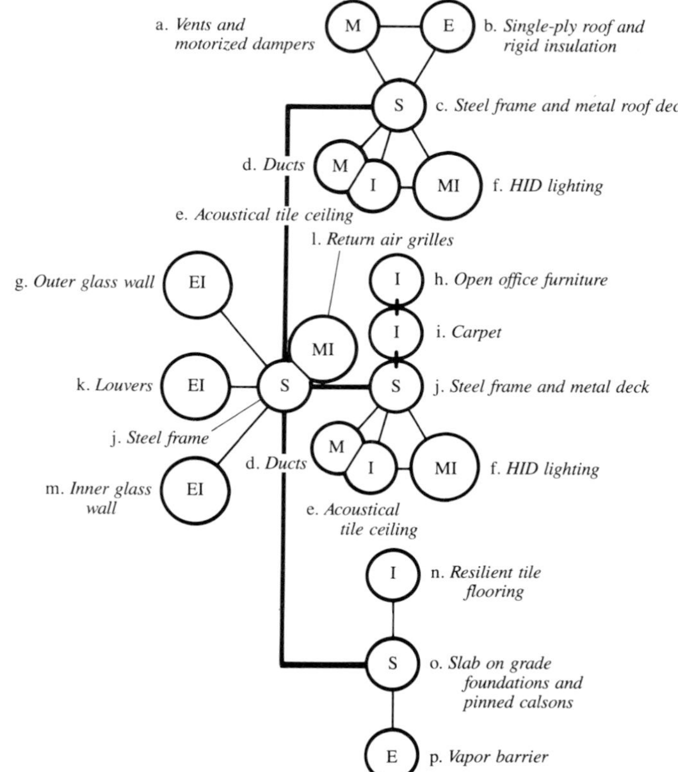

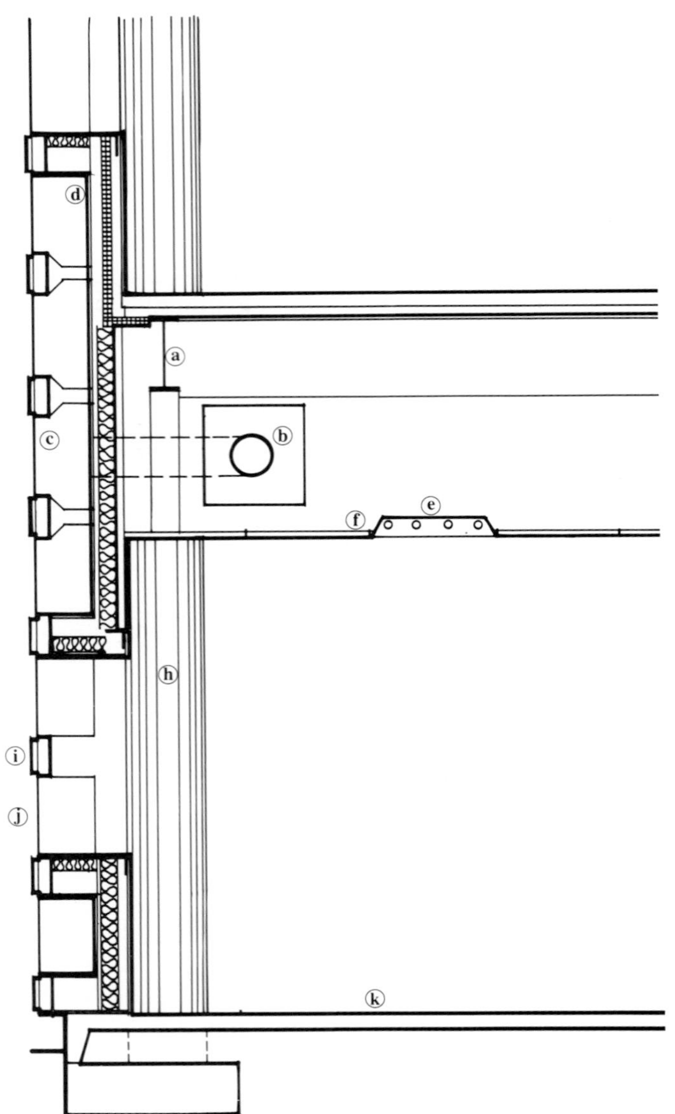

Equitable Life

Creation of "solar belts" between the exterior glass and an aluminum-panelled exterior wall gives the Southern Service Center for the Equitable Life Assurance Society its ability to balance thermal demands and conserve energy. As in the Occidental Chemical building, the double wall system creates a solar-heated air plenum serviced by ducts to the interior space. In essence, the envelope is transformed into a duct, a creative act of integration that transcends simple system description. To further conserve energy, the interior wall is lined with batt insulation.

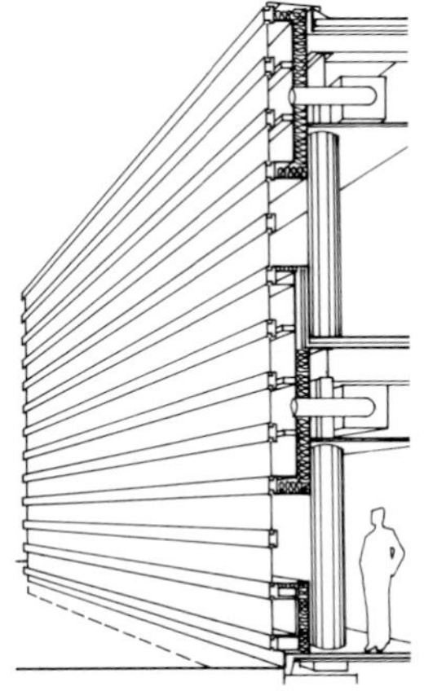

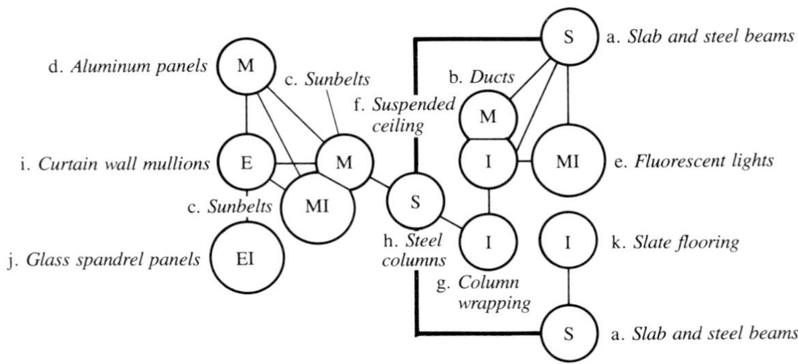

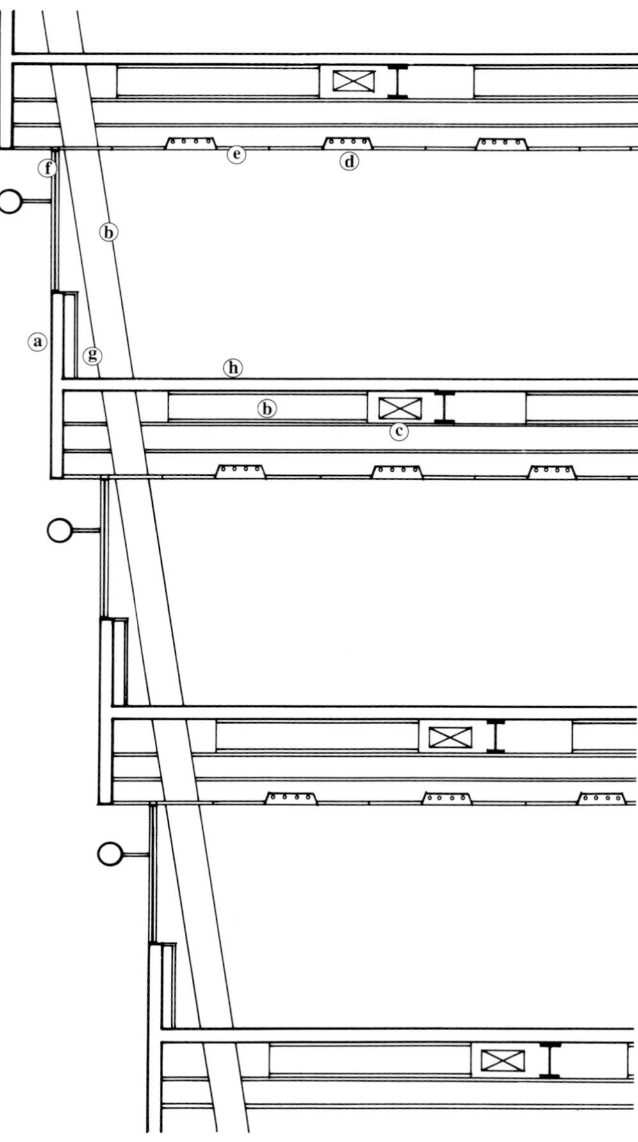

Georgia Power

The steel stub girder system chosen for the floor structure of the Georgia Power Company Corporate Headquarters saves space in the office tower by allowing ducts and conduits to be *meshed* with the structure. In this respect, stub girders serve the same purpose as wood trusses; they also produce savings in overall building height. The steel frame supports a suspended ceiling which is *connected* to high-pressure sodium lamps chosen for their low energy use.

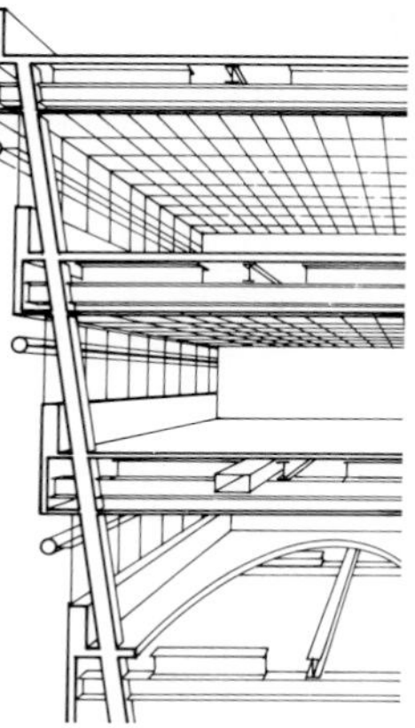

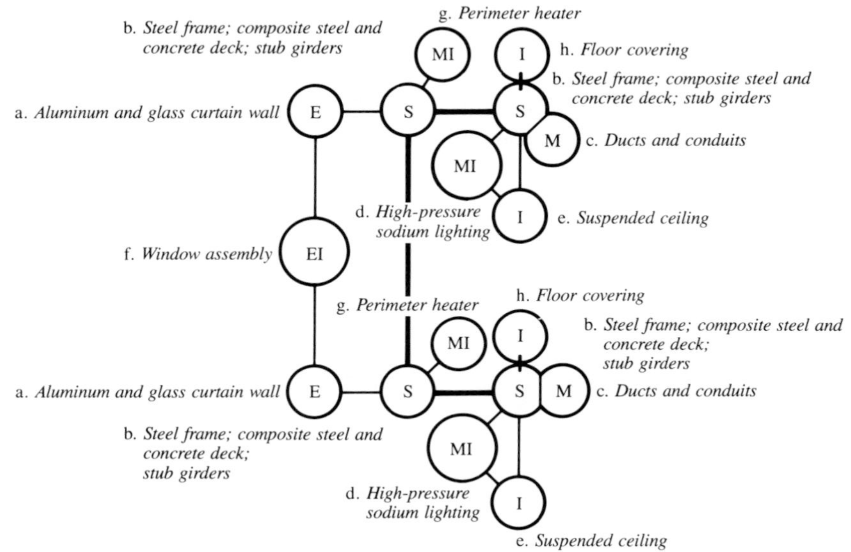

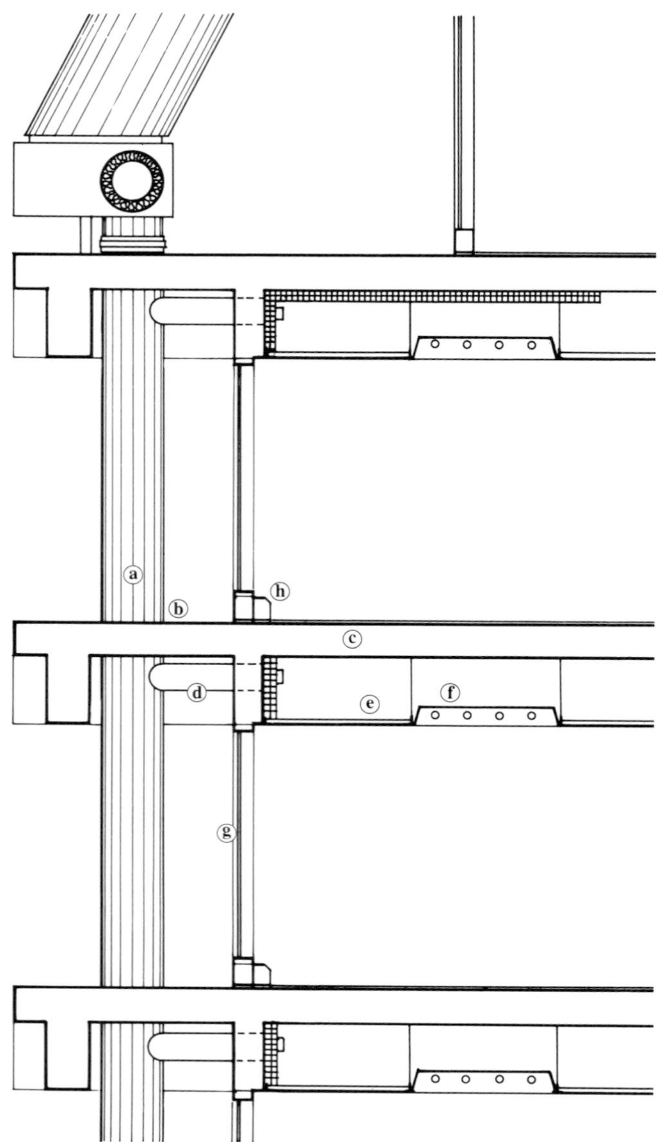

National Permanent

The exterior exposure of the black metal ducts and concrete columns of the National Permanent Building is an example of integration governed by visual coordination. Functionally, the columns diminish in size as they rise and carry less load; the supply ducts decrease in size as they descend from the rooftop and carry less air. To prevent heat loss, the ducts are lined with insulation, painted black, and moved to the interior on the north facade. Also for energy conservation, the gray-glass windows are recessed and shaded by grill overhangs on the south and west facades. The interior finish is drywall, and baseboard heaters provide supplemental heat.

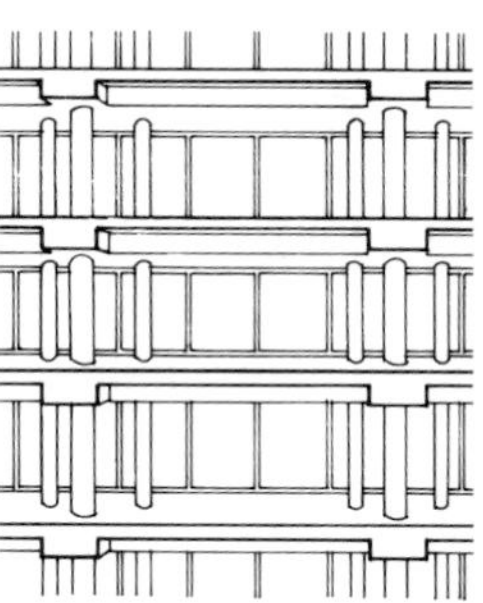

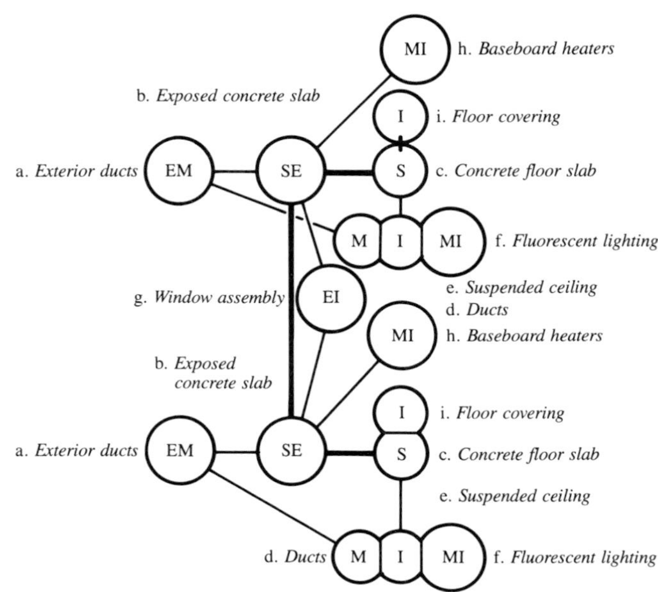

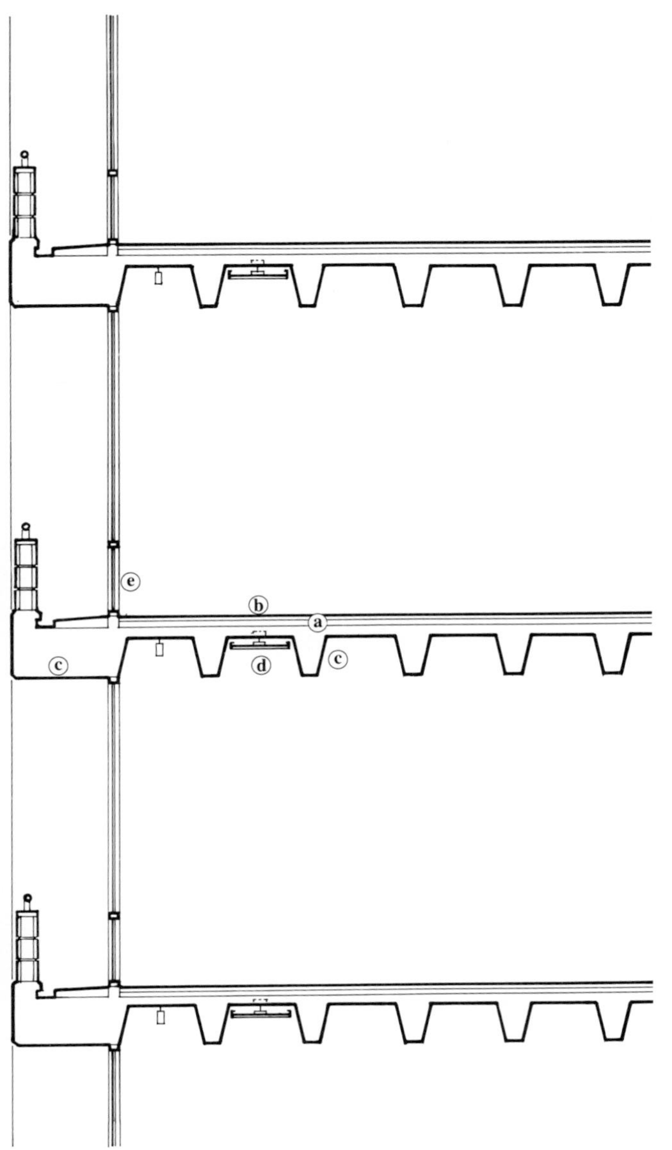

Pike and Virginia

The concrete waffle slab structure of the Pike and Virginia Building is an integrating element for the ceiling and the space below it, and for the floor and the space above it. The waffle slab is exposed as the finish ceiling, with implications for the interior arising from its thermal mass, as well as from its hard, resonant surface and the possibility of structure-borne sound. Its coffers provide recesses into which radiant heat panels and light fixtures can be *meshed*. As a floor, it is topped with rigid insulation and a lightweight concrete slab through which wiring is routed. The occupant chooses the floor finish.

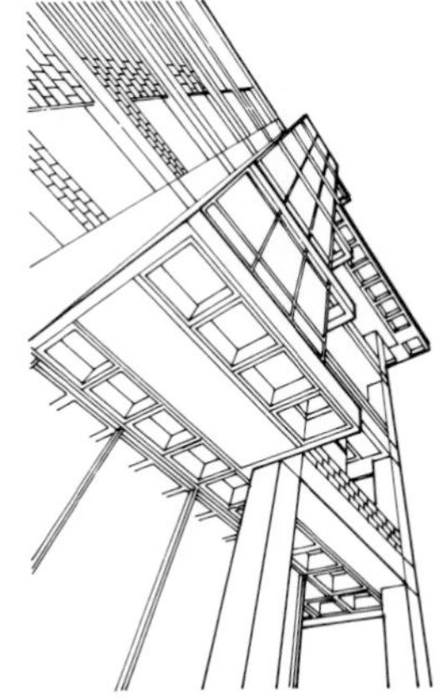

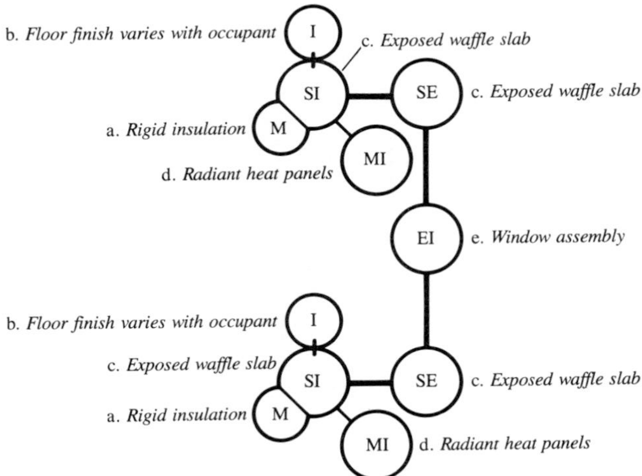

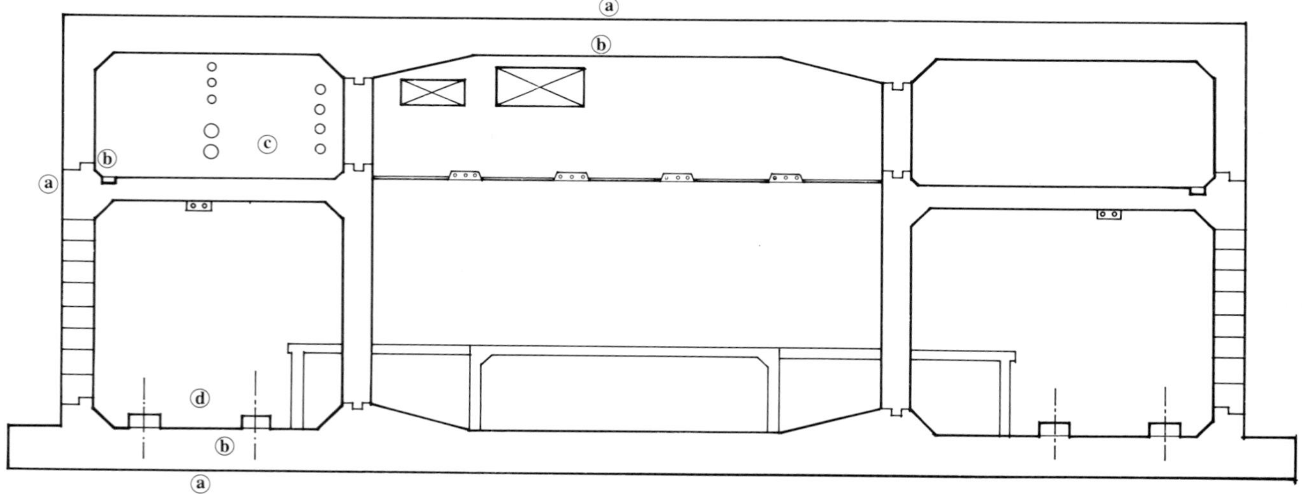

Atlanta Airport

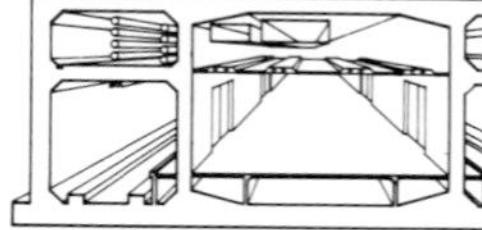

Precast insulated concrete panels *unify* structure and envelope in the underground spine of the Atlanta International Airport. This combination produces a relatively simple ball diagram. The panels form what amounts to a horizontal elevator shaft for the people-mover. The distances involved are very demanding on the HVAC system, and on the passenger who decides to walk them. The car interiors of the people-mover are visibly integrated with the stations as elevator cars are with the lobbies they serve. As in Walter Reed, a separation of mechanical space from human space is evident in the section.

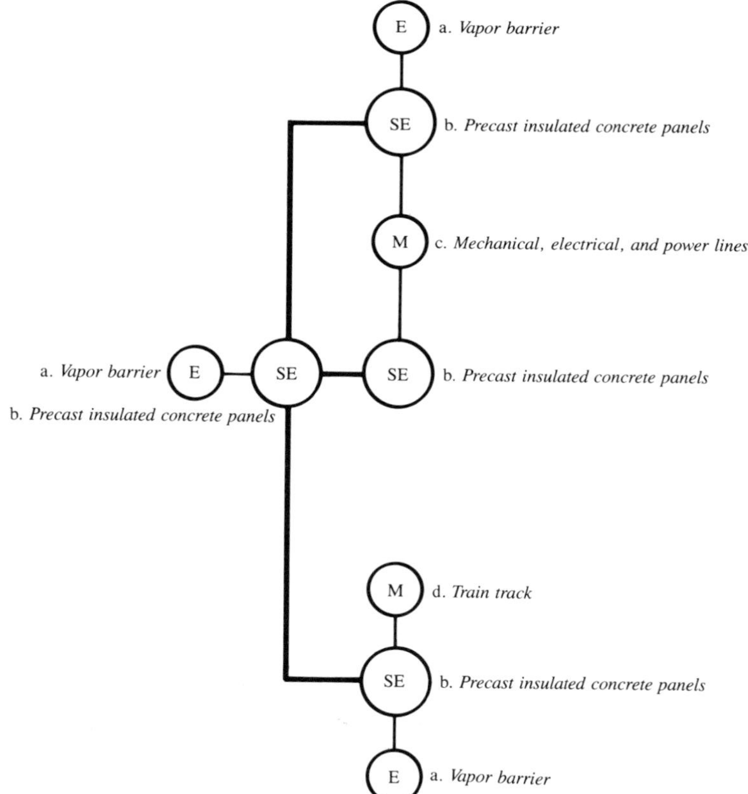

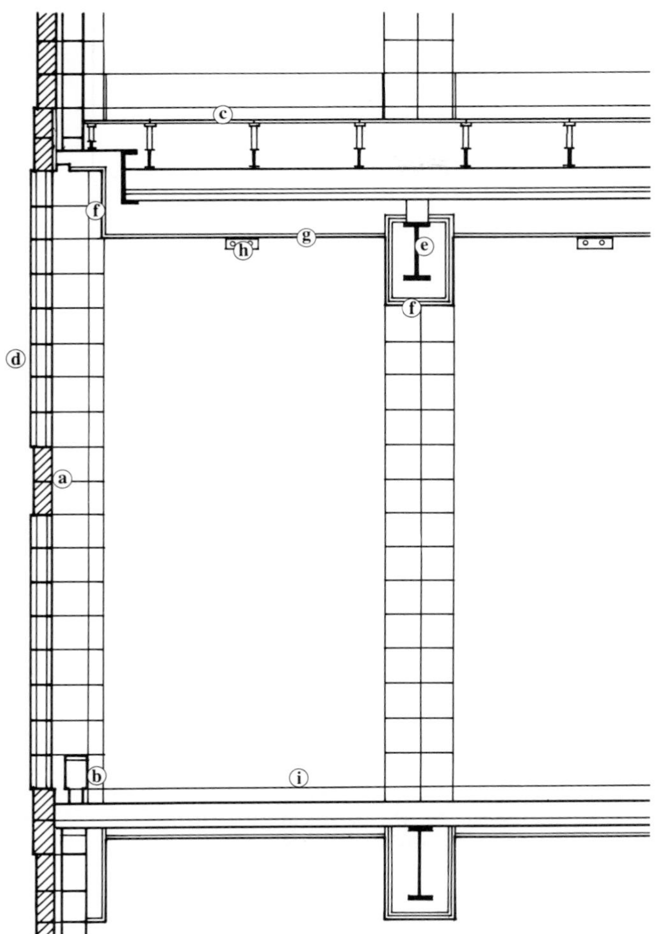

Addition to Submarine Training Facility

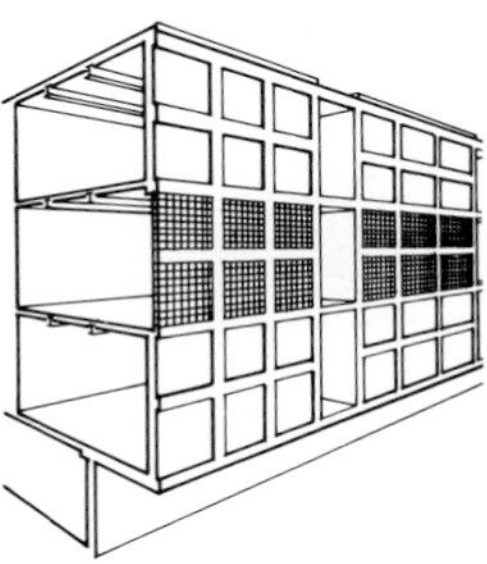

An interior floor in the addition to the Submarine Training Facility at Groton features a drop floor slab to accommodate an access floor; computer and electrical equipment is not shown in the diagram. The access floor *touches* the structure and possesses structural characteristics itself. It is also one of the few interior products with a *touching* relationship to the substrate which are nevertheless permanent parts of the building. This condition facilitates change in the event of future remodeling. The glass block panels, like window glass, *unify* envelope and interior.

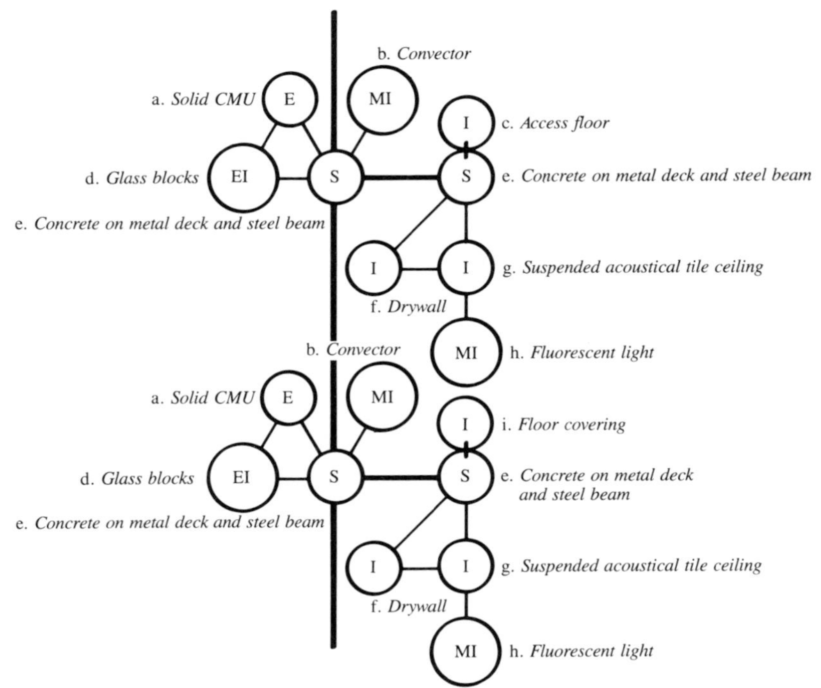

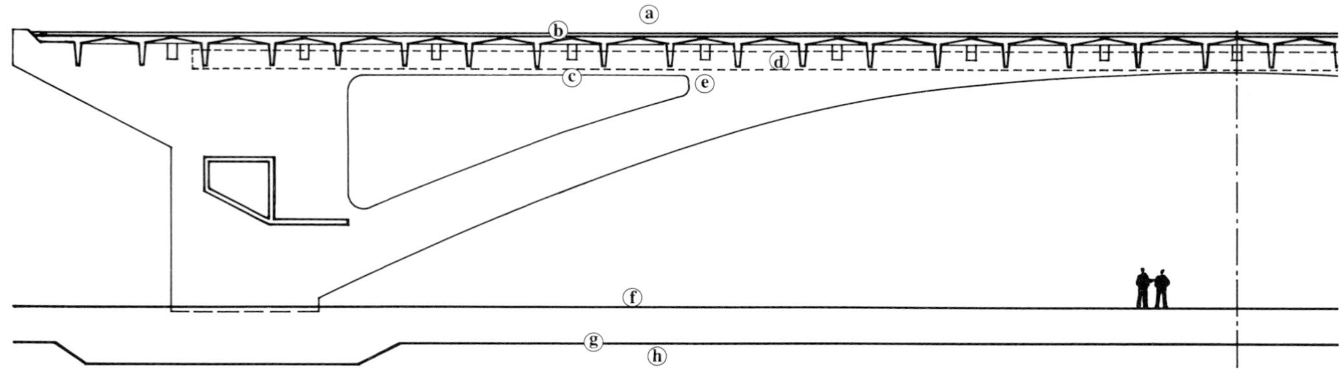

Moscone Center

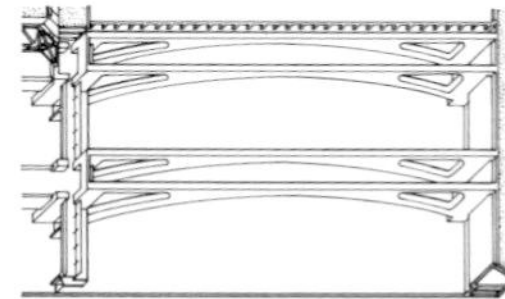

The five acre roof of the George R. Moscone Convention Center is supported by pairs of huge concrete arches exposed to and *unified* with the interior exhibition space. The roof itself is cast-in-place concrete topped with a protected membrane roof. Earth serves as the roof ballast. It should be noted that paired arches are not structurally more efficient than single ones; the task of nesting the ducts was a very strong visible integration criterion. The exposed ducts in the exhibition space are *meshed* between the pairs of arches, which also support the fluorescent lighting system and sprinklers.

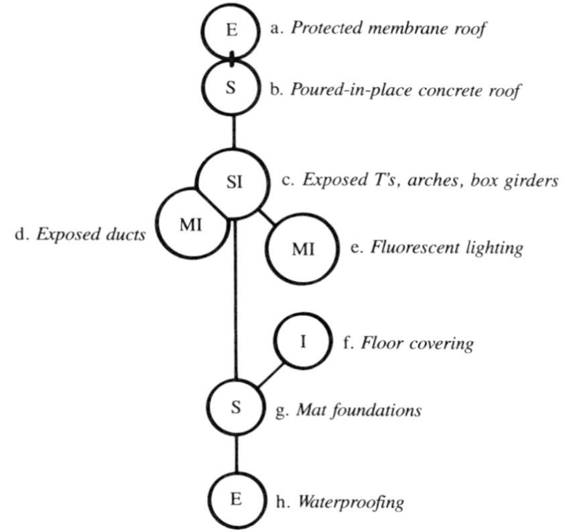

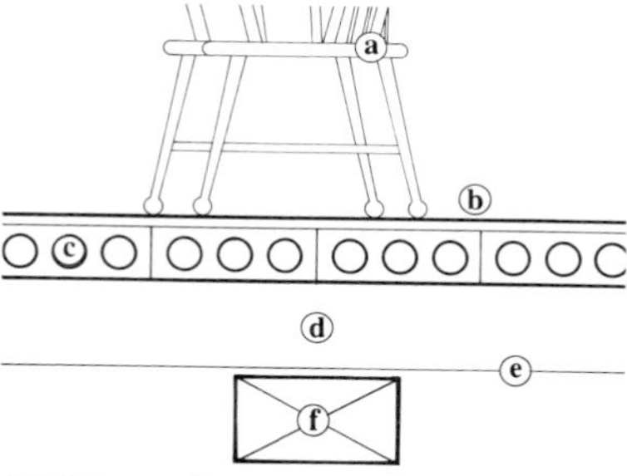

Illinois Regional Library

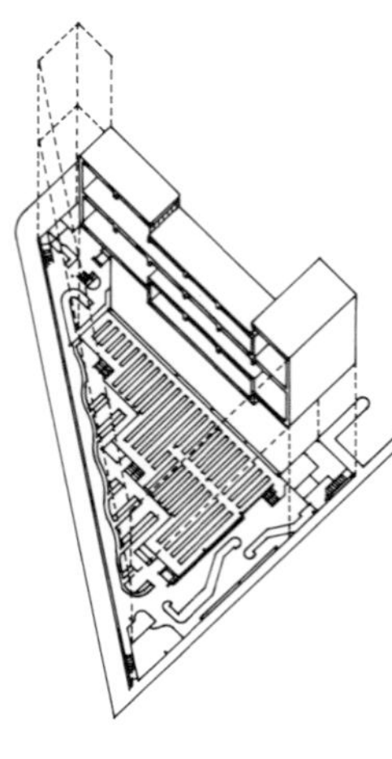

In the Illinois Regional Library for the Blind and Physically Handicapped, the integration interest stems from the unique class of building users. The result is expressed primarily in plan and in small-scale detailing. Exposed and brightly painted structural and mechanical elements are *unified* with the interior, as are precast concrete planks visible in the ceiling. The latter are used together with steel beams, a material combination which does not strongly affect the ball diagram.

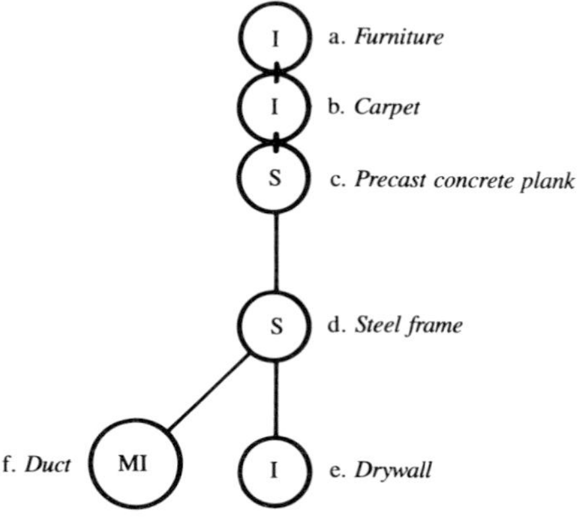

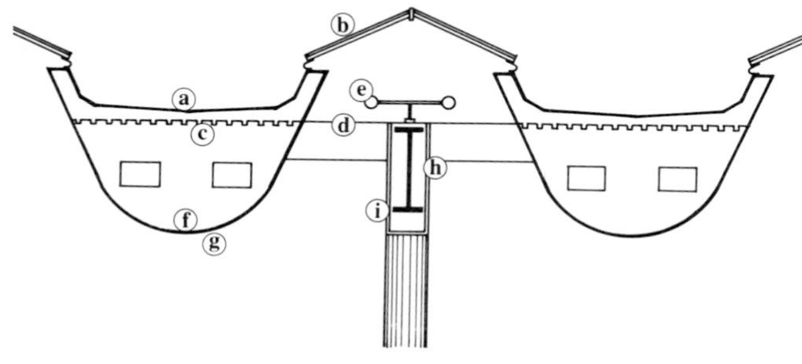

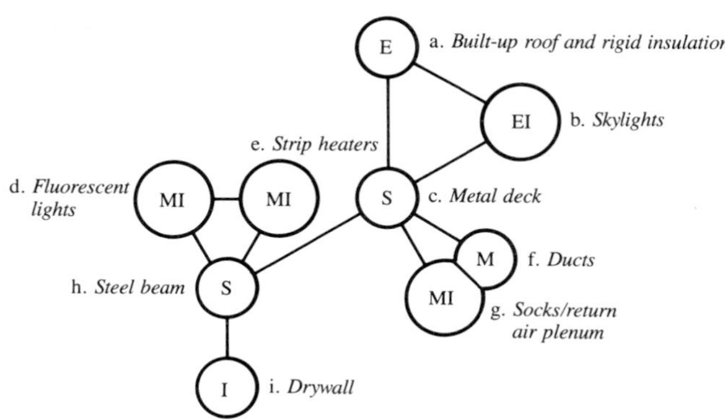

Aid Association for Lutherans

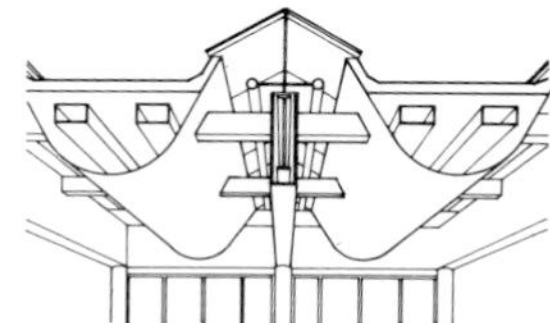

The ceiling composition of the Aid Association for Lutherans Headquarters incorporates all four building systems into a specialized, integrated design. The white fiberglass "socks," designed to diffuse light and sound, act as return air plenums and hide ducts and air-handling equipment. The socks are hung from a metal deck and encased steel beams, which also support fluorescent light fixtures and strip heaters. The deck is covered with rigid insulation and built-up roofing. Skylights span the areas between the socks.

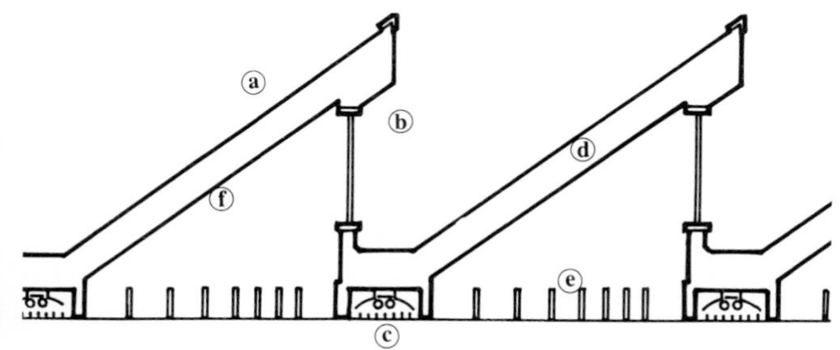

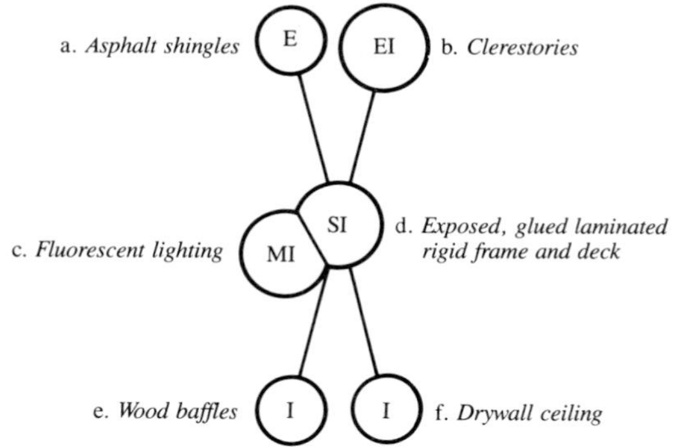

Trust Pharmacy

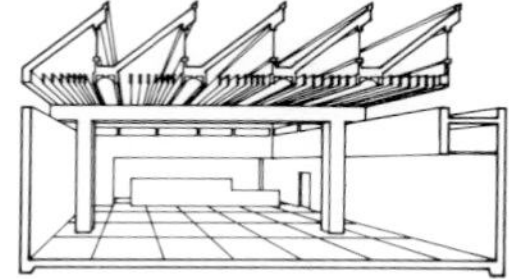

The roof of the Trust Pharmacy provides much of the heating and cooling in a building specially designed to be climate-responsive. A series of clerestories admit sunlight to the interior; wood baffles at the ceiling are positioned to enhance solar gain in winter and limit it in summer. An asphalt shingle roof covers the roof deck and the glued laminated rigid roof frame, both of which are exposed to and *unified* with the interior. The frame supports the wood baffles and fluorescent lighting over the space.

John Nutting Apartments

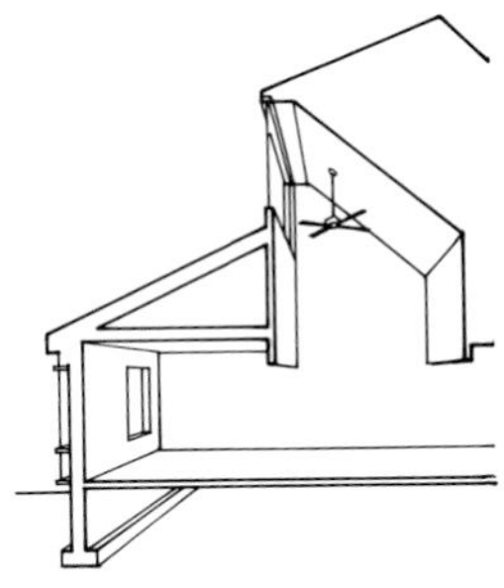

Energy conservation through the use of Trombe walls is a major integration theme in the wall assemblies of the John C. Nutting Apartments. The glass and masonry Trombe wall stores solar heat which is released to the interior space through damper-controlled registers. Outside-mounted canvas awnings shade the Trombe walls and double-glazed window assemblies when solar heat gain is undesirable. Other wall structures are wood stud frame, with batt insulation *meshed* between the studs and drywall *connected* to the interior side. A unique character and regional flavor are achieved by means of commonplace systems and connections.

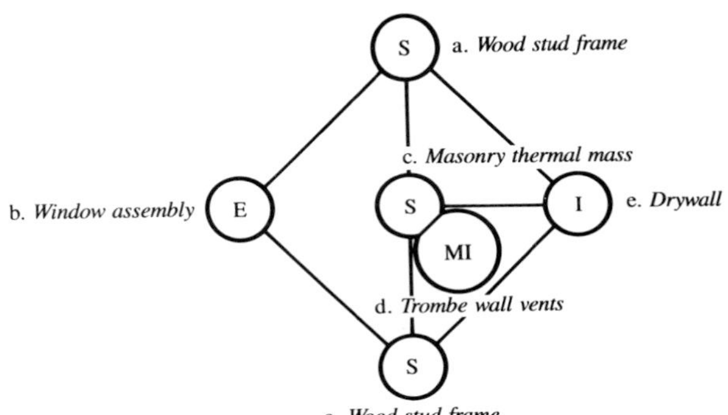

Visible Integration

Throughout the history of architecture, the esthetics of systems integration have varied widely. Expression of structure alone can be traced historically from Egypt to Las Vegas. Today, each building type can emphasize a different attitude. Similarly, every architect has his or her own unique perceptions of the way the building should look when it is completed. Some personal styles are so distinctive as to be immediately recognizable as the work of a particular architect.

To many lay people, it might appear that an architect's primary purpose is to order the environment visually. The question of whether the visual result originates in the mind of the architect or within the problem itself, or both, is one that could be, and is, argued constantly. At any given time in history, or even within the practice of a single architect, the pendulum of emphasis swings between formal domination and functional domination in the design process.

Buildings, while far from being exclusively visual experiences, always contain visual experience. There are buildings perceived as ugly which may work very well in other respects. There is probably a like number of buildings perceived as beautiful which do not function very well. Most buildings fall somewhere between these extremes. How well the finished building corresponds to the intended visual experience of the participants in the design is one measure of its performance. Each perception by each person who uses the building will in fact be different. Such performance is therefore extremely difficult to evaluate.[23]

23. Integration for performance, pp. 232–233.

In addition to more readily quantified performance criteria, systems integration is influenced by the visual qualities of the result. The functioning of the systems and the workability of the integration itself are affected when decisions made about the way a system looks affect its performance. Therefore, the question of the visual aspects of buildings must be addressed. Our purpose is not to propagate a particular esthetic, but rather to discuss the influence of esthetics on building systems integration.

In defining the types and levels of system combinations, we have limited ourselves as far as possible to describing readily observable physical conditions. Questions such as whether or not two systems are in contact, are connected, or occupy the same space should be sufficiently clear to yield objective answers. We have tried to define our own assumptions clearly enough to help make these evaluations universal. It is not necessary that each individual come to the same conclusion about integration levels. What is important is that the distinctions are made and that they are made consistently. In short, we have tried to invent a system that is consistent and that works. What should be clear is that in order to discuss integration, the distinctions must be made as to how systems combine. The real task is to define the context in which esthetics can be created.

Like the system combinations themselves, the physical results of an esthetic decision, as distinct from its underlying rationale, can be described in terms of a hierarchy of observed conditions. We define five levels of visible integration, three of which may occur simultaneously:

Level One: *Not visible, no change.* The system or subsystem in question is not in view to the building user, and therefore modification of its physical form is esthetically irrelevant. Example: HVAC equipment in a mechanical room.[24]

Level Two: *Visible, no change.* The system is exposed to public view but not altered or improved in any way from what the purely functional application requires. Example: Exposed structure in a parking garage or warehouse.[25]

Level Three: *Visible, surface change.* The system is visible to the building's occupants and has had only surface alteration made to it, with its other physical aspects remaining unchanged. Example: Brightly colored pipes or ductwork.[26]

Level Four: *Visible, with size or shape change.* The system is visible to the user of the building and has been given a size and/or shape other than what is simplest and most economical. The surface treatment and position may remain unchanged. Example: Octagonal columns or triangular light fixtures.[27]

Level Five: *Visible, with location or orientation change.* The system is exposed to the view of the occupants of the building, but its position has been altered from what is functionally optimal. The shape or surface, however, may remain unchanged. Example: Relocation of columns or ducts.[28]

THE FOUR SYSTEMS

Structural: The most efficient structural loading condition is tension. When a tensile member fails, it is fully stressed. A column can fail before all of the material contained in the section has been stressed to ultimate compressive capacity. A bending member (and columns sometimes take bending) contains both tension and compression. When one thinks of optimizing structure, it is usually in the context of minimizing the amount of material contained in it.[29] Structural efficiency therefore has a very strong innate geometry and orientation, as well as preferred proportions and dimensions. The physical form that results from purely structural criteria may not satisfy all visual criteria. For example, a space may suffer from a visible structure that is thought to be too dominant. For this reason, the architect may choose to hide the pattern created by a structure. A masonry wall may be made to deviate from the structural optimum in pattern, dimension, or geometry while maintaining its structural function. A fabric structure is one example of a situation where the structure is very demanding upon the experience of a space.

Envelope: The visual characteristics of an envelope provide varying degrees of transparency, translucence, or opacity. Its surface may also have color, texture, pattern, or reflective qualities. Since the function of the envelope is to act as a barrier to the natural elements, one might conclude that, at one extreme, the optimal envelope is no envelope at all. Another extreme might depict an underground building as making optimal use of the natural environ-

24. Walter Reed General Hospital, pp. 82–85.

25. Herman Miller Seating Plant, pp. 56–59.

26. Museum of Science and Industry, pp. 74–77.

27. Illinois Regional Library, pp. 70–73.

28. National Permanent Building, pp. 90–91.

29. Conservation of material, pp. 236.

Structure is emphasized in the National Permanent Building (top left), mechanical in the John Nutting Apartments (top right), envelope in the Herman Miller Seating Plant (above), and interior in the Atlanta International Airport (above left). Photos, clockwise from top left: Warren Cox, D. Randolph Foulds, Balthazar Korab, Hursley/Lark/Hursley.

ment.[30] Obviously these two extremes enclose a range of opportunity for integration. What happens more frequently is that the surfaces employed as parts of the building envelope are constructed of a set of components. The result is frequently a texture or pattern. Exterior surface materials may be chosen to harmonize with adjacent buildings, plant life, or other aspects of the landscape, and envelope geometry may also serve this purpose.

30. Moscone Center, pp. 112–115.

Mechanical: While the actual machinery of the building must be separated from ready public access for security and safety reasons, there is frequently a need to expose lines running from machinery to the point of application or use. Escalators, elevators, and sprinkler heads, for example, are usually visible in some way. Beyond this, there is a conflict between mechanical systems and their visual characteristics. The more visible and accessible they are, the easier they are to maintain and monitor; at the same time, it is seldom considered desirable to leave them on view in their purely functional form. To maintain a consistent proportional and geometrical relationship to other building members, visible ductwork is frequently oversized (meaning that the duct size is constant through the length of its run). The geometry of ductwork can create disharmony in context with elements of other systems. The treatment of exposed pipes and ducts frequently involves color-coordination with the rest of the space.[31] Similarly, it is not unusual to find elevators in hotels that have been customized to reflect the geometry or shapes of adjacent systems. All five levels of visible integration are common for mechanical systems.

31. Illinois Regional Library, pp. 70–73; Museum of Science and Industry, pp. 74–77.

Interior: Chairs and tables are frequently rounded or proportioned for strictly utilitarian reasons; chairs composed of triangles and squares are rarely comfortable. Surface, color, and pattern can be construed as a maintenance issue. Interior systems are the least permanent and by far the most convenient to change. By contrast, structural beams can be hidden but not easily altered.

Since surface, shape, and location are part of every interior design decision, the distinction between a purely visual decision and one that has functional connotations is often hard to discern. Historical allusions in furnishings are perhaps the easiest to recognize as having a purely visual motivation. One could argue that even these decisions are the result of psychological needs.

THE COMBINATIONS

In the context of this book, we define the interior as everything in view on the inside of the building. Similarly, the envelope (in addition to its other functions and characteristics) is defined as everything in view on the exterior of the building. By this definition, the structure and mechanical systems are *never* independent when they are in view. For example, when a structural slab is visible from within the building, it is *unified* with the interior. When a load-bearing masonry wall is on the outside of the building, it is *unified* with the envelope; the converse is also true. Obviously, neither interior nor exterior systems can be hidden from view.

Any given system has a surface, a shape, and a specific location. When a system is in view, these characteristics become more immediate to the building user; furthermore, any system can be resurfaced, reshaped, or relocated (or all three). It should be noted that the surface condition of a structural or mechanical system rarely affects function in a major way. Shape and location changes carry greater impact.

Structure + Envelope: When structural systems are exposed to exterior view, they are also exposed to the climate. Also, whatever changes in surface, shape, or location are made, maintenance, safety, and security issues must always be addressed.

Structure + Mechanical: In order for one or both of these systems to be in view, one or both of them must be *unified* with either interior or envelope systems (or both). Since mechanical systems are either *meshed* or *connected* to structure, the chances are that a mechanical system would unify separately with an interior system, while the structure could conceivably be *unified* with both the interior and the envelope; an exterior column is an example of this.

Structure + Interior: As stated above, the structure must be *unified* with the interior in order to be seen. When this occurs, it is common practice to adjust the shape and position of structural members to comply with interior needs.

Envelope + Mechanical: This situation implies mechanical equipment or lines which are located outside the building. When they are in view, they are immediately *unified* with the envelope and take on all of the characteristics of an envelope system.

Envelope + Interior: The combination of envelope and interior systems is universal, in the form of glass in windows. This exemplifies a *unified* relationship.

Mechanical + Interior: In order for mechanical subsystems to be visible, they must be *unified* with the interior in some way. Exposed ductwork is the most common example.

SUMMARY

The visible properties discussed here play some role in every building system application; the question is one of degree. Visual questions as to relationship are by nature integrative. The act of composition is an integrative act, as is the act of constructing a pattern.

Low levels of physical systems integration can embody high levels of visible integration. Physical integrations at the *touching* or *connected* levels can be composed and proportioned almost at will. Paradoxically, as the physical integration of the systems approaches either the *remote* level or the *unified* level, the task of visible integration becomes more difficult. In each case there are only a few possibilities; in the former because there exists almost no interrelationship, and in the latter because of the close interaction of the various systems.

A physical systems integration can be visually destroyed through the choice of the appropriate surface, shape, size, or location. The architect has that option, consciously or unconsciously. It is also possible that the user may not in fact see the results as intended. Intentional physical integration is sometimes formally perceived as inadequate visible integration.

Because architecture is an art as well as a science, designing a building provides an opportunity for expression and visual communication. Because it has a physical presence, a building will stimulate reactions that reflect ideas and values not anticipated by the designer. This book's focus on systems integration includes the importance of surface, shape, and location as part of that process, and the form they take. What follows is a series of examples drawn from the Chapter 3 case studies of ways in which visible integration influences system design and integration.

Example 1: The Occidental Chemical building (pp. 94–97) vividly illustrates how the environment can visibly affect the design of a building envelope. The site, one of America's most spectacular, is unusual in itself. The design strategy of using a double skin determines both visual and formal qualities, and integrates envelope and interior at a relatively high level. The facade is repeated on all four sides of the cube-like building, achieving visual symmetry.

Example 2: Stockton State College (pp. 78–81) responds to a different set of visual issues. The site's location away from existing architectural contexts permits the buildings to open into the surrounding forest, and the envelope is influenced by the view from the interior to the outside. The program required that an entire campus be produced within a year; hence, overriding concerns during the design phase were economy and speed of construction.

Facing page: *Occidental Chemical Company Corporate Office Building, Niagara Falls, New York. Photograph: Barbara Elliott Martin.* Above: *Stockton State College, Pomona, New Jersey. Photograph: GBQC.*

Above: *Pike and Virginia Building, Seattle, Washington. Photograph: Dick Busher.*
Facing page: *National Permanent Building, Washington, DC. Photograph: Robert Lautman.*

Example 3: The structural system dominates the design of the Pike and Virginia Building (pp. 92–93), and visibly integrates the building with its nineteenth-century waterfront surroundings. Large areas of glass integrate dwelling unit interiors with the environment, providing views of both Puget Sound and the Pike Place Market historic district.

Example 4: The National Permanent Building (pp. 90–91) exemplifies visual response to formal and environmental requirements. The building fits appropriately into the existing visual context of highly modeled buildings; the mansard-like setback was chosen to comply with the National Capital Planning Commission's height and zoning requirements. Columns and ducts, pulled out of the building's mass and emphasized, have been treated in a highly integrated way; their size, shape, and location have all been uniquely designed to suit the formal context.

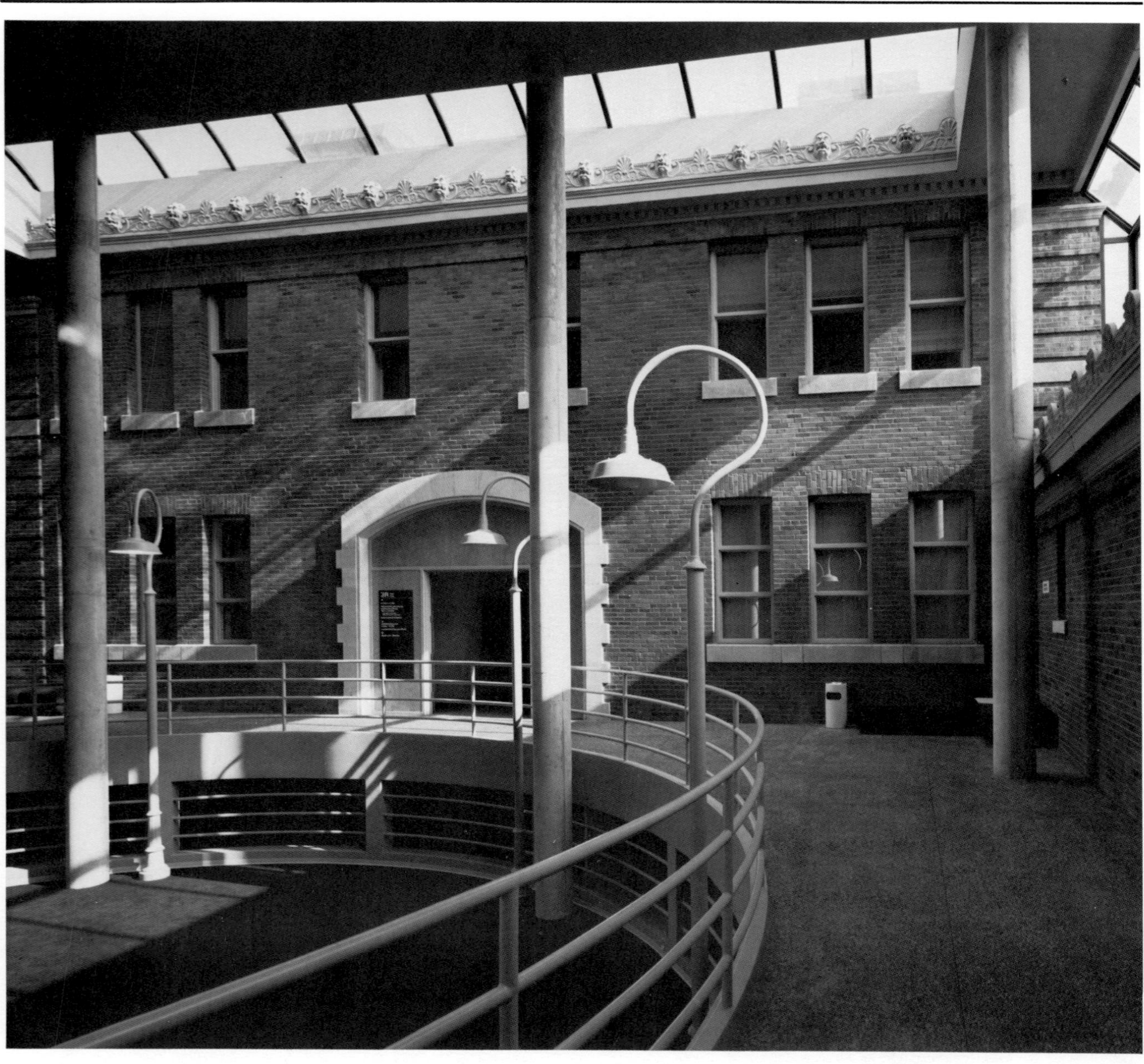

Above: *Vocational Technical Education Facility, University of Minnesota, St. Paul, Minnesota. Photograph: Franz C. Hall.*
Facing page: *Georgia Power Company Corporate Headquarters, Atlanta, Georgia. Photograph: Hursley/Lank/Hursley.*

Example 5: The design of the atrium connecting new and existing portions of the Vocational Technical Education Facility (pp. 98–101) represents a visual response to the requirements of preserving the original building and making the transition between it and the addition.

Example 6: Curtain wall selection requires consideration of energy properties as well as attention to glare and daylighting, while color and surface texture are visible integration choices. In this respect, the Georgia Power building (pp. 86–89) suggests that harmony with the materials and scale of the existing cityscape was not a priority except at street level.

HOTEL
HOTEL FRANCES
STEAKS
BURGERS
Domino

Example 7: The 8 in. square glass block used in the addition to the Submarine Training Facility at Groton (pp. 106–107) unifies envelope and interior and helps to generate the form of the building, a series of grids that visibly integrate structure, envelope, mechanical, and interior systems. The largest grid articulates the building's steel frame.
Example 8: Visible integration of the envelopes of the John Nutting Apartments (pp. 68–69) with their context embodies a response to a vernacular building vocabulary. The building envelopes also accommodate passive solar features, integrating mechanical and interior systems at a high level.
Example 9: The abstract and geometrical envelope design of the Equitable Life building (pp. 102–105) creates a strong formal identity for the building in preference to a direct reponse by elevation to orientation and climatic factors.
Example 10: Another view of the National Permanent Building (pp. 90–91) shows the corner where the north and west facades meet. The sunshading and recesses of the west and south sides are undesirable on the north. All of the facades must visibly integrate into a single whole.

Facing page, top: *Addition to Submarine Training Facility, Groton, Connecticut. Photograph: Nick Wheeler.*
Facing page, bottom: *John C. Nutting Apartments, Amherst, Massachusetts. Photograph: D. Randolph Foulds.*
Below: *Southern Service Center for the Equitable Life Assurance Society, Charlotte, North Carolina. Photograph: Ezra Stoller, ESTO.*
Left: *National Permanent Building, Washington, DC. Photograph: Warren Cox.*

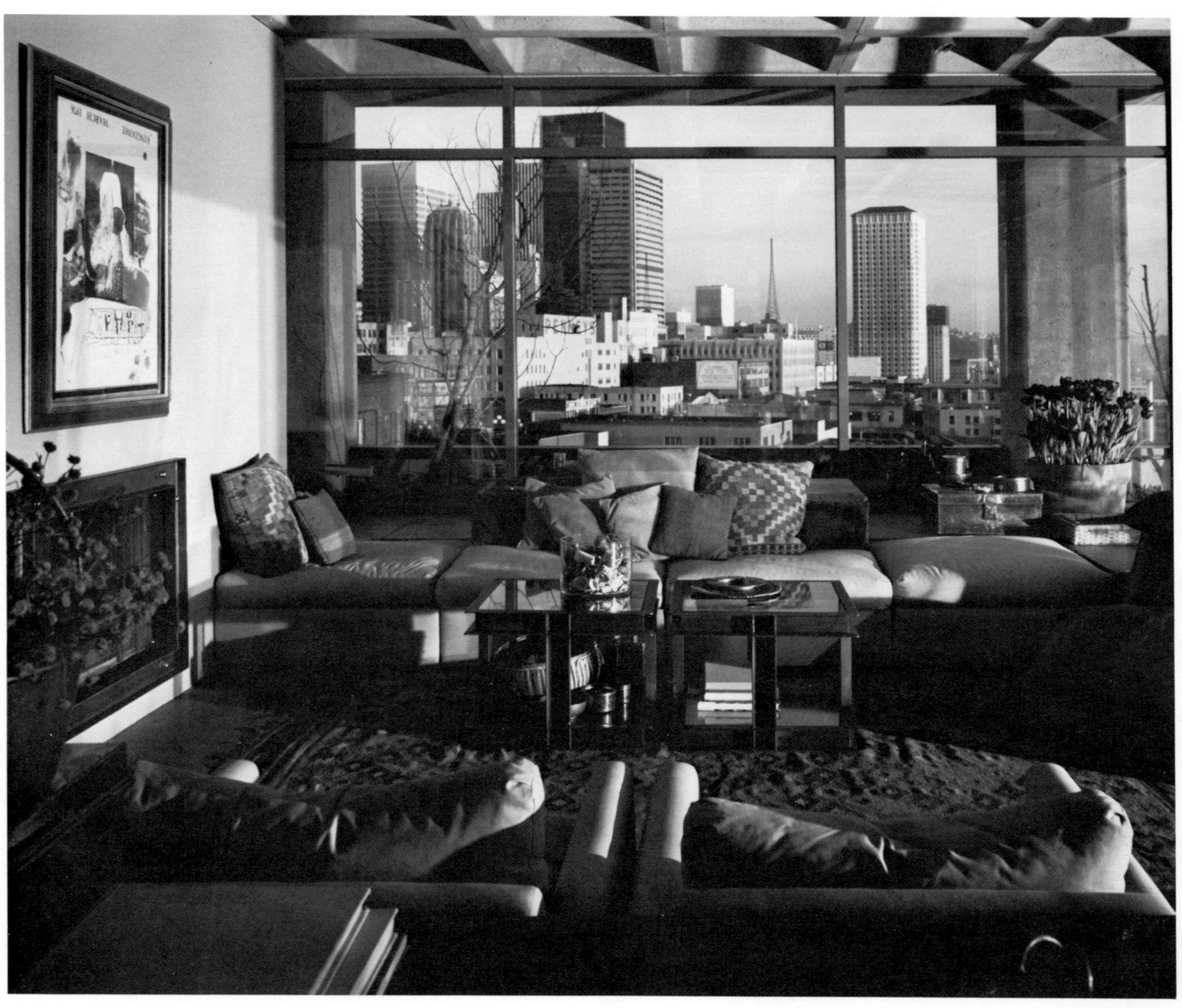

Above: *Pike and Virginia Building, Seattle, Washington. Photograph: Dick Busher.*
Facing page: *George R. Moscone Convention Center, San Francisco, California. Photograph: Peter Aaron, ESTO.*

Example 11: The concrete and glass elements of the Pike and Virginia Building (pp. 92–93) comprise structure, envelope, and interior finishes, and provide each dwelling unit with terraces and views. The unfinished concrete seen in each unit represents the simplest level of visible integration, where a system is left exposed and unaltered. The extensive use of glass not only provides views but helps to define envelope and interior.

Example 12: The Moscone Center's (pp. 112–115) glassed-in lobby relates the building visually to its surroundings and allows natural light to penetrate to the underground levels. The exposed space frame unifies structure with interior.

refreshments
Chris Craft

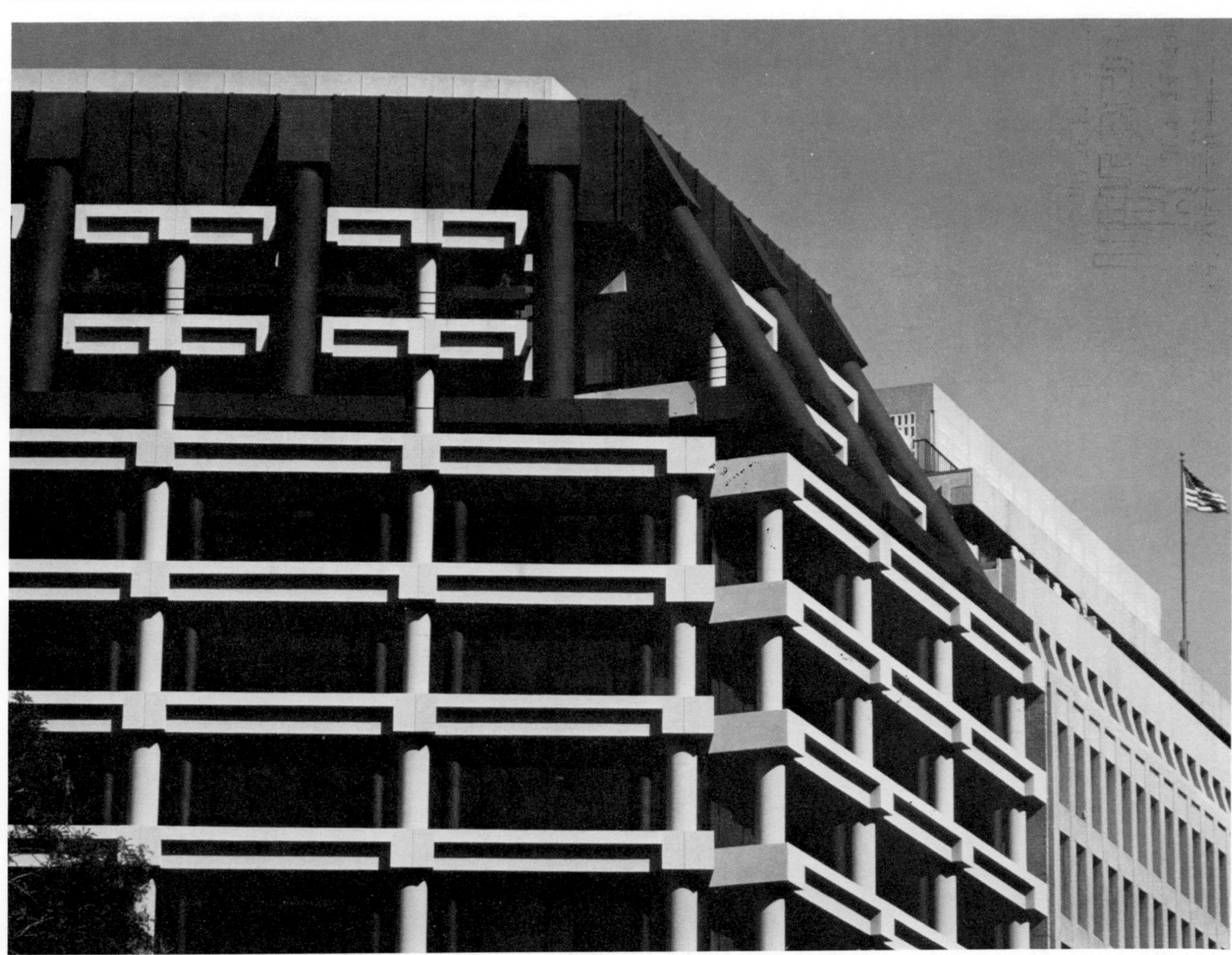

Example 13: The pairs of giant post-tensioned concrete arches supporting the Moscone Center's (pp. 112–115) roof structure partially conceal sets of exposed ducts. The height and scale of the space permits the use of exposed ducts without the effect of machine-like detailing visible at closer range.

Example 14: The finish ceiling of the Aid Association for Lutherans Headquarters (pp. 62–63) incorporates a series of half-cylindrical "socks" slung between the skylights. These modulate and diffuse natural light, and also conceal air-handling equipment, roof drains, sprinkler lines, and sound-masking speakers. This unique solution causes the concealing element to itself become visually prominent.

Example 15: The two heavily modeled facades of the National Permanent Building (pp. 90–91) have been "pulled out" from the building. Note that the columns decrease in size as they ascend the building while the ducts (painted black) increase in size as they ascend. The resulting interplay between structure and mechanical systems provides a conscious visual theme for the facade while accurately depicting its engineering logic.

Facing page, top: *George R. Moscone Convention Center, San Francisco, California. Photograph: Peter Aaron, ESTO.*
Facing page, bottom: *Aid Association for Lutherans Headquarters, Appleton, Wisconsin. Photograph: Harr, Hedrich-Blessing.*
Above: *National Permanent Building, Washington, DC. Photograph: Robert Lautman.*

Above: *Illinois Regional Library, Chicago, Illinois. Photograph: Howard N. Kaplan.* Facing page: *Museum of Science and Industry, Tampa, Florida. Photograph: Gordon H. Schenck, Jr.*

Example 16: In the Illinois Regional Library (pp. 70–73), ducts can be seen in the corridor and in one of the classrooms. In each case, the ducts have been consciously positioned to visually complement the characteristic geometry of the space.

Example 17: Whereas the ducts in the Illinois Regional Library are carefully composed in the space, function dictates the placement of ductwork in the Museum of Science and Industry (pp. 74–75). The ductwork in the museum has also been left exposed, with some elements color-coded and others left bare. These elements are in fact part of the technological character of the formal design, and many of them are parts of museum exhibits. In this level of visible integration, the concrete walls have been left exposed and unfinished, serving as a background for the other systems.

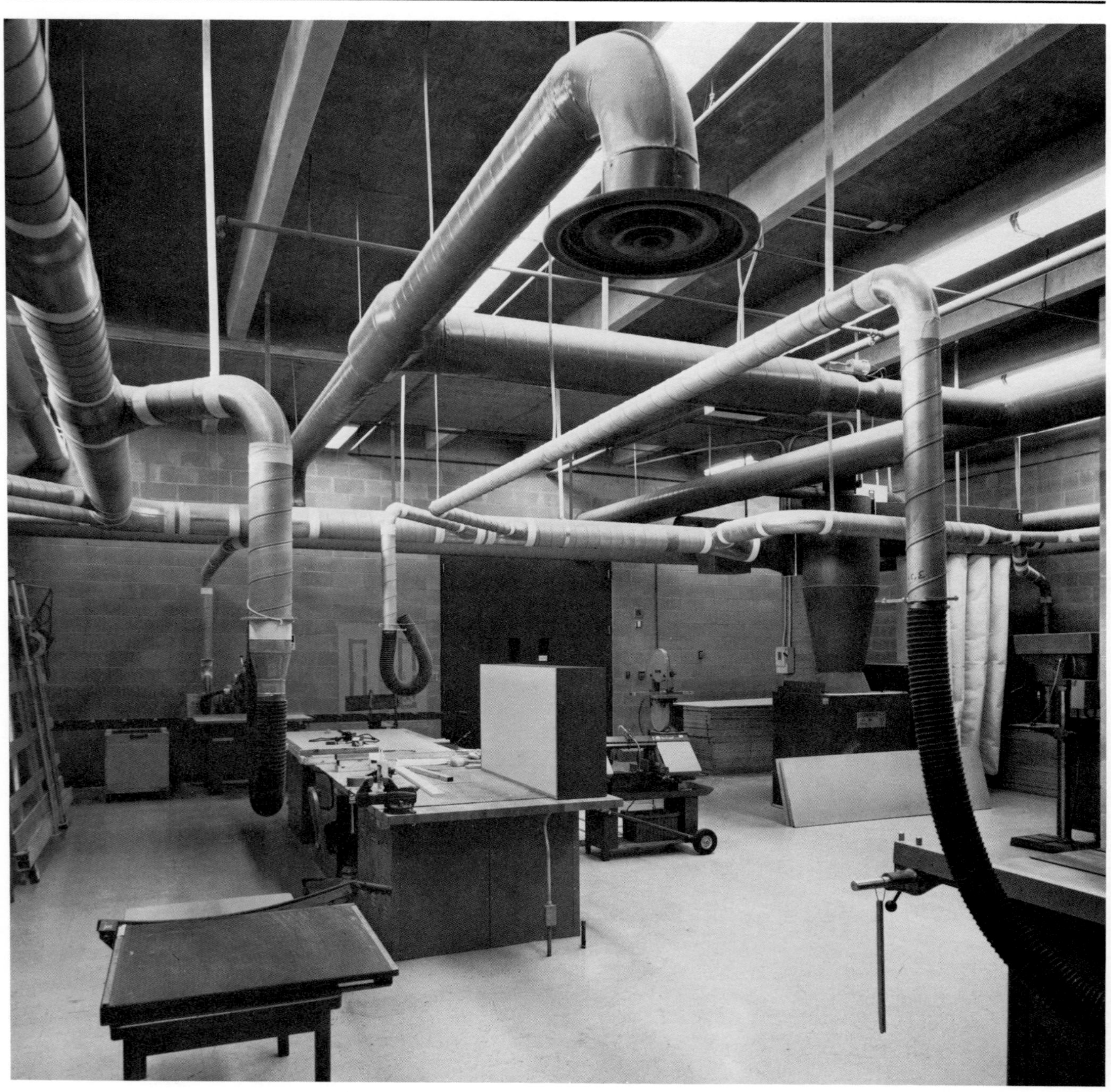

Above: *Museum of Science and Industry, Tampa, Florida. Photograph: Gordon H. Schenck, Jr.*

Example 18: The exposed structural members, ducts, pipes, and conduits of the Museum of Science and Industry (pp. 74–75) result in a functionally flexible and utilitarian environment. Mechanical and electrical equipment can be easily repaired or replaced without upsetting the visual order. The unfinished concrete block interior walls and exposed light fixtures have not been rearranged for visual reasons; however, a consistent geometry and character results from their exposure and surface treatment.

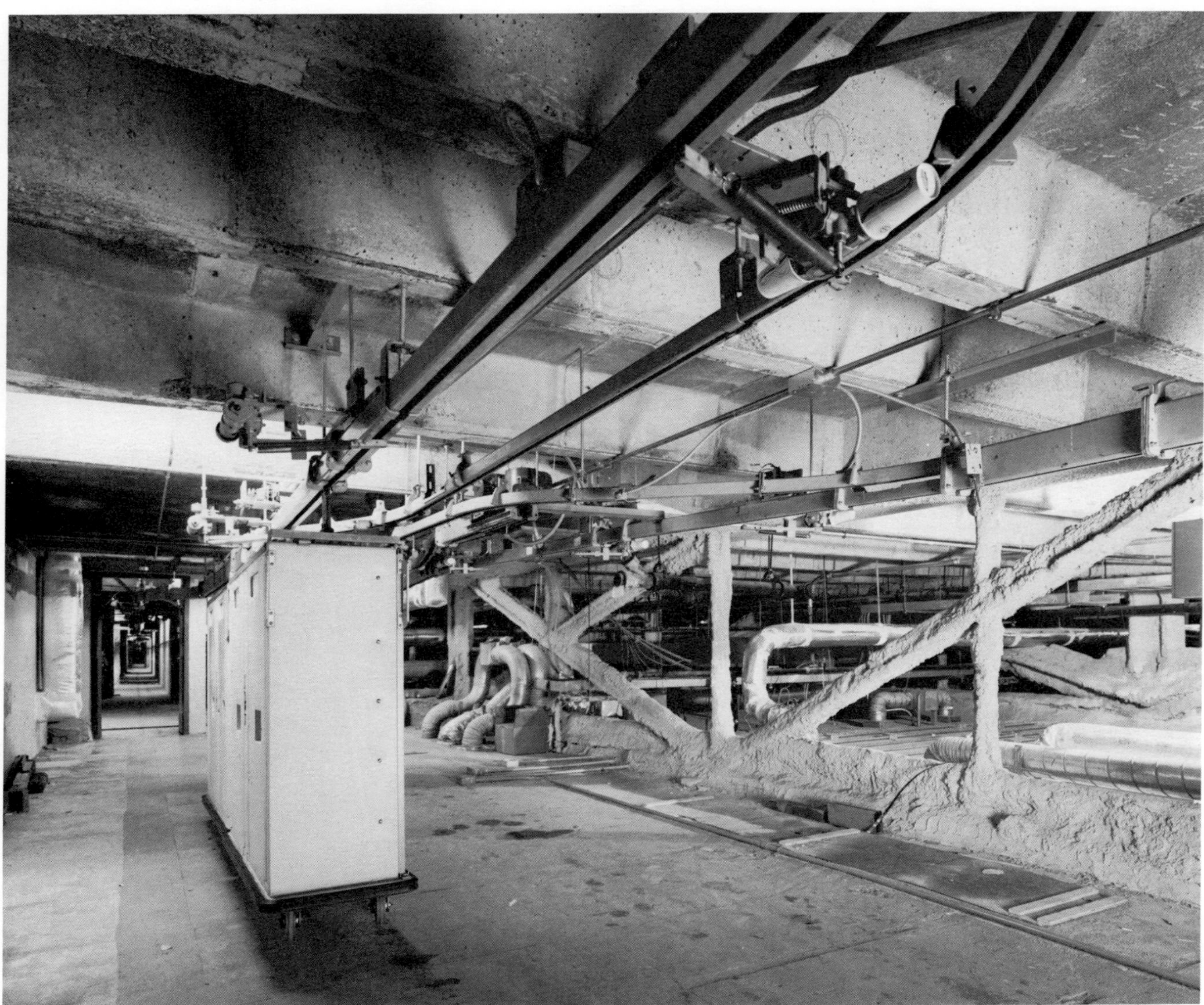

Example 19: The view of an interstitial floor at Walter Reed Hospital (pp. 82–85) shows one of the automated dumbwaiter/monorail carts that serve both vertical and horizontal transportation needs. Interstitial floors alternate with occupied floors and house many of the mechanical systems. Structural trusses sprayed with insulating material are on view, as are electrical system components. No attempt has been made to alter any system component for visual reasons, since the function of the space is a utilitarian one. Only the maintenance staff or repair crews would normally work there. A visual order, however, is imposed on the mechanical and electrical runs, the communications equipment, and the materials handling subsystems by the strict rectilinearity of the structural grid that dominates the design. As in the Museum of Science and Industry, flexibility is a key aspect of the design; necessary repairs and changes can be made to the hospital space from above or below without interrupting activities on occupied floors.

Above: *Walter Reed General Hospital, Washington, DC. Photograph: Harlan Hambright.*

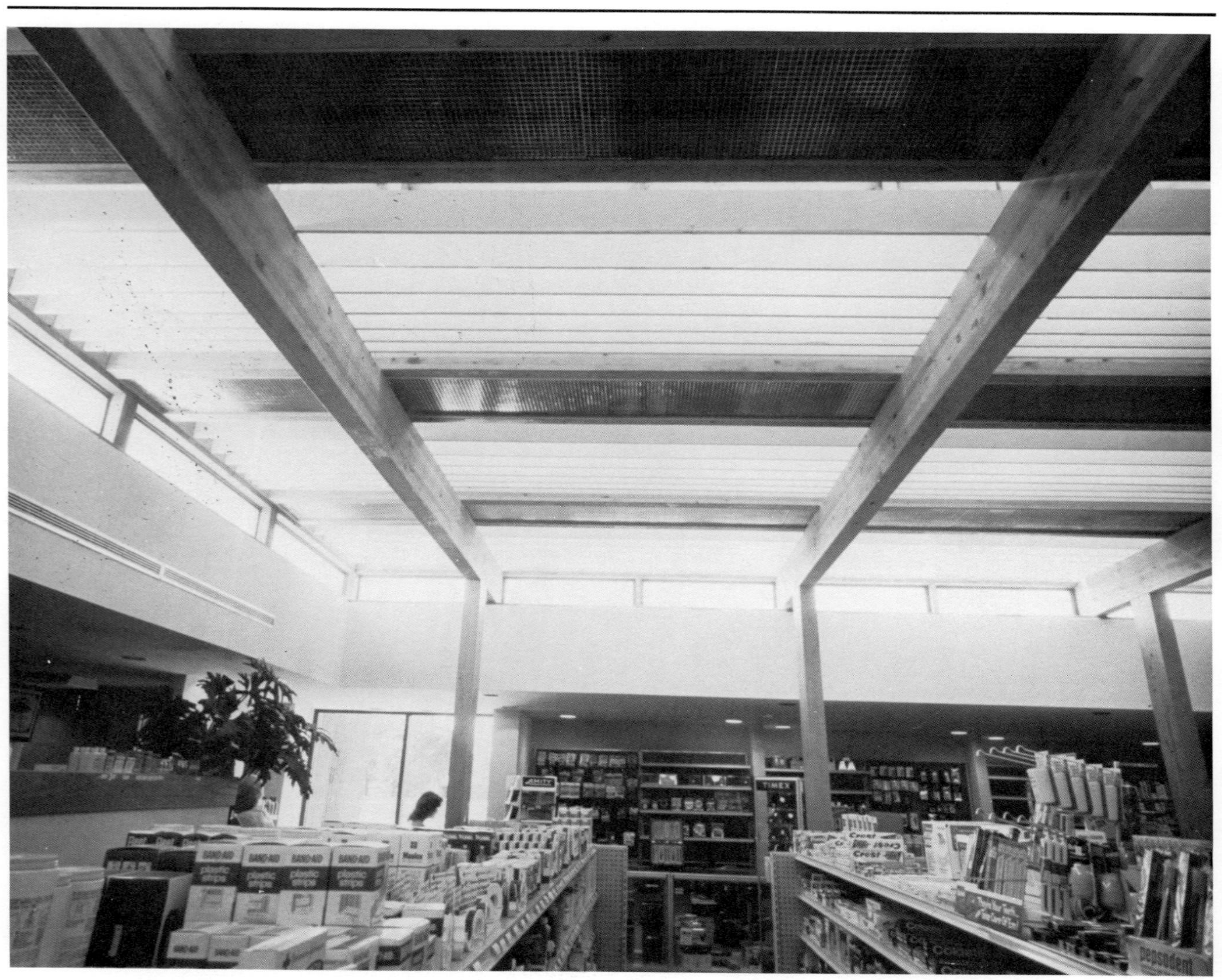

Above: *Trust Pharmacy, Grants, New Mexico. Photograph: Mazria/ Schiff & Associates.* Facing page: *Illinois Regional Library, Chicago, Illinois. Photograph: Howard N. Kaplan.*

Example 20: Trust Pharmacy's (pp. 60–61) high, naturally lighted central space takes light from the four sawtooth clerestories that give the roof its form; masonry walls and wood columns support the glued laminated wood beams. The building's design exemplifies a formal, visible integration of structural, envelope, and interior systems in its wood structure, which not only supports elements of the daylighting system but helps to diffuse light. Both the wooden structural elements and the concrete masonry exterior walls have been exposed without paint.

Example 21: Exposed lighting and mechanical systems are on view in a reading area of the Illinois Regional Library (pp. 70–73). In contrast with Trust Pharmacy, lighting is completely artificial in this space. Structure, ductwork, and electrical runs are color-coded, and ductwork and lighting have been formally organized to respond to the layout. Ductwork has undergone the most radical treatment, being visually sized, positioned, and colored.

EXIT
Vintage
Vintage

Above: *Herman Miller Seating Manufacturing Plant, Holland, Michigan. Photograph: Balthazar Korab.* Facing page : *Kimbell Art Museum, Fort Worth, Texas. Photograph: Bob Wharton.*

Example 22: As in Illinois Regional Library, the exposed structural, mechanical, and electrical systems in the Herman Miller plant (pp. 56–59) have each been painted various colors. With their surface alterations, the exposed systems complement the natural factory quality of the interior, which is further decorated with the furniture systems seen in various stages of manufacture, as well as in use in the office areas.

Example 23: A gallery in the Kimbell Museum (pp. 64–67) demonstrates a mode of visible integration unique to this building. Natural light, relating envelope and interior, is diffused throughout the interior space from the skylight splitting the crown of the concrete shell. In contrast with the Herman Miller plant, mechanical and electrical equipment is concealed, a visual decision in keeping with the formal qualities of a traditional art museum. The exposed structural concrete surfaces are smooth and precise.

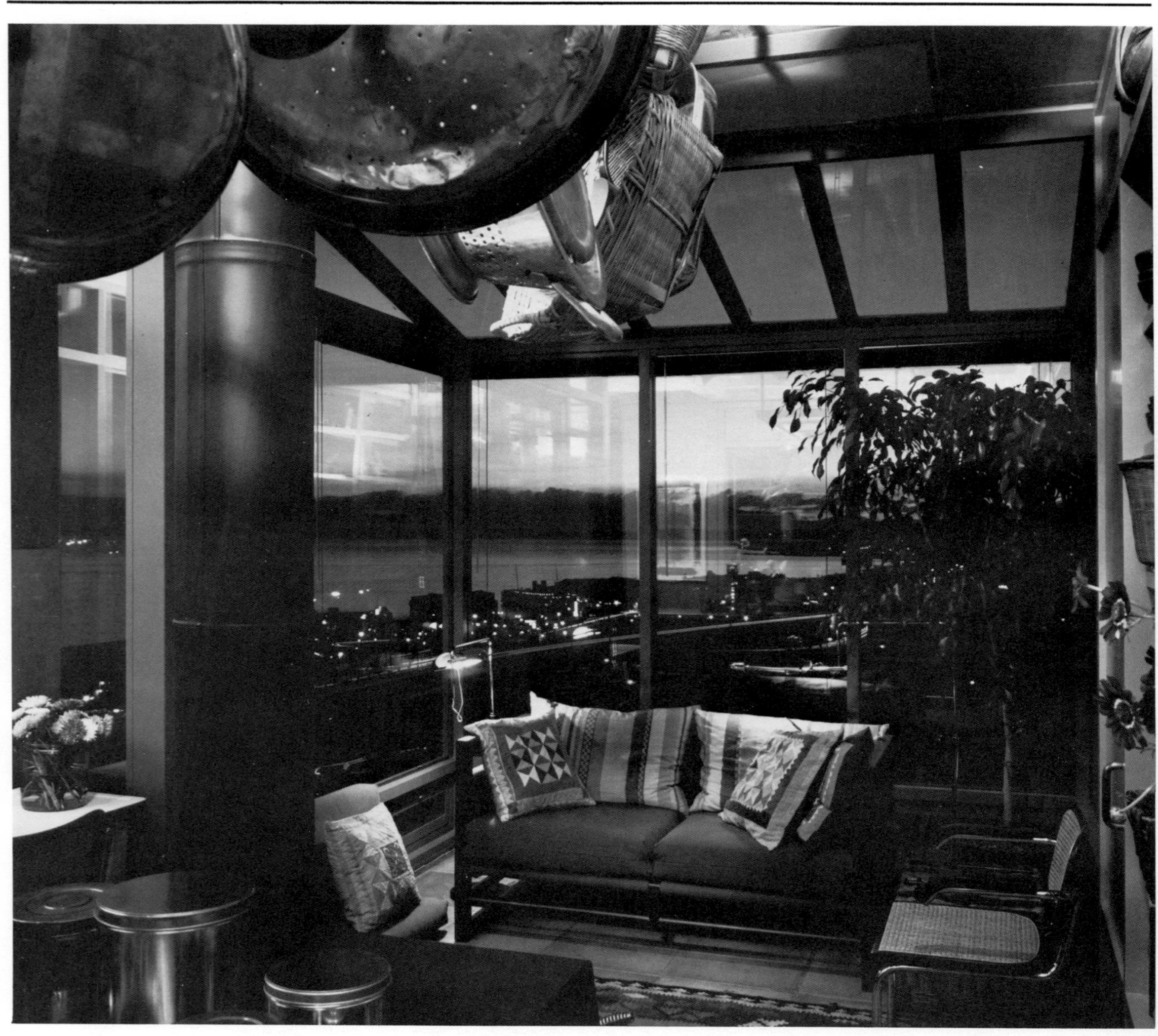

Above: *Pike and Virginia Building, Seattle, Washington. Photograph: Dick Busher.*
Facing page: *Museum of Science and Industry, Tampa, Florida. Photograph: Gordon H. Schenck, Jr.*

Example 24: In the Pike and Virginia Building (pp. 92–93), structural elements such as the waffle slab ceilings are left in view with their surfaces unaltered. Interiors contribute to the informal quality of the living space and permit chimney flue and plant life to coexist.

Example 25: The lobby of the Museum of Science and Industry (pp. 74–75), although quite different in building type, shares many characteristics with the living room from the Pike and Virginia Building shown on the opposite page. The attitude toward material finish and geometry are similar. The contrast is most thoroughly felt in the difference between private and public space.

auditorium

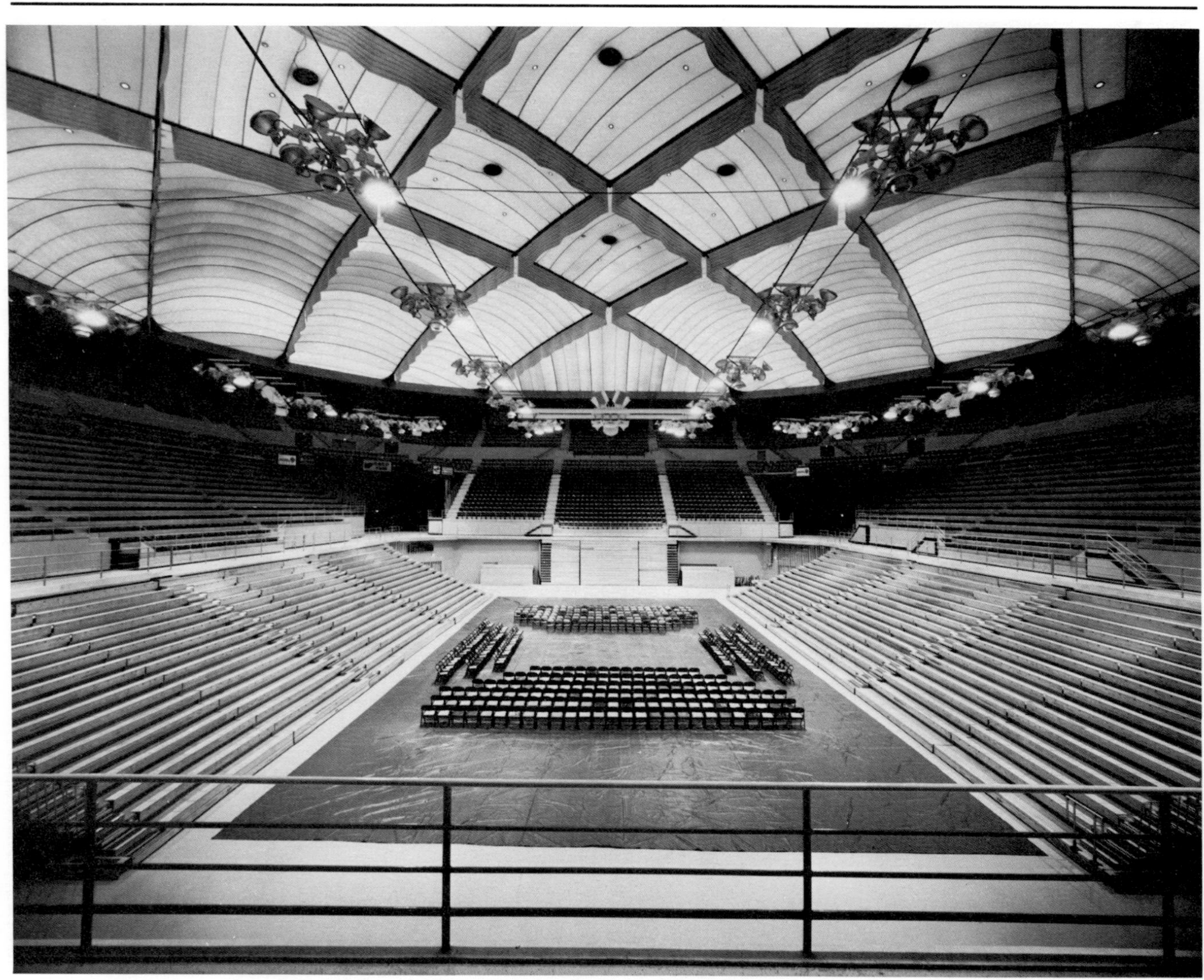

Above: *Stephen C. O'Connell Activities Center, University of Florida, Gainesville, Florida. Photograph: Balthazar Korab.*

Example 26: Because the air-supported fabric roof of the O'Connell Center (pp. 108–111) offered no convenient point of attachment for artificial lighting equipment, light fixtures are suspended and exposed. The treatment is similar to that of exposed ductwork. During the day, the envelope's translucency controls the interior environment visually and thermally; the air supporting the structure is of course invisible. The fabic roof represents a complicated level of integration, with structural, lighting, and acoustical needs all satisfied by the roof. A strong visual element in the main arena space is the curved grid at the ceiling level formed by acoustical baffles. The alternating line patterns in view on the ceiling are functional and help the roof to avoid a favored direction for stress failure.

Example 27: The design of the Atlanta International Airport (pp. 116–119) is of necessity integrated with transportation systems that serve the needs of both planes and passengers. The building shape is determined by the circulation requirements of the planes, resulting in large internal distances. A moving sidewalk, one of a number of service modes whose functions involve conservation of time, connects adjacent concourses. The difficulty in designing such a space is that people are always moving in it; the quantity of wall, roof, and floor is so great that visible integration, if it is a high priority, must be accomplished inexpensively. Locating the lighting near the walls allows the space to be lighted and the walls dramatically patterned at the same time. The signage is important for orientation, yet cannot be permitted to dominate the spatial experience.

Above: *William B. Hartsfield Atlanta International Airport, Atlanta, Georgia. Photograph: Balthazar Korab.*

Appendix

The 15 drawings that follow are the generic examples from Chapter 4, enlarged and with captions and callouts deleted. This book began with a pure fascination for the inner workings of buildings; it seems only appropriate that it end in the same fashion.

Illustration has been done by Darrell Downing Rippeteau, AIA, Architect with Richard J. Vitullo, designer in charge.

1. Access Floor and Curtain Wall

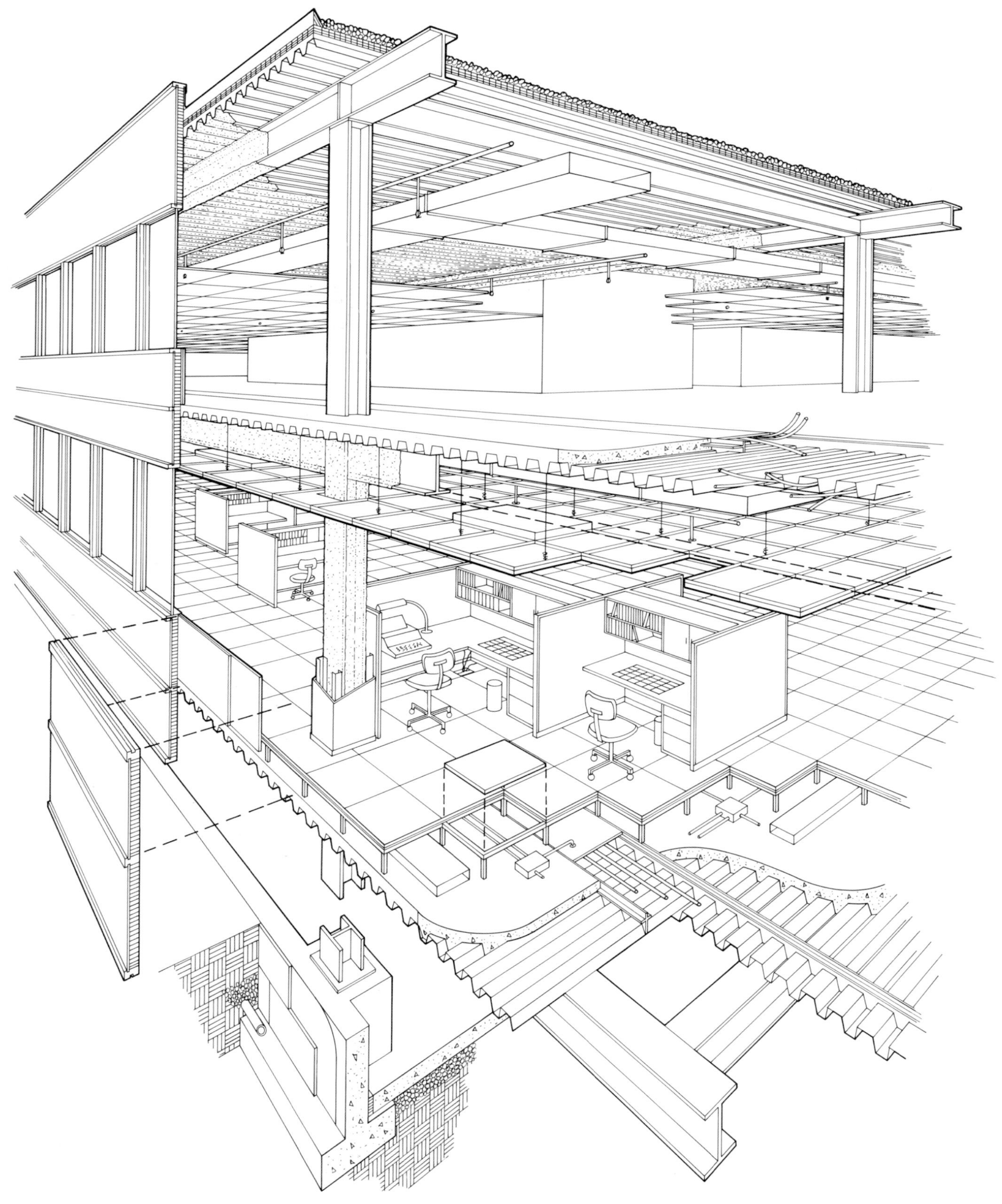

2. Post-Tensioned Concrete

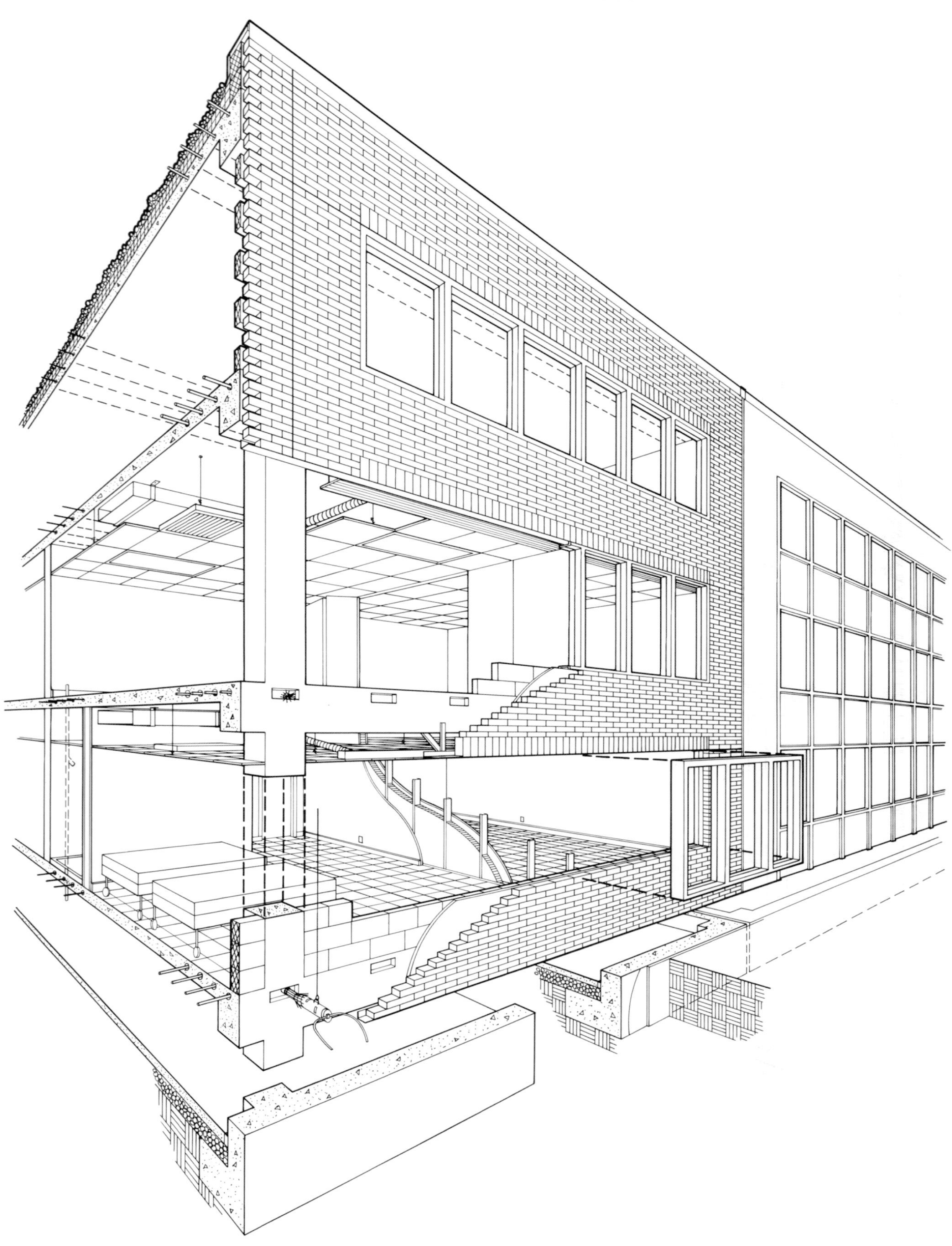

3. Flying Form

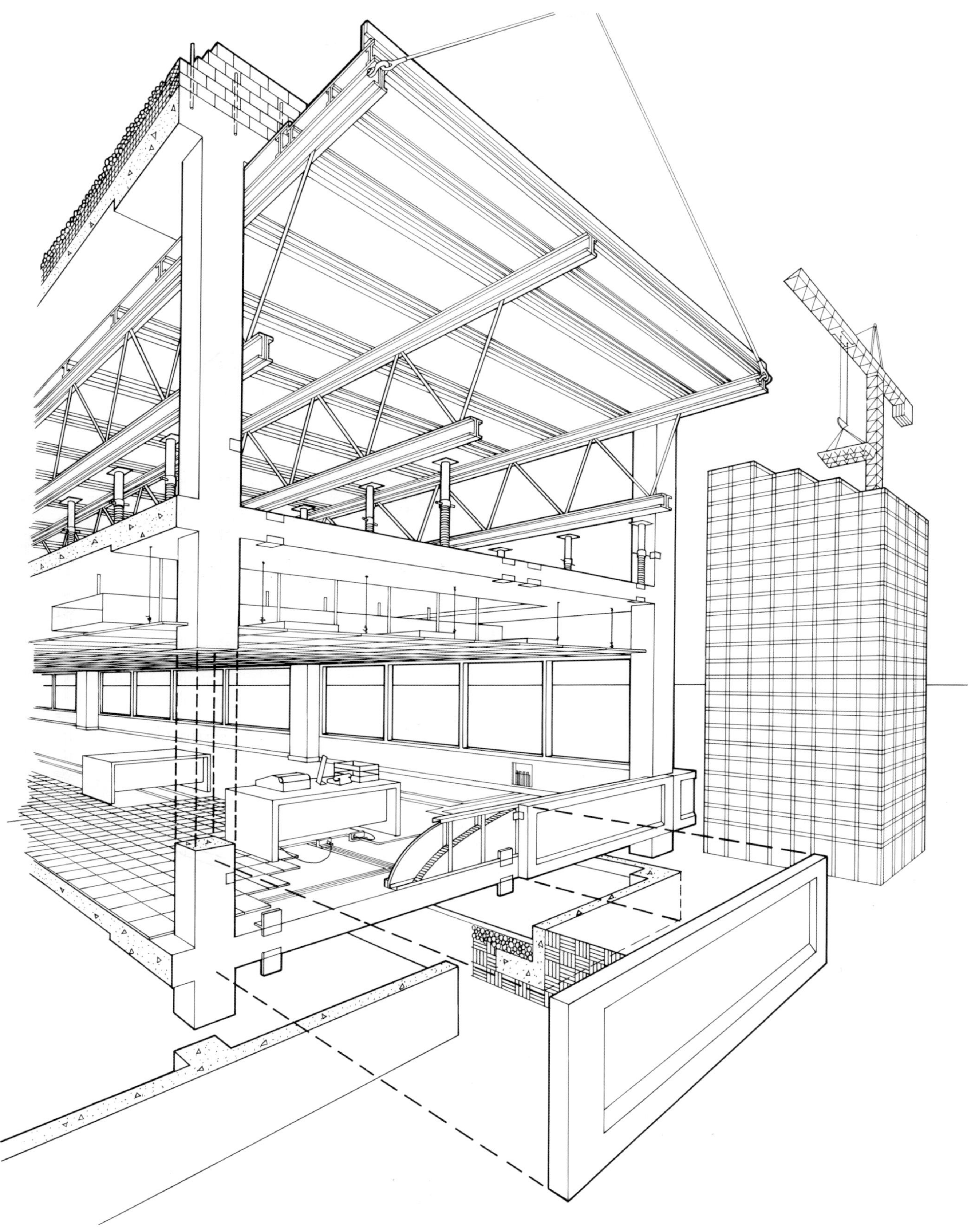

4. Flat Plate

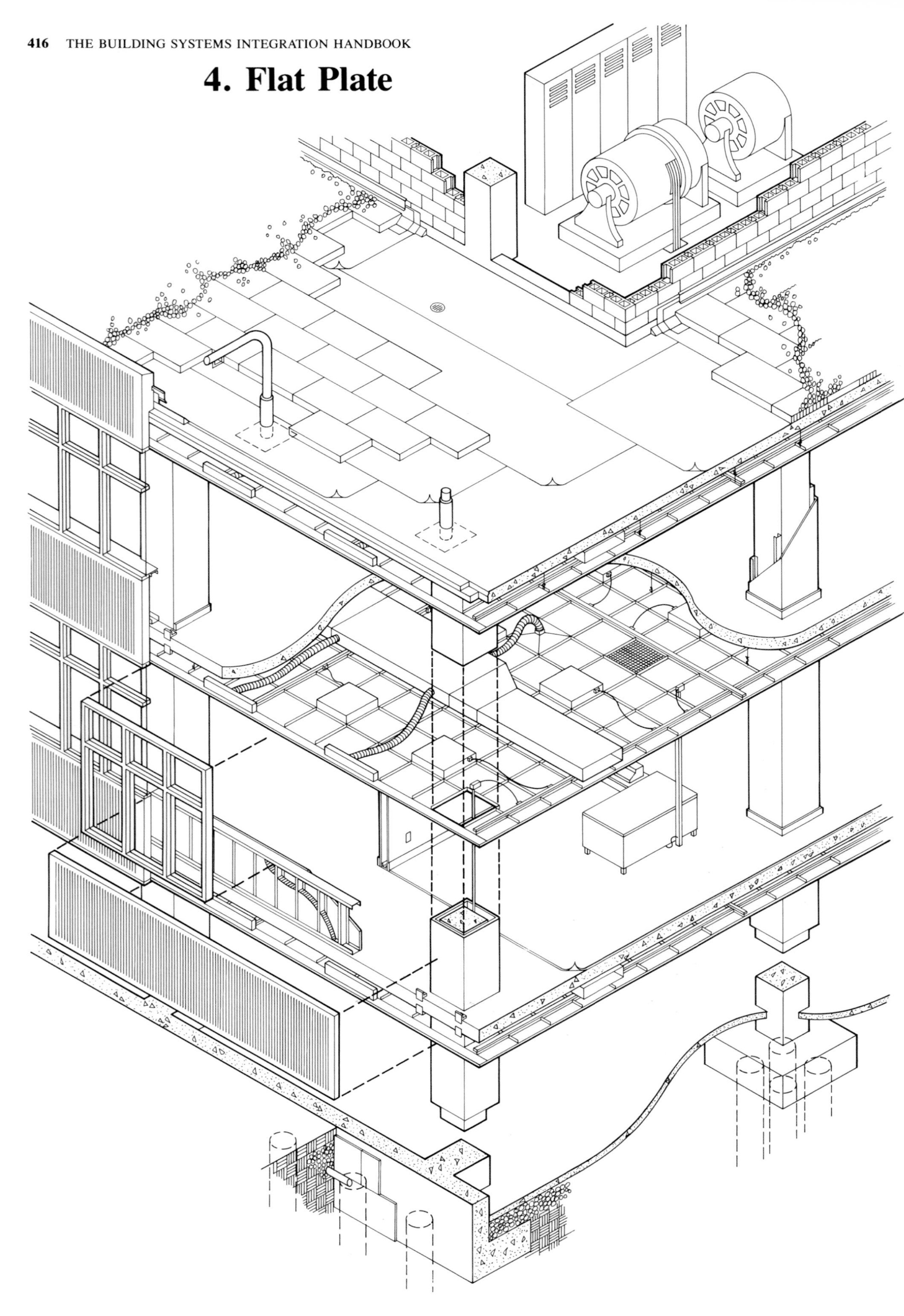

5. Precast Frame

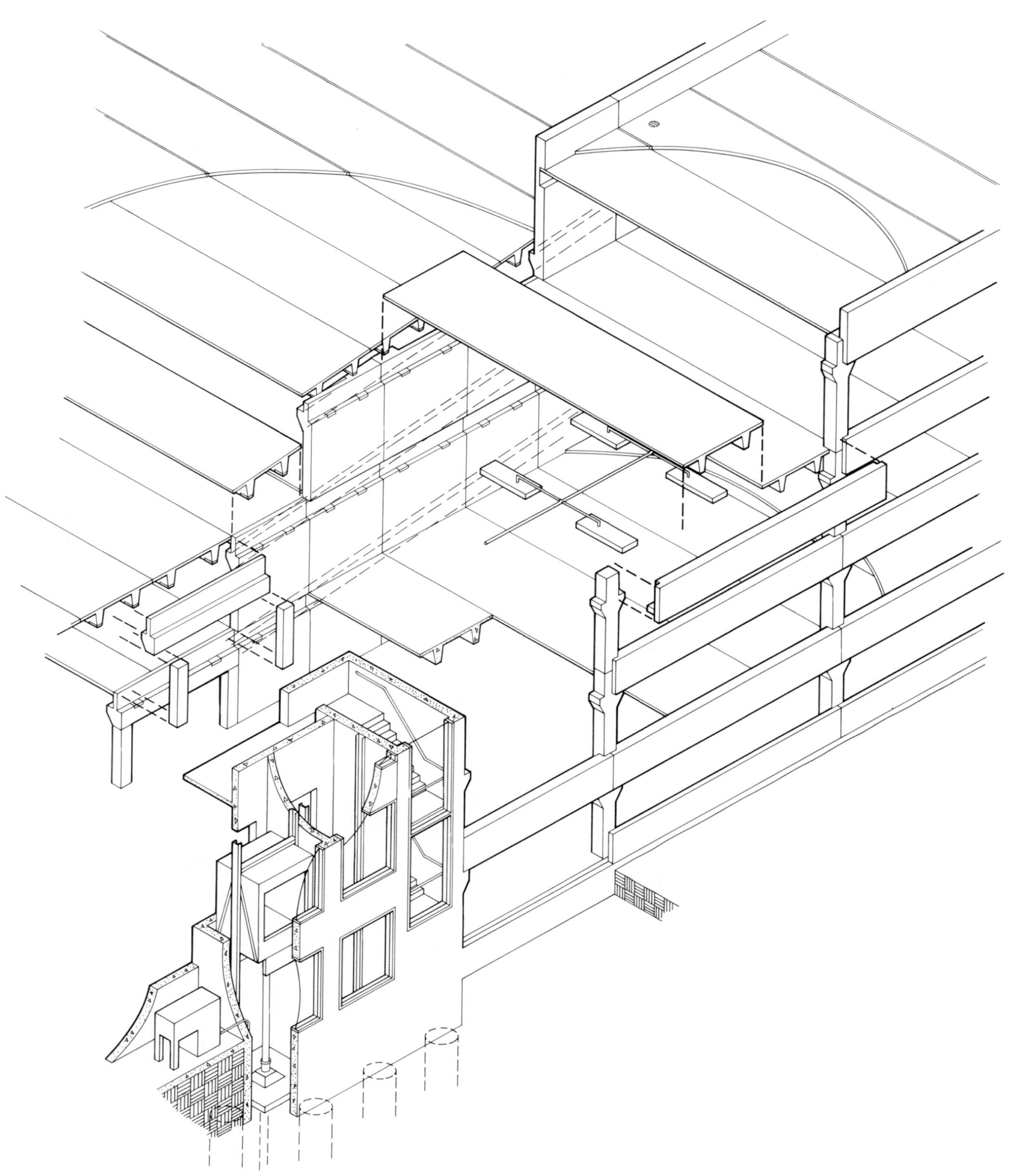

6. Staggered Truss

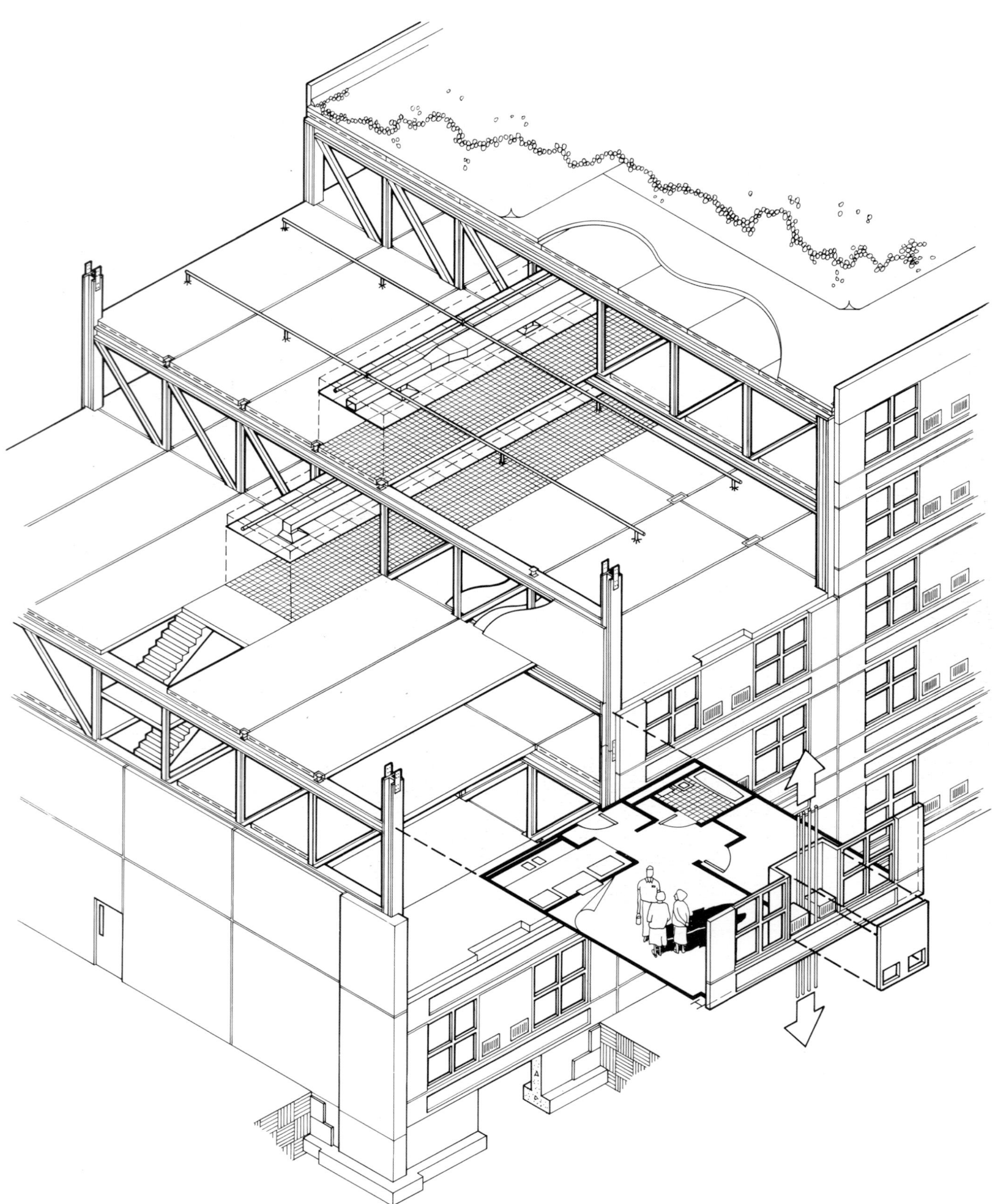

7. Tilt-up Wall

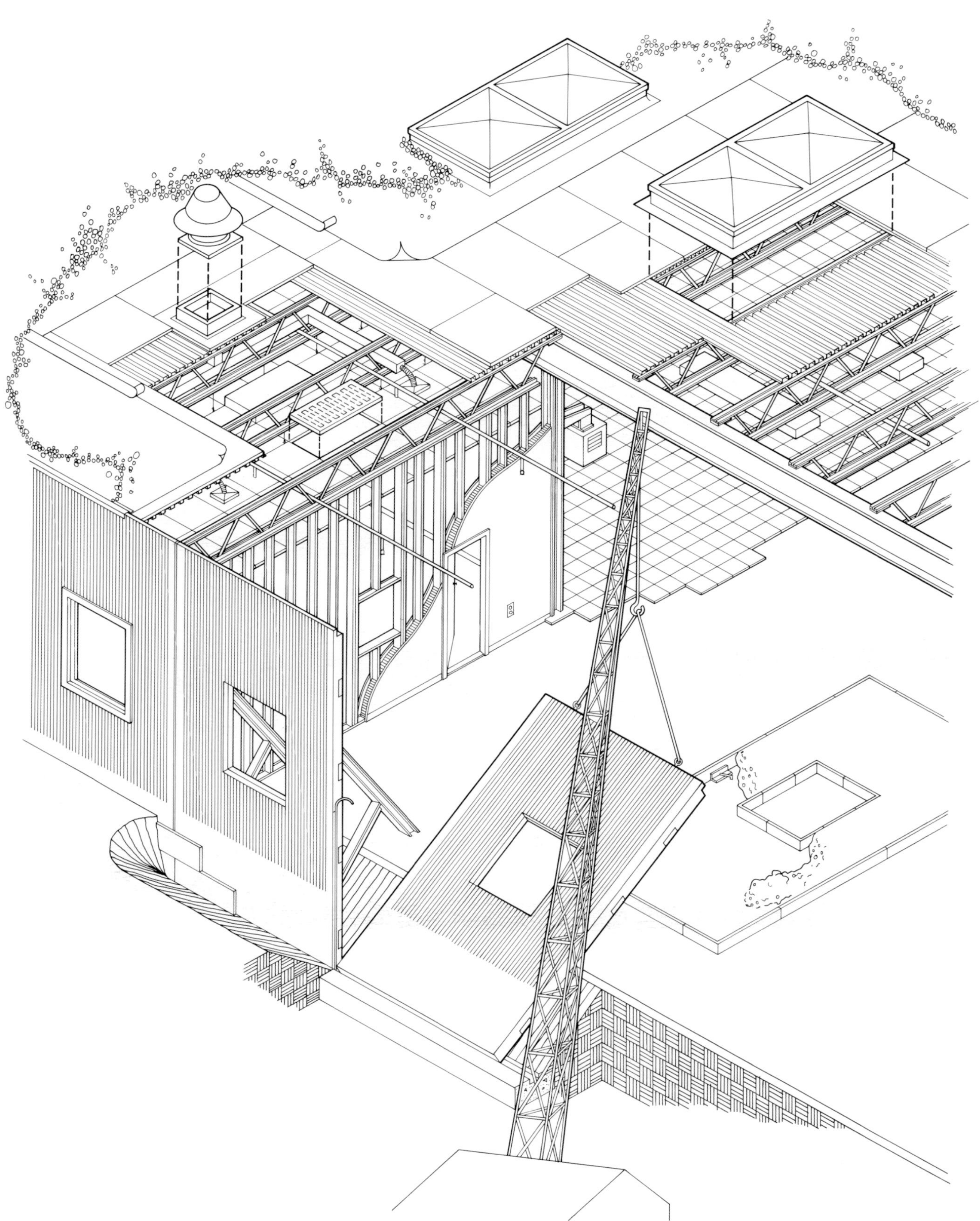

8. Bearing Wall and Bar-Joist Roof

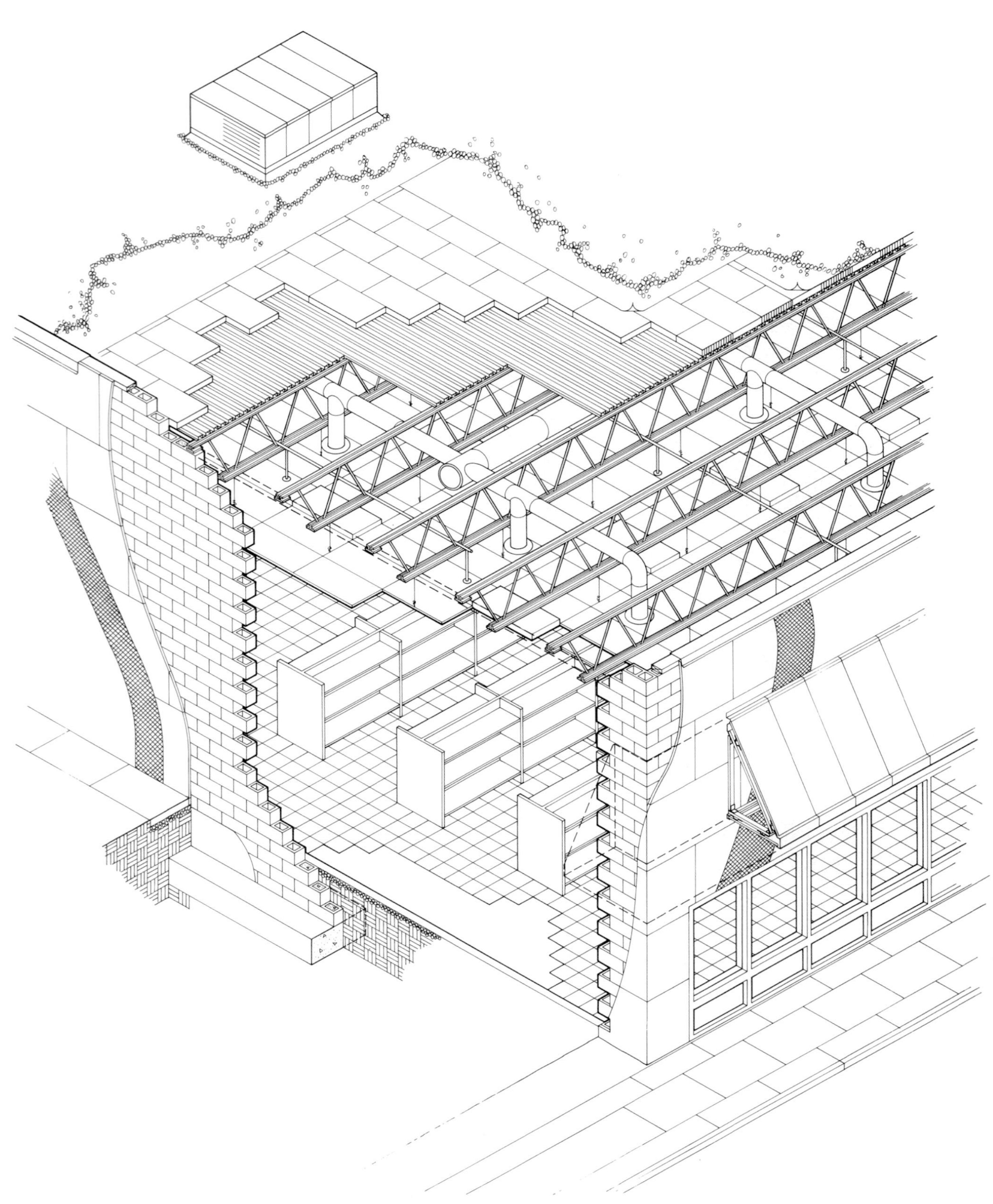

9. Lightweight Steel Frame and Brick Veneer

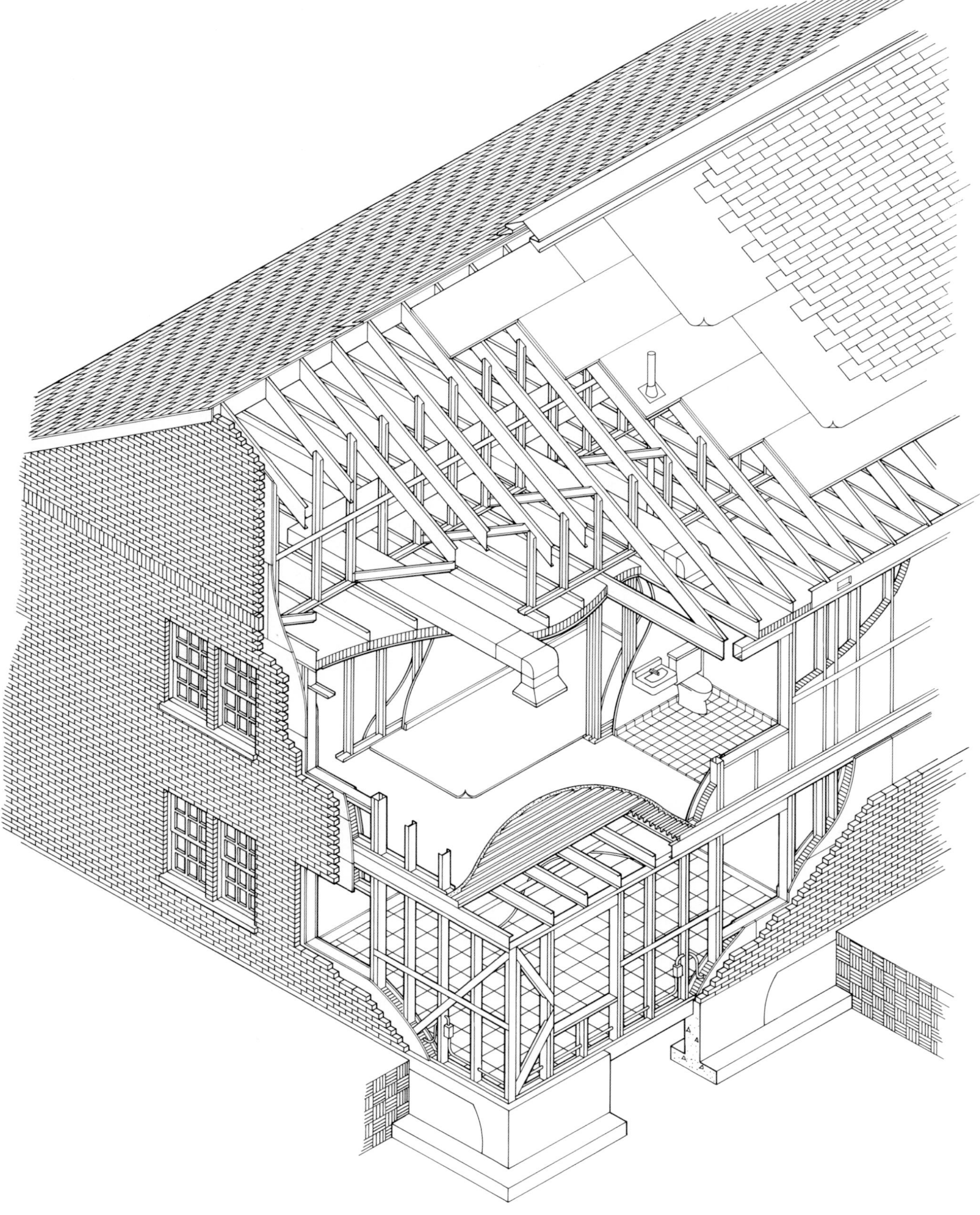

10. Wood Floor and Roof Truss

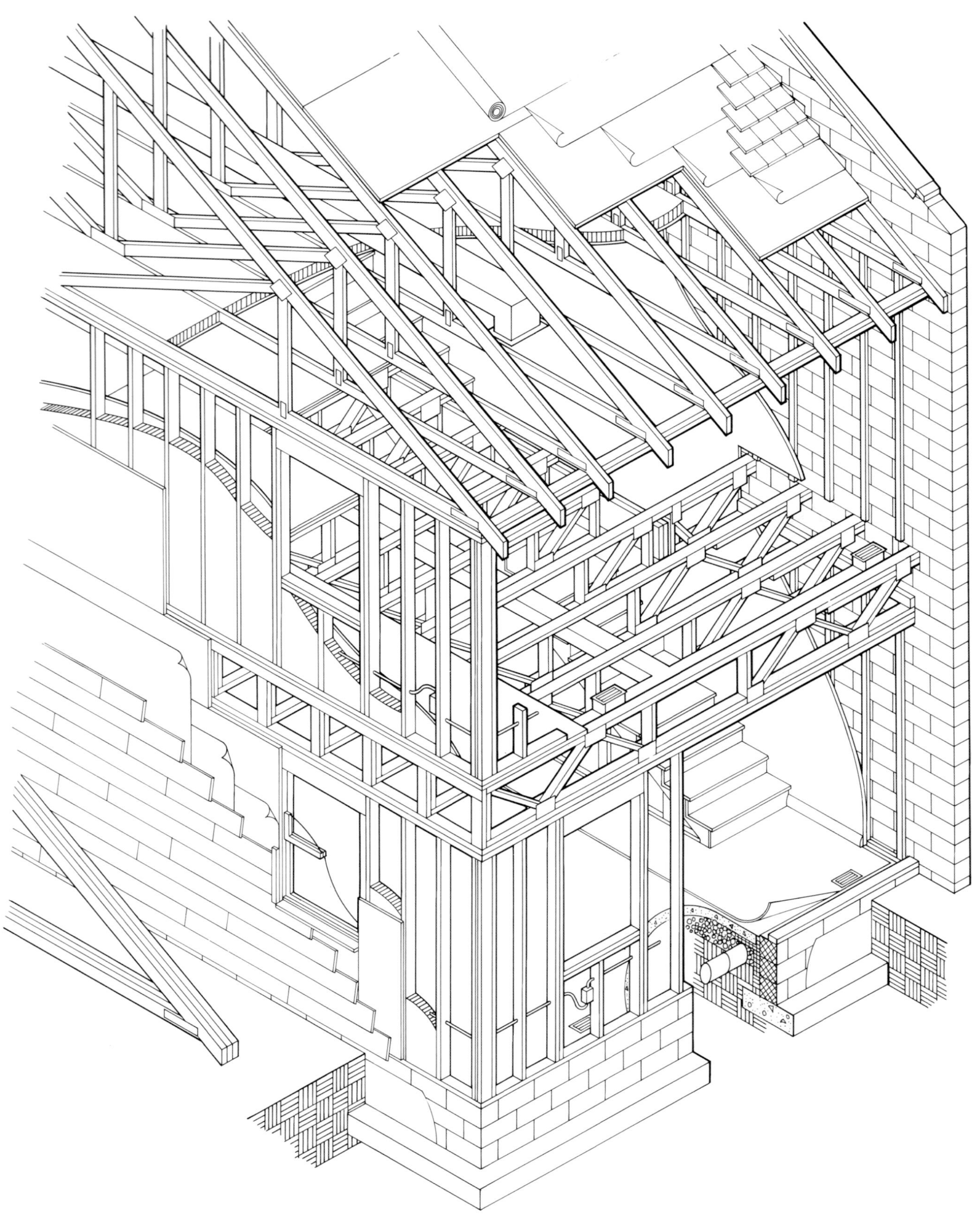

11. Laminated Wood Post and Beam

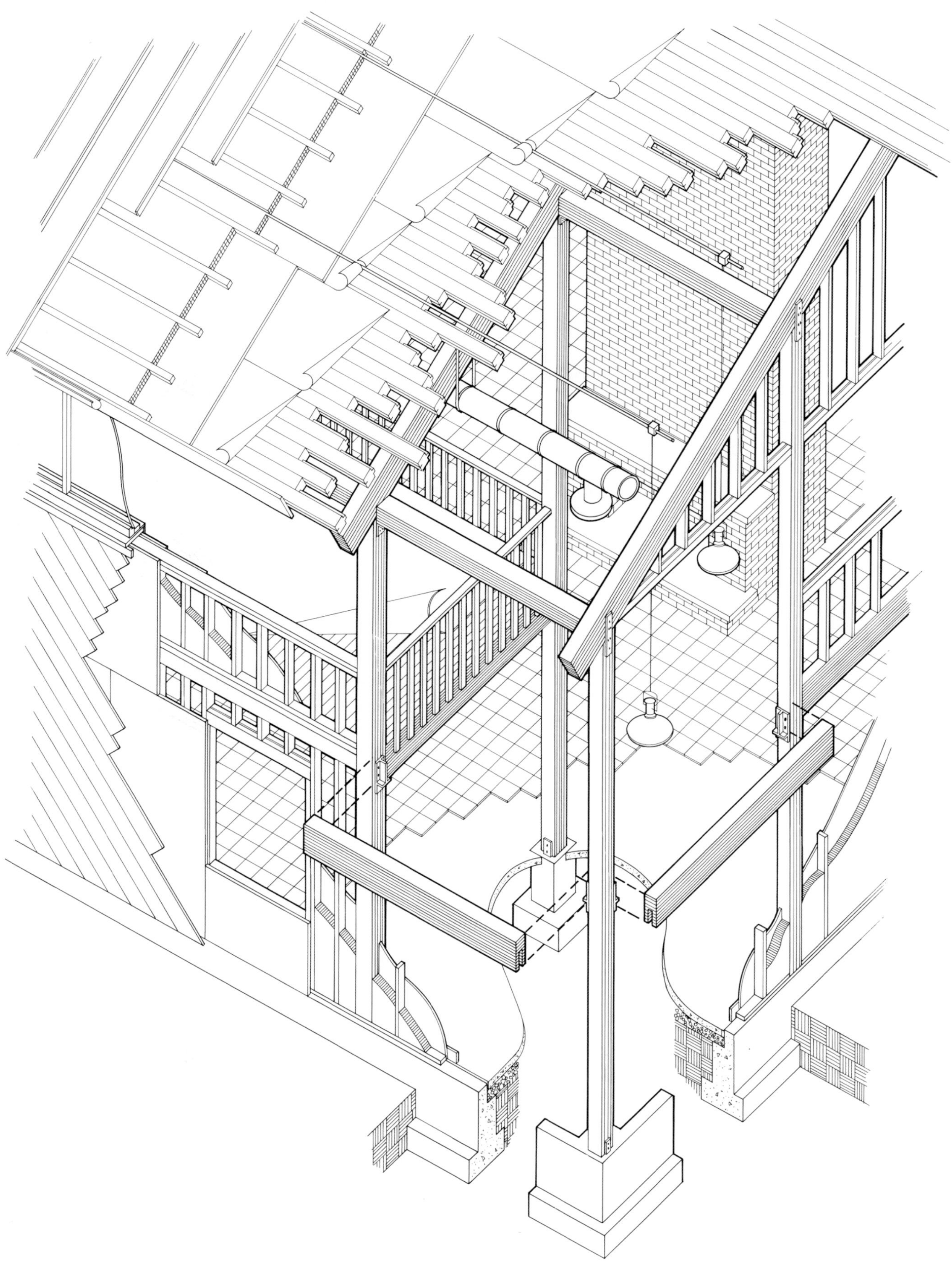

12. Lightweight Mobile Modular Buildings

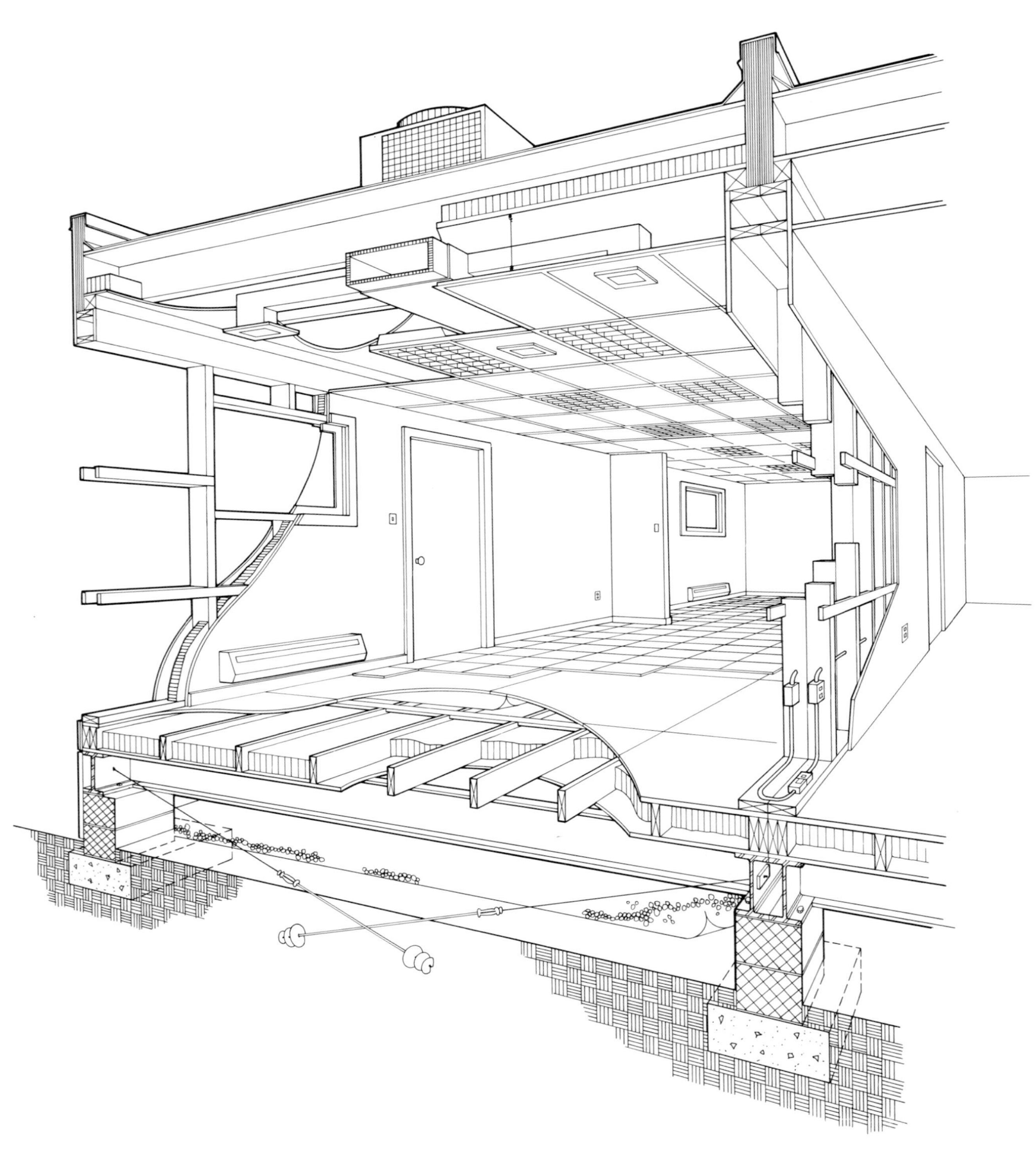

13. Space Frames

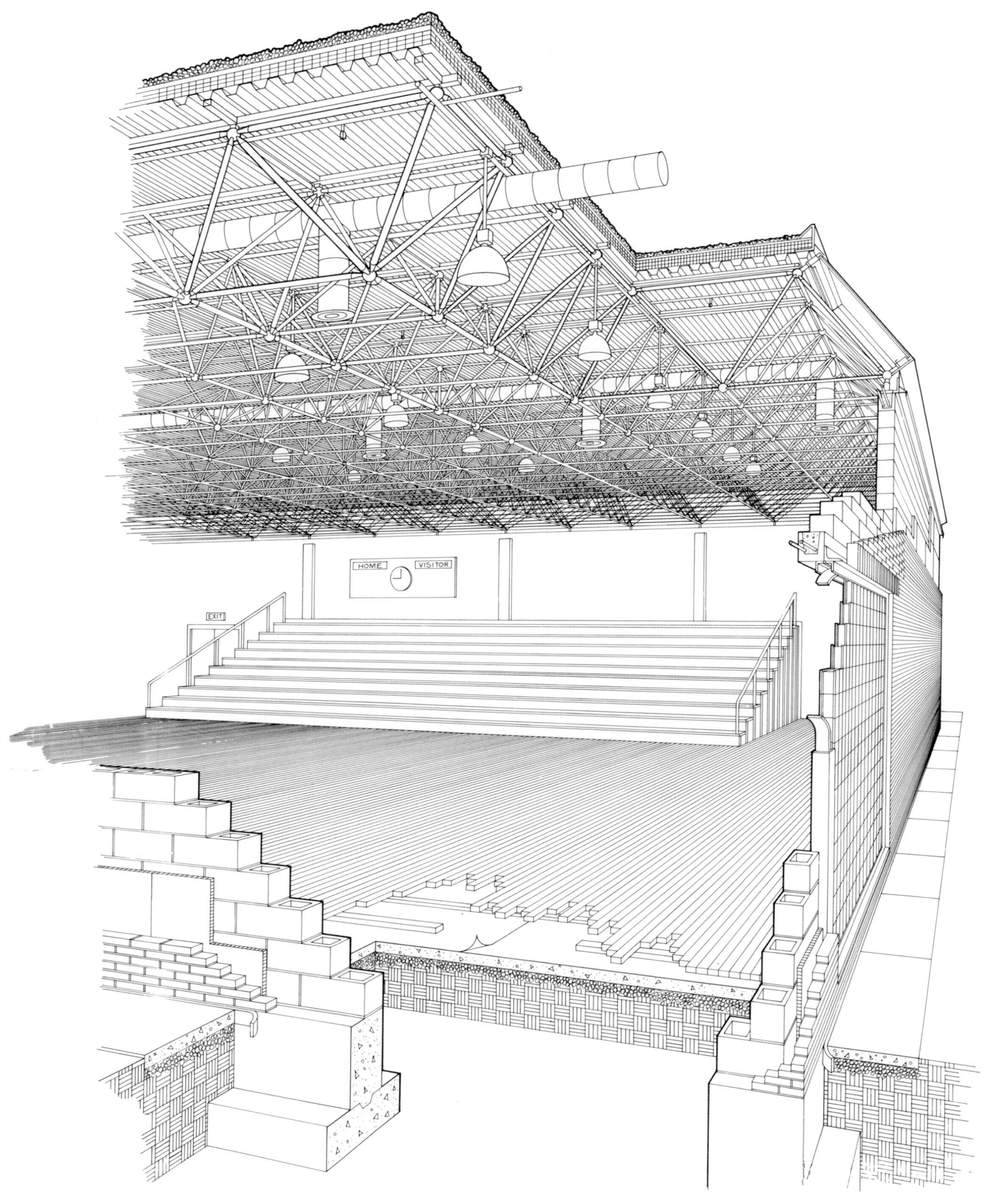

14. Metal Building Systems

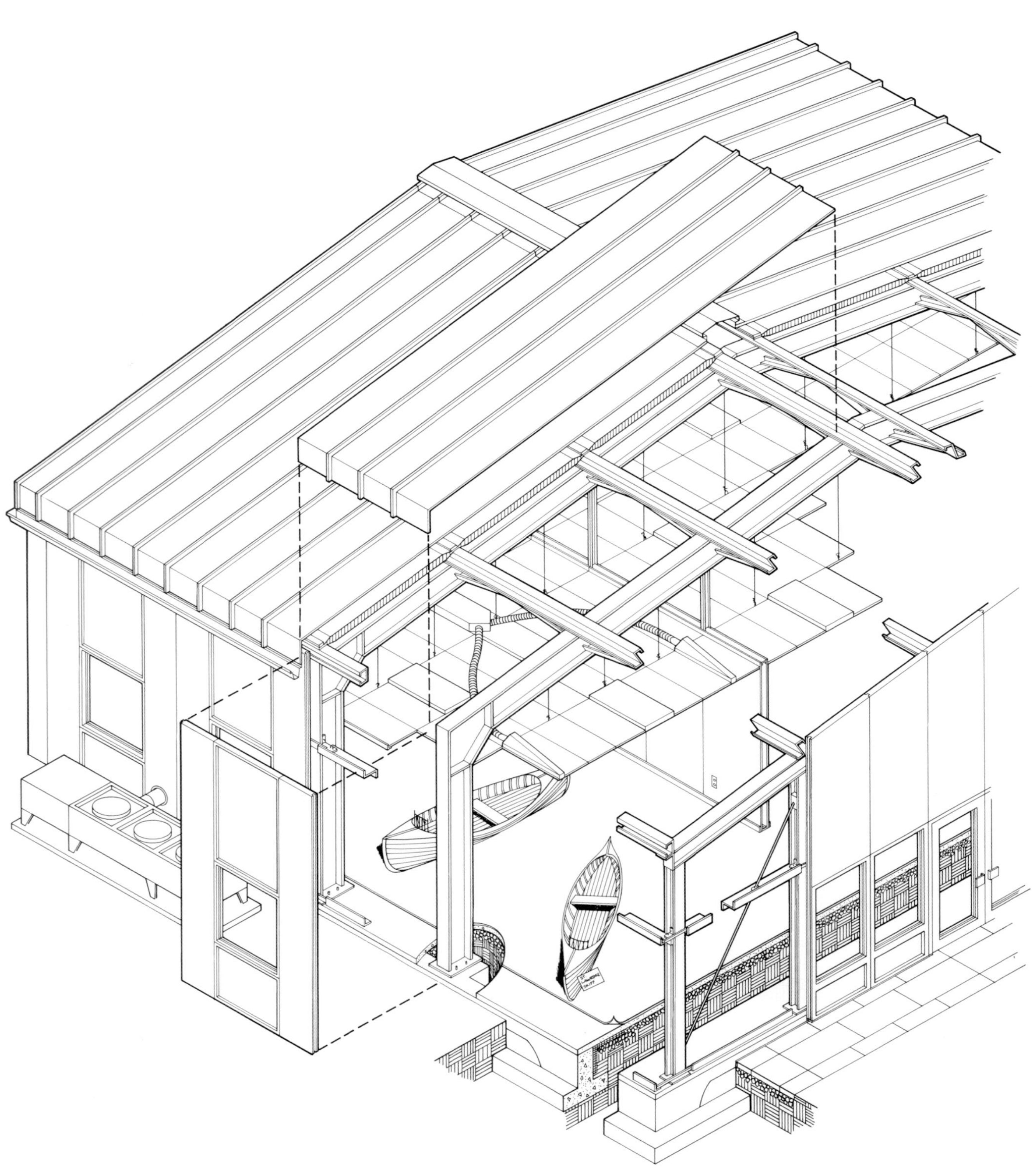

15. Tension Fabric Structures

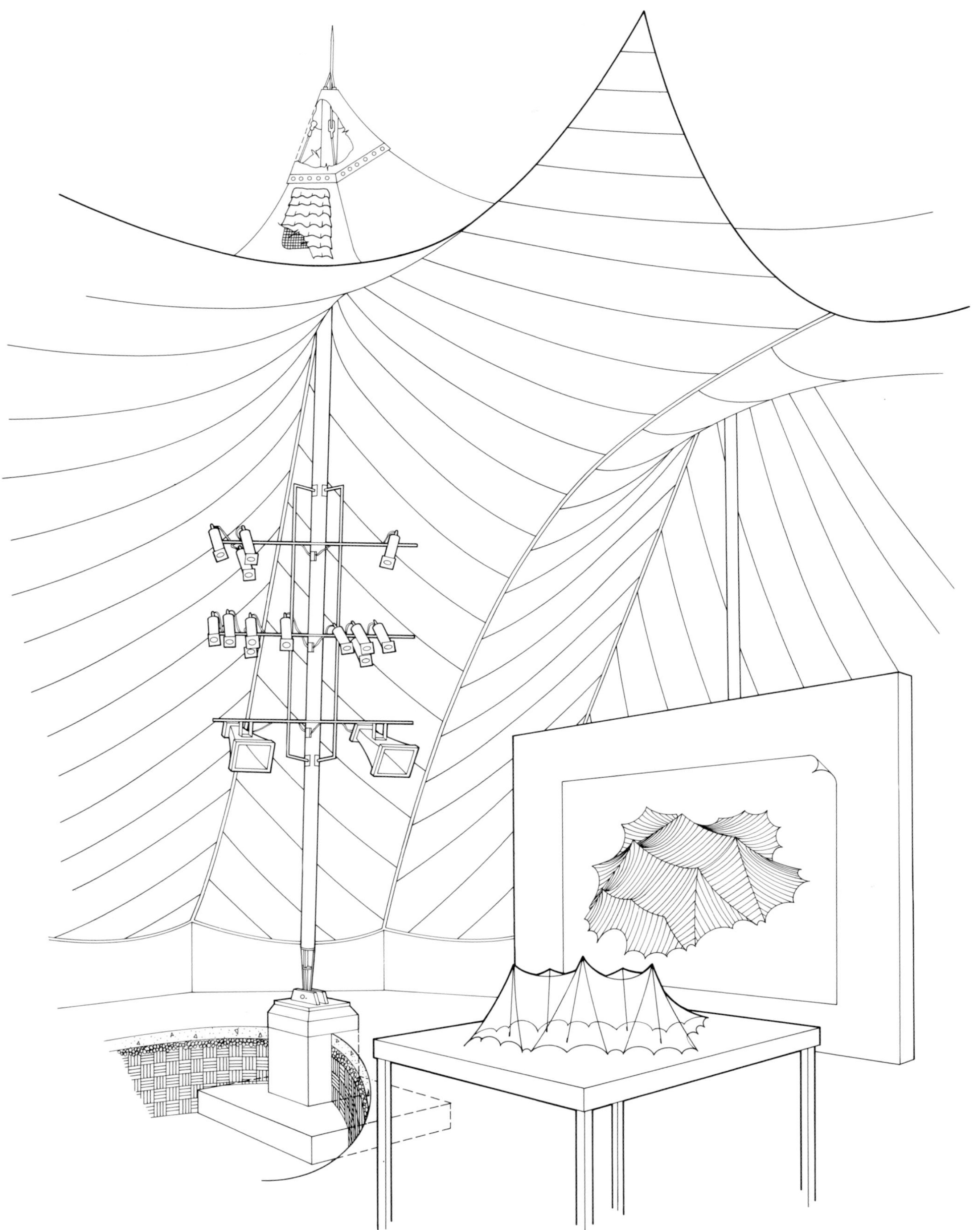

Author Biographies

Richard D. Rush, AIA, is a registered architect and consultant practicing in Arlington, Virginia. During his three years as editor of *The Building Systems Integration Handbook,* Mr. Rush was director of technical information for the American Institute of Architects. Prior to that he served for four years as senior editor in charge of technics for *Progressive Architecture* and wrote numerous articles on a broad range of subjects. The editorial experience culminated five years of teaching design and technical subjects in schools of architecture at Carnegie-Mellon University and Lawrence Institute of Technology. Mr. Rush has lectured nationally at industry conventions and has served as a juror for five national competitions. He received a B.Arch. from M.I.T. and a M.Arch. from the Cranbrook Academy of Art.

Robert Miller, AIA, is an architect and public relations consultant to design professionals in Washington, DC and New York. His writing has appeared in *Architecture, Progressive Architecture, Architectural Record, Skyline, Express, Design Action,* and *Mimar,* and he has served as a visiting critic at the University of Maryland and Catholic University. Formerly an account executive with Hill and Knowlton, Inc., he was an associate of Arthur Cotton Moore/Associates in Washington, DC. He holds a M.Arch. with honors from Yale University.

Thomas Vonier, AIA, manages his own architectural practice in Washington, DC, and has served as a correspondent for *Progressive Architecture* since 1981. He is a member of the AIA's National Energy Committee and a program advisor for the Association of Collegiate Schools of Architecture. He holds the AIA's Henry Adams Award for Excellence in Architecture and was a program director with the AIA Research Corporation for three years. His publications include *Natural Ventilation and Passive Cooling, New Design Concepts for Energy-Conserving Buildings,* and numerous articles in professional journals. He received his M.Arch. from the University of Wisconsin-Milwaukee in 1974.

Barbara Golter Heller, AIA, is a registered architect and principal of Heller Associates Inc., a specifications consulting firm in Washington, DC. Ms. Heller has done specifications writing for the past six years and contributes periodically to *Architectural Technology,* the AIA's quarterly magazine dealing with issues of technology. She holds a B.S. in architecture from the University of Illinois at Champaign/Urbana.

Volker Harkopf is professor of architecture at Carnegie-Mellon University, where he has developed one of North America's first multidisciplinary graduate programs in architecture, engineering, building sciences, and urban affairs, established with grants from the National Science Foundation and the building industry. He has also been principal investigator for several research contracts and demonstration projects. Since 1981, at the Architectural and Building Sciences Directorate of Public Works Canada, Mr. Hartkopf has worked on developing a generic methodology for evaluating overall building performance. He has written numerous articles and technical publications. He holds the following degrees: Vordiplom Architecture, University of Stuttgart; Diplom Ingenieur, University of Stuttgart; M.Arch. and Business Administration, University of Texas at Austin.

Vivian E. Loftness is a principal of VLH Associates and adjunct associate professor at Carnegie-Mellon University. She is an international energy consultant for commercial and residential building design, and has edited and written numerous publications on energy conservation, passive solar design, climate, and regionalism in architecture. Under contract to the Greek and German governments she completed the energy conservation and passive solar design of a 400-unit low-income community, now under construction in Athens, Greece. Most recently Ms. Loftness has worked with the Architectural and Building Sciences Directorate of Public Works Canada. She received both her B.S. and M.Arch. from M.I.T.

Peter A. D. Mill is director of the Architectural and Building Sciences Directorate of Public Works Canada. His work on the development of non-destructive diagnostic testing for buildings, ranging from thermography to occupancy and use analysis, has broadened the definition and capabilities for assessing total building performance. He is an associate fellow of the Center for Building Diagnostics at Carnegie-Mellon University, and for four years was associate professor of building science in the graduate program at the University of Calgary. Mr. Mill is currently the building science advisor at Public Works Canada for the new National Gallery of Canada. His degrees include a B.Arch. from the University of Glasgow in Scotland and a M.Arch. from the State University of New York at Buffalo.

M. Stephanie Stubbs maintains her own practice, Archisearch, in Arlington, VA, which offers architectural research, environmental design, and technical writing services for the architectural community and related disciplines. Before establishing her own company, Ms. Stubbs served as project manager and research associate at the American Institute of Architects Foundation. She holds a M.Arch. in design from the State University of New York at Buffalo, where she also served as an instructor. Her publications include monographs in the *Handbook of Energy Practice, A National Agenda for the Planning and Design of Cost-Effective Health Care Facilities,* and several articles in *Architectural Technology.*

Index